Linux User's Guide

Using the Command Line & GNOME with Red Hat Linux 9.0

Carolyn Z. Gillay

Saddleback College

Franklin, Beedle & Associates, Inc.
8536 SW St. Helens Drive, Suite D
Wilsonville, Oregon 97070
503-682-7668
www.fbeedle.com

Dedication

To Mike Estes, whose exceptional intelligence, combined with his outstanding technical knowledge and skills in managing our network and classroom computers, is surpassed only by his wonderful attitude and personality, which always puts the needs of the students first. His willingness to help me provide the best classroom experiences for my students, regardless of the extra work it creates for him, makes working with him a joy—my heartfelt thanks!

—C.Z.G.

President and Publisher	Jim Leisy (jimleisy@fbeedle.com)
Production	Tom Sumner
	Stephanie Welch
	Dean Lake
Cover	Ian Shadburne
Marketing	Christine Collier
Order Processing	Krista Brown

Printed in the U.S.A.

Library of Congress Cataloging-in-Publication data available from the publisher.

Contents

Preface ix

Chapter 1 • Getting Started • 1

Chapter Overview 1
Learning Objectives 1
Student Outcomes 2
1.1 What Is an Operating System? 2
1.2 What is Unix/Linux? 3
1.3 What Is Red Hat Linux? 5
1.4 Overview of Files and Disks 6
1.5 File Names, File Types,
    and Directories 7
1.6 Interfaces 9
1.7 Linux and Users 11
1.8 Booting the System 11
1.9 Activity: Booting the System 12
1.10 Shutting Down the System 13
1.11 Activity: The Linux Shut Down
     Procedure 13
1.12 The GNOME Desktop 14
1.13 Windows 17
1.14 Pointing Devices 17
1.15 Activity: Using the Main Menu 18
1.16 The Nautilus File Manager 23
1.17 Activity: Exploring
     the Nautilus File Manager 25
1.18 Manipulating the Panel 32

1.19 Activity: Working with the Panel 33
1.20 The Taskbar and the
     Workspace Switcher 37
1.21 Activity: Using the Taskbar
     and Workspace Switcher 37
1.22 Customizing the Panel 41
1.23 Activity: Customizing the Panel 41
1.24 Customizing the Desktop 47
1.25 Activity: Customizing the Desktop 47
1.26 gEdit and OpenOffice 50
1.27 Activity: Using gEdit
     and OpenOffice.org Writer 51
Chapter Summary 55
Key Terms 56
Discussion Questions 56
True/False Questions 57
Completion Questions 57
Multiple Choice Questions 58
Application Assignments 58
Problem Set I—At the Computer:
    Multiple Choice 58
Problem Set II—At the Computer:
    Short Answer 61
Problem Set III—Brief Essay 62

Chapter 2 • The Linux File System • 63

Chapter Overview 63
Learning Objectives 63
Student Outcomes 64
Commands Introduced 64
2.1 Understanding the Linux File System . 64
2.2 Activity: Looking at
    the File System 66
2.3 Introducing the Bash Shell 72
2.4 Command Syntax 73
2.5 What Are Options and Arguments? 73
2.6 Reading a Syntax Diagram 74
2.7 Introducing Commands
    and the Terminal Window 74
2.8 Activity: Looking at the Shell 74
2.9 Navigating in the Shell 78

2.10 Activity: Navigating the Shell 78
2.11 The date and cal commands 83
2.12 Activity: Using the date
     and cal Commands 83
2.13 Mounting File Systems 86
2.14 Activity: Mounting
     and Unmounting File Systems 87
2.15 Filename Expansion 94
2.16 Activity: Filename Expansion 94
2.17 The ls Command 101
2.18 Activity: Using Options with the ls
     Command 102
2.19 The locate Command 105
2.20 Activity: The locate Command 105
2.21 The find Command 107

2.22	Activity: The find Command 108
2.23	Redirection 110
2.24	Activity: Redirecting Output to a File and a Device 111
2.25	The whereis Command..................... 112
2.26	Activity: Using the whereis Command 112
Chapter Summary 113
Key Terms 114
Discussion Questions 114

True/False Questions 115
Completion Questions 115
Multiple Choice Questions 115
Writing Commands 116
Application Assignments 116
Problem Set I—At the Computer:
Multiple Choice 116
Problem Set II—At the Computer:
Short Answer 120
Problem Set III—Brief Essay 122

Chapter 3 • Getting Help • 123

Chapter Overview 123
Learning Objectives 123
Student Outcomes 124
Commands Introduced 124
3.1   Help 124
3.2   Types of Help 124
3.3   Red Hat Help 125
3.4   Activity: Using Help 126
3.5   The GNOME Help Browser Manual Pages 132
3.6   Activity: Using Manual Pages with GNOME 134
3.7   The Command Line man Pages 136
3.8   Activity: Using man, whatis, and apropos 138
3.9   Info Pages 143
3.1   Activity: Using Info Pages in the GNOME Help Browser 144
3.11   The info Command 146
3.12   Activity: Using the info Command 147
3.13   Internet Support 149
3.14   Red Hat and Internet Support 150

3.15   Activity: Using Red Hat Internet Support 151
3.16   Internet Support 152
3.17   Activity: Using Internet Support 153
3.18   Newsgroups 159
3.19   Activity: Adding and Using a News Server 161
3.20   Mailing Lists and User Groups 167
Chapter Summary 167
Key Terms 167
Discussion Questions 168
True/False Questions 168
Completion Questions 169
Multiple Choice Questions 169
Writing Commands 169
Application Assignments 170
Problem Set I—At the Computer:
Multiple Choice 170
Problem Set II—At the Computer:
Short Answer 173
Problem Set III—Brief Essay 174

Chapter 4 • Directory Commands • 175

Chapter Overview 175
Learning Objectives 175
Student Outcomes 176
Commands Introduced 176
4.1   The Hierarchical Filing System (Tree-structured Directories) 176
4.2   Managing Files and Directories 182
4.3   Viewing Files and Directories 183
4.4   Activity: Viewing Files and Directories 183

4.5   Creating Directories 188
4.6   Activity: How to Create Directories . 189
4.7   The Current Directory 192
4.8   Activity: Changing Directories 193
4.9   Building a Structure 194
4.10   Activity: Creating More Directories.. 195
4.11   The dot (.) and double-dot (..)— Dot Addressing 200
4.12   Activity: Using the Double-dot 200
4.13   Changing the Names of Directories .. 202

4.14 Activity: Renaming Directories 202

4.15 Removing Directories 204

4.16 Activity: Removing Directories 204

4.17 Removing Directories
      Recursively—Using rm and rmdir 207

4.18 Activity: Removing
      Directories 207

4.19 Variables....................................... 210

4.20 The PROMPT Variable 211

4.21 Activity: Changing the Prompt.......... 211

4.22 Understanding the PATH Variable ... 214

4.23 Activity: Using the
      PATH Variable 215

4.24 Understanding the
      CDPATH Variable 216

4.25 Activity: Using the
      CDPATH Variable 216

Chapter Summary 217

Key Terms 218

Discussion Questions 218

True/False Questions 219

Completion Questions 219

Multiple Choice Questions 219

Writing Commands 220

Application Assignments 220

Problem Set I—At the Computer:
      Multiple Choice 220

Problem Set II—At the Computer:
      Short Answer 225

Problem Set III—Brief Essay 226

Chapter 5 • File Management Commands • 228

Chapter Overview 228

Learning Objectives 228

Student Outcomes 229

Commands Introduced 229

5.1 Why Learn Commands? 229

5.2 Copying Files 230

5.3 Activity: Making Copies of Files
     Using the Nautilus File Manager 230

5.4 Copying Files at
     the Command Line 235

5.5 Activity: Making Copies of Files
     Using cp 236

5.6 Classifying Files.................................. 238

5.7 Activity: Using the file Command 238

5.8 Using Wildcards with
     the cp Command 240

5.9 Activity: Using Wildcards
     with the cp Command 240

5.10 The cat, less, and more Commands.. 241

5.11 Activity: Displaying Files Using
      the cat, more, and less Commands ... 242

5.12 The cp and ls Commands with
      Directories and Dot Addressing........ 247

5.13 Activity: Using cp and ls with
      Directories Dot Addressing............... 247

5.14 Overwriting Files............................... 250

5.15 Activity: Overwriting Files
      Using the cp Command and
      Using the -b, -p, and -i Options 251

5.16 Creating Files and Combining
      Text Files with the cat Command..... 255

5.17 Activity: Combining and Creating
      Files Using the cat Command 255

5.18 The touch Command 258

5.19 Activity: Using the
      touch Command 259

5.20 Changing File Names 260

5.21 Activity: Using the mv
      Command to Rename Files 261

5.22 Moving Files and Renaming
      Directories 264

5.23 Activity: Moving Files
      and Directories 265

5.24 Eliminating Files 267

5.25 Activity: Deleting Files 268

5.26 Deleting Files with Wildcards
      and Using Other Options 271

5.27 Activity: Using the rm Command
      with Options and Wildcards 272

5.28 Printing Files 275

5.29 Activity: Printing Files with lpr 275

Chapter Summary 276

Key Terms 277

Discussion Questions 277

True/False Questions 278

Completion Questions 278

Multiple Choice Questions 278

Writing Commands 279

Application Assignments 279
Problem Set I—At the Computer:
    Multiple Choice 279

Problem Set II—At the Computer:
    Short Answer 284
Problem Set III—Brief Essay 286

Chapter 6 • Editors • 287

Chapter Overview 287
Learning Objectives 287
Student Outcomes 288
6.1   Editors 288
6.2   The vi Editor 288
6.3   Activity: Creating a File 289
6.4   Moving and Searching in a File 293
6.5   Activity: Moving
        and Searching in a File 296
6.6   Getting Help 300
6.7   Activity: Using Help 301
6.8   Adding Text to a File 304
6.9   Activity: Adding Text to a File 305
6.10 Correcting Text 307
6.11 Activity: Correcting Text 307
6.12 Searching and Replacing 310
6.13 Activity: Replacing Text
        and Printing the File 311
6.14 Copying, Pasting,
        and Moving Text 314

6.15 Activity: Copying, Pasting,
        and Moving Text 315
6.16 Multiple Windows and Multiple Files 317
6.17 Activity: Manipulating Files
        and Windows 318
6.18 Emacs 322
6.19 Activity: Using Emacs 324
Chapter Summary 334
Key Terms 334
Discussion Questions 334
True/False Questions 335
Completion Questions 335
Multiple Choice Questions 336
Writing Commands 336
Application Assignments 337
Problem Set I—At the Computer:
    Multiple Choice 337
Problem Set II—At the Computer:
    Short Answer 340
Problem Set III—Brief Essay 342

Chapter 7 • Pipes, Filters, and Redirection • 343

Chapter Overview 343
Learning Objectives 343
Student Outcomes 344
Commands Introduced 344
7.1   Standard Input and Output—
        The Terminal as a File 344
7.2   Activity: Using Standard Input and
        Output and the Terminal as a File 346
7.3   Standard Input and Output—
        Standard I/O 349
7.4   Activity: Using the
        Redirection Symbols 350
7.5   Linux Files and File Structures 355
7.6   The cut and paste Commands 357
7.7   Activity: Using the cut and paste
        Commands 358
7.8   Filters 363
7.9   Activity: Using sort and wc 364
7.10 Pipes 369
7.11 Activity: Using Pipes 369

7.12 Introducing grep, egrep, and fgrep ... 372
7.13 Activity: Using grep,
        egrep, and fgrep 374
7.14 Formatting a Document with pr 378
7.15 Activity: Using pr 379
7.16 Introducing tee, tr, and ispell 381
7.17 Activity: Using tee, tr, and ispell 382
7.18 Introducing head and tail 386
7.19 Activity: Using head and tail 387
7.20 Introducing uniq, diff, and comm 389
7.21 Activity: Using uniq,
        diff, and comm 390
7.22 File Compression and Archiving 394
7.23 File Compression
        and Archiving Tools 395
7.24 Activity: Using bzip2, bunzip2, gzip,
        gunzip, zcat, tar, and File Roller 398
Chapter Summary 405
Key Terms 405
Discussion Questions 405

True/False Questions 406
Completion Questions 406
Multiple Choice Questions 407
Writing Commands 407
Application Assignments 408

Problem Set I—At the Computer: Multiple
    Choice.. 408
Problem Set II—At the Computer: Short
    Answer 412
Problem Set III—Brief Essay 414

Chapter 8 • File Systems, File Ownership, Permissions, and Links • 415

Chapter Overview 415
Learning Objectives 416
Student Outcomes 416
Commands Introduced 416
8.1   File Ownership
    and Permissions 416
8.2   Activity: Looking
    at Permissions 418
8.3   File Systems 421
8.4   Activity: Creating an
    ext2 File System 423
8.5   Disk Use 427
8.6   Activity: Using du and df 428
8.7   Groups 435
8.8   Activity: Looking at
    Users and Groups 437
8.9   Permissions 444
8.10 Activity: Using Permissions 447
8.11 Octal Permissions 453

8.12 Activity: Using
    Numeric Permissions 456
8.13 Linking Files—Hard Links 461
8.14 Activity: Using Hard Links 462
8.15 Linking Files—Symbolic Links 467
8.16 Activity: Using Symbolic Links 468
Chapter Summary 471
Key Terms 472
Discussion Questions 472
True/False Questions 473
Completion Questions 473
Multiple Choice Questions 473
Writing Commands 474
Application Assignments 475
Problem Set I—At the Computer:
    Short Answer 475
Problem Set I—At the Computer:
    Short Answer 477
Problem Set III—Brief Essay 478

Chapter 9 • Processes, Shell Scripts, Variables, and Command Line Substitution • 479

Chapter Overview 479
Learning Objectives 480
Student Outcomes 480
Commands Introduced 480
9.1   The Shell 481
9.2   The Role of the Shell 481
9.3   Process Structure 483
9.4   Processes 484
9.5   Activity: Looking at Processes 488
9.6   The kill and killall commands 493
9.7   Activity: Using the kill and killall
    Commands with Processes 494
9.8   The fg, bg, and jobs commands 497
9.9   Activity: Using the fg, bg,
    and jobs commands 497
9.10 Shell Scripts 500

9.11 Activity: Writing Shell Scripts 501
9.12 Command Types 506
9.13 Activity: Using alias,
    type, and help 507
9.14 Manipulating the Directory Stack
    with Built-in Commands 511
9.15 Activity: Using the Built-in
    Commands dirs, pushd, and popd..... 513
9.16 Variables and the set Command 516
9.17 Activity: Using the set Command 517
9.18 User-created Variables 518
9.19 Activity: Creating and
    Removing User-created Variables 518
9.20 export and declare............................. 523
9.21 Activity: Using
    export and declare............................. 523

9.22 Command Line Expansion
      and Quoting 525
9.23 The Single Quote, the
      Double Quotes, and the Backslash ... 526
9.24 Activity: The Single Quote, the
      Double Quotes, and the Backslash ... 527
9.25 More on Command Line Expansion .. 530
9.26 Activity: More on
      Command Line Expansion 530
9.27 The Initialization Files and Sourcing . 535
9.28 Activity: Altering the .bashrc File 535
Chapter Summary 538

Key Terms 539
Discussion Questions 539
True/False Questions 540
Completion Questions 540
Multiple Choice Questions 540
Writing Commands 541
Application Assignments 542
Problem Set I—At the Computer:
      Short Answer 542
Problem Set II—At the Computer:
      Short Answer 545
Problem Set III—Brief Essay 546

Chapter 10 • Shell Scripts • 547

Chapter Overview 547
Learning Objectives 547
Student Outcomes 548
Commands Introduced 548
10.1 Commands, Comments,
      and Executing Shell Scripts 548
10.2 Commands, Comments,
      and Executing Shell Scripts 549
10.3 Activity: Writing a Shell Script 550
10.4 The read Command 553
10.5 Activity: Using the read Command ... 554
10.6 Positional Parameters 557
10.7 Activity: Using
      Positional Parameters 558
10.8 The shift Command 562
10.9 Activity: Using the shift Command ... 562
10.10 The set Command 564
10.11 Activity: Using the set Command 564
10.12 Exit Status 567
10.13 Activity: Using the Exit Status 567
10.14 The test and let commands 568
10.15 Activity: Using the test
      and let commands 571
10.16 The if ... then commands
      and Logical Operators 573

10.17 Activity: Using the
      if ... then commands 574
10.18 The if ... then ... else commands
      and the exit Command 579
10.19 Activity: Using the
      if ... then ... else commands 580
10.20 The if ... then ... elif commands 583
10.21 Activity: Using the
      if ... then ... elif commands 584
10.22 The case Command 587
10.23 Activity: Using the case command 589
10.24 Loops—the for, while,
      and until Commands 593
10.25 Activity: The for, while,
      and until Commands 595
Chapter Summary 600
Key Terms 601
Discussion Questions 601
True/False Questions 602
Completion Questions 602
Multiple Choice Questions 602
Writing Commands 603
Application Assignments 604
Problem Set I—At the Computer 604
Problem Set II—Brief Essay 606

Appendix A   Master Accounts 607
Appendix B   ASCII Collating Sequence 610
Glossary 615
Index 623

Preface

This textbook gives students a solid foundation in the fundamentals of the Linux operating system. Although it uses Red Hat Linux 9 as the platform, the concepts and activities can be used with almost every Linux and Unix variant. Students gain system-level experience through problem-solving exercises at the command line and in the graphical user interface (GUI). The subject matter is approached through both the graphical user interface and the command line so students easily transition from the Windows environment to the Linux environment. By the end of the course, the students will have learned the major, essential, command-line commands necessary to be accomplished users of their Linux workstations, as well as be able to use the GUI when appropriate. It is written for use as the core textbook for a course that focuses exclusively on Linux/Unix, for the Linux/Unix portion of a network or programming class, or as the Linux/Unix supplement in a multi-platform operating systems course.

Why Learn Linux When It Is a Windows World?

With Windows dominating the desktop computer marketplace, many people are unaware that there are other commonly used computer operating systems. There is no question that Unix/Linux plays a crucial role in academic and corporate computing. In fact, Unix/Linux powers more Internet servers and corporate networks than Microsoft Windows NT and 2000 combined. The rise of heterogeneous network computing makes a knowledge of Unix/Linux crucial to being a well-rounded network administrator or network technician. Networks that interconnect with diverse operating systems (i.e., Windows, Unix/Linux, Mac OS, and Palm OS) are becoming the norm, not the exception. It is important to note that this text incorporates many operating system concepts, such as file systems, that apply to any operating system.

Begins with the Basics and Leads to the Advanced

Today, most students are familiar with a GUI environment (Windows). Since the leading Linux distributions include a GUI, this text introduces Linux using the GNOME desktop GUI. The approach provides a comfort level for many students as they begin to interact with Linux in a manner already familiar to them from their use of Windows. It also allows students to begin to appreciate the fact that all operating systems serve the same purpose and have shared functionality. Although the students begin with using the GUI to perform operating system tasks, they quickly move to using character-based commands to perform the same tasks. The students also begin to appreciate the power of character-based commands rather than rely all of the time on a GUI interface.

This text leads students from a basic to a sophisticated use of Linux. They will learn commands that allow them to accomplish simple personal tasks, such as managing their files and directories, dealing with permissions, and shell programming. Each chapter has questions for both novice and advanced students, so it challenges advanced students without sacrificing the needs of beginning students. Furthermore, this text stresses the concepts, theory, and understanding of operating systems in general. Thus, important operating system concepts are covered, such as an understanding of file systems, pipes, filters, redirection, variables, and permissions. This critical understanding of operating system functions enables students to transfer their knowledge of these operating system functions to other Unix/Linux environments (Solaris, Mandrake, and so on) as well as to operating systems in general.

The text demonstrates the command line interface and explains when and why one would use it instead of a graphical user interface such as GNOME. It provides numerous examples to allow students to master operating systems. This text teaches these concepts using both the GNOME desktop and the terminal window. By the end of the text, tasks are almost completely performed in a terminal window with text-based commands. Thus, although this text deals primarily with those text commands and functions that are available in a terminal window, it also deals with commands and functions necessary to understand, maintain, and use the GUI where using the GUI is easier and makes more sense.

Focuses on Real-World Skills and Conceptual Mastery

The text is designed to be a tutorial with extensive hands-on practice to tie the practical with the theoretical. The students learn by working with concrete examples that promote understanding of universal operating system concepts. The advanced material covers elementary shell scripting and the ability to customize the student's desktop environment. This is an enduser's guide, so students do not operate at the root access level, but learn the tools necessary to manage their workstation (as they would in a real-world work environment). The student has also acquired the knowledge necessary to move to the next level, basic system administration. Thus, after working carefully through the material in this textbook, students should know the how and why of the enduser functions of the Linux operating system. Further, students are encouraged to understand that the primary function of Linux, as of any operating system, is the management of the entire computer system (hardware, software, and files).

An Integrated Presentation of Concepts and Skills

Each section of the book is presented in a careful, student-oriented, step-by-step approach. Numerous screens shots show the expected results of each step. This not only minimizes the need for assistance in a lab environment, but also eases the difficulties of those working on their own computers at home or work. Interspersed between the steps in the exercises are the reasons for and results of each action. A student activities disk is bundled with the textbook. This disk, labeled BOOK, contains the files that are needed to successfully complete the step-by-step activities in each chapter. The BOOK disk is a FAT disk, but students will format a new disk, called BOOK2, with the ext2 file system and copy files from the FAT disk to the ext2 disk. Not only is this a great exercise in understanding file systems, it also allows hands-on experience with file and directory permissions.

In a lab environment, certain accounts, groups, and files must be created so that the activities work. These accounts and files are provided in Appendix A. These instructions may also be used by students working on their own computer.

Publisher's Edition of Red Hat Linux 9

Included within the packaging of this book is a copy of Red Hat Linux Publisher's Edition, Version 9, on a CD. All, or portions, of this software is copyrighted by Red Hat and others (not including Franklin, Beedle & Associates, Incorporated). Neither Red Hat nor Franklin, Beedle & Associates, Incorporated, is under obligation to provide technical support to purchasers of this textbook. Furthermore, neither Red Hat nor Franklin, Beedle & Associates, Incorporated, can be held responsible for any loss, personal injury, or property damage that may result from the use of this software.

Uses a Self-Mastery Approach

Each chapter includes a chapter overview, learning objectives, student outcomes, commands introduced, a list of key terms, a chapter summary, discussion questions, true-and-false questions, completion questions, multiple-choice questions, and problems where students are asked to write the commands.

At the end of each chapter are homework assignments that allow students to apply their knowledge and prove mastery of the subject area through critical-thinking skills. Each chapter also includes three sets of application assignments that focus on the skills learned in the chapter. The first problem set requires students to complete activities on the computer. The problem sets in the first five chapters and Chapter 7 require students to complete activities on the computer and write the resulting answers on a Scantron form. The problem sets in Chapters 6, 8, 9, and 10 require students to use the computer and print out the answers. The second set of questions asks for short written answers. These require the students to complete the activities on a computer and then answer the questions. The third set of application assignments asks brief essay questions that encourage students to integrate what they have accomplished in the chapter. All of these assignments reinforce critical-thinking skills. The instructor can use all of the assignments or any part of them as homework assignments. These application assignments are intended to be turned in as homework.

Instructor Support Material

Instructor support material has been prepared that consists of chapter outlines, teaching suggestions for each chapter, answers for every question and application exercise for each chapter, a complete PowerPoint presentation for each chapter, a quiz for each chapter, and two tests (a mid-term covering Chapters 1–5 and a final covering Chapters 6–10). This support is available without charge to the instructor upon adoption of the textbook for a course.

Acknowledgments

A project of this scope is difficult to complete successfully without the contributions of many individuals. Thank you to all who contributed. A special thanks to

* Kathryn Maurdeff for providing questions, answers, and PowerPoint presentations, and whose heroic efforts in completing this project are greatly appreciated.
* Lars Sunberg, who has been so helpful to me in setting up the lab environment so everything works correctly—and who is a great student.
* Nicholas Markiw, who is my Linux guru and always knows the answer when no one else does.
* Pat Sullivan, who is my friend and my colleague, and one very gracious lady.
* Sean Wilson, for all his help in seeing this project to completion.
* Aleesha Hunter, for all her assistance on this project.
* Robert Ruby, Edison Community College, for his generous contributions.
* My students at Saddleback College, who make writing worthwhile.
* My colleagues in the Computer Information Management Department at Saddleback College.
* A big thanks to everyone at Franklin, Beedle & Associates for all their time and effort—Tom Sumner, Stephanie Welch, Ian Shadburne, Chris Collier, Krista Brown, Dean Lake, and Bran Bond.

- A big thanks to Jim Leisy—my publisher and my friend.
- Linus Torvalds, thank you for leading and inspiring so many people to join together in the development of the world-class (Open Source Software) desktop operating system, Linux.
- And, as always, to my husband, Frank Panezich. If I can locate any more love, it's yours.

Anyone who wants to offer suggestions or improvements or just share ideas can reach me at **czg@bookbiz.com**.

—C.Z.G.

CHAPTER 1

Getting Started

Chapter Overview

The Unix operating system, the precursor to Linux, has been in use since the 1970s and is a major operating system in the scientific, business, and Internet worlds. Linux is a Unix-like operating system. In this chapter, you will be introduced to the functions and purposes of an operating system such as file and disk management as well as an understanding of a multi-tasking, multi-user operating systems in general, and specifically of Red Hat Linux 9.0.

You will also be introduced to how a user interacts with the operating system, with either a text-based command line or graphical user interface (GUI). The windowing environment will be examined. In this chapter, focus will be on the GNOME desktop, which is "wrapped" in the Bluecurve theme, provided with Red Hat Linux 9.0. This includes use of the features of the GNOME desktop as well as the features of the Nautilus file manager. You will learn to boot the system, log in, and properly shut down your computer. You will also customize the GNOME panel and desktop and use the text editor gEdit and the word processor OpenOffice, provided with the GNOME desktop.

Learning Objectives

1. Explain the purpose and function of an operating system.
2. List and explain five features that the Linux operating system supports.
3. Compare and contrast Red Hat with Red Hat Professional distributions.
4. Explain the purpose and function of files and disks.
5. List and explain Linux rules for naming files.

6. List and explain the purpose and function of the three major types of computer files.
7. Compare and contrast the two major ways Linux provides for the user to interact with the computer.
8. Compare and contrast the super user with the ordinary user.
9. Locate and explain the purpose and function of the objects found on the GNOME desktop.
10. Explain the purpose and function of a window and how pointing devices are used.
11. Locate and explain the purpose and function of the objects found in the Nautilus file manager.
12. Explain how to manipulate and customize the panel.
13. Explain how to customize your desktop.
14. Explain the purpose and function of the Tasklist and the Workspace Switcher.
15. Explain the purposes and functions of gEdit and OpenOffice programs.

Student Outcomes

1. Boot the system.
2. Properly shut down Linux.
3. Use the menus and mouse to navigate within the GNOME windowed environment.
4. Use the mouse to navigate within the Nautilus file manager.
5. Use the Workspace Switcher to create virtual desktops and alter the properties of the tasklist.
6. Manipulate and customize the panel.
7. Customize the desktop.
8. Use gEdit to create, manipulate, and edit a Linux text file.
9. Use OpenOffice to create, manipulate, and edit a simple word-processing document.

1.1 • What Is an Operating System?

A computer is a tool that lets you more easily accomplish tasks such as managing your checkbook, writing letters and reports, or playing games. Today, a vital part of owning a computer is to be able to use the Internet; if for nothing else, so email can be sent or received. Users are also interested in the tools (application software) they may install on their computer. Furthermore, today there is almost no business that does not use computers as an integral part of their business. When computers are used in business, employees need to share resources such as printers or information. This is done by connecting computers (networking). The sharing of resources and information brings to light new concerns such as security, privacy, and control of those resources.

Computer users do not purchase a computer to use an operating system. However, it is—at least at this point in time—impossible to use a computer without an operating system (OS). An operating system supervises the processing of application programs and all the input/output of the computer. A network operating system (NOS) additionally controls and manages resources and users.

Running a computer is somewhat analogous to producing a concert. The hardware is like the musicians and their instruments. They do not change. The application software is like the score the musicians play, anything from Mozart to the Dixie Chicks. The computer hardware can "play" any type of application software, from accounting to a game. Like the conductor who tells the violins or trumpets when to play and how loudly, the operating system makes the computer work. It is the first and most important program on the computer and must be loaded into memory (RAM) before any other program. You, the user, communicate what you want the computer to do through the operating system. These commands are issued by pointing and clicking in the GUI or by keying in commands such as **ls** or **clear** at the command line.

An operating system is a software program that acts as a set of instructions between the hardware (disks, memory, and so on) and the software (application programs such as word processors or web browsers). The heart of an operating system is called the kernel. A *kernel* performs the most basic computing functions, such as memory management, process administration, and management of the hardware. A *process* is an executing program or a task. Besides the kernel, an operating system provides other essential services. These include the following:

- *file systems*—The file system determines how information is stored on storage media such as the hard disk. All information is stored as files. Information consists of program files, system files, user data files, and so on.
- *device drivers*—A device driver is a program that interfaces with hardware devices connected to your computer. It allows a program to access or write to a device without needing to know the details of how that piece of hardware is implemented.
- *user interface*—A user interface allows a user to run programs and to access the file system on the computer. User interfaces are either text based or graphical. A text-based interface (a shell command interpreter, usually just called the *shell*) requires the user to key in commands and any options or arguments that might apply. A text-based interface requires that the user know the commands and how to use them. A graphical user interface, commonly referred to as a GUI (pronounced "gooey") allows a user to click and point at objects to execute the programs and perform routine computer tasks such as copying or moving files.
- *system services*—System services are services that are run by the computer. These include processes such as those that will mount a file system, start a network, and run scheduled tasks.

There are many different operating system "brand names." The most popular operating system in use today on personal computers that are Intel or Intel clones has been Windows, owned and licensed by Microsoft. Windows is a proprietary operating system. To use Windows on your computer, you must purchase it. An operating system determines which version of application software may be purchased, installed, and used on a computer. Application software is OS (operating system) dependent. If for instance, you have a Macintosh computer, which uses a Motorola processor, it runs its unique proprietary operating system as well as application software designed for the Mac.

1.2 • What is Unix/Linux?

Long before Windows or the Mac operating system, there was Unix. Unix was developed by researchers, primarily by Bell Laboratories, which offered it to educational institutions at a very minimal cost. In addition, the University of California at Berkeley made significant additions and changes to Unix. The two most popular versions of Unix are the Berkeley Software Distribution (BSD) and Unix System V, which was developed by AT&T and the Unix System Laboratory. Unix also migrated into industry. However, the proliferation of different versions of Unix required a standard. The Institute of Electrical and Electronics Engineers (IEEE) developed an independent Unix standard for the American National Standards Institute (ANSI). This standard is called the Portable Operating System Interface for Computer Environments (POSIX). A *standard* defines how a Unix-like system needs to work and specifies details such as system calls and interfaces. POSIX is considered a universal standard and most versions of Unix are POSIX compliant. Nonetheless, even with the POSIX standards, the hardware costs of running Unix as well as the complexity of its user interface did not make it a very popular operating system for the average user.

In 1991, Linus Torvalds, a student at the University of Helenski, wanted a Unix-like operating system for his desktop computer. He did not care for DOS nor could he afford Unix. Thus, he and a team of programmers created the core operating system, the kernel, which was named Linux. Linux adheres to the POSIX standard. By 1994 Linux became available for public use.

Linux was designed to provide personal computer users with a free or low-cost operating system comparable to Unix. Torvalds and the other team members made use of other system components developed by members of the Free Software Foundation (FSF) for the GNU project. (*GNU* is an acronym for GNU's Not Unix.)

The GNU Project was started in 1983 by Richard Stallman and others who believe that users should be free to do whatever they want to the software they acquire, including making copies and modifying the source code. The FSF uses a stipulation called *copyleft*, which states that anyone redistributing the free software must also pass along the freedom to copy and change the program, ensuring that no one can claim ownership for future versions or place restrictions on users. The "free" does mean "freedom," but does not necessarily mean "no charge." The FSF does charge an initial distribution price for GNU. Redistributors can also charge for copies either for cost recovery or for profit. However, anyone can download Linux from the Internet and install it at no charge. Linux is a full-featured operating system that supports the following:

- multitasking—Concurrent execution of several processes. This means that not only can a user run many programs at the same time, but Linux itself can be running programs in the background.
- multiusers—Concurrent use by many individuals on a network or by different users on a single computer. Each user can customize his environment without affecting other users.
- portability—Works on a wide range of hardware platforms including Intel processors (386 to the Pentium III), IBM, Motorola Power PC, DEC, Alpha, and Sun SPARC workstations.
- hardware support—Linux supports nearly all common PC hardware such as common CD-ROMs, Zip drives, ISA, EISA and PCI busses, and so on.
- security—Linux is a secure stand-alone or network operating system that protects unauthorized users from using resources or even looking at data.
- network connectivity/interoperability (open systems)—Allows different types of computers on a network to communicate. Linux offers support for a wide variety of LAN (local area network) cards, modems, and serial devices. In addition, most LAN protocols, such as Ethernet or Token Ring, can be built in, along with most upper-level networking protocols such as TCP/IP. Linux is fully compliant with POSIX, which provides application portability between Unix variants.
- network servers—Provides networking services to client computers. The common software packages are available, which allow you to use Linux as a print server, a mail server, a Web server, an FTP server, and so on.
- graphical user interface (X Window System)—This is a framework for working with graphical applications. It is commonly referred to as X. X handles the functions of opening any

X-based GUI applications and displaying them on an X server process, which manages the screen, mouse, and keyboard.

- SMP (symmetric multiprocessing)—Allows users who have multiple processors to be able to use them.

Today, most people who purchase a desktop/home computer find that Microsoft's proprietary Windows operating system is installed on it. Most users would not even know to ask for a different operating system than Windows. In fact, some version of Windows (95, 98, 2000, or XP) is installed on over 95 percent of home computers.

Is Unix/Linux a viable operating system? The answer to that is a resounding yes. Where Unix/Linux is a powerful influence is behind the scenes. Linux has a good share of the server market and is making even further inroads. Server computers are those that are used for such things as managing printing, files, and Web pages for a company. The combined Unix/Linux operating system is on over 40 percent of the world's servers, while Windows is on 50 percent of the world's servers. Linux is increasing its share every day. Major search engines for the Internet, such as Google (**www.google.com**), are running their servers on Linux. Government, academic institutions, and commercial companies are increasingly turning to Linux to run their operations.

Linux was designed as a network operating system and as such provides stability, security, and reliability, at low or no cost. In addition, if a feature of the operating system is not working on the server, rather than having to wait for a fix from Microsoft, since Linux/Unix is an open-source operating system, the network administrator can directly alter the code to solve the problem. If a home user has minimal needs such as wanting to use email or write simple documents, then using Windows is fine. However, if one wishes to have a career in the IT (Information Technology) world, then learning Linux is an absolute necessity.

1.3 ◦ **What Is Red Hat Linux?**

Although Linux can be downloaded for free from the Internet, many people choose to purchase a distribution of Linux. Because operating systems tend to be very large, downloading from the Internet can be a lengthy process. A *distribution* is a combination of the kernel and additional programs. A distribution is sold on CDs and allows a relatively quick installation of Linux. Distributions usually include additional software, technical support, and documentation. Popular distributions include Red Hat, Caldera, SuSE, and so on.

Red Hat Linux is one of the best maintained Linux distributions available and is especially dominant in the United States marketplace. Red Hat features two major desktop-distribution versions—Red Hat Linux 9 and Red Hat Linux 9 Professional. Red Hat offers an operating system that provides everything needed for a personal productivity workstation from installation through system maintenance. Red Hat Professional is designed for small networks and small businesses. It provides everything needed for a small business to provide a stable and secure working environment. This includes personal productivity workstations and additional necessary elements such as basic web serving. Table 1.1, "Differences in Red Hat Linux Versions," delineates the major differences between the two versions. Red Hat also has a product called Red Hat Enterprise, formerly called Advanced Server, which is Red Hat's version of an enterprise platform for mission-critical Information Technology (IT) deployments. Red Hat Enterprise has been specifically designed for IT solutions that require the highest level of application availability and performance.

Red Hat Linux 9	Red Hat Linux 9 Professional
The operating system CDs	The operating system CDs The operating system on a DVD
The source code CDs	The source code CDs
30-day web-based installation support	60-day web-based installation support 60-day telephone installation support
Written documentation	Additional written documentation
Red Hat Network Basic Service—30-day subscription support. The basic service level subscriptions allow individuals to register one or more systems, manage these systems independently, receive priority access to Red Hat Network, and download Instant ISOs (full versions of Red Hat Linux), as well as other system features.	Red Hat Network Basic Service—60-day subscription support. The basic service level subscriptions allow individuals to register one or more systems, manage these systems independently, receive priority access to Red Hat Network, and download Instant ISOs (full versions of Red Hat Linux), as well as other system features.
Application software including OpenOffice, an application suite that features programs such as a word processor, a spreadsheet, a database, and so on.	Application software including OpenOffice, an application suite that features programs such as a word processor, a spreadsheet, a database, and so on.
Simplified installation that uses a GUI to assist you in installing it.	Simplified installation that uses a GUI to assist you in installing it.
Red Hat Package Manager (RPM)	Red Hat Package Manager (RPM)
	Additional multimedia application software
	System administrator tools CD

Table 1.1 • Differences in Red Hat Linux Versions

Both Red Hat Linux 9 and Red Hat Linux 9 Professional, in addition to providing the command-line interface, include a GUI for the user interface that is Windows/Mac-like. The two most popular GUIs in the Linux environment are GNOME and KDE. Red Hat Linux provides both GUIs. GNOME is the default GUI when you install either version of Red Hat Linux. This text assumes that Red Hat Linux 9 or Red Hat Linux 9 Professional is installed on the computer using the GNOME desktop.

1.4 • Overview of Files and Disks

You need a way to store information permanently. In the computer world, the primary way to save data and programs permanently is to store them on a disk. After you have booted your computer, Linux reads the programs or data it needs from the disk back into its memory. However, in order for Linux to find this information, it has to have a way of organizing it,

which it does by keeping programs and data in files on the disk. Just as you organize your written work in files, Linux organizes computer information in disk files.

A disk file is much like a file folder stored in a file cabinet. The file cabinet is the floppy disk or the hard disk. A file consists of related information stored on the disk in a "file folder" with a unique name. All information a computer works with is contained and stored in files on the disk (see Figure 1.1, "Disks and Files").

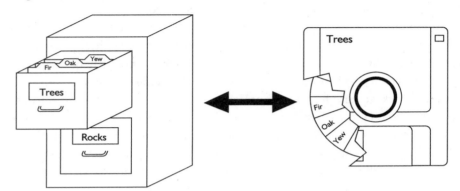

Figure 1.1 • Disks and Files

1.5 • File Names, File Types, and Directories

Because Linux must follow very specific rules, there are rules for file names:

- File names must be unique.
- File names cannot exceed 255 characters.
- Linux is case sensitive in the native Linux file system. This means that **ONE**, **One**, and **one** are considered three unique and separate files.
- You may use special characters such as a period (.) or an underscore (_) in file names. You may have multiple special characters in a file, such as **my.file.txt** (for those users familiar with DOS or Windows, the **.txt** is a familiar file extension; Linux also considers **.txt** a file extension). Although Linux does not require or need file extensions, the characters following the last period are considered a file extension in Linux and may be used to associate document files with a specific program. However, certain assumptions in the Windows file system are not true in Linux. For instance, .exe in Windows always means an executable program. This is not necessarily true in Linux.
- Spaces may be used in a file name. However, when referencing that file, you must enclose its name in quotation marks. Thus, the file **my file** would be referenced as **"my file"** or **'my file'**.
- Reserved characters that should not be used in file names include " , ' * &) (! ? / \ > < ; and |.
- Any file that begins with a dot is considered a hidden file.

There are three major types of computer files: user data files, program (executable) files, and system files. User data files contain information generated usually from an application program. Most often, only an application program can use the data file directly. Program files are application programs that allow the user to perform specific tasks; for example, a payroll program that lets you create and maintain a payroll system for a company. System files contain information that is used by executable programs or by the operating system.

You do not purchase a computer to run Linux. You purchase a computer so that you may do useful tasks such as writing letters, managing your checkbook, doing your taxes, or creating a budget. If you needed to employ someone to do these tasks for you, you might go to a temporary employment agency and hire a secretary to write your letters or an accountant to manage your checkbook and taxes. You would employ a temporary secretary or accountant because you do not need the employee on a full-time basis.

In the computer world, you instead may purchase application packages. For Linux, many of these application programs are free and can be downloaded from the Internet. These application packages fall into generic categories such as word processing or spreadsheet programs, much like you refer generically to secretaries or accountants. Of course, you may be specific and wish to use a specific secretary such as Mr. Woo or a specific accountant such as Ms. Brown. Software application packages also have brand names such as WordPerfect (the secretary) or AccountiX (the accountant) or Xess Spreadsheet (the budget manager). You can choose among a variety of employees—instead of choosing WordPerfect, you may prefer OpenOffice, or instead of AccountiX, you may prefer Emma. These application packages are the "employees" who know how to do the job. However, you must be sure to only use applications designed for Linux. You cannot use or install programs such as Microsoft Office that are designed to work under the Windows operating system.

In order for these application programs to do work, they must be placed in RAM, the workspace of the computer. They are "temporary" employees because you only call on them when you need to do a specific task that only they can accomplish. When they are not working, they are kept on the disk in files. Linux is like the office manager. You tell Linux what work you want to do, and Linux goes to the disk to get the correct file and place it in RAM. This process is known as loading the program from disk into memory. Linux then lets the program do its job. This is known as executing the program. Program files are step-by-step instructions that direct the computer to "do" something—the task that you required.

Even though the secretary, WordPerfect, can create letters for anyone, you are interested only in the letters you create—the information that you want. Once you create your data, you also want to keep it permanently. Remember, all the work is occurring in RAM, and RAM is volatile (temporary). In order to keep the information permanently, you direct WordPerfect to write (save) the information to disk as a data file. WordPerfect actually does not save the data; instead, it turns to Linux, which does the actual work of writing the file to disk. When you need to retrieve the information to alter it, WordPerfect again turns to Linux to retrieve the file. Linux then reads the disk to retrieve the appropriate data file and gives it to WordPerfect.

In order to be able to identify each file, a unique name must be assigned to the file. Program files have predetermined names. Keying in the file name, choosing it from a menu, or double-clicking its icon informs Linux to retrieve the program from the disk and place it in memory so you may work. Data files, on the other hand, are named by you, the user. You may call the file anything that you want. For instance, a good file name for a letter to your sister might be **sister.let**, or a name for your budget file might be **budget04**.

Data files are generated by specific application programs, and the information or data in them can be altered or viewed only with the application package. It is the same concept as not giving your tax information to the secretary to have the secretary make changes to it. You would give that data only to the accountant.

Data files do not stand alone. They can be used only in conjunction with an application program. Again, the job of Linux is to fetch and carry both program files and data files in and out of memory and to and from the disk (reading and writing). In addition, since Linux is the "office manager," you may also use Linux to do office-related tasks such as copying a file or deleting a file. Linux does not know what is in the file folder, nor can it make changes to the information in the file folder. It can manipulate the file folder by accomplishing such tasks as copying the information in it or by throwing it away.

To assist you in organizing your information further, Linux structures your disks into what are called directories. *Directories* are containers that store files. Directories allows you to group related files so they will be easy to locate at a later date. For instance, you might group any data files you created with WordPerfect for writing school reports, such as a project and a term paper, in a directory you called **school**. This would allow you to know that when you wanted to locate your file called **project**, it would be in the directory called **school**. Directories may be further divided into other directories. For instance, you could divide the **school** directory into your classes such as **history** and **computers**. Then your term paper would be located in the directory called **school/history**.

A primary directory (root) is automatically created when you prepare a disk to store information. It is named the root, but its symbol is / (the forward slash). There are also many other directories created when Linux is installed. You can create additional directories of your own.

1.6 • Interfaces

Linux provides two major ways of interacting with the computer—the command line and the GUI. The command line is a character-based interface, where you will see a command prompt, key in commands, and press **Enter** for the commands to execute. When you key in commands, you are interacting with a command interpreter that interprets and executes the commands you key in. The interface is the *shell*. There are actually many shells, such as the Bourne shell, Korn shell, and C Shell. Red Hat Linux uses the Bash shell (Bourne Again shell, named after Stephen Bourne, who helped create it). If you ever worked with DOS, the command prompt will also seem familiar to you. It is virtually impossible to work in Linux and not use the shell.

The other alternative is a GUI (graphical user interface), which—as its name suggests—is a graphical environment. In Microsoft Windows and the Macintosh GUI, the graphical system is tightly integrated into the operating system. You must use the environment that those operating systems provide. Linux and Unix systems divide the GUI into three separate components: the X Window System, also known as X and X11; a window manager; and a desktop environment.

The X Window System is a network-oriented graphics program that runs on top of the Linux kernel. The X Window System (X for short) is the standard graphical user interface for Linux. X uses a client-server protocol, the X protocol. The server is the computer (X terminal) with the monitor, keyboard, mouse, and server programs. The clients are application programs. Clients may run on the same computer as the server or on a different computer communicating over Ethernet via TCP/IP protocols. This can be confusing because X clients often run on what people think of as their server, in a networked environment; but in X, it is the screen and keyboard that are being "served out" to the client application. This means that users could run a program on a high-powered computer located in a different building but see the results on their own local computer. Most Linux users, including users of Red Hat Linux, use the version of X Window System called XFree86, which comes from the XFree86 project. The XFree86 Project is a group of programmers who maintain the free version of the X Window System for Intel-based computers.

X Window System is not tied to any specific desktop interface. It provides an underlying set of graphical operations that user interfaces, such as window managers, can use (more about window managers later). Thus, the X Window System is essentially a collection of functions to draw points, open windows, and display other graphics on a screen. X has a server component and a client component. The X server provides the fundamental services that create and manage the graphical interface. These services include controlling the video adapter, interpreting input from input devices such as the keyboard and the mouse, drawing and moving windows, and responding to requests from X clients on your computer. An X client is an application, such as a word processor, that runs in the graphical environment. X clients communicate with the X server when they need to display output on the screen. X server runs on your computer and controls the monitor, the keyboard, and the mouse or other pointing device. An X client may run locally or on a remote system. In addition, since the X server is the interface between the X Window System and the hardware (graphics card, mouse) on your system, there are many configuration utilities provided with X, such as redhat-config-xfree86, that allow you to set up the graphical display to specify such elements as monitor resolution or available colors.

But X server does not provide the menus or the mechanisms for such functions as switching windows, minimizing windows, or maximizing windows. These types of features are provided by another application, an X client called a window manager. A ***window manager*** is essentially the component that controls the appearance of windows and provides the means by which the user can interact with them. Virtually everything that appears on the screen in X is in a window; X makes it possible to have windows on the screen. The placement of windows, the borders, and the decoration (the appearance of the window frames and the placement and design of the controls such as buttons in a dialog box) of any window are managed by the window manager. It allows the manipulation of the windows themselves so that you may move, minimize, maximize, or switch windows using a mouse.

There are many window managers available in Linux. Red Hat Linux 6.x used the window manager called Enlightenment. Many users felt that Enlightenment required too much overhead (system resources), so with the release of Red Hat Linux 8.x and above, the Red Hat distribution of Linux now uses the window manager called Metacity.

There is one more component to a GUI—the desktop environment. A desktop is a user interface to system services, usually using icons and menus that allow a user to run programs and use a file system through a file manager without directly keying in commands, using techniques such as dragging and dropping. Although X can be run without a desktop, it is much easier to run with a desktop. A desktop includes common utility programs for tasks users commonly need such as a text editor, a calendar, or calculator. Most desktop components, such as background colors on the screen, can usually be changed by using dialog boxes. The two major desktops used with Linux are GNOME and KDE.

The default desktop environment used in Red Hat Linux is GNOME. However, Red Hat modified the look and feel of GNOME. Red Hat felt that it wanted to take responsibility for the default user experience with the user interface. This set of decisions is called the "Bluecurve look-and-feel." Bluecurve serves as a style guide that says how any given desktop environment or application should be configured by default, what its widgets and icons should look like, and so on. This look is configured for the GNOME desktop as well as the KDE desktop (and other types of programs) so that they all follow these guidelines. Bluecurve can also be considered a theme.

GNOME does not have a window manger of its own but can be used with any window manager. In Red Hat Linux, Metacity is the window manager that is used with GNOME. The user can easily change the look of applications by using the GNOME control center. GNOME provides desktop themes, which allow the user to change the way their desktop looks based on the user choice; for instance, the user could choose the ThinIce desktop theme, so all their windows and text are in some shade of pale blue and gray. In addition, many applications are included in GNOME—a graphics manipulation package, a spreadsheet program, an address book, and so on. Furthermore, GNOME provides the extensive support of drag and drop, which allows the user to perform such tasks as dropping a file onto the desktop, or onto a printer icon to print the file. GNOME also remembers the state of the desktop between logins so when users log on they will see the same desktop and applications they were using the last time they logged off. Also, GNOME applications can work together using such features as a common clipboard, where items can be saved and then pasted into any other GNOME applications. One of the important functions of a desktop is the management of files. GNOME provides this tool, and the file manager that GNOME uses is Nautilus.

1.7 ● Linux and Users

Since Linux is a secure operating system, you must log in in order to use the computer. There are two parts to the login—your user name and your password. If you are using your own computer, you should know what user name you gave yourself, as well as your password. If you are in lab environment, your system administrator will need to give you your user name and your password. By keying in your user name and confirming it with the password, you are identifying yourself to the operating system and ensuring you are an authorized user.

Linux provides for two types of users—the first is the *super user*, also called the *root user*. The second is the ordinary user. The super user, usually the system administrator, is the only user who can totally control the computer. The super user can also be referred to as the privileged user. The login name for the super user is root. The super user can do anything to the computer, including such items as adding other users or restricting rights to files and folders. The super user's login name is always *root*. The password is determined for the root at the time of installation, although it can be changed. It can be exceedingly dangerous to log in and use the computer as the root user. Normally, you only log in as root when you have specific computer or operating-system functions to alter. Even if you are working on your own computer, and hence are the system administrator for your own computer, you should normally log in as an ordinary user. The installation procedure should lead you through creating a user other than root.

The ordinary user has fewer privileges than the root user. In fact, the root user determines what privileges each user on the computer system has. Normally, the ordinary user can perform all essential tasks on the computer, such as running programs, copying files, or printing files. Thus, if you are working on your own computer, when you plan on doing ordinary computer-related tasks, you would not log in as root. If you are in a lab environment, you normally will not be able to log in as root, only as a regular user. You will need to get your login name and password in order to use the computer.

1.8 ● Booting the System

You need to know how to get the operating system files from the bootable disk into memory (RAM) so that you can use the computer. This process is known as "booting the system." These files reside on the hard disk. The following activity allows you to have your first hands-on experience with the computer. You are going to load Linux (or "boot the system").

Note: Since laboratory procedures will vary, check with your instructor before proceeding with these activities. A special process may be needed to boot the system if you are on a network.

1.9 • Activity: Booting the System

Note: The activities in this book assume Linux is installed at run level 3. See the Installation section of Appendix A for details.

STEP 1   Turn on the monitor, if necessary.

STEP 2   Be sure there is no disk in Drive A. If your Drive A has a door that shuts or latches, be sure it is open. (Remember that your instructions may be different if you are booting to a network. You may need a floppy disk, depending on your network setup.) Power on the computer by locating the power button and pressing it. The power button location can vary, depending on the design of the computer.

WHAT'S HAPPENING? The system checks itself in the diagnostic routine. You see information on the screen about your computer. After the system check is complete, Linux then begins its loading process. How it loads depends on which boot loader was selected when Red Hat Linux was installed. Introduced in Red Hat 7.2 was the boot loader called GRUB (GRand Unified Bootloader (GNU)). LILO (Linux Loader) is the legacy boot loader. In this text, GRUB is selected as the boot loader. So when you boot, you see the GRUB boot. Linux first boots the kernel, which in turn loads the device drivers for all of your peripherals, such as your hard drives, sound card, network card, and so on. As each driver is loaded and initialized, you will see a confirmation message and a green OK, indicating that the device loaded successfully. Next, the *init* program begins executing. It runs a variety of programs and scripts that configure your specific computer. If your system is configured to automatically start X Window System and GNOME, you are taken directly to a dialog box that questions your login name and then your password. You will then be taken to the screen following Step 5. Otherwise, you will see the following screen:

```
Red Hat Linux release 9 (Shrike)
Kernel 2.4.20-6 on an i686


RedHat9 login:
```

STEP 3   Key in your login name and press [Enter].

```
Password:_
```

STEP 4   Key in your password and press [Enter]

```
Last login: Tue Jun 10 09:32:46 on tty1
[cgillay@RedHat9 cgillay]$
```

WHAT'S HAPPENING? You have logged onto the system. The $ prompt tells you that you are logged in as an ordinary user. If you saw the # prompt, you would know that you were logged in as the root user.

STEP 5   Key in the following: **startx** [Enter]

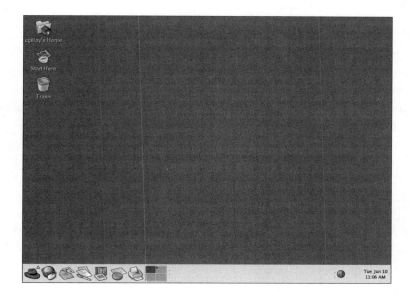

WHAT'S **HAPPENING?** You have successfully booted the system, loaded X Window System, loaded the window manager, Metacity, and loaded the desktop environment, GNOME with the Bluecurve theme.

1.10 ● Shutting Down the System

It is *critical* that you shut down Linux correctly every time. When you go through the shut-down process, Linux writes certain information to the disk. If you simply turn off the computer, Linux will not have an opportunity to take care of the process it needs to go through to shut down, and that could "crash" the system so you will be unable to boot the next time it is turned on.

1.11 ● Activity: The Linux Shut Down Procedure

STEP 1   Click the GNOME main menu button, the red hat, , usually in the lower-left corner of the screen.

WHAT'S HAPPENING? You have opened the GNOME menu. The bottom choice is Log Out.

STEP 2   Click **Log Out**.

WHAT'S HAPPENING? If when you booted your computer, you did not have to key in **startx**, but instead were directly taken to the GNOME desktop, when you click Log Out, go to Step 5. Otherwise, you will see a dialog box that gives you three choices under Action: Log Out, Shut Down, and Restart the computer. Log Out will leave the computer running and return you to the text interface. At the text interface, you will key in **exit**. This will then display the login prompt. This will allow another user to log in but not access any of the files or folders you were working with. The Shut Down choice will shut down the computer. Not everyone has the privilege to shut down the computer. If you click Shut Down, it may then request your password to ensure that you have the privilege of shutting down. The last choice is to Restart the computer or reboot. If your computer "hangs" (freezes during the process of shutting down), you may have to choose **Restart the computer** to get your system again operational. Before proceeding with Step 3, find out what the procedures are in your lab. You may be required only to log out, not to shut down the system.

STEP 3   Click **Shut Down**. Click **OK**.

WHAT'S HAPPENING? You may see a dialog box asking for your password to be sure that you are authorized to shut the system down.

STEP 4   If necessary, key in your password. Press ⎡Enter⎤

WHAT'S HAPPENING? Just as you got a confirmation message when you logged on, you also get a confirmation message as each process is shut down. Wait until you see the confirmation message, **Halting system** followed by **md: stopping all md devices** at the bottom of the screen. It is now OK to turn off your computer. On a computer that automatically shuts down, the screen will simply go blank, and you may only need to turn off the monitor.

STEP 5   Turn off the monitor. If necessary, turn off the power switch.

WHAT'S HAPPENING? You have successfully shut down Linux.

1.12 • The GNOME Desktop

Once you have logged onto the computer and keyed in startx, the GNOME workplace, called the desktop, appears on the monitor screen. The *desktop* is your primary work area. (See Figure 1.2, "The GNOME Desktop") Like your desk, it is a convenient location to place objects such as your tools, your program files, document files, and your devices. It can also provide access to a network or to the Internet.

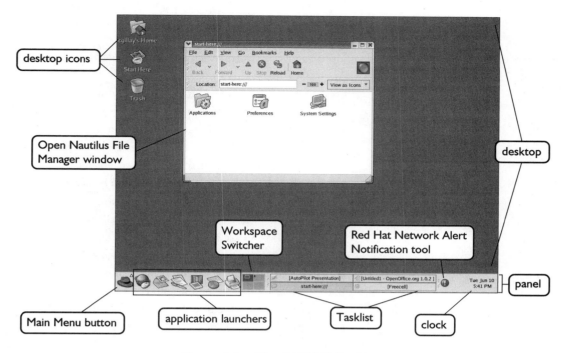

Figure 1.2 • The GNOME Desktop

Although the desktop varies depending on what objects have been placed on it, certain items are always present:

panel The focal point of GNOME is the panel. The *panel* is a graphic taskbar used to select, via the mouse, GNOME menus and applications. Typically located at the bottom of the screen, the taskbar contains the *Main Menu button*. Clicking this button displays a *menu* that allows you to accomplish such tasks as launching programs or altering the look of the desktop. It is also where you find commands for shutting down the computer and logging on as a different user.

application launchers Buttons that will start an application program. The default application launchers that are on the panel are shown in Figure 1.3, "Application Launchers."

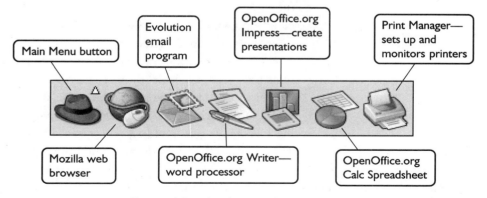

Figure 1.3 • Application Launchers

Main Menu button Opens the main menu.

Mozilla Browser	Used to open the web browser, use email, and so on. Mozilla replaces Netscape Navigator as the default browser.
Evolution Email	Used to send and receive email and manage your schedule.
OpenOffice.org Programs	An application suite of programs that include a word processor, spreadsheet program, and presentation manager (Writer, Calc, and Impress).
Tasklist	When you open a program, a document, a window, or a folder, a labeled button is placed on the taskbar. There will be a button on the taskbar to represent each open program, window, or folder. You can use the *taskbar buttons* to move between open windows. By clicking the desired button on the taskbar, you easily switch to a different task. All open windows are represented on the taskbar. The active window is identified by its button looking indented.
Icon	An *icon* is a pictorial representation of an object. An icon may represent a program, a document, or a folder that holds programs or documents. Shortcut icons provide convenient access to objects that are stored elsewhere. Icons can appear on the desktop and in windows; they can also open windows. The primary place you work and interact with data is in a window. One icon that will appear is an icon called *the username's Home*. This is your *home directory*, an area that is automatically set up for each user account. This is the default location where files you create will be stored. Also, by default two other icons appear: the Start Here icon, which launches the file manager, Nautilus, and the Trash icon.
clock	An applet that shows the current date and time.
Workspace Switcher	This applet shows a view of the multiple desktops areas of your GNOME desktop. A desktop is the collection of windows, toolbars, icons, and buttons that appear on your display screen (monitor). If you are working in a complex environment where you have many windows open running many programs simultaneously, it is useful to divide up your desktop into several areas, each appearing to be its own desktop. These areas are a virtual extension to your single desktop. By default, there are four quadrants (desktops) available. Each square represents each workspace (desktop) and shows the applications running in it. You may change to a different desktop by clicking the appropriate quadrant in the Workspace Switcher.
pointer	The *pointer* is the visual representation of your location on the screen.
Red Hat Alert Notification Tool	A tool that will allow you an easy method to ensure your system is up to date with current errata and bug fixes from Red Hat. If you click on the icon, a list of available

updates will be displayed. To update the system, you would click the button to launch the Red Hat Update Agent. If you have not yet registered with Red Hat, it will lead you through the registration component.

Print Manager   Allows you to manage your print job so you may view your current print jobs or cancel a print job. If you have not yet set up your printers, you will be led through a series of steps to set up your printer.

1.13 ● Windows

The GNOME desktop uses specially delineated areas of the screen called *windows*. A window is a defined work area (a rectangular frame) on the screen that is moveable and sizable; in it information is displayed with which you, the user, can interact. All windows-based programs run in windows. Some programs use windows that are split vertically or horizontally. The resulting window divisions are called *panes*. Figure 1.4, "A Window Divided into Panes," shows a window divided vertically into panes.

Figure 1.4 ● A Window Divided into Panes

A window can be moved freely around the desktop and can be minimized (called "iconified" in Linux) to a button, or maximized to fill the entire screen.

1.14 ● Pointing Devices

A graphical user interface allows you to select and manipulate objects on the screen. In Linux, an arrow, called the *mouse pointer* or *cursor*, tells you where you are on the screen. You manipulate the pointer by moving the pointing device. The most common pointing device is the mouse. As you move the mouse on a flat surface, it responds by moving the arrow on the screen. When you position the arrow over an object, you are *pointing* to it.

When you position the arrow over an object and click the left mouse button, you are selecting or activating that object. *Clicking* is the process of pressing and then immediately releasing the left mouse button once. *Double-clicking* means quickly pressing and releasing the left mouse button twice. When you double-click an object, you are usually about to act upon it. The left mouse button is called the *primary mouse button*. Whenever you press the right mouse button—the secondary mouse button—it is called *right-clicking*. Thus, an instruction to click means press and release the left mouse button. Remember, *click* refers to the left mouse button; *right-click* refers to the right mouse button. In addition, you may *mid-click* the item, which means you point to it and press the middle button. If you have a wheel mouse, you press the wheel for a mid-click. If you do not have a three-button mouse or a wheel mouse, you may emulate a mid-click by pressing the left and right button simultaneously. However, this feature must be enabled when installing Linux or configured later.

When you select an object and then press and hold the left mouse button, you are preparing to drag the object across the screen. Dragging is the process of moving an object. When you release the mouse button, you place the object in another location. The entire process is called *drag and drop*. *Dragging* means holding the left mouse button while you drag. *Right-drag-ging* means holding the right mouse button while you drag.

This textbook will refer to a mouse, but the same instructions may be followed for a trackball or integrated pointer. In addition, when the textbook refers to placing the mouse pointer on an object, it will use the term mouse, though technically it is a cursor.

1.15 • Activity: Using the Main Menu

STEP 1   Log on to your computer.

STEP 2   Click the Main Menu button, the red hat.

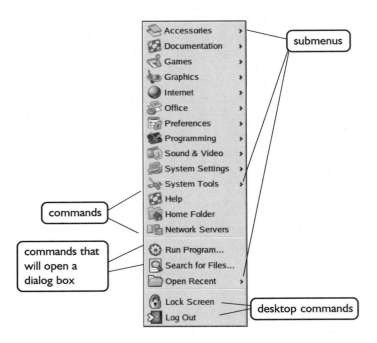

WHAT'S **HAPPENING?** You have opened a menu that presents a list of items from which you may choose. The Main menu lists the major functions on your system. The Main menu is divided into commands and submenus.

The commands include Help, which is help with GNOME; Home Folder, which will open your home directory in the Nautilus file manager; Run Program, which opens a dialog box allowing you to key in the specific name of a program; Network Servers, which allow you to see your network servers in the Nautilus file manager; Search for Files, which will open a dialog box that will allow you to key in a file name that you are looking for; and the desktop commands. The desktop commands include Lock Screen and Log Out. Lock Screen allows you to leave your computer with GNOME running and not allow other users to use or view your GNOME desktop. Log Out lets you log out, stop the system, or reboot it. Both the Run Program and Search for Files choices have three dots following them. These three dots are called an *ellipsis*. Any time you see a menu choice followed by an ellipsis that choice will open a dialog box so you may take further action.

In addition, Linux uses submenus. A *submenu* is a menu that opens another menu. In a submenu structure, the first in a series is a *parent menu* to the menu that follows. Each subsequent *child menu* becomes a parent to the next menu. Thus, a submenu is also referred to as a *hierarchical menu*; each time you make a choice, another menu opens. Since not all menus are cascading menus, a right-pointing triangular arrow appears to the right of any menu that can be cascaded. You can easily identify a submenu by the triangular arrow on its right, as shown below:

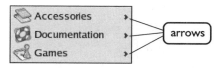

Your choices on the menu may vary, depending on what packages you decided to install when you installed Red Hat. If you are missing items on the menu, do not be concerned. In this textbook, during the installation process, all packages were installed. Within the submenus (in a complete installation), you see the following choices:

Accessories	This menu includes such programs as a calculator and a dictionary. One program you will use that is found on this menu is the Text Editor.
Documentation	All the printed manuals that come with the purchase of Red Hat Linux 9 Professional were installed here so that these manuals are available online. In addition, other documentation that was installed includes a glossary, a book called "Maximum RPM" that tells you how to use the Red Hat Package manager, a security guide, and a System Administration Primer.
Games	Many games can be selected from this menu.
Graphics	The graphic packages that allow you to use your digital camera, take screen shots, use a scanner, read PDFs (Portable Document Files) with Adobe Acrobat, and so on.
Internet	Access to Evolution Email, Instant Messenger, the Mozilla web browser, and so on.
Office	All the OpenOffice programs as well as programs such as a project management application and a mini-word-processor (AbiWord).
Preferences	Here is where you may customize your desktop by altering menus and toolbars, choosing a screen saver, or choosing a theme.
Programming	These are the tools for programming and include other text editors such as Vi Improved (vim) and Emacs.
Sound & Video	These are the programs that allow you to play a CD, control your volume, and other such items.
System Settings	Here you can configure your system, including items such as adding and removing application packages, configuring your display (monitor) or mouse, and managing users and groups. However, in order to use these tools, you will need to be root or have root privileges.

System Tools	These include items such as the programs to write to a CD, mount your floppy or CD-ROM drive, and open a character-based window (Terminal).
Help	Will access help about GNOME.
Home Folder	Will open the Nautilus file manager with your home directory as the default directory.
Network Servers	Will allow you to access any network servers that you have permission to access.
Run Program	Will present you with a dialog box where you may key in the name of a specific program you wish to run or choose from a list. Most programs that are installed on your system will be listed here.
Search for Files	Will present you with a dialog box where you may key in the name of a file you are looking for.
Open Recent	Will list the most recent programs you have used.

As you move the mouse pointer through the menu, you can tell which item is selected on a menu because it is highlighted. The purpose of highlighting is to identify a selected item. *Highlighting* alters the appearance of a selection, usually by displaying the selected item in a different or inverse color.

STEP 3   Move the mouse pointer to **Games** on the Main menu.

WHAT'S **HAPPENING?** To point is to place the mouse pointer on a specified item. You have opened the submenu for Games. Now all the installed games are displayed. To choose one of the games, you must click the game you wish to play.

STEP 4   Click **FreeCell**.

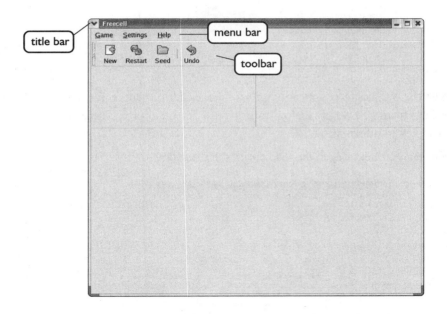

FreeCell is an application program. When you clicked it, you loaded the program files into memory. When a program is in memory, it may be used. You can now play a card game called FreeCell. Playing this game will allow you to become familiar with your mouse as well as introduce you to some of the common elements of an application program.

Every application program has a *title bar* with its name in it. In addition, an application program will usually have a *menu bar*. The FreeCell menu bar has three menu choices: Game, Settings, and Help. Each has its first letter underlined. Whenever you see an underlined letter on a menu bar, you may open, or *drop down*, the menu by pressing the **Alt** key and the underlined letter, or you may select the menu by clicking it. Most people prefer clicking the mouse. Many windows will also have a toolbar. A toolbar button allows you to click a button that is a shortcut to a menu item.

STEP 5   Click **Game**.

You have several choices on the menu. If an item is dimmed, it is unavailable. Most of the choices have a underlined letter. Pressing the underlined letter will select that choice. Also, many choices have a keystroke, or a combination of keystrokes, next to the menu choice. Rather than clicking the mouse, you may use the keyboard commands. You are going to select a specific game to play.

STEP 6   Click **New game with seed...**

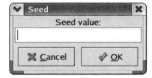

WHAT'S HAPPENING? A dialog box appears. A *dialog box* either presents information to you or requests information from you. Many dialog boxes have a default choice. There is also a text box where you can key in information.

STEP 7   Click in the text box. Key in the following: **100**. Click **OK**.

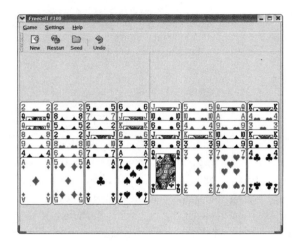

WHAT'S HAPPENING? Now you may play the game. The object of the game is to place all the cards in the four empty right-hand squares above the cards. The cards should be separated by suit and stacked in order of rank, beginning with the ace, then the two, etc. You may temporarily place cards in the left-hand empty squares as you move the cards around. On the playing field, you must place the red and black cards in alternate order.

STEP 8   Click the ace of diamonds. Click the empty square farthest to the right above the cards.

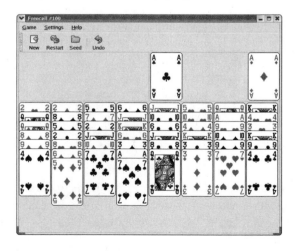

WHAT'S HAPPENING? You moved the ace of diamonds to the top. At the same time, the ace of clubs also moved. At this point, you are going to close the program and return to the desktop.

STEP 9   Click **Game**. Click **Quit**.

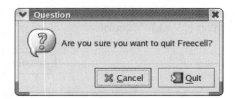

WHAT'S **HAPPENING?** You are presented with a message box. A *message box* is a box that informs you of a condition. It interrupts your current task to alert you to a problem with your system, to inform you of an error you have made, to request a confirmation of a command that could have serious consequences, or to explain why the command you have chosen will not work. Often a message box will have a default choice.

Message boxes most often ask you to confirm, cancel, or retry an action after you have corrected the problem. Both message boxes and dialog boxes provide command buttons to accomplish these tasks.

A *command button* is an example of a *control* because it controls what happens. In this case, you have two choices—Quit, which acknowledges that you do wish to carry out your command of exiting FreeCell, and Cancel, which cancels your command to quit the game. Command buttons also have default values. If you look carefully at the Cancel command button, you will see that it looks indented or pressed in and has a dotted border, indicating that it is the default choice.

STEP 10 Click **Quit**.

WHAT'S **HAPPENING?** You have closed FreeCell and returned to the desktop.

1.16 • The Nautilus File Manager

When you use GNOME, there are no open windows. However, there is an icon on the desktop labeled **Start Here**. When you double-click the icon, you open a window that is the Nautilus file manager as well as a File Transfer Protocol (FTP) client application for transferring files between your computer and an FTP site.

FTP stands for *File Transfer Protocol*, one of the standard protocols defined for the Internet. It is a client/server-based protocol, whereby a client program on one system (usually your computer) sends requests to a server program on another computer system (an FTP site) and receives replies from the site. FTP allows the fastest and safest means of file transfers on the Internet. FTPing files is much better and faster than simply attaching a file as an attachment to an email message.

An FTP client is a computer that is running FTP client software. When you use FTP to download files from an FTP site, you are actually running an FTP client (such as the Nautilus file manager) on your computer. An FTP site consists of an FTP server program located on an Internet host computer. Many companies and organizations maintain FTP sites (also known as "FTP servers").

These servers allow you to copy files such as free programs and evaluation versions of software or to place files for use by others; for example, a site on which you place your web site pages for your Internet Service Provider (ISP) or a site on which you place a photograph file for use in an online auction.

The Nautilus file manager supports standard file management features such as copying files and directories. Nautilus is an attempt to integrate your access to your files, your applications, any media applications you have, and the web so that you have one location for all the resources that you use. See Figure 1.5, "The Nautilus Window."

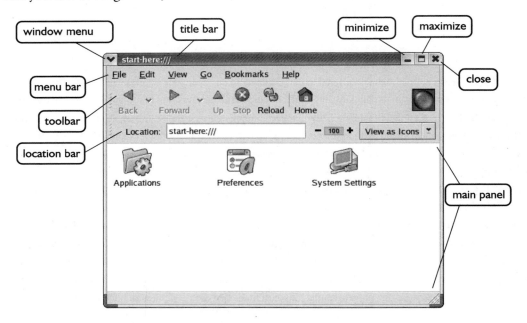

Figure 1.5 · The Nautilus File Manager Window

window menu	When clicked, it will drop down a menu for controlling the operation of the window, sometimes called a system or operations menu.
title bar	The name of the window and the handle for moving the window around on the desktop.
Minimize button	When clicked, it will keep the window open but minimize it. The window will still appear on the panel as a button. In Linux, minimize is also referred to as "iconify."
Maximize button	When clicked, it acts as a toggle switch, making the window fill the entire screen or return to its default size.
Close button	When clicked, it will close the window and the application. Since the application will be closed, it will no longer have a button on the panel.
menu bar	Contains available menus for this window. Clicking on a menu choice will open a menu with more choices. These choices in the Nautilus file manager window contain choices for most of your file- and directory-management tasks and also allow you to customize how you wish to view your files and folders.
toolbar	Toolbars contain buttons, usually with icons (small images) to identify each button. Each button performs some function. Toolbar buttons can be graphical shortcuts to items on a menu or are navigational tools for the window. In general, in the Nautilus file manager, these toolbar buttons are primarily navigational and allow you to browse and search your directories. An important button on the toolbar is the Home button. This will display your home directory.
location bar	Allows you to view your current location or key in a new location in the file system or an FTP site.

main panel   This is where your files, folders, and applications are displayed. You may customize your view.

1.17 ● Activity: Exploring the Nautilus File Manager

STEP 1   Double-click the Start Here icon on the desktop.

STEP 2   On the menu bar, click **View**.

WHAT'S HAPPENING? By default, Toolbar, Location Bar, and Status bar are checked. Side Pane is not checked. A check mark means that a feature is enabled whereas an unchecked item is not available. Each time you click an item, you enable or disable the chosen feature and the menu closes.

STEP 3   Click **Side Pane**. If Toolbar, Location Bar, and Status bar are not checked, click **View** and check each one to set it.

STEP 4   In the right pane of the Start Here window, click **Applications**.

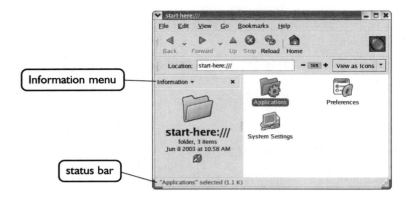

WHAT'S HAPPENING? When you select an object, the status bar gives information about that object. It names the object and gives the size of the selected object. In addition, there is a drop-down Information menu that displays different types of information in the start-here window.

STEP 5   On the Information drop-down list box, click the down arrow.

WHAT'S HAPPENING? Each of these choices represents a different look in the right pane. An *emblem* is a small icon that you can add to a file or folder so you may visually mark the item. The available emblems are listed here. The History selection will allow you to review where you have been. The Notes is like a note that you can attach to a file or folder with information that will further identify the contents of the file or folder.

STEP 6   Click **Tree** in the menu.

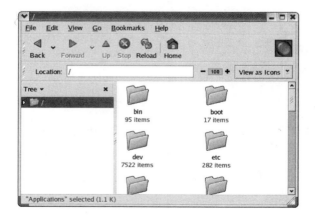

WHAT'S HAPPENING? By clicking **Tree** in the side pane, you opened a display of the hierarchical structure of your disk. The slash (/) is the root or top of the hierarchy. There is a chevron (right-pointing arrow) indicating that this item can be expanded.

STEP 7   Click the right-pointing arrow next to the / (root folder). Click the **etc** folder to select it. Do not expand the **etc** directory.

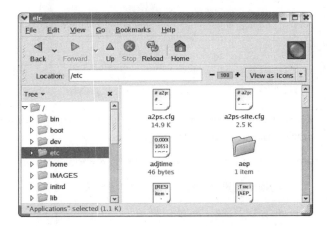

WHAT'S HAPPENING? When you clicked the chevron, you expanded the root directory. When you clicked the **etc** folder, you selected the folder. When you expand an entry, then select a directory—in this case, the **etc** directory in the sidebar window—you see the files and directories that are in that directory. Note that now the root directory has a downward pointing arrow indicating that it can be collapsed.

STEP 8   Click the downward-pointing arrow at the top of the tree next to the / folder.

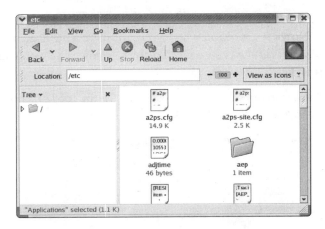

WHAT'S HAPPENING? Although you collapsed the tree in the sidebar window, note that the Main panel display still shows the files located in the **etc** directory. The location bar states that you are in the /**etc** directory.

STEP 9   Click the root directory folder.

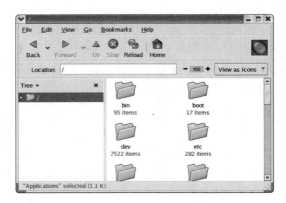

WHAT'S HAPPENING? Now the display in the right pane is of the files and directories in the root directory. Again, the location bar indicates the root directory (/).

STEP 10 Click the down arrow on the information menu and choose **Notes**.

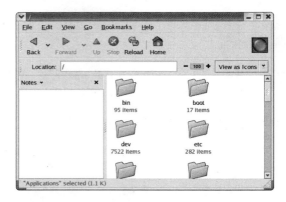

WHAT'S HAPPENING? **Notes** is a location where you can create a message, a "note" to yourself about the contents of what is in the right pane. To create a note, you would click inside the note and key in your information.

STEP 11 Click the X in the information menu to close it. On the toolbar, click the **Home** button. On the menu bar, click **View**. Click **Side Pane** to set it.

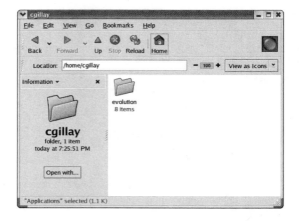

WHAT'S HAPPENING? In this example, you have opened a window with one object in it. The object is a folder. Your home directory may be empty. If you look at the panel, you will see that your user name appears in the Tasklist. If you look at the Location in the window, you will see

/home/cgillay. Instead of **cgillay**, you will see your user login name. Each user will have a **/home** directory. The name following **/home** will be the name you logged on as. Again, in this example, it is **/home/cgillay**. Your display will differ. It will be referred to as **/home/*user*** where **user** will vary, depending on the login name. On the Tasklist, the button looks indented, indicating that it has the focus or is active. The title bar states **user**, and the location bar displays the location, **/home/user**. The home directory is created when the user is created and is populated with a default set of files. However, the files are hidden. In this example, there is one folder that was created by the user **cgillay** when she activated her email account. The home directory is the default location where the logged-in user stores user-created files and directories.

Windows programs are composed of what are called widgets. **Widgets** are graphic control elements for specific tasks. There are widgets for items such as text fields or command buttons. The items that were delineated in Figure 1.5 listed the various controls (widgets).

STEP 12   Click the Minimize button on your user window.

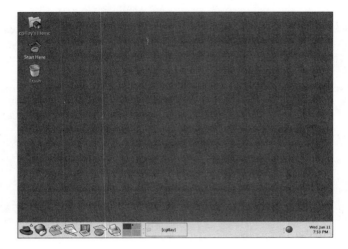

WHAT'S **HAPPENING?** You have minimized the window. It is now in the Tasklist on the panel. The home directory window is open but not the focus, nor is it active.

STEP 13   Click the home directory button in the Tasklist.

WHAT'S **HAPPENING?** You have restored the window to its previous size. It is now open and the focus. The button in the Tasklist also is indented, further telling you that **/home/user** is the focus.

STEP 14 Double-click the **/home/*user*** title bar.

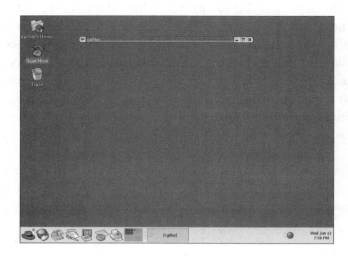

WHAT'S HAPPENING? When you double-click the title bar you shade or unshade the focused window. As you can see, the window "rolled" up like a window shade. To unroll it, you double-click the title bar again

STEP 15 Double-click the **/home/*user*** title bar to unshade it. Click the Maximize button on the **/home/*user*** title bar.

WHAT'S HAPPENING? The window now fills the entire screen.

STEP 16 Click the Maximize button.

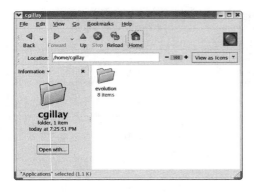

WHAT'S HAPPENING? ▷ The Maximize button is a toggle that alternates between full screen and restored size. By clicking it, you restored the window to its previous size

STEP 17   Click the windows menu down arrow on the **/home/*user*** title bar.

WHAT'S HAPPENING? ▷ You have dropped down the Windows menu. You can choose any selection on the menu by clicking. The menu selections are as follows:

Minimize	Minimizes a window to appear on the panel as part of the Tasklist. You may also click the Minimize button on the title bar to achieve the same effect.
Maximize	Enlarges the window to fill the entire screen. You may also click the Maximize button on the title bar to achieve the same effect.
Roll Up	Rolls up the window into a "shade." You may also double-click the title bar to achieve the same effect.
Move	Immediately places the mouse pointer in the current window so you may move the window about the screen. You may click the title bar with the mouse and drag the window to achieve the same effect.
Close	Closes a window. You may also click the Close button on the title bar to achieve the same effect.
Put on All Workspaces	The Workspace Switcher, as mentioned previously, shows your entire virtual desktop as separate rectangles in a box on the Panel. Open windows appear as small colored rectangles in each workspace. This choice on the Window Menu allows you to have a specific window appear in all of your workspaces.

Move to Workspace 1   This is your current workspace and is dimmed since it is the current default choice.

Move to Workspace 2, 3 and 4   Allows you to move the current window to a specific workspace.

Here is where you can see differences in the window manager you are using. This computer is running Metacity, the default window manager. Metacity is a "minimalist" window manager, and hence has minimal choices. If you were running the Sawfish window manager, which offers more bells and whistles, you would have many more choices on this menu, such as Frame type, which would offer you choices on how you wish your window to appear; for instance, as a Title only or Frame style, which would let you choose the style of the borders around each window. Even though you are running GNOME, the window manager still determines the look and feel of how windows and menus appear.

STEP 18 Minimize the window. On the panel, right-click your *user* name button.

WHAT'S HAPPENING? The right-click menu on the panel opens a menu, which also can control the window. The choices are almost identical to the drop-down Window menu except your only choice for Workspaces is for all of them. Again, if you were using a window manager such as Sawfish, you would have more choices such as Kill app which forces a window to close, usually when an application is not responding.

STEP 19 Click **Unminimize**. Click the Close button on the /home/*user* title bar.

WHAT'S HAPPENING? You have closed the /**home**/*user* window and have returned to the desktop.

1.18 • Manipulating the Panel

If you have worked with Microsoft Windows or the Macintosh desktops, you will find many similarities between those desktops and GNOME. However, there are features you may not have used or are not available in any desktop but the GNOME desktop. One difference you may find is working with onscreen windows. In GNOME, in order to accomplish any task, you must first move the *keyboard focus*, simply called focus, to the window of interest. The keyboard focus determines where your keystrokes show up when you key in information. Although most often just placing the mouse pointer in a window or dialog box will move the focus to that window, sometimes you may need to take an additional step and click in the window or dialog box to make the window active. Also remember that you will use the mid-mouse button to accomplish some tasks.

In addition, you may customize the panel and have different types of panels. You may change its size or location. You may also manipulate the panel in other ways. You may hide it, have it always on top, or enable or disable the *hide buttons*. To manipulate the panel settings, you use a property sheet.

A *property sheet* is more complex version of a dialog box. Remember, a dialog box is a window in which you provide information to a program. Many objects in Linux (folders, files, the desktop, the panel, etc.) have properties associated with them that can be viewed or altered. The settings in an object's property sheet affect how the object looks and, sometimes, how it works. A property sheet allows you to look at or change information about an object. It can be accessed easily by right-clicking an object and then clicking Properties on the shortcut menu. When you open a property sheet, there may be multiple sheets. Each sheet has its name on a tab, much like the tabs on file folders. To access a sheet of interest, click its tab.

1.19 • Activity: Working with the Panel

STEP 1   Right-click the Main Menu button.

WHAT'S HAPPENING? You have opened a right-click menu. A *right-click menu* provides an efficient way for you to perform an operation on an object. Right-click menus are displayed at the location of the pointer. They eliminate the need to move the pointer to the menu bar and then select from the menu. What you can do with an object selected from the panel depends on what the object is. In this case, you can receive help or move the main menu or remove it from the panel. Since this is the main panel (and you must have one panel), removing it is not a good idea.

STEP 2   Right-click the calendar object on the right side of the panel.

WHAT'S HAPPENING? With the calendar object, you have more choices available.

STEP 3   Click **Preferences**.

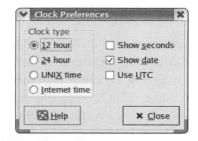

WHAT'S HAPPENING? Here you can choose to display the clock in many different formats.

STEP 4   Click **Close**. Left-click the calendar icon.

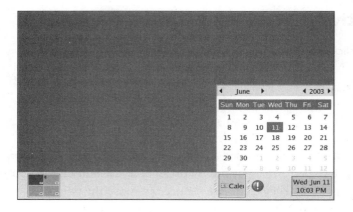

WHAT'S HAPPENING? Here you opened a calendar for the current month and date. If you look at the Workspace Switcher, you see that this calendar appears in every workspace as you see a small rectangle representing the calendar.

STEP 5   Right-click the calendar icon on the Panel.

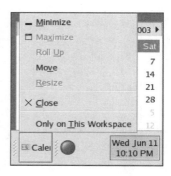

WHAT'S HAPPENING? You may manipulate the calendar as well. One of the choices is Only on **This Workspace**. If you made that choice, then the calendar would only appear in your current workspace.

STEP 6   Click **Close**. Right-click the panel in an empty spot. Click **Properties**.

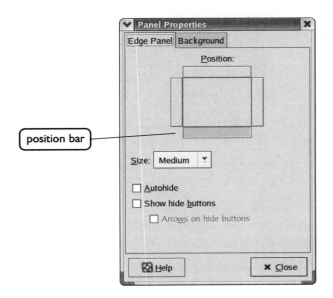

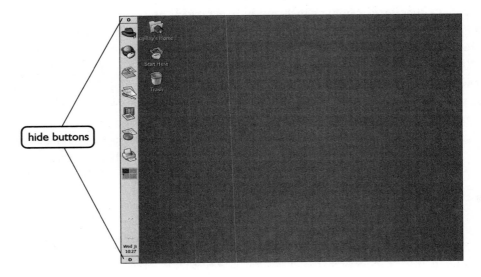

WHAT'S HAPPENING? Here is where you determine how you want this panel to behave. You can change the location of the panel by clicking one of the position bars. You can change the size of the panel itself using the Size drop-down list box. You can Autohide the Panel, which means that the panel will disappear until your mouse gets near it and you can enable the hide buttons with or without arrows.

STEP 7   Click the left-most position bar. Click the **Show hide buttons** check box to set it. Click the **Arrows on hide buttons** check box to set it. Click **Close**.

WHAT'S HAPPENING? You have moved the panel to the left side of the screen and enabled the hide buttons.

STEP 8   On the panel, click the hide button, the top arrow.

WHAT'S HAPPENING? The panel was moved off the screen. To return it to view, you simply click the visible down arrow.

STEP 9   Click the visible arrow. Right-click the panel in an empty spot. Click **Properties**. Clear the **Show hide buttons** and **Arrows on hide buttons** check boxes. Click **Close**. Right-click in an empty spot on the panel. Point to **New Panel**.

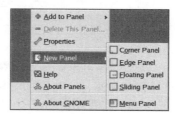

WHAT'S HAPPENING? You have returned the panel to its original location and configuration. You then opened the panel menu. Here is where you can choose to add additional panels to your desktop. You must have at least one panel running at all times. However, you may have more than one panel and/or you choose the type of panel you wish. The selection of panels includes Edge panel, Corner panel, Sliding panel, and Floating panel. An edge panel is like the main panel that you have seen when you started GNOME. It stretches along the whole length of one of the screen edges. You may add another edge panel to another edge of the screen. A corner panel is also along the edge of the screen. However, it will stretch only as much as necessary to show the icons and applets it contains. A sliding panel is like an aligned panel, except it may be positioned anywhere and is not tied to an edge. As you add objects, it grows in only one direction. A floating panel can "float" anywhere on the desktop.

In addition, icons on any panel may be moved anywhere on the panel by either right-clicking the icon and choosing Move or by selecting the item on the panel with a mid-click and then dragging it to the location you wish.

STEP 10   Right-click the Workspace Switcher icon. Click **Move**.

WHAT'S HAPPENING? You see a four-headed arrow, ⊕ , that allows you to move the Workspace Switcher icon.

STEP 11   Left-click the Workspace Switcher icon to set it in position. Mid-click the Workspace Switcher icon. Again, the four-headed arrow appears, allowing you to move the object.

STEP 12   Release the mid-click button to set the Workspace Switcher icon in position.

WHAT'S HAPPENING? You have returned the panel to its original configuration.

1.20 • The Taskbar and the Workspace Switcher

On the panel is the GNOME Workspace Switcher. In order to understand the Workspace Switcher settings, you first need to know what it is. Essentially, the desktop is larger than it looks. A workspace is a part of the desktop that occupies the entire display screen. Using this applet allows you to have many open windows and applications but be able to treat each as a separate desktop, minimizing clutter. You are creating virtual desktops. A *virtual desktop* is one that is larger than the dimensions of your computer's screen. The Workspace Switcher applet allows you to move between the desktops. Workspaces are divided into columns and rows. Each workspace on your desktop contains the same desktop background, panels, and menus. However, you can run different applications and open different windows in each workspace. But you can display only one workspace at a time. The default setup of the desktop is to have four workspaces. Figure 1.6, "The Workspace Switcher," shows four pages in a small display area on the panel.

Figure 1.6 • The Workspace Switcher

Each quadrant represents a desktop area for each virtual desktop equal to the size of the display screen. To go to a different screen, you click in one of the squares. Open windows in the desktop show up as colored rectangles in those squares.

The Taskbar, also called the Window List, shows currently open applications. There is a button for each open window. A task can be a program that is running or a window that is displaying files and directories. As you have seen, clicking a button moves you to that window, and a right-click allows you to choose whether to open, close, or kill the window. The Taskbar can also be configured using its properties menu.

1.21 • Activity: Using the Taskbar and Workspace Switcher

STEP 1   Double-click the **Start Here** icon on the desktop.

STEP 2   Double-click your home directory icon on the desktop to open it.

STEP 3   Click the Main Menu button. Point to **Games**. Click **GNOME Tetravex**.

STEP 4   Click the Main Menu button. Point to **Accessories**. Click **Text Editor**.

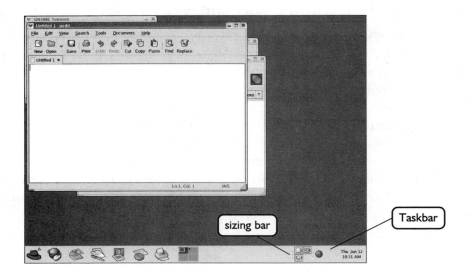

WHAT'S HAPPENING? You have opened four windows. One is the Start Here window, another your home directory, yet another is a game, and the last is a simple text editor. If you look at the panel, you will see all four open windows listed in the Taskbar. If you cannot see all of the titles of the open windows, you can alter the display of the Taskbar so it is larger.

STEP 5   Click on the sizing bar to the left of the Taskbar and drag to the left until you can see the entire title of each open window. *Note:* depending on the positioning of the items on the panel, you may need to move the icons so that you may stretch the Window List.

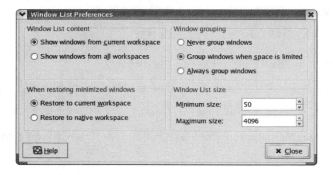

WHAT'S HAPPENING? Now you can see all your open windows.

STEP 6   Right-click the sizing bar. Click **Preferences**.

WHAT'S HAPPENING? You have opened the Window List (Taskbar) properties sheet. Here you may alter the properties of the Windows List, how you want it to display, what you want on it, and even determine the size.

STEP 7   Click **Close**. Right-click the gedit title bar.

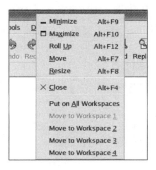

WHAT'S HAPPENING? Right-clicking the title bar of a window is another way to access the Window Menu. Here you may move this window to another workspace.

STEP 8   Click **Move to Workspace 2**.

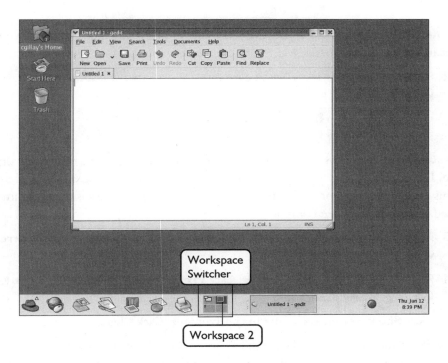

WHAT'S HAPPENING? You are now in a different workspace or virtual desktop. You have only one open window in this area. You moved your application to a different workspace. The Window List only displays the open window in this workspace, not all your open windows.

STEP 9   Right-click the Workspace Switcher on the panel. Click **Preferences**.

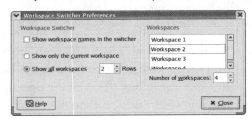

WHAT'S HAPPENING? Here is where you can customize the Workspace Switcher. You may name each workspace and display the names as well as choose how many workspaces you want to have.

STEP 10 In the Workspaces list box, click **Workspace 2** twice. Key in the following: **GAMES**

WHAT'S HAPPENING? You now have named Workspace 2.

STEP 11 Click the checkbox for **Show workspace names in the switcher**. Click **Close**.

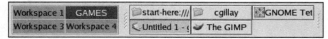

WHAT'S HAPPENING? Now your workspaces are named. But you still do not see all your open programs in the other workspaces.

STEP 12 Right-click the sizing bar. Click **Preferences**. Click **Show windows from all workspaces** to set it. Click **Close**.

WHAT'S HAPPENING? Now you can see all your open windows regardless of which workspace each is in. If you cannot see all the names of all the open windows, you need to size the window list. In this example, there is one more program open—The GIMP. This is the program that is being used to capture the screen output.

STEP 13 Right-click the sizing bar. Click **Preferences**. Click **Show windows from current work space** to set it. Click **Close**.

STEP 14 Right-click the Workspace Switcher. Click **Preferences**. Click **GAMES** twice. Key in the following: **Workspace 2**

STEP 15 Clear **Show workspace name in the switcher**. Click **Close**.

WHAT'S HAPPENING? You have returned the values to their defaults. To move objects from one workspace to another, you drag the object in the Workspace Switcher to the desired window.

STEP 16 In the Workspace Switcher, drag the rectangle in Workspace 2 to the left to Workspace 1. Click Workspace 1. If you were in Workspace 1, then you could move objects from Workspace 1 to Workspace 2 and so on.

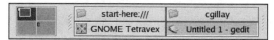

WHAT'S HAPPENING? Now all of your windows and applications are in one workspace. In addition to separate desktops, you may also have *virtual consoles*. A console, also called the *terminal*, is a device with which a user communicates with the operating system, usually the keyboard and monitor that is working with Linux. Although you have only one physical terminal, Linux allows you to access up to 63 virtual consoles. Some are set so that you may log in as a different user or even the same user. Virtual consoles exist outside of the GUI, each with its own shell command prompt. You cannot start another session of X Window System in the virtual console, but you can do so using the command prompt. You may actually log in again.

If, for instance, you had a lengthy job, you could create a virtual console, start the job, and then switch back to your other consoles. Or if you had a problem shutting down, you could switch to a virtual console and shut down the system. There are seven virtual consoles by default. You can move among them by pressing **Ctrl** + **Alt** and Function keys **F1** through **F7**. Console 1 is the system console, and console 7 is the GUI.

If your computer is running any type of virtual software such as Vmware, you will not be able to do the next steps. A virtual machine software package allows an operating system such as Windows to be installed on a computer but then allows a different operating system, such as Linux, to run on top of the base operating system without altering the base operating system.

STEP 17   Press **Ctrl** + **Alt** + **F2**.

```
Red Hat Linux release 9 (Shrike)
Kernel 2.4.20-6 on an i686


RedHat9 login:
```

WHAT'S **HAPPENING?** As you can see, you can log in again and create a new session. Your prompt will be different. In the last line, **RedHat9 login: , RedHat9** is the name of this specific computer.

STEP 18   Press **Ctrl** + **Alt** + **F7**.

WHAT'S **HAPPENING?** You are returned to the GUI. If you do create virtual consoles, you must be sure to close the console session. If, in fact, you had logged in, to close the console, you would key in **exit Enter**.

STEP 19   Close all open windows.

WHAT'S **HAPPENING?** You have returned to the desktop.

1.22 ● Customizing the Panel

As you saw when you opened the Main menu, included with Red Hat are a large variety of small, useful programs, called applets. Some of the programs are GNOME-specific; others are utility programs that are packaged with Red Hat, but not GNOME-specific. You can create a Panel button for any item on the menus or any other applications you have installed.

1.23 ● Activity: Customizing the Panel

STEP 1   Right-click the Panel. Point to **Add to Panel**.

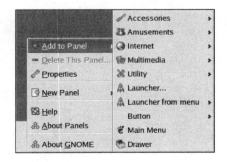

WHAT'S **HAPPENING?** Here are programs that you can add to the panel. One choice is to add a Log Out button to the panel. This saves you the trouble of opening the menu.

STEP 2   Point to **Button**. Click **Log Out**.

Log out button

WHAT'S **HAPPENING?** On the panel you now have a new button: a door. Now when you wish to log out, you may click this button.

STEP 3   Click the Log Out button.

WHAT'S **HAPPENING?** By clicking a panel button, you can quickly log out.

STEP 4   Click **Cancel**.

STEP 5   Right-click the Log Out button. Click **Help**.

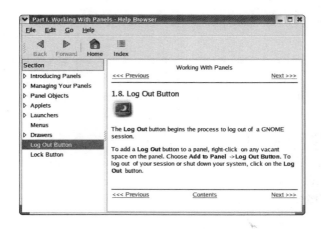

WHAT'S **HAPPENING?** Here you find the purpose of the Log Out button. If you forget or do not know what an item does on the panel, you may right-click it and choose **Help**.

STEP 6   Close the open window.

STEP 7   Click the Main menu. Point to **Games**. Right-click **FreeCell**.

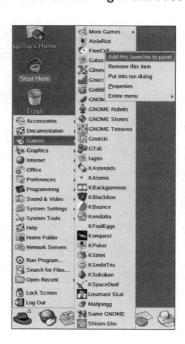

WHAT'S **HAPPENING?** You may add FreeCell to the panel. This type of button is called a launcher, as it "launches" a program.

STEP 8 Click **Add this launcher to panel**. Click outside the menu to close it.

FreeCell button

WHAT'S **HAPPENING?** Now you have a panel button for the **FreeCell** game. You can add some built-in utilities. One of the most common things you will want to do is to use the command line. You need to have access to the terminal window. Rather than using the menus, you can add a button to the panel.

STEP 9 Click the Main Menu. Point to **System Tools**. Right-click **Terminal**. Click **Add this launcher to panel**. Click outside the menu to close it.

Terminal command line button

WHAT'S **HAPPENING?** Now you see a terminal window icon on the panel. Another useful utility is a text editor. You also can place a button on the panel for this utility program.

STEP 10 Click the Main menu. Point to **Accessories**. Right-click **Text Editor**. Click **Add this launcher to panel**. Click outside the menu to close it.

Text Editor button

WHAT'S **HAPPENING?** Now you see a text editor icon on the panel. As you can see, the Panel is becoming cluttered with icons. You can use a drawer. A drawer can contain applets and launchers but takes up only one slot on the panel.

STEP 11 Right-click the panel. Point to **Add to Panel**. Click **Drawer**.

Drawer button

WHAT'S **HAPPENING?** A drawer is a secondary panel that extends perpendicular to the Panel. You can see the arrow above the drawer that opens it.

STEP 12 Left-drag-and-drop the Log Out icon on the drawer.

STEP 13 Left-drag-and-drop the Text Editor icon on the drawer.

STEP 14 Left-drag-and-drop the FreeCell icon on the drawer.

WHAT'S HAPPENING? You now have your icons neatly grouped. To close the drawer, you click the down arrow. Once closed, there is an up arrow to open the drawer. One of the important reasons for having a text editor available to you is that in the Linux/Unix world, **configuration files** are plain text files. In computers and in computer networks, a *configuration* often refers to the specific hardware and software details in terms of devices attached, capacity or capability, and exactly what the system is made up of. The configuration information for Linux is stored in a file called **fstab**.

STEP 15   Click the Text Editor icon. Click **File**. Click **Open**.

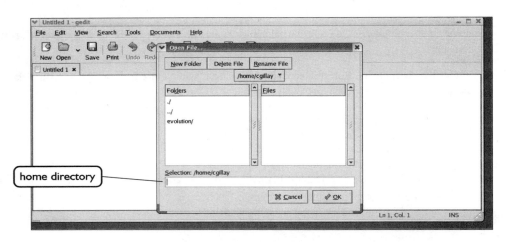

WHAT'S HAPPENING? You have opened the text editor called gedit. When you try to open an existing file or save a file, gedit, like most application programs, will first look in your home directory. In this example, it is **/home/cgillay**. In this example there are no files in the home directory, but there is one named folder, evolution. In addition, the **./** represents the current directory (**/home/cgillay**) and the **../** represents the parent of the current directory. The file you are interested in is the **fstab** file which is located in the **/etc** directory.

The **etc** directory is a very important directory in Linux. It contains most of the system configuration files for your specific computer. These are the files that are used when you start your computer. The file called **fstab** lists the file systems that are mounted automatically when the system starts. An **fstab** file contains several fields, each field separated by a space or tab. They are as follows:

```
<device> <mountpoint> <filesystemtype> <options> <dump> <fsck>
```

\<device\>	The first field is the name of the device to be mounted
\<mountpoint\>	The directory in your file system structure where you want the file system on this device to be attached.
\<filesystemtype\>	The type of file system that is going to be mounted.

\<options\>	Different options for that file system, such as not being automatically mounted (noauto).
\<dump\>	A value that is used by the dump command to determine whether a file system needs to be dumped, backing up the file system.
\<fsck\>	A value that determines whether the file system needs to be checked at reboot and in what order. If the field has a value of 1, it indicates a boot partition; other partitions have a value of 2. If there is a 0, it means that **fsck** does not need to check the file system.

Users familiar with the concept of disk drives being assigned a letter of the alphabet, with the first hard drive called C: and the first floppy drive A:, and so on, will find a completely different mind set in Linux.

Every piece of hardware that is connected to your computer is a device. Each device has a piece of software, called a device driver, that allows the system to interact with the device. In Linux, each device is identified by the location of the driver in the file system. Thus, all disks are united into a single file system. Some naming conventions are listed in Table 1.2: "Device Names."

Device	Description
fd0	First floppy drive
cdrom	CD-ROM drive
hda1	First partition on the first IDE (Integrated Device Electronics) hard drive.
hda2	Second partition on the first IDE hard drive.
hdb1	First partition on the second IDE hard drive
sda1	First partition on the first SCSI (Small Computer System Interface) hard drive.
sda2	Second partition on the second SCSI hard drive.

Table 1.2 · Device Names

Devices listed as None are really not devices, but this method is used by Linux to provide to programs and users information found in computer memory.

However, having a device name is not sufficient for Linux. In order to access the file systems on each device, they must each be mounted. *Mount* means to connect the file system to the directory tree structure. The root file system (/), **swap**, and /**boot** (a directory that usually contains the bootstrap loader—the utility that starts the operating system as well as the kernel images) are mounted automatically when you start the system. The swap partition supports virtual memory and provides disk space for the swap file.

In addition, each removable drive has a mount point, which is simply another directory in the file system. Typically, temporary mount points are kept in the directory called /**mnt**. When Linux is installed, it automatically creates two mount points, /**mnt/floppy** and /**mnt/cdrom**. Thus, /**dev/fd0** refers to the device drive for the floppy disk, whereas /**mnt/floppy** refers to the location in the file system where you can view the contents of that device. If you wanted to see what was on the disk in the floppy drive, you would first have to mount it, then open the directory **/mnt/floppy**. As you will learn, in Linux you do not simply place a disk in the drive or remove it at any time; you must mount and unmount every disk every time. Now you are going to take a look at your **fstab** file.

STEP 16 In the **Selection** text box, key in the following: **/etc/fstab**. Click **OK**.

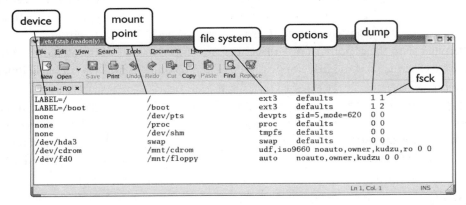

WHAT'S HAPPENING? The Device column lists the name for the device. The mount point is where the device is mounted. The File System tells which file system is being used on that device. The file system **ext3** is the native file system for Linux, whereas **vfat** is for accessing Windows or DOS disks. Options determine whether, for instance, the mounting is automatic. If the option is **Auto**, the device is mounted automatically. If the option is **noauto**, it must be mounted manually. Options also includes such items as who has what permission for what devices and whether the file system needs to be checked. Figure 1.7 shows another example of an **fstab** file.

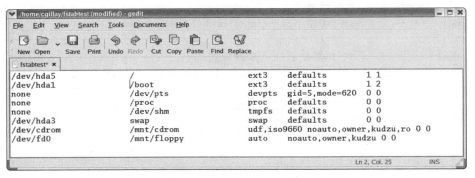

Figure 1.7 • Another fstab File

WHAT'S HAPPENING? However, when you compare the example after Step 16 and Figure 1.7, there are some major differences. In the screen capture that follows Step 16, Device shows **LABEL=/** for the mount point of the root directory / instead of a device statement (**/dev/hda5** for the root directory as shown in Figure 1.7 and **/dev/hda1** for the **/boot** partition). Beginning with Red Hat 7.2, instead of explicitly stating the device point (**/dev/hda1**), the **fstab** file may indicate the file system that is to be mounted by its UUID (user id) or volume label. The advantage of using this system is that the system administrator can swap out or change drives, giving them a volume label so Linux will know where to boot based on the volume label or UUID. The hardware change will become transparent to the operating system.

STEP 17 Click **File**. Click **Quit**.

WHAT'S **HAPPENING?** > You have closed gedit and returned to the desktop. It is easy to remove items from the panel.

STEP 18 Right-click the drawer.

WHAT'S **HAPPENING?** > To remove the drawer and all of the objects in the drawer, you simply choose **Remove From Panel**.

You successfully removed the drawer. However, you left the Terminal icon on the panel. You will find that throughout the text, you will constantly be using the terminal. Thus, it is faster to select it from the panel rather than using the menu. But a word of warning: When you log out, there is a checkbox called **Save current setup**. If you want to retain this icon on the panel, you must click this checkbox. If you are in a lab environment that does not allow you to save your changes, you will have to add the icon to the panel each time you boot into the system or choose it from the menu.

1.24 • Customizing the Desktop

You may also customize the look and feel of your desktop. You can change colors and alter the properties of the mouse and keyboard. You can choose your own screen saver. You can decide whether you prefer single- or double-clicking objects to activate them. You can choose a theme. A theme is simply an organized collection of icons, colors, pointer styles, and so on. Bluecurve is the default theme. If you are using the Metacity window manager, a few themes are available. If you are using Sawfish, many more themes are available.

1.25 • Activity: Customizing the Desktop

STEP 1   Click the Main menu. Point to **Preferences**.

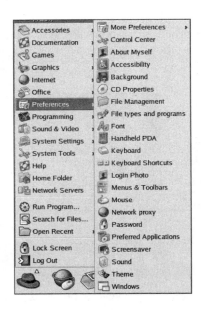

WHAT'S HAPPENING? Here is a list of all the items you can alter to suit your needs.

STEP 2   Click **Mouse**.

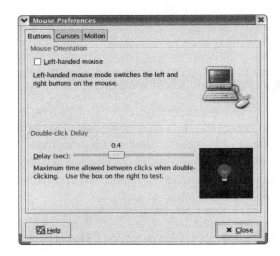

WHAT'S HAPPENING? You are looking at a tabbed property sheet. Each tab has different options to customize your mouse. On this property sheet, you may alter the mouse for a left-handed individual.

STEP 3   Click the **Cursors** tab.

WHAT'S HAPPENING? Here you may choose your cursor type.

STEP 4 Click **Close**. Click the Main menu. Click **Preferences**. Click **More Preferences**. Point to **More Preferences**. Click **Sawfish window manager**.

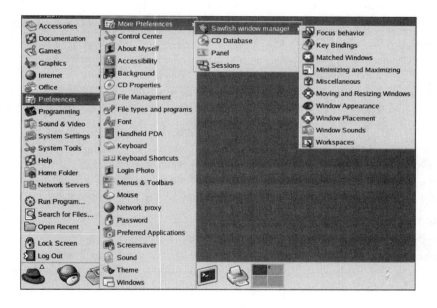

WHAT'S HAPPENING? You may not have the the Sawfish window manger available, but if you do, here are more choices. It appears that you can customize the Sawfish window manger. However, you should be aware that when you install "everything," items appear on the menu that are not necessarily available to you. On this computer system, Metacity is the window manager, not Sawfish. So, on this computer, although you could select any item on the menu, it would not have any impact. If you changed window managers to Sawfish, then these choices would work.

STEP 5 Click **Panel**.

WHAT'S HAPPENING? Since this dialog box refers to the GNOME panel, you could make changes here that would affect the operation of any drawers you created.

STEP 6   Click **Close**.

WHAT'S HAPPENING? You have returned to the desktop. You can experiment with these different items on the **Preferences** menu to alter the desktop to suit your needs. Just remember that what you can change is dependent not just on GNOME but on which window manager you are using.

1.26 • gEdit and OpenOffice

One of the items that all users need in an operating system is an editor, specifically a text editor. A text editor allows you to create any ASCII text document. An ASCII or text file is any file that has no special embedded codes in it. Most word-processing programs place those codes in documents so you may perform such functions as creating columns, tables, and so forth. Text files do not have such embedded codes. Many files in Linux are text files, such as **fstab**. If you need to make changes to it, you must use a text editor. Red Hat Linux provides an editor called gEdit.

However, text editors are not as useful when you want a fully formatted document such as a résumé, a research paper, or a report. For this you need a word processor. Red Hat includes, in the programs it supplies, a suite of applications that most users need: a word processor, a spreadsheet, a presentation manager, and a drawing package. This suite is OpenOffice.org and is both an Open Source product and a project. The product is a multi-platform office productivity suite. It includes the key desktop applications, such as a word processor, spreadsheet, presentation manager, and drawing program, with a user interface and features set similar to other office suites. OpenOffice is part of the Open Source movement. In general, *open source* refers to any program whose source code is made available for use or modification as users or other developers see fit. Historically, the makers of proprietary software (such as Microsoft Office) have generally not made source code available. Open source software is usually developed as a public collaboration and made freely available. The idea is very similar to the "copyleft" concept of the Free Software Foundation. Open Source is the result of a long-time movement toward software that is developed and improved by a group of volunteers cooperating together on a network. Many parts of the Unix operating system were developed this way, including today's most popular version, Linux.

gEdit and OpenOffice.org Writer allow you to create and manipulate text in a document. gEdit is a full-featured text editor with such common functions as copying, pasting, and searching through a document for text, whereas Writer is a full-featured word processor. Each allows you to open multiple documents and allows easy switching among open documents. gEdit also provides many plug-ins. A *plug-in* is a small software program that plugs into a larger application program to provide added functionality. Plug-ins include such useful features as a spell-checker and the ability to directly email your current document. Writer, as a full-featured word processor, includes such features as a thesaurus, outlining, and other powerful options that allow you to create professional-looking documents.

1.27 ● Activity: Using gEdit and OpenOffice.org Writer

STEP 1   Click the Main Menu button. Point to **Accessories**. Click **Text Editor**.

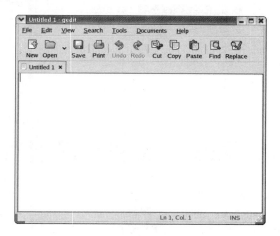

WHAT'S HAPPENING? You have opened gEdit. It has the normal window components, such as a menu bar and title bar. GNOME-compliant applications have some interesting features, one of which is a floating menu. The menu can be torn off from the usual menu and can be displayed anywhere in the window or on the desktop. You can identify a tear-off menu by the dotted line. See Figure 1.8, "Tear-off Line."

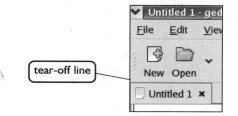

Figure 1.8 ● Tear-off Line

STEP 2   Click and hold the dotted line next to **New**.

WHAT'S HAPPENING? You see a four headed arrow. You can drag this menu anywhere in the window or on the desktop. The File menu can appear in its own window. You may drag it anywhere on the desktop.

STEP 3   Click in the window. Key in the following but do not key in Enter. Press the Enter key when you see Enter:

> **This is a test.** Enter
> **This is a test.** Enter

STEP 4   Click **File**. Click **Print**.

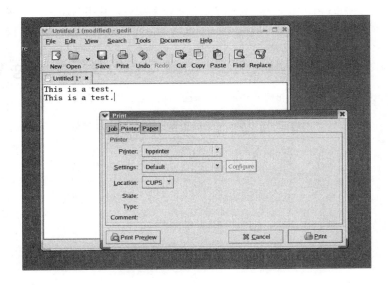

WHAT'S HAPPENING? The Print Document dialog box appears. In the dialog box, you see the name of the printer (hpprinter), the settings (default), and the location (CUPS). Beginning with Red Hat 9, Red Hat defaults to the CUPS printing system. The printer is named and the default settings are chosen when the system administrator runs the printer configuration utility. The Common Unix Printing System (CUPS) is a cross-platform printing solution for all Unix environments. It is based on the Internet Printing Protocol (IPP) and provides complete printing services to most PostScript and raster printers. CUPS is provided under the GNU GPL. It provides a portable printing layer for Unix-based operating systems. The Line Printer Daemon (lpd), Server Message Block (smb), and other printing protocols are also supported with reduced functionality.

When you print a document, the print command does not send your file directly to the printer, but instead sends your file to the printer spool queue. The print spooler essentially is a directory containing the files that need to print. Normally, a print daemon looks at the print spooler directory to see if any files are waiting to be printed. If it finds any, it sends them to the printer as the printer is ready to print another print job. A *print job* is a request to print one file. If you had three files waiting to print, you would have three print jobs. The print daemon gets information about which printers are available from a configuration file called **/etc/printcap** (*print*er *cap*abilities) or the **/etc/cups/cupsd.conf** file. Printers are treated as files and also have mount points. Printer mount points are in the **/dev** directory. The first parallel printer is usually called **/dev/lp0**, which would correspond to the DOS/Windows name of LPT1.

At the heart of Linux is the concept of a *process*. A process is an independently run program with its own set of resources. A process can run and control another program, which is then referred to as a subprocess. As you will see, every process is assigned an identification number (pid).

A *daemon* (pronounced "demon") is a background process that takes a predefined action when certain events occur. It does not need to be called by the user. A daemon sits in background and is activated only when needed. Thus, the printer daemon, **lpd** or **cupsd**, manages the print queue in background. You may notice that many daemon commands end in "d," for daemon.

STEP 5   Click **Print**.

WHAT'S HAPPENING? Your file should print.

STEP 6   Close the **gedit** window.

WHAT'S HAPPENING? You are asked if you want to save this file.

STEP 7   Click **Don't Save**.

WHAT'S HAPPENING? You have returned to the desktop.

STEP 8   Click the Main Menu button. Point to **Office**. Click **OpenOffice.org Writer**.

tear-off point

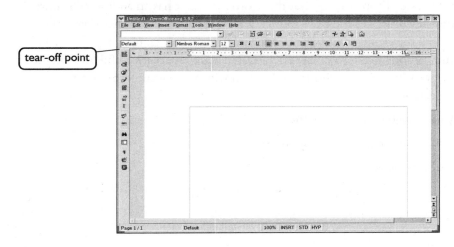

WHAT'S HAPPENING? You have opened Writer. It has the normal window components such as a menu bar and title bar. Since this is a GNOME-compliant application, it too has floating toolbars (sometimes called tear-off toolbars).

STEP 9   Click in the window. Key in the following, but do not key in `Enter`. Press the `Enter` key when you see `Enter`:

> **This is a test.** `Enter`
> **This is a test.** `Enter`

STEP 10   Click **File**. Click **Print**.

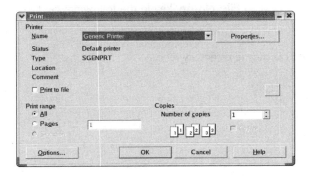

WHAT'S HAPPENING? You see that Generic Printer is in the Name drop-down list box.

STEP 11 Click the down arrow in the Name drop-down list box.

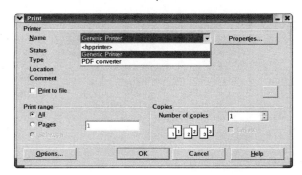

WHAT'S HAPPENING? If you choose Generic Printer, your document will print but you might lose any special formatting features such as a specific font. You would normally choose your default printer, in this case **<hpprinter>**. But this word processor has an additional feature. It lets you convert your document to the PDF format. ***PDF (Portable Document Format)*** is a file format that captures all the elements of a printed document as an electronic image that you can view, navigate, print, or forward to someone else. PDF files are especially useful for documents such as magazine articles, product brochures, or flyers in which you want to preserve the original graphic appearance online.

STEP 12 Select your default printer. Click **OK**.

WHAT'S HAPPENING? Your document should print.

STEP 13 Click **File**. Click **Save**.

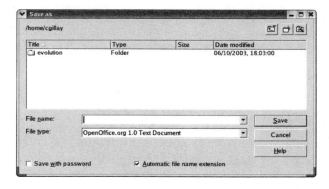

WHAT'S HAPPENING? In this case, since you chose to save the file, you are asked where you want to save it. By default, it will be saved to your home directory.

STEP 14 In the text box next to **File Name**, key in the following: **test**

STEP 15 Click **Save**. Close the OpenOffice.org window.

STEP 16 Double-click your home directory icon.

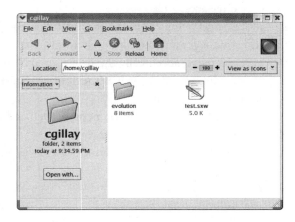

WHAT'S HAPPENING? You now have a file called **test.sxw** in your home directory. You want to delete this file.

STEP 17 Right-click **test.sxw**.

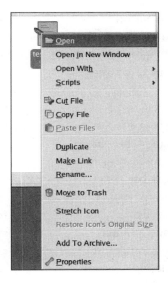

WHAT'S HAPPENING? You have opened a menu with the right-click. One of the choices is **Move to Trash.**

STEP 18 Click **Move to Trash**.

WHAT'S HAPPENING? You have eliminated the **test** file.

STEP 19 Close your home directory window.

Chapter Summary

In this chapter you were introduced to the following:
* An overview of the purpose and function of operating systems in general.
* An explanation of a distribution of an operating system with specific focus on Red Hat Linux 9.
* The purpose and function of files and directories, including major file types.
* The rules for naming files and directories.

- An overview of types of user interfaces.
- The purpose and function of a windowing environment, including the purposes of the X Window System, a window manager and a desktop environment.
- The differences between types of users, specifically the root user and an ordinary user.
- The ability to boot and log into the system, as well as the ability to start the GUI.
- The ability to properly shut down the system.
- The ability to navigate the GNOME desktop environment, as well as explain and use features of the desktop such as dialog boxes and menus.
- The ability to navigate the Nautilus file manager and understand the purpose and function of a file manager.
- The ability to customize the GNOME Panel.
- The ability to customize the desktop.
- The importance of the **fstab** file and an overview of assigned device names.
- The ability to use two programs, the text editor gEdit and the word processor Writer (OpenOffice.org).

Key Terms

child menu	hide button	print job
clicking	hierarchical menu	process
command button	highlighting	property sheet
configuration	home directory	right-click menu
configuration files	icon	right-clicking
control	kernel	right-dragging
copyleft	keyboard focus	root
cursor	Main Menu button	root user
daemon	menu	shell
desktop	menu bar	standard
device drivers	message box	submenu
dialog box	mid-click	super user
directories	mouse pointer	system services
distribution	open source	taskbar buttons
double-clicking	pane	terminal
drag and drop	panel	title bar
dragging	parent menu	user interfaces
drop down	plug-in	virtual consoles
ellipsis	pointer	virtual desktop
emblem	pointing	widgets
file systems	Portable Document Format	window manager
File Transfer Protocol (FTP)	(PDF)	window menu
GNU	primary mouse button	windows

Discussion Questions

1. What is the function of an operating system?
2. "The heart of an operating system is the kernel." Explain.
3. Explain the origin of the Linux operating system.
4. List and explain four of the features that the Linux operating system supports.
5. What is a distribution?

6. Compare and contrast the two major desktop distribution versions of Red Hat—Red Hat 9 and Red Hat 9 Professional.
7. What is a file? A directory?
8. List Linux rules for naming files.
9. List and compare the three major types of computer files.
10. Compare and contrast the two major ways Linux provides for the user to interact with the computer.
11. Linux divides the GUI into three separate components. List and briefly describe these components.
12. What is an interface?
13. What is X Window System?
14. Compare and contrast the super user with the ordinary user.
15. What does it mean to boot the system?
16. List the steps to boot a Linux system.
17. Why is it necessary to follow the Linux shutdown process instead of just turning off the computer?
18. List and explain the purpose and function of five of the features found on the GNOME Desktop.
19. What is a window?
20. Explain the purpose and function of a pointing device.
21. What is the difference between a menu and a submenu (hierarchical menu)?
22. Explain the purpose and function of the Nautilus file manager.
23. The Side Pane allows you to choose Emblems, History, Notes, and Tree. List and explain the purpose and function of each of these items.
24. In what ways can you customize the panel? What is used to manipulate the panel?
25. What is a property sheet?
26. What kinds of panels may you have? How may you access them?
27. Explain the purpose and function of the Window List? The Workspace Switcher?
28. How can you place a launcher for an application program on the panel?
29. What is purpose and function of the **fstab** file? Name and explain the purpose of at least three items found in the **fstab** file.
30. Compare and contrast a text editor with a word processor.

True/False Questions

For each question, circle the letter T if the question is true and the letter F if the question is false.

T   F   1. Red Hat is the only distribution of Linux.
T   F   2. A distribution is a combination of the Linux kernel and additional programs.
T   F   3. A window is a defined work area that is moveable and sizable.
T   F   4. User data files contain information on executable programs.
T   F   5. Programs designed to work in a Windows operating system can be installed and used in the Linux environment.

Completion Questions

Write the correct answer in each blank space.

6. In Linux the three parts to the GUI are the _____, the _____, and the _____.

7. Linux provides for two types of users: the _____ user and the _____ user.

8. Linux provides two ways of interacting with the computer: _____ and _____ .

9. A graphical representation of an object is known as a(n) _____.

10. In Linux, to access files on a specific drive, the drive must first be _____.

Multiple Choice Questions

For each question, write the letter for the correct answer in the blank space.

11. An operating system
  a. determines how the user interacts with the computer.
  b. supervises the hardware.
  c. supervises all the input/output of the computer.
  d. All of the above.

12. Red Hat Linux distribution include many application programs. Which of the following is *not* included?
  a. GIMP
  b. gEdit
  c. Microsoft Excel
  d. OpenOffice

13. A drawer on the panel is
  a. created when you boot the system.
  b. a location you can create on the panel that can hold several application launchers.
  c. a quick way to log out.
  d. the means to access the Internet.

14. When logging onto the system the
  a. $ prompt indicates that you logged in as the root.
  b. # prompt indicates that you logged in as an ordinary user
  c. both a and b
  d. neither a nor b

15. The native file system for Linux is
  a. ext2 or ext3
  b. FAT32
  c. NTFS
  d. vfat

Application Assignments

Problem Set I—At the Computer: Multiple Choice

Problem A

- Click the Main Menu button.

  1. You have opened a
    a. menu.
    b. dialog box.

- Open **FreeCell**.

    2. To open **FreeCell**, you used
        a. cascading menus.
        b. only a dialog box.

- Choose game number 555.

    3. The only ace among the fully exposed cards is the
        a. ace of clubs.
        b. ace of diamonds.
        c. ace of hearts.
        d. ace of spades.

- Play **FreeCell** if you wish. When you are finished, you must exit or close the program. Before you close **FreeCell**, begin a new game, but do not finish it.

    4. Which button must you click to close **FreeCell**?
        a. [_]
        b. [▢]
        c. [✖]

    5. When you close **FreeCell**, you are
        a. immediately returned to the desktop
        b. first presented with a message box.

Problem B

- Double-click the **Start Here** icon. Maximize the window.

    6. The title bar contains the word(s):
        a. **start-here:///**
        b. **File**

    7. The menu bar contains the word(s):
        a. **start-here:///**
        b. **File**

- Restore the window.

- Double-click the title bar of the **start-here:///** window.

    8. The **start-here:///** window
        a. became only a title bar
        b. became a title bar and an additional window
        c. closed.

- Right-click the **Start Here** button on the panel.

    9. One choice available on this menu is
        a. **Reactivate**
        b. **Restore**
        c. **Shade**
        d. **Unroll**

- Double-click the title bar of the **start-here://** window.

- Minimize the **start-here:///** window.

- Right click the **start-here** button on the panel.

10. One choice *not* available on the right-click menu is
    a. Unminimize.
    b. Minimize.
    c. Maximize.
    d. Resize.

- Click **Close**.
- Double-click the **Home** icon on the desktop.
- Click **View**. Be sure Side Pane is checked.
- Choose **Tree** in the information drop-down list box.

11. Your location is the _____ directory.
    a. /
    b. /etc
    c. /home
    d. /home/*yourusername*

- Locate the /**home** directory in the tree. Make it the default directory.
- Double-click the **student9** directory.

12. When you double-clicked the /**home/student9** directory, you
    a. displayed the contents of the /**home/student9** directory.
    b. were denied viewing the contents because you did not have the correct permissions.
    c. were immediately returned to your home directory.

- Choose **Emblems** in the information drop-down list box.

13. The Emblem displayed for Cool is a picture of a(n)
    a. ice cube.
    b. refrigerator.
    c. pair of sunglasses.
    d. person surfing.

- Close the window.

Problem C

- Open the Panel Properties.
- Click the down-arrow in the Size drop-down list box.

14. One size that is *not* available is
    a. **Tiny**.
    b. **XX Small**.
    c. **Large**.
    d. **XX Large**.

- Click the **Background** tab. Click the **Type** drop-down list box.

15. Available background types include
    a. **Standard**.
    b. **Color**
    c. both a and b
    d. neither a nor b

- Click outside the menu to close it. Close the dialog box.

Problem D

- Open **Start Here**.
- Open **FreeCell**.
- Send **FreeCell** to Workspace 2.

  16. In order to accomplish this, you clicked the _____ and pointed to **Move to Workspace 2**.
      a. **File** menu (or right-clicked the menu)
      b. **Window** menu (or right-clicked the menu)
      c. **Forward** arrow (or right-clicked the menu)

  17. In your current desktop,
      a. only the **start here:///** window is visible.
      b. only **FreeCell** is visible.
      c. both **FreeCell** and the **start here:///** window are visible.

- Close **FreeCell**.
- Click the top left quadrant of the workspace switcher.

  18. The **start here:///** window _____ open and visible.
      a. is
      b. is not

- Close any open windows.
- In **Add to Panel/Amusements**, there are two application buttons you can add to the panel.
- Create a panel button for **Fish**.
- Create a panel button for **Geyes**.
- Open Preferences for **Fish**.

  19. What is the fish's name?
      a. Wanda.
      b. Carolyn.
      c. Walter.
      d. Kyle.

  20. What is the purpose of the **Geyes** applet?
      a. To play a game.
      b. To track the movement of the mouse pointer on the screen.
      c. To track the mouse pointer in an application program.
      d. To do nothing useful.

- Remove the **Fish** and **Geyes** buttons from the panel.

Problem Set II—At the Computer: Short Answer

Note: In order for these activities to work correctly, it is assumed that a complete installation of Red Hat Linux 9 Professional was completed.

1. Open the game called **Iango**. How did you accomplish this? What is **Iagno**? How did you find out this information?
2. Open the Nautilus file manager. Open **Applications**. How did you accomplish these tasks? Name two items in the open window. How would you find out what windows you have visited in this file manager session?

3. You want to look at the files in the **bin** directory using the Nautilus file manager. How can you accomplish this task? What is the name of the first file listed in the /**bin** directory? Does the /**bin** directory have any directories beneath it? How did you find out this information?

4. Add a corner panel. How did you accomplish this task? Where does the corner panel first appear on the screen? Add a **FreeCell** application launcher to the new panel. How did you accomplish this? Position the new corner panel on the right side of the screen in the center. How did you accomplish this? What difference do you notice between the panel at the bottom of the window and the one you just created? Delete the corner panel. How did you accomplish this task?

5. Double-click your home directory icon. Open **FreeCell**. Move your home directory window to Workspace 3. How did you accomplish this task? Place your home directory window so that is appears in all the workspaces. How did you accomplish this? Open the Window menu. What choices are now available to you on this menu? Close all open windows in all workspaces.

6. Create a drawer on the panel. How did you do this? In your new drawer add application launchers for the text editor and for **FreeCell**. How did you accomplish this? Remove the drawer. How did you accomplish this?

7. Open your **fstab** file. How did you accomplish this? What device is mounted for the swap device? What file system is on the **swap** device? What file system is listed for the **cdrom** device? Close any open windows.

8. What font is the desktop using? The Terminal window? How did you locate this information? Close any open windows.

9. What keyboard shortcut will allow you to move a window on workspace to the right? How did you locate this information?

10. Using the text editor, briefly describe what item or information you had the most difficulty in understanding in this chapter. Using OpenOffice, briefly describe your favorite feature of the GNOME graphical user interface.

Problem Set III—Brief Essay

Use gEdit or OpenOffice.org Writer to write and print your response. Be sure to put your name as well as what day and time your class is. Include the number of the question you are answering.

a. Describe the purpose and function of the Workspace Switcher. Would you or would you not use this feature? Document your reasons for either position.

b. Open the **fstab** file. List and describe each entry in the file. What kind of information is available from the entries in this file? How could you use this information?

c. Compare and contrast X Window System, a window manager, and a desktop environment.

CHAPTER 2

The Linux File System

Chapter Overview

A major component of any operating system is its file system. Linux, like any operating system has a file system and an organization to that file system. You will learn about file systems and about the native Linux file system (ext2 and ext3) as well as other file systems that Linux supports. Furthermore, you will learn the purpose and function of the standard directories that are installed in a Linux file system.

You will learn to navigate the file system both in the Nautilus file manager and at the command prompt, the Bash shell. You will discover that to communicate with the operating system at the command line prompt, you need to learn the operating system's language. You must follow the syntax of the language and use punctuation marks the computer understands. As in mastering any new language, new vocabulary words must be learned, word order (syntax) must be determined, and the method of separating statements into syntactic units must be understood.

In this chapter, you will learn some basic operating system commands and their syntax. In addition, you will learn the difference between arguments and options and how they affect commands. You will learn to use wildcards, called globbing, to affect the outcome of commands. Since you will want to access drives, you will learn what drives are named in Linux, why you must mount them, and how to mount them. Redirection will be introduced.

Learning Objectives

1. Explain the purpose and function of a file, a directory, and a file system.

2. List at least three file systems Linux supports.

3. Compare and contrast the Linux ext2 and ext3 file system.

4. List at least five common Linux directories and describe the types of files found in those directories.

5. Explain the hierarchical filing system of a tree-structured directory.

6. Explain the purpose and function of the Bash shell.

7. Explain how to navigate within the Bash shell using keystrokes and the **history** command.

8. Explain the importance of command syntax.

9. Explain how options and arguments are used with commands.

10. Be able to read a syntax diagram.

11. Compare and contrast the absolute path with the relative path.

12. Explain why and how file systems are mounted.

13. Explain the purpose and function of globbing.

14. Explain the purpose and function of the **pwd**, **cd**, **history**, **cal**, **date**, **ls**, **locate**, **find**, and **whereis** commands.

15. List and explain five options that can be used with the **ls** command and with the **find** command.

16. Explain when and why you would use redirection.

Student Outcomes

1. Start GNOME and traverse the tree structure.

2. Read a syntax diagram and be able to name and explain what each part signifies.

3. Run the terminal window (Bash shell) in GNOME.

4. Navigate within the terminal window using the absolute path and the relative path.

5. Mount and unmount file systems.

6. Use the **history**, **cal**, **date**, **pwd**, and **cd** commands.

7. Use wildcards, arguments and options with the **ls** command.

8. Use the **locate** command.

9. Use wildcards and options with the **find** command.

10. Redirect output to a file and a device.

11. Use the **whereis** command to display the location of commands in the directory structure.

Commands Introduced

cal	echo	ls
cat	exit	mount
cd	find	pwd
chsh	history	startx
clear	locate	umount
date	lpr	whereis

2.1 • Understanding the Linux File System

Files and directories are the most fundamental components of any operating system. No matter what you use your computer for, you will deal with files and directories. Files and directories will be created on your computer, or they will be added to your computer when you install software. The minute you decide to save your work, you will create files and directories.

A *file* is a named and stored collection of related information, such as a program, a set of data used by a program, or a user-created document. It is the basic unit of storage that enables a computer to distinguish one set of information from another. Remember as well that in Linux, everything is a file: data you store and devices, such as the keyboard or settings that you have created for devices.

Because of all the files that come with Linux and the different application programs you use, not to mention the files that you create, your hard disk can contain hundreds, if not thousands, of files. If you are on a network, you could have access to millions of files. There would be no way to keep track of all these files if they were not organized in some way. The fundamental way to organize and track files in Linux is using directories.

A *directory* is a means of organizing programs and documents. It can hold both files and additional directories. Technically, a directory is just a special kind of file that contains a list of the locations of other files. In Linux, the directories are hierarchical with the system root directory at the top. The system root is simply called root and its symbol is the / (the forward slash). All other directories and files are beneath the root. This hierarchical arrangement is called the directory tree. Technically, there is only one directory, the root (/). All other directories are subdirectories. However, the terms "subdirectory" and "directory" are used interchangeably. In this text, the term directory will be used to refer to subdirectories. To locate a specific item in the directory tree, you must use the path. The *path* is the complete list of directories that Linux follows to locate, save, or retrieve a file. A path begins at the root. If you had a file called **myfile**, located in the **/home/cgillay** directory, the path to the file would be **/home/cgillay/ myfile**. The slashes in the path act as a delimiter. A *delimiter* indicates one item is ending and another is beginning. There is one exception—the first slash indicates the root directory, not a delimiter.

Every file and directory has a unique name. In Linux, if you are using the native Linux file system (ext2 or ext3), remember that everything is case sensitive, so that **my file** and **MY FILE** are two separate and unique files. In general, most Linux users tend to use all lowercase letters and avoid using spaces in file and directory names.

A *file system* is the way any operating system names, stores, and organizes the files on storage devices such as hard disk or floppy disks. Thus, a file system consists of files and directories and the information needed to locate and access those objects. In addition, under Linux, storage devices—such as hard disks, hard disk partitions, floppy disks, Zip disks, and CD-ROMs—are united into a single file system, all branching off from the root directory. The current native Linux file system is called ext3 (extended file system version 3). The ext3 file system is installed by default. The file system ext3 was introduced in Red Hat Linux 7.2. Prior to that release, the native file system was ext2. The ext2 and ext3 are very similar. The major difference between the two is that ext3 is a journaling file system. A *journaling file system* is one that in general writes meta data to a journal on the disk before it is actually used to modify the file. Thus, if there is a system problem or system crash, there is enough uncorrupted data available to finish writing to the original file. *Meta data* is data about data. It is definitional data that provides information about or documentation of other data managed within an application or environment, such as the operating system.

Linux supports many other foreign file systems, such as msdos (reading and writing of old MS-DOS partitions with the 8.3 file names), umsdos (builds on the MS-DOS file system and allows the reading and writing of DOS partitions with long file names), vfat (builds on the Windows 95/98 file system and allows the reading and writing of vfat32 partitions) and ntfs (read access to the Windows NT NTFS file system). In addition, Linux supports network file systems. Network file systems are physically somewhere else but look as though they are mounted on your local computer. Two major examples of network file system are NFS (Network File System) and SMB (System Message Block). The Linux implementation of SMB is known as Samba.

Since Linux is a secure operating system, users can protect their data and determine who can and cannot view or alter files and directories, but only if the Linux file system is ext2 or ext3. If, for instance, you were using a floppy disk with the MS-DOS file system on it, you would not be provided this protection. In the Linux file system, files and directories are owned and have permissions assigned to them. Many files and directories, such as system configuration files and password files, are only accessible by the system administrator, the super user (root user).

Under the ext2 and ext3 file systems, a file is usually owned by the person who creates it, considered the user. The file permissions specify who else may do what to any file. There are three categories of file owners: user, group, and other. When user accounts are created, groups can be created that consist of one or more users. For instance, a group could be created called **class**, and all class members could be assigned membership in that group. Then, the owner of a file could grant permissions to the group called **class**, rather than on a user-by-user basis.

There are three types of permissions to be granted: read, write, and execute. The owner of a file, has, by default, read, write, and execute permissions to files he owns. If a file has read permission, it can be viewed but not altered. If a file has write permission, it can be read, altered, or deleted. If a file has execute permission, a program or script can be launched (executed). When execute permission is applied to a directory, it gives access to that directory. Executable programs have two additional permission types called "set userid" (Set UID) and "set group userid" (Set GUID). These permissions, used by the system administrator, specify that a program will start with the permissions available to the owner of a file.

2.2 • Activity: Looking at the File System

Note: The activities in this book assume Linux is installed at run level 3. See the Installation section of Appendix A for details.

STEP 1   Boot the system, and if necessary, start GNOME (startx).

STEP 2   Double-click your Home directory icon on the desktop. Click **View** and click **Side Pane**, if it is not checked. On the menu bar, click **View**. Click **View as Icons**.

STEP 3   In the information drop-down list box, click **Tree**. If necessary, in the side pane, expand the root directory. In the side pane, scroll until you locate the **home** directory. Expand the **home** directory. Then click your user name.

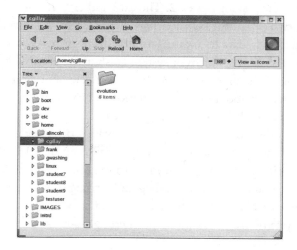

WHAT'S HAPPENING? Your directory may appear to be empty or it may have more files and directories than are shown here. In this example, in the side pane, you are looking at the tree, which is a hierarchical view of your computer's directories. Each user on your system will have a directory with his user name. You may have more or fewer users. Your default directory is your home directory—in this case **/home/cgillay**. When you use the Nautilus file manager, there are hidden files and directories.

STEP 4   Click **Edit**. Click **Preferences**. Click the **Behavior** tab.

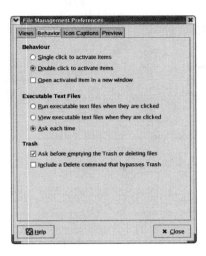

WHAT'S HAPPENING? Here you have different options to change the behavior of objects in your window. You may choose to open your icons (activate) with a single or double-click or open them in a new window. You may also change your options for executable programs and alter how deleted files are handled (**Trash**).

STEP 5   Click the **Views** tab.

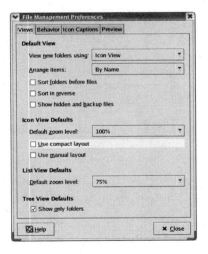

WHAT'S HAPPENING? One of the choices in the **Views** tab allows you to see your hidden files and backup files. Hidden files in Linux always begin with a dot.

STEP 6   Click the **Show hidden files and backup files** check box to set it. Click **Close**.

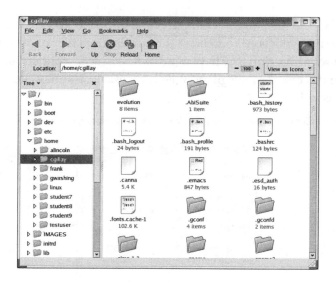

WHAT'S HAPPENING? For the GNOME desktop, these are the various configuration files that are now visible.

STEP 7   Click **Edit**. Click **Preferences**. Click the **Views** tab. Click the **Show hidden and backup files** check box to clear it. Click **Close**.

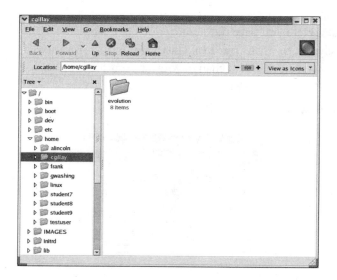

WHAT'S HAPPENING? You have returned to your home directory window with the hidden files hidden. If you look at the tree, the root directory (/)is at the top. Below that are the top-level directories such as **bin** and **boot**. If you see a right pointing arrow next to a directory name, that directory can be expanded to show further directories under it. On the other hand, if you see a downward pointing arrow, it means the directory is expanded. You may navigate within the window by using the mouse and clicking the arrow to expand or contract a directory. You may also use the navigation icons—**Back**, **Forward**, and **Up**. **Up** moves you to the parent directory of the current directory. Currently the **Back** and **Forward** buttons are not available (dimmed), since you have not yet looked at any other directories or windows. Once you have looked at another directory or window, **Back** will take you to a previously viewed directory or window. Continually clicking **Back** will move you through all your previously viewed windows or directories. After you have been "back," clicking the **Forward** icon will redisplay a directory or window you went back from. **Home** will take you to your home directory.

When you logged in, you used your user name. Every user on the system has a default home directory. In this example, the home directory is **/home/cgillay**. The home directory is normally used to store all your data files, as well as any configuration choices you made to run GNOME, Metacity, and various applications. When you are connected to the Internet, this directory will also store your mail, bookmarks, and any cached web documents. In the example shown, there is one directory—**evolution**. This directory was created when the email program was started. The default directory, **/home/cgillay**, is the *working directory* or *current directory*. The working directory will change as you move within the structure. The working directory is simply your current location.

STEP 8   Click the **bin** directory.

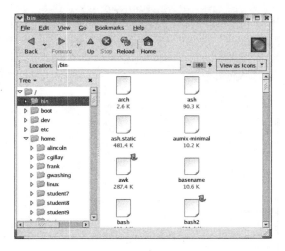

WHAT'S HAPPENING? ➢ Now the **bin** directory is the default or working directory. Note now that your Back arrow is available. If you click **Back**, you would be returned to your last visited directory.

STEP 9   Click the Up arrow.

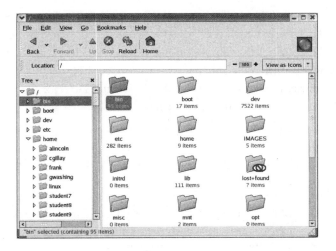

WHAT'S HAPPENING? You have moved to the parent of the **bin** directory. You will hear the terms parent and children to define the relationships among directories. A *parent directory* is one that contains other directories. In the above example, the parent of **bin** is the root (/). Thus, **bin** is a child to /. In the first screen capture, **cgillay** is a child to **home**, which is a child to /. Thus, **home** is parent to **cgillay** but child to /.

You are in icon view. In the Nautilus file manager, the icons try to represent what is in the file. Thus, by looking at the icon, you may be able to determine what the contents of the file are. You will find that the Bluecurve theme used with the GNOME desktop has many styles of icons.

STEP 10 Click the down arrow next to the home directory to collapse it. Expand the size of the directory window so that you may see the structure.

STEP 11 Click the root directory to make it the working directory.

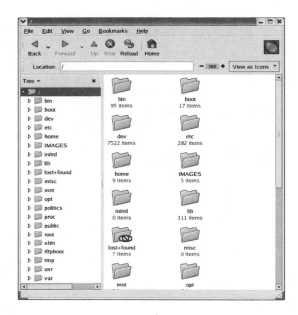

WHAT'S HAPPENING? When Linux is installed, it creates many directories. The directory names the *File System Hierarchy Standard (FHS)*. This is a collaborative document that defines the names and locations of many files and directories. Most Linux distributions follow this standard. This standard determines which files are typically stored in which directories. Within this standard are required directories as well as optional directories. The complete standard is available at **http://www.pathname.com/fhs**. In addition, Red Hat extends the FHS slightly to accommodate some special files. Table 2.1, "Common Linux Directories," lists these directories and the types of files that are kept in those directories.

Directory name	Files
/	Root—The root of the entire file system; it contains all other directories.
/bin	Contains binary files that are part of Linux. Binary files are programs, also called executables.
/boot	Contains the kernel and files that the bootstrap loader (utility that starts the operating system) needs.

/dev	Contains all device drivers for connected hardware.
/etc	Contains most system configuration files that are used when the computer is started. Generally reserved for the system administrator.
/home	Contains a directory for each user on the system. All these user directories are under /home.
/initrd	Red Hat specific—an empty directory, but is used as a critical mount point during the boot process.
/lib	Contains shared library images, which are files that programmers use to share code rather than having to create code in their programs. Many of these files are symbolic links to files in system libraries. "Symbolic links" is a name that points to and allows access to a file located in a directory other than the current directory. These files are needed for the execution of programs.
/lost+found	Contains any files that get lost in the file system, for whatever reason.
/mnt	Contains mount points (directories) for removable media such as floppy disks.
/opt	Contains additional packages that can be installed at a later date. In many systems, commercial programs are installed here. Another popular location is /usr/local.
/proc	Used by Linux for handling processes. It occupies no space on the disk. It is a virtual file system allocated in memory only. Files located here refer to various processes that are running on the system.
/root	Home directory for the root user—usually the system administrator. Do not confuse this directory with the /—the root directory.
/sbin	Directory reserved for the super user (usually the system administrator). Programs that start the system, any programs needed for file system repair and any essential network programs are kept in this directory and only the system administrator can run these programs.
/tmp	Contains any temporary files that programs must create during processing. Any files in this directory are deleted when the system is rebooted or started.
/usr	Contains files that are accessible to all users.
/var	Contains files whose contents change, such as error logs or other system performance logs that are useful to the system administrator.

Table 2.1 • Common Linux Directories

Other directories shown in this example were those created either by the user or by the installation of an application program.

STEP 12 Expand the **/usr** directory. Click **bin**.

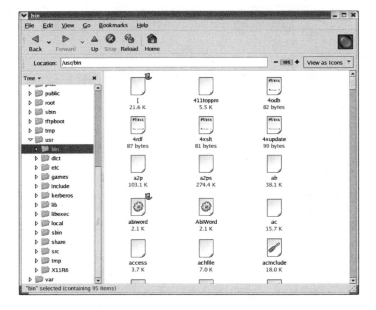

WHAT'S HAPPENING? You have been looking at the structure of the directories at the root level, which is fairly straightforward. Many subdirectories are created beneath the root level. As you can see in the above example, the subdirectory names are similar, such as **/usr/bin**. This directory contains binary files that are available to all users. Remember, if you use the entire path name, it is clear to see the difference between **/bin** and **/usr/bin**. Directories that you expand will remain expanded the next time you open your home directory window.

STEP 13 Collapse the **/usr** directory. Collapse the **/home** directory. Collapse the / directory. Click the / to select it. Close the home directory window.

2.3 • Introducing the Bash Shell

Although using a GUI such as GNOME is visual and fairly easy, you will find that in Linux many tasks are best accomplished at the command line. The command line is the character-based interface that interacts with the operating system. To access the command line, you use a shell. A *shell* is a program that interprets keyboard commands and acts as a buffer between you and the operating system. Once you log in, you are communicating with the shell. If you needed to key in **startx** to use GNOME, you issued a command. Once in GNOME, you can access the character-based interface with a terminal-emulation program, which in GNOME is called Terminal. If, when you boot the system, you never start GNOME (startx), you are at the command line and in the Bash shell.

There are three main reasons for using the shell: to allow interactive use, to customize your Linux session, and for programming. There are many flavors of shells, such as the Bourne shell, the Korn shell, the C shell and so on; Red Hat uses the Bash shell (Bourne Again shell) as the default shell.

When you use the shell interactively, it waits for you to issue commands via the keyboard. In Linux, a command is simply a file that is a program that you run. You key in the command, and the shell processes and executes it. Shells generally have a set of commands, known as built-ins, to supplement Linux commands. A shell defines such variables as your home directory. Although some variables are set by the operating system, you may define others in startup files that the shell reads when you log in. In addition, you can combine a series of commands into one program called a shell script. If you are familiar with creating batch files in the DOS environment, you will see that shell scripts are a similar concept.

2.4 • Command Syntax

All languages have rules or conventions for speaking or writing. The syntax—the word order and punctuation—of a language is important. For example, in English the noun (person, place, or thing) is followed by the verb (the action). In another language, however, the syntax or order might be different: first the verb, followed by the noun. When you learn a language, you learn its syntax.

Anything you key into the computer must be something the computer understands. What you key in is actually a command to the computer to perform a specific task. Any command you issue must also be in the correct order; that is, it must have the proper syntax. The computer cannot guess what you mean. People can understand "Going I store," but if you key in an incorrect word or put correct words in the wrong order, a computer will respond with the message **bash: unknowncommand: command not found**. This statement is the computer equivalent of "I do not understand." In computer language, a command can be compared to a verb, the action you wish to take.

Using a graphical user interface such as GNOME does not change things—there are still syntax and rules. When you double-click on icon on the desktop or panel or when you choose a program from a menu, you are initiating a command. If you were at the command line, you would key in **/usr/bin/freecell** to launch the freecell program. The menu choice that launches a program is based on the rules of syntax. Certainly, it is easier from a user's perspective to choose an item from a menu or double-click an icon to accomplish the task than to know and key in the command and syntax. However, when things do not work, and often they do not in the computer world, you, the user, need to know how to go under the hood, so to speak, and fix the problem so that you can "click" successfully. Furthermore, in the Linux world, many tasks can only be accomplished at the command line.

2.5 • What Are Options and Arguments?

An *option* is information you can use to modify or qualify a command. An option is a way to request that Linux carry out a specific command in a specific variation. Some commands require options, while other commands let you add them when needed. Options follow a command name, separated by a space. A space is a delimiter. Remember, a delimiter is a character that identifies the beginning or the end of a character string (a contiguous sequence of characters). The delimiting character is not part of the character string. In command syntax, a space, a backslash (\), or a forward slash (/) is often a delimiter, depending on the rules of the command language. The program—in this case the Bash shell—interpreting the character string knows what the delimiters are. Options always begin with a - (hyphen). Options are case sensitive. In Linux, **ls** is a command to list the files in a directory. One option is **-a**, which means to show all the files. There is also an option **-A**, which means "almost all": it does not list the implied . (a single dot to represent the directory you are in) and .. (a double dot to represent the parent directory of the directory you are in). Thus, you would issue two different commands—one would be **ls -a** and the other would be **ls -A.**

An argument follows command options separated by a space (a delimiter). Command arguments are usually file or directory names. Thus, to see the files in the **/bin** directory, the command would be issued as **ls   /bin.** The **/bin** is the argument and is what the **ls** command will act upon. You can combine options and arguments. For instance, **ls** has the option **-l** for "long listing." The long listing includes such information as permissions and owner of the file. To see a long listing of the files in the **/bin** directory, the command would be **ls   -l   /bin. ls** is the command, **-l** is the option and **/bin** is the argument.

2.6 ● Reading a Syntax Diagram

A command line interface is a language that has a vocabulary, grammar, and syntax. To use the language of the command line, you must learn the vocabulary (commands) and understand the grammar (punctuation) and syntax (order). The syntax information is provided through online help, either via **man** *command name* or *commandname* **- -help**. The command syntax diagrams tell you how to enter the command with its options and allowable arguments. However, you need to be able to interpret these syntax diagrams.

Here is an example of the part of the formal command syntax diagram for the **ls** command:

```
ls [OPTION]...[FILE]...
```

The first entry is the command name. You must use this name only. You cannot substitute another word such as **LS** or **list**. The [OPTION] that follows the command is in brackets, indicating that this is optional. Because [OPTION] is in brackets, the **ls** command does not require the use of options. Following the command would be a list of the available options. Brackets are never keyed in. The [FILE] notation indicates that you may use a file or directory argument with the **ls** command to locate a specific file or directory.

2.7 ● Introducing Commands and the Terminal Window

In order to use Linux commands, you must either not have started GNOME or opened a terminal window in GNOME. You must know what command to use and what are allowable options and arguments. You must key in the command and press **Enter** when you have completed the command. The **Enter** key indicates you have completed your command and you are sending the signal for the shell to execute it. You will also find that the character-based interface allows you to use command line history. You may use the up and down arrows to scroll through the commands that you keyed in.

2.8 ● Activity: Looking at the Shell

Note: In Chapter 1, you placed the **Terminal** button on the panel. If you did not do so, or if you did not save your settings or your lab environment does not allow you to save your settings, you may access the **Terminal** by clicking the Main menu, pointing to **System Tools** and clicking **Terminal**. If you want the Terminal button on the panel, right-click **Terminal** and click **Add this launcher to panel**. For the remainder of the text, it will be assumed that you know how to access the **Terminal**.

STEP 1   Click the **Terminal** button [icon] on the panel

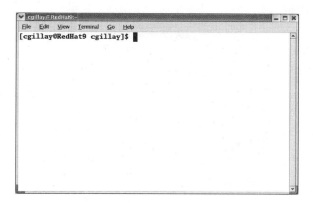

WHAT'S HAPPENING? You have opened the terminal window. You may find it difficult to read because of colors or font size. This can be altered. When you start the GNOME terminal for the first time, this application opens with a group of default settings. These settings are kept in what is called a *profile*. Your initial launching of the **Terminal** application with these default settings is called the Default profile. You can alter this profile or create a new profile. This is one advantage to using the Terminal in GNOME because you can easily customize the settings.

STEP 2   Click **Edit**. Click **Current Profile**. Click the **General** tab.

WHAT'S HAPPENING? As you can see, you are looking at the Default profile. If you want a different font, you need to clear the **Use the same size font as other applications** check box.

STEP 3   Clear the **Use the same size font as other applications** check box. Click the **Font** drop-down list box.

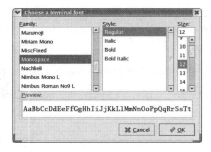

WHAT'S HAPPENING? You may pick a font and a font style that you find easier to read.

STEP 4   Click **Cancel**. Click the check box in **Use the same size font as other applications** to set it.

STEP 5   Click the **Colors** tab.

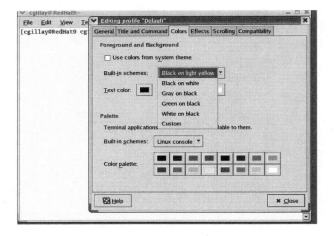

WHAT'S HAPPENING? Currently the choice is using the colors from the system theme (Bluecurve). But here you may choose other built-in schemes or choose your own colors that may be easier to read.

STEP 6   Clear the check box in front of **Use colors from system theme** to clear it. Click the **Built-in schemes** drop-down list box.

WHAT'S HAPPENING? If you look at the Terminal window in the background, you can see black text on a yellow background. You may find this easier to read. If you make changes to any of these items, such as fonts or colors, depending on how your system is set up, your settings should be retained each time you log on. However, in some lab environments, each time you log in, you have a "fresh" environment, so if you like different color and font choices, you will need to make those changes each time.

STEP 7   Click the check box in front of **Use colors from system theme** to set it. Click **Close**.

STEP 8   Click the Main Menu button. Point to **System Tools**. Click **Terminal**.

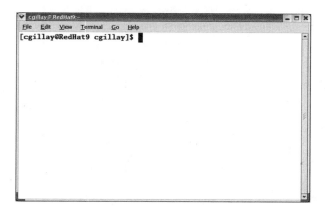

WHAT'S HAPPENING? This is another way to access the terminal window using the menu system. If you made any changes, they would be reflected here.

STEP 9 Close the terminal window you just opened. In the open terminal window, key in the following: **chsh -l** Enter

```
[cgillay@RedHat9 cgillay] $ chsh -l
/bin/sh
/bin/bash
/sbin/nologin
/bin/bash2
/bin/ash
/bin/bsh
/bin/tcsh/bin/csh
/bin/ksh
/bin/zsh
[cgillay@RedHat9 cgillay] $
```

WHAT'S HAPPENING? Before there was a GUI, there was and is the command line, where you key in commands to run your computer and the programs on it. When you run the terminal window in GNOME, you are running a program, called the shell, that is used to interpret and manage commands. A shell is a way to run your programs, manage your files and directories, compile code, and, in general, manage your computer. The shell is the user interface between the computer and the operating system. The shell interprets commands and passes them on to the operating system. After verifying that the keyed-in command is valid, the shell sends it to another part of the command processor to be executed. A shell can be called a command interpreter, but in the Unix/Linux world command interpreters are usually known as shells. They can also be referred to as the Terminal or the Command line.

You cannot interact with the operating system directly. You must have some user interface so that you may interact with the OS. Although shells are much less user-friendly than a GUI, most Linux/Unix administrators and power users feel that the shell is much more powerful than a GUI. In addition, since shells have been around much longer than GUIs, there are many powerful features built into them. You must communicate with the operating system through the shell. As a matter of fact, when you boot into Linux and before you start X, you are in a shell.

When you executed the **chsh -l** command, you were asking for a list of the available shells provided in this system. There are many popular shells. Examples include **sh**, which is the

Bourne shell; **csh**, which is the Cshell, **tcsh**, which is a look-alike C shell; **ash**, which is a look-alike Bourne shell and **ksh**, the public domain Korn shell. The Korn shell is a comprehensive combined version of other major shells. It incorporates all the features of C shell (**csh**) and Tab C-shell (**tcsh**) with the script language features similar to that of the **Bourne** shell. Many users consider **ksh** the most efficient shell. Korn, Bourne, and C are the three most commonly used Unix shells. The default shell used by Red Hat Linux is **Bash**, the Bourne Again shell. You can verify what shell you are running.

STEP 10 In the open terminal window, key in the following: **echo $SHELL** [Enter]

```
[cgillay@RedHat9   cgillay]$ echo $SHELL
/bin/bash
[cgillay@RedHat9   cgillay]$
```

WHAT'S HAPPENING? The **echo $shell** command you keyed in told you which shell you were using. You displayed the full path name with where the shell is located (/**bin**) and which shell you are using (**bash**). Figure 2.1, "Command Prompt," dissects the command prompt.

```
[cgillay@RedHat9   cgillay]$ _
```

Figure 2.1 • Command Prompt

WHAT'S HAPPENING? Your prompt will, of course, look different. If you were logged in as the root user, your prompt symbol will be a # instead of a $.

STEP 11 Key in the following: **bash --version** [Enter]

```
[cgillay@RedHat9   cgillay]$ bash --version
GNU bash, version 2.05b.0(1)-release (i386-redhat-linux-gnu)
Copyright (C) 2002 Free Software foundation, Inc.
[cgillay@RedHat9 cgillay]$
```

WHAT'S HAPPENING? When you used the option **--version** with the **bash** command, you saw what version of Bash you were using. Note the double --. Some options allow the use of two hyphens, and some commands require two hyphens with an option.

STEP 12 Close the terminal window.

WHAT'S HAPPENING? You have returned to the desktop.

2.9 • Navigating in the Shell

When you use the GNOME desktop, Nautilus is the file manager you use to locate files and directories. You may also locate files and directories and execute commands in the shell. However, when you use the shell, you must know what command you wish to use and the syntax of the command. Furthermore, you need to be aware of your location in the hierarchy of the file system.

2.10 • Activity: Navigating the Shell

STEP 1 Open a terminal window.

```
[cgillay@RedHat9 cgillay]$
```

WHAT'S HAPPENING? As indicated by Figure 2.1, **cgillay** is the current directory. It is where you are located in the file system hierarchy. In Linux, the prompt shows only the current local or working directory, not the entire path.

STEP 2 Key in the following: **pwd** Enter

```
[cgillay@RedHat9   cgillay]$ pwd
/home/gillay
[cgillay@RedHat9   cgillay]$
```

WHAT'S HAPPENING? The command **pwd** (print working directory) shows you the absolute path to your current directory. It is important to understand the difference between the terms "absolute path" and "relative path." The *absolute path* is the complete and total hierarchical structure. You start at the top and work your way down through every directory without skipping a directory. The absolute path is always absolutely correct. The *relative path* is the designation of the location of a file in relation to the current working directory.

As an analogy, if you were living in Los Angeles, California, you could get bus ticket to Santa Barbara. It would not be necessary to ask for a ticket to the United States, California, Los Angeles, and then Santa Barbara—you could use the "relative" path of just Santa Barbara. But, if you were in London, England, and were flying to Los Angeles, and needed to buy your connecting bus ticket before you left England, you would need to give the English ticket broker complete information about the ticket that you wanted. You would need to give the absolute path of where you wanted to leave from, and where you wanted to go to—you would ask for a ticket to the USA, state of California, city of Los Angeles, and then the city of Santa Barbara.

Just as the ticket salesperson in Los Angeles knew where Santa Barbara was, the current directory also knows information about its immediate surroundings. However, a directory knows only about the directories immediately beneath it and the directory immediately above it. There can be many directories beneath it (many child directories), but only one directory immediately above it (the parent directory). Each directory knows only its immediate child directories and its parent directory—no more. If you want to move to a different parent directory, you must return to the root. The root is the common "ancestor" of all the directories on the disk.

The command to navigate through your directories is **cd** followed by the directory to which you wish to move. **cd** keyed in alone will return you to your home directory.

STEP 3 Key in the following: **cd /usr** Enter

```
[cgillay@RedHat9   cgillay]$   cd /usr
[cgillay@RedHat9   usr]$
```

WHAT'S HAPPENING? You can see by the prompt that you are in the **/usr** directory. You used an absolute path. In the following step, be sure to use the lower case l, not the number 1.

STEP 4 Key in the following: **ls** Enter

```
[cgillay@RedHat9   usr]$   ls
bin        etc    include    lib      local    share    tmp
dict       games  kerberos   libexec  sbin     src      X11R6
[cgillay@RedHat9   usr]$
```

WHAT'S HAPPENING? By using the **ls** command, you asked to display all the files and directories in the **/usr** directory. On most Linux systems, the **ls** command is allowed to display file names of different types of files in different colors. Frequently used colors are navy blue for directory names; white (or black) for ordinary text files; green for executable files; cyan (a turquoise blue) for symbolic links; and red for compressed or archived files. This information is kept in a file called **/etc/DIR_COLORS** and can be customized. If this file does not exist, there will be no color differentiation.

STEP 5   Key in the following: **cd   share/apps/carddecks** [Enter]

```
[cgillay@RedHat9   usr]$   cd share/apps/carddecks
[cgillay@RedHat9   carddecks]$
```

STEP 6   Key in the following: **pwd** [Enter]

```
[cgillay@RedHat9   carddecks]$ pwd
/usr/share/apps/carddecks
[cgillay@RedHat9   carddecks]$
```

WHAT'S HAPPENING? Here you used a relative path to move to the **carddecks** directory. Linux also has some shortcuts. The single period (.) indicates the current directory, and two periods (..) is the parent directory. The parent directory is always one level higher than the current directory.

STEP 7   Key in the following: **cd ../..** [Enter]

STEP 8   Key in the following: **pwd** [Enter]

```
[cgillay@RedHat9   carddecks]$ cd ../..
[cgillay@RedHat9 share]$ pwd
/usr/share
[cgillay@RedHat9 cgillay]$
```

WHAT'S HAPPENING? The **../..** moved you from **carddecks** to the parent of **carddecks** (**apps**) and then to the parent of **apps** (**share**).

STEP 9   Key in the following: **cd** [Enter]

```
[cgillay@RedHat9   cgillay]$ cd
[cgillay@RedHat9   cgillay]$
```

WHAT'S HAPPENING? Whenever you key in **cd** with no options or arguments, you are moved to your home directory. Bash also supports command-line editing. You may use your left and right arrow to move on the command line, and you may also use the up arrow and down arrow to scroll through your command history.

STEP 10 Press the Up arrow key five times.

```
[cgillay@RedHat9   cgillay]$ cd share/apps/carddecks
```

WHAT'S HAPPENING? You have moved to the fifth command you keyed in. You may execute this command by pressing [Enter] *Note:* You may need to "up" arrow or "down" arrow a different number of times depending on if you entered any other commands. Just be sure that the command displayed is the one indicated under Step 10.

STEP 11 Press [Enter]

```
[cgillay@RedHat9   cgillay]$ cd share/apps/carddecks
bash: cd: share/apps/carddecks: No such file or directory
[cgillay@RedHat9   cgillay]$
```

WHAT'S HAPPENING? Since you are in your home directory, the command did not start at the root. There is no **share/apps/carddecks** directory in your home directory. That directory is located under the **/usr** directory. Thus, you need to add the **/usr** in order to go to the root and then to the **usr** directory.

STEP 12 Press the Up arrow once. Press [Alt] + **b** three times.

```
[cgillay@RedHat9   cgillay]$   cd share/apps/carddecks
```

WHAT'S HAPPENING? The [Alt] + **B** moved you back a word at a time.

STEP 13 Press the /. Key in **usr/**

```
[cgillay@RedHat9   cgillay]$ cd /usr/share/apps/carddecks
```

WHAT'S HAPPENING? You have edited this line. To execute, you only would need to press [Enter]. Table 2.2, "Common Editing Keys," gives some common command-line editing keys. You will find that these editing keys are common to most shells and also are used in the vi text editor.

Keys	Description
[←]	Moves back one character at a time without deleting characters.
[→]	Moves forward one character at a time without deleting characters.
[Backspace] or [Delete]	Deletes one character backward.
[Alt] + d	Deletes next forward word.
[Alt] + b	Moves backwards one word at a time.
[Alt] + f	Moves forward one word at a time.
[Ctrl] + a	Moves to beginning of line.
[Ctrl] + d	Deletes one character forward.
[Ctrl] + e	Moves to the end of the line.
[Ctrl] + k	Deletes everything forward from position of cursor.
[Ctrl] + w	Deletes previous word.
[Ctrl] + t	Transposes characters left of and under the cursor.

Table 2.2 • Common Editing Keys

STEP 14 Press `Ctrl` + **a**. Press `Ctrl` + **k**.

```
[cgillay@RedHat9   cgillay]$
```

WHAT'S HAPPENING? Pressing `Ctrl` + **a** moved you to the beginning of the command line. Pressing `Ctrl` + **k** deleted the line. You may also use the **history** command to recall commands that you have keyed in. This command, as its name indicates, lists your command line history with the line number of the commands. You can recall commands by using the number listed in the history or by using special characters. The syntax of the history command is **history**. One useful option is **-c**. This option clears the history list.

STEP 15 Key in the following: **history** `Enter`

```
[cgillay@RedHat9   cgillay]$   history
      1   pwd
      2   cd   /usr
      3   ls
      4   cd   share/apps/carddecks
      5   pwd
      6   cd ../..
      7   pwd
      8   cd
      9   cd   share/apps/carddecks
     10   history
[cgillay@RedHat9   cgillay]$
```

WHAT'S HAPPENING? You can see that each command you keyed in is prefaced by a number. To select a command by number, you key in the **!** (exclamation point) followed by the command number of interest.

STEP 16 Key in the following: **!2** `Enter`

```
[cgillay@RedHat9   cgillay]$   !2
cd /usr
[cgillay@RedHat9   usr]$
```

WHAT'S HAPPENING? You executed the **cd /usr** command. Note that you did not have to press `Enter`; the command just executed. As you can imagine, though, if you have keyed in many commands, when you key in history to get the command number, you would have a very long listing of commands. There is a more efficient way of using the history file, and that is to search for a specific command. You may use the following syntax if what you are looking for is in the command string: **!?*string*?**. Otherwise, you may simply key in the name of the command prefaced by the **!**. In the next step, you are going to look for the character string **apps**. Thus, you need to surround it by the question marks.

STEP 17 Key in the following: **!?apps?** `Enter`

```
[cgillay@RedHat9   usr]$   !?apps?
cd share/apps/carddecks
[cgillay@RedHat9   carddecks]$
```

WHAT'S HAPPENING? You were taken to the command that had **apps** in it. Next you will use the **history** command to execute the **pwd** command as an example of using the name of a command. You will see that you can use a partial command. As soon as the history command finds the first characters, it will complete the rest of the command.

STEP 18 Key in the following: **!pw** [Enter]

```
[cgillay@RedHat9  carddecks]$  !pw
pwd
/usr/share/apps/carddecks
[cgillay@RedHat9  carddecks]$
```

WHAT'S HAPPENING? The shell completed your command. It found the first instance of **pw** and completed the rest of the command (**pwd**) and executed it.

2.11 • The date and cal commands

The operating system keeps track of the current date and time. Date and time indicate the system date, which is the date and time used when files are opened and closed (last date/time accessed), or when a program asks for the date and time. The system administrator usually maintains the date and time and is the only one who can alter them unless the administrator has given the user permission to alter the date. The way the system date and time is displayed can be altered. The command is simply **date**.

Another useful command is the **cal** command. This command displays a calendar. The syntax for the **cal** command is

```
cal [-mjy13]  [[month] [year]
```

With no options, the calendar command displays the current month and year. Table 2.3, "cal Options," lists some of the more useful options.

Option	Name	Result
-m	Monday	Displays Monday as the first day of the week.
-j	Julian	Displays Julian dates. A Julian date is the number of elapsed days since the beginning of a particular year. The Julian date for the calendar date of 2004-02-28 would be day 59.
-y	Year	Displays a calendar for the current year.
-1	Single	Displays single month output.
-3	3 months	Displays previous, current, and next month.

Table 2.3 • cal Options

2.12 • Activity: Using the date and cal Commands

STEP 1 Key in the following: **date** [Enter]

```
[cgillay@RedHat9  cgillay]$ date
Wed Jun 18 09:20:01 PDT 2003
[cgillay@RedHat9  cgillay]$
```

WHAT'S **HAPPENING?** As you can see, the current day, date, time, and time zone are displayed. Look at the notification area of the panel in the lower right corner.

WHAT'S **HAPPENING?** The system date and time are the same since it is the same computer system.

STEP 2   Key in the following: **cal** Enter

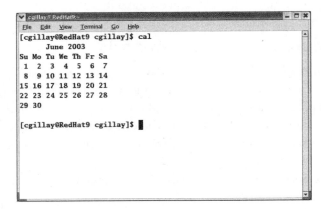

WHAT'S **HAPPENING?** The calendar for the current month and year, starting on a Sunday, is displayed. If you want a calendar for a specific month, you must specify the month and year numerically. You must use the entire year. You cannot, for instance, abbreviate 1999 as 99 or 2004 as 04.

STEP 3   Key in the following: **cal -m** Enter

```
cgillay@RedHat9:~                                         _ □ ×
File  Edit  View  Terminal  Go  Help
[cgillay@RedHat9 cgillay]$ cal
        June 2003
Su Mo Tu We Th Fr Sa
 1  2  3  4  5  6  7
 8  9 10 11 12 13 14
15 16 17 18 19 20 21
22 23 24 25 26 27 28
29 30

[cgillay@RedHat9 cgillay]$ cal -m
        June 2003
Mo Tu We Th Fr Sa Su
                 1
 2  3  4  5  6  7  8
 9 10 11 12 13 14 15
16 17 18 19 20 21 22
23 24 25 26 27 28 29
30
[cgillay@RedHat9 cgillay]$
```

WHAT'S **HAPPENING?** Using the **-m** option now displays the calendar starting with Monday rather than Sunday.

STEP 4   Key in the following: **cal 5 1998** Enter

```
                                                cgillay@RedHat9:~                              _ □ x
File   Edit   View   Terminal   Go   Help
Su Mo Tu We Th Fr Sa
 1  2  3  4  5  6  7
 8  9 10 11 12 13 14
15 16 17 18 19 20 21
22 23 24 25 26 27 28
29 30

[cgillay@RedHat9 cgillay]$ cal -m
       June 2003
Mo Tu We Th Fr Sa Su
                   1
 2  3  4  5  6  7  8
 9 10 11 12 13 14 15
16 17 18 19 20 21 22
23 24 25 26 27 28 29
30
[cgillay@RedHat9 cgillay]$ cal 5 1998
       May 1998
Su Mo Tu We Th Fr Sa
                1  2
 3  4  5  6  7  8  9
10 11 12 13 14 15 16
17 18 19 20 21 22 23
24 25 26 27 28 29 30
31
[cgillay@RedHat9 cgillay]$
```

WHAT'S **HAPPENING?** You asked for a calendar for the fifth month (May) for the year 1998.

STEP 5   Key in the following: **date;cal;cal 5 2004** Enter

```
                                                cgillay@RedHat9:~                              _ □ x
File   Edit   View   Terminal   Go   Help
[cgillay@RedHat9 cgillay]$ date;cal; cal 5 2004
Fri Jun 20 10:32:28 PDT 2003
       June 2003
Su Mo Tu We Th Fr Sa
 1  2  3  4  5  6  7
 8  9 10 11 12 13 14
15 16 17 18 19 20 21
22 23 24 25 26 27 28
29 30


       May 2004
Su Mo Tu We Th Fr Sa
                   1
 2  3  4  5  6  7  8
 9 10 11 12 13 14 15
16 17 18 19 20 21 22
23 24 25 26 27 28 29
30 31
[cgillay@RedHat9 cgillay]$ ▮
```

WHAT'S **HAPPENING?** You do not need to key in each command on a separate line. You may key in multiple commands on one command line, provided you separate each command with the semicolon (;). You may notice that your screen is becoming cluttered with commands and output. You can eliminate what is on the screen using **clear** command.

STEP 6   Key in the following: **clear** Enter

```
[cgillay@RedHat9  cgillay]$ clear
[cgillay@RedHat9  cgillay]$
```

WHAT'S **HAPPENING?** You have cleared your terminal window.

STEP 7   Close the terminal window.

2.13 ● Mounting File Systems

In Linux, a file system is a device, such as a hard disk or a floppy disk, that is formatted to store files. The file system is organized in a hierarchy, beginning from the root (/) and continuing downward, off the root directory. The organization of the file system begins when Linux is installed. Part of the installation procedure is to divide the hard disk or disks into partitions. A *partition* is a logical portion of the disk. Each partition normally has its own file system. Linux tends to treat partitions as though they were separate physical entities. These partitions can then be assigned to a part of the Linux file system or swap space for Linux or other file system types. If you are logged on as root (the super user), you may run the command **fdisk -l,** which will list the partitions on your system. See Figure 2.2, "The fdisk Command."

```
Disk /dev/hda: 80.0 GB, 80000000000 bytes
255 heads, 63 sectors/track, 9726 cylinders
Units = cylinders of 16065 * 512 bytes = 8225280 bytes


   Device Boot     Start       End     Blocks   Id  System
/dev/hda1    *         1        13     104391   83  Linux
/dev/hda2             14      9661   77497560   83  Linux
/dev/hda3           9662      7297    522112+   82  Linux swap
```

Figure 2.2 • The fdisk Command

You can see that, in this example, the partition labeled **/dev/hda2** has most of the space available for data and is the root partition (/) . The partition labeled **/dev/hda3** is dedicated to the Linux swap file. A *swap file* is a space on a hard disk used as the virtual memory extension of a computer's physical memory (RAM). Having a swap file allows the operating system to pretend that there is more RAM than there actually is. The least recently used files in RAM can be "swapped out" to the hard disk until they are needed later so that new files can be "swapped in" to RAM. The partition labeled **/dev/hda1** is the boot partition, which is the smallest partition.

In order to access the files on the device (the partition or file system), you must mount the device. In the Linux/Unix world, all files are arranged in a single tree which begins with the root directory (/). The files can be spread out over several devices. Mounting a device checks its status and readies it for access and attaches the file system found on the mounted device to the / directory.

In the DOS/Windows world, devices are also mounted, but the process is more transparent to the user. In the DOS/Windows world, each partition gets a drive letter and then, to access the files and directories on a partition, the user refers to the correct drive letter. In the Unix/ Linux world, instead of a drive letter, the device is mounted at a mount point, which is simply some directory in the file system. Once the file system is mounted, the device appears as a directory on the tree to the user, who can then access those files on that device. Normally, hard drives are mounted automatically when you boot. However, removable devices such as a floppy disk, CD-ROM, or Zip drive are not. You must mount the device in question each time you wish to use it, and, just as importantly, unmount it when you are finished. You cannot insert or remove removable media such as a floppy disk without using the mount and umount commands. One mistake users often make is to key in **unmount** instead of **umount**.

Only the root user (system administrator) can execute the **mount** command to establish the mount point. However, when the mount is set up, the root user can allow other users to mount or unmount the device. The syntax of the **mount** command is

```
mount -t  type device mount-point
```

The type is the name of the file system, such as ext2, ext3, or vfat. The device is the physical device and its location, such as **/dev/fd0**. mount-point is the name of the directory where the file system is mounted. A common directory name for a removable device is **/mnt**. Under the **/mnt** directory would then be each removable device, such as **/mnt/cdrom** or **/mnt/floppy**. The directory must be created prior to issuing the mount command. When you start Linux, one of the startup files reads the **/etc/fstab** file and mounts any file systems listed in the file. Thus, if there is a line in the fstab file that reads:

```
/dev/fd0 /mnt/floppy auto          noauto,owner,kudzu
```

any user can mount the specified device (**/dev/fd0**) at the mount point (**/mnt/floppy**) by using the command **mount /mnt/floppy**. This will then attach the file system found on the floppy disk to the root directory. The **auto** indicates that the mount command will identify the file system on the device; **noauto** means that the device is not automatically mounted; **owner** means that the user who mounts the device is the only one who can unmount; and **kudzu** is a program that detects and configures hardware. The syntax for the **umount** command is:

```
umount   dir   device
```

A file system (device) cannot be unmounted when it is busy; for instance, if you have open files on the device or when some process has its working directory on the device.

In order to allow ordinary users to mount and unmount removable devices, the root user must, in the **/etc/fstab** file, include the user option. This allows any user to use the **mount** and unmount commands. You can mount and unmount devices through either the GUI or at the command line.

2.14 • Activity: Mounting and Unmounting File Systems

STEP 1   Double-click your Home directory icon. In the Information drop-down list box, click **Tree**. Locate and expand the **mnt** directory. Click the **mnt** directory to make it the default directory.

WHAT'S HAPPENING? On this system, there are two mount points: **cdrom** and **floppy**. Most Linux systems will have at least **cdrom** and **floppy** and most will be located under the **/mnt** directory.

STEP 2   Place the floppy disk that comes with this book (labeled BOOK disk) in the drive. Click **floppy** in the directory tree.

WHAT'S HAPPENING? Because the floppy disk file system has not been mounted, you cannot read the disk. It appears as an empty directory.

STEP 3   Close the window. Right-click the desktop. Point to **Disks**.

WHAT'S HAPPENING? As you can see, the right-click lists the peripheral devices on your system. When you click a device—in this case, **Floppy** or **CD-ROM**—you are instructing Linux to mount the device.

STEP 4   Click **Floppy**.

WHAT'S HAPPENING? You now have a floppy icon on your desktop. You have mounted the disk, or in Linux terminology, added the file system to the root.

STEP 5 Double-click the floppy icon.

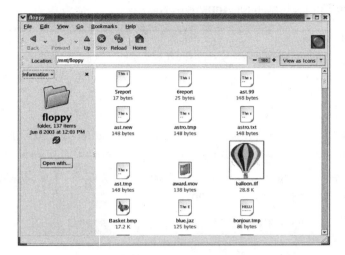

WHAT'S HAPPENING? At first the window appears empty. Be patient. It takes time for the OS to read the disk. You can tell if the system is reading the floppy disk, either by the noise the system makes as it begins reading the disk or by the light that flashes for the floppy disk drive. Once the disk has been read, the files appear in the window.

STEP 6 Close the floppy window. Right-click the floppy icon on the desktop.

WHAT'S HAPPENING? The right-click menu now presents the choice of **Eject**. If you chose that item, you would be unmounting the floppy disk. With a floppy disk, it will not be physically ejected. However, if the device were a CD-ROM, it would be physically ejected.

STEP 7 Click **Eject**. Click the Main Menu button. Point to **System Tools**. Click **Disk Management**.

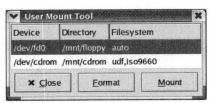

WHAT'S HAPPENING? This is the GUI User Mount Tool. On it, you can see what removable devices are already mounted or need to be unmounted. In this case, no device is mounted since the **Mount** button is available.

STEP 8   Click the **Mount** button for **/mnt/floppy.**

WHAT'S HAPPENING? You now know the floppy disk is mounted, because the choice in the dialog box is **Unmount**. In addition, the floppy disk icon appears on the desktop.

STEP 9   Click **Close**. Double-click your home directory icon. Click **Tree** . Locate the **/mnt** directory and expand it. Click **floppy.**

WHAT'S HAPPENING? Because the floppy is mounted, it appears as just another directory on the directory tree. You can access any file on the disk. Again, be patient. It takes time to read a floppy disk.

STEP 10   Double-click **astro.txt**.

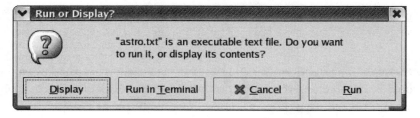

WHAT'S HAPPENING? The OS thinks that **astro.txt** is an executable text file. As you will see, shell scripts are text files and act as executable programs. In this example, **astro.txt** is simply a text file and all you want to do is to open or display the contents of the file.

STEP 11   Click **Display**.

WHAT'S HAPPENING? When you chose to display the file, you opened the file and displayed the contents of the file.

STEP 12 Close the **astro.txt** window. Right-click the desktop. Point to **Disks**.

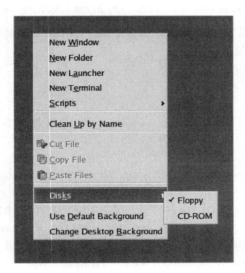

WHAT'S HAPPENING? Here is another way to unmount the floppy disk. Floppy has a check mark by it, indicating it is mounted.

STEP 13 Click **Floppy**.

WHAT'S HAPPENING? You have successfully unmounted the floppy. You can tell it is unmounted, as the floppy drive icon is no longer on your desktop. You must always unmount before you remove the media; in this case, the floppy disk.

STEP 14 Double-click your Home directory icon. Click **Tree** . Expand the **/mnt** directory. Click **floppy**.

WHAT'S HAPPENING? Note that even though the disk is still in the drive, the contents are no longer available to you because you unmounted it.

STEP 15 Close the floppy window. Open **gedit**. (Main menu/Accessories/Text Editor). Click **File**. Click **Open**. In the selection text box, key in the following: **/etc/fstab**. Click **OK**.

WHAT'S HAPPENING? In the **fstab** file, the line **/dev/fd0** tells you what the device is. **/mnt/ floppy** tells you the mount point. **noauto** tells Linux that the device must be mounted manually, and the owner is the user who has the permissions to mount and unmount the device. The **kudzu** option is the result of the actions of the **updfstab** file, which keeps **fstab** consistent with removable device on your system such as CD-ROMs, Zip drives, and so on.

STEP 16 Close the window. Open the Terminal. Key in the following: **mount** $\boxed{\text{Enter}}$

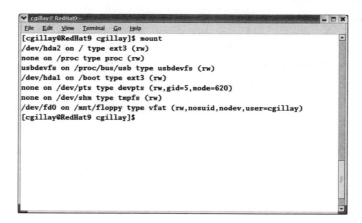

WHAT'S HAPPENING? The **mount** command, with no options or arguments, tells you what file systems are mounted and where they are mounted.

STEP 17 Key in the following: **mount /mnt/floppy** Enter

STEP 18 Key in the following: **ls /mnt/floppy** Enter

```
File  Edit  View  Terminal  Go  Help
exp01jan.dta    LONGFILENAMING.TXT    titan.txt
exp01mar.dta    media                 ven.99
exp02feb.dta    mer.99                ven.new
exp02jan.dta    mercury.tmp           ven.tmp
exp02mar.dta    mercury.txt           venus.tmm
exp03feb.dta    mer.new               venus.txt
exp03jan.dta    mer.tmp               wild1.xxx
exp03mar.dta    middle.red            wild2.yyy
exp201feb.dta   middle.up             wild3.zzz
exp201jan.dta   mikereport            wildone
exp201mar.dta   music                 wildone.dos
file2.czg       NEW AUTOS.txt         wildthr.dos
file2.fp        newprson.fil          wildtwo.dos
file2.swt       newreport             world.tif
file3.czg       new-suvs.xls          y.fil
file3.fp        oldauto.mak           zodiac.fil
file3.swt       Old Automobiles
[cgillay@RedHat9 cgillay]$
```

WHAT'S HAPPENING? The first command mounted the floppy disk. The second command displayed the contents of that disk.

STEP 19 Key in the following: **cat /etc/mtab** Enter

```
File  Edit  View  Terminal  Go  Help
[cgillay@RedHat9 cgillay]$ cat /etc/mtab
/dev/hda2 / ext3 rw 0 0
none /proc proc rw 0 0
usbdevfs /proc/bus/usb usbdevfs rw 0 0
/dev/hda1 /boot ext3 rw 0 0
none /dev/pts devpts rw,gid=5,mode=620 0 0
none /dev/shm tmpfs rw 0 0
/dev/fd0 /mnt/floppy vfat rw,nosuid,nodev,user=cgillay 0 0
[cgillay@RedHat9 cgillay]$
```

WHAT'S HAPPENING? You are looking at the **mtab** file. The **mtab** file lists all file systems that are currently mounted and the options they were mounted with. You can see that the floppy disk was mounted from the mount point **/mnt/floppy**, that the filesystem type is **vfat**, that there are read and write privileges ("rw" for privileges, and the user is the current logged-on user). **cat** stands for concatenate files and print to the standard output. The standard output device is the monitor. In essence, **cat** displays text files. In the next command, be sure you key in **umount**, not unmount

STEP 20 Key in the following: **umount /mnt/floppy** Enter

STEP 21 Key in the following: **ls /mnt/floppy** Enter

```
[cgillay@RedHat9  cgillay]$ umount /mnt/floppy
[cgillay@RedHat9  cgillay]$ ls
[cgillay@RedHat9  cgillay]$
```

WHAT'S HAPPENING? Since you unmounted the device, you cannot access the file system.

STEP 22 Close the window.

2.15 ● Filename Expansion

When you are using the Bash shell or the **Search for Files** menu choice in the GUI, rather than selecting one file at a time, you may give the shell or the Search for Files dialog box abbreviated file names that contain special characters, sometimes called metacharacters. ***Metacharacters*** are those characters that have special meaning to the shell. For instance, you may use the **ls** command with an argument of a specific file name. When you key in **ls myfile**, you locate the one specific file that matches what you keyed in. Every time you wish to locate a file, you can key the entire file name. Often, however, you wish to work with a group of files that have similar names or a group of files whose names you do not know. There is a "shorthand" system that allows you to operate on a group of files rather than a single file. These special characters are also called ***wildcards***. Conceptually, they are similar to playing cards, where the joker can stand for another card of your choice. This feature of the shell is also called *globbing*.

In Linux, the question mark (**?**) , the asterisk (*****), and square brackets (**[ ]**) are wildcards. When one of these symbols appears in an argument on the command line , the symbol is expanded into a list of file names and passes the list to the program that you used. File names that contain these special characters are called ***ambiguous file references***, since they do not reference a specific file. The ***** represents or substitutes for a group or "string" of characters; the **?** represents or substitutes for a single character. A pair of square brackets enclosing a list of characters allows the shell to match individual characters. It is important to realize that the commands do not do the expansion. The shell does and passes the information to the command.

Many commands allow globbing. You will use the **ls** command in the shell, and you will use the **Search for Files** menu choice to demonstrate the use of wildcards.

2.16 ● Activity: Filename Expansion

Note: Although when in the shell the instructions use the term *Key in the following:*, remember that you may use the editing keys.

STEP 1 Mount the BOOK floppy disk. Double-click the user Home icon. Click **Tree**. Click **/mnt/floppy** to select it.

WHAT'S HAPPENING? You are looking at the files on the floppy disk in icon view. In Red Hat Linux 9, the Nautilus file manager 2.2.1 has no find utility. You may check which version of a program you are using in a GUI by clicking **Help** and then **About**.

STEP 2   Click **Help**. Click **About**.

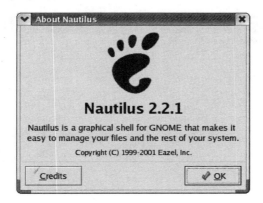

WHAT'S HAPPENING? In this example, this is version 2.2.1 of Nautilus, which does not support a find operation. However, you can move about the window using key strokes or the scroll bar.

STEP 3   Click **OK**. Click in the contents side of the window. Press the **G** key.

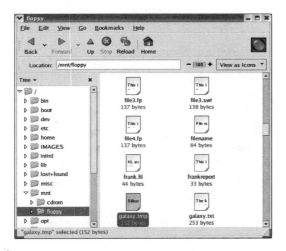

WHAT'S HAPPENING? You moved to the first file that begin with the letter G. You are looking at the files and directories on the floppy disk. However, unless you know the exact name of your file or directory, locating a group of files or a file for which you are unsure of the name is a laborious task. In this case, it is easier to use the command line or the Search for Files menu choice.

STEP 4   Close the **floppy** window. Open the Terminal.

STEP 5   Key in the following: **ls /e**

STEP 6   Press the **Tab** key.

```
[cgillay@RedHat9  cgillay]$  ls/etc/
```

WHAT'S HAPPENING? The shell provides word completion. The criterion for completing a file name is minimal completion. In other words, you must key in enough characters so the shell will find the name and complete it. If it is a directory, the shell will add the /.

STEP 7 Key in the following where the cursor is located: **p**. Then press the ⌈**Tab**⌋ key twice.

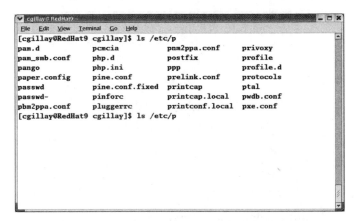

WHAT'S HAPPENING? There was no file named "**p**," but there were multiple files that began with the letter p. Pressing the ⌈**Tab**⌋ key twice displayed all the possible files that matched the letter p.

STEP 8 Press ⌈**Ctrl**⌋ + **a**. Press ⌈**Ctrl**⌋ + **k**.

STEP 9 Key in the following: **cd /mnt/floppy** ⌈**Enter**⌋

```
[cgillay@RedHat9  cgillay]$ cd  /mnt/floppy
[cgillay@linux72  floppy]$
```

WHAT'S HAPPENING? You first cleared what you had keyed in. Then you issued a new command. You have changed the default directory to the floppy disk. If you wanted to locate a file and all you remembered about the file name was that it began with the letter **e** and that it was located on the default drive and directory, you could try the following command.

STEP 10 Key in the following: **ls e** ⌈**Enter**⌋

```
[cgillay@linux72  floppy]$  ls  e
ls: e: No such file or directory
[cgillay@linux72  floppy]$
```

WHAT'S HAPPENING? You could not locate the file, as you have insufficient information. First, note how the prompt reflects the only the current directory (**floppy**), not the entire path (/**mnt/ floppy**). When you keyed in **ls e**, you were correct, but only somewhat. You first entered the work you wanted done, the command **ls**. You did not need to enter the path name, since **ls** assumed the default directory (/**mnt/floppy**). However, **ls** specifically looked for a file called **e**. There was no file called e; that was simply the first letter of the file name. You can find files that begin with **e** by using the wildcard symbol * to represent all other characters—both the file name and the file extension.

STEP 11 Key in the following: **ls e*** ⌈**Enter**⌋

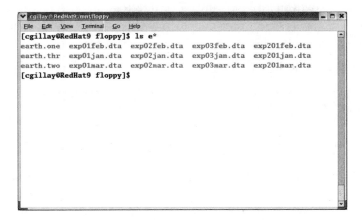

WHAT'S HAPPENING? In this example, you asked **ls** to find files beginning with the letter **e** in the default directory. You did not know anything else about the file names or even how many files you might have that began with the letter "e." You represented any and all characters following the letter **e** with the asterisk. Now, **ls** could look for a match.

STEP 12 Key in the following: **ls report*** Enter

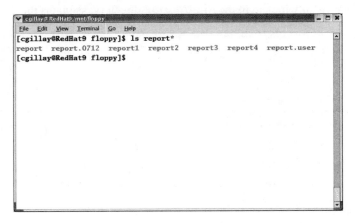

WHAT'S HAPPENING? You asked for any file that began with the word **report**. However, this does not show you all the files with **report** in their name, only those that begin with **report**.

STEP 13 Key in the following: **ls *report*** Enter

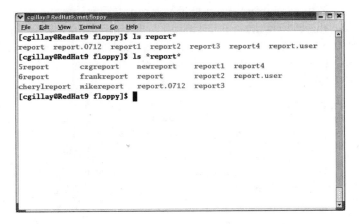

WHAT'S HAPPENING? Now you asked for any file or directory that had **report** anywhere in its name. The next activities will demonstrate the differences between * and ?. Whereas the * represents a group of characters, the ? represents a single character.

STEP 14 Key in the following: **ls *.?** Enter

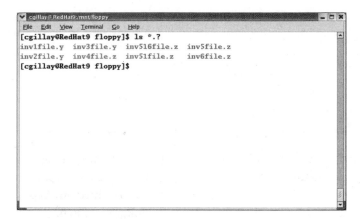

WHAT'S HAPPENING? You asked **ls** for any file that had any character but had a one-character file extension. Remember, **ls** only looked in the **/mnt/floppy** directory, as that is the default.

STEP 15 Key in the following: **ls exp*jan.dta** Enter

```
[cgillay@RedHat9   floppy]$   ls   exp*jan.dta

exp01jan.dta      exp02jan.dta      exp03jan.dta      exp201jan.dta

[cgillay@RedHat9   floppy]$
```

WHAT'S HAPPENING? You asked for every file that began with **exp**, had any number of characters in the middle, but had **jan** at the end of the file name and had **.dta** as an extension. If you wanted to see the files that had only two characters in the middle, you could use the ?.

STEP 16 Key in the following: **ls exp??jan.dta** Enter

```
[cgillay@RedHat9   floppy]$   ls   exp??*jan.dta
exp01jan.dta      exp02jan.dta      exp03jan.dta
[cgillay@RedHat9   floppy]$
```

WHAT'S HAPPENING? You were more specific, so you saw a more specific display. You eliminated the file that had three characters in the middle (**exp201jan.dta**) since you specified only two characters with the ??. When you use the square brackets, they surround a group of specific, individual characters. The brackets define a character class, and if any single character within the brackets matches a file, the file is selected.

STEP 17 Key in the following: **ls inv*.*** Enter

```
[cgillay@RedHat9    floppy]$   ls inv*.*
inv1file.y     inv3file.y     inv516file.z     inv5file.z
inv2file.y     inv4file.z     inv51file.z      inv6file.z
[cgillay@RedHat9    floppy]$
```

WHAT'S HAPPENING? Eight files are displayed when you used the *.*. To view specific files, you may use the brackets.

STEP 18 Key in the following: **ls inv[123]*** **Enter**

```
[cgillay@RedHat9  floppy]$  ls  inv[123]*
inv1file.y    inv2file.y    inv3file.y
[cgillay@RedHat9  floppy]$
```

WHAT'S HAPPENING? Only files that began with **inv** and had a **1**, **2**, or **3** in their file name were displayed.

STEP 19 Key in the following: **ls inv[15]*** **Enter**

```
[cgillay@RedHat9  floppy]$  ls  inv[15](
inv1file.y    inv516file.z    inv51file.z    inv5file.z
[cgillay@RedHat9  floppy]$
```

WHAT'S HAPPENING? Now only files that began with **inv** and had a **1** or a **5** were displayed anywhere in their name.

STEP 20 Key in the following: **ls project[a-c]** **Enter**

```
[cgillay@RedHat9  floppy]$  ls project[a-c]
projecta    projectb    projectc
[cgillay@RedHat9  floppy]$
```

WHAT'S HAPPENING? Now only files that had an **a**, **b**, or **c** and that followed **project** were displayed.

STEP 21 Key in the following: **ls project[x-z]** **Enter**

```
[cgillay@RedHat9  floppy]$  ls project[x-z]
projectx    projecty    projectz
[cgillay@RedHat9  floppy]$
```

WHAT'S HAPPENING? Now only files that had an **x**, **y**, or **z** and that followed **project** were displayed. You may also use globbing (wildcards) in the Search for Files menu choice. You may also look for a specific file.

STEP 22 Close the Terminal. Click the Main menu. Click **Search for Files ...**

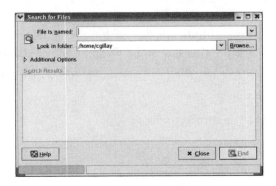

WHAT'S HAPPENING? The Search for Files dialog box has a location (currently blank) where you key in your file specification. The **Look in folder:** text box assumes the default, in this case your home directory (/**home/cgillay**).

STEP 23   In the **File is named:** box, key in the following: **galaxy.txt.**

STEP 24   In the **Look in folder:** text box, key in the following: **/mnt/floppy**.

STEP 25   Click **Find**.

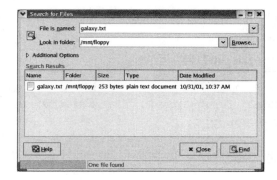

WHAT'S HAPPENING? The file, **galaxy.txt**, was located. You also see other information about the file—its size, type and the date and time it was last modified. You may also use ambiguous file references with this tool.

STEP 26   In the **File is named:** text box, highlight **galaxy.txt**. Then, key in the following: **g*.***. Click **Find**.

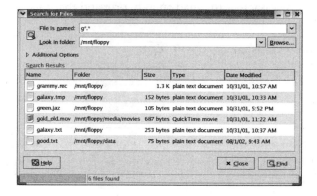

WHAT'S HAPPENING? By highlighting the entry in the **File is named:** text box, you selected it. Then, what you keyed in replaced what was there. This is known as "typing replaces selection." This feature saves you the trouble of individually deleting the characters that are there. If you look at the display, you will also see that this utility program found all the files that began with **g** on the floppy disk—even those in another directory (/**mnt/floppy/media/movies**).

STEP 27   Click the **Close** button.

WHAT'S HAPPENING? You have returned to the desktop.

2.17 • The ls Command

You have seen that you can use the **ls** command with wildcards. By default, when you simply key in **ls**, **ls** sorts the files based on the value of the characters. In Linux, uppercase letters come before lowercase letters, and numerals or symbols come before any letters at all. The **ls** command also has more than 40 options that can be combined to format listings. Table 2.4, "Options Used with ls," lists some of the more useful options.

Option	Name	Purpose
-1	lists	Lists files in a single column. Note that the option is the number 1, not the lower case l.
-C	columns	Lists files in columns vertically.
-F	flags	Lists files and directories with visual clues as to what items are in a directory. Some classify flags include the following: / for directories, * for executable files, and @ for symbolic links
-R	recursive	Lists recursively so that it will list the directories and files in the subdirectories of the current directory.
-S	size	Lists files by size, from largest to the smallest.
-X	extension	Lists files in file extension order. Files with no extensions appear first.
-a	all	Lists all the files in the current or specified directory, including any hidden files or directories.
-d	directory names	Lists directory name, not the contents of the directory.
-k	kilobytes	Lists files sizes in kilobytes. Needs to be combined with the **-s** option (**-sk**).
-l	long	Provides a long format, which includes file details such as the size, time stamp, owner, and permissions.
-m	commas	Lists filenames separated by commas.
-r	reverse	Lists files in reverse name order. When combined with the **-t**, lists in reverse time order.
-s	size	Lists size of files in blocks.
-t	time	Lists files by last time created or modified. Most recent files are listed first.
-x	horizontally	Lists files horizontally in rows.

Table 2.4 • Options Used with ls

2.18 • Activity: Using Options with the ls Command

Note: The BOOK disk should be mounted.

STEP 1   Open a terminal window.

STEP 2   Key in the following: **ls -1 /mnt/floppy** [Enter]

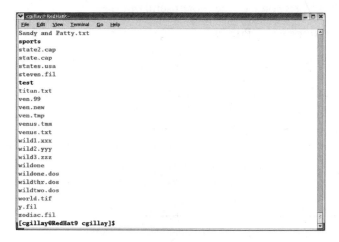

WHAT'S HAPPENING? Here you used the **-1** option, and your files that are located on the BOOK disk are listed in a single column.

STEP 3   Key in the following: **ls -R /mnt/floppy** [Enter]

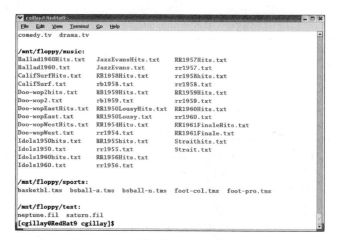

WHAT'S HAPPENING? Here you listed the contents of the floppy disk recursively. ***Recursively*** means that the command traverses the directory tree from the top down and shows all the directories as well as the files in those subdirectories.

STEP 4   Key in the following: **ls -l /mnt/floppy** [Enter]

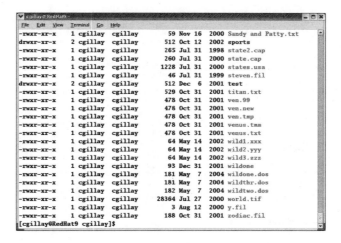

WHAT'S HAPPENING? Here you used a long listing (you used the lower case ell, not the number 1). The information here tells you what the file is, whether it is a directory or file, what permissions are set for the file, what links there are to the file, the owner of the file, name of the group the file belongs to, the size of the file, the time and the date the file was last modified, and the name of the file. Permissions are **r** for **read**, **w** for **write** and **x** for **execute**. If there is a hyphen in a permission slot, that means that the user does not have that right. Figure 2.3, "Long Listing," dissects the listing.

File type & permissions	Links	Owner	Group	Size last	Date and time modified		File name
-rwxr-xr-x	1	cgillay	cgillay	181	May 7	2004	wilddone.dos
drwxr-xr-x	2	cgillay	cgillay	512	Oct 12	2002	sports

Figure 2.3 • Long Listing

Looking at **wildone.dos**, the first listing in the Figure 2.3, the first character, the -, is the file type. The hyphen means an ordinary file. Compare that with the second entry, the directory **sports**. Its first character is a **d** for directory. Following type, the file permissions are listed in blocks of three. Looking at **wildone.dos**, the owner has **rwx** (read, write, execute permissions for this file); the next group of three, **r-x** (read, execute), means that any groups that are associated with this file have the same permissions. The last three permissions, **r-x**, are for any other users. Any other user can read or execute the file but cannot write to it. Whenever you see a - in a file permission set, it means that permission is not available. A link is a pointer to a file or directory. This column indicates how many links there are. The next two columns list the owner of the file and any groups. In this example, the owner and the group are the same. The next column lists the size of the file in bytes. In the case of the **sports** directory, the size refers to the size of the directory file itself, not what it contains. The last column contains the date the file was created or modified if it was in the previous year and the day and time if it was modified in the current year.

STEP 5   Key in the following: **ls -t /mnt/floppy** ‹Enter›

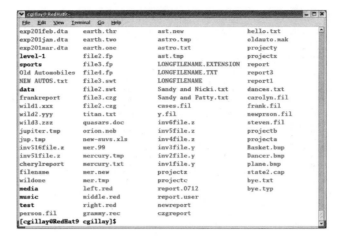

```
exp201feb.dta    earth.thr      ast.new                hello.txt
exp201jan.dta    earth.two      astro.tmp              oldauto.mak
exp201mar.dta    earth.one      astro.txt             projecty
level-1          file2.fp       ast.tmp               projectx
sports           file3.fp       LONGFILENAME.EXTENSION report
Old Automobiles  file4.fp       LONGFILENAME.TXT      report3
NEW AUTOS.txt    file3.swt      LONGFILENAME          report1
data             file2.swt      Sandy and Nicki.txt   dances.txt
frankreport      file3.czg      Sandy and Patty.txt   carolyn.fil
wild1.xxx        file2.czg      cases.fil             frank.fil
wild2.yyy        titan.txt      y.fil                 newprson.fil
wild3.zzz        quasars.doc    inv6file.z            steven.fil
jupiter.tmp      orion.neb      inv5file.z            projectb
jup.tmp          new-suvs.xls   inv4file.z            projecta
inv516file.z     mer.99         inv3file.y            Basket.bmp
inv51file.z      mercury.tmp    inv2file.y            Dancer.bmp
cherylreport     mercury.txt    inv1file.y            plane.bmp
filename         mer.new        projectz              state2.cap
wildone          mer.tmp        projectc              bye.txt
media            left.red       report.0712           bye.typ
music            middle.red     report.user
test             right.red      newreport
person.fil       grammy.rec     czgreport
[cgillay@RedHat9 cgillay]$
```

WHAT'S HAPPENING? Here you listed the files in order of the last time they were modified. The oldest files are at the end. However, right now, since you cannot see the dates of the files, you cannot confirm that the oldest files were at the end of display. The **-l** option allows you to see this information. Now, if you want to see the oldest files first, you can combine **-t** with **-r** and add the **-l** to actually see the dates.

STEP 6   Key in the following: **ls -ltr /mnt/floppy** Enter

```
File  Edit  View  Terminal  Go  Help
-rwxr-xr-x   1 cgillay  cgillay        64 May 14  2002 wild2.yyy
-rwxr-xr-x   1 cgillay  cgillay        64 May 14  2002 wild1.xxx
-rwxr-xr-x   1 cgillay  cgillay        33 Jul 30  2002 frankreport
drwxr-xr-x   2 cgillay  cgillay       512 Aug  1  2002 data
-rwxr-xr-x   1 cgillay  cgillay       159 Aug 24  2002 NEW AUTOS.txt
-rwxr-xr-x   1 cgillay  cgillay       183 Aug 24  2002 Old Automobiles
drwxr-xr-x   2 cgillay  cgillay       512 Oct 12  2002 sports
drwxr-xr-x   3 cgillay  cgillay       512 Nov 16  2002 level-1
-rwxr-xr-x   1 cgillay  cgillay       290 Jun 16 11:15 exp201mar.dta
-rwxr-xr-x   1 cgillay  cgillay       304 Jun 16 11:15 exp201jan.dta
-rwxr-xr-x   1 cgillay  cgillay       297 Jun 16 11:15 exp201feb.dta
-rwxr-xr-x   1 cgillay  cgillay       292 Jun 16 11:15 exp02mar.dta
-rwxr-xr-x   1 cgillay  cgillay       294 Jun 16 11:15 exp02jan.dta
-rwxr-xr-x   1 cgillay  cgillay       295 Jun 16 11:15 exp02feb.dta
-rwxr-xr-x   1 cgillay  cgillay       292 Jun 16 11:15 exp01mar.dta
-rwxr-xr-x   1 cgillay  cgillay       294 Jun 16 11:15 exp01jan.dta
-rwxr-xr-x   1 cgillay  cgillay       295 Jun 16 11:15 exp01feb.dta
-rwxr-xr-x   1 cgillay  cgillay       292 Jun 16 11:16 exp03mar.dta
-rwxr-xr-x   1 cgillay  cgillay       294 Jun 16 11:16 exp03jan.dta
-rwxr-xr-x   1 cgillay  cgillay       295 Jun 16 11:16 exp03feb.dta
-rwxr-xr-x   1 cgillay  cgillay       182 May  7  2004 wildtwo.dos
-rwxr-xr-x   1 cgillay  cgillay       181 May  7  2004 wildthr.dos
-rwxr-xr-x   1 cgillay  cgillay       181 May  7  2004 wildone.dos
[cgillay@RedHat9 cgillay]$
```

WHAT'S HAPPENING? Now the oldest files are listed first and the newest file listed last, which you can confirm, since the date appears in the display. You listed files in the long file format, in reverse order by date/time. You could have keyed in the command as **ls -l -t -r /mnt/floppy**, using the hyphen before each option but it is not necessary. You can use one hyphen and then combine the options.

STEP 7   Key in the following: **ls -F /mnt/floppy** Enter

WHAT'S HAPPENING? Here you see the classification flags. Directories are indicated by the / following their name, whereas files are indicated by the *. As you can see, there are many ways to look at your files and directories. The **ls** command is also a little different from other commands. It will allow you to place the options after the arguments, as in **ls /mnt/floppy -lrt** or **ls /mnt/floppy -F.**. Since all **ls** does is list files, it is a very forgiving command. However, since most commands require that options precede arguments, it is best to get in the habit of placing options first on the command line.

STEP 8   Close the Terminal window.

2.19 ● The locate Command

Since everything in Linux is a file, one of the things you will often need to do is find the location of a file. The **locate** command is the fastest way to search for a file or files in the entire directory tree. The **locate** command is a link or a "shortcut" to the **slocate** (secure locate) command. The **locate** command looks in a pre-defined database, which contains a list of all the files on your system. This database is indexed for rapid searching. Obviously you will add or delete files to your system, so the database can quickly become obsolete. Because of this, the database is automatically updated every day. It can be updated manually using the **updateb** or **slocate -u** command, but only the root user can use these two commands. The basic syntax for the command is:

```
locate [FILE]
```

where FILE can be preceded by a directory name to limit your search. The **locate** command will find all or part of the file name you specified.

2.20 ● Activity: The locate Command

Note: The BOOK disk should be mounted.

STEP 1   Open a terminal window.

STEP 2   Key in the following: **locate ls** `Enter`

STEP 3   Quickly press `Ctrl` + **c**

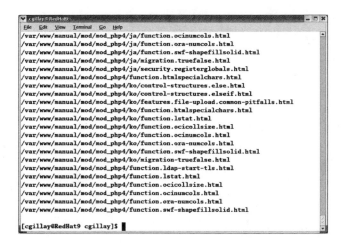

WHAT'S HAPPENING? This is a case of too much information. The locate command located any file in any directory starting with the root (/) that had **ls** somewhere in its name. Using **Ctrl** + **C** was a quick way to break into the command and stop it from executing. You can be more specific.

STEP 4   Key in the following: **locate /bin/ls** **Enter**

WHAT'S HAPPENING? Now your display is more manageable. You may use wildcards with the locate command as well.

STEP 5   Key in the following: **locate /politics/t*** **Enter**

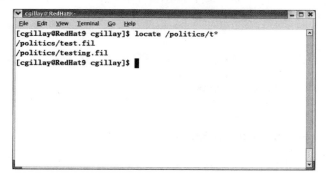

WHAT'S HAPPENING? Remember, if you are working on your own computer, you needed to refer to Appendix A and set up users, groups, directories, and files. Here you are looking for all files that begin with a **t** that are located in the **/politics** directory.

STEP 6 Key in the following: **ls /mnt/floppy/r*** Enter

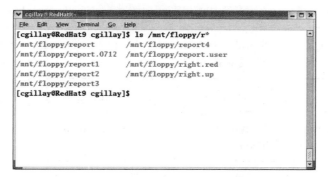

WHAT'S HAPPENING? You used the **ls** command to confirm that there were files on **/mnt/floppy** that began with an "r." Now you are going to try the **locate** command with the same argument.

STEP 7 Key in the following: **locate /mnt/floppy/r*** Enter

```
[cgillay@RedHat9   cgillay]$   locate /mnt/floppy/r*
[cgillay@RedHat9   cgillay]$
```

WHAT'S HAPPENING? The **locate** command did not find any files that began with an **r** even though the **ls** command did find those files. The problem is that the database that **locate** searched was not updated to include the files on **/mnt/floppy** and therefore found no files. If you were a root user, you could manually update the database. However, normally you would not want to include removable media as part of the database.

STEP 8 Close the Terminal window.

WHAT'S HAPPENING? You have returned to the desktop.

2.21 • The find Command

Although understanding file name expansion is useful for searching for files, it does not assist you when you want to know where a specific file or group of files are located. The find command is an extremely powerful and useful command to locate files. Unlike the locate command, it does not rely on a database, but instead searches the directory tree for files that meet the criteria that you specified. To locate a file by name, you use the basic syntax of

```
find pathname  -name  filename
```

The command is **find**, and *pathname* is where you want the search to begin. The option **-name** states you want to locate a file by name, and filename is the name of the file you are searching for. You may use wildcards in the filename statement. The **find** command searches recursively. In this instance, recursive means that the find command starts in the named directory and searches down through the directory tree through all the files and directories under the directory name you specified. The **-name** option is actually only one of many options that can be used with find. Table 2.5, "**find** Options," lists some helpful options.

Option	Purpose
-atime <+t, -t, t>	Searches for a file last accessed in a certain period of time. The **t** stands for time. You would substitute a numerical value. **+t** is more than a specific number of days ago, **-t** is less than a specific number of days ago, and t is a specific number of days ago.
-ctime <+t, -t, t>	Searches for a file last changed in a certain period of time. The **t** is time.
-iname	Searches for a specific file name ignoring case.
-mtime <+t, -t, t>	Searches for a file last modified in a certain period of time. The **t** is time.
-name	Searches for a specific file name.
-print	Some versions of Unix/Linux will not display the output of the find command unless **-print** is added.
-type <type>	Searches for any files of a specified type. Two popular choices are **d** for directories and **f** for files.
-user	Searches for files belonging to a specific user.

Table 2.5 • find Options

2.22 • Activity: The find Command

Note: The BOOK disk should still be mounted.

STEP 1   Open a terminal window.

STEP 2   Key in the following: **find -name astro.tmp** Enter

```
[cgillay@RedHat9   cgillay]$ find -name astro.tmp
[cgillay@RedHat9   cgillay]$
```

WHAT'S **HAPPENING?** Since you did not specify a path name, **find** looked only in the default directory, your home directory.

STEP 3   Key in the following: **find /mnt/floppy -name astro.tmp** Enter

```
[cgillay@RedHat9   cgillay]$ find /mnt/floppy -name astro.tmp
/mnt/floppy/astro.tmp
[cgillay@RedHat9   cgillay]$
```

WHAT'S **HAPPENING?** Your file was located. You may use wildcards with the **find** command as well.

STEP 4   Key in the following: **find /mnt/floppy -name *.tmp** Enter

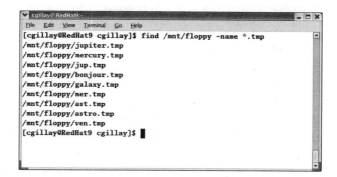

WHAT'S HAPPENING? ⟩ By using a wildcard, you located all the files in the **/mnt/floppy** directory (floppy disk) that matched the criterion of any with a file extension of **.tmp**.

STEP 5   Key in the following: **find /mnt/floppy -type d** ⟨Enter⟩

```
[cgillay@RedHat9 cgillay]$ find /mnt/floppy -type d
/mnt/floppy
/mnt/floppy/test
/mnt/floppy/music
/mnt/floppy/media
/mnt/floppy/media/tv
/mnt/floppy/media/movies
/mnt/floppy/media/books
/mnt/floppy/data
/mnt/floppy/sports
/mnt/floppy/level-1
/mnt/floppy/level-1/level-2
/mnt/floppy/level-1/level-2/level-3
[cgillay@RedHat9 cgillay]$
```

WHAT'S HAPPENING? ⟩ Now you have located all the directories on the floppy disk. You asked for a specific type of file (**-type**), and the **d** indicated that the type of file you were looking for was a directory.

STEP 6   Key in the following: **find /mnt/floppy -mtime 20** ⟨Enter⟩

```
[cgillay@RedHat9  cgillay]$ find /mnt/floppy -mtime 20
[cgillay@RedHat9  cgillay]$
```

WHAT'S HAPPENING? ⟩ No file on the floppy disk was modified exactly 20 days ago.

STEP 7   Key in the following: **find -mtime 5** ⟨Enter⟩

```
[cgillay@RedHat9 cgillay]$ find -mtime 5
./.gnome2/gedit-print-config
./.nautilus/metafiles/start-here:%2F%2F%2F.xml
./.nautilus/metafiles/file:%2F%2F%2Fhome%2Fcgillay%2F.Trash.xml
./.openoffice/user/config/registry/instance/org/openoffice/Office/
Views.xml
./.openoffice/user/config/inethist.dat
./.openoffice/user/basic
./.openoffice/user/basic/dialog.xlc
./.openoffice/user/basic/script.xlc
./.Trash
./.Trash/test.sxw
[cgillay@RedHat9 cgillay]$
```

WHAT'S HAPPENING? ⟩ Your display will differ. You looked in your home directory to see what files have been modified within the past five days. Although you may not have personally modified the files listed, the operating system is always changing and modifying files. You are looking recursively in your home directory. The **.** in front of a directory or file name means that it is hidden. You can see hidden directories and files with the **-a** (all) used with **ls**.

STEP 8   Key in the following: **ls   -a** Enter

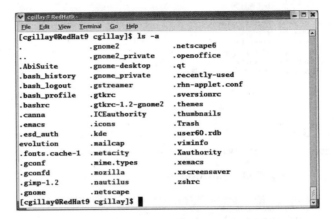

WHAT'S HAPPENING? You are now looking at your home directory with its hidden files and directories. Your display will vary.

STEP 9   Key in the following: **find / -iname gedit** Enter

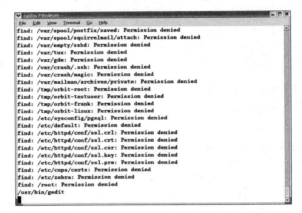

WHAT'S HAPPENING? You were looking for a file named **gedit**. The **iname** option told the command to ignore case. You began at the root directory with the /. There are many directories that you do not have permission to access. This is why on many of the lines, you see the message **Permission denied**. If you wanted to filter out some of this information, you could use redirection.

STEP 10 Close your terminal window.

2.23 • Redirection

The operating system knows what you want to do because you key commands. Input is expected from the console keyboard, which is considered the standard input device (**stdin**). In addition, the results of a command's execution are written to the screen. The console screen is considered the standard output device (**stdout**). In addition, if there are error messages, they are written to what is called standard error (**stderr**), which is usually written to the console screen.

You can change this through a feature called *redirection*, which allows you to tell the operating system to, instead of writing the output to the standard output device (the screen), write the information somewhere else. Typically, this is to a file or to a device. Redirection does not make sense with all commands, since all commands, after executing, do not write to the monitor. Redirection does work with the **ls** and **find** commands because both commands get their input from the standard input device, the keyboard, and write to the standard output device, the screen. The syntax is **command > destination**. The command is what you key in, such as **ls *.txt**. You then use the greater-than symbol (**>**) to redirect the results of that command to where you specify instead of to the screen. The command would be keyed in as **ls *.txt > my.fil** to send the results or output to a file named **my.fil**. You may also redirect standard error so you do not see it. You redirect it to a device called **/dev/null**. A null device means the output goes "nowhere" and you do not see it. So, to redirect the error messages in the find command, you could key in **find / -iname gedit 2>/dev/null**. The **2** preceding the greater-than sign indicates that you only want to redirect standard error, which is file type **2**.

2.24 ● Activity: Redirecting Output to a File and a Device

Note: The BOOK disk should be mounted.

STEP 1   Open a terminal window.

STEP 2   Key in the following: **ls /mnt/floppy/*.txt > my.file** [Enter] .

STEP 3   Key in the following: **ls** [Enter]

```
[cgillay@RedHat9   cgillay]$   ls /mnt/floppy/*.txt > my.file.
[cgillay@RedHat9   cgillay]$   ls
evolution  my.file
[cgillay@RedHat9   cgillay]$
```

WHAT'S HAPPENING? You could have more or fewer files in your home directory. What you did was take the output from the **ls** command and redirect to a file called **my.file** located in your home directory.

STEP 4   Key in the following: **ls /mnt/floppy/*.txt** [Enter]

STEP 5   Key in the following: **cat my.file** [Enter]

```
[cgillay@RedHat9 cgillay]$ ls /mnt/floppy/*.txt
/mnt/floppy/astro.txt      /mnt/floppy/mercury.txt
/mnt/floppy/born.txt       /mnt/floppy/NEW AUTOS.txt
/mnt/floppy/bye.txt        /mnt/floppy/planets.txt
/mnt/floppy/dances.txt     /mnt/floppy/Sandy and Nicki.txt
/mnt/floppy/galaxy.txt     /mnt/floppy/Sandy and Patty.txt
/mnt/floppy/hello.txt      /mnt/floppy/titan.txt
/mnt/floppy/jupiter.txt    /mnt/floppy/venus.txt
[cgillay@RedHat9 cgillay]$ cat my.file
/mnt/floppy/astro.txt
/mnt/floppy/born.txt
/mnt/floppy/bye.txt
/mnt/floppy/dances.txt
/mnt/floppy/galaxy.txt
/mnt/floppy/hello.txt
/mnt/floppy/jupiter.txt
/mnt/floppy/mercury.txt
/mnt/floppy/NEW AUTOS.txt
/mnt/floppy/planets.txt
/mnt/floppy/Sandy and Nicki.txt
/mnt/floppy/Sandy and Patty.txt
/mnt/floppy/titan.txt
/mnt/floppy/venus.txt
[cgillay@RedHat9 cgillay]$
```

WHAT'S HAPPENING? Here you first issued the command to display all the files that had **.txt** as an extension on the floppy disk. You then used the **cat** command to look at the contents of the file you created when you redirected the output of the **ls /mnt/floppy/*.txt** command. The **cat** command will display text files on the screen. It is analogous to the **type** command in DOS.

STEP 6   Key in the following: **rm my.file** [Enter]

STEP 7   Key in the following: **find / -iname gedit 2>/dev/null** [Enter]

```
[cgillay@RedHat9  cgillay]$  rm my.fil
[cgillay@RedHat9  cgillay]$ find / -iname gedit 2>/dev/null
/usr/bin/gedit
/usr/share/gnome/help/gedit
/usr/share/omf/gedit
[cgillay@RedHat9  cgillay]$
```

WHAT'S **HAPPENING?** First you eliminated the file you created, **my.file**, using the **rm** command. Be patient. It does take time for **find** to search the directory tree. Then you filtered out all the error messages that you saw when you ran the command without redirecting the error messages to the null device. You ignored case, began your search at the root directory, and displayed the output on the screen.

STEP 8   Unmount the BOOK disk. Close all open windows.

2.25 • The whereis Command

You have used the **ls**, **locate**, and **find** command to locate files of general interest to you. The **whereis** command is not for looking for files in general, but is used to locate and display the locations of program (binaries), source, and manual page files for a specific command. Manual pages are the documentation and instructions for using the various commands. The **whereis** command will determine the directory path of programs or their source files. When you use the **whereis** command, the shell searches a list of directories for the program you are looking for. The list of directories is called a *search path*. Unless you alter the search path, the standard set of Linux directories is searched. The **whereis** command is faster than the **find** command since your search path is built in. It also is more specific than the locate command since it looks specifically for a command name, not any characters that appear. However, remember it is searching for files that are programs.

2.26 • Activity: Using the whereis Command

STEP 1   Open a terminal window.

STEP 2   Key in the following: **whereis ls** [Enter]

```
[cgillay@RedHat9  cgillay]$ whereis ls
ls: /bin/ls  /usr/share/man/man1/ls.1.qz
[cgillay@RedHat9  cgillay]$
```

WHAT'S **HAPPENING?** You now know that the **ls** command is located in the **/bin** directory and the manual pages for **ls** are located in the **/usr/share/man/man1** directory.

STEP 3   Key in the following: **whereis gedit** [Enter]

```
[cgillay@RedHat9  cgillay]  $ whereis gedit
gedit: /usr/bin/gedit /usr/share/man/man1/gedit.1.qz
[cgillay@RedHat9  cgillay]$
```

WHAT'S **HAPPENING?** Here **gedit** is located in the **/usr/bin** directory. You should begin to realize that most binary programs that the ordinary user can use are located in the **/usr/bin** directory. You may also note that most documentation is located in the **/usr/share/man** directory.

STEP 4   Key in the following: **whereis find** [Enter]

```
[cgillay@RedHat9   cgillay]$ whereis find
find: /usr/bin/find /usr/share/man/man1/find.1.gz /usr/share/man/
mann/find.n.gz
[cgillay@RedHat9   cgillay]$ _
```

WHAT'S **HAPPENING?** Now you know that **find** is located in the **/usr/bin** directory as well.

STEP 5   Key in the following: **whereis fdisk** [Enter]

```
[cgillay@RedHat9   cgillay]$ whereis fdisk
fdisk: /sbin/fdisk /usr/share/man/man8/fdisk.8.gz
[cgillay@RedHat9   cgillay]$ _
```

WHAT'S **HAPPENING?** In this case, **fdisk** is not located in the **/usr/bin** directory. It is located in the **/sbin** directory. You cannot execute a command unless it is in your search path. Normally, **sbin** is not in the search path for the ordinary user. Thus, if you were trying to execute a command and got the message **bash: commandname: command not found**, it does not necessarily mean that the command is not available. You may have to change directories to where the command is located and execute it from that location. There is also another wrinkle to running commands. You must have permission to execute the command. **fdisk** is an example of a command that may only be run by root (the super user).

STEP 6   Close the terminal window.

Chapter Summary

In this chapter you were introduced to the following:
* The purpose and function of file systems was described.
* Definitions of files and directories was provided.
* The differences between the Linux ext2/ext3 native file systems were explained.
* The purpose and function of the File System Hierarchy standard was described.
* In accordance with the FSH standard, the major directories that are created when Linux is installed with the types of files kept in those directories was described.
* You learned about command syntax and how to read a syntax diagram.
* The difference between commands, options, and arguments was explained.
* The importance of the shell was discussed, as well as how to find which shell you are using with the **echo $SHELL** command.
* The differences between the relative and absolute path was discussed.
* You learned how to use the **cd** and **pwd** commands.
* You learned how to use the editing keys in the Bash shell, as well as use the **history** command to recall previously used commands.
* Some basic commands such as **cal** and **date** were introduced.
* The mounting of file systems was implemented and the purpose and function of the **fstab** and **mtab** files was discussed.

- Essential commands for navigating the Bash shell were used such as **ls** and **find**.
- You explored filename expansion with those commands that support globbing in both the Bash shell and the GUI.
- You used the GUI Search for Files menu choice to locate files.
  Techniques for using the Nautilus file manager to move through the files and directories was implemented.
- You added options and arguments to commands using **ls** as an example.
- You learned how to redirect the output to devices and files and learned about the null device (**/dev/null**).
- You learned about the **find**, **locate**, and **whereis** commands.

Key Terms

absolute path	globbing	profile
ambiguous file references	home directory	recursively
current directory	journaling file system	redirection
delimiter	meta data	relative path
directory	metacharacters	search path
file	option	shell
file system	parent directory	swap file
File System Hierarchy	partition	wildcards
Standard (FHS)	path	working directory

Discussion Questions

1. What is a file? A directory? A file system?
2. Compare and contrast the Linux ext2 file system with the Linux ext3 file system.
3. List and describe five file systems that Linux supports.
4. What is the function of the working directory?
5. List five common directories and explain the types of files that will be found in each of the directories.
6. What is a command line? A shell?
7. The shell can be used interactively. Explain.
8. What is a shell script?
9. Explain the importance of command syntax.
10. Briefly describe the purpose and function of options and arguments. Give one example of each.
11. How are options and arguments used with commands?
12. How would you use a syntax diagram?
13. Explain each part of the following syntax diagram:

        ls [OPTIONS]...[FILE]...

14. How can the command line history be used? The **history** command?
15. Why would you use a terminal window in GNOME?
16. How can you access the terminal window from GNOME?
17. Explain the function of the **pwd** command.
18. Compare and contrast the absolute path with the relative path.
19. Explain the purpose and function of partitions.
20. What does it mean to mount a partition?
21. If you were in the GUI how would you mount a floppy drive? In the Bash shell?

22. How and why would you use wildcards?
23. Explain each part of the following syntax diagram: **ls inv[123]***
24. Define recursively as it is used in Linux.
25. What are the advantages/disadvantages to using the **locate** command to find a file?
26. Explain how the **find** command can be used to locate a file by name.
27. If you key in **find /mnt/floppy –type d,** what are you looking for?
28. Explain why you would use redirection.
29. When would you use the **whereis** command?
30. Why is the "search path" important when using the whereis command?

True/False Questions

For each question, circle the letter T if the question is true and the letter F if the question is false.

T   F   1. FHS refers to the standard location for common directories and files in Linux.
T   F   2. **ls -a** and **ls -A** are identical commands and will produce the same output.
T   F   3. When execute permission is applied to a directory, it gives access to that directory.
T   F   4. Hidden files in Linux always begin with a dot (.)
T   F   5. You can use either an option or an argument but not both with a single command.

Completion Questions

Write the correct answer in each blank space.

6. To go directly to either a parent or child directory, you may use the _____ path.
7. The device called **/dev/null** is where you may direct _____ that you do not wish to see displayed in the terminal window.
8. Before a device can be accessed it must first be _____.
9. A "shorthand" system that allows the operation on a group of files rather than a single file is called _____.
10. Items used to modify or qualify a command are called _____.

Multiple Choice Questions

For each question, write the letter for the correct answer in the blank space.

11. Which of the following is a syntax diagram?
    a. **ls [OPTIONS] [FILE]**
    b. **ls -a**
    c. **ls -A**
    d. **man find**

12. Using filename expansion you can
    a. make use of wildcards such as * and ?.
    b. use globbing.
    c. perform an operation on a group of files rather than a single file.
    d. all of the above

13. If you do not know what directory a file is in, you should
    a. begin at the system root.
    b. begin in your home directory.
    c. both a and b.
    d. neither a nor b.

14. A parent directory
    a. contains other directories.
    b. is always located at the root directory.
    c. both a and b.
    d. neither a nor b.

15. The **whereis** command
    a. is used to list the locations of program files and their manual pages.
    b. follows a relative path to locate manual pages.
    c. can be used to locate a data file.
    d. is slower than the find command.

Writing Commands

Write the correct steps or commands to perform the required action as if you were at the computer. You will assume that there is a terminal window open. The prompt will indicate the current working directory.

16. You wish to verify which shell you are using.

    ```
    [mestes@RedHat9 mestes]
    ```

17. You want to know the absolute path of your current working directory.

    ```
    [lars@linux72 mail]
    ```

18. You want to display a calendar for December 2004, and you want the calendar to begin with Monday.

    ```
    [fpanezich@RedHat9 fpanezich]
    ```

19. You want to know what file systems are mounted and where they are mounted.

    ```
    [cgillay@RedHat9 cgillay]
    ```

20. You want to locate all the files in the **/mnt/floppy** directory that begin with an **a**, **b**, or **c** and have **report** anywhere in the file name. None of the files you are looking for have a file extension.

    ```
    [bhewitt@RedHat9 bhewitt]
    ```

Application Assignments

Problem Set I—At the Computer: Multiple Choice

Note: In all exercises, username in italics represents your user name. For example, I would substitute cgillay for username.

Problem A

- Open a terminal window

  1. You have opened a
     a. GUI interface.
     b. character-based interface.

  2. You may open a terminal window in this way:
     a. Click the Main menu. Point to Accessories. Click Terminal.
     b. Click the Main menu. Point to System Tools. Click Terminal.
     c. both a and b
     d. neither a nor b

- In the open Terminal window, locate the Color settings.

  3. If the **Use colors from system theme** check box is cleared, one valid Built-in
     schemes Color choice *not* available is
     a. White on black
     b. Black on white
     c. Green on black
     d. Green on white

Problem B

- The terminal window should be open.
- Key in the following: **cd /usr**

  4. You keyed in a(n)
     a. absolute path.
     b. relative path

- Key in the following: **cd include**

  5. You keyed in a(n)
     a. absolute path.
     b. relative path

- Key in the following: **pwd**

  6. What is displayed?
     a. **/usr**
     b. **/usr/include**
     c. **/home/username/usr**
     d. **home/username/usr/include**

- Key in the following: **cd**

  7. You have
     a. displayed the current path.
     b. moved to the root directory.
     c. moved to your home directory.
     d. moved to the **/bin** directory.

Problem C

- The terminal window should be open.
- Display the current system date and time.

8. The command you used was
    a. **date**
    b. **date -t.**
    c. **DATE**
    d. **time**

- You want to know if 1988 was a leap year. (February has 29 days in a leap year.)

    9. In 1988, February had 29 days.
        a. true
        b. false

- You want to know if 1978 was a leap year. (February has 29 days in a leap year.)

    10. In 1978, February had 29 days.
        a. true
        b. false

    11. In 1983, New Year's Day (January 1) fell on a
        a. Wednesday.
        b. Thursday.
        c. Friday.
        d. Saturday.

- Close all open windows.

Problem D

Note: It is assumed that **/mnt/floppy** is the device name for your floppy disk.

- Mount the BOOK floppy disk.

    12. You may mount a floppy disk from
        a. System Tools/Disk Management using the GNOME menu.
        b. the Bash shell.
        c. both a and b
        d. neither a nor b

    13. One command you may use to see all your mounted devices is
        a. **mount**
        b. **mount /mnt/floppy**
        c. **ls /mnt/floppy**
        d. **cat /mnt/floppy**

    14. One command you may use to see the files on the floppy disk is
        a. **mount**
        b. **mount /mnt/floppy**
        c. **ls /mnt/floppy**
        d. **cat /mnt/floppy**

- On the BOOK floppy disk, locate all the files with **project** anywhere in their name.

    15. How many files did you locate?
        a. two
        b. four
        c. six
        d. ten
        e. fourteen

- On the BOOK floppy disk, locate all the files with **report** anywhere in their name.

  16. How many files did you locate?
      a. two
      b. four
      c. six
      d. ten
      e. fourteen

- On the BOOK floppy disk, locate all the files with **.tif** as an extension.

  17. How many files did you locate?
      a. two
      b. four
      c. six
      d. ten
      e. fourteen

- On the BOOK floppy disk, locate all the files with any file name but only a four-character file extension.

  18. How many files did you locate?
      a. two
      b. four
      c. six
      d. ten
      e. fourteen

- On the BOOK floppy disk, locate only files that begin with **inv** and have a **1** or **6** in their file names.

  19. Which command did you use?
      a. **ls /mnt/floppy/inv*.***
      b. **ls /mnt/floppy/inv[1-6]***
      c. **ls /mnt/floppy/inv[16]***
      d. **ls /mnt/floppy/inv*[16]***

- On the BOOK floppy disk, display the files by size from the largest to the smallest so that the smallest file is the last one displayed on the screen.

  20. Which file appeared last?
      a. **y.fil**
      b. **italy.tif**

- You want to know the permissions in the **/usr** directory for the directories.

  21. In the **/usr** directory, for the directory called **bin**, other users have the permissions of
      a. **rwx**
      b. **--x**
      c. **r-x**
      d. **---**

- Close all open windows.

- Be sure to unmount the floppy disk if you are no longer going to use it.

Problem E

● Change your working directory to your home directory.

● You want to find the **fstab** file but you do not know where it is located. You also do not want to see any error messages

22.   Which command can you use?
   a. **ls fstab**
   b. **find / fstab 2>/dev/null**
   c. **find / -name fstab 2>/dev/null**
   d. **find -name fstab 2>/dev/null**

23.   What directory is the **cat** command file located in? Do not use the **find** command.
   a. **/bin**
   b. **/usr/bin**
   c. **/**
   d. **/etc**

24.   Were any manual pages located as well?
   a. yes
   b. no

25.   What directory is the **ip** command file located in?
   a. **/bin**
   b. **/sbin**
   c. **/**
   d. **/etc**

Problem Set II—At the Computer: Short Answer

Note: In order for these activities to work correctly, it is assumed that a complete installation of Red Hat Linux 9 Professional was completed.

1. In the Nautilus file manager you want to single click rather than double-click to activate an item. How would you accomplish this task? What other items can you change in behavior?

2. Using the Nautilus file manager, expand the tree. Locate the device folder. Locate the **i2o** folder. How did you accomplish this task? Describe the parent/child relationships in this specific hierarchy. Name two files found in the **i2o** directory. What do most of the icons look like? What does this tell you about this directory?

3. Open a terminal window. You want to change the font for this window. How would you accomplish this task? What is the initial title of the terminal? How did you find out this information? What shells could you use? How did you find out this information? What shell are you running? How did you find out this information?

4. Open a terminal window. Change directories to **/usr/share/nautilus** using an absolute path. Change directories to the **/usr/share/nautilus/patterns** directory using a relative path. What commands did you use? What does the prompt look like? What information does the prompt give you? Change to your home directory. What command did you use? You now want to change directories to the **/usr/bin** directory. Using the command line editing keys, how could you quickly accomplish this? Using the **history** command, locate the command number for the command you used to change to the **/usr/share/nautilus**

directory. What is the number? Use the command number to change to this directory. How did you accomplish this? Key in **!?usr?** two times. What directory did you end up in? What was the purpose of the **!?usr?** command?

5. Open a terminal window. What is the Julian date for the first day of the current month? How did you find this information? What day of the week does your birthday fall on in 2006? How did you find out this information? Close the terminal window.

6. Mount the BOOK disk that came with the textbook. Name two ways you can accomplish this task. Using the **Search for Files** tool, locate every file on the BOOK disk that has **hits** in its name. How many files did you find? What directory were they located in? How did you accomplish this task? Close the window.

7. The BOOK disk is still mounted. Open a terminal window. Locate every file on the BOOK disk in the **music** directory that has **Idols** in its name. How many files were located? How did you accomplish this task? Locate every file on the BOOK disk that begins with **exp02**. How many files were found? How did you accomplish this task? Locate every file on the BOOK disk that has a **1** or a **5** in its name. Were any directories found? If so, what is the directory name? How did you accomplish this task?

8. The BOOK disk is still mounted. The terminal window is still open. Display every file on the BOOK disk in file extension order—or ascending order—A to Z. You also want to look at the file permissions. What is the last file to appear on the screen? What permissions does the group have for the last file displayed? What do those permissions mean? How did you accomplish this task? Now you want the files displayed in file extension order but in descending order. What is the last file to appear on the screen? How did you accomplish this task?

9. The terminal window is still open. You want to find every occurrence of the text string **ed** in the **bin** directory. What files did you find? How did you accomplish this task?

10. The BOOK disk is still mounted. The terminal window is still open. On the BOOK disk, you want to find every directory that has **level** in its name. What directories did you find? How did you accomplish this task? On the BOOK disk, you want to find every file whose name begins with **rr**. What is the last file displayed? How did you accomplish this task? You want to issue the same command but you want to be sure that you also find any files that begin with **RR** or **Rr**. What is the last file displayed? How did you accomplish this task?

11. The BOOK disk is still mounted. The terminal window is still open. Your home directory is the default directory. On the BOOK disk, locate every file that begins **ca** regardless of case and redirect the output to a file in your home directory called **this.fil**. How many files were found? How did you accomplish this task? You want to see the contents of this file. How did you accomplish this task? You want to delete **this.fil**. How did you accomplish this task? Unmount the BOOK disk. How did you accomplish this task?

12. You want to find the location of the **cat** command and any manual references. What directory is the **cat** command located in? Where are its manual pages? How did you accomplish this task? You want to find the location of the **cal** command and any manual references. What directory is the **cal** command located in? Where are its manual pages? How did you accomplish this task?

Problem Set III—Brief Essay

Use gEdit or OpenOffice.org Writer to write and print your response. Be sure to put your name as well as what day and time your class is. Include the number of the question you are answering.

    a. Why is the Linux file system referred to as a hierarchical (tree-like) file system? What advantages or disadvantages do you see to such a structure?

    b. Define command syntax. Why is syntax important when using a command?

    c. What is a shell? How does it differ from a graphical user interface such as GNOME? Discuss advantages and disadvantages to using a shell.

CHAPTER 3

Getting Help

Chapter Overview

Linux is a complex operating system. In order to assist you, there is much help available. Red Hat Linux provides extensive help on commands. In addition, the main menu bar of each application program in the GUI includes help on how to use the specific application. If you purchased Red Hat Linux 9 Professional, you received printed documentation plus documentation on CD. If you purchased the Red Hat Linux 9, you received the documentation on CD only. If you install the documentation, rather than having to look up how to accomplish a task in a printed manual, you can access the information directly from information stored on your computer. The help available in GNOME is a hypertext utility, which means you can jump between logically connected items with a click of a mouse.

A wide variety of types of help is available to you. These include man pages, FAQs, HOWTOs, mini-HOWTOs, and guides maintained by the Linux Documentation Project. Much of this help is accessed through the Internet. But you may also access help directly through the GNOME help features as well as use tools such as man pages and info pages in GNOME and in the terminal window. You will find that man pages provide descriptions and syntax for commands.

In addition, you may receive further help through the Internet, including newsgroups, user groups, and mail lists.

Learning Objectives

1. Explain the purpose and function of online Help capabilities.
2. Explain the types of help available in Red Hat documentation and types of help available online.
3. Explain the purpose and function of a hypertext utility.
4. List two ways of accessing man pages

123

5. Explain the purpose and function of man pages and list and explain three options that can be used with **man**.
6. Explain the purpose and function of Info pages.
7. List and explain five keyboard movements that can be used with the info command.
8. Explain the purpose and function of HOWTOs and FAQs
9. List and explain the types of Internet help resources available and how to access them.
10. Explain the purpose and function of newsgroups, mailing lists, and user groups.

Student Outcomes

1. Access Red Hat Manuals online and use the browser to display and use various help options.
2. Locate the appropriate section in which to search for an item using manual pages with GNOME.
3. Use the **man**, **whatis**, and **apropos** commands in the Bash command line shell.
4. Access information about commands using info pages.
5. Use the **info** command with keyboard movements in a terminal window.
6. Use Internet help resources to locate and use various web sites including GNOME and Red Hat Linux, and Linux Support Services.
7. Add and use a news server.

Commands Introduced

apropos	info	more
clear	less	whatis
--help	man	

3.1 ● Help

It is difficult to know everything about your computer system, much less everything about the commands and programs. There are hundreds of commands and programs that come with your installation of Linux. The difference between commands and programs is mostly linguistic. All commands are programs. However, commands are usually considered smaller programs that are necessary to use the Linux operating system effectively. Usually a program is considered more complex and has commands of its own that can be used only within the program.

To assist you, Linux comes with a built-in help system. The help system is *online*. "Online" has two meanings: 1) in a local sense, it means that the Help files you need are located on your hard disk and you can call them up and use them without having to refer to a printed manual, and 2) in a global sense, it means that you are on a network and connected to other computers. The network can be a company network or a worldwide network such as the Internet. In this chapter, you are going to look at both the local online help as well as some Internet sites for more extensive help.

3.2 ● Types of Help

Linux provides help in the form of man pages (manual pages), FAQs (Frequently Asked Questions), HOWTOs, mini-HOWTOs, and Guides. These resources are located in a variety of locations. Some of the help is built into GNOME as well as into the command line interface. Some of it is supplied with the Red Hat distribution, and other help is available through the Internet. Manual help pages provide the basic construct of a command with the command's name, purpose, options, and arguments. Manual pages can be accessed locally as well as through Internet sites. FAQs are those common questions that nearly everybody asks. They are available in the Red Hat documentation as well as online. HOWTOs are document files that describe how to use or configure some aspect of Linux. Mini-HOWTOs are documents on short, specific subjects. The lines blur between a mini- and full-fledged HOWTO, so if you are seeking help, you should look at both HOWTOs and mini-HOWTOs. HOWTOs and mini-HOWTOs tend to be step-by-step oriented. Guides tend to be full-fledged books that provide detailed and in-depth coverage of a variety of topics.

Internet sites are a valuable resource for finding help. Red Hat provides such help. The Red Hat Support site (**http://www.redhat.com**) contains documentation and online resources and allows you to register so you may have your own personal support page. **www.redhat.com** is the general site for Red Hat. Furthermore, you may locate the most recent information about important updates, bug fixes, and any corrections to Red Hat Linux. There is also a GNOME web site (**http://www.gnome.org**), which is supported by the GNOME project and is part of the GNU project. Special mention needs to be made of the LDP, or the Linux Documentation Project site.

The LDP is a collection of efforts to document Linux. Its goal is to provide good, reliable documentation for Linux. Anyone who wishes can contribute to the LDP. Many of the FAQs, HOWTOs, mini-HOWTOs, and guides come directly from the LDP. The LDP is hosted on mirrored sites throughout the world. A *mirror site* is a file server that contains duplicate sets of files. Mirror sites exist to spread the distribution burden over more than one server to provide faster access to the files you want to use. In addition to these major sites, there are also hundreds of other sites that deal specifically with Linux available on the Internet.

3.3 ● **Red Hat Help**

In order to use help in an application program in GNOME, you open the program and then click Help on the Main Menu bar. You may also seek help by clicking the Main Menu button and clicking **Help**. You can access help through the hypertext utility choices in the window that you open. A hypertext utility means that topics are linked together logically, allowing you to jump rapidly from one topic to another. The GNOME Help Browser gives you access to the GNOME User's Guide, GNOME Desktop documents, the man pages, and the Info Pages. There are links indicated by an underline in the Help window. The navigation buttons allow you to move back and forth between the links you have viewed. See Figure 3.1, "Help Browser Window."

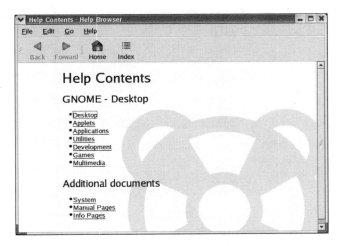

Figure 3.1 ● Help Browser Window

Under **GNOME - Desktop** are links to the documentation for various GNOME utilities such as gEdit. The man pages contains most of the Linux manual pages converted to HTML. The **Info Pages** link is also in HTML. HTML (Hypertext Markup Language) is the format used by most documents on the World Wide Web. The **System** link refers to the standards for writing documentation.

If you purchased a Red Hat Linux 9 distribution, you received a hard copy of the *Red Hat Getting Started Guide* and the *Red Hat Installation Guide*. They are also both available online as well as on your system, provided you installed the documentation. If you purchased the professional version of Red Hat, you also received a hard copy of the *Red Hat Linux Reference Guide* and the *Customization Guide*. The *Red Hat Linux Reference Guide* is further documentation related to Red Hat Linux. The *Customization Guide* is obviously a more detailed guide to various configuration issues such as network configuration issues. Regardless of which version of Red Hat you purchased, the documentation is available on your system, provided you installed the documentation as part of your install process. When you install the documentation on your system, you also receive additional documentation—a Glossary, a book called *Maximum RPM*, a Security Guide and a System Administration Primer. To access the documents on your system, you click the Main menu and point to **Documentation**. You then choose the manual of interest. See Figure 3.2, "Accessing Red Hat Manuals."

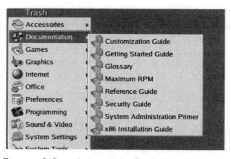

Figure 3.2 • *Accessing Red Hat Manuals*

Many of the activities in this chapter assume either the installation of the documentation and/or access to the Internet. If you have neither of those capabilities, you will not be able to do some of the activities. If that is the case, read the activities you cannot do.

3.4 • Activity: Using Help

Note: The activities in this book assume Linux is installed at run level 3. See the Installation section of Appendix A for details.

STEP 1   Click the Main menu button. Point to **Documentation**. Click **Reference Guide**.

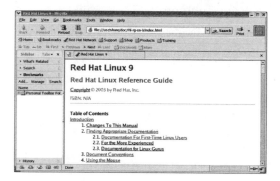

WHAT'S HAPPENING? If the Sidebar is not visible, press the ⌗F9⌗ key. Here is the Reference Guide for Red Hat Linux. Note that it opens in the Mozilla browser. *Browser* is short for "web browser." A browser is a software application used to locate and display web pages. Browsers were designed to look at and interact with the information on the World Wide Web. The browser gives some means of viewing the contents of web pages and of easily navigating from one web page to another. However, since a browser is a program that allows a person to read hypertext, many application windows use browser techniques to move among hypertext pages that may or may not connect to the Internet. A browser has navigation buttons, a location bar, and so on.

STEP 2 Scroll through the window, if necessary, and click the link **Finding Appropriate Documentation.**

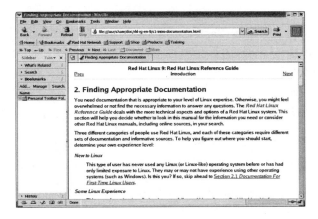

WHAT'S HAPPENING? The hypertext link tries to lead you to the documentation that is appropriate for you.

STEP 3 Click the link the section called **Section 2.1 Documentation for First Time Linux Users**.

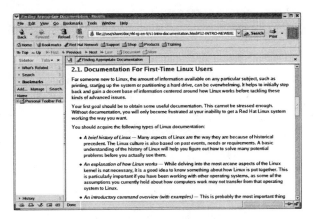

WHAT'S HAPPENING? Again, the documentation tries to lead you to the documentation that is appropriate for you

STEP 4 Click the **Back** button twice.

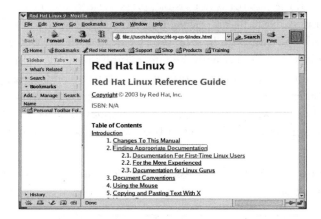

WHAT'S **HAPPENING?** You used the **Back** button to return you to the opening window of the Mozilla browser. Note that the **Back** button is dimmed, indicating that you can go no further back, but the **Forward** button is available.

STEP 5   Close the **Mozilla** window.

STEP 6   Click the Main menu. Point to **Documentation**. Click **Glossary**.

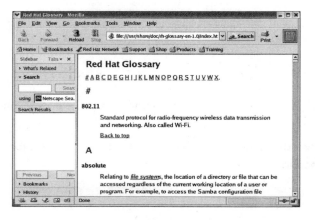

WHAT'S **HAPPENING?** If the Sidebar is not visible, press the [F9] key. One of the options that is very useful is the glossary. Having definitions of terms is very valuable.

STEP 7   Click the **D**.

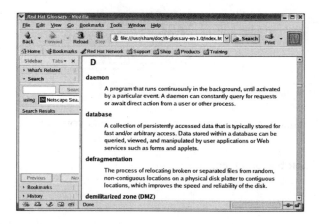

WHAT'S HAPPENING? When you clicked the "D," you were taken to all the terms that begin with a D. The first term to appear is "daemon." **Daemon** (pronounced "demon") is defined. The term comes from Greek mythology, in which daemons were guardian spirits. Later, the term was rationalized as an acronym; **D**isk **a**nd **E**xecution **Mon**itor. One of the features of the Mozilla browser is that you can bookmark pages you wish to return to.

STEP 8   Click **Bookmarks** on the toolbar. Click **Bookmark This Page**.

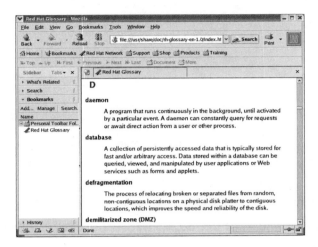

WHAT'S HAPPENING? You marked help on daemon.

STEP 9   Click the **Back** button. In the Sidebar, click **Red Hat Glossary**.

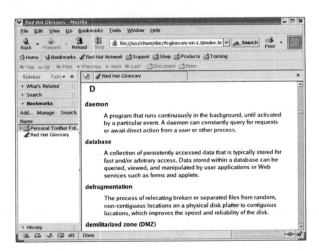

WHAT'S HAPPENING? To return to it, you clicked your bookmark selection.

STEP 10   Right-click **Red Hat Glossary** in the Sidebar. Click **Delete**.

STEP 11   In the Sidebar, click **History**. Expand the plus sign in front of **Today**.

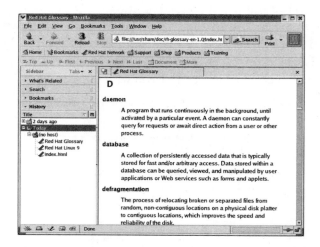

WHAT'S HAPPENING? You first removed your bookmark. Mozilla keep track of the sites and locations you have visited. It is exactly what it says—a history. If you wanted to return to a particular location, you could choose it from the history list.

STEP 12 Close the **Red Hat Glossary - Mozilla** window.

STEP 13 Click the Main menu. Point to **Documentation**. Click **Getting Started Guide**.

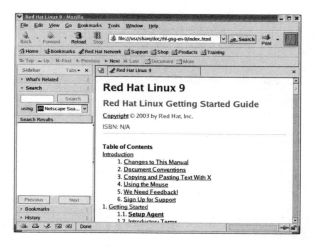

WHAT'S HAPPENING? You opened the Getting Started Guide in Mozilla as well. Again, if you are new to Linux, this documentation will give you useful information.

STEP 14 Scroll in the right pane until you locate the link labeled **4.1.1 - Mounting and Unmounting a Diskette**. Click the link.

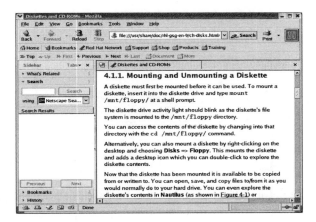

WHAT'S HAPPENING? Here you get an explanation of mounting and unmounting diskettes. As you can see, there is extensive help and explanations of many aspects of Linux in the documentation. You can get help on GNOME as well.

STEP 15 Close the open window. Click the Main menu. Click **Help**.

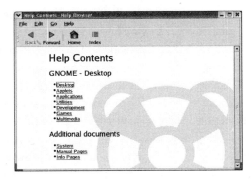

WHAT'S HAPPENING? Here you may get help on the various aspects of the GNOME desktop.

STEP 16 Click **Applications**. Click **Accessories**. Click **gedit**.

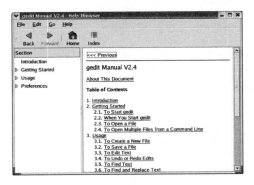

WHAT'S HAPPENING? Here is help for **gedit**. Rather than having to scroll thorough the entire document, you may click a link to take you directly to your area of interest.

STEP 17 Click **Introduction**.

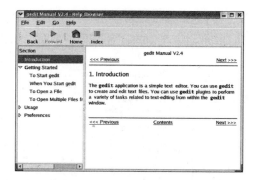

WHAT'S HAPPENING? The **Introduction** section begins by telling you the purpose of the **gedit** editor.

STEP 18 Close the **gedit Manual** window.

3.5 • The GNOME Help Browser Manual Pages

The GNOME Help Browser provides a link to the manual pages. The manual pages, called man pages, provide detailed but brief information on commands. These pages provide the name and a description of the purpose of the command, as well as the syntax, arguments, and options for the command of interest. Notes are included that provide additional information about the command, as well as any warnings. If appropriate, the location and names of files that are relevant to the command are included. There are also included "See Also" references to refer you to other relevant commands. Commands are provided for the root user as well as the ordinary user. However, the manual page does not usually specify who may use the commands. There are also man pages for important files, library functions, shells, languages, devices and other features.

The manual pages are written by many different authors, so some are better written or more complete than others. Most man pages are presented in a concise format with information grouped under well-known standard headings such as those shown in Table 3.1, "Standard man page Settings." In general, manual pages try to follow the following organization, although there may be more or fewer headings.

Heading	Description
Name	Name of the command and a brief description of the command.
Synopsis	Short overview of the command. Often the syntax or usage of command is located here.
Description	A more detailed explanation of the command.
Options	Detailed information on each command line option for commands.
Return values	Information on function return values (for programming references).
Files	A list of important files related to the item such as configuration files.
Environment	Lists any *environmental variables* that affect the program. A *variable* is a value that can change, depending on conditions or on information passed to the program. Data consists of constants or fixed values that

never change and variable values that do change. The *environment* is, in essence, an area in memory where data can be stored. When evaluating an expression in some environment, the evaluation of a variable consists of looking up its name in the environment and substituting its value. In programming, an *expression* is any legal combination of symbols that represents a value. Most programming languages have some concept of an environment, but in shell scripts for Linux/Unix, it has a specific meaning slightly different from other contexts. In shell scripts, environment variables are one kind of shell variable. A *shell variable* is one accessible to a Linux/Unix shell process. These variables are used by commands or shell scripts to discover things about the environment they are operating in. Environmental variables can be changed or created by the user or a program.

Diagnostics	Overview of any error messages you might receive.
Bugs	Known problems.
Copying or copyright	A description of how the item is to be distributed or protected.
Author	Who wrote the documentation.
See also	Any other related commands.

Table 3.1 • Standard man page Settings

Based on the Linux file system standard and the file system hierarchy standard, man pages are divided into sections. There are times when you should know the appropriate section in which to search for an item. Manual sections are numbered 1 through 9 and N. They are searched in the order shown in Table 3.2, "man page Sections."

1	User Commands—Executable programs or shell commands.
8	System Administration Commands—usually only for the root user.
2	System Calls—functions provided by the kernel.
3	Library Calls - subroutines—functions within system libraries such as programming language functions.
4	Special Files—usually found in /**dev** as they relate to device files
5	File Formats and Conventions, such as /**etc passwd** and other configuration files.
6	Games
7	Macro packages and conventions (man page formats and so on), sometimes called "Miscellaneous."

9	Kernel Routines—kernel internal variable and functions.
N	New—sometimes called mann or Tcl/Tk command. Tcl is really two things, a scripting language and an interpreter for that language that is designed to be embedded into an application. Tcl and its associated graphical user interface toolkit, Tk, were designed by Professor John Ousterhout of the University of California at Berkeley.

Table 3.2 • man page Sections

In many texts and other documentation, the commands will be followed by their man numbers. For instance, if you see the command **apropos (1)**, that tells you that the subject area is User Commands. Most users find the information they need in Section 1 (User Programs), Section 8 (System Administration Commands), Section 6 (Games) and Section 7 (Miscellaneous). Programmers and system administrators more typically use the other sections. You should become familiar with the general layout of the manual sections numbering as well as the standard man page settings.

In the GNOME help browser, rather than grouping the man pages in numerical order, the man pages are grouped logically by topic. However, once you access the man page of interest, you will see that it follows the standard schema.

3.6 • Activity: Using Manual Pages with GNOME

STEP 1   Click the Main menu. Click Help. Click the **Manual Pages** link.

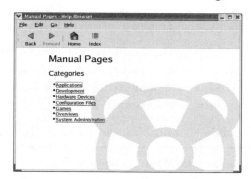

WHAT'S HAPPENING? Here you see the man pages organized by topic. However, they do relate to the nine manual sections described above.

STEP 2   Click **Applications**.

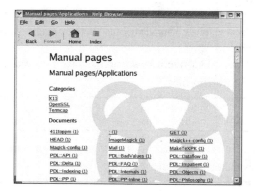

WHAT'S HAPPENING? The GNOME Help Browser begins by dividing the topic into **Categories** and **Documents**. Then it next lists commands in uppercase letters. If you look at the number following each item, you see a **(1)**, indicating that you are in Section 1 (**User Commands**).

STEP 3   Scroll until you locate **cal**. Click **cal**.

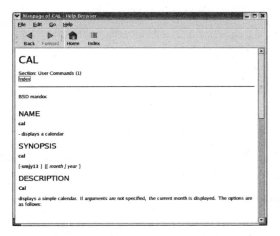

WHAT'S HAPPENING? Again, note at the top of the window, it states that you are in **User Commands (1)**. The manual page begins with the name of the command, which gives a brief description of the purpose of the command, the synopsis (the syntax), and the description, which give a fuller description of the command, followed by the options.

STEP 4   Scroll through the command window until you reach the bottom.

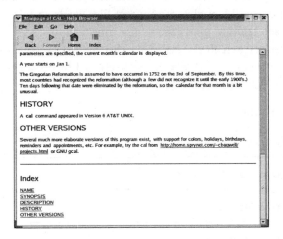

WHAT'S HAPPENING? Here you have additional categories: **History**, which tells you when the command first appeared, and **OTHERS VERSIONS**, which offers you places to locate more elaborate versions of this program. The links also allow you to move to any section in the manual page you are looking at.

STEP 5   Click the **Back** button to return you to the **Topics** page. Click **Configuration Files**. Scroll until you locate **fstab**. Click **fstab**.

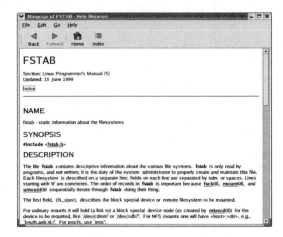

WHAT'S HAPPENING? Here the location is FSTAB and its location in **section 5 - Section 5, File Formats (configuration files)**. Here you learn about the purpose and function of this file.

STEP 6   Close the **GNOME Help Browser** window.

3.7 • The Command Line man Pages

You may access the manual pages from the command line as well. The pages provide good, concise help. The man pages are especially useful when you know the command you are looking for but have either forgotten the syntax or wish to review the syntax. The syntax of **man** is **man** *commandname* (*commandname* is the name of the command you are looking for). Unless you specify a manual section, **man** displays the first occurrence of the *commandname* that you specified in the command line. Manual pages are text files written using a special formatting program displayed one screenful of information at a time. Manual pages send the output though what is called a pager, which is a utility for displaying one page of information at a time. Usually the utility is a command called **less**. Some keyboard shortcuts help you move around in a manual page. See Table 3.3, "Keyboard Shortcuts."

Keys	Movement
←	Moves to left one tab stop.
→	Moves to right one tab stop.
↑	Moves up one line.
↓	Moves down one line.
y	Moves up one line.
e	Moves down one line.
u	Moves one page up.
d	Moves one page down.
g	Moves to beginning of text.

Shift + g	Moves to end of text.
b	Moves back one screen at a time.
Ctrl + u	Moves back one-half a screen at a time.
/string	Searches forward for a specific string. *String* is a sequence of characters.
?string	Searches backward for a specific string.
n	Repeats search forward.
Shift + n	Repeats search backwards.
q	Quit.
h	Displays help with additional keyboard shortcuts.

Table 3.3 • Keyboard Shortcuts

man, like almost all Linux commands, has many options. Table 3.4, "Options Used with man," lists some of the more useful options.

Option	Purpose
-a	Displays all manual pages matching a specified string.
-f	Displays a short description of a command.
-k	Displays a list of all available man texts where a specified string occurs.
n intro	A number that indicates a specific section followed by intro will give you an introduction to that section. You must be in the **/sbin** directory.
n	A number that limits a search to a specific section.
-w	Displays the path name of a location of a manual page.

Table 3.4 • Options Used with Man

Commands related to the **man** command include **whatis**, **apropos**, and **manpath**. The **whatis** command is exactly the same as **man -f** *command*. The **whatis** command is built on the **whatis** database. It searches the short manual page descriptions for each keyword and prints a one-line description to standard output (the monitor) for each match. **whatis** searches for complete words only. Its syntax is **whatis** *keywords*

An almost-equivalent command to **whatis** is the **apropos** command. **apropos** is also a command that allows you to search for each occurrence of the string in the database. **apropos** searches the short manual pages for the occurrence of each string and displays the results on the screen. This means that if you are unsure of the command name, **apropos** will look for any manual page that contains that string. However, **apropos** also needs the **whatis** database to search. **apropos** is like **whatis**, except it searches for strings instead of keywords. The syntax is **apropos** *string*. **apropos** is equivalent to **man -k** *string*.

The **manpath** command tries to determine the path to the manual pages. There are options (**-d** for debug and **-h** for help). The **manpath** command is a symbolic link to **man**.

3.8 • Activity: Using man, whatis, and apropos

STEP 1   Open a terminal window. Key in the following: **cd /sbin** ⏎Enter

STEP 2   Key in the following: **man 1 intro** ⏎Enter

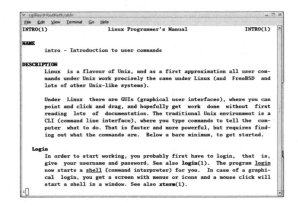

WHAT'S HAPPENING? By using the **man** command with a section number, the number 1, and the intro option, you get a description of what the section is about. Not all versions of Linux support this feature.

STEP 3   Key in the following: **q**

STEP 4   Key in the following: **cd** ⏎Enter

STEP 5   Key in the following: **man ls** ⏎Enter

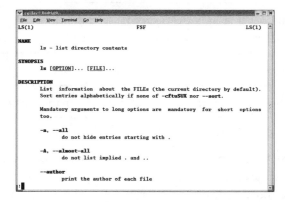

WHAT'S HAPPENING? First you returned to your home directory. The **cd** command with no argument always returns you to your home directory. Then you keyed in the command for the manual page for the **ls** command. As you can see, you are looking at the command ls. It is in manual section 1 because you see the notation **LS(1)**. **NAME** gives a brief description of the purpose of the command. **SYNOPSIS** gives the syntax of the command. Then follows **DE-**

SCRIPTION, which lists the various available options. The **:** at the bottom of the window is the prompt.

STEP 6   Press **h**.

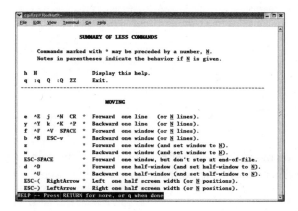

WHAT'S HAPPENING? Since the man pages use the **less** command, you see further keyboard shortcuts for the **less** command.

STEP 7   Press **q**. At the prompt, key in the following: **/c** ⟨Enter⟩

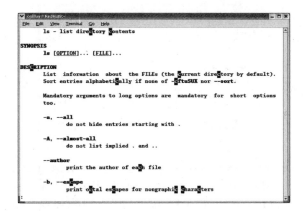

WHAT'S HAPPENING? You see that you moved forward through the document. Every occurrence of **c**, both upper- and lowercase, is highlighted. You can get help with **man** itself.

STEP 8   Press **q**.

STEP 9   Key in the following: **man man** ⟨Enter⟩

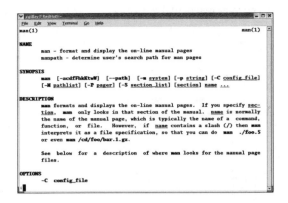

WHAT'S HAPPENING? Included in the **NAME** section is also the command called **manpath**. Remember, **manpath** determines which directories man will search for the man page you requested.

STEP 10 Press the PgDn key.

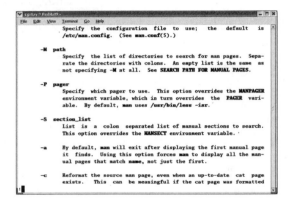

WHAT'S HAPPENING? You may need to press the PgDn key more times, depending on the size of your terminal window. Also, you may need to use the PgDn key in the directional section of the keyboard as opposed to the numeric keypad. Look at the **-a** option. As it describes, once **man** has found the first occurrence of your command, it exits. A command may be listed in more than one section because there are different tools and commands with the same name. If you want all the manual pages referring to that term, called *homonymous man texts*, you need to use the **-a** option.

STEP 11 Press **q**. Key in the following: **man mount** Enter

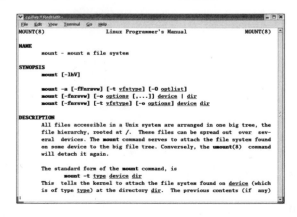

WHAT'S HAPPENING? You are looking at the manual page for **mount** which is in Section 8 (System Administration). When you press **q** to exit the man page, you will be at the command prompt. You only saw one entry for **mount**.

STEP 12 Press **q**. Key in the following: **man -a mount** Enter. Press **q**.

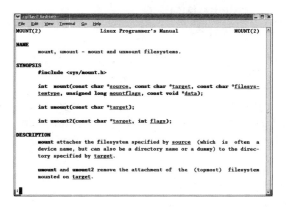

WHAT'S HAPPENING? You are now looking at the manual page for **mount** in Section 2. This time, when you pressed **q** to exit the man page, the next manual page dealing with **mount** was displayed.

STEP 13 Press **q**. Key in the following: **man 8 mount** Enter

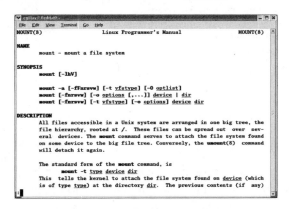

WHAT'S HAPPENING? You limited your search to Section 8 (System Administration).

STEP 14 Press **q**. Key in the following: **man -f ls** Enter

```
[cgillay@linux72  cgillay]$ man -f ls
ls                           (1) - lists directory contents
[cgillay@linux72  cgillay]$
```

WHAT'S HAPPENING? If you see the message, **ls: nothing appropriate**, it means that the database the command uses has not been built. Depending on your version of Unix/Linux, the database of commands and keywords may not be installed automatically. The database is created by what is called a cron job. A **cron job** is a job that runs automatically at some specific time, usually at night. If you always turn off your computer, the database will never be built, and if there is no database, **whatis** cannot find anything. If you are a root user, you can create the database at any time by keying in **/usr/sbin/makewhatis**. If you are an ordinary user, you will not be allowed to create this database, and if you try to execute the command, you will see the message, **Permission denied**.

In Red Hat Linux, 7.2 and above, the **whatis** database is automatically built during your installation of Red Hat. Assuming that the database has been built, using the **-f** option gave you a brief description of what the **ls** command does. There is an equivalent command to **man - f**. It is **whatis**. The **whatis** command also uses the whatis database. The syntax is **whatis** *string*.

STEP 15   Key in the following: **whatis   ls** ⌷Enter⌷

```
[cgillay@linux72   cgillay]$ whatis ls
ls                              (1) - lists directory contents
[cgillay@linux72   cgillay]$
```

WHAT'S HAPPENING? The **whatis** command is exactly the same as the **man -f ls** command. It searches the short manual pages for the keyword. An almost-equivalent command to **whatis** is the **apropos** command. Remember, **apropos** is also a command that allows you to search for each occurrence of the string in the database.

STEP 16   Key in the following: **apropos   whatis** ⌷Enter⌷

STEP 17   Key in the following: **man   -k   whatis** ⌷Enter⌷

STEP 18   Key in the following: **man   -f   whatis** ⌷Enter⌷

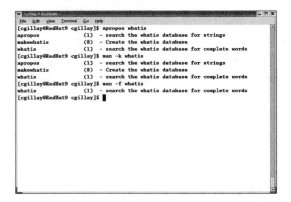

WHAT'S HAPPENING? In each case, provided the database has been built, each command found the keyword you were looking for and indicated in what section of the man pages it is located. Note that **man –f** only gave a you a brief description of the command. Sometimes, if you just want the syntax of a command, the command followed by **--help** will show you just the syntax. Not all commands support the **--help** option. Note that there are two hyphens.

STEP 19   Key in the following: **man   --help** ⌷Enter⌷

WHAT'S HAPPENING? ⊱ The **man** command does support the **--help** function. Here you got a summary of the syntax for **man**. You can also look for the search path of the man pages themselves using the **-w** option.

STEP 20 Key in the following: **man -w** Enter

```
[cgillay@linux72   cgillay]$ man -w
/usr/share/man:/usr/X11R6/man
[cgillay@linux72   cgillay]$
```

WHAT'S HAPPENING? ⊱ Here you see the search path man uses when looking for man pages. You may also use the **manpath** command for the same information.

STEP 21 Key in the following: **manpath** Enter

```
[cgillay@linux72   cgillay]$ manpath
/usr/share/man:/usr/X11R6/man
[cgillay@linux72   cgillay]$
```

WHAT'S HAPPENING? ⊱ The search path for man pages was again shown. In the next step, if your manpath is different, use what path appeared. In its standard configuration, man searches the directories listed above.

STEP 22 Close the terminal window. Double-click your Home directory icon on the desktop. Click **Information**. Click **Tree**.

STEP 23 Locate and expand **/usr**. Locate and expand **/usr/kerberos**.

STEP 24 Locate and expand **man**. Click **man1** in the tree.

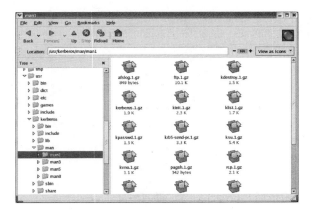

WHAT'S HAPPENING? ⊱ Here you can see the directory structure of the man pages. You can see all the man sections and the man files.

STEP 25 Collapse **man**. Collapse **kerberos**. Collapse **usr**. Close the window.

3.9 • Info Pages

Info is a program for reading documentation. It is a GNU hypertext reader that displays information from a previously built textinfo input. Textinfo is a documentation system that uses a single source file to produce both online information and printed output. You can use textinfo to build your own info pages. However, at this point, you are going to look at those info pages that are built in. Info pages are yet another way to access information about commands. Info pages tend to be more explanatory than man pages and contain more general, conceptual information than man pages. You may access info pages from either the GNOME Help Browser or from the command line. The GNOME Help Browser is not as complete as using the command line.

3.10 • Activity: Using Info Pages in the GNOME Help Browser

STEP 1   Click the Main menu. Click **Help**. In the GNOME Help Browser window, click the **Info Pages** link.

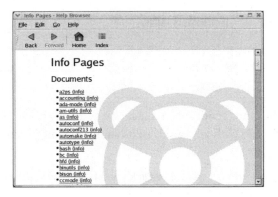

WHAT'S HAPPENING?   A list of the Info Pages appears. To access any page, you simply click the link. If you scrolled through the list of commands, you would see that **ls** is not one of the commands that has an info page that can be accessed here.

STEP 2   Scroll until you locate **find**. Click **find**.

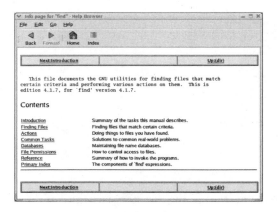

WHAT'S HAPPENING?   The contents are much more extensive than the display available with man pages. In addition, the info pages offer navigation tools that are hypertext links. At the top of the window, you see a link called **Next: Introduction** and a link called **Up(dir)**. **Next** takes you to the next item in the table of contents, **Introduction**, whereas **Up:(dir)** takes you to the first directory listing for **Info Pages**. These same links appear at the bottom of the window, if you have it sized to see the entire window.

STEP 3   Click the **Finding Files** link.

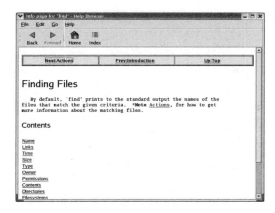

WHAT'S HAPPENING? You are taken to your link of interest. Now the navigation tools include **Next: Actions,** your previous action (**Prev:Introduction**) and a link to take you back to the table of contents (**Up:Top**).

STEP 4   Click the **Name** link.

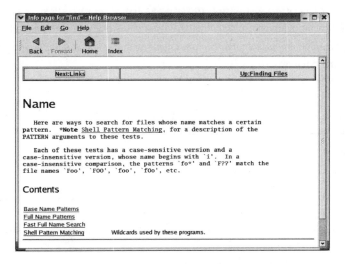

WHAT'S HAPPENING? If you cannot see the entire display, you can resize the window. You have further links to explanations about Name. The explanations are much more in depth than those provided by the man pages. When you see an * (asterisk) in front of a command, it indicates the beginning of a menu item.

In the explanation, the term "foo" is used. A note about the word "foo": *Foo* is a sample name for absolutely anything, especially for programs and files. Foo is often used for any name used in an example and is understood to stand for whatever thing is under discussion. It is used similar to the way "x"or "John Doe" might be used. For instance, if you wanted to show the syntax for an email address, you would say "Send email to **foo@anywhere.com**," where the user would substitute a real name for *foo*.

STEP 5   Click the **Shell Pattern Matching** link.

WHAT'S HAPPENING? You see a full discussion of how to use wildcards.

STEP 6   Close the GNOME Help Browser window.

3.11 • The info Command

The syntax for **info** is **info** *subject*, with the subject being the command you are interested in. The subject tells the info command which file to look for. The info files are usually kept in the **/usr/share/info** directory. Moving around in the info window can be somewhat disconcerting. Extensive help is provided to assist you. Some important movement keys are provided in Table 3.5, "Keyboard Movement in Info."

Keys	Movement
Space Bar	Scrolls text down one screen.
Backspace	Scrolls text up one screen.
b	Moves to the beginning of the text.
e	Moves to the end of the text.
Tab	Moves to the next cross reference. A cross reference is preceded by an asterisk.
Enter	Continues the cross-reference.
n	Moves to next unit of the same hierarchy level.
p	Moves to previous unit of the same hierarchy level.
u	Moves one hierarchy up.
l	Moves back to the last text displayed.
h	Provides detailed instructions on movement keys in window.
? or **Ctrl** + h	Provides brief overview of movement keys in window.
q	Quits the info window.

Table 3.5 • Keyboard Movement in Info

3.12 • Activity: Using the info Command

STEP 1   Open a terminal window. Key in the following: **info find** ⎣Enter⎦

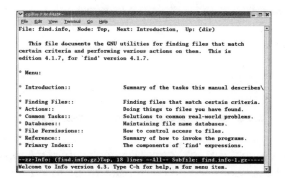

WHAT'S HAPPENING? The info pages are organized into nodes. Each node represents information grouped on a specific topic. If the node takes more than one screen, you can move forward a screen by pressing the ⎣**Space Bar**⎦ and back a screen by pressing the ⎣**Backspace**⎦ key. The bottom of the window has a status line that tells you how many lines are in the file and where you are. Pressing **n** takes you to the next node (or menu item), "Introduction."

STEP 2   Press **n**

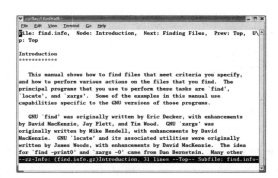

WHAT'S HAPPENING? You moved to the next node, **Introduction**. To move through this window, you may press the ⎣**Space Bar**⎦.

STEP 3   Press the ⎣**Space Bar**⎦.

WHAT'S HAPPENING? At the bottom of the window, the status line tells you that you are at the bottom(—**Bot**—).

STEP 4   Press the [Backspace] key. Press **p**

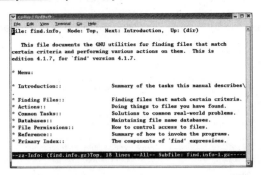

WHAT'S **HAPPENING?** Pressing the [Backspace] key took you to the top of the window. Pressing **p** took you to the previous node. You can directly go to a menu item by using the **m** command followed by the node or menu name you wish. The info screen also has a completion feature. When you key in enough letters, it will try to complete the phase for you.

STEP 5   Press **m**. Key in the following: **Fin**. Press [Tab].

WHAT'S **HAPPENING?** The m brought up the command **Menu** item; Keying in F, then i, then n gave the menu command enough to work with so that when you pressed [Tab], it completed your request for Finding Files.

STEP 6   Press [Ctrl] + **g**. Press [Ctrl] + **g**. Press [Ctrl] + **h**

WHAT'S **HAPPENING?** Pressing the first [Ctrl] + **g** canceled your menu choice of **Finding Files** but still left you in menu mode. The second [Ctrl] + **g** cancelled the **Menu** command. [Ctrl] + **h** took you into some basic help commands. As you can see, the command to quit this help is l.

STEP 7   Press l. Press **h**

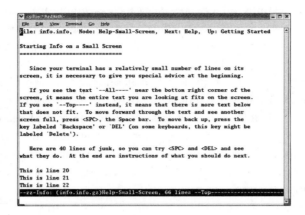

WHAT'S HAPPENING? There is extensive help for help. The tutorial here describes and walks you through how to work through many of the features of using info. Work through all the directions and steps to familiarize yourself with the info screens. When you are done, you press **q** to quit the program.

STEP 8   Press **q**. Key in the following: **info ls** [Enter]

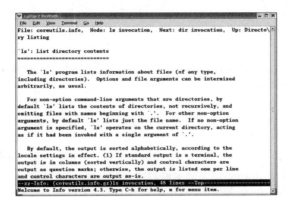

WHAT'S HAPPENING? When you pressed **q**, you quit your last command, **info find** as well as the **Help window**. Keying in **info ls** gives you detailed help for **ls**. Remember, in the GNOME Help Browser, **ls** was not available as an info page, but it is available at the command line.

STEP 9   Key in the following: **q**

STEP 10 Close the terminal window.

3.13 • Internet Support

In order to use the Internet, you must have a connection to the Internet as well as a browser. Remember that a browser is a program that allows a user to read hypertext and gives the user some means of viewing web page and of navigating from one page to another. Popular graphical web browsers include Mozilla, Galeon, and Nautilus, all of which come with the Red Hat distribution. The default browser is Mozilla. Mozilla is used primarily as a web browser and as the tool to set up your newsreader, although you can also use it to locate files on your computer. However, if you—in addition to searching the web—also want the ability to send and receive email, you need to use either Evolution Mail or Mozilla Mail. The default graphical email program provided with Red Hat is Evolution, which includes other features such as a calendaring feature. Mozilla comes from the same source code that is the core of Netscape, and it has many of the same features as Netscape. Netscape Communicator source code is open source code. Mozilla.org was formed to coordinate the development of the new browser from that code. There are also text-based tools that can be used for web browsing and mail, although those tools will not be explored in this text.

Mozilla is the default newsreader tool as well. A *newsreader* allows a user to read articles posted to Usenet. *Usenet* is a distributed bulletin board that is supported by people who post and read articles on the bulletin board. Usenet is probably one of the largest decentralized information utilities available. It encompasses government agencies, universities, high schools, businesses of all sizes, and home computers of all descriptions. It hosts many thousands of newsgroups. A *newsgroup* is where users of different interests can chat, communicate, post, and read articles of common interest to the group.

In order to use a browser, you must have a connection to the Internet. There are three common ways to connect to the Internet: by a direct connection, by a dial-up connection using a modem, or by a cable modem or DSL (Digital Subscriber Line) connection. A direct connection is a high-speed dedicated connection to the Internet using a high-speed line such as a T-1 or T-3. A direct connection is fast and reliable, but very expensive. Many business organizations and schools have direct connections. If you are in such an environment, you are always connected to the Internet and you only need to access it via your browser. A modem using your telephone line is also a viable way to connect to the Internet. In order to access the Internet, you need an ISP (Internet Service Provider). An ISP is a company that provides individuals or companies access to the Internet and other related services such as web site building and virtual hosting. On the Internet, virtual hosting is the provision of web server and other services so that users do not have to purchase and maintain their own web server host. Often, using a modem and an ISP is referred to as a dial-up account. There are many commercial ISP companies, such as UUNet and Earthlink, that charge a user a fee. In addition, there are free ISPs available. Cable and DSL connections use special modems and are much faster than dial-up accounts, but slower than direct lines. Availability of cable connection or DSL is dependent on your cable or phone company. In addition, many cable and DSL services do not directly support Linux, but since most cable and DSL providers use standard network protocols, you may connect to the Internet using Linux. How you connect to the Internet is beyond the scope of this text, but the assumption is made that you do have a connection.

3.14 ● Red Hat and Internet Support

Red Hat has extensive Internet support for its products and offers links to general Linux sites. Red Hat provides all of its documentation on its site at no charge. After purchasing Red Hat Linux, once you activate your product, you receive support via email or phone for a specified length of time. You may also purchase a support package called the Red Hat Network . This service, which has an annual charge, provides an easy way for Red Hat to email you when errata has been released. *Errata* are errors either in a printed work discovered after printing and shown with its correction on a separate sheet or, when used with software, bug fixes or enhancements. A *bug* is an error in a computer program or in the computer's hardware that causes repeated malfunctions. The identification and removal of bugs in a program is called *debugging*. Errata releases from Red Hat either tell you where to down load patches (fixes to the operating system) or provide *workarounds*. A workaround is either something that works for the wrong reason or is a way to "work around" the problem. With Red Hat Network installed, it will automatically confirm your updates. Red Hat Network will also let you download each new release of Red Hat Linux as well as provide technical support.

3.15 ● Activity: Using Red Hat Internet Support

Note: Web sites are ever-changing, so your screens may differ from those shown here. You may need to look in another location, or the web site may no longer be available.

STEP 1 Click the Mozilla ⊕ icon on the panel.

WHAT'S HAPPENING? ➤ If the Sidebar is not visible, press the **F9** key. You may also access Mozilla from the menu by clicking the Main menu, pointing to Internet, and clicking Mozilla Web Browser. If this is the first time you have activated Red Hat, you are give instructions on how to activate the product. You are not required to do so. You may still use Red Hat Internet support without product activation.

STEP 2 Click the **Support** button on the links bar.

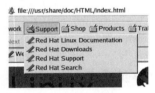

WHAT'S HAPPENING? ➤ Here you have listed all the official Red Hat sites. You can find documentation, locate downloads, find support, and search the Red Hat site.

STEP 3 Click **Red Hat Support**. Maximize the window.

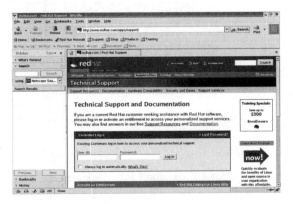

WHAT'S HAPPENING? ➤ On this web page, you may log in to get personalized support. First, however, you would have to activate your product

STEP 4 Scroll until you see **Product Support Guides**. Click the down arrow in the **Select a product** drop list box.

WHAT'S HAPPENING? Here is the available documentation for supported products. Once you select a product, the Official Manuals & Guides for a specific Red Hat version will be available. *Note:* If you have activated your product, you may not find the drop-down box. In that case, go to **www.redhat.com**, click **Support and Docs** and scroll until you see the drop-down box.

STEP 5   Click **Red Hat Linux 9**. Click **Go**. Click **Continue**. Scroll to see what is in the window.

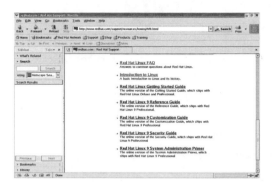

WHAT'S HAPPENING? You may see more or less, depending on your monitor resolution. But here you see errata and FAQs specifically for Red Hat Linux, as well as hardware-compatibility lists and all the documentation. You could have gone directly to the documentation.

STEP 6   Click the **Support** button on the toolbar. Click **Red Hat Linux Documentation**.

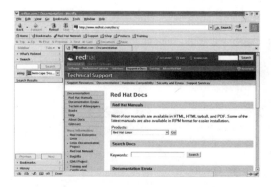

WHAT'S HAPPENING? Here you find another way to locate the manuals of interest.

STEP 7   Restore the Mozilla window. Close the Mozilla window.

3.16 • Internet Support

Besides the support that Red Hat offers for its own products, it also provides other sites for general information on Linux and provides common search engines for locating information about anything on the web. A *search engine* is a remotely accessible program that lets you do keyword searches for information on the Internet. Popular search engines include *google.com*, *askjeeves.com*, and *dogpile.com*. There are several types of search engines: the search may cover titles of documents, URLs, headers, or the full text. A *URL (Uniform Resource Locator)* identifies the location of resources on the web. The URL form is as follows: **protocol://host-domain/path**. The protocol identifies the kind of content you are requesting. The most common protocol you see is *HTTP (Hypertext Transfer Protocol)*. Thus, a typical URL looks like *http://www.redhat.com* where *http* is the protocol, *www* is the host computer name and *redhat.com* is the path.

3.17 • Activity: Using Internet Support

Note: Web sites are ever-changing, so your screens may differ from those shown here. You may need to look in another location, or the web site may no longer be available.

STEP 1   Open Mozilla. In the sidebar, click **Search**. In the **Search** text box, key in the following: **gnome**.

STEP 2   In the **using** drop down list box, click **Google**. Click **Cancel**.

WHAT'S **HAPPENING?** ⟩ You are using the Google search engine to locate information about GNOME.

STEP 3   Click **Search**.

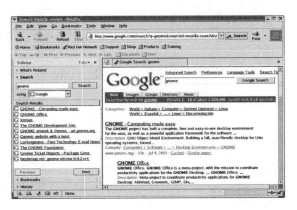

WHAT'S **HAPPENING?** ⟩ In the Search Results box, there are many links to information about GNOME. If you wanted to go to the official GNOME web site, you could use their URL, **gnome.org**. Non-profit organizations usually use **.org**. If you look at the location bar, you see that the URL became more complicated as you went further into the web site.

STEP 4   In the **Search** text box, add **.org** so that the entry reads **gnome.org.** Click **Search**.

STEP 5   In the **Search Results** box, click **GNOME - Computing made easy.**

STEP 6   Click the **Support** button. Click **Red Hat Search**.

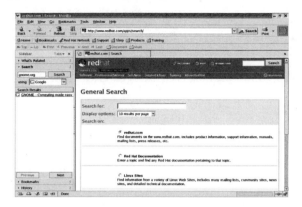

WHAT'S HAPPENING? You may search for general terms in a variety of locations. The default location is redhat.com.

STEP 7   In the **Search for:** text box, key in **URLs**. Press **Enter**. Click **Continue**.

STEP 8   Click **Helpful URLs list**.

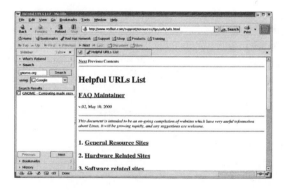

WHAT'S HAPPENING? Here is a list of sites that relate to general questions about Linux

STEP 9   Scroll until you see the link **6. Commercial Support Sites**. Click it.

STEP 10   Click **Linux Support Services**.

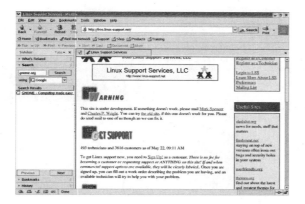

WHAT'S HAPPENING? ≫ Here are listed some particularly good sites, specifically **http://www.slashdot.com**, **http://www.freshmeat.com**, and **http://www.linux.org**. Each of these sites has problem-solving tools and excellent resources for assisting you in learning Linux. One site that provides some good tutorials is **linux.org**.

STEP 11 Scroll in the window until you see **linux.org**. Click **linux.org**. Scroll until you see **Linux 101**.

WHAT'S HAPPENING? ≫ Particularly valuable to new users (often called "newbies") is **Linux 101**.

STEP 12 Click the **more** link under **Linux 101**.

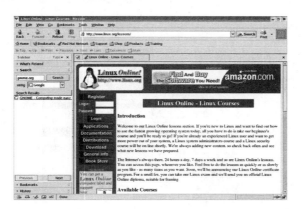

WHAT'S HAPPENING? ≫ Here you have online lessons that can assist you in learning Linux.

STEP 13 If necessary, scroll until you see the link **Getting Started with Linux - Beginner's Course**. Click **Getting Started with Linux**.

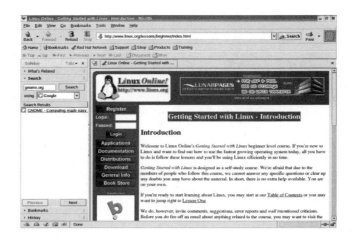

WHAT'S HAPPENING? This is a complete online course in Linux.

STEP 14   Click the **Table of Contents** link. Scroll to **Lesson 4**. Click the **Linux file system** link. Then locate **Getting in and out of directories with 'cd'**.

WHAT'S HAPPENING? This online lesson gives specific instructions. You could open a terminal window and practice the steps and commands that are shown to you.

STEP 15   Click **Next** located at the bottom of the window.

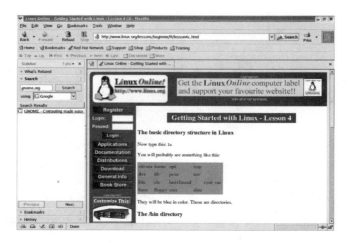

WHAT'S HAPPENING? Again, you are offered a command and description of what happens when you use the command.

STEP 16 Click **Next**.

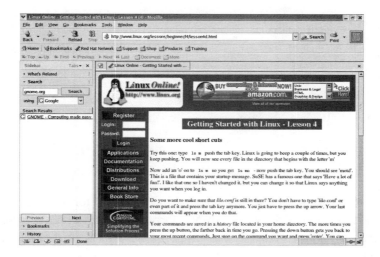

WHAT'S HAPPENING? As you can see, you are led through a series of lessons with examples of how to use Linux. There are many excellent sites—too many to list—but as you explore the links to the different sites, you will find sites that are useful to you.

STEP 17 Click the **Support** button. Click **Red Hat Documentation**. Scroll to the bottom of the screen. Click the **Linux Documentation Project** link.

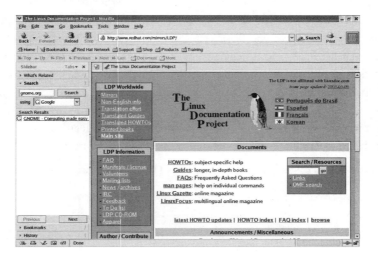

WHAT'S HAPPENING? One of the ways that users get help is with what are called HOWTOs. A HOWTO, as it name implies, is a step-by-step guide to performing a specific task. Since most users face similar problems and have similar questions, the Linux/Unix community has developed answers to those types of questions and problems. They are documented in what are called FAQs (frequently asked questions). The Guides are longer, in-depth books. The Linux Documentation Project maintains the Guides, FAQs, HOWTOs, man pages, an online journal called the *Linux Gazette*, and another online journal, the *LinuxFocus*.

STEP 18   Click the **HOWTOs** link. Scroll until you see the table below.

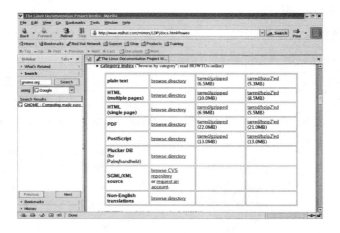

WHAT'S HAPPENING? ▷ Linux documentation comes in a variety of formats. The plain text documents can be read by any editor. The HTML format is for use with a browser such as Nautilus or Netscape. PDF (Portable Document Format) is a file format developed by Adobe Systems. PDF captures formatting information from a variety of desktop publishing applications, making it possible to send formatted documents and have them appear on the your monitor or printer as they were intended to look. People viewing a PDF file (or document) with the Acrobat Reader see the document in the exact layout intended by the author. This is its main advantage over other electronic formats, such as HTML, where the layout can vary depending on the software being used. To view a file in PDF format, you need Adobe Acrobat Reader, a free application distributed by Adobe Systems. PostScript files are a page description language (PDL) also developed by Adobe Systems. PostScript is primarily a language for printing documents on laser printers. PostScript is the standard for desktop publishing. Now there is also a format for Palm and other hand-held PDAs (personal digital assistants). You need a special application to read PostScript files. Standard generalized markup language (SGML) is a generic markup language for representing documents. SGML is an international standard that describes the relationship between a document's content and its structure. SGML allows document-based information to be shared and re-used across applications and computer platforms. Files listed as "tarred" and "gzipped" are files that have been compressed.

STEP 19   Click the link **browse directory** next to **HTML (single page)**.

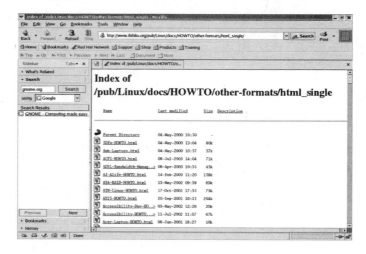

WHAT'S HAPPENING? Here are links to all the HTML HOWTO pages.

STEP 20 Scroll until you locate the link **HOWTO-INDEX.html**. Click it.

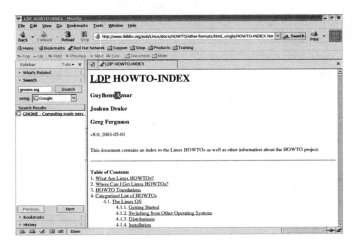

WHAT'S HAPPENING? You have the HOWTO-INDEX from the LDP available in your browser.

STEP 21 Scroll until you see the link **5. Single list of HOWTOs**. Click it.

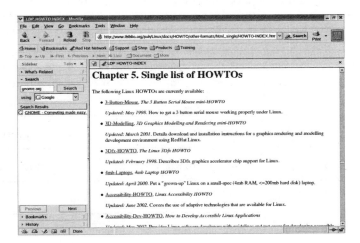

WHAT'S HAPPENING? Here you have a HOWTO list on a variety of topics.

STEP 22 Restore your window then close the open window.

3.18 • Newsgroups

A newsgroup is a discussion group on the Internet. The discussion takes place by having users post and respond to messages. You can participate in a newsgroup by subscribing to it and reading and commenting on the articles (messages). An original article has a subject line, and all postings to that subject constitute a **threaded discussion**.

Usenet is the most popular set of newsgroups. It is a worldwide network of Unix systems that has a decentralized administration and is used as a bulletin board system by newsgroups. Usenet, which is considered part of the Internet (although Usenet predates it), is composed of thousands of newsgroups, each devoted to a particular topic. Its address list, maintained by the

Massachusetts Institute of Technology, contains the name and email address of everyone who has posted to Usenet.

Usenet is organized by topic. Each newsgroup has a name that consists of a series of words, separated by periods, indicating the newsgroup's subject in increasingly narrow categories, such as **rec.crafts.textiles.needlework**. The name is hierarchical; the first part describes the major topic, and the later parts describe the subtopics. Table 3.6, "Usenet Categories," describes the most common categories.

Category	Topic
alt	A wide variety of topics. These are topics that are carried by local Usenet servers at their own risk. Although many alt groups have interesting and useful information, they can also have adult or objectionable material.
biz	Business and commerce.
comp	Computer science and related topics, including operating systems, hardware, and artificial intelligence.
k12	Subjects for teachers and students in grades K–12.
misc	Anything that does not fit into the other topics.
news	Information about Usenet itself. Topics covered include new groups being formed and other types of announcements.
newusers	A place for new users. If you are a new user, starting here will assist you with updated information on how to use Usenet groups.
rec	Recreational activities such as hobbies, the arts, music, movies, and books.
sci	Scientific topics such as math, physics, and engineering.
soc	Social issues, culture, trends, and current events.
talk	Topics include controversial subjects such as gun control and politics.

Table 3.6 • Usenet Categories

There may also be local newsgroups for subjects of interest to people in the local area. In addition, there are private newsgroups for businesses and industries. These private newsgroups usually require a password and are limited to special purposes. Some newsgroups are **moderated**. In a moderated newsgroup, before anything gets posted, it first goes to the moderator, who decides whether the post is appropriate and makes the decision to post it. For an extensive listing of newsgroups, you can visit the web site **http://groups.google.com**.

Newsgroups are hosted on news servers, also called NNTP (Network News Transport Protocol) servers. Your Internet service provider will usually give you access to at least one news server. Not all newsgroups are carried on all servers. In order to access newsgroups, you must have a program called a newsreader. A newsreader is a program that allows you to read newsgroup postings and post your own messages. Mozilla is an example of such a program.

3.19 ● Activity: Adding and Using a News Server

Note 1:   If you have already installed newsgroups, you do not need to do this activity. If you are in a lab environment, check with your instructor before proceeding with this activity. Depending on your lab environment, you may not be able to do this activity.

Note 2:   You may not be able to do this activity in a lab or on your own computer if you do not have a valid email address.

STEP 1   Open **Mozilla**. Click **Window**. Click **Mail & Newsgroups**.

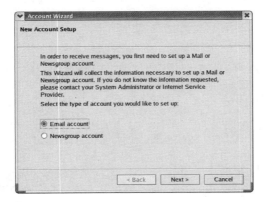

WHAT'S HAPPENING? ◦ A wizard opens so you may easily set up your newsgroups and email. If you have already set up your mail and newsgroups accounts, go to Step 7.

STEP 2   Click **Newsgroup account**. Click **Next**.

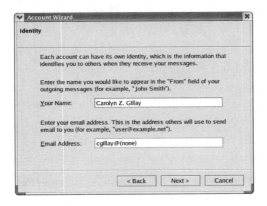

WHAT'S HAPPENING? ◦ Here you need to fill in the name you wish to appear in the From field as well as your email address. Note that Your Name comes from the comments field of the /etc/ **passwd** file. However, a word of warning here. Spam has become epidemic. *Spam* is unsolicited e-mail on the Internet. From the sender's point-of-view, it's a form of bulk mail, often to a list of users that are subscribers to a Usenet discussion group or obtained by companies that specialize in creating e-mail distribution lists. To the receiver, it usually seems like and is junk e-mail, and much of it is offensive. It is generally concluded that the term spam was derived from a famous Monty Python sketch ("Well, we have Spam, tomato & Spam, egg & Spam, Egg, bacon & Spam...") that was current when spam first began arriving on the Internet. Spam is a trademarked Hormel meat product that was well-known in the U.S. Armed Forces during World War II.

One way to try to minimize spam is to have several email addresses. Most ISPs allow you more than one email address. Hence, you can have a "public" email address for responding to ads or participating in newsgroups and have a "private" email address for friends and family. When your public email address becomes an overwhelming target for spam, you can abandon it and choose a new public email address. There are also commercial programs that try to filter out spam.

STEP 3   Change your name if you wish, fill in your email address, and click **Next.**

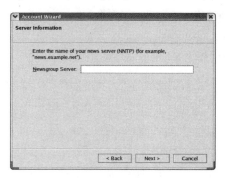

WHAT'S HAPPENING? You would key in the name of your newsgroups server. You get this information from your ISP. Typically, the name is *news.ispname.com*, where *ispname* is the name of your Internet service provider.

STEP 4   Key in the name of your newsgroup server. Click **Next.**

WHAT'S HAPPENING? Here you can give your newsgroup account a friendly name.

STEP 5   Key in a name that you like for your news server. Click **Next.**

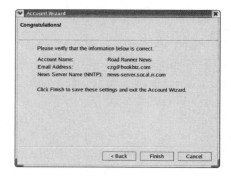

WHAT'S HAPPENING? The information you provided is displayed in a summary sheet.

STEP 6   Click **Finish.**

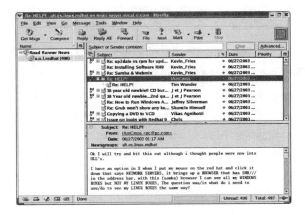

WHAT'S HAPPENING? You have opened the **Mail & Newsgroups** window, where your newsgroup should be listed.

STEP 7   Right-click your newsgroup and click **Subscribe**.

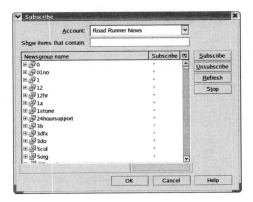

WHAT'S HAPPENING? You have selected your news account. In order use Mozilla as your newsreader, you first needed to download the list of what groups are available to you. The bottom of the window shows newsgroups being downloaded. Once you have downloaded the list, you must choose which newsgroups interest you. Once you subscribe, you can participate in the newsgroups, browse the topics in the newsgroups, sort the messages, manage the threads, track what you have and have not read, and post your messages to the newsgroups. You can also download newsgroups while online and view them later offline. The list is comprehensive. Rather than scrolling through the entire list, you can search by topic.

STEP 8   In the **Show items that contain:** text box, key in the following: **linux**

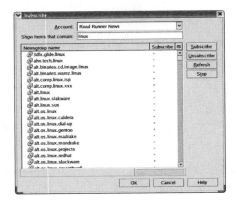

WHAT'S HAPPENING? ⇝ You moved to the **alt.os.linux** heading. There should be an entry for **alt.os.linux.redhat**. You may need to scroll down to see this entry.

STEP 9   Double-click **alt.os.linux.redhat**. If that is not available, choose another newsgroup.

STEP 10   Click **OK**. Click **a.o.l.redhat (498)** in the sidebar.

WHAT'S HAPPENING? ⇝ When you click the newsgroup, it tells you how many messages there are to download.

STEP 11   Click **Download**. Click a message in the **Subject** area.

WHAT'S HAPPENING? ⇝ Now that you have subscribed and downloaded this newsgroup, you see that there are 496 unread postings for this group. Your display will be different. However, the left pane indicates which newsgroups you are looking at. The right pane lists the postings. As you select an item in the message box, the text appears in the pane below. If an item has a plus, it can be expanded. This is a threaded discussion.

STEP 12   Click your newsgroup name.

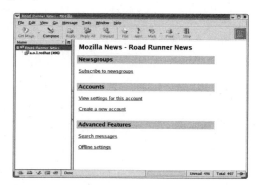

WHAT'S HAPPENING? You can subscribe to more than one newsgroup.

STEP 13   Click **Subscribe to newsgroups**. In the **Show items that contain:** text box, key in the following: **comp.os.linux.help**.

STEP 14   In the **Newsgroup name** list box, click **comp.os.linux.help**. Click **Subscribe**. Click **OK**. Click **c.o.i help (217)** in the sidebar.

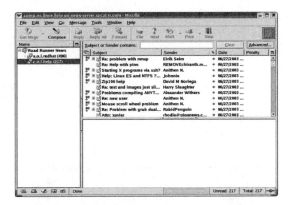

WHAT'S HAPPENING? *Note:* Your display will be different. When you see an arrow or a message that beings with Re:, you are looking at a threaded discussion. The entries are listed in date order. Each time you click a column heading, you will arrange items by that column type. Thus, if you click the **Subject** heading, you will arrange the listing by subject.

STEP 15   Click the **Subject** column heading.

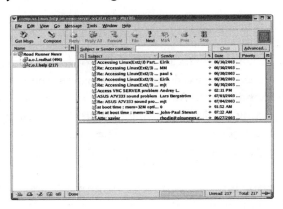

WHAT'S HAPPENING? The listings are now arranged alphabetically by subject.

STEP 16   Double-click an item.

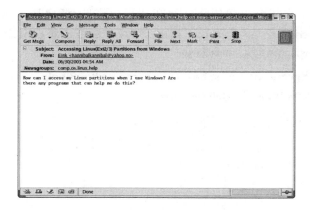

WHAT'S HAPPENING? You are looking at the message.

STEP 17 Click **Reply**.

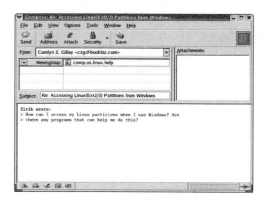

WHAT'S HAPPENING? Here you would create the posting of an article to the entire group. You would be continuing the thread. You would key in information where the cursor is located. Then you would click the **Send** button. Although there is no formal governing body that determines the rules for posting articles or replying to posts, there is an informal code of ethics, called *netiquette*, that most considerate users follow. These include:

* Before you post anything, read what is there to get a sense of that group's style.
* Be succinct (brief).
* Never assume that a person is speaking for an entire group or organization.
* If you want to respond to an individual, use email rather than just posting a follow-up post to the entire group.
* Avoid "me-too" postings where you are simply agreeing with what someone else has said.
* Be careful about what you say.
* Use descriptive titles in your Subject line.
* Be careful with humor. Not everyone has the same sense of humor.

STEP 18 Close the windows until you return to the Mozilla New Server window.

STEP 19 Right-click a newsgroups that you subscribed to and click **Unsubscribe**.

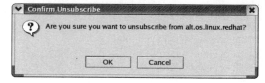

WHAT'S **HAPPENING?** You are asked to confirm.

STEP 20 Click **OK**

STEP 21 Unsubscribe to any other newsgroups you subscribed to.

WHAT'S **HAPPENING?** You no longer are subscribed to that newsgroup. Some good places to start for newsgroups include **comp.os.linux**; **linux**, and **os.linux**.

STEP 22 Close the all open windows.

3.20 • Mailing Lists and User Groups

Mailing lists are similar to newsgroups, but instead of your searching for articles of interest, mailing lists send messages directly to your email address. If you send a question to a mailing list, every subscriber to that mailing list will receive your question in their email. The recipient can respond directly to you or to everyone on the mailing list. The same etiquette that applies to newsgroups applies to mailing lists. There are many mailing lists that deal with Linux.

User groups have been formed so that people can get together to share ideas, share their knowledge, get help from other users, and see new products. User groups are not limited to computer user groups. There are user groups for everything from sewing enthusiasts to model plane enthusiasts. Linux User Groups (LUGs) are very important to Linux users. Users can rely on other users and experts that can help them find real solutions to problems. LUGs typically get together on a monthly basis. Meeting topics can range from trading software to installation issues. Sometimes, depending on the group, the meetings are social in nature, allowing you to share your common interests. Some LUGs have their own newsletters, web sites, and mailing lists. To see if there are any LUGs in your area, you can check out **http://www.linux.org/users/index.html** or **http://www.ssc.com:8080/glue** for groups in your area.

Chapter Summary

In this chapter you were introduced to the following:
* The extensive help resources available for the Linux operating system.
* The types of help available in GNOME.
* Using the help browser in GNOME and at the command line.
* Using man pages in the GUI and at the command line.
* How man pages are set up and the meaning of the various sections in man pages.
* The **info**, **whatis**, and **apropos** commands used in the GUI and at the command line.
* The use of HOWTOs and FAQs.
* Descriptions of and uses for online resources.
* The purpose and function of newsgroups and news servers.
* The purpose and function of user groups.
* The purpose and function of the Linux Documentation Project.

Key Terms

browser	environmental variables	HOWTO
bug	errata	HTTP (Hypertext Transfer
command name	expression	Protocol)
cron job	FAQs	mirror site
debugging	foo	moderated
environment	homonymous man texts	newsreader

newsgroup	spam	Usenet
newsreader	string	variable
online	threaded discussion	workaround
search engine	URL (Uniform	
shell variable	Resource Locator)	

Discussion Questions

1. Explain what is meant by online help capabilities.
2. What is the Linux Documentation Project (LDP)?
3. What is a mirror site? What purpose does a mirror site serve?
4. List the necessary steps to access the installed man pages in the Red Hat Linux's Gnome interface.
5. What is a hypertext utility?
6. Explain the purpose and function of man pages.
7. man pages are divided into manual sections. List and explain the purpose of three of these sections.
8. What are man pages?
9. What is the difference between **apropos** and **whatis**?
10. What will be the result of keying in each of the following commands?
    1. **man 1 intro**
    2. **/usr/sbin/makewhatis**
    3. **apropos whatis**
11. Explain the purpose and function of the **info** command.
12. Compare and contrast info pages with man pages.
13. When would you use the term **foo**?
14. Give the syntax for the **info** command and explain each part of the syntax.
15. Explain the purpose and function of HOWTOs and **FAQ**s.
16. What is a browser? A newsreader? Usenet? A newsgroup?
17. List three ways to connect to the Internet. Compare and contrast two of the ways listed.
18. List at least two online sites that have excellent resources for assisting you in learning Linux. Which do you prefer and why?
19. Linux documentation comes in a variety of formats. Compare and contrast three of the formats.
20. What is a newsgroup? A threaded discussion?
21. Explain the purpose and function of Usenet.
22. Some newsgroups are *moderated*. Explain.
23. List five of the eight informal codes of ethics that most considerate users follow.
24. What is the difference between mailing lists and newsgroups?
25. Why would you join a Linux User Group (LUGs)?

True/False Questions

For each question, circle the letter T if the question is true and the letter F if the question is false.

T	F	1. man pages can be accessed only through Internet sites.
T	F	2. Using **man** at the command line gives different information than using the man pages through the GNOME help browser.
T	F	3. A workaround is often used to bypass bugs.
T	F	4. Spam is considered junk email.
T	F	5. Mozilla is an example of a newsreader.

Completion Questions

Write the correct answer in each blank space.

6. Linux provides _____ help, which minimizes the need for printed manuals.

7. A file server that contains duplicate sets of files is called a(n) _____ site.

8. Document files that describe how to use or configure some aspect of Linux are called _____.

9. The command that determines which directories **man** will search for the requested man page is _____.

10. The Info pages are organized into _____.

Multiple Choice Questions

For each question, write the letter for the correct answer in the blank space.

11. To search using whatis or apropos you need to
    a. key in the exact command name you want help with.
    b. key in completely different command names.
    c. have the whatis database built.
    d. none of the above

12. LDP is an abbreviation for
    a. Linux Developer's Program.
    b. Linux Device Project.
    c. Linuxlike Development Program.
    d. Linux Documentation Project.

13. The purpose of the **-w** option used with **man** is to
    a. display all manual pages matching a specific string.
    b. display path name for the location of the man pages.
    c. display short description of the command.
    d. display the purpose of the **-w** option.

14. Documentation is provided by Red Hat
    a. in printed manual.
    b. on the Red Hat web site.
    c. both a and b
    d. neither a nor b

15. When using info pages, pressing **n** takes you to
    a. the next node.
    b. the next page.
    c. the next screen.
    d. help with the info command.

Writing Commands

Write the correct steps or commands to perform the required action as if you were at the computer. You will assume that there is a terminal window open. The prompt will indicate the current working directory.

16. You wish to find help on the **less** command. You want the name of the command, a brief overview of the command, the syntax, and options.

```
[cgillay@RedHat9 cgillay]$_
```

17. You want to find every man page on the command **ls**.

    [tsumner@RedHat9 mail]$_

18. You want to only display a brief description of the **mount** command.

    [jleisy@RedHat9 jleisy]$_

19. You want a description of the purpose and function of the **fstab** file.

    [swhang@RedHat9 swhang]$_

20. You wish to locate the path where the manual pages are located.

    [cgillay@RedHat9 cgillay]$_

Application Assignments

Problem Set I—At the Computer: Multiple Choice

Note 1:   In all exercises, *username* in italics represents your user name. For example, I would substitute **cgillay** for *username*.

Note 2:   If you are working in a lab environment, your home directory may be freshened each time you boot, which means your work will not be saved from session to session.

Problem A

- Click the Main Menu button. Point to **Documentation**.
- Open the **Reference Guide**.
- Locate and open the link **For the More Experienced**
    1. The more experienced user will already
        a. have a basic grasp of the most frequently used commands.
        b. have acquired some useful documentation.
        c. be able to read the source code and/or configuration files.
        d. realize that they do not have any need for documentation.
- Return to the opening page.
    2. You may return to the opening page by
        a. Clicking the **Reload** button.
        b. Clicking the **Back** button until you reach the opening page.
        c. both a and b
        d. neither a nor b
- Click the Main menu.
- Click **Help**.
- Choose **Manual Pages**.
- In **Applications**, locate **date**.
    3. The **date** command allows you to
        a. print the system date and time.
        b. set the system date and time.
        c. both a and b
        d. neither a nor b

4. In what section does **date** appear?
    a. 1.
    b. 2.
    c. 3.
    d. 4.

* In User **Applications**, locate **clear**.

    5. The **clear** command allows you to
        a. clear the desktop.
        b. clear the terminal screen.
        c. clear the home directory.
        d. none of the above

* Close all open windows.

Problem B

* Open a terminal window and locate the man page for **startx**.

    6. The synopsis for **startx** is
        a. **startx [[client] options ....] [-- [server] options ....]**
        b. **startx [[server] options ....] [-- [client] options ....]**
        c. **startx [[client] options ....]**
        d. **startx [[server] options ....]**

* Locate the man page for **man**.

    7. What two options will not display the man pages, but do print the location(s) of
        the files that would be formatted for display?
        a. **-w** or **manpath**
        b. **-w** or **--path**
        c. **-W** or **--PATH**
        d. none of the above

    8. You are interested in a one-line summary of the command **logout**. What command
        could you use?
        a. **whereis logout** or **man logout**
        b. **whatis -f logout** or **man -w logout**
        c. **where logout** or **manual logout**
        d. **whatis logout** or **man -f logout**

    9. Using the correct command from Question 8, what section does **logout** appear in?
        a. **1**
        b. **2**
        c. **3**
        d. **4**

    10. Using the correct command from Question 8, what description appears for **logout**?
        a. logs out user.
        b. bash built-in commands
        c. both a and b
        d. neither a nor b

* Close all open windows.

Problem C

* Use the **info** command in the terminal window for the following questions.

* Locate info about **cat**.

* Press the **n** key.

    11. What node are you in?

        a. **"od" :Write files in octal or other formats.**

        b. **"nl": Number lines and write files.**

        c. **"op" Output of entire files.**

        d. **"tac": Concatenate and write files in reverse.**

* Press `Ctrl` + h. If necessary, scroll until you see the entry for TAB.

    12. What does the `Tab` key do?

        a. Skips to the next hypertext link within this node.

        b. Follows the hypertext link under cursor.

        c. Moves to the Top node.

        d. Moves to the last node seen in this window.

* Close the window.

* Locate info about **pwd**.

    13. What options are available?

        a. **-d** or **-x**

        b. **--help** or **--version**

        c. only **--help**

        d. no options are available.

* Close the window. Locate info about **echo**.

    14. The purpose of **echo** is to

        a. **Print to the printer.**

        b. **Print a document.**

        c. **Print help.**

        d. **Print a line of text.**

* Locate info about **lpd**.

    15. Under NAME, it states **lpd -**

        a. **line**

        b. **line printer**

        c. **line printer spooler**

        d. **line printer daemon**

    16. Is there a definition given for only the term **daemon**?

        a. yes

        b. no

* Close all open windows.

Problem D

* Use your browser to go to the Linux Documentation Project site.

* Choose **Guides**.

17. *Securing and Optimizing Linux Red Hat Edition: The Ultimate Solution* by Gerhard Mourani is available in
    a. HTML format.
    b. Text format.
    c. PDF format.
    d. all of the above

* Use your browser to go to Red Hat Products.

* Locate the link **for Red Hat Linux 9.0, 7.3, or 8.0** under **Community Products**.

* Choose **Technical Details**

18. How much hard disk space is recommended on a PC for the complete (everything) installation of Red Hat Linux?
    a. 475 MB
    b. 1.7 GB
    c. 2.1 GB
    d. 5 GB

* Locate the online resources for Red Hat 9.

19. Is there an errata document that deals with the security of a Red Hat Linux System?
    a. Yes.
    b. No.

* Go to the site **http://counter.li.org**

20. What is counted on this site?
    a. Number of registered Linux users
    b. Number of registered machines
    c. both a and b
    d. neither a nor b

* Close all open windows.

Problem Set II—At the Computer: Short Answer

1. Red Hat Linux 9.0 has been released. Are there major differences between 7.2, 7.3, 8.0, and 9? If so, identify them. What are the pros/cons of updating? How did you come to your conclusions? What tools did you use?
2. What is Red Hat Enterprise Linux AS? Who do you think would use this product? Why? How did you come to your conclusions? What is the cost of this product? How did you locate this information?
3. What are the five window managers shipped with Red Hat Linux 9? List two ways that a window manager differs from a desktop manager. How did you locate this information?
4. Find a HOWTO on how to install a Zip drive on a Linux system. Where did you go to find this information? Was the information useful to you? Why or why not?
5. What is **http://www.faqs.org**? Can you use it to find information about Linux? What kind of information will you find? Do you think that this is a useful site? Why or why not?
6. What is **http://www.gnu.org/manual/info/info.html**? Can you use it to find information about Linux? What kind of information will you find? Did you find this information useful? Why or why not?
7. You want to know how to safely shut down Linux from the command line. Use the man pages to investigate the halt command and to answer these questions:

a. In what section is halt located? Why?

b. Is it safe to use the halt command to shut down Linux?

c. Which command(s) can be used to shut down the system instead of halt?

d. Which is the best and safest command to shut down the system?

e. What other commands are given in the **See Also** section? Do you think that they are relevant?

8. Are there any Linux user groups in your geographic area? If so, where and when do they meet? How did you find out this information? How would you set up a local LUG?

9. You want to know about file systems and which file systems Linux supports. Find at least two locations that will give you this kind of information. What did you learn about file systems? Where did you look?

10. You are interested in the FSH (File System Hierarchy). What is the most current version? Does Red Hat vary at all from the FSH standard? If so, where? Where did you find this information?

Problem Set III—Brief Essay

Use gEdit or OpenOffice.org Writer to write and print your response. Be sure to put your name as well as what day and time your class is. Include the number of the question you are answering.

a. Compare and contrast the man pages in the GNOME Help Browser and using man at the command line. What are the disadvantages/advantages of each method? Which do you prefer using and why?

b. *Documentation such as FAQs, HOWTOs, and mini HOWTOs are vital to using and understanding Linux.* Agree or disagree with this statement and explain your answer. In your discussion, include brief descriptions of each type of documentation.

c. Locate and subscribe to a Linux newsgroup. Read some postings. Which newsgroup did you select? How did you locate it? Why did you select it? What did you learn from it? Would you want to subscribe to newsgroups? Why or why not?

CHAPTER 4

Directory Commands

Chapter Overview

When you work with a computer, you will accumulate many files. If you are going to be an efficient user of your computer, you need to have a way to manage those files. But first you need to understand how Linux names your devices, particularly if you have only encountered a Windows environment where drives are assigned letters. As you will discover, devices are identified very differently in Linux.

You may manage your files in the GUI, using the Nautilus file manager, or you may manage your files from the command prompt. Linux provides tools that give you the ability to create directories, remove directories, and move about the hierarchical structure using the Nautilus file manager and at the command prompt. You will learn several essential commands, as well as shortcuts that can be used with those commands, such as dot addressing techniques. In addition, Linux also provides an environment in which you work. Linux keeps track of your environment by the means of variables.

In this chapter, you will learn how to use the Nautilus file manager to create and remove directories, and you will learn how to do this at the command prompt using **mkdir**, **cd**, **mv**, **rmdir**, and **rm**. You will also learn the important options that can be used with these commands. You will also learn how to use the dot and double dot to easily move about in your directory structure. You will explore several important variables such as **path**, **ps1**, and **cdpath**.

Learning Objectives

1. Explain the purpose and function of partitions and extended partitions.
2. Explain the hierarchical filing system of a tree-structured directory.

175

3. Explain the purpose and function of a root directory and tell how and when it is created.
4. Explain what directories are and tell how directories are named, created, and used.
5. Define the purpose and function of the **cd** and **mkdir** commands.
6. Compare and contrast the absolute path with the relative path.
7. Explain the purpose and use of directory markers (the dot addressing techniques).
8. Explain how to change the names of directories.
9. List the steps to remove a directory and the steps to delete directories recursively.
10. Explain the purpose and function of shell environmental variables.
11. Explain the purpose of the **PROMPT** variable.
12. Explain the purpose and function of the **PATH** variable and the **CDPATH** variable.

Student Outcomes

1. Display and sort files and directories in different sequences using the Nautilus file manager and in the terminal window.
2. Create directories using the Nautilus file manager and in a terminal window.
3. Change directories using the **cd** command.
4. Use the dot addressing techniques with commands.
5. Rename a directory using the **mv** command.
6. Eliminate a directory.
7. Use **rm** and **rmdir** to remove directories recursively.
8. Use the **PROMPT** command to change the display of the prompt.
9. Use the **PATH** variable and **CDPATH** variable to execute specific commands.

Commands Introduced

cd
ls
mkdir
mv
printenv
pwd
rmdir
set

4.1 • The Hierarchical Filing System (Tree-structured Directories)

In Linux, as in all operating systems, nearly all information is stored in files. Programs, data, system settings, and other information is stored in files. As you can imagine, if everything were stored in one location, it would be extremely difficult to locate any item. As an example of what you are faced with, imagine you own 10 books. By reading each title, you can quickly peruse the authors and titles and locate the book you wish to read. Suppose your library grows and you now have 100 books. You do not want to have to read each author and title looking for a specific book, so you classify the information. A common classification scheme is to arrange the books alphabetically by the author's last name. Now you have shortened your search time. If you are looking for a book by Gillay, you go to the letter G. You may have more than one book by an author that begins with G, but by going to the letter G, you have narrowed your search. Now imagine you have 10,000 books—arranging alphabetically by author is still not enough. You may have 200 books by authors whose last names begin with G. So you further classify your books. You first divide them into categories like computer or fiction. Then, within the category, you arrange alphabetically by last name. So, if you wanted a computer book by Gillay, you would first go to the computer section, then to the letter G. If you wanted a novel by Grafton, you would first go to the fiction section and then the letter G. As you can see, you are classifying and categorizing information so that you can find it quickly.

This process is exactly what you want to do with files. You have many files. You want to be able to locate them quickly and group them logically. The way you do this is by the means of directories and subdirectories. How those files and directories are stored on disk is dependent on the file system of the operating system. As you learned in Chapter 2, every disk must have a file system. But in addition, the disk itself must be organized.

A hard disk has one major purpose, which is to store and retrieve data. In order to do so, a disk is divided into *partitions*. Each partition can be accessed as if it were a separate disk. This is done through a *partition table*. Each partition must have a file system installed on it so that the operating system may save and retrieve information. Each physical disk can be divided into a maximum of four partitions. See Figure 4.1, "Total Disk Space."

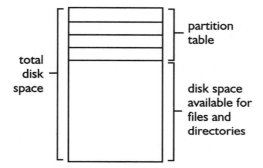

Figure 4.1 • Total Disk Space

The partition table contains several important characteristics of the partition. It states where each partition begins and ends, whether the partition is active, and the partition type. The starting and ending points of the partition define the size and location on a disk. The active partition tells some operating systems that the active partition is the one that is booted from. The type indicates the anticipated use of that partition. The type can include a file system type, a flag that associates the partition with a specific operating system or to indicate that the partition is a boot partition, or any combination of these types. Many computers purchased with the Windows operating system use only a single partition. See Figure 4.2, "Typical Computer with Windows."

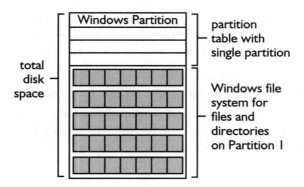

Figure 4.2 • Typical Computer with Windows

A disk drive may have more than one operating system on it. See Figure 4.3, "Dual Booting System."

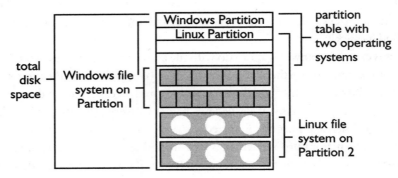

Figure 4.3 • Dual Booting System

Here there are two operating systems, each with a corresponding file system that the designated operating system can read and write to. To access these partitions, there must be a partition-naming scheme. In the Windows world, each partition type is checked to see if it is a file system compatible with Windows. If it is, then it is assigned a drive letter. The hard drive letters start with C. That drive letter can then be used to refer to that partition as well as the file system on that drive. In the Linux world, the naming scheme is file based on the syntax of /dev/xxyN. See Table 4.1, "Linux Partition-naming Scheme."

Syntax	Meaning
/dev	The name of the directory where all device files are located. Partitions are on hard disks, and hard disks are devices. The files that represent all possible partitions are located in this directory.
xx	The *xx* string represents the type of device on which the partition resides. Normally you will see **hd** for IDE drives and **sd** for any SCSI drives.
y	This *y* string represents the device that the partition is on. Thus, /**dev/hda** would indicate the first IDE hard drive, and /**dev/hdb** would represent the second hard drive. If they were SCSI drives, the notation would be /**dev/sda** or /**dev/sdb**.
N	The *N* string indicates the partition. The first four primary or extended partitions have the numbers 1 through 4. Logical partitions begin with 5.

Table 4.1 • Linux Partition-naming Scheme

This brings up the discussion of extended partitions. Although there can be only four primary partitions, one partition type may be set to extended. Then, an extended partition table is created. An extended partition is a partition within a partition, and you can also create one or more partitions, *logical partitions*, which reside entirely within the extended partition. See Figure 4.4, "Windows and Linux Using an Extended Partition."

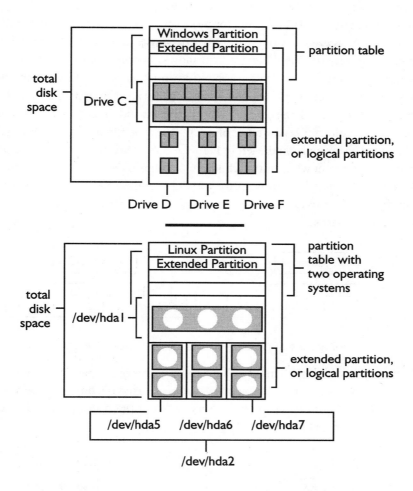

Figure 4.4 · Windows and Linux Using an Extended Partition

To access the file system in the Windows-DOS world, each partition is assigned a drive letter. Within that partition, a separate hierarchy is created, beginning with the drive letter (**C:**) and the root directory (\). Thus, in the DOS-Windows world, for every drive letter, there is a root directory. When you use a peripheral device such as a floppy device, you are connecting the device and the files on the device to the file system tree managed by the operating system. That device is also assigned a drive letter such as **A:**, and it also has a root directory (\).

The Linux world is quite different. In Linux, partitions are identified by device names such as **hda1**, **hda2**, **hdb1** and so on. **hda** describes the first IDE hard drive, and **1** is the first partition on the first IDE drive. **hda2** would then be the first IDE drive, but the second partition on that drive. **hdb1** then describes the first partition on the second IDE drive. Peripheral devices are also named; for example, the first floppy drive would be **fd0**. To access the file system on the partition, each partition is used to form part of the storage necessary to support a single set of files and directories. This is accomplished by associating a partition with a directory through *mounting*. When you mount a partition, you make the files and directories available starting at the *mount point*. You are adding the device and its files to the directory tree. The directories in Linux are still a hierarchy, but Linux provides a single hierarchy that includes every mounted partition and mounted peripheral device. Thus, to access the floppy disk, as you learned in Chapter 2, you mount it at the mount point in the hierarchy (/**mnt/floppy**). Now your floppy disk is part of the hierarchical structure. The topmost directory of the directory tree is the root directory, the / (forward slash).

The hierarchical or tree-structured filing system allows not only for files but also for other directories, called subdirectories, which can contain any number of entries, including other subdirectories. The terms "directory" and "subdirectory" are used interchangeably. The directory structure is like a family tree with the root directory at the top and the subdirectories branching off from the root. The root directory is the point of entry—the mount point—in the hierarchical directory structure. The example on the left in Figure 4.5, "A Directory Is Like a Family Tree," is a family tree showing a parent who has two children; the one on the right is the root directory with two directories. One directory is the **home** directory for user files; the other is the **usr** directory, which contains files that are accessible to all users. Again, what you are doing is classifying and further classifying information.

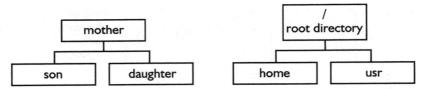

Figure 4.5 • A Directory Is Like a Family Tree

A child can have only one biological mother, but a child can become a parent and have children. Those children can also become parents and have children. Likewise, **home** can be a child directory of the root directory, but also a parent directory to directories beneath it (see Figure 4.6, "Hierarchical Structure of a Directory").

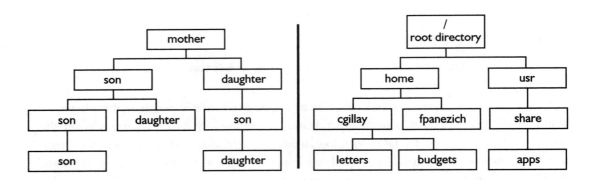

Figure 4.6 • Hierarchical Structure of a Directory

The children are dependent on the parent above. Each directory is listed in its parent directory, but not in any directory above the parent. Note the absolute hierarchical structure. You cannot skip a directory any more than you can have a grandparent and grandchild with and no parent between. You move around in the directories via the path, which tells the operating system where to go for a particular file.

Since it is difficult to find things when they are scattered about a large room, you want to put up walls (directories) so that like things can be grouped together. When the walls go up, the root directory is the main lobby—the forward slash (/). Under the **home** directory, you have your own specific home directory (**cgillay**), and you plan to have **games** and **classes**. You further want to break up each of those directories. The **games** directory will have the **kids** and **adults** subdirectories. The **classes** directory will have two classes (**history**, a directory, and **linux**, another directory). You in essence are setting up who can "live" in each room. You post a sign indicating what you plan to put inside each room. See Figure 4.7, "Directories as Rooms."

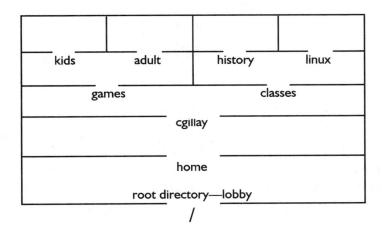

Figure 4.7 • Directories as Rooms

Each room is off the main lobby, the /. You cannot go from the **games** room to the **classes** room without first going through **cgillay**. The lobby (/) sees the entryways to the **home** room only. It does not know what is in the room, only that there is a room (directory). Each new room (directory) is off another room (directory). The **home** room only knows that has one room, **cgillay** (directory). When you move inside the **cgillay** room, it only knows that it has a **games** room and a **classes** room. The **games** room has two rooms—**kids** and **adults**. The **games** room (directory) now becomes a lobby. You can get to the **kids** and **adult** rooms (directories) only through the **games** lobby. Furthermore, in order to get to the **games** room, you must pass through the main lobby (/, the root directory), then the **home** directory, then **cgillay**.

The **games** lobby knows that there are two new rooms but does not know what is inside each. **cgillay** knows the **games** room, but does not know what is inside **games**. The **kids** and **adult** rooms know only the **games** lobby.

The same relationship exists for all other new rooms (directories). A directory knows only its parent lobby and any children it may create. There are no shortcuts. If you are in the **kids** room and wish to go the **history** room, you must return to the **games** lobby, then you must pass through the **cgillay** lobby to the **classes** lobby. Although these rooms are subdivided, it is not mandatory that you subdivide them. The purpose of these rooms is to hold files. The files are like the furniture. See Figure 4.8, "Files in Subdirectories."

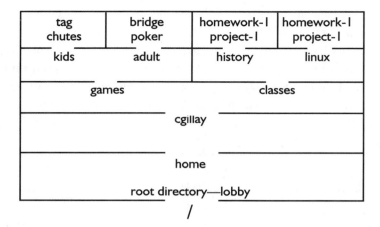

Figure 4.8 • Files in Subdirectories

You now have not only created the rooms (directories), but you have also filled them with furniture (files). Thus, using directories is a way to manage the numerous files and programs you collect and create. Again, this is a classification scheme, and you expect some logic to it. Just as you would not expect to find a stove in a room called bedroom, you would not expect to find a file called **jeopardy** in a subdirectory called **history**. This does not mean there cannot be a mistake—that someone could indeed place the stove in the bedroom—but that would make the stove very hard to find. And although it may appear that you have duplicate file names (**project-1** and **homework-1**), in fact they are unique file names because of their location. For example, one file is **/home/cgillay/history/project-1** and the other file is uniquely identified as **/home/cgillay/linux/project-1**.

There is another component to using directories. When you use directories, you can change your work area, much like using a room. If you are going to cook, you will go to the kitchen because you expect the tools you need to be in that location. You expect not only the stove to be there but also all the tools you need—the sink, the spices, the pots and pans. If you want to go to sleep, you will go to the bedroom because that is where you expect the to find the bed. Directories have names that you or a program choose. The only exception is that the root directory is always known as / (forward slash). The root directory is *always* at the top of the hierarchical structure.

4.2 • Managing Files and Directories

Remember, a computer is a tool to perform work, such as accessing the Internet to do research, managing a project budget, or writing a report. This is analogous to any business. The purpose of the business may be to sell insurance or to provide medical care. Whatever the purpose of the business, prior to actually performing the work, there are office-related tasks to be accomplished in order to manage the business. These tasks range from the purchase of file cabinets to the organization of the filing system. These business housekeeping tasks are ongoing. In order to successfully run a business, you need to know where your documents are, how to file them, and how to retrieve them so you may actually do business.

A computer is no different. You must manage your files so you may efficiently do your work. Once you understand that the organization and structure of a disk is dependent on the file system used by the operating system, the next task is to use that structure for saving and retrieving files. Thus, an important function of an operating system is to provide the tools to manage files and directories. These tools are the housekeeping tasks of the operating system, and they include the commands you use to copy files, create directories, rename files and directories, delete files and directories, and view and locate files and directories.

4.3 • Viewing Files and Directories

As you accumulate files and directories, you need to see what files are on your computer system. In addition to viewing them, you may also wish to sort them in different sequences, such as by last time modified. You may alter your view in the Nautilus file manager in GNOME. In addition, there are options available for use with the ls command that also allow you to alter your view.

4.4 • Activity: Viewing Files and Directories

Note 1:   In Nautilus file manger, your view may not match the text. If you want it to match the text, you may change your view by clicking **View as Icons** or **View as List** in the drop-down list box on the Location bar.

Note 2:   The activities in this book assume Linux is installed at run level 3. See the Installation section of Appendix A for details.

STEP 1   Place the BOOK disk in the floppy disk drive. Mount the disk.

STEP 2   Double-click the **Start Here** icon on the desktop. Click **Information**. Click **Tree**. Expand **mnt** in the tree. Click **floppy** in the tree.

STEP 3   On the location bar, confirm that View as Icons is selected.

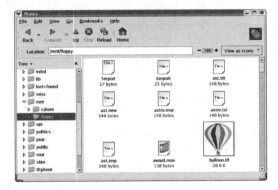

WHAT'S HAPPENING? This is the default view in Nautilus. Your files and directories are displayed.

STEP 4   Click **Edit**. Click **Preferences**. Click the **Views** tab.

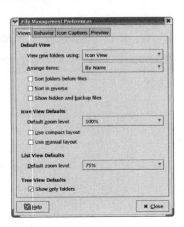

WHAT'S HAPPENING? The directory listings are intermixed with the file listing. Usually, users want to see the directories listed first. Here the directories are called folders.

STEP 5   Under **Arrange items**, check **Sort folders before files**. Click **Close**.

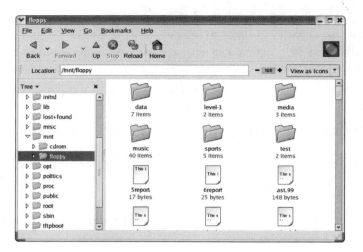

WHAT'S HAPPENING? Now the directory icons are listed first. Directory icons are shown as folders.

STEP 6   Double-click the **data** folder in the right pane.

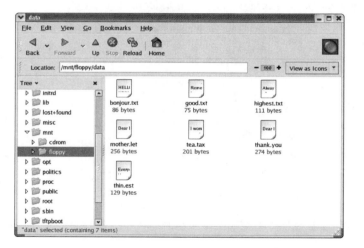

WHAT'S HAPPENING? You are looking at the files in the **data** directory. The same task can be accomplished at the command line.

STEP 7   Open a terminal window. Key in the following: **ls /mnt/floppy/data** Enter

WHAT'S HAPPENING? You see your files and folders as you did in the display following Step 6.

STEP 8 Click your user button on the Panel make it active. Click the **Back** button.

STEP 9 On the toolbar, click the down arrow of **View as Icons**. Click **View as List**.

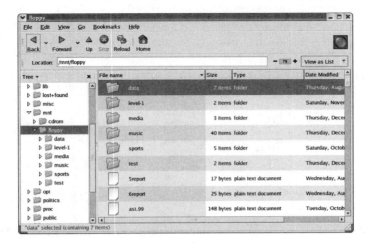

WHAT'S HAPPENING? You are looking at your files in a list view in Nautilus. Here you see your files and folders, but with the size, the file type, and the date and time the last time the file was modified. If you cannot see the date and time, you can size the window. In addition, if there are any emblems, Nautilus will show them. An *emblem* is a graphical symbol that Nautilus adds to icons for files and folders that are read only, and any links. Links are like shortcuts in Windows. The emblems vary depending on the theme you are using.

STEP 10 In the tree, click the **home** directory folder.

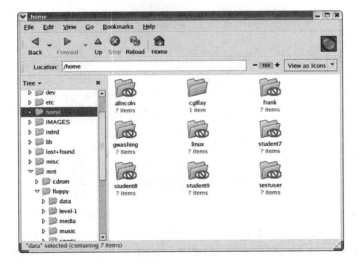

WHAT'S HAPPENING? Here you see the emblem for no read, no write, and no execute for all the folders except your own home directory.

STEP 11   Make the terminal window active. Key in the following: **ls -l /mnt/floppy** Enter

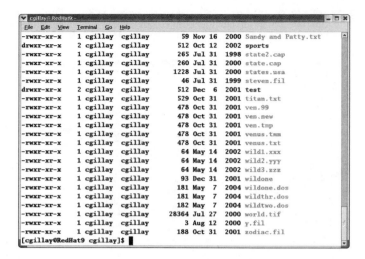

WHAT'S HAPPENING? Here you see the file names, file sizes, date, and time; but you also see the file permissions, the number of links to the file, and the owner of the file.

STEP 12   Click the **home** button on the toolbar to make the Nautilus window active. In the tree, click **floppy**. On the menu bar of the Nautilus file manager, click **Edit**. Click **Preferences**. Click the **Views** tab. Click the down arrow in the **Arrange items** drop-down list box.

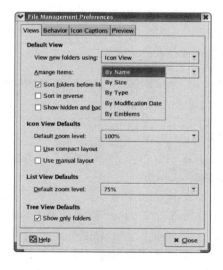

WHAT'S HAPPENING? Here you may choose which default view you prefer. You may choose to see your files and directories sorted by name, size, type (file extension), modification date, or by the emblem. You may also sort in ascending order or descending order (reverse).

STEP 13   Click **By Type**. Check the **Sort in reverse** check box. Click **Close**.

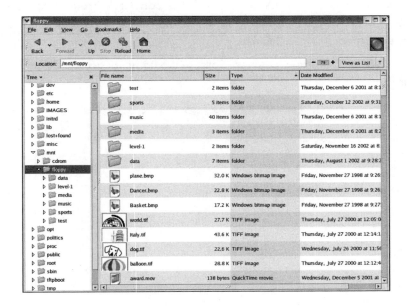

WHAT'S HAPPENING? Your files are now sorted by file type, in descending order (z to a). Directories are listed first. However, when you requested to sort by file type (extension), you may have thought that you were sorting by the actual extension such as **.bmp**, **.tif**, or **.mov**. If you look at the display, you see that you are actually sorting by the Type name given to the file, such as Windows bitmap image. Thus, if you actually want to sort in file extension order, using the command line is more accurate.

STEP 14 Make the terminal window active. Key in the following: **ls -Xr /mnt/floppy** Enter

```
report.user       world.tif      exp201jan.dta    projectz
states.usa        italy.tif      exp201feb.dta    projecty
right.up          dog.tif        exp03mar.dta     projectx
middle.up         balloon.tif    exp03jan.dta     projectc
dress.up          earth.thr      exp03feb.dta     projectb
bye.typ           file3.swt      exp02mar.dta     projecta
born.typ          file2.swt      exp02jan.dta     Old Automobiles
LONGFILENAMING.TXT right.red     exp02feb.dta     newreport
LONGFILENAME.TXT  middle.red     exp01mar.dta     music
LONGFILENAMED.TXT left.red       exp01jan.dta     mikereport
venus.txt         granny.rec     exp01feb.dta     media
titan.txt         earth.one      wildtwo.dos      LONGFILENAME
Sandy and Patty.txt ven.new      wildthr.dos      level-1
Sandy and Nicki.txt mer.new      wildone.dos      frankreport
planets.txt       jup.new        quasars.doc      filename
NEW AUTOS.txt     ast.new        file3.czg        data
mercury.txt       orion.neb      file2.czg        czgreport
jupiter.txt       award.mov      state.cap        cherylreport
hello.txt         oldauto.mak    state2.cap       6report
galaxy.txt        green.jaz      plane.bmp        5report
dances.txt        blue.jaz       Dancer.bmp
bye.txt           file4.fp       Basket.bmp
born.txt          file3.fp       ven.99
[cgillay@RedHat9 cgillay]$
```

WHAT'S HAPPENING? The **-X** instructs **ls** to sort in file extension order. The **r** is the reverse option (descending order). As you saw, you may combine the two options. In this display, directories are intermixed with files as any file with no extension is listed last. Using Nautilus or using the command line allows you to accomplish many of the same tasks. You may choose which method works best for you.

STEP 15 Close the terminal window.

STEP 16   In the tree, click **floppy**. On the toolbar, click **Edit**. Click **Preferences**. Click the **Views** tab. In the **Arrange items** drop-down list box, choose **By Name**. Clear the **Sort in reverse** check box. Click **Close**.

STEP 17   Click **View**. Click **View as Icons**. Collapse the **floppy** directory. Collapse the **mnt** directory.

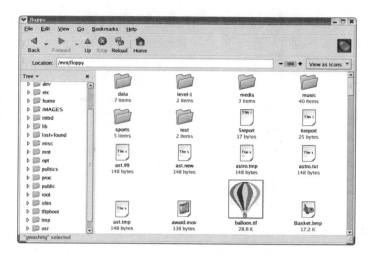

WHAT'S HAPPENING? You have returned the window to its default values.

STEP 18   Close the floppy window.

4.5 • Creating Directories

When you create a directory, you are setting up an area where files can be stored. You must have write permission in the parent directory in order to create a directory. You may create directories using the Nautilus file manager or from the command line using the **mkdir** command. When you create a new directory, it is empty. When you create a directory, you are preparing it to hold a logical group of files. The syntax of the command is:

```
mkdir [options] directoryname
```

Table 4.2, "mkdir Options," lists the major options for the **mkdir** command.

Option	Name	Description
-p	Parent	If you use the command **mkdir –p foo/foo1**, both **foo** and **foo1** will be created.
-v	Verbose	Displays the steps that are being taken for every directory that is created.

Table 4.2 • mkdir Options

In the following activity, you will create three directories on the BOOK disk. These directories will be for three classes: one in astronomy, one in physical education, and one in operating systems. You are creating a directory tree.

4.6 ● Activity: How to Create Directories

STEP 1   Mount the BOOK disk if it is not mounted. Open your home directory on the desktop by double-clicking the ***username*** **Home** icon. Click **Information**. Click **Tree**. Expand the **/mnt/floppy** directory. Click **floppy** to make it the working directory.

STEP 2   On the menu bar, click **File**. Click **New Folder**.

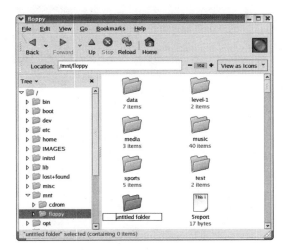

WHAT'S HAPPENING? ▷ You are using the GUI file manager—the Nautilus file manager. The **File** menu allowed you to create a new folder (directory). Since **/mnt/floppy** was selected, that was the location of where you wanted your new directory created. You are at the top of the hierarchical tree for the floppy disk, but in the hierarchical tree of the Linux file system your location is **/mnt/floppy**.

STEP 3   In the highlighted rectangle labeled **untitled folder**, key in **ASTRONOMY**. Delete the remaining characters by pressing the Delete key. Press Enter

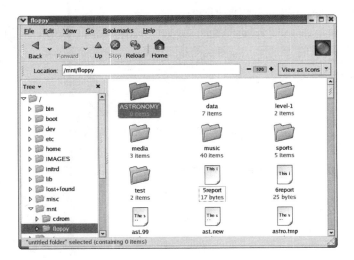

WHAT'S HAPPENING? ▷ Your directory is now visible and selected in the right pane of the file manager. Since you used uppercase letters, the directory **ASTRONOMY** appears first in the window. Uppercase comes before lowercase. *Note:* If you made an error in naming the directory, click the directory that you want to rename. Click **Edit**. Click **Rename**. You can then rename the directory. However, be sure that you have deleted all the old characters before keying in the new characters.

STEP 4   In the **floppy** window, in the right pane, right-click. Click **New Folder**.

STEP 5   In the highlighted rectangle labeled **untitled folder**, hold the $\boxed{\text{Shift}}$ key and press $\boxed{\rightarrow}$ until **untitled folder** is selected. Then key in the following: **physed** $\boxed{\text{Enter}}$

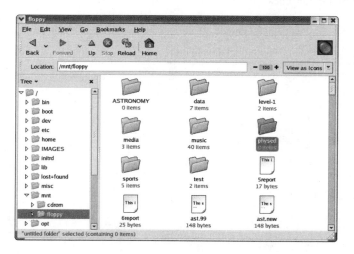

WHAT'S HAPPENING? By highlighting the characters **untitled folder** and then keying in your new folder name, you automatically deleted the characters you selected. This is known as "typing replaces selection." You created two directories, one called **ASTRONOMY** and the other called **physed** at the top of the hierarchy of the floppy disk, but remember **floppy** is under **mnt**, which is under / (the root directory). You used uppercase for **ASTRONOMY** and lowercase for **physed**. Linux retained the case that you choose. **ASTRONOMY** will hold all the files that involve classes in astronomy, and **physed** will hold files that involve classes in physical education. Although you have created the directories to hold the files, they are now "empty" file cabinets. Creating a directory from a terminal window is just as easy.

STEP 6   Open a terminal window. Key in the following: **mkdir /mnt/floppy/os** $\boxed{\text{Enter}}$

```
[cgillay@RedHat9   cgillay]$ mkdir /mnt/floppy/os
[cgillay@RedHat9   cgillay]$ _
```

WHAT'S HAPPENING? When you used **mkdir** in a terminal window, all you saw on the screen was the prompt. How do you know that you created a directory? You can see the directories you just created by using the **ls** command.

STEP 7   Key in the following: **ls /mnt/floppy** $\boxed{\text{Enter}}$

```
cgillay@RedHat9:~                                                    _ □ ✕
File   Edit   View   Terminal   Go   Help
bonjour.tmp     file4.fp        mer.tmp          Sandy and Patty.txt
born.txt        filename        middle.red       sports
born.typ        frank.fil       middle.up        state2.cap
bye.txt         frankreport     mikereport       state.cap
bye.typ         galaxy.tmp      music            states.usa
carolyn.fil     galaxy.txt      NEW AUTOS.txt    steven.fil
cases.fil       grammy.rec      newprson.fil     test
cherylreport    green.jaz       newreport        titan.txt
czgreport       hello.txt       new-suvs.xls     ven.99
Dancer.bmp      inv1file.y      oldauto.mak      ven.new
dances.txt      inv2file.y      Old Automobiles  ven.tmp
data            inv3file.y      orion.neb        venus.tmm
dog.tif         inv4file.z      os               venus.txt
dress.up        inv516file.z    personal.fil     wild1.xxx
earth.one       inv51file.z     person.fil       wild2.yyy
earth.thr       inv5file.z      physed           wild3.zzz
earth.two       inv6file.z      plane.bmp        wildone
exp01feb.dta    italy.tif       planets.txt      wildone.dos
exp01jan.dta    jup.99          projecta         wildthr.dos
exp01mar.dta    jupiter.tmp     projectb         wildtwo.dos
exp02feb.dta    jupiter.txt     projectc         world.tif
exp02jan.dta    jup.new         projectx         y.fil
exp02mar.dta    jup.tmp         projecty         zodiac.fil
[cgillay@RedHat9 cgillay]$
```

WHAT'S HAPPENING? You may not see all the files and directories, depending on the size of your terminal window. The **ls** command displayed the contents of the disk. You can identify the directories because they are in a different color. If colors are not available, you could key in **ls -F /mnt/floppy** where the **-F** marks each directory name by appending an **/** at the end of its name. What if you wish to see the names of the files inside the directory? Since **ASTRONOMY** is a directory, not just a file, you can display the contents of the directory with the **ls** command. Again, the syntax of the **ls** command is **ls [OPTION][FILE]**. You use the subdirectory name for FILE. Depending on your location, you use the absolute path or relative path.

STEP 8 Key in the following: **pwd; ls /mnt/floppy/ASTRONOMY** Enter

```
[cgillay@RedHat9   cgillay]$ pwd; ls /mnt/floppy/ASTRONOMY
/home/cgillay
[cgillay@RedHat9   cgillay]$ _
```

WHAT'S HAPPENING? Remember, you can key in more than one command on a line, provided you use a semicolon (;) to separate the commands. Your response to **pwd** (print working directory) told you what your default directory was (**/home/cgillay**). However, there appeared to be no response to the next command, **ls /mnt/floppy/ASTRONOMY**. There are no files yet in this directory.

STEP 9 Key in the following: **ls -a /mnt/floppy/ASTRONOMY** Enter

```
[cgillay@RedHat9   cgillay]$ ls -a /mnt/floppy/ASTRONOMY
.  ..
[cgillay@RedHat9   cgillay]$ _
```

WHAT'S HAPPENING? Even though you just created the directory **ASTRONOMY**, in the terminal window it seems to have two directories in it already, **.** (one period, also called "the dot") and **..** (two periods, also called "the double dot"). Every directory, except the root directory, always has two named directories. The directory named **.** is another name or abbreviation for the current directory, **ASTRONOMY**. The directory named **..** is an abbreviation for the parent directory of the current directory, in this case **/mnt/floppy**. If you went up the tree, **floppy**'s parent is **mnt** and **mnt**'s parent is the root. **.** (dot) and **..** (double dot) can be called *subdirectory markers* or *directory markers*.

STEP 10   Click the **floppy** button on the Panel.

STEP 11   In the right pane, double-click **ASTRONOMY**.

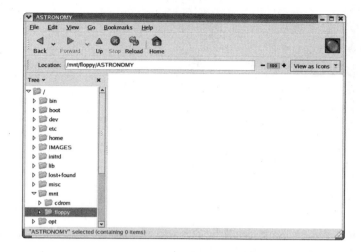

WHAT'S HAPPENING? Your default directory is now **ASTRONOMY**. In the Nautilus file manager, you do not see the dot or double dot notation. But you can move up the hierarchical tree by using the Up button on the toolbar.

STEP 12   Click the **Up** button on the toolbar.

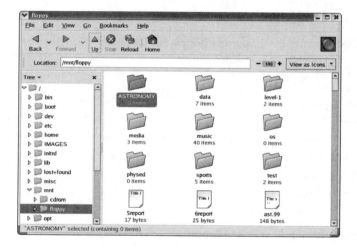

WHAT'S HAPPENING? You have moved to the parent of **ASTRONOMY**—/**mnt/floppy**, and you have also changed the default directory from /**mnt/floppy/ASTRONOMY** to /**mnt/floppy**.

4.7 ● The Current Directory

The operating system keeps track of the current directory, or default directory. When you boot the system, the default directory is usually /**home**/*username*. You can change the default directory, and doing so makes a specific subdirectory the default. In previous chapters you used the **cd** command.

The change directory command (**cd**) has two purposes. If you key in **cd** with no parameters, you are returned to your home directory. If you include a directory name after the **cd** command, the default directory will be changed to the directory you requested. The syntax is **cd [dir]**.

In the Nautilus file manager, changing your default directory is as simple as clicking the location in the tree that you want to be your default. You can tell that it is the default directory, since it is highlighted in the left pane, the hierarchical tree, and its name is displayed in the location text box.

4.8 ● Activity: Changing Directories

Note: The BOOK disk is mounted. The floppy Nautilus file manager window is open. The terminal window is open.

STEP 1   In the tree of the Nautilus file manager window, double-click **ASTRONOMY**.

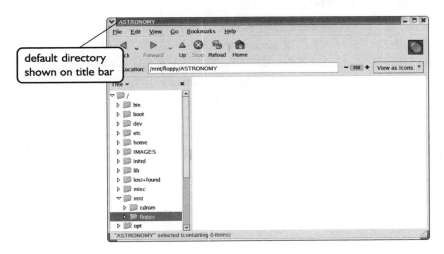

WHAT'S HAPPENING? In the Nautilus file manager, **ASTRONOMY** is now the current directory. You can tell not only because **ASTRONOMY** is highlighted in the tree, but if you look at the title bar of the window, you see **ASTRONOMY**, another indication that it is the default. And if you look in the Location bar, it tells you your location as well: **/mnt/floppy/ASTRONOMY**.

STEP 2   Activate the terminal window. Key in the following:
    cd /mnt/floppy/ASTRONOMY; pwd [Enter]

```
[cgillay@RedHat9  cgillay]$ cd /mnt/floppy/ASTRONOMY; pwd
/mnt/floppy/ASTRONOMY
[cgillay@RedHat9  ASTRONOMY]$ _
```

WHAT'S HAPPENING? You issued two commands; the first (**cd /mnt/floppy/ASTRONOMY**) changed your default directory. The second (**pwd**) showed you your current working directory. Any command you enter will apply to this directory, which is the default directory, so **cd** followed by the name of the directory changed the default to the directory **ASTRONOMY**. Since you changed the default directory, the prompt now says **[cgillay@RedHat9 ASTRONOMY]**. Remember that the prompt only displays the current directory, not the entire path name. However, **pwd** displays the entire path.

STEP 3   Key in the following: **ls -a** [Enter]

```
[cgillay@RedHat9  ASTRONOMY]$ ls -a
.  ..
[cgillay@RedHat9  ASTRONOMY]$ _
```

WHAT'S HAPPENING? You are displaying the contents of the current default directory, **/mnt/floppy/ASTRONOMY**. When you use a command, in this case **ls** with the **-a** option, it always assumes the default directory, unless you specify another drive and/or subdirectory.

STEP 4   Key in the following: **cd** **Enter**

```
[cgillay@RedHat9  ASTRONOMY]$ cd
[cgillay@RedHat9  cgillay]$ _
```

WHAT'S HAPPENING? By keying in **cd**, you moved to your home directory.

4.9 • Building a Structure

You are going to add directories to the tree structure so that the levels will look like those in Figure 4.9, "Directory with Subdirectories." To create these additional subdirectories, you may use the Nautilus file manager or use the **mkdir** command in the terminal window. A directory structure is built from the top so that before you can create **homework** in the **linux** directory, you must first create its parent, **linux**. However, **mkdir** allows you to create your structure in a single command rather than having to create each directory in linear fashion. Each will create the intervening directories if they do not exist. When using **mkdir**, you use the **-p** option (parents) to create the parent directories. In addition, in the command syntax **mkdir [options]** *directory*, since directory is not in brackets, you must include a directory name when you use the command.

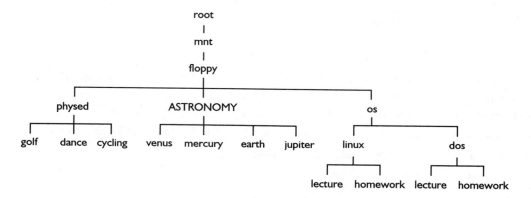

Figure 4.9 • Directory with Subdirectories

Remember the concept of the absolute path and the relative path. The absolute path is the complete and total hierarchical structure. You start at the top and work your way down through every directory without skipping a directory. The absolute path is *always* absolutely correct. The relative path is your location relative to where you are.

Thus, if you wanted to go from directory **golf** in the above figure to the directory **venus**, the absolute path with the **cd** command would be **cd /mnt/floppy/ASTRONOMY/venus**. However, if you wanted to use a relative path, you would need to go up two levels, through **physed**, up to **floppy**, and then down to **ASTRONOMY** in order to reach **venus**. Once you get to the proper directory, you can choose where you want to go. There are many places to go. It is like a subway—you must pass through all the stations along the path to get to your destination.

4.10 • Activity: Creating More Directories

Note: The BOOK disk is mounted. The Nautilus file manager window is open. The terminal window is open. You should be in Icon view.

STEP 1   Make the Nautilus file manager the active window. Click **ASTRONOMY** in the tree pane.

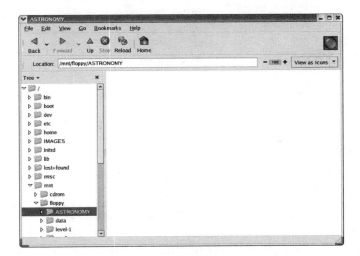

WHAT'S HAPPENING? > You confirmed that the default directory is **ASTRONOMY**. To create the directory under **ASTRONOMY**, you will use the right-click menu to create a directory called **earth**.

STEP 2   Right-click in the **ASTRONOMY** window. Click **New Folder**. In the text box, select **untitled folder** and then key in the following: **earth** [Enter]

STEP 3   Click **View**. Click **View as List.**

STEP 4   Right-click in the **ASTRONOMY** window. Click **New Folder**. Right-click **untitled folder**. Click **Properties**.

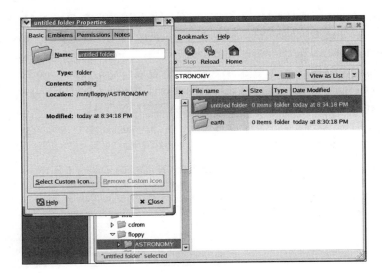

WHAT'S HAPPENING? > When you are in list view, you may open the properties for the untitled folder.

STEP 5   In the text box of Properties, key in **venus**. Click **Close**.

WHAT'S HAPPENING? Since **ASTRONOMY** was the default directory, both the **earth** and **venus** directories were created in **ASTRONOMY**. You were using the *relative path*.

STEP 6   Make the terminal window the active window. Key in the following:
         mkdir /mnt/floppy/ASTRONOMY/mercury Enter

STEP 7   Key in the following: **ls /mnt/floppy/ASTRONOMY** Enter

```
[cgillay@RedHat9   cgillay]$ mkdir  /mnt/floppy/ASTRONOMY/mercury
[cgillay@RedHat9   cgillay]$ ls  /mnt/floppy/ASTRONOMY
earth   mercury   venus
[cgillay@RedHat9   cgillay]$ _
```

WHAT'S HAPPENING? You created the directory **mercury** under **ASTRONOMY**. You used the *absolute path* to create the directory. You gave absolute instructions as to where to create the directory. You issued the **mkdir** command and then you keyed in the location. (Go to the root (/), then go to **mnt**, then go to **floppy**, then go to **ASTRONOMY**, and then create a directory called **mercury**.) The first / was the root directory. Every other slash was a delimiter to separate the entries from one another. **mercury** cannot exist until **ASTRONOMY** exists because it is hierarchy. In your display, you see the **mercury** directory as well as the other two directories you created. You are now going to create the directory called **jupiter**.

STEP 8   Key in the following: **cd /mnt/floppy/ASTRONOMY; pwd; ls** Enter

```
[cgillay@RedHat9   cgillay]$ cd /mnt/floppy/ASTRONOMY; pwd; ls
/mnt/floppy/ASTRONOMY
earth     mercury     venus
[cgillay@RedHat9   ASTRONOMY]$ _
```

WHAT'S HAPPENING? You have changed the default directory to **ASTRONOMY**. It is under the **floppy** directory, which is under the **mnt** directory, which is under the root directory. You are going to create one more directory, **jupiter**, under **ASTRONOMY** using a relative path. Remember, you are in **ASTRONOMY**, so all you need to do is use a relative path name—relative to where you are.

STEP 9 Key in the following: **mkdir jupiter; ls** Enter

```
[cgillay@RedHat9  ASTRONOMY]$  mkdir jupiter; ls
earth    jupiter    mercury    venus
[cgillay@RedHat9  ASTRONOMY]$ _
```

WHAT'S **HAPPENING?** You needed only to key in **jupiter**. The path was assumed from the position relative to where you were, **/mnt/floppy/ASTRONOMY**. In other words, the current directory as displayed, **ASTRONOMY**, was where the new directory **jupiter** was added. Because you gave no other path in your command, the default drive and directory were assumed.

STEP 10 Key in the following: **mkdir /mexico; mkdir /floppy/mexico** Enter

```
[cgillay@RedHat9  ASTRONOMY]$  mkdir /mexico; mkdir /floppy/mexico
mkdir: cannot create directory '/mexico': Permission denied
mkdir: cannot create directory 'floppy/mexico': No such file or directory
[cgillay@RedHat9  ASTRONOMY]$
```

WHAT'S **HAPPENING?** You could not create the directory **mexico** for two different reasons. The first command, **mkdir /mexico**, told the operating system to go to the root (the first slash). You do not have permission to create files at the root (**Permission denied**). The second command did not work because there is no such directory as **/floppy**. Since there is no such directory, you cannot create another directory (**mexico**) under a nonexistent directory. Remember, the absolute path would be **/mnt/floppy**, not just **/floppy**.

STEP 11 Key in the following: **mkdir ../mexico; ls** Enter

```
[cgillay@RedHat9  ASTRONOMY]$  mkdir ../mexico; ls
earth    jupiter    mercury    venus
[cgillay@RedHat9  ASTRONOMY]$ _
```

WHAT'S **HAPPENING?** You created the subdirectory **mexico**, but where is it? Because you used the **../** preceding **mexico**, that told the operating system to move up one level from **ASTRONOMY** and create **mexico** under **floppy**. The slash in the command was simply a delimiter separating **mexico** from the **...**

STEP 12 Key in the following: **ls /mnt/floppy** Enter

WHAT'S HAPPENING? By keying in **ls /mnt/floppy**, you followed the absolute path to the **floppy** directory. As you can see, looking at the screen display, **mexico** is under the **floppy** directory, which is under the **mnt** directory which is under the root directory. Linux simply followed your instructions. Remember, there are no files in the newly created directories. You have made "rooms" for "furniture." As of now, they are empty. You can create directories wherever you wish, as long as the proper path is included. You *must* pay attention to where you are and whether you are keying in an *absolute* path or a *relative* path. If you key in an absolute path, you will always be correct. If you key in a relative path, you must remember that you will create the directory relative to where you are in the hierarchy.

STEP 13   Key in the following: **mkdir /mnt/floppy/physed/tennis** [Enter]

```
[cgillay@RedHat9   ASTRONOMY]$   mkdir /mnt/floppy/physed/tennis
[cgillay@RedHat9   ASTRONOMY]$ _
```

WHAT'S HAPPENING? Since the default ("working" or "current" directory) at this time is **AS-TRONOMY**, you first had to tell the operating system to follow the absolute path (**/mnt/floppy/physed**) to create the directory **tennis** in **physed**. Remember, the relative path only looks down or under **ASTRONOMY**. The first slash indicates the root. Any other slashes in the line are delimiters. This is *always* true. The **mkdir** command does not change the default directory. You can verify that you created the subdirectory **tennis** under the directory **physed** by using the **ls** command with the path name.

STEP 14   Key in the following: **ls /mnt/floppy/physed** [Enter]

```
[cgillay@RedHat9   ASTRONOMY]$   ls /mnt/floppy/physed
tennis
[cgillay@RedHat9   ASTRONOMY]$ _
```

WHAT'S HAPPENING? The directory **physed** is displayed with the **tennis** directory listed. It was important to key in the absolute path in order to tell **ls** to go up to the root (/) and then down to the directory **mnt/floppy/physed**. If you had not included the slash (/) and had keyed in **ls physed** or **ls mnt/floppy/physed**, you would have seen the message *No such file or directory* because **ls** would have looked below **ASTRONOMY** only. **physed** is under the **/mnt/floppy** directory, not under the directory **ASTRONOMY**.

STEP 15   Key in the following: **cd /mnt/floppy** [Enter]

```
[cgillay@RedHat9   ASTRONOMY]$   $ cd /mnt/floppy
[cgillay@RedHat9   floppy]$
```

WHAT'S HAPPENING? You have returned to the parent of **ASTRONOMY**, **floppy**. Although you have been building your structure from the top down, Linux allows you to create the intervening parent directories if they do not exist. You may do so from the command line. Referring back to Figure 4.9, you created the directory **os** under **floppy**. You want to create a **lecture** and **home-work** directory under both a **linux** and a **dos** directory. At this point, neither the **linux** nor **dos** directory exists.

STEP 16   Key in the following: **mkdir -p os/linux/lecture; mkdir os/linux/homework** [Enter]

```
[cgillay@RedHat9  floppy]$ mkdir -p os/linux/lecture; mkdir os/linux/homework
[cgillay@RedHat9  floppy]$
```

WHAT'S HAPPENING? By using the **-p** (the "create parent" option in the first command) you created **linux**, the intervening parent, the same time that you created **lecture**. Since the parent directory, **linux**, was already created, the second command did not need the **-p** option. You used a relative path. The absolute path would have been:

```
/mnt/floppy/os/linux/lecture
```

STEP 17   Key in the following: **ls os os/linux** Enter

```
[cgillay@RedHat9  floppy]$ ls os os/linux
os:
linux

os/linux
homework    lecture
[cgillay@RedHat9  floppy]$ _
```

WHAT'S HAPPENING? As you can see, you did indeed create the intervening parent, **linux**. Now you want to do the same for the **dos** directory.

STEP 18   Key in the following: **cd** Enter

STEP 19   Key in the following: **mkdir -p /mnt/floppy/os/dos/lecture** Enter

STEP 20   Key in the following: **mkdir /mnt/floppy/os/dos/homework** Enter

STEP 21   Make the Nautilus file manager window active. In the ASTRONOMY window, click **View**. Click **View as Icons**.

STEP 22   In the tree pane, expand **os**. Expand **dos**. Expand **linux**. Click **os** in the tree to make it the default directory.

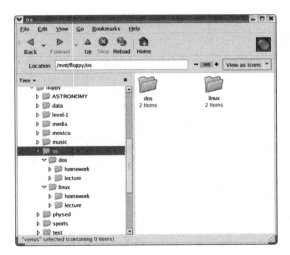

WHAT'S HAPPENING? First you returned to your home directory. Then, as you can see, you did indeed create the intervening parent directory, **dos**. But in Steps 19 and 20, you used an absolute path. You will also note that it is easier to see the hierarchical structure in the Nautilus file manager than at the command line.

4.11 • The dot (.) and double-dot (..)—Dot Addressing

The single **.** (one period or one dot) in a directory is the specific name of the current directory, which is a way to refer to the current subdirectory. The **..** (two periods or two dots) is the specific name of parent directory of the current directory. There are no spaces between the dots. The parent directory is the one immediately above the current directory. You can use the **..** as a shorthand version of the parent directory name to move up the directory tree structure. You can move up the hierarchy because a child always has only one parent. However, you cannot use a shorthand symbol to move down the hierarchy because a parent directory can have many child directories. This method of using dots, also called "dot" and "dot dot," to refer to directories is called sometimes called *dot addressing*.

4.12 • Activity: Using the Double-dot

Note: The BOOK disk is mounted. The terminal window is open with your home directory as the default directory. Your home directory window is open using the **Tree** with **/mnt/floppy/OS** selected. You are in icon view.

STEP 1   In the Nautilus file manager window, click the Up button until **floppy** is selected. Click **floppy** to select it in the tree.

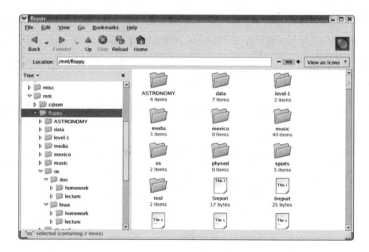

WHAT'S HAPPENING? The Nautilus file manager does not show the dot dot for moving up the directory tree. But clicking the up arrow is the equivalent. You did move to the parent of **os**, which is **floppy.**

STEP 2   Make the terminal window active. Key in the following:
   cd /mnt/floppy; mkdir physed/golf Enter

```
[cgillay@RedHat9   cgillay]$   cd /mnt/floppy; mkdir physed/golf
[cgillay@RedHat9   floppy]$
```

WHAT'S HAPPENING? You created a directory called **golf** under the directory called **physed** under the directory called **floppy**, which is under the directory **mnt** under the root (/). Since your working directory was **floppy**, you used a relative path. You could have correctly keyed in

mkdir /mnt/floppy/physed/golf and used the absolute path. However, if you move to the **physed** directory and make it the default, you do not need to include the path name of **physed**.

STEP 3 Key in the following: **cd physed** Enter

```
[cgillay@RedHat9   physed]$   cd physed
[cgillay@RedHat9   physed]$
```

WHAT'S **HAPPENING?** **physed** is now the default or working directory. Any activity that occurs will automatically default to this directory, unless otherwise specified. You may use a relative path name.

STEP 4 Key in the following: **mkdir dance; ls** Enter

```
[cgillay@RedHat9   physed]$   mkdir dance; ls
dance   golf   tennis
[cgillay@RedHat9   physed]$
```

WHAT'S **HAPPENING?** You used the relative path name. You did not have to key in **/mnt/floppy/physed**, which you would have needed to do if you wanted to use an absolute path name. If **floppy** were your working directory, you would have needed to key in **physed/dance**. Since **physed** was the default directory, you only needed to use the directory name of **dance**. **dance** is now under the directory called **physed**.

STEP 5 Key in the following: **cd dance** Enter

```
[cgillay@RedHat9   physed]$   cd dance
[cgillay@RedHat9   dance]$
```

WHAT'S **HAPPENING?** You used the relative path to move to the subdirectory **dance** under **physed**. You are going to create one more directory under **physed** called **cycling**, but you are going to use the dot-addressing technique.

STEP 6 Key in the following: **mkdir ../cycling; ls ; ls ..** Enter

```
[cgillay@RedHat9   dance]$   mkdir ../cycling; ls; ls ..
cycling   dance   golf   tennis
[cgillay@RedHat9   dance]$
```

WHAT'S **HAPPENING?** When you used the **mkdir** command, you first used **..** (the directory marker) to go to the parent of **dance**, which is **physed**. You then used the delimiter (/) to tell the operating system that you wanted to go down from **physed** and create **cycling**. When you keyed in the **ls** command, you were looking at the default directory **dance**. **cycling** does not appear there because you did not put it in **dance**. When you keyed the **ls** command followed by **..** you looked at the parent directory of **dance**, which was **physed**. **cycling**, indeed, appeared there.

STEP 7 Key in the following: **cd ../..** Enter

```
[cgillay@RedHat9   dance]$   cd ../..
[cgillay@RedHat9   floppy]$
```

WHAT'S HAPPENING? You used the double dot to move to the parent of **dance** (**physed**). The / was a delimiter you used to separate the next **..** which then moved to the parent of **physed**, which is **floppy**.

4.13 • Changing the Names of Directories

Sometimes you will want to change the name of a directory. You may find a name you like better or correct a spelling error. You may rename a directory in either the Nautilus file manager or at the command line. The command to change the name of a directory is **mv**. The syntax is as follows:

```
mv [OPTION]  SOURCE  DEST
```

Since neither **SOURCE** nor **DEST** are bracketed, you must use these arguments. The **SOURCE** is the "old" name and the "**DEST**" is the new name. Table 4.3, "mv Options," lists the major options for the **mv** command.

Option	Name	Description
-i	Interactive	Prompts you before overwriting a file.
-v	Verbose	Displays the steps that are being taken.

Table 4.3 • mv Options

4.14 • Activity: Renaming Directories

Note: The BOOK disk is mounted. The terminal window is open with **/mnt/floppy** as the default directory. Your home directory window is open using the **Tree** with **/mnt/floppy** selected. You are in icon view.

STEP 1   Make the Nautilus file manager window active. Collapse dos. Collapse linux. Collapse os. Click **floppy** in the left pane to make it the default directory. In the right pane, right-click **physed**. Click **Properties**.

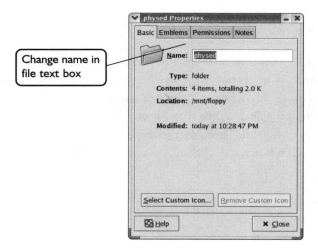

WHAT'S HAPPENING? You opened the properties of **physed**. One of the properties is the name of the file. Remember, a directory is also a file—a special kind of file, but a file nonetheless.

STEP 2   The name **physed** should be highlighted. Key in **gym**. Click **Close**.

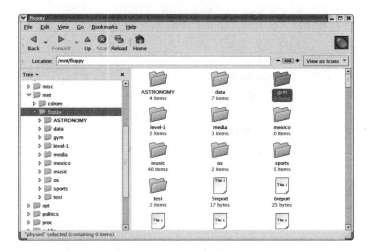

WHAT'S HAPPENING? › When a phrase is highlighted, you do not need to delete it. You simply key in your new information and the old information is deleted. Remember, this feature is called *typing replaces selection*. Indeed, the file folder now states **gym** instead of **physed**.

STEP 3   Right-click **gym**.

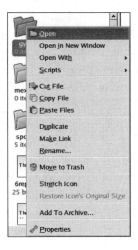

WHAT'S HAPPENING? › You may also rename a file with the right-click menu.

STEP 4   Click **Rename**.

WHAT'S HAPPENING? › You would key in your new name inside the highlighted box.

STEP 5   Click anywhere in the window to deselect **gym**. Make the terminal window active.

STEP 6   Key in the following: **cd /mnt/floppy** Enter

STEP 7   Key in the following: **mv gym/cycling gym/biking; ls gym** Enter

```
[cgillay@RedHat9  floppy]$    cd /mnt/floppy
[cgillay@RedHat9  floppy]$    mv gym/cycling gym/biking; ls
biking  dance  golf  tennis
[cgillay@RedHat9  floppy]$
```

WHAT'S **HAPPENING?** You first ensured you were in the correct directory (**cd /mnt/floppy**). You could have verified that by looking at the prompt. You then used the **mv** command to change the name of the **cycling** directory under **gym** to **biking**. As long as you give the correct path name, either absolute or relative, you can be anywhere and rename a directory. You then used **ls** to confirm the name change. Indeed, **cycling** is no longer there, but **biking** is.

4.15 • Removing Directories

In the same way a directory can be cluttered with files, it be cluttered with directories. Removing directories can be accomplished with either the Nautilus file manager or with the command line command **rmdir**. At the command line, if a directory has files in it, you cannot remove it until it is empty of files or child directories. This two-step process prevents you from accidentally wiping out not only a directory but also the files inside. Thus, if a directory has files in it, you must delete (**rm**) the file(s) first, then remove (**rmdir**) the directory. At the command line, you cannot delete a directory that contains hidden or system files with the **rmdir** command. However, if you are using the Nautilus file manager, you can delete a directory that has other directories and has hidden files. At the command line or in the Nautilus file manager, you cannot remove the default directory—the current directory. In order to remove a directory, you must be in another directory. At the command line, since you created the directories from the top down, to remove them, you must remove them from the bottom up. This means using **rmdir** one directory at a time, unless you use the **–p** option. You cannot use wildcards with **rmdir**. The command syntax is:

```
rmdir [options] directories
```

If you do not include the path designator, the default path will be used. The remove directory command will not remove the directory you are currently in (the default directory), nor will it ever remove the root directory. Table 4.4, "rmdir Options," lists the major options for the **rmdir** command.

Option	Name	Description
-p	Parent	If you use the command **rmdir –p foo/fool**, both **foo** and **fool** will be removed.
-v	Verbose	Displays the steps that are being taken for every directory that is removed.

Table 4.4 • rmdir Options

4.16 • Activity: Removing Directories

Note: The BOOK disk is mounted. The terminal window is open with **/mnt/floppy** as the default directory. Your Nautilus file manager window is open using the **Tree**. In the tree, **/mnt/floppy** is selected.

STEP 1   Make your home directory floppy window active. Right-click **mexico** in the right pane. Click **Move to Trash.**

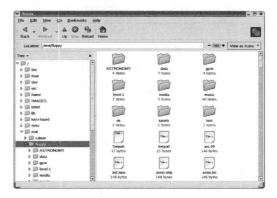

WHAT'S HAPPENING? Your folder was moved to Trash and is no longer in the **floppy** window. The directory **mexico** is deleted—almost.

STEP 2   Double-click the **Trash** icon on the desktop.

WHAT'S HAPPENING? The "trash" is a folder in your home directory that retains the files and folders you delete until you empty the trash—the **Empty Trash** button. If you wanted to retrieve this folder, you could drag and drop it back to your home directory, your desktop, or wherever you wanted to place it.

STEP 3   Close the Trash window.

STEP 4   Click **File** in the floppy window.

WHAT'S HAPPENING? In order to actually delete what you moved to the trash, you must empty the trash. Until you delete the trash, you can recover what files and folders are in the trash. This is another way to empty the trash. In this case, you do want to delete the folder **mexico**, so you will choose **Empty Trash**.

STEP 5   Click **Empty Trash**.

WHAT'S HAPPENING? You get one more opportunity not to remove what is in the trash.

STEP 6   Click **Empty**.

WHAT'S HAPPENING? You saw a quick message that what was in the trash was being deleted.

STEP 7   Make the terminal window active.

STEP 8   Key in the following: **cd ASTRONOMY/mercury** Enter

STEP 9   Key in the following: **rmdir mercury** Enter

```
[cgillay@RedHat9   floppy]$   cd ASTRONOMY/mercury
[cgillay@RedHat9   mercury]$   rmdir mercury
rmdir: 'mercury' No such file or directory
[cgillay@RedHat9   mercury]$
```

WHAT'S HAPPENING? **rmdir** did not remove the directory **mercury**. You got an error message. There is a directory called **mercury** and it is empty of files or other directories. The problem is that you cannot remove a directory you are in, nor will **rmdir** ever remove the default directory.

STEP 10   Key in the following: **cd ..; ls; rmdir mercury; ls** Enter

```
[cgillay@RedHat9   mercury]$   cd ..; ls; rmdir mercury; ls
earth   jupiter   mercury venus
earth   jupiter   venus
[cgillay@RedHat9   ASTRONOMY]$
```

WHAT'S HAPPENING? You moved to the parent of **mercury**, which is **ASTRONOMY**. You used the **ls** command to see that **mercury** was there. You then used the **rmdir** command and the **ls** command again. The directory entry **mercury** is not displayed. You did, indeed, remove it. Remember, you create directories in a hierarchical fashion, top-down, and you must remove directories from the bottom up. So, if **mercury** had a subdirectory beneath it, such as **ASTRONOMY\mercury\surface**, you would have needed to remove the **surface** directory before you could remove the **mercury** directory.

STEP 11   Key in the following: **cd ..** Enter

```
[cgillay@RedHat9   ASTRONOMY]$   cd ..
[cgillay@RedHat9   floppy]$
```

WHAT'S HAPPENING? You have moved to the parent of **ASTRONOMY**, floppy.

4.17 • Removing Directories Recursively— Using rm and rmdir

As you can see, removing directories one at a time can be a very laborious process when you have a complex directory structure. You would like to be able to delete directories recursively. Remember, recursive (to call oneself) refers to the parent and all its child directories. Thus, deleting recursively would delete the parent directory and all the directories and files in the directories beneath the parent. You may use the Nautilus file manager to delete a directory structure.

You may also use the command **rmdir -p** *directories* as mentioned above. The **-p** option will delete any intervening parent directories. However, the directory must be empty. If the directory has files in it or other directories, you will not be able to use **rmdir**. However, you have another command that you may use. If the directory is not empty, you may use the **rm** command to remove files. The syntax for the **rm** (remove files) command is as follows:

```
rm [options] files
```

It will delete one or more files. If you use the **-r** (recursive) option, and if *file* is the name of a directory, it will remove the entire directory structure and all its contents including directories. Beware when you **rm -r.** Although very useful, it can also be *very* dangerous. It is a command that deletes the directory structure and all the files in the directories from the top down. It is fast, but it is also fatal! Use it cautiously. The same is true of the **–f** option, which will delete even read-only files without prompting. Table 4.5, "rm Options," lists the major options for **rm.**

Option	Name	Description
-f	Force	Never prompts you and "force" the deletion.
-i	Interactive	Prompts you before deleting files or directories.
-r -R	Recursive	Removes the directory tree.
-v	Verbose	Displays steps it is taking.

Table 4.5 • rm Options

4.18 • Activity: Removing Directories

Note: The BOOK disk is mounted. The terminal window is open with **/mnt/floppy** as the default directory. Your home directory window is open, using Tree with **/mnt/floppy** selected.

STEP 1 Make your user window (**floppy**) active. Expand **gym** in the tree. Click **floppy** in the tree to confirm it as the default directory.

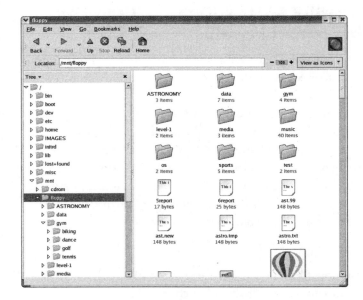

WHAT'S **HAPPENING?** You can see that **gym** has four directories beneath it: **biking**, **dance**, **golf**, and **tennis**. There are no files in those directories.

STEP 2   In the right pane, right-click **gym**. Click **Move to Trash**.

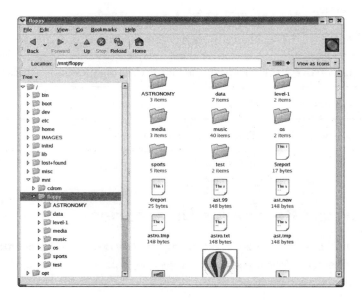

WHAT'S **HAPPENING?** Even though the directory called **gym** was not empty, because it had directories in it, it was removed from the floppy window. Remember, to actually delete this structure, you need to empty the trash.

STEP 3   Click **File**. Click **Empty Trash**. Click **Empty**.

WHAT'S HAPPENING? Again, you saw a confirmation message box. The directory **gym** and its subdirectories have been deleted. They were deleted recursively.

STEP 4   Make the terminal window active. Key in the following:
rmdir -p ASTRONOMY/venus Enter

```
[cgillay@RedHat9  floppy]$  rmdir -p ASTRONOMY/venus
rmdir: `ASTRONOMY': Directory not empty
[cgillay@RedHat9  floppy]$
```

WHAT'S HAPPENING? **ASTRONOMY** has two other directories in it: **earth** and **jupiter**. But what happened to **venus**?

STEP 5   Key in the following: **ls ASTRONOMY** Enter

```
[cgillay@RedHat9  floppy]$  ls ASTRONOMY
earth   jupiter
[cgillay@RedHat9  floppy]$
```

WHAT'S HAPPENING? The **rmdir** command did remove the directory **venus**. However, the **–p** option was not invoked since **ASTRONOMY** was not empty.

STEP 6   Key in the following: **rmdir -v ASTRONOMY/jupiter; ls ASTRONOMY** Enter

```
[cgillay@RedHat9  floppy]$  rmdir -v ASTRONOMY/jupiter;ls ASTRONOMY
rmdir: removing directory, ASTRONOMY/jupiter
earth
[cgillay@RedHat9  floppy]$
```

WHAT'S HAPPENING? Using the **–v** option allows you to see what is occurring. You removed the **jupiter** subdirectory. Now you can use the **–p** option since there is only one subdirectory left in **ASTRONOMY - earth**.

STEP 7   Key in the following: **rmdir -p ASTRONOMY/earth; ls ASTRONOMY** Enter

```
[cgillay@RedHat9  floppy]$ rmdir -p ASTRONOMY/earth; ls ASTRONOMY
ls: ASTRONOMY: No such file or directory.
[cgillay@RedHat9  floppy]$
```

WHAT'S HAPPENING? Since there was only one directory, you successfully used the **-p** option to remove both **earth** and its parent, **ASTRONOMY**. Now you are going to use the **rm** command with the **dos** directory under the **os** directory. Remember, **dos** has two directories, **homework** and **lecture**.

STEP 8   Key in the following: **ls os/dos; rm -r -f os/dos** Enter

```
[cgillay@RedHat9  floppy]$ ls os/dos; rm -r -f os/dos
homework   lecture
[cgillay@RedHat9  floppy]$
```

WHAT'S HAPPENING? You have confirmed the directory structure for **os/dos**. You then forced the removal of the **dos** directory and its subdirectories, **homework** and **lecture**. The **-f** option showed those directories as being force deleted.

STEP 9   Key in the following: **ls os; ls os/linux** Enter

```
[cgillay@RedHat9  floppy]$  ls os; ls os/linux
linux
homework    lecture
[cgillay@RedHat9  ·floppy]$ _
```

WHAT'S HAPPENING? Indeed, the **dos** directory is gone. Now you are going to delete the entire **os** directory.

STEP 10 Key in the following: **rm -r os; ls os** Enter

```
[cgillay@RedHat9  floppy]$  rm -r os; ls os
ls: os: No such file or directory.
[cgillay@RedHat9  floppy]$
```

WHAT'S HAPPENING? You removed **os** and all its subdirectories with one command. As you can see, **rm -r** is very useful, very fast, and very dangerous.

4.19 • Variables

Since Linux, and any operating system, always uses default values unless you specify otherwise, knowing the current default directory is very important. Recognizing the default directory is easy because the operating system, in a terminal window, displays your current location in the prompt. The Bash shell can give you this information by the use of environmental variables.

The Bash shell is a programming language in its own right. In programming, a *variable* is a value that can change depending on conditions or on information passed to the program. A symbol or name is used to represent a value. The functionality of the shell, as well as many other Linux commands, is controlled by what are called shell variables. *Shell variables* are those that you create at the command line or in a shell script. A *shell script* is a text file that contains a sequence of commands. Shell variables are widely used because they provide an easy way of transferring values from one command to another. Programs can get the value of a shell variable and use it to modify their operation, much as you can use a value in a command line argument.

The shell has the ability to store data. The stored data takes the form of two strings—one is the name of the variable and the other is the value of the variable. An *environmental variable* is a name assigned to a string (value) of data. You can set your own environmental variables. However, there are some common shell environmental variables that are set when starting the shell by either logging in or opening an xterm window. These environmental variables are set by the default configuration file used when you log in. There are commonly used environmental variables that usually have short, easy-to-remember names. These environmental variables store information such as the location of your home directory (**HOME**), the search path the shell uses to look for commands (**PATH**), and what is displayed in your prompt (**PS1**). By convention, environmental variables are all uppercase. In addition, the $ is used to display the contents of a variable rather than the literal string that is the variable's name.

4.20 • The PROMPT Variable

The command prompt is configured automatically when you log in. How the prompt looks depends on what is set in the configuration files. The environmental variables **PS1** and **PS2** contain the text of the prompt displayed in your terminal window. **PS1** is the primary prompt. When you see it displayed, it is asking you to key in a command. **PS2** is the secondary prompt and shows up on continuation lines of commands that are longer than one line. The environmental variable has special characters that will return a specified value. These special characters are preceded by a \ and followed by a character indicating what is to be displayed. You may also use literal text in a prompt. Table 4.6, "Formatting Characters for Prompt," shows the special characters for formatting your prompt.

Character	Display
\!	number of current command in command history
\#	number of the command in the current session
\d	date
\h	hostname
\n	new line
\s	shell name
\t	time
\u	user name
\w	entire path of working directory
\W	only working directory

Table 4.6 • Formatting Characters for Prompt

The default Red Hat prompt is [\u@\h \W]\$. The \$ character will print a # if the user is logged as root user or a $ if the user is logged on as an ordinary user. Thus, a default Red Hat default prompt for an ordinary user named **cgillay** would be **[cgillay@localhost cgillay]$** . In the next activity, you are going to look at some environmental variables and change the prompt at the command line.

4.21 • Activity: Changing the Prompt

Note: The BOOK disk is mounted. Your home directory window is open using **Tree**. The terminal window is open and **/mnt/floppy** is the default directory.

STEP 1   Make the terminal window active. Key in the following: **printenv** Enter

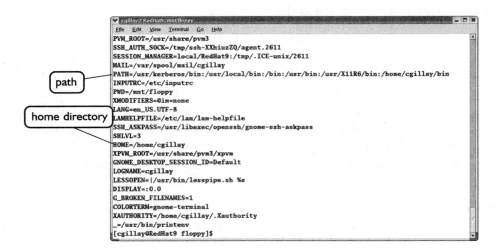

WHAT'S HAPPENING? The **printenv** command prints all or part of what is in the environment. Your display will be different. However, in this display, you see some common environmental variables, both the name and the value associated with it. In this example, two important variables—**PATH** and **HOME**—have values assigned to them. **PATH** is what directories will be searched for a command when a command is keyed in. **HOME** is what is the home directory—in this case, the value is **/home/cgillay**.

STEP 2   Maximize your terminal window. Key in the following: **set** Enter

WHAT'S HAPPENING? The **set** command with no arguments or options will print all the values of all variables known to the shell. **set** has many options which can be enabled or disabled. Options can also be set when the shell is invoked. However, at this point, you are simply looking at the environmental variables on your computer. You should be able to see the value for the environmental variable under **PS1**. Table 4.6, "Formatting Characters for Prompt," shows you what is displayed with those values. You may look at the value of any environmental variable by using **echo,** the dollar sign (to indicate that you wish to see the value contained in that variable), and then the variable name.

STEP 3   Restore the terminal window. Key in the following: **echo $PS1; echo $HOME**
[Enter]

```
[cgillay@RedHat9   floppy]$   echo $PS1
[\u@\h \W]\$
/home/cgillay
[cgillay@RedHat9   floppy]$
```

WHAT'S HAPPENING? Here you see the contents of the **PS1** variable. Table 4.6, "Formatting Characters for Prompt," shows you what is displayed using these values. You also saw the value for your home directory. You may change the way your prompt looks.

STEP 4   Key in the following: **PS1="hello \$"; cd data; ls** [Enter]

```
[cgillay@RedHat9   floppy]$   PS1="hello \$" cd data; ls
bonjour.txt good.txt highest.txt mother.let tea.tax thank.you
thin.ext
hello $
```

WHAT'S HAPPENING? You changed the prompt so that it simply had text in it, **hello** followed by the ordinary user prompt, **$**. You then changed directories to the **data** directory (**/mnt/floppy/data**) and listed the contents of **data**. However, your prompt now gives you no information about where you are in the hierarchy. You can see that having the default directory displayed on the screen is very important. You might also prefer to have the entire path in the prompt, rather than just the current working directory.

STEP 5   Key in the following: **PS1="[\u@\h \w]\$ "** [Enter]

```
hello $ PS1="[\u@\h \w]\$ "
[cgillay@RedHat9   /mnt/floppy/data]$
```

WHAT'S HAPPENING? By using the **\w** instead of the **\W**, you displayed the entire path to the directory you are in.

STEP 6   Key in the following: **cd** [Enter]

```
[cgillay@RedHat9   /mnt/floppy/data]$ cd
[cgillay@RedHat9   ~]$
```

WHAT'S HAPPENING? When you see the tilde (the ~ symbol) alone, it is shorthand for the home directory of the currently logged in user. You can use the ~ as a shorthand for your home directory no matter where you are in the system.

STEP 7   Key in the following: **cd /mnt/floppy/data; ls ~** [Enter]

```
[cgillay@RedHat9   ~]$   cd /mnt/floppy/data; ls ~
evolution
[cgillay@RedHat9   /mnt/floppy/data]$
```

WHAT'S HAPPENING? Even though your default directory is **/mnt/floppy/data**, the shorthand command of **ls ~** displayed the contents of your home directory. Your display may be different, especially if you have no files or directories in your home directory.

STEP 8   Key in the following: **cd ; PS1="[\u@\h \W]\$ "** [Enter]

```
[cgillay@RedHat9   /mnt/floppy/data]$ cd ; PS1="[\u@\h \W]\$ "
[cgillay@RedHat9   cgillay]$
```

WHAT'S **HAPPENING?** You have returned to your home directory and returned the prompt to your default value. Even if you change your prompt at the command line, it will not retain those settings the next time you log in. If you wanted a permanent change in the way your prompt is displayed, you would need to make changes in the configuration files. You must be the root user to make those changes. Typical Red Hat Linux Bash configuration files are listed in Table 4.7, "Red Hat Linux/Bash Configuration Files." Remember that the ~ stands for the user's home directory.

Location and File Name	Processing order	Contents
/etc/profile	First	System-wide environment variables and start-up programs.
/etc/bashrc	Second	System-wide functions and aliases.
~/.bash_profile	If exists, third	User-specific environmental variables and start-up programs.
~/.bashrc	If exists, fourth	User-specific functions and aliases; is invoked by the .bash_profile.

Table 4.7 • Red Hat Linux/Bash Configuration Files

4.22 • Understanding the PATH Variable

Every command you key in is an executable file. Executable files are stored in different directories. Some directories where programs are stored are common to nearly all Linux/Unix systems, such as **/bin** or **/usr/bin**. Other directories where executables are specific to your own computer or can vary depending on the distribution of Linux you are using. If you wish to execute a command, and you have execute permission and you know the location of the command, you can always use the absolute path. For instance, if you wanted to use **ls**, you could key in **/bin/ls**. The **bin** directory is where the **ls** command is located. You do not need to key in **/bin/ls**, only **ls** because the operating system searches the set path for executable commands. When you log in, the shell assigns a value to the **PATH** variable, which is set in the **/etc/profile** directory. Usually your home directory is searched, then specific directories such as **/bin** and **/usr/bin**, which usually hold the most common commands used. The **PATH** variable specifies the directories to be searched as well as the order in which they will be searched for any command that you key in. Each directory in the **PATH** variable must be separated by colons.

The process of executing a program is simple and always the same. You key in the file name of the program, and in the specified search path the operating system looks for what you keyed in. It stops when it finds the first occurrence of the program name you keyed in. If your **PATH** variable was set to **/usr/bin:/home/cgillay** and you had two programs called **ls**—one located in each directory—the search path would dictate that the **ls** program located in **/usr/bin** would be executed, not the one located in **/home/gillay**.

4.23 • Activity: Using the PATH Variable

Note: The BOOK disk is mounted. The terminal window is open with **/mnt/floppy** as the default directory. Your home directory window is open using Tree with your home directory selected.

STEP 1   Key in the following: **cd ; echo $PATH** [Enter]

```
[cgillay@RedHat9  cgillay]$ cd; echo $PATH
/home/kerberos/bin:/usr/local/bin:/bin:/usr/bin:/usr/X11R6/bin:
/home/cgillay/bin
[cgillay@RedHat9  cgillay]$
```

WHAT'S HAPPENING? You confirmed that you were in your home directory by keying in **cd**. You then displayed the value for **PATH** on your system. The directories listed are the ones that will be searched, in order from left to right, for each command you key in. The delimiter used to separate one directory name from another is the colon (:). Your display will be different depending on what your configuration file sets as the default value for **PATH**. If you wanted to add a directory to your search path each time you logged in, the configuration file would have to be changed. However, if during a work session you want to add a directory you need to search, you can do so. This addition to your search path will last only as long as you are in a work session. For instance, certain commands are kept in the **/sbin** directory. If you were using many commands (and you had execute permission for those commands), you could add it temporarily to your **PATH** variable.

STEP 2   Key in the following: **PATH=$PATH:/sbin** [Enter]

```
[cgillay@RedHat9  cgillay]$  PATH=$PATH:/sbin
[cgillay@RedHat9  cgillay]$
```

WHAT'S HAPPENING? You have added **/sbin** as the last directory to be searched in your current path. You used the command **PATH**. Then you said the new path would be equal to (=) the old path (**$PATH**) with the addition of the new directory to be searched (**:/sbin**).

STEP 3   Key in the following: **echo $PATH** [Enter]

```
[cgillay@RedHat9  cgillay]$ echo $PATH
/home/kerberos/bin:/usr/local/bin:/bin:/usr/bin:/usr/X11R6/bin:
/home/cgillay/bin:/sbin
[cgillay@RedHat9  cgillay]$
```

WHAT'S HAPPENING? You see that **/sbin** has been added to your search path.

STEP 4   Close the terminal window. Open the terminal window. Key in the following: **echo $PATH** [Enter]

```
[cgillay@RedHat9  cgillay]$  echo $PATH
/home/kerberos/bin:/usr/local/bin:/bin:/usr/bin:/usr/X11R6/bin:
/home/cgillay/bin
[cgillay@RedHat9  cgillay]$
```

WHAT'S HAPPENING? The directory **/sbin** is no longer appended to your search path. The addition lasted only as long as your work session.

4.24 • Understanding the CDPATH Variable

CDPATH is another variable, like **PATH**. It is a list of directories separated by colons. Normally, when you key **cd** *directory* name, the **cd** command will look in the default directory. If you have long path names for a directory you often use, you can set the **CDPATH** variable so that the shell has a list of directories to search for the directory name you keyed in. You will then not need to include the entire path name for the directory. There is normally no value set for **CDPATH** when you log in. Again, this is a variable whose value only lasts as long as your terminal session.

4.25 • Activity: Using the CDPATH Variable

Note: The BOOK disk is mounted. The terminal window is open with your home directory as the default directory.

STEP 1   Key in the following: **echo $CDPATH** (Enter)

```
[cgillay@RedHat9   cgillay]$ echo $CDPATH

[cgillay@RedHat9   cgillay]$
```

WHAT'S **HAPPENING?** Currently there is no value set for **CDPATH**.

STEP 2   Key in the following: **ls /mnt/floppy/media /mnt/floppy/level-1** (Enter)

```
[cgillay@RedHat9  cgillay]$ ls /mnt/floppy/media /mnt/floppy/level-1
/mnt/floppy/level-1
hello.txt  level-2

/mnt/floppy/media
books       movies       tv
[cgillay@RedHat9  cgillay]$
```

WHAT'S **HAPPENING?** As you can see, the **level-1** directory has one file, **hello.txt**, and a directory called **level-2**. The **media** directory has three directories in it: **books**, **movies**, and **tv**. If you were using these directories constantly, each time you wanted to change directories to **books**, you would have to key in **cd /mnt/floppy/media/books**. By using the **CDPATH** variable, you can set it up so that all you would need to key in would be **cd books**. The **CDPATH** would know to look in **/mnt/floppy/media** for the **books** directory.

STEP 3   Key in the following: **CDPATH= ˜ :/mnt/floppy/media:/mnt/floppy/level-1** (Enter)

```
[cgillay@RedHat9   cgillay]$  CDPATH=~:/mnt/floppy/media:/mnt/
floppy/level-1
[cgillay@RedHat9   cgillay]$
```

WHAT'S **HAPPENING?** You have now set the search path for directories with the **CDPATH** variable. The first entry was a tilde (˜). Remember, that is the shorthand notation for your home directory. You then keyed in a colon and entered your next directory, **/mnt/floppy/media**. You then keyed in a colon as a delimiter and entered your last directory, **/mnt/floppy/level-1**. Now you can test your settings.

STEP 4   Key in the following: **cd books** (Enter)

```
[cgillay@RedHat9   cgillay]$   cd books
/mnt/floppy/media/books
[cgillay@RedHat9   books]$
```

WHAT'S HAPPENING? Indeed, just using **cd** with **books** took you to the **/mnt/floppy/media/books** directory.

STEP 5   Key in the following: **cd level-2** Enter

```
[cgillay@RedHat9   cgillay]$   cd level-2
/mnt/floppy/level-1/level-2
[cgillay@RedHat9   level-2]$
```

WHAT'S HAPPENING? Again, just using **cd** with **level-2** took you to **/mnt/floppy/level-1.**

STEP 6   Key in the following: **cd** Enter

```
[cgillay@RedHat9   level-2]$   cd
[cgillay@RedHat9   cgillay]$
```

WHAT'S HAPPENING? Since you included the ~ in your **CDPATH**, **cd** still took you to your home directory.

STEP 7   Close the terminal window. Open the terminal window.

STEP 8   Key in the following: **echo $CDPATH** Enter

STEP 9   Key in the following: **cd books** Enter

```
[cgillay@RedHat9   cgillay]$ echo $CDPATH

[cgillay@RedHat9   cgillay]$ cd books
bash: books: No such file or directory
[cgillay@RedHat9   cgillay]$
```

WHAT'S HAPPENING? Since your **CDPATH** variable is no longer set, the **cd** command looked for **books** only in your home directory.

STEP 10   Close the terminal window.

STEP 11   In your **floppy** window, collapse **floppy**. Collapse **mnt**. Close the window.

STEP 12   Unmount the BOOK disk.

STEP 13   After the BOOK disk is unmounted, remove it from the drive.

STEP 14   Unmount the BOOK disk and remove it from the drive.

Chapter Summary

In this chapter you were introduced to the following:
* The disk partitioning scheme.
* The process Linux follows to name partitions and what naming scheme Linux uses to identify the devices attached to the system.
* The relationship of tree-shaped hierarchical nature of the file system.
* Different methods of viewing your files and folders in both the Nautilus file manager and in the terminal window.

- The ability to create directories in the Nautilus file manager and in the terminal window.
- The ability to navigate in the directory structure using **cd** and using the dot addressing technique.
- The differences between relative and absolute paths.
- The methods for renaming a directory.
- The various methods for removing directories, both empty directories and directories that contain files.
- The power (and danger) of removing directories recursively.
- Viewing and manipulating environmental variables.

Key Terms

absolute path	mount point	shell script
directory markers	mounting	shell variables
dot addressing	partition table	subdirectory markers
emblem	partitions	typing replaces selection
environmental variable	relative path	variable
logical partition		

Discussion Questions

1. What is the purpose and functions of directories?
2. What is the function of the partition table?
3. What is an extended partition? A logical partition?
4. How do you access a partition in Linux?
5. Explain the purpose and function of a directory tree.
6. Why is it important to identify the file system that is used by the operating system of your computer?
7. In what ways can you sort your files and directories? In the Nautilus file manager? At the command prompt?
8. How can you create a directory?
9. Identify two purposes of the **cd** command.
10. Compare and contrast the absolute path with the relative path.
11. Before you can create a subdirectory you must first create its parent. How can you do this with just one command in the terminal window?
12. If you keyed in the following command:

       mkdir /michigan; mkdir /floppy/michigan

    and the following messages were displayed:

       mkdir: cannot create directory '/michigan': Permission denied

       mkdir: cannot create directory 'floppy/michigan': No such file or directory

    Explain why each command failed.
13. What is the difference between the single dot (.) and the double dot (..)?
14. What is meant by "dot addressing"?
15. What is the result of keying in **ls ..**?
16. How can you rename a directory at the command line?
17. Compare and contrast removing directories using the Nautilus file manager with removing directories at the command line.
18. What is the difference between the **rm** command and the **rmdir** command?
19. When using the **rmdir** command, what is the function of the **–p** option? The **–v** option?
20. What does it mean to remove directories recursively?

21. Why is the **rm –r** command considered to be very dangerous?
22. When using the **rm** command, compare the -**f** option with the -**r** option.
23. How can you determine your current default directory?
24. What is a shell script?
25. What is the purpose and function of shell variables?
26. Explain the purpose and function of an environmental variable.
27. Why is it important to have the default directory displayed on the screen?
28. What is the function of the **PATH** variable?
29. Explain the purpose and function of the **CDPATH** variable.
30. What is the function of the tilde (~)?

True/False Questions

For each question, circle the letter T if the question is true and the letter F if the question is false.

T   F   1. A logical partition resides entirely in the extended partition.

T   F   2. An important function of the operating system is to provide tools to manage files and directories

T   F   3. The prompt displays the entire path name.

T   F   4. You can use the double dot (..) as a shorthand method to move up and down the hierarchy tree structure.

T   F   5. Environmental variables are not case sensitive.

Completion Questions

Write the correct answer in each blank space.

6. The point of entry in the hierarchical directory is called the _____.
7. The organization and structure of a disk in dependent on the _____ used by the operating system.
8. To create a directory from the command line you would use the _____ command.
9. When you are deleting a parent directory and all the child directories/files below it you are removing directories _____.
10. Each directory in the **PATH** variable must be separated by _____.

Multiple Choice Questions

For each question, write the letter for the correct answer in the blank space.

11. When using Linux, /**dev** is the
    a. type of device on which partition resides.
    b. device that partition is on.
    c. partition.
    d. name of directory where all device files are located.

12. The directory named . (dot) is
    a. another name for the current directory.
    b. an abbreviation for the parent directory of the current directory.
    c. both a and b
    d. neither a nor b

13. The **set** command with no arguments or options will display
    a. only the PATH and HOME variables.
    b. all the values of all variables known to the shell.
    c. only shell variables you created.
    d. the commands necessary to change variables.

14. If you are user **juan**, your hostname is **linux** and your default directory is /mnt/floppy/music, and you key in **PS1="[\s]\$"**, your prompt will look as follows:
    a. **[bash]$**
    b. **[juan@linux /mnt/floppy/music]$**
    c. **[juan@linux bash]$**
    d. **[linux /mnt/floppy/music]$**

15. In the Nautilus file manager, you may view your files
    a. in icon view.
    b. in list view.
    c. both a and b
    d. neither a nor b

Writing Commands

Write the correct steps or commands to perform the required action as if you were at the computer. You will assume that there is a terminal window open. The prompt will indicate the current working directory.

16. You wish to display your files in the **/home/sharifi/books** directory sorted in file extension order.

```
[sharifi@RedHat9 sharifi]$
```

17. You want to create the directory structure **colleges/letters** under your home directory. Neither directory exists. Write the command that is the quickest way to create this structure.

```
[xu@RedHat9 xu]$
```

18. Your directory structure is **/home/jimenez/classes/music/piano**. You want to change directories to the **classes** directory. Use dot addressing techniques.

```
[jimenez@RedHat9 piano]$
```

19. Your directory structure is **/home/jimenez/classes/music/piano**. You want to remove the **piano** directory. **piano** has files in it. Write the command that is the quickest way to delete **piano**.

```
[jimenez@RedHat9 classes]$
```

20. You want to change the name of a directory from **IMAGES** to **images**. **IMAGES** is located in your home directory.

```
[xu@RedHat9 xu]$
```

Application Assignments

Problem Set I—At the Computer: Multiple Choice

Note: If you are working in a lab environment, your home directory may be freshened each time you boot into Linux. This means that any work you do will not be saved from work session to work session.

Problem A

- Mount the BOOK disk if it is not already mounted.
- Open a terminal window and use the terminal window for Problem A.
- Change the default directory to **/mnt/floppy**.
- Use the *relative* path to create a directory called **new**.

  1. What command did you use to create the directory?
      a. **mkdir new**
      b. **mkdir /home/new**
      c. **cd new**
      d. **cd /mnt/floppy/new**

- Use the *relative* path to make **new** the default directory.

  2. What command did you use to make **new** the default directory?
      a. **mkdir new**
      b. **mkdir /home/new**
      c. **cd new**
      d. **cd /mnt/floppy/new**

- Do a directory listing of the default directory showing *all* files.

  3. What was displayed?
      a. **new**
      b. . ..
      c. both a and b
      d. neither a nor b

- Remove the **new** directory using the **rmdir** command.

  4. What command did you execute *first*?
      a. **rmdir new**
      b. **cd ..**
      c. **rmdir /**
      d. **ls new**

Problem B

- Open a terminal window and use the terminal window for Problem B.
- Change the prompt so it reads only **HELLO THERE**.

  5. What command did you use?
      a. **PS1=HELLO THERE**
      b. **PS1=$HELLO THERE**
      c. **PS1="HELLO THERE"**
      d. none of the above

- Key in the following: **PS1="[\u@\h \d]\$"** [Enter]

  6. What appears in the prompt?
      a. The current version of Linux.
      b. The current date.
      c. The current time.
      d. The current shell name.

- Key in the following: **PS1="[\u@\h \W]\$ "** [Enter]

Problem C

- Get help on **environ**. Remember, you may need to scroll to see all of help.

    7. What environmental variable name is used for the terminal type for which output is to be prepared?
        a. **TERM**
        b. **TERMINAL**
        c. **SHELL**
        d. **HOME**

- Using the terminal window, make **/mnt/floppy** the active directory.

- Key in the following **cd astro** `Enter`

    8. What message appears?
        a. **Incorrect bash shell**
        b. **bash: cd: astro: command not found**
        c. **bash: cd: astro: invalid directory**
        d. **bash: cd: astro: No such file or directory**

Problem D

- Open a terminal window and use the terminal window for Problem D.

- Make the default directory **/mnt/floppy**.

- You want to create the structure shown to the right.

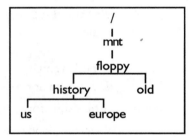

    9. What would be the *fastest* way to create the **us** directory?
        a. **mkdir history/us**
        b. **mkdir -p history/us**
        c. **mkdir /history/us**
        d. **mkdir -p /history/us**

- Create the remaining structure.

- Make **old** the default directory.

- With **old** selected as the default directory, create the subdirectory called **letters** under **history/us.**

    10. What command could you use to create **letters** under the **us** directory, assuming **/mnt/floppy/old** was the default?
        a. **mkdir /mnt/floppy/history/us/letters**
        b. **mkdir ../history/us/letters**
        c. both a and b
        d. neither a nor b

    11. The parent of **old** is
        a. **floppy**
        b. **history**
        c. **letters**
        d. **mnt**

- Remove the subdirectory called **letters** that you just created.

- Remove the subdirectory called **old.**

Problem E

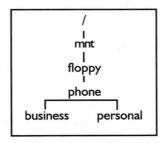

- Open a terminal window and use the terminal window for Problem E.
- Change the default directory to **/mnt/floppy**.
- You want to create the structure shown to the right, and you want to create **personal** first.

    12. What would be the *fastest* way to create the **personal** directory?
        a. **mkdir phone/personal**
        b. **mkdir -p phone/personal**
        c. **mkdir /mnt/floppy/phone/personal**
        d. **mkdir -p /mnt/floppy/phone/personal**

- Create the rest of the structure.
- Using the relative path, change the default directory to **phone**.

    13. The command you used was
        a. **cd phone**
        b. **cd /phone**
        c. **mkdir phone**
        d. **rmdir phone**

- Using the relative path, change the default directory to **business**.

    14. The command you used was
        a. **cd phone**
        b. **cd business**
        c. **cd phone/business**
        d. **cd /phone/business**

- Use the dot technique to move to the parent directory of **business**.

    15. The command you used was
        a. **cd /**
        b. **cd ../phone**
        c. **cd ../..**
        d. **cd ..**

    16. The parent of **business** is
        a. **personal**
        b. **phone**
        c. **root**
        d. **floppy**

- Make **/mnt/floppy** the default directory.

    17. Which of the following command(s) could you have used to change directories to **/mnt/floppy**?
        a. **cd ..**
        b. **cd /mnt/floppy**
        c. either a or b
        d. neither a nor b

Problem F

- Open a terminal window and use the terminal window for Problem F.
- Be sure the default directory is **/mnt/floppy**.
- Create a directory called **books** under **/mnt/floppy**.

    18. Which of the following command(s) could you have used to create **books**?
        a. **mkdir books**
        b. **mkdir /mnt/floppy/books**
        c. either a or b
        d. neither a nor b

- With the **/mnt/floppy** as the default directory, create two directories called **mystery** and **scifi** under the **books** directory.

    19. With **/mnt/floppy** as the default, which of the following command(s) could you have used to create **mystery**?
        a. **md mystery**
        b. **mkdir mystery**
        c. either a or b
        d. neither a nor b

- With **/mnt/floppy** as the default directory, rename **scifi** to **horror**.

    20. With **/mnt/floppy** as the default, which of the following commands could you have used to rename **scifi** to **horror**?
        a. **mv books/scifi horror**
        b. **mv books/scifi books/horror**
        c. **mv scifi horror**
        d. **mv horror scifi**

- Use the **rmdir** command to remove the **books** directory.

    21. What steps do you have to complete *first*?
        a. Remove only the **horror** directory.
        b. Remove only the **mystery** directory.
        c. Remove both the **mystery** and **horror** directories.
        d. None. Just key **rmdir books**.

    22. If you used the command **rm -r** to remove the **books** directory, what steps would you have had to complete *first*?
        a. Remove only the **horror** directory.
        b. Remove only the **mystery** directory.
        c. Remove both the **mystery** and **horror** directories.
        d. None. Just key **rm -r books**.

- You want to remove the **phone** directory and see what is occurring during the removal

    23. Which of the following command(s) could you have used to accomplish this task?
        a. **rm -v -r phone**
        b. **rmdir -v -r phone**
        c. **rm -r phone**
        d. **rmdir -v phone**

Problem G

- Open a terminal window and use the terminal window for Problem G.

24. If you wanted to know the value of the **PATH** variable, what command would you use?
 a. **PATH**
 b. **echo $PATH**
 c. **echo PATH**
 d. none of the above

- Change the default directory to your home directory.

- Set up your **CDPATH** variable so that from anywhere, you can key in **cd history** and have the default directory be **/mnt/floppy/history**.

25. Which command did you use?
 a. **CDPATH= ~ :/mnt/floppy**
 b. **CDPATH= ~ :/mnt/floppy/history**
 c. **PATH= ~ :/mnt/floppy**
 d. **PATH= ~ :/mnt/floppy/history**

- Close your terminal window. Close your home directory window.

- Unmount the BOOK disk. Remove it from the floppy disk drive. Close any open windows.

Problem Set II—At the Computer: Short Answer

1. Imagine that you have the following files in your home directory:

venus.tmm	titan.txt	ast.new
astro.txt	earth.one	states.usa
born.txt	thunderbird	autos
dances.txt	expenses-01feb.dta	ulit
earth.two	expenses-02mar.dta	ven.99
expenses-03feb.dta	grammy.rec	bonjour.tmp
expenses-04jan.dta	jup.tmp	carolyn.fil
hello.txt	mer.new	dress.up
jupiter.tmp	newprson.fil	expenses-03jan.dta
mercury.tmp	new-suvs.xls	expenses-04feb.dta
orion.neb	personal.fil	galaxy.tmp
quasars.doc	mercury.txt	green.jaz
jupiter.txt	planets.txt	jup.new
mer.tmp	state.cap	ven.tmp
expenses-01mar.dta	ven.new	earth.thr
expenses-02mar.dta	mystery-bks	expenses-02jan.dta
galaxy.txt	astro.tmp	award.mov
jup.99	steven.fil	mer.99
bestpictures	venus.txt	vwbug
bestsongs	italy.tif	person.fil
ame-lit-bks	goldenoldmovies	addressfile
dog.tif	plane.bmp	goldenglobemovies
eng-lit-bks	world.tif	pulitzer-prize-bks
amhistory	balloon.tif	

2. Based on the file names, plan what directories you would need to logically group these files.

3. In your home directory, create the structure you designed in the most expedient method possible.

4. Write a brief report on what directories you created and your rationale for those decisions. Include in your discussion what files would go in what directories.

5. Create the following directory structure:

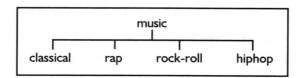

a. What command(s) did you use?

b. Rename **rock-roll** to **rock**. What command did you use?

c. Create a directory under each subdirectory called **composer**. What command(s) did you use.

d. Make **music/classical/composer** the default directory. What command did you use?

e. Move to the parent of **composer** using dot-addressing techniques. What command did you use? What does the prompt display?

f. Make **music/hiphop/composer** the default directory. What command did you use? What does the prompt display?

g. With **music/hiphop/composer** as the default directory, rename **music/rap/composer** to **music/rap/artist**. What command did you use?

h. Set a CDPATH variable so that you can always move to the **music/rap/artist** directory by keying in only **cd artist**.

i. Remove the **music** directory in your home directory with all its subdirectories. How did you accomplish this task?

6. Change the prompt so it contains the following information on separate lines:

   current date
   user name @ machine
   entire path]$

   How did you accomplish this?

7. Return the prompt to its default value. How did you accomplish this task?

Problem Set III—Brief Essay

Use gEdit or OpenOffice.org Writer to write and print your response. Be sure to put your name as well as what day and time your class is. Include the number of the question you are answering.

a. A friend is watching you work at the command line. You key in the following:

```
cd /mnt/floppy
cd house/utils
ls
ls ../linux/homework
```

Your friend asks you how you know when and where to place the slashes. She also wants you to explain the double dot you used. Explain to her how to determine the positioning of the slashes, what the double dot represents, and the difference between the placements. Include a brief description of relative and absolute paths.

b. You may manage your directories from either the Nautilus file manager or the command line. Describe the differences between the Nautilus file manager and the command line. What are the advantages and disadvantages of either method? Which do you prefer and why?

c. *Environmental variables are an important part of the Linux environment*. Agree or disagree with this statement. Support your argument. In your discussion, be sure to define environmental variables. Name at least two environmental variables and the purpose each serves.

CHAPTER 5

File Management Commands

Chapter Overview

In this chapter you will learn essential commands that will help you manage and manipulate your files. These are known as housekeeping commands. You will learn to copy files using the Nautilus file manager and the **cp** command, allowing you to make backup copies. You will learn the consequences of overwriting files and of combining the contents of files. You will copy and create files on your BOOK disk and in your home directory so that you can have experience creating files with the **cat** command. You will view the contents of your files with the **less** and **more** commands. You will learn how to change the name of a file using the Nautilus file manager or using the **mv** command. You will find that the **mv** command, which can also move your files from one location to another. You will also understand why removing files is important in managing your files, and you will delete files with the Nautilus file manager and with the **rm** command. You will use the **file** command to help you identify different file types. You will find that you can create an empty file or change a file date with the **touch** command. The **lpr** command will let you print your files. Learning these commands will allow you to manage your files in effective and efficient ways.

Learning Objectives

1. Explain why copies of files are made.
2. Determine what type of data is in a file.
3. Compare and contrast copying files in the GUI and copying files using the **cp** command with wildcards.
4. Explain the purpose and function of the following commands: **cat**, **less**, and **more**.
5. Explain how and why files are overwritten.

228

6. Explain why dummy files are created and why files are concatenated.
7. Explain the purpose and function of the **touch** command.
8. Explain why and how you would change a file name.
9. Compare and contrast moving and renaming files and directories using the **mv** command with the Nautilus file manager.
10. Compare and contrast eliminating files using the Nautilus file manager with using **rm** at the command line.
11. Explain how to delete files using wildcards and other options.
12. Compare and contrast the **lpr** command, the **lpq** command, and the **lprm** command.

Student Outcomes

1. Copy files using the Nautilus File Manager and the **cp** command (with and without wildcards).
2. Use the **file** command to determine if a file is executable and what type of data is in a file.
3. Display files using **cat, more,** and **less** commands.
4. Use **cp** and **ls** commands with subdirectories dot addressing to place and then view files in subdirectories.
5. Overwrite a file using the **cp** command without options and with the **b, p,** and **i** options.
6. Create and combine files using the **cat** command.
7. Use the **touch** command to create an empty file and to change a file's modification date.
8. Use the **mv** command to move and rename files and directories.
9. Delete files using the Nautilus file manager, the **rm** command, and the **rm** command with wildcards and options.
10. Print a file using the **lpr** command.

Commands Introduced

cat
cp
file
less
more
touch

5.1 • Why Learn Commands?

In the last chapter, you learned how to manipulate directories. You learned to use the Nautilus file manager to create, rename, and remove directories, as well as move around in the directory structure. You learned the shell commands **mkdir** to create directories, **cd** to change directories, **mv** to rename directories, **rmdir** to remove directories, and **rm –r** to remove directories that are not empty. All of these procedures dealt with directory management commands, which handle directories and subdirectories. However, directories are places to hold files. With the directory management commands, you built the book shelves, but you have not as yet put any books on them. If shelves are directories, the books are the files. In a library, you are interested in locating, reading, and using the books, not admiring the shelves. In the same way, on your computer you are interested in locating, reading, and using files—not admiring the directories you created.

You will have many files and directories on a disk. The directories will be used to organize both your program and your data files. Directories are the largest units of information management, but you need to manage information in smaller quantities—at the file level. You will generate many data files with your programs. You will need a way to perform what are called *housekeeping tasks*, such as copying files from one directory or one disk to another or eliminating files you no longer need. These tasks are different from creating or changing the data in the files. To create the data, you need to use an application program such as OpenOffice.org Writer. You must then use the application program that created the data file to change the data in the file. You may also create files simply using the shell and other Linux commands.

You may use the Nautilus file manager in GNOME to manage your files. You can drag files from one place to another, cut and paste them, rename them, and delete them with the click of a mouse button. However, it is critical in Linux to use the command line. Everything you can do in the Nautilus file manager can also be done at the command line. And, as you will discover, there are even more tasks you can accomplish at the command line. File-management commands include such commands as **ls**, **cp**, **rm**, and **cat**, which help you manage your files. Normally, your search path is set to allow you to use these commands.

5.2 • Copying Files

Copying a file does exactly what it says—it takes an original source file, makes an identical copy of that file, and places the copy where you want it to go. In a sense, it is similar to a photocopy machine. You place your original on the copy plate, press the appropriate button, and receive a copy of your document. Nothing has happened to your original document. If it has a smudge on it, so does your copy. The same is true with the copying files—an exact copy of the file is made, and the original file remains intact. Copying a file does not alter the original file in any way.

Why would you want to copy files? You might want to copy a file from one disk to another. For example, you might create an inventory of all your household goods for your homeowner's insurance policy. It would be stored as a file on your disk. If your home burned down, so would your disk with your inventory file. It makes sense to copy this file to another disk and store it somewhere else, perhaps in a safe-deposit box.

You might want to make a second copy of an existing file on the same disk. Why would you want to do this? If you are going to be making changes to a data file with the program that created it, you might like a copy of the original just in case you do not like the changes you made to the data file. If you are going to make a change to a configuration file, you would like a copy of the original file so that if your change does not work, you can return to the original configuration file.

The Nautilus file manager has a copy command on its **Edit** menu and on the right-click menu. Some users prefer to use Nautilus file manager because it allows dragging and dropping files from one location to another.

5.3 • Activity: Making Copies of Files Using the Nautilus File Manager

Note 1:   In the examples shown below, **cgillay** is used as the user name. Whenever **cgillay** is used as an example, substitute your user name.

Note 2:   The activities in this book assume Linux is installed at run level 3. See the Installation section of Appendix A for details.

STEP 1   Place the BOOK disk in the floppy disk drive. Mount the disk.

STEP 2   Open your home directory window by double-clicking your **Home** icon on the desktop. Click **Information**. Click **Tree**. Place the window in icon view.

STEP 3   Click **File**. Click **New Window**. Click **Information**. Click **Tree**. In the window you just opened, select **/mnt/floppy**. Place it in icon view.

STEP 4   In the **floppy** window, locate the file called **astro.tmp**. Click it to select it.

WHAT'S HAPPENING? You have opened two windows. You can see the files on the BOOK disk as well as your home directory. You are going to copy the **astro.tmp** file from the BOOK disk (source) to your home directory (destination).

STEP 5   Click **Edit**. Click **Copy File**. Click your home directory window to make it active. Click **Edit**. Click **Paste Files**.

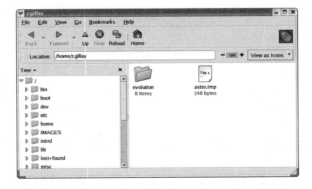

WHAT'S HAPPENING? You successfully copied the file. You may use drag-and-drop techniques as well. However, if you are dragging a file from a removable media type such as a floppy disk, the default action is a copy. But if you are in your home directory and dragging from one directory to another, you will have performed a move operation. Moving the file means that you will remove it from one location and place it in another location. If you right-click a file, you will open a shortcut menu that allows you the choice of various file operations such as copying, cutting, or creating a link to the file (like a shortcut in Windows).

STEP 6   Make the **floppy** window active and locate the file called **galaxy.tmp**. Click it to select it. Drag and drop it into your home directory window. Make your **user (cgillay)** directory window active.

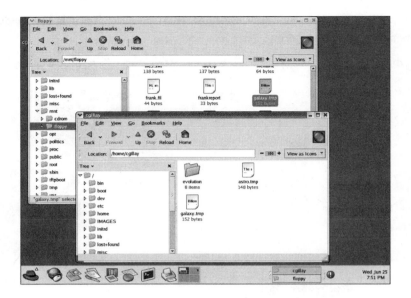

WHAT'S HAPPENING? You saw a symbol attached to the **/mnt/floppy/galaxy.tmp** file as you dragged it to **/home/cgillay**—a plus sign—indicating that it was a copy operation. You see that you have **galaxy.tmp** in both directories. You copied the file successfully.

STEP 7   Right-click in your home directory window. Click **New Folder**. Name it **test**.

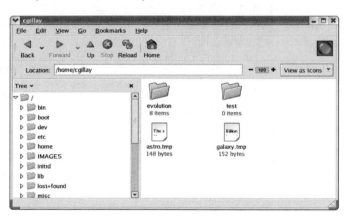

WHAT'S HAPPENING? In your home directory, you now have at least a directory called **test** and two files, **astro.tmp** and **galaxy.tmp**.

STEP 8   Drag and drop **astro.tmp** on the **test** folder.

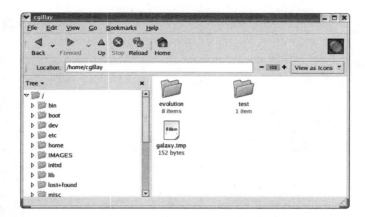

WHAT'S HAPPENING? In your home directory structure, when you dragged and dropped, you moved the file **astro.tmp** from **/home/cgillay** to **/home/cgillay/test**.

STEP 9   In the tree, locate your home directory. Expand it. Click **test**.

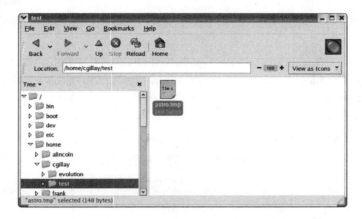

WHAT'S HAPPENING? Indeed, your file **astro.tmp** is now located in the **/home/cgillay/test** directory.

Note 1:   If you are working on your own computer, you will need to set up the users and directories to make the activities work. See Appendix A for the necessary users, directories, and files.

Note 2:   In your lab environment, **politics** may be in a different location.

STEP 10   In the current window, in the tree, click your home directory to make it active. Click the other window (**floppy**) to make it active. In the tree, locate the **politics** directory (**/politics**). Size the windows so you can see both the **politics** window and your home directory. Click your home directory window.

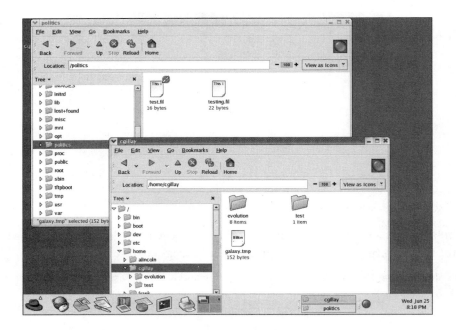

WHAT'S HAPPENING? You should see that you have files called **test.fil** and **testing.fil** in the **politics** directory. The file called **test.fil** has an emblem indicating that it is protected from deletion. You are going to drag and drop the file called **testing.fil** into your home directory window.

STEP 11 Drag and drop **testing.fil** into your home directory window.

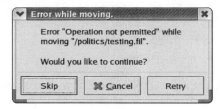

WHAT'S HAPPENING? You do not have permission to move the file. A drag-and-drop operation within the hierarchical structure is a move. You do not have the correct permissions to move this file.

STEP 12 Click **Cancel**. Right-click **testing.fil**. Click **Copy File**.

STEP 13 Click your home directory window. Right-click. Click **Paste Files**.

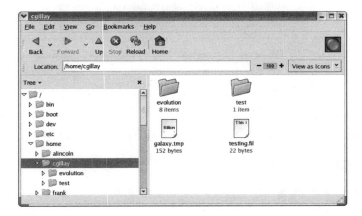

WHAT'S HAPPENING? You do have permission to copy the file. You successfully copied **testing.fil** to your home directory.

STEP 14 Close your home directory window. Close the **politics** window.

5.4 • Copying Files at the Command Line

At the command line, **cp** has many options, such as the use of wildcards, that make it more powerful than using the Nautilus file manager. At the command line, **cp** has a specific syntax. Its basic syntax is always:

```
cp   [options]  file1 file2
cp   [options]  files directory
```

or conceptually:

```
cp   source   destination
```

cp is the command or the work you want the system to do. The *source* is what you want copied, your original. The *destination* is where you want it copied. The command, the source, and the destination are separated by spaces. You must specify the path if you are not using the default directory. Table 5.1, "**cp** Options," lists some of the major options that can be used with the **cp** command.

Option	Name	Result
-b	Backup	If copying a file would overwrite an existing file, using this option would make a backup of the file that is to be overwritten. The backup file name is the same as the destination file name but has a tilde (~) added to its name.
-f	Force	If an existing destination file cannot be opened, remove it and try again.
-i	Interactive	Prompts the user when a file would be overwritten.
-p	Preserve	Preserves each file's owner, group, and modification dates, or as much information as it can, depending on the user.
-r, -R	Recursive	Usually used when destination is a directory. If any of the files named as the source are a directory, this will copy the

> directory and any of the directories to the destination directory. Directories and their files are copied.

-v	Verbose	Displays the name of each file before copying it.

Table 5.1 • cp Options

5.5 • Activity: Making Copies of Files Using cp

Note: The BOOK disk is mounted.

STEP 1   Open a terminal window. Your home directory is your default directory.

STEP 2   Key in the following:
           cp /mnt/floppy/jup.tmp ~ ; ls -l [Enter]

```
[cgillay@RedHat9   cgillay]$ cp /mnt/floppy/jup.tmp ~ ; ls -l
total 20
drwx------   4  cgillay  cgillay  4096  Jun 10  18:03  evolution
-rwxr-xr-x   1  cgillay  cgillay   152  Oct 31   2001  galaxy.tmp
-rwxr-xr-x   1  cgillay  cgillay   190  Jun 25  22:14  jup.tmp
drwxrwxr-x   2  cgillay  cgillay  4096  Jun 25  19:58  test
-rwxrwxrwx   1  cgillay  cgillay    22  Jun 25  22:06  testing.fil
[cgillay@RedHat9   cgillay]$
```

WHAT'S **HAPPENING?** You may have more or fewer files in your home directory. You used the syntax **cp** *source destination*. The command was **cp**. The source file was **/mnt/floppy/jup.tmp**. You must have a destination. You used the ~, the tilde, the shorthand notation for your home directory. Since you did not state a file name, the default was used, **jup.tmp**. When you used **ls** with the -l, (**ls -l**) you saw that the file was successfully copied. Remember, using the **-l** option with **ls** shows you the permissions, the owner, the size, and the date and time the file was modified or created. In this case, you used a relative path name, but remember, you may always use the absolute path name. Remember to use your login name, not **cgillay**.

STEP 3   Key in the following: **cp /mnt/floppy/mer.tmp /home/cgillay; ls** [Enter]

```
[cgillay@RedHat9   cgillay]$ cp /mnt/floppy/mer.tmp /home/cgillay;
ls
evolution   galaxy.tmp   jup.tmp   mer.tmp   test   testing.fil
[cgillay@RedHat9   cgillay]$
```

WHAT'S **HAPPENING?** You successfully copied the file. You will next give the destination file a different name and override the defaults. If you were dragging and dropping in the Nautilus file manager, you could copy the files, but you could not give them a new name at the same time. You would drag and drop, then have to rename the file. At the command line, you can copy and give a file a new name at the same time.

STEP 4   Key in the following: **cp /mnt/floppy/mer.tmp   ~/mercury.fil; ls** Enter

```
[cgillay@RedHat9   cgillay]$ cp /mnt/floppy/mer.tmp ~/mercury.fil;
ls
evolution      jup.tmp        mer.tmp       testing.fil
galaxy.tmp     mercury.fil    test
[cgillay@RedHat9   cgillay]$
```

WHAT'S HAPPENING? You executed the **cp** command and used **ls** to confirm that you copied the file. Following the syntax diagram, **cp** is the command. **/mnt/floppy/mer.tmp** is the source file or what you want to copy. **~/mercury.fil** is the new destination file name in your home directory. You used the / as a delimiter to separate the file name from the directory names. You also used the ~ to represent your home directory. In this case, you overrode the defaults by telling the **cp** command to call the destination file in your home directory, **mercury.fil**. If you want to copy a directory structure, you can do so with the recursive option (**-r**).

STEP 5   Key in the following: **ls /mnt/floppy/media /mnt/floppy/media/books** Enter

```
[cgillay@RedHat9   cgillay]$ ls /mnt/floppy/media /mnt/floppy/media/books
/mnt/floppy/media
books   movies   tv


/mnt/floppy/media/books
ame-lit.bks    mystery.bks    pulitzer.bks
[cgillay@RedHat9   cgillay]$
```

WHAT'S HAPPENING? On the BOOK disk, the directory **media** has three subdirectories, **books**, **movies**, and **tv**. Each directory has files in it. You looked at the **book** directory and saw that indeed there were files in it. You want to copy this entire directory structure to your home directory.

STEP 6   Key in the following: **cp -r /mnt/floppy/media media** Enter

STEP 7   Key in the following: **ls media media/books** Enter

```
[cgillay@RedHat9   cgillay]$  cp -r /mnt/floppy/media media
[cgillay@RedHat9   cgillay]$  ls media media/books
media:
books    movies    tv


media/books:
ame-lit.bks    mystery.bks    pulitzer.bks
[cgillay@RedHat9   cgillay]$
```

WHAT'S HAPPENING? By using the **-r** option, you did copy the entire media directory structure including all the files in the directories.

5.6 ● Classifying Files

As you have seen, a computer system contains a huge number of files. Files can be classified according to type, such as text files, program files (binary programs), shell scripts, graphic images, and so on. Sometimes you can identify what is in the file by the file extension (file type). This is not foolproof. You can also use the **file** command to determine what the file is. The **file** command can open a file and try to find a matching entry in the **/usr/share/magic** file. The **file** command identifies the type of file using, among other tests, a test for whether the file begins with a certain "magic" number. The **/usr/share/magic** file specifies what magic numbers are to be used to be tested for, what message to print based on the magic number found, and any additional information that can be extracted if a specific magic number is found. The output from the **file** command is only as good as the database in the magic file. Most Linux distributions contain good versions of **magic**. The magic file entries have been collected from various sources, mostly from Usenet. The syntax is:

```
file argument
```

Table 5.2, "**file** Options," lists some of the major options that can be used with the **file** command.

Option	Description
-b	Brief mode.
-i	Outputs mime type strings instead of the more human readable ones. **MIME** (Multipurpose Internet Mail Extension) types are a standard way to identify files so that they can be transmitted over the Internet. Each kind of file is assigned a specific **MIME** type. For example, a jpeg file would have a MIME type of image/jpeg. The **MIME** type tells Internet applications such as email or browser programs what type of file is being exchanged, and how to code (on sending) and decode it (on arrival).
-s	Normally, **file** determines file type only for ordinary files. Using this option causes the file command to read block or character special files. This can be useful for determining the file system types of the data in raw disk partitions (block-specific files). A block device file is one that reads or writes in blocks. A typical block device file is a disk drive. A character device file is one that reads or writes a character at a time. A typical character device file is a printer.
-v	Version of file and location of magic file.
-z	Tries to look inside compressed files.

Table 5.2 ● file Options

5.7 ● Activity: Using the file Command

Note: A terminal window is open. Your home directory is your default directory. The BOOK disk is mounted.

STEP 1   In your terminal window, key in the following: **file /bin/ls** ⌜Enter⌝

```
[cgillay@RedHat9   cgillay]$   file /bin/ls
/bin/ls: ELF 32-bit LSB executable, Intel 80386, version 1,(SYSV)
for GNU/Linux 2.2.5, dynamically linked (uses shared libs),
stripped
[cgillay@RedHat9   cgillay]$
```

WHAT'S HAPPENING? Indeed the **ls** command is an executable file.

STEP 2   Key in the following: **file mer.tmp; file -b mer.tmp** Enter

```
[cgillay@RedHat9   cgillay]$   file  mer.tmp; file -b mer.tmp
mer.tmp: ASCII English text, with CRLF line terminators
ASCII English text, with CRLF line terminators
[cgillay@RedHat9   cgillay]$
```

WHAT'S HAPPENING? The **mer.tmp** file is a simple text file. **CRLF** is a shorthand way of referring to carriage return (CR); i.e., Enter at the end of a line and line feed (LF), the beginning of a new line.

STEP 3   Key in the following: **file /mnt/floppy/balloon.tif** Enter

STEP 4   Key in the following: **file /mnt/floppy/plane.bmp** Enter

STEP 5   Key in the following: **file -i /mnt/floppy/balloon.tif** Enter

```
[cgillay@RedHat9   cgillay]$   file  /mnt/floppy/balloon.tif
/mnt/floppy/balloon.tif: TIFF image data, little-endian
[cgillay@RedHat9   cgillay]$ file  /mnt/floppy/plane.bmp
/mnt/floppy/plane.bmp: PC bitmap data, Windows 3.x format, 344 x 92 x 8
[cgillay@RedHat9   cgillay]$ file  -i /mnt/floppy/balloon.tif
/mnt/floppy/balloon.tif: image/tiff
[cgillay@RedHat9   cgillay]$
```

WHAT'S HAPPENING? The term *endian* refers to the ordering of bytes in a multi-byte number. *Little-endian* is an order in which the little end (least significant value in the sequence) is stored first. This is in contrast to *big-endian*, in which the big end (most significant value in the sequence) is stored first. In this example, both **balloon.tif** and **plane.bmp** are graphic or image files. The MIME type for balloon.tif is **image/tiff**. Although you could assume files with a **.tif** and **.bmp** extension are graphic files, if a file were misnamed, the **file** command could help you determine what is really in the file. For instance, the file type **.mov** is used to denote a QuickTime movie file, but file extensions can be deceiving.

STEP 6   Key in the following: **file -b /mnt/floppy/media/movies/bestpic.mov** Enter

```
[cgillay@RedHat9   cgillay]$ file -b  /mnt/floppy/media/movies/bestpic.mov
ASCII text, with CRLF line terminators.
[cgillay@RedHat9   cgillay]$
```

WHAT'S HAPPENING? Although the **.mov** extension seemed to indicate a QuickTime movie file, in fact, this specific file, **bestpic.mov** is a text file.

5.8 ● Using Wildcards with the cp Command

In Chapter 3, you used global file specifications, or wildcards (*, ?, and [ ]), with the **ls** command so that you could display a group of files. You can also use the wildcards to copy files. In the previous activity you copied one file at a time; for example, **cp /mnt/floppy/jup.tmp ~** . You then keyed in a command for each file you wanted copied. Since each of the files you wished to copy had the same file extension, **.tmp**, instead of keying in each source file and destination file, you could have used the wildcards to key in the command line and reduced three commands to one. This is also a case where you need to use the command line. There is no way to quickly select a group of files to be copied in the GUI.

5.9 ● Activity: Using Wildcards with the cp Command

Note: The BOOK disk is mounted. You are using a terminal window. Your home directory is your default directory.

STEP 1   Key in the following: **cd /mnt/floppy; mkdir class** [Enter]

STEP 2   Key in the following: **cp *.tmp class; ls class** [Enter]

```
[cgillay@RedHat9   cgillay]$ cd /mnt/floppy; mkdir class
[cgillay@RedHat9   floppy]$  cp *.tmp  class; ls class
astro.tmp      bonjour.tmp  jupiter.tmp   mercury.tmp  ven.tmp
ast.tmp        galaxy.tmp   jup.tmp       mer.tmp
[cgillay@RedHat9   floppy]$
```

WHAT'S HAPPENING? Your command line instructed the operating system to copy any file in the **/mnt/floppy** directory that has the file extension **.tmp**, regardless of its file name, to a new directory called **class**. You could have keyed in the absolute path name, **cp /mnt/floppy/*.tmp /mnt/floppy/class**, but once again, it is unnecessary to specify the absolute path. You may use the relative path.

STEP 3   Key in the following: **mkdir ~/class; cp -v class/* ~/class; ls ~/class** [Enter]

```
cgillay @ RedHat9:/mnt/floppy                                          _ □ x
File  Edit  View  Terminal  Go  Help
[cgillay@RedHat9 floppy]$ mkdir ~/class; cp -v class/* ~/class; ls ~/class
`class/astro.tmp' -> `/home/cgillay/class/astro.tmp'
`class/ast.tmp' -> `/home/cgillay/class/ast.tmp'
`class/bonjour.tmp' -> `/home/cgillay/class/bonjour.tmp'
`class/galaxy.tmp' -> `/home/cgillay/class/galaxy.tmp'
`class/jupiter.tmp' -> `/home/cgillay/class/jupiter.tmp'
`class/jup.tmp' -> `/home/cgillay/class/jup.tmp'
`class/mercury.tmp' -> `/home/cgillay/class/mercury.tmp'
`class/mer.tmp' -> `/home/cgillay/class/mer.tmp'
`class/ven.tmp' -> `/home/cgillay/class/ven.tmp'
astro.tmp  bonjour.tmp  jupiter.tmp  mercury.tmp  ven.tmp
ast.tmp    galaxy.tmp   jup.tmp      mer.tmp
[cgillay@RedHat9 floppy]$
```

WHAT'S HAPPENING? Here you created a directory in your home directory. You used the **-v** (verbose) option to see the results of your copy command. **class/*** said to copy all the files in the **class** directory to the **/home/cgillay/class** directory. How can you tell if the contents of the files are the same? You can use the **cat** command.

STEP 4   Key in the following: **cd** [Enter]

```
[cgillay@RedHat9  floppy]$ cd
[cgillay@RedHat9  cgillay]$
```

WHAT'S **HAPPENING?** You have returned to your home directory.

5.10 • The cat, less, and more Commands

The **ls** command allowed you to determine that, indeed, there are "file folders" with the **.tmp** extension on the BOOK disk and your home directory in the **class** directory. Using the **ls** command is like opening your file drawer (the disk) and looking at the labels on the file folders. **ls** does not show you what is in the file folder. The **cat** command opens the file folder and displays the contents of the file on the screen. The **cat** command displays the file on the screen without stopping (scrolling). It actually copies each file to standard output (the screen). The **cat** command name is derived from concatenate, which means to join together one after another. The syntax is:

```
cat [options] [filename]
```

Table 5.3, "**cat** Options," lists some of the major options that can be used with the **cat** command.

Option	Description
-A	Shows all—this will display even nonprinting characters. It is equivalent to **-vET**.
-b	Numbers nonblank output lines.
-e	Equivalent to **-vE**.
-E	Displays a $ at the end of each line.
-n	Numbers all output lines.
-t	Equivalent to **–vT**.
-T	Displays tab characters as ⌃I.
-v	Uses the ⌃ and the **M** to show nonprinting characters except for line feeds and tabs.

Table 5.3 • cat Options

cat is the command (the work) you want the system to perform. The brackets ([ ]) indicate that what is between the brackets is optional. You do not key in the brackets, only what is inside them. The options are fixed. In addition, the **cat** command will display the contents of any file, but unless it is a text file it is not readable.

If you have a text file that is more than one screenful, you may use the **more** or **less** commands in place of **cat** to display the file one screenful at a time. The **more** command displays the file a screenful at a time and returns you to the shell prompt. The **less** command also displays a file one screenful at a time, but requires you to key in **q** before it will return to the shell prompt. Both commands allow you to use the ⟨Space Bar⟩ to move one screenful at a time. Both commands allow the use of the ⟨Enter⟩ key to move one line at a time. The **less** command allows you to move backward through the file one screen at a time (**b**) or one half a screen at a time (**u**), whereas the **more** command only allows you to move forward. The syntax for the **more** and **less** command follow the same format:

```
less [options] [filename]
more [options] [filename]
```

5.11 • Activity: Displaying Files Using the cat, more, and less Commands

Note: The BOOK disk is mounted. You are using a terminal window. Your home directory is your default directory.

STEP 1   Key in the following: **cd /mnt/floppy; cat basket.bmp** ⟨Enter⟩

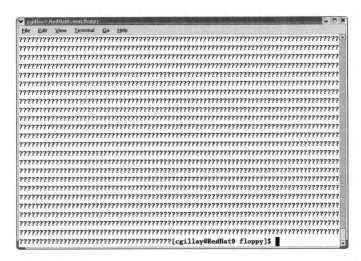

WHAT'S HAPPENING? Your display could be slightly different, depending on your system. What you see on the screen is, indeed, the contents of a file named **basket.bmp** on the BOOK disk. This file is in machine language and not meaningful to you in this format. Since this is a graphic file, it can be read only by a graphics program. Furthermore, since there is no CRLF at the end of this file, the prompt immediately follows the end of the file and does not return to a new line.

STEP 2   Press ⟨Enter⟩

STEP 3   On the desktop, double-click your home directory icon. Click **Information**. Click **Tree**. In the directory structure, select **/mnt/floppy**. Be in icon view. Scroll until you can see the **basket.bmp** icon.

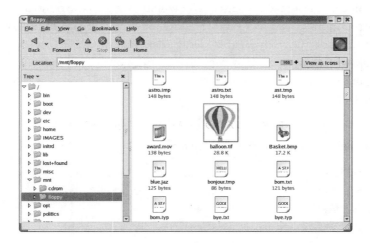

WHAT'S HAPPENING? In icon view, the Nautilus file manager will show graphics as thumbnails. A *thumbnail* is a term used by graphic designers for a small image representation of a larger image. It is a miniaturized version of an image. You could also open this with the two graphic programs included with Red Hat—Eye of Gnome and the Gimp.

STEP 4   Right-click **Basket.bmp**. Point to **Open With**. Click **Eye of Gnome**.

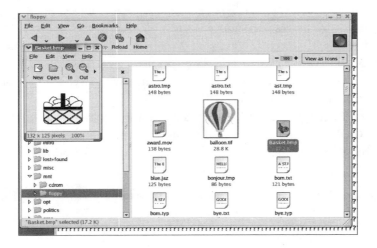

WHAT'S HAPPENING? When you used Eye of Gnome, the data now becomes meaningful. The **cat** command will open any file, but as you saw, the contents were not meaningful unless the data was text. The **cat** command will do whatever you ask, even if it means displaying nonsense. A file must be a text file to be readable.

Another name for a text file is an ASCII (pronounced ask-ee) file. *ASCII* is an acronym for American Standard Code for Information Interchange. ASCII is a code that translates the bits of information into readable letters. All you need to remember is that an ASCII file is a readable text file. ASCII files are a common language that almost all programs can recognize.

The data files that programs generate are usually not readable either. Each program has a special way of reading and writing the information in the data file so that the program knows what to do with the data. Usually no other program can read the data file except the program that generated it. It would be like wanting to write a letter in Japanese if you didn't speak, read, or write Japanese. You would hire a translator (the program). He would write the letter (the data file). You still could not read the letter. You would give it to the translator to know what is in the letter. Furthermore, if you had another translator—say a French translator (another program), you could not give your Japanese letter (data file) to the French translator. She would not be able to read it either. However, in this text, you are not going to be dealing with application programs, but with the Linux commands. Thus, most files you will be looking at and creating will be text files.

STEP 5   Close the Eye of Gnome window. Make the terminal window active.

STEP 6   Key in the following: **clear; cat ast.tmp; cat -n ast.tmp** [Enter]

```
[cgillay@RedHat9  floppy]$ cat ast.tmp; cat -n ast.tmp
The study of Astronomy came from Astrology.
Most scientists no longer believe in
Astrology.  The science of Astronomy is
changing every day.
     1
     2   The study of Astronomy came from Astrology.
     3   Most scientists no longer believe in
     4   Astrology.  The science of Astronomy is
     5   changing every day.
[cgillay@RedHat9  floppy]$
```

WHAT'S **HAPPENING?** In this case, the above is a text file (ASCII file), so you can read it. You first cleared the screen with the **clear** command. You then, using the **cat** command, "opened" your file, **ast.tmp**, and saw the contents displayed on the screen. The second iteration of **cat** used the **-n** option, which placed line numbers in your file. Whenever a file is readable on the screen, as this one is, you know it is an ASCII file.

This was one of the files you copied to the **class** directory, both in your home directory as well as to your BOOK disk. Is the content of the file the same wherever you copied it? If it is, you will know that the **cp** command makes no changes to any information in a file when it copies it.

STEP 7   Key in the following: **cat ast.tmp class/ast.tmp ~/class/ast.tmp** [Enter]

```
[cgillay@RedHat9  floppy]$ cat  ast.tmp  class/ast.tmp  ~/class/ast.tmp
The study of Astronomy came from Astrology.
Most scientists no longer believe in
Astrology.  The science of Astronomy is
changing every day.

The study of Astronomy came from Astrology.
Most scientists no longer believe in
Astrology.  The science of Astronomy is
changing every day.

The study of Astronomy came from Astrology.
Most scientists no longer believe in
Astrology.  The science of Astronomy is
changing every day.
[cgillay@RedHat9  floppy]$
```

WHAT'S HAPPENING? The contents of the files are the same. Copying the file from one location to another had no impact on the contents. With the **cat** command, you may also display multiple files. When you are using the same command with multiple arguments, you need only spaces between the file names—you do not need to reenter the command and separate the commands and arguments using a semi-colon. You only need to do that when the commands are different. You may also use wildcards with the **cat** command.

STEP 8 Key in the following: **cat *.tmp** Enter

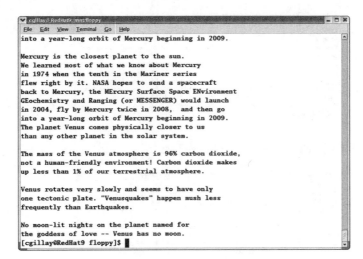

WHAT'S HAPPENING? You saw the contents of all the files that have **.tmp** as an extension. However, the files scrolled by so quickly that you could not see them all. The same is true if you had a text file that was longer than one screen.

STEP 9 Key in the following: **cat personal.fil** Enter

```
cgillay@RedHat9:/mnt/floppy                                          _ □ x
File   Edit   View   Terminal   Go   Help
Babchuk     Nicholas  13 Stratford   Sun City West   AZ   Professor
Babchuk     Bianca    13 Stratford   Sun City West   AZ   Professor
Rodriguez   Bob       20 Elm         Ontario         CA   Systems Analyst
Helm        Milton    333 Meadow     Sherman Oaks    CA   Consultant
Suzuki      Charlene  567 Abbey      Rochester       MI   Day Care Teacher
Markiw      Nicholas  354 Bell       Phoenix         AZ   Engineer
Markiw      Emily     10 Zion        Sun City West   AZ   Retired
Nyles       John      12 Brooks      Sun City West   AZ   Retired
Nyles       Sophie    12 Brooks      Sun City West   CA   Retired
Markiw      Nick      10 Zion        Sun City West   AZ   Retired
Washingon   Tyrone    345 Newport    Orange          CA   Manager
Jones       Steven    32 North       Phoenix         AZ   Buyer
Smith       David     120 Collins    Orange          CA   Chef
Babchuk     Walter    12 View        Thousand Oaks   CA   President
Babchuk     Deana     12 View        Thousand Oaks   CA   Housewife
Jones       Cleo      355 Second     Ann Arbor       MI   Clerk
Gonzales    Antonio   40 Northern    Ontario         CA   Engineer
JONES       JERRY     244 East       Mission Viejo   CA   Systems Analyst
Lo          Ophelia   1213 Wick      Phoenix         AZ   Writer
Jones       Ervin     15 Fourth      Santa Cruz      CA   Banker
Perez       Sergio    134 Seventh    Ann Arbor       MI   Editor
Yuan        Suelin    56 Twin Leaf   Orange          CA   Artist
Markiw      Nicholas  12 Fifth       Glendale        AZ   Engineer
[cgillay@RedHat9 floppy]$
```

WHAT'S HAPPENING? The **cat** command does not allow you to scroll through the files one screenful at a time. The **more** or **less** commands do allow you to scroll one screen at a time. The **more** command is a filter for paging through text one screenful at a time, but only forward. You may not page back through a file using the **more** command. The **less** command is similar to **more** but allows backward movement as well as forward movement through a file.

STEP 10 Key in the following: **more personal.fil** <kbd>Enter</kbd>

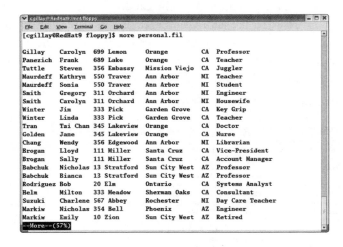

STEP 11 Press <kbd>Enter</kbd> twice. Press the <kbd>Space Bar</kbd>.

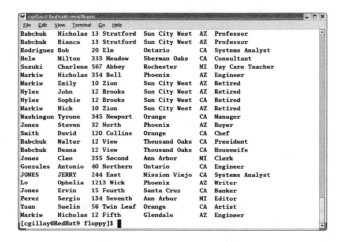

WHAT'S HAPPENING? Pressing the <kbd>Enter</kbd> key moved you a line at a time. Pressing the <kbd>Space Bar</kbd> took you to the end of the file and returned you to the prompt.

STEP 12 Key in the following: **more *.tmp** <kbd>Enter</kbd>. Press <kbd>Enter</kbd> twice. Press the <kbd>Space Bar</kbd> twice.

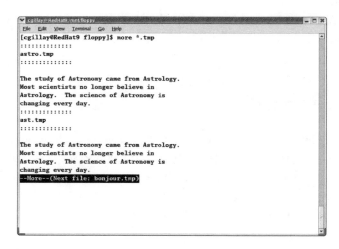

WHAT'S HAPPENING? Pressing [Enter] moved you one line at a time. Pressing the [Space Bar] took you to the next file.

STEP 13 Press **q**. Key in the following: **less personal.fil** [Enter]. Press **b**. Press **f**. Press the [↑] arrow key three times.

```
cgillay@RedHat9:/mnt/floppy
File   Edit   View   Terminal   Go   Help
Chang       Wendy     356 Edgewood  Ann Arbor      MI  Librarian
Brogan      Lloyd     111 Miller    Santa Cruz     CA  Vice-President
Brogan      Sally     111 Miller    Santa Cruz     CA  Account Manager
Babchuk     Nicholas  13 Stratford  Sun City West  AZ  Professor
Babchuk     Bianca    13 Stratford  Sun City West  AZ  Professor
Rodriguez   Bob       20 Elm        Ontario        CA  Systems Analyst
Helm        Milton    333 Meadow    Sherman Oaks   CA  Consultant
Suzuki      Charlene  567 Abbey     Rochester      MI  Day Care Teacher
Markiw      Nicholas  354 Bell      Phoenix        AZ  Engineer
Markiw      Emily     10 Zion       Sun City West  AZ  Retired
Nyles       John      12 Brooks     Sun City West  AZ  Retired
Nyles       Sophie    12 Brooks     Sun City West  CA  Retired
Markiw      Nick      10 Zion       Sun City West  AZ  Retired
Washingon   Tyrone    345 Newport   Orange         CA  Manager
Jones       Steven    32 North      Phoenix        AZ  Buyer
Smith       David     120 Collins   Orange         CA  Chef
Babchuk     Walter    12 View       Thousand Oaks  CA  President
Babchuk     Deana     12 View       Thousand Oaks  CA  Housewife
Jones       Cleo      355 Second    Ann Arbor      MI  Clerk
Gonzales    Antonio   40 Northern   Ontario        CA  Engineer
JONES       JERRY     244 East      Mission Viejo  CA  Systems Analyst
Lo          Ophelia   1213 Wick     Phoenix        AZ  Writer
Jones       Ervin     15 Fourth     Santa Cruz     CA  Banker
:
```

WHAT'S HAPPENING? The **less** command allows you forward and backward movement through a file. If you wanted to know all the movement keystrokes, you could key in **less --help**.

STEP 14 Press **q**.

WHAT'S HAPPENING? You have returned to the system prompt. The **less** command requires you to use the **q** to quit the program, whereas **more** pages through the file and returns you to the prompt, although you can use **q** to exit more quickly.

5.12 • The cp and ls Commands
with Directories and Dot Addressing

You are going to see how commands work with directories by using the **cp** command to place files in the directories and by using the **ls** command to see that the files were copied. Because the command line can get unwieldy, using the dot and the double dot is a convenient shorthand way of writing commands. Remember, the dot (.) represents the current directory, and the double dot (..) represents the parent of the current directory. The only directory that does not have a parent is the root directory, because it is the ultimate parent of all the directories on a disk. You are going to use **cp** as an example, but many commands work with the dot and double-dot.

5.13 • Activity: Using cp and ls
with Directories Dot Addressing

Note: The BOOK disk is mounted. You are using a terminal window. Your **/mnt/floppy** directory is your default directory.

STEP 1 Key in the following: **cp data/good.txt** [Enter]

```
[cgillay@RedHat9  floppy]$  cp data/good.txt
cp: missing destination file
Try 'cp -help' for more information.
[cgillay@RedHat9  floppy]$
```

WHAT'S HAPPENING? You must have a destination when you use the **cp** command. The destination in this case is **/mnt/floppy**. However, the single dot represents the current directory, which is **/mnt/floppy**. Thus, as a destination you may use the **.**, the single dot.

STEP 2   Key in the following: **cp data/good.txt . ; ls good.txt** Enter

```
[cgillay@RedHat9  floppy]$  cp  data/good.txt  . ; ls  good.txt
good.txt
[cgillay@RedHat9  floppy]$
```

WHAT'S HAPPENING? Using the single dot (.) meant that you did not have to key in **cp data/good.txt /mnt/floppy** since the . represented the current directory.

STEP 3   Key in the following: **mkdir -p astronomy/earth; cd astronomy/earth; ls** Enter

```
[cgillay@RedHat9  floppy]$ mkdir -p astronomy/earth; cd astronomy/earth; ls
[cgillay@RedHat9  earth]$
```

WHAT'S HAPPENING? You created both the **astronomy** and **earth** directories. You could do so because you used the **mkdir** command with the **-p** option. You changed the default directory to the **earth** directory, which is under the **astronomy** directory under /**mnt/floppy** directory. The prompt displays **[cgillay@RedHat9 earth]** as the default directory. Remember: *All activities will occur in the directory* /**mnt/floppy/astronomy/earth**, *unless you specify another path*. When you keyed in **ls**, it showed you the contents of only the current default directory. The directory is empty of files.

STEP 4   Key in the following: **cp /mnt/floppy/class/ast.tmp final.rpt; ls** Enter

```
[cgillay@RedHat9  earth]$ cp /mnt/floppy/class/ast.tmp  final.rpt; ls
final.rpt
[cgillay@RedHat9  earth]$
```

WHAT'S HAPPENING? The file called **ast.tmp** in the subdirectory **/mnt/floppy/class** was successfully copied to the subdirectory **/mnt/floppy/astronomy/earth**, but is now called **final.rpt**. You used the absolute path. Remember that the first / in any command line always means the root directory. Any other / in the command line is simply a delimiter. Next, you are going to make a copy of the file in the current directory, so you do not need to include the absolute path name; here, you can use the relative path name.

STEP 5   Key in the following: **cp final.rpt note2.tmp; cp final.rpt note3.tmp; ls** Enter

```
[cgillay@RedHat9  earth]$ cp final.rpt note2.tmp; cp final.rpt note3.tmp; ls
final.rpt  note2.tmp  note3.tmp
[cgillay@RedHat9  earth]$
```

WHAT'S HAPPENING? You copied two files. You did not have to include the absolute path name because the default path was assumed. You used the relative path name. The operating system always assumes the default directory, unless you tell it otherwise. Technically, the commands looked like this:

```
cp  /mnt/floppy/astronomy/earth  /mnt/floppy/astronomy/earth/note2.tmp
```

and

```
cp  /mnt/floppy/astronomy/earth/final.rpt  /mnt/floppy/astronomy/earthnote3.tmp
```

You can see that using the relative path eliminates a lot of typing. You see only the files that are in the default directory. You can create directories from the current directory. You may use the dot technique to save keystrokes.

STEP 6   Key in the following: **mkdir -p ../../work/clients; mkdir ../../work/ads** [Enter]

STEP 7   Key in the following: **ls ../../work** [Enter]

```
[cgillay@RedHat9  earth]$ mkdir -p ../../work/clients; mkdir ../../work/ads

[cgillay@RedHat9  earth]$ ls ../../work
ads  clients
[cgillay@RedHat9  earth]$
```

WHAT'S HAPPENING? The first command said to create a directory called **clients** under **work**. Since **work** did not exist, you used the **-p** option to create it first. The **../..** said to go to the parent of **earth** (**astronomy**), then go to the parent of **astronomy** (**/mnt/floppy**) and there create a directory called **work**, then create the directory called **clients** under **work**. Since you already created the **work** directory, the second command said create a directory called **ads**. The **../..** said to go to the parent of **earth** (**astronomy**), then go to the parent of **astronomy** (**/mnt/floppy**) and there create a directory under **work** called **ads**. Now that you have created the directories of interest, you can use wildcards to copy files to them.

STEP 8   Key in the following: **cp * ../../work/clients; ls ../../work/clients** [Enter]

```
[cgillay@RedHat9  earth]$  cp * ../../work/clients; ls ../../work/clients
final.rpt   note2.tmp   note3.tmp
[cgillay@RedHat9  earth]$
```

WHAT'S HAPPENING? The syntax is the same: the command, **cp**, copies the source, * (all the files in the default directory, **/mnt/floppy/astronomy/earth**), to the destination, **/mnt/floppy/work/clients**. Since you used the double dots to move up the directory tree, you did not have to use the absolute path. The operating system used or *defaulted* to the current file names. You can copy files from anywhere to anywhere provided you give the source and destination location. If you use the relative path, be sure you are aware of the current default directory.

STEP 9   Key in the following: **cp final.rpt ../first.tst; ls ..** [Enter]

```
[cgillay@RedHat9  earth]$  cp final.rpt ../first.tst; ls ..
earth   first.tst
[cgillay@RedHat9  earth]$
```

WHAT'S HAPPENING? You copied the file called **final.rpt** located in the current directory, **earth**, to the parent of **earth**, which is **astronomy**. You gave it a new name, **first.tst**. Instead of having to key in **/mnt/floppy/astronomy/first.tst** as the destination file path, you used the shorthand name for **/mnt/floppy/astronomy**, which is **..**, meaning the parent of **earth**. You included **/** as a delimiter between the **..** and **first.tst**.

STEP 10 Key in the following: **mkdir ../venus** [Enter]

STEP 11 Key in the following: **cp ../first.tst ../venus/last.tst; ls ../venus** [Enter]

```
[cgillay@RedHat9  earth]$  mkdir ../venus
[cgillay@RedHat9  earth]$  cp ../first.tst ../venus/last.tst; ls ../venus
last.tst
[cgillay@RedHat9  earth]$
```

WHAT'S HAPPENING? You first created a directory called **venus** under the **/mnt/floppy/astronomy** directory. You then copied the file called **first.tst** from the **astronomy** directory to the **venus** directory, which is a child directory of **astronomy**. The long way to key in the command is to use the absolute path. If you issued the commands using the absolute path, they would look like the following:

```
mkdir  /mnt/floppy/astronomy/venus
```

and

```
cp  /mnt/floppy/astronomy/first.tst   /mnt/floppy/astronomy/venus/last.tst
```

Because you used the double dots in creating the directory, the first **..** represented the parent of **earth** (**astronomy**), and the **venus** directory was created in the parent (**astronomy**). When you copied the source file, the first **..** represented the parent of **earth**. You did not have to key in **/mnt/floppy/astronomy**. However, you did need to key in the **/** preceding the file name. This **/** is a delimiter. You also did not need to key in **/mnt/floppy/astronomy** in the destination file. Instead you used the **..**, the directory markers. You did need to key in the **/** preceding **venus** and the **/** preceding **last.tst** because they were needed as delimiters to separate directory names and file names. You can use relative pathnames to save keystrokes.

STEP 12 Key in the following: **cd ../..** [Enter]

WHAT'S HAPPENING? You have returned to the **/mnt/floppy** directory.

5.14 ● Overwriting Files

When you made copies of files, you gave unique names to files in the same directory. One of the reasons for doing this is that, when you tried to use the same file name in the same directory, you got this error message: **cp: 'filename' and 'filename' are the same file.** The operating system would not permit you to make that error.

However, the rule of unique file names is true only if the files are in the same directory. If you are using more than one directory, the system *will* let you use the same file name. In reality, although the file names seem to be the same, they are not. The full file name contains the path. Thus, **/mnt/floppy/this.fil** and **/mnt/floppy/data/this.fil** are actually unique names because of the path. There have been no problems so far in the activities you have been doing because, when you copied the source file from one directory to another, it was a unique file in that new directory.

Overwrite means just what it says; it writes over or replaces what used to be in that file. If the content of the source file is different from the content of the destination file, overwriting the destination file will change its content. Both files will now have not only the same file *name* but also the same file *contents*. The previous content of the destination file will be gone. Overwriting also happens on the same disk when the destination file name already exists. The same rules apply to directories.

The overwrite process seems dangerous because you could lose the data in a file. Why are you not protected from this error? Because, in working with computers, typically, you *do* want to overwrite files. That is, you do want to replace the old contents of a file with the new, revised contents.

Data changes all the time. For example, if you have a customer list stored as a file named **customer.lst** in a directory, the information in the file (the data) changes as you add customers, delete customers, and update information about customers. When you have completed your work for the day, you want to back up your file because you are working with it on a daily basis. Typically you back it up to another disk, but in the Linux file system, the other disk is simply a directory off the root directory. So you might have a file called **customer.lst** in your home directory and want to copy it to your **/mnt/floppy** directory as a backup. Since **customer.lst** is clearly a descriptive file name, you really do not want to create a new file name every time you copy the file to your backup because creating new file names and then tracking current files can be time consuming and confusing. In addition, if you are working with a file on a daily basis, you could end up with hundreds of files. In reality, you do not care about last week's or yesterday's customer information, or the old file; you care about the current version and its backup file. When copying a file for backup purposes, you do want the source file to overwrite the destination file.

If you do not, you have some options that can be used that can protect you. These include **-b**, **-p**, and **-i**. See Table 5.2, "cp Options." In other editions of Linux, you will automatically be prompted before you attempt to overwrite a file, and you will not need to use the **-i** option.

5.15 ● Activity: Overwriting Files Using the cp Command and Using the -b, -p, and -i Options

Note: The BOOK disk is mounted. You are using a terminal window. Your **/mnt/floppy** directory is your default directory.

STEP 1   Key in the following: **cat bye.txt good.txt** [Enter]

```
[cgillay@RedHat9  floppy]$  cat bye.txt good.txt
GOODBYE ALL.
IS THIS ALL THERE IS?
YES!


Remember, whenever you are doing your
best, you are doing a GOOD job!
[cgillay@RedHat9   floppy]$
```

WHAT'S HAPPENING? You have displayed the contents of two files and can see that each file contains different data.

STEP 2 Key in the following: **cp bye.txt good.txt** [Enter]

```
[cgillay@RedHat9  floppy]$  cp bye.txt  good.txt
[cgillay@RedHat9  floppy]$
```

Note: If you see a prompt asking you if you want to overwrite the file, key in **y**.

WHAT'S HAPPENING? The file **bye.txt** was successfully copied to the file called **good.txt**, but what about the contents of the file? Did anything change?

STEP 3 Key in the following: **cat bye.txt good.txt** [Enter]

```
[cgillay@RedHat9  floppy]$ cat bye.txt  good.txt
GOODBYE ALL.
IS THIS ALL THERE IS?
YES!

GOODBYE ALL.
IS THIS ALL THERE IS?
YES!

[cgillay@RedHat9  floppy]$
```

WHAT'S HAPPENING? The file contents are now identical. What used to be inside the file called **good.txt** located in the **/mnt/floppy** directory has been overwritten or replaced (gone forever) by the contents of the file called **bye.txt**. You should be aware of how this works so that you do not overwrite a file accidentally. You cannot overwrite or copy a file when the source file and the destination file in the same subdirectory have exactly the same file name.

STEP 4 Key in the following: **cp ast.99 ast.99** [Enter]

```
[cgillay@RedHat9  floppy]$  cp ast.99  ast.99
cp: 'ast.99'and 'ast.99' are the same file
[cgillay@RedHat9  floppy]$
```

WHAT'S HAPPENING? You tried to copy (overwrite) a file onto itself and got an error message. However, what if you did want to protect yourself from accidentally overwriting a file? You can do so by using the **-i** option—the interactive mode, which will ask you if you want to overwrite an existing file or not.

STEP 5 Key in the following: **cp -i data/good.txt good.txt** [Enter]

```
[cgillay@RedHat9  floppy]$  cp  -i  data/good.txt  good.txt
cp: overwrite 'good.txt'?
```

WHAT'S HAPPENING? Here you are informed that you have an existing file by the name of **good.txt** in the **/mnt/floppy** directory. If you want to overwrite it with the contents of the file **/mnt/floppy/data/good.txt**, you key in y. If not, you key in **n**.

STEP 6 Key in the following: **y** [Enter]

STEP 7 Key in the following: **cat good.txt** [Enter]

```
cp: overwrite 'good.txt'? y
[cgillay@RedHat9  floppy]$ cat good.txt


Remember, whenever you are doing your
best, you are doing a GOOD job!
[cgillay@RedHat9  floppy]$
```

WHAT'S HAPPENING? You had the choice of overwriting the file or not. In this case you choose to overwrite it. You can also use the **-b** option to create a backup copy of a file when you overwrite it.

STEP 8 Key in the following: **cp -b bye.txt good.txt** [Enter]

```
[cgillay@RedHat9  floppy]$  cp -b  bye.txt  good.txt
[cgillay@RedHat9  floppy]$
```

WHAT'S HAPPENING? The file **bye.txt** was successfully copied to the file called **good.txt.** The **good.txt** file was overwritten, but you now have a backup copy with the original contents called **good.txt ˜** .

STEP 9 Key in the following: **ls good.*; cat good.txt good.txt ˜** [Enter]

```
[cgillay@RedHat9  floppy]$ ls good.*; cat good.txt  good.txt~
good.txt     good.txt~


GOODBYE ALL.
IS THIS ALL THERE IS?
YES!


Remember, whenever you are doing your
best, you are doing a GOOD job!
[cgillay@RedHat9  floppy]$
```

WHAT'S HAPPENING? Although you overwrote **good.txt** with the contents of **bye.txt**, you still have a copy of the original file with the original, but the name now has a tilde at the end. Another useful option that can be used with **cp** is the **-p** option. The **-p** option will preserve the attributes of the original file, such as the permissions and the date.

STEP 10 Key in the following: **cd; ls -l /mnt/floppy/titan.txt** [Enter]

```
[cgillay@RedHat9  floppy]$ cd; ls -l  /mnt/floppy/titan.txt
-rwxr-xr-x  1 cgillay  cgillay  529 Oct 31 2001 /mnt/floppy/titan.txt
[cgillay@RedHat9  cgillay]$
```

WHAT'S HAPPENING? You changed directories to your home directory. You then looked at the attributes of the **titan.txt** file on the BOOK disk. Since you mounted the floppy disk, you are the owner of the file with certain specific permissions. The date of the file is **Oct 31 2001**.

STEP 11 Key in the following: **cp /mnt/floppy/titan.txt . ; ls -l titan.txt** [Enter]

```
[cgillay@RedHat9  cgillay]$ cp  /mnt/floppy/titan.txt  .  ; ls -l  titan.txt
-rwxrwxr-x  1  cgillay  cgillay       529 Jun 27 10:33 titan.txt
[cgillay@RedHat9  cgillay]$
```

WHAT'S HAPPENING? You copied the **titan.txt** file to your home directory. You used the single dot as your destination instead of having to key in **/home/*username***. The file permissions and owner remained the same, but the file date changed. The file used the current date, not the date of the original file.

STEP 12 Key in the following: **cp -p /mnt/floppy/titan.txt . ; ls -l titan.txt**

```
[cgillay@RedHat9  cgillay]$ cp -p  /mnt/floppy/titan.txt  .; ls -l  titan.txt
-rwxr-xr-x  1  cgillay  cgillay  529 Oct 31 2001 titan.txt
[cgillay@RedHat9  cgillay]$
```

WHAT'S HAPPENING? Because you used the **-p** option (preserve), it preserved some of the attributes of the file. This option will also preserve the original owner and permissions.

STEP 13 Key in the following: **ls -l /politics/test.fil** Enter

```
[cgillay@RedHat9  cgillay]$ ls -l  /politics/test.fil
-rwxrwxr--  1  alincoln  alincoln   16 Jun 9 09:34  /politics/test.fil
[cgillay@RedHat9  cgillay]$
```

WHAT'S HAPPENING? This file has a set of permissions, is owned by the user **alincoln**, and has a specific date.

STEP 14 Key in the following: **cp /politics/test.fil .; ls -l test.fil** Enter

```
[cgillay@RedHat9  cgillay]$ cp /politics/test.fil .; ls  -l  test.fil
-rwxrwxr--  1  cgillay  cgillay   16 Jun 27 10:47 test.fil
[cgillay@RedHat9  cgillay]$
```

WHAT'S HAPPENING? When you copied the file to your home directory, the new copy of the file took the ownership attributes (user and group ownership). The date became the current date.

STEP 15 Key in the following: **cp -p /politics/test.fil .; ls -l test.fil** Enter

```
[cgillay@RedHat9  cgillay]$ cp -p /politics/test.fil .; ls  -l  test.fil
-rwxrwxr--  1  cgillay  cgillay       16 Jun 9 09:34 test.fil
[cgillay@RedHat9  cgillay]$
```

WHAT'S HAPPENING? The date remained the same as the original file in the **politics** directory, but **test.fil** still took your ownership attributes (user and group ownership), even though you used the -p option. Only the root user can change the ownership of a file—an ordinary user cannot. When you copy a file into your home directory, you become the owner. However, **-p** did preserve the original file date. When you, as an ordinary user, use the **-p** option with the **cp** command, it will preserve what attributes it can for the ordinary user.

5.16 • Creating Files and Combining Text Files with the cat Command

You may want to create some simple text files for practice purposes. You are going to use some dummy files. "Dummy" means that these files have no particular meaning. You can use these files to practice file-management commands. The concept of dummy files and/or dummy data is common in data processing. Often, data-processing professionals wish to test different portions of systems or programs. For instance, if you were writing a program about employee benefits, rather than looking at every employee, you would create dummy files and data in order to have a smaller representative sample that is manageable and easily tested. Not only are the files smaller, they are samples. If the data gets harmed in any way, it has no impact on the "real" data. You use the **cat** command and redirection. The syntax is **cat > filename**. Once you key in this command, you are taken to the next line. You keep keying in data until you are finished. Once you are finished, you press Ctrl + D to tell Linux you are done entering data. The file then gets written to disk.

You may also combine the contents of two or more text files. This process is known as *concatenation* of files. To concatenate means to put together. You might wish to concatenate when you have several short text files that would be easier to work with if they were combined into one file. When you combine files, nothing happens to the original files; they remain intact. You just create another new file from the original files.

5.17 • Activity: Combining and Creating Files Using the cat Command

Note: The BOOK disk is mounted. You are using a terminal window. Your home directory is your default directory.

STEP 1   Key in the following: **cd /mnt/floppy** Enter

STEP 2   Key in the following: **cat earth.one earth.two** Enter

```
[cgillay@RedHat9  floppy]$  cat earth.one earth.two

This is the first Earth file.

Did you know that the Earth's
inner-most region is called
the core?  Did you know it is
made up primarily of iron and nickel?


This is the second Earth file.

Did you know that there is a
region around the earth filled
with charged particles having
high energy? Two such regions are
called the VAN ALLEN BELTS, named
for James Van Allen who helped to
detect them in 1958.
```

```
[cgillay@RedHat9    floppy]$
```

WHAT'S HAPPENING? You have displayed the contents of two files on the screen. Each file is unique, with different file names and different file contents. You are going to place the contents of these two files into a new file called **joined.sam**, which will consist of the contents of the first file, **earth.one**, followed by the contents of the second file, **earth.two**. The new file will reside in the **/mnt/floppy** directory.

STEP 3   Key in the following: **cat   earth.one earth.two > joined.sam** Enter

STEP 4   Key in the following: **cat joined.sam** Enter

```
[cgillay@RedHat9    floppy]$ cat earth.one earth.two > joined.sam
[cgillay@RedHat9    floppy]$ cat joined.sam

This is the first Earth file.

Did you know that the Earth's
inner-most region is called
the core?  Did you know it is
made up primarily of iron and nickel?

This is the second Earth file.

Did you know that there is a
region around the earth filled
with charged particles having
high energy? Two such regions are
called the VAN ALLEN BELTS, named
for James Van Allen who helped to
detect them in 1958.

[cgillay@RedHat9    floppy]$
```

WHAT'S HAPPENING? You are making one destination file out of two source files. What you did here was to say **cat** (the command) the contents of the file called **earth.one** *and* the contents of the file called **earth.two** (source) and redirect (**>**) the contents to a new file called **joined.sam**, which will reside in the default directory. The content of the file **joined.sam** consists of the content of the file **earth.one**, followed by the content of the file **earth.two**. The content in **joined.sam** does not show any file names. You do not know where one file ended and the next began. **joined.sam** is a new file, but you did not destroy or in any way alter the two original source files, **earth.one** or **earth.two**. You can prove this by using the **cat** command.

STEP 5   Key in the following: **cat earth.one earth.two** Enter

```
[cgillay@RedHat9    floppy]$  cat earth.one earth.two

This is the first Earth file.
```

```
Did you know that the Earth's
inner-most region is called
the core?  Did you know it is
made up primarily of iron and nickel?

This is the second Earth file.

Did you know that there is a
region around the earth filled
with charged particles having
high energy? Two such regions are
called the VAN ALLEN BELTS, named
for James Van Allen who helped to
detect them in 1958.

[cgillay@RedHat9  floppy]$
```

WHAT'S **HAPPENING?** As you can see, you created a third file from the contents of two files, but the original files remained unchanged. You can also use wildcards to join files. If you wanted to join all the files that began with **ast** and place them into a new file called **allastro**, you can do so using wildcards.

STEP 6   Key in the following: **cat ast*.* > allastro; cat allastro** [Enter]

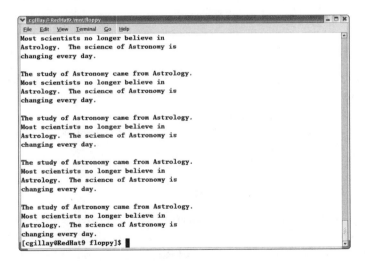

WHAT'S **HAPPENING?** As you can see, you joined together the contents of all the files that had **ast** as the first three letters in their file names into a new file called **allastro**. Since these are text files, they are readable on the screen. You may also create a new text file using the syntax **cat > *newfile***. In the next example, press [Enter] at the end of each line. Do not key in [Enter]. At the completion of data entry, press [Ctrl] + D.

STEP 7   Key in the following:
      cat > cities [Enter]

Orange Enter
Mission Viejo Enter
Laguna Beach Enter
Tustin Enter
Irvine Enter
Pasadena Enter
Los Angeles Enter
Altadena Enter
Whittier Enter
Villa Park Enter
Ctrl + **d**

STEP 8   Key in the following: **cat cities** Enter

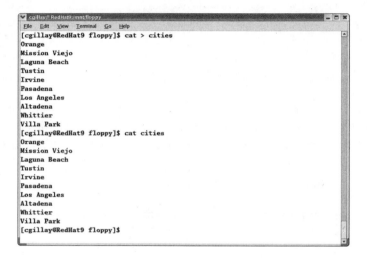

WHAT'S HAPPENING? In Step 7, you took the input from the keyboard (standard input). The redirect output symbol (>) causes the shell to associate the standard output with the file specified on the command line, **cities**. In Step 8, the **cat** command "copied" the file **cities** to standard output, the terminal. Since the shell directs standard output to the terminal, the end result is that the content of the file is displayed on the terminal.

5.18 • The touch Command

Sometimes you will want to change the modification date and time of a file without actually changing the content of the file. This task often occurs while administering the system where the administrator will want to tell a process to reload a configuration file, and this can only occur if the date/time stamp of the file is updated. You can reset the modification date stamp of an existing file to the current date and time by using the **touch** command.

Another common use of the **touch** command is to create an empty file. An empty file can be useful when a program or a script needs to create a temporary file to indicate a special state. The only difference is that you use the **touch** command with a new file name. The syntax is

```
touch  [option]  file
```

Table 5.4, "**touch** Options," lists some of the major options that can be used with the **touch** command.

Option	Description
-a	Only changes the access time.
-c	Prevents **touch** from creating the file if it does not already exist.
-m	Only changes the modification time.

Table 5.4 • touch Options

5.19 • Activity: Using the touch Command

Note: The BOOK disk is mounted. You are using a terminal window. The **/mnt/floppy** directory is your default directory.

STEP 1   Key in the following: **touch foo-a; ls -l foo-a; cat foo-a** Enter

```
[cgillay@RedHat9  floppy]$ touch  foo-a; ls  -l foo-a; cat  foo-a
-rwxr-xr-x 1   cgillay   cgillay   0   Jun 27 11:38   foo-a
[cgillay@RedHat9  floppy]$
```

WHAT'S HAPPENING? You have just created a file called **foo-a**. You can see it is an empty file, as it has 0 bytes. When you used the **cat** command, nothing was displayed since the file was empty.

STEP 2   Key in the following: **cat dress.up** Enter

STEP 3   Key in the following: **ls -l dress.up; touch dress.up; ls -l dress.up** Enter

```
[cgillay@RedHat9  floppy]$ cat dress.up

There are so many beautiful things that
dress up our universe. The nebulas appear
to be "dressed" in lovely veils of translucent
clouds.  Wonderful pictures of our universe
can be seen at http://antwrp.gsfc.nasa.gov/apod/astropix.html
Take a look at the archive files to see!
[cgillay@RedHat9  floppy]$ ls -l dress.up; touch dress.up; ls -l dress.up
-rwxr-xr-x  1   cgillay   cgillay   284   Oct 30 2001    dress.up
-rwxr-xr-x  1   cgillay   cgillay   284   Jun 27 11:41   dress.up
[cgillay@RedHat9  floppy]$
```

WHAT'S HAPPENING? By using the **touch** command, you changed the date on the **dress.up** file. Did you affect the contents?

STEP 4   Key in the following: **cat dress.up**

```
[cgillay@RedHat9  floppy]$ cat dress.up

There are so many beautiful things that
dress up our universe. The nebulas appear
to be "dressed" in lovely veils of translucent
```

```
clouds.  Wonderful pictures of our universe
can be seen at http://antwrp.gsfc.nasa.gov/apod/astropix.html
Take a look at the archive files to see!
[cgillay@RedHat9  floppy]$
```

WHAT'S **HAPPENING?** Nothing changed but the date.

STEP 5   Key in the following: **ls -l foo-a; touch -m foo-a; ls -l foo-a** ⊡Enter⊡

```
[cgillay@RedHat9  floppy]$ ls -l foo-a; touch -m foo-a; ls  -l foo-a
-rwxr-xr—x 1       cgillay cgillay        0        Jun 27 11:38   foo-a
-rwxr-xr—x 1       cgillay cgillay        0        Jun 27 11:52   foo-a
[cgillay@RedHat9  floppy]$
```

WHAT'S **HAPPENING?** By using the **-m** option with **touch**, you only changed the modification time for **foo-a**.

5.20 • Changing File Names

Often when working with files, you want to change a file name. For example, you may wish to change the name of a file to indicate an older version. You might also think of a more descriptive file name. As the contents of a file change, the old name may no longer reflect the contents. When you make a typographical error, you want to be able to correct it. One way to change the name of a file is to copy it to a different name. The **cp** command can, in this way, help to change the name of a file. You could, for example, copy the file **ast.99** to **/mnt/floppy/trip/ast.99**. But this would not actually change the name of an existing file—it would create a new file with the same contents under a different name.

You follow the same procedures to change a file name as you did to change a directory name, which you accomplished in Chapter 4. In the GUI, you right-click the file of interest, choose **Properties** and change the name in the text box or right-click the file and choose **Rename**. You may also use the **mv** command at the command line. The **mv** command does change the name of a file. The contents of the file do not change, only the name of the file. The syntax for this command is:

```
mv [option] source target
```

Table 5.4, "**mv** Options," lists some of the major options that can be used with the **mv** command.

Option	Name	Result
-f	Force	Forces the move even if the target file exists.
-i	Interactive	Queries the user before removing files.
-u	Update	Does not remove a file or link if its modification date is the same or newer than that of its replacement.
-v	Verbose	Displays each file name before removing it or renaming it.

Table 5.4 • mv Options

5.21 • Activity: Using the mv Command to Rename Files

Note: The BOOK disk is mounted. A terminal window should be open with the **/mnt/floppy** directory as your default directory.

STEP 1   Open your home directory window by clicking the **Home** icon on the desktop. Click **Information**. Click **Tree**. Select **/mnt/floppy** as the current working directory.

STEP 2   Locate **states.usa** in the right pane. Right-click **states.usa**. Point to **Open With**. Click **gedit**.

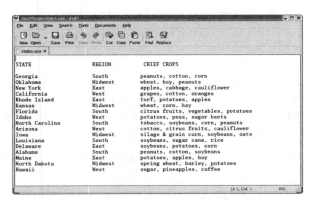

WHAT'S HAPPENING? The contents of this file deal with agricultural crops in specific states. You want to change this name to more accurately reflect this.

STEP 3   Close the gedit window. Right-click **states.usa**. Click **Properties**.

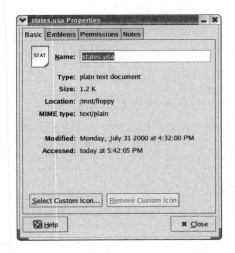

WHAT'S HAPPENING? Just as you changed a directory name in Chapter 4, you may change your file name in the same dialog box.

STEP 4   Change the file name from **states.usa** to **crops.txt**. Click **Close**.

STEP 5   Locate **crops.txt**. Right-click **crops.txt**. Point to **Open With**. Click **gedit**.

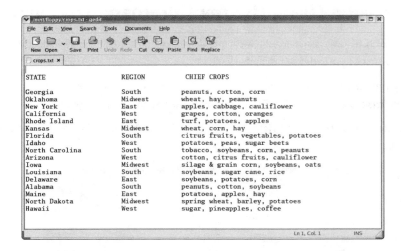

```
/mnt/floppy/crops.txt - gedit
File   Edit   View   Search   Tools   Documents   Help

New Open   Save Print   Undo Redo   Cut Copy Paste   Find Replace

crops.txt ×

STATE              REGION         CHIEF CROPS

Georgia            South          peanuts, cotton, corn
Oklahoma           Midwest        wheat, hay, peanuts
New York           East           apples, cabbage, cauliflower
California         West           grapes, cotton, oranges
Rhode Island       East           turf, potatoes, apples
Kansas             Midwest        wheat, corn, hay
Florida            South          citrus fruits, vegetables, potatoes
Idaho              West           potatoes, peas, sugar beets
North Carolina     South          tobacco, soybeans, corn, peanuts
Arizona            West           cotton, citrus fruits, cauliflower
Iowa               Midwest        silage & grain corn, soybeans, oats
Louisiana          South          soybeans, sugar cane, rice
Delaware           East           soybeans, potatoes, corn
Alabama            South          peanuts, cotton, soybeans
Maine              East           potatoes, apples, hay
North Dakota       Midwest        spring wheat, barley, potatoes
Hawaii             West           sugar, pineapples, coffee

                                                      Ln 1, Col. 1          INS
```

WHAT'S HAPPENING? As you can see, you changed the file name from **states.usa** to **crops.txt**, but the contents of the file did not change.

STEP 6   Close gedit. Close the floppy window. Make the terminal window active. Be sure **/mnt/floppy** is the active directory.

STEP 7   Key in the following: **cat green.jaz** Enter

```
[cgillay@RedHat9  floppy]$  cat green.jaz
High temperatures on Venus are caused by the
green house effect.

CO2 causes the green house effect
[cgillay@RedHat9  floppy]$
```

WHAT'S HAPPENING? You are looking at the contents of a file called **green.jaz**.

STEP 8   Key in the following: **mv green.jaz greener.jaz** Enter

STEP 9   Key in the following: **ls green.jaz greener.jaz; cat greener.jaz** Enter

```
[cgillay@RedHat9  floppy]$  mv green.jaz greener.jaz
[cgillay@RedHat9  floppy]$  ls green.jaz greener.jaz; cat green.jaz
ls: green.jaz: No such file or directory
greener.jaz

High temperatures on Venus are caused by the
green house effect.

CO2 causes the green house effect
[cgillay@RedHat9  floppy]$
```

WHAT'S HAPPENING? The **mv** command successfully renamed the file and the file contents did not change. However, you must be careful when you use **mv** with directories. In fact, the command name says it all—**mv** for move. When you use **mv** between directories, the command actually removes the file from the current directory and copies it to the new directory, overwriting any existing file.

STEP 10 Key in the following:

    cd; cat > greener.jaz `Enter`
    This is my greenest file. `Enter`
    I am going to move it from one location to another. `Enter`
    `Ctrl` **+ d**

```
[cgillay@RedHat9  floppy]$  cd; cat > greener.jaz
This is my greenest file.
I am going to move it from one location to another
[cgillay@RedHat9  cgillay]$
```

WHAT'S HAPPENING? You changed the directory from **/mnt/floppy** to your home directory. You then created a new file called **greener.jaz** with contents that are different from **greener.jaz** in the **/mnt/floppy** directory.

STEP 11 Key in the following: **mv greener.jaz /mnt/floppy** `Enter`

STEP 12 Key in the following: **cat greener.jaz /mnt/floppy/greener.jaz** `Enter`

```
[cgillay@RedHat9  cgillay]$  mv greener.jaz /mnt/floppy
[cgillay@RedHat9  cgillay]$  cat greener.jaz /mnt/floppy/greener.jaz
cat: greener.jaz: No such file or directory
This is my greenest file.
I am going to move it from one location to another.
[cgillay@RedHat9  cgillay]$
```

WHAT'S HAPPENING? The file **greener.jaz** is no longer in your home directory, but in the **/mnt/floppy** directory. Furthermore, the contents were replaced. If you are working with different directories, you must be careful. There is an option—the **-i** (interactive)option— that queries you prior to overwriting. Again, if you have a different version of Linux, you may find that the interactive mode is on automatically.

STEP 13 Key in the following:

    cat > greener.jaz `Enter`
    I am changing the contents of this file so that it `Enter`
    is not the same as the file in the /mnt/floppy directory. `Enter`
    `Ctrl` **+ d.**

STEP 14 Key in the following: **mv -i greener.jaz /mnt/floppy/greener.jaz** `Enter`

```
[cgillay@RedHat9  cgillay]$  cat > greener.jaz
I am changing the contents of this file so that it
is not the same as the file in the /mnt/floppy directory.
[cgillay@RedHat9  cgillay]$  mv -i greener.jaz  /mnt/floppy/greener.jaz
mv: overwrite '/mnt/floppy/greener.jaz'?
```

WHAT'S HAPPENING? Since you used the **-i** option, you were queried prior to overwriting the file.

STEP 15 Key in the following: **n** `Enter`

STEP 16 Key in the following: **cat greener.jaz /mnt/floppy/greener.jaz** `Enter`

```
[cgillay@RedHat9  cgillay]$  cat greener.jaz /mnt/floppy/greener.jaz
I am changing the contents of this file so that it
is not the same as the file in the /mnt/floppy directory.
This is my greenest file.
I am going to move it from one location to another.
[cgillay@RedHat9  cgillay]$
```

WHAT'S HAPPENING? In fact, you did not move the file, nor did you overwrite the file.

5.22 ● Moving Files and Renaming Directories

You learned in Chapter 4 that you could use the Nautilus file manager or the **mv** command to rename a directory. In this chapter, you also learned to use the Nautilus file manager and the **mv** command for renaming files. In reality, the **mv** command allows you to move files and directories from one location to another. In the Nautilus file manager, you can rename a file or directory by using the **Rename** command on the menu. But when you use drag and drop from one physical medium to another, your operation is a copy. When you drag and drop on the same physical medium, your operation is a move. If you want to move a directory or a single file on the same physical medium, using Nautilus file manager to drag and drop is effective. However, if you want to move or rename a group of files, using the Nautilus file manager is not as effective as using the command line.

You may always use the **mv** command from the command line. Table 5.5, "**mv** Results," specifies the results of using the **mv** command. The source column refers to what you have selected. The target column is where you are moving/renaming, and the results column is what transpires when you use the command.

Source	Target	Results
File	*newfilename* (new file that doesn't exist)	Renames file to *newfilename*.
File	File that already exists	Overwrites the contents of the existing file with the source file contents.
Directory	*newdirectoryname* (directory that doesn't exist)	Renames current source directory to *newdirectoryname*.
Directory	Directory that already exists	Moves directory to become a subdirectory of existing directory.
One or more files	Existing directory	Moves selected files to existing directory—removes those files from current location (rm) and places them in existing directory.

Table 5.5 ● mv Results

5.23 • Activity: Moving Files and Directories

Note: The BOOK disk is mounted. Your home directory is your default directory.

STEP 1   Open your home directory window by double-clicking the Home icon on the desktop. Click **Information**. Click **Tree**. Select **/mnt/floppy** as the current working directory. Expand **/mnt/floppy** in the tree.

STEP 2   Select the **data** folder in the right pane. Drag and drop **data** on the **class** folder in the tree pane. Expand **class** in the tree pane.

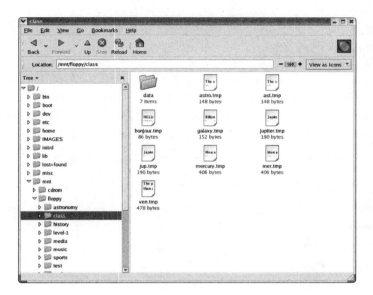

WHAT'S HAPPENING? When you dragged and dropped the **data** folder to the **class** folder, you moved it and all its files from **/mnt/floppy/data** to **/mnt/floppy/class/data**.

STEP 3   In the tree pane, click **class** to make it active. Expand it if necessary. In the right pane, drag **data** to **floppy** in the tree pane. Click **floppy** to make it active.

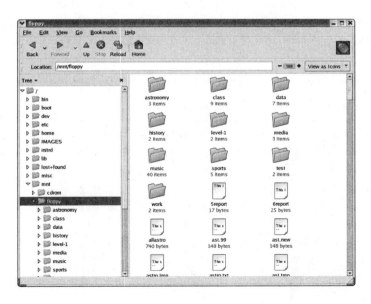

WHAT'S **HAPPENING?** You moved the **data** folder back to its original location. When you dragged and dropped the **data** folder to the **floppy** folder, you moved it and all its files from **/mnt/floppy/class** to **/mnt/floppy**.

STEP 4 Close the window. Make your terminal window active.

STEP 5 Key in the following: **cd /mnt/floppy; mkdir files** [Enter]

STEP 6 Key in the following: **cp *.99 files** [Enter]

STEP 7 Key in the following: **cd files; ls** [Enter]

```
[cgillay@RedHat9  cgillay]$  cd /mnt/floppy; mkdir  files
[cgillay@RedHat9  floppy]$  cp *.99  files
[cgillay@RedHat9  floppy]$  cd files; ls
ast.99   jup.99   mer.99   ven.99
[cgillay@RedHat9  files]$
```

WHAT'S **HAPPENING?** You created a new directory called **files** and copied all the files with a **99** extension to that directory. You then changed directories to the **files** directory.

STEP 8 Key in the following: **mkdir room; mv ast.99 jup.99 room** [Enter]

STEP 9 Key in the following: **ls . room** [Enter]

```
[cgillay@RedHat9  files]$ mkdir  room; mv ast.99 jup.99 room
[cgillay@RedHat9  files]$  ls  .   room
.:
mer.99 room  ven.99

room:
ast.99  jup.99
[cgillay@RedHat9  files]$
```

WHAT'S **HAPPENING?** Indeed, the two selected files—**ast.99** and **jup.99**—have been moved from **files** to the **room** directory. Note that when you used **ls**, you used the dot to see the listing of the current directory. You can move a directory with its files from one location to another, as well as change the name of directory. Be sure to use the double dot in front of **class/place**.

STEP 10 Key in the following: **mv room ../class/place** [Enter]

STEP 11 Key in the following: **ls . ../class/place ../class** [Enter]

```
[cgillay@RedHat9  files]$  mv room ../class/place
[cgillay@RedHat9  files]$  ls  .  ../class/place  ../class
.:
mer.99  ven.99

../class:
astro.tmp   bonjour.tmp   jupiter.tmp   mercury.tmp   place
ast.tmp     galaxy.tmp    jup.tmp       mer.tmp       ven.tmp
```

```
../class/place:
ast.99    jup.99
[cgillay@RedHat9  files]$
```

WHAT'S HAPPENING? The directory **room** was moved from **/mnt/floppy/files** to **/mnt/floppy/class**, and its name was changed from **room** to **place**. In addition, the files were moved with the directory. Again, note how you used the dot and the double dot to view your listings and move files. You can move entire directory structures, along with the files in them, with one command.

STEP 12 Key in the following: **cd ..; mkdir -p start/next** [Enter]

STEP 13 Key in the following: **cp *.jaz start/next; ls start/next** [Enter]

```
[cgillay@RedHat9  files]$  cd ..; mkdir -p start/next
[cgillay@RedHat9  floppy]$  cp *.jaz start/next; ls start/next
blue.jaz    greener.jaz
[cgillay@RedHat9  floppy]$
```

WHAT'S HAPPENING? You first moved to the **/mnt/floppy** directory. You then created a new directory, **start**, which contains a child directory, **next**, in which there are two files with the **.jaz** extension. You used the **-p** option to create **start** at the same time you created **next**. You decide that you want to place this entire directory structure beginning with **start** under the directory **files**. You can move the entire structure with the **move** command.

STEP 14 Key in the following: **mv start files** [Enter]

STEP 15 Key in the following: **ls files/start/next** [Enter]

```
[cgillay@RedHat9  floppy]$  mv start files
[cgillay@RedHat9  floppy]$ ls files/start/next
blue.jaz    greener.jaz
[cgillay@RedHat9  floppy]$
```

WHAT'S HAPPENING? As you can see, the **start** directory is no longer in the **/mnt/floppy** directory, but is now in the **files** directory. In addition, the entire structure with all the files has been moved.

STEP 16 Key in the following: **cd** [Enter]

WHAT'S HAPPENING? You returned to your home directory.

5.24 • Eliminating Files

In the various activities completed previously, you copied or created many files and directories. As you have been working, the number of files on the disk has increased dramatically—typical when working with computers. There is a kind of Murphy's Law that says you create as many files as you have disk space. However, you do not want to keep files forever. The more files and directories you have, the harder it is to keep track of what directories have which files and which files are the ones you need. Often, you are not quite sure what files are where. By keeping only the files you need, you will decrease the number of files you have to manage.

Logic should tell you that if you can copy, create, and move files, you should be able to eliminate files by deleting or erasing them. You can do these tasks using the Nautilus file manager or using **rm** at the command line. If you use the Nautilus file manager and move your files to the trash or select a file and press the $\boxed{\text{Delete}}$ key, you can recover those files in the trash by opening the Trash icon on the desktop, dragging the files from the trash, and placing them elsewhere. The files remain in the Trash directory until you choose **Empty Trash**.

When you are at the command line, you do need to be careful with the **rm** command. Once you have deleted a file, the file is gone forever. The operating system does not ask you if this is really the file you want to get rid of; it simply obeys your instructions. There is no trash folder using the command line.

The syntax of the **rm** command is:

```
rm [options] filename
```

Table 5.6, "**rm** Options," lists some of the major options that can be used with the **rm** command.

Option	Name	Result
-f	Force	Removes write-protected files without prompting.
-i	Interactive	Prompts the user for a **y** or **n**. **y** would delete the file, **n** would not.
-r, -R	Recursive	If the file is a directory, removes the entire directory and all its contents. This is a very powerful and dangerous option.
-v	Verbose	Displays the name of the file before deleting it.

Table 5.6 • rm options

5.25 • Activity: Deleting Files

Note: The BOOK disk is mounted. Your home directory is your default directory.

STEP I   Open your home directory window by double-clicking the Home icon on the desktop. Click **Information**. Click **Tree**. Be sure your home directory is the current working directory.

STEP 2   On your home directory window menu, click **File**. Click **Empty Trash**.

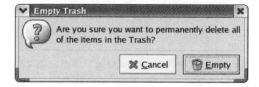

WHAT'S **HAPPENING?** If your **Empty Trash** was dimmed on the menu, there was no trash to empty. In this example, there were files in the trash. The Nautilus file manager is confirming that you do want to get rid of all in your trash. The trash is simply a directory that stores the files you have deleted on the hard drive.

STEP 3   If necessary, click **Empty**.

STEP 4   In your home directory window, right-click **galaxy.tmp**. Click **Move to Trash**.

STEP 5   In your home directory window, click **media**. Hold the Ctrl key and click **test**. While holding the Ctrl key, click **greener.jaz**; **mercury.fil**, **test.fil**, **testing.fil** and **titan.txt**.

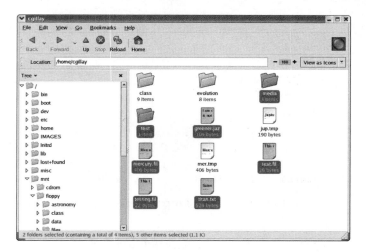

WHAT'S **HAPPENING?** When you right-clicked **galaxy.tmp** and selected **Move to Trash**, you moved it to the **trash** folder. You then selected other files, beginning with the **media** folder. You then held down the Ctrl key and selected the other files, as shown above. These files are noncontiguous (not next to one another). If the files you wished to select were contiguous (next to one another), in List view, you could select the first file, and then press the Shift key as you click the last contiguous file. You would have selected all the files between the first click and the Shift click.

STEP 6   Press the Delete key.

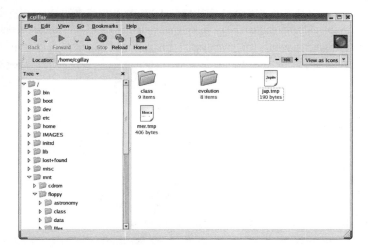

WHAT'S **HAPPENING?** You quickly deleted the files. However, the files are not deleted yet—they are in the trash.

STEP 7   Double-click the Trash icon on the desktop.

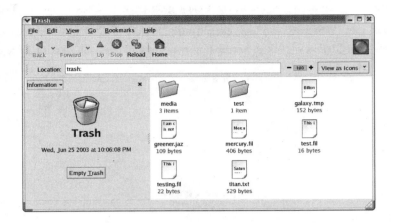

WHAT'S HAPPENING? The files are in the trash. To get rid of them, you must empty the trash.

STEP 8   Click the **Empty Trash** button. Click **Empty**. Close the Trash window. Close your home directory window.

WHAT'S HAPPENING? The files are really deleted now. It is just as easy to delete files from the command line.

STEP 9   Make the terminal window active. Key in the following: **cd** **Enter**

STEP 10   Key in the following: **ls** **Enter**

```
[cgillay@RedHat9   cgillay]$ cd
[cgillay@RedHat9   cgillay]$ ls
class   evolution   jup.tmp   mer.tmp
[cgillay@RedHat9   cgillay]$
```

WHAT'S HAPPENING? You first confirmed that you were in your home directory by keying in **cd**. Your display may be different; you may have more or fewer files and directories, but you should have the **class** directory and the two files, **jup.tmp** and **mer.tmp**, in your home directory. You are looking at the files and directories in your home directory. You want to remove the **jup.tmp** and **mer.tmp** files that you created in that directory.

STEP 11   Key in the following: **rm jup.tmp mer.tmp; ls** **Enter**

```
[cgillay@RedHat9   cgillay]$   rm jup.tmp mer.tmp; ls
class   evolution
[cgillay@RedHat9   cgillay]$
```

WHAT'S HAPPENING? You asked the **rm** command to remove the two files you specified (**jup.tmp** and **mer.tmp**). You only needed to issue the **rm** command once followed by the names of the files you wanted to delete. You placed the semi-colon just before the **ls** command since you were introducing a new command.

STEP 12   Key in the following: **cd /mnt/floppy/class; ls** **Enter**

```
[cgillay@RedHat9   cgillay]$   cd /mnt/floppy/class; ls
astro.tmp   bonjour.tmp   jupiter.tmp   mercury.tmp   place
ast.tmp     galaxy.tmp    jup.tmp       mer.tmp       ven.tmp
[cgillay@RedHat9   class]$
```

WHAT'S HAPPENING? You changed your default directory to **/mnt/floppy/class** and looked at the files that are in the directory. You want to remove the **astro.tmp** file.

STEP 13 Key in the following: **rm astro.tmp; ls** Enter

```
[cgillay@RedHat9   class]$   cd /mnt/floppy/class; ls
ast.tmp        galaxy.tmp    jup.tmp        mer.tmp   ven.tmp
bonjour.tmp   jupiter.tmp   mercury.tmp    place
[cgillay@RedHat9   class]$
```

WHAT'S HAPPENING? You asked the **rm** command to eliminate the file called **astro.tmp** located in the **class** directory. You did not need to include the path because the default directory was assumed. However, it appeared that nothing happened. You then issued the **ls** command to see if the file was deleted. The **ls** command confirmed that the file is gone. You now know that the **rm** command was executed and it removed the file called **astro.tmp**. It is no longer on the BOOK disk. What if the file you wanted to delete was not on the disk?

STEP 14 Key in the following: **rm nofile.xxx** Enter

```
[cgillay@RedHat9   class]$   rm   nofile.xxx
rm: cannot lstat 'nofile.xxx': No such file or directory
[cgillay@RedHat9   class]$
```

WHAT'S HAPPENING? In order for **rm** command to execute, it must be able to find the file to delete. Here, the file was not found.

STEP 15 Key in the following: **rm** Enter

```
[cgillay@RedHat9   cgillay]$   rm
rm: too few arguments
Try 'rm --help" for more information
[cgillay@RedHat9   class]$
```

WHAT'S HAPPENING? Not only must the operating system find the file, it must also know what file to look for. Remember, the syntax is **rm** *filename*. The message *Too few arguments* is the shell's way of saying "Get rid of what file?"

STEP 16 Key in the following: **cd ..** Enter

```
[cgillay@RedHat9   class]$   cd ..
[cgillay@RedHat9   floppy]$
```

WHAT'S HAPPENING? You have moved to the parent of **class**, which is **/mnt/floppy**.

5.26 • Deleting Files with Wildcards and Using Other Options

Using the **rm** command to eliminate files works exactly the same in other directories as it did in the previous activity. The syntax of the command remains **rm [options]** *filename*. The only difference is that you must specify the path. The operating system will follow your instructions exactly as you key them in. It does not check with you to see if you are deleting the correct file.

You have deleted individual files one file at a time. Often you want to erase many files. It is tedious to erase many files one at a time. Just as you can use the global file specifications with the **ls** and **cp** commands, you can also use the wildcards with the **rm** command. Wildcards allow you to erase a group of files with a one-line command. Remember wildcards are also called ambiguous file references and, in general, referred to as globbing. Although you can certainly delete files in the Nautilus file manager, you must select each file to be deleted. This takes more time than simply deleting the files from the command line. However, at the command line be *exceedingly* careful when using wildcards with the **rm** command. Once again, the strength of wildcards is also their weakness. Global means global. You can eliminate a group of files very quickly. If you are not careful, you could erase files you want to keep. In fact, you probably will some day. "Oh, no—not *those* files gone." However, this does not mean you should never use wildcards. They are far too useful. Just be very, *very* careful.

If you use the **-i** option, which queries you for each file deletion, you can make the use of wildcards with **rm** safer. This option allows you to tell the **rm** command to prompt you with the file name prior to deleting the file. You can also use the **-v** option, which displays each file as it is deleted. The most global (and dangerous) option is using **-r**. It is fast and deletes everything, but is extremely useful.

5.27 ● Activity: Using the rm Command with Options and Wildcards

Note: The BOOK disk is mounted. In the terminal window, the **/mnt/floppy** directory is the default directory.

STEP 1   Make the terminal window active with **/mnt/floppy** as the default directory.

STEP 2   Key in the following: **mkdir trip; cp *.99 *.txt trip; ls trip** Enter

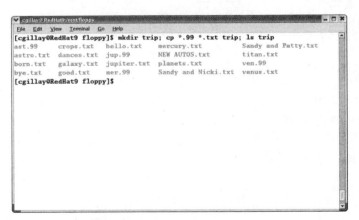

```
cgillay@RedHat9:/mnt/floppy
File  Edit  View  Terminal  Go  Help
[cgillay@RedHat9 floppy]$ mkdir trip; cp *.99 *.txt trip; ls trip
ast.99      crops.txt  hello.txt     mercury.txt      Sandy and Patty.txt
astro.txt   dances.txt jup.99        NEW AUTOS.txt    titan.txt
born.txt    galaxy.txt jupiter.txt   planets.txt      ven.99
bye.txt     good.txt   mer.99        Sandy and Nicki.txt venus.txt
[cgillay@RedHat9 floppy]$
```

WHAT'S HAPPENING? You created another directory on the BOOK disk called **trip**. You then copied files to the directory called **trip**. You first used the **mkdir** command to create the directory, then used the **cp** command with two arguments (***.99** and ***.txt**). All of those files were located in the **/mnt/floppy** directory. The destination for those files was the directory **trip** that you created. Using the **ls** command showed that all the files you requested were successfully copied to the **trip** directory.

STEP 3   Key in the following: **rm trip/ast.99; ls trip/ast.99 ast.99** Enter

```
[cgillay@RedHat9  floppy]$ rm  trip/ast.99; ls  trip/ast.99   ast.99
ls: trip/ast.99: No such file or directory
ast.99
[cgillay@RedHat9  floppy]$
```

WHAT'S HAPPENING? You had to provide the proper syntax to tell the **rm** command the location of the **ast.99** file that you wanted to delete. It was in the directory **trip**. Since the default directory is **/mnt/floppy**, you used the relative path of **trip**. You did not need to key in **/mnt/floppy/trip**. You did need to use the / between the subdirectory **trip** and the file name **ast.99** because it is used as a delimiter between the directory name and the file name. The use of the **ls** command showed **ast.99** is gone from the directory called **trip** but is still in the **/mnt/floppy** directory.

STEP 4 Key in the following: **rm -v trip/jup.99 trip/hello.txt** Enter

```
[cgillay@RedHat9  floppy]$  rm -v  trip/jup.99  trip/hello.txt
removing 'trip/jup.99'
removing 'trip/hello.txt'
[cgillay@RedHat9  floppy]$
```

WHAT'S HAPPENING? The use of the **-v** option allowed you to see what was being deleted. But it only lets you see what is going on, not change the outcome. If you want to use wildcards, which saves keystrokes, it is wise to use the **ls** command to see what files you will be deleting. Furthermore, the use of the **-v** option does not allow you to interrupt the process if you did not want to delete a file. This is where the **-i** option is useful.

STEP 5 Key in the following: **ls trip/*.99; rm -i trip/*.99** Enter

```
[cgillay@RedHat9  floppy]$  ls trip/99; rm -i trip/*.99
trip/mer.99  trip/ven.99
rm: remove regular file 'trip/mer.99'?
```

WHAT'S HAPPENING? You first confirmed which files in **trip** had a **.99** extension. Prior to doing a global erase, it is always wise to key in **ls** with the same global file specification you are going to use with the **rm** command. In this way, you can see ahead of time exactly which files will be deleted. This process allows you to confirm visually that you are not going to erase a file you want to retain. Let it be emphasized that before you use a wildcard to delete groups of files, you should use the **ls** command to see the files you are going to delete. For instance, if you had a file called **testing.99**, the command **rm trip/*.99** would remove **mer.99**, **ven.99**, and **testing.99**. Using the **ls** command with wildcards will let you display on the screen all the files that have been selected by *.99, which would include the **testing.99** file that you did not want to erase. If you had keyed in **rm trip/*.99**, all the *.99 files in the **trip** directory would have been deleted. Remember, the operating system does not come back and tell you, "Oh, by the way, **testing.99** is included with the *.99 files; did you want to erase that file?" The **rm** command simply eliminates all the .99 files in the **trip** directory because that is what you told it to do.

In addition to displaying the files you are going to delete, an even safer choice is to use the **-i** option. Then, you are acting interactively with the **rm** command. It is waiting for a **y** or **n**. **y** means yes, you do want to delete the file; **n** means no, you do not want to delete the file.

STEP 6 Key in the following: **y** Enter

```
[cgillay@RedHat9  floppy]$  ls trip/*.99; rm -i trip/*.99
trip/mer.99    trip/ven.99
rm: remove regular file `trip/mer.99'? y
rm: remove regular file `trip/ven.99'?
```

STEP 7   Key in the following: **n** [Enter]

STEP 8   Key in the following: **ls trip/*.99** [Enter]

```
[cgillay@RedHat9  floppy]$  ls trip/*.99 rm -i trip/*.99
trip/mer.99    trip/ven.99
rm: remove regular file `trip/mer.99'? y
rm: remove regular file `trip/ven.99'? n
[cgillay@RedHat9  floppy]$ ls trip/*.99
trip/ven.99
[cgillay@RedHat9  floppy]$
```

WHAT'S HAPPENING? The **y** choice removed **mer.99**, and the **n** choice retained the **ven.99** file in the **trip** directory. The most powerful, but dangerous option is using **-r**. Remember, when you perform any task recursively, you are dealing with the entire directory structure.

STEP 9   Key in the following: **rm -r trip; ls trip** [Enter]

```
[cgillay@RedHat9  floppy]$  rm -r trip; ls trip
ls:trip: no such file or directory
[cgillay@RedHat9  floppy]$
```

WHAT'S HAPPENING? As you can see, recursive means recursive. You quickly removed the **trip** directory and all its files. Had there been other directories beneath **trip**, those too would have been deleted. Using the **-r** option is very useful, but be very careful with it because it is so powerful. Once you have deleted the structure, you cannot recover those files or directories from the command line.

STEP 10   Key in the following: **cd; ls class** [Enter]

```
[cgillay@RedHat9  cgillay]$  cd; ls class
astro.tmp    bonjour.tmp  jupiter.tmp  mercury.tmp    ven.tmp
ast.tmp      galaxy.tmp   jup.tmp      mer.tmp
[cgillay@RedHat9  cgillay]$
```

WHAT'S HAPPENING? You moved to your home directory. The home directory has a directory **class**, with many files in it. The fastest way to delete it is to use the **rm -r** command.

STEP 11   Be sure you are in your home directory (**cd**). **DO NOT DELETE THE class DIRECTORY on the BOOK disk.** If your prompt has **floppy** in it, you are in the wrong directory!

STEP 12   Key in the following: **rm -r class; ls class** [Enter]

```
[cgillay@RedHat9  cgillay]$  rm -r class; ls class
ls: class: No such file or directory
[cgillay@RedHat9  cgillay]$
```

WHAT'S HAPPENING? You indeed removed the **class** directory and all the files in your home directory, not on the BOOK disk, with one command.

5.28 ● Printing Files

So far, you have only printed the contents of a file in gedit or OpenOffice.org Writer. In these application programs, you used the Print command from the menu. You may print from the command line as well. The command to print from the command line is **lpr**. You may use the **lpr** command to print one or more files from the command line. The **lpr** command does not actually print the file, but it places the file or files you wish to print in the print queue. If you have more than one printer on your system and if you know the name of the printer, you can specify it using the **-P** option, followed by the name of the printer. If, for instance, you had a printer named **color** and a file you wished to print on that printer called **this.file**, the command would be issued as **lpr   -Pcolor this.fil**. You may print multiple files with **lpr.** If you wish to see what is in the print queue, you may use the **lpq** command. The **lpq** command without any options reports on any print jobs currently in the print queue. There is also the **lprm** command, which will remove jobs from the line printer spooling queue. The **lpr, lpq**, and **lprm** commands have many options. However, at this time you are going to use the commands only in their simplest forms.

5.29 ● Activity: Printing Files with lpr

Note: The BOOK disk is mounted. You are using a terminal window. Your home directory is your default directory.

STEP 1   Key in the following: **cd /mnt/floppy; cat planets.txt** ⌨Enter⌨

```
[cgillay@RedHat9  cgillay]$  cd /mnt/floppy; cat planets.txt
POSITION,PLANET,# of MOONS,DIAMETER
1,MERCURY,,3030
2,VENUS,,7523
3,EARTH,1,7026
4,MARS,2,4222
5,JUPITER,16,89424
6,SATURN,20,74914
7,URANUS,15,31770
8,NEPTUNE,18,31410
9,PLUTO,1,1444
[cgillay@RedHat9  floppy]$
```

WHAT'S HAPPENING? The contents of the **planets.txt** file is written to the standard output device, the screen.

STEP 2   Be sure the printer is on and online.

STEP 3   Key in the following: **lpr planets.txt; lpq** ⌨Enter⌨

```
[cgillay@RedHat9  floppy]$ lpr planets.txt; lpq
hpprinter is ready and printing
Rank      Owner     Job          File(s)          Total Size
active  cgillay    7            planets.txt     1024.bytes
[cgillay@RedHat9  floppy]$
```

WHAT'S HAPPENING? In this example, **cgillay** has a job that is currently being printed, and there are no other jobs in the queue. You see the rank (status), the file owner, the job number, the name of the file, and the size. The job number—7 in this example—can be used with the **lprm** utility to remove a job from the print queue. The command would be issued as **lprm 7**. However, since the file being printed is so small, you could not delete the file before it printed. Remove the printout from the printer. It should look as follows:

```
POSITION,PLANET,# of MOONS,DIAMETER
1,MERCURY,,3030
2,VENUS,,7523
3,EARTH,1,7026
4,MARS,2,4222
5,JUPITER,16,89424
6,SATURN,20,74914
7,URANUS,15,31770
8,NEPTUNE,18,31410
9,PLUTO,1,1444
```

STEP 4   Key in the following: **lpr cities ast.tmp mer.99; lpq** Enter

```
[cgillay@RedHat9  floppy]$ lpr cities ast.tmp mer.99; lpq
hpprinter is ready and printing
Rank      Owner     Job          File(s)          Total Size
active  cgillay    12           cities          3072.bytes
[cgillay@RedHat9  floppy]$
```

WHAT'S HAPPENING? Again, depending on how fast your system is, you may not see the message. Note that it shows the total size of all the files and the job number is different. Each file will be printed on a separate page.

STEP 5   Key in the following: **cd** Enter

STEP 6   Close all open windows.

STEP 7   Unmount the BOOK disk and remove it from the drive.

Chapter Summary

In this chapter you were introduced to the following:
* Copying files using the Nautilus file manager and the **cp** command.
* Determining the type of file using the **file** command.
* Using wildcards with the **cp** command.
* Displaying files using the **cat**, **less**, and **more** commands.
* Using dot addressing with the **cp** and **ls** commands.
* Overwriting files using the **cp** command using the **b**, **p**, and **i** options.

- Creating and combining files with the **cat** command.
- Using the **touch** command to create empty files and to modify a file attributes.
- Changing file names using the Nautilus file manager and the **mv** command.
- Moving files and renaming directories using the Nautilus file manager and the **mv** command
- Eliminating files using the Nautilus file manager and with the **rm** command
- Removing files and directories using wildcards.
- Printing files and using the **lpr** and **lpq** commands.

Key Terms

ASCII
big-endian
concatenation
defaulted
housekeeping tasks
little-endian
thumbnail

Discussion Questions

1. When dealing with a file system, what is the purpose and function of housekeeping tasks?
2. What does it mean to copy a file?
3. Give one reason why you might make a copy of a file on the same disk.
4. When in Nautilus compare and contrast the results of dragging a file from the floppy disk to your home directory and dragging a file from your home directory to a directory under your home directory.
5. Give the syntax for the **cp** command and explain each part of the syntax.
6. List and explain two options that can be used with the **cp** command.
7. How can you recognize a text file? An executable file?
8. When would you use wildcards with the **cp** command?
9. What is the purpose and function of the **cat** command?
10. Compare and contrast the **more** command with the **less** command.
11. What is an ASCII file?
12. When working with directories, what is the function of the **cp** command? The **ls** command?
13. When you are in the root (/)directory why will "dot addressing" not work?
14. What does it mean to overwrite a file?
15. How can you protect yourself from accidentally overwriting a file?
16. What is a "dummy" file?
17. Explain the purpose and function of concatenating files.
18. When you concatenate two files, what happens to the original files?
19. What is the purpose and function of the **touch** command?
20. When using the touch command, what is the function of the **a**, **c**, and **m** options?
21. Give two reasons why you would want to change a file name.
22. Explain two ways to change a file name.
23. List and explain two options that can be used with the **mv** command.
24. Why must you be very careful when using the **mv** command with directories?

25. Compare and contrast moving a file within Nautilus and moving a file at the command line.

26. How would you rename a file within Nautilus? At the command line?

27. Compare and contrast eliminating files using the Nautilus file manager with using **rm** at the command line.

28. When would you use a wildcard with the **rm** command? Why is this method considered dangerous?

29. List and explain the options that can be used with the **rm** command. Which option is considered the most dangerous? Why?

30. What is the purpose and function of the **lpr** command? The **lpq** command? The **lprm** command?

True/False Questions

For each question, circle the letter T if the question is true and the letter F if the question is false.

T   F   1. When a user copies a file and makes changes to the copy, the original file is also altered.

T   F   2. Copying files in the Nautilus file manager is more powerful than using the **cp** command at the command line.

T   F   3. You may use the **touch** command to modify an existing file's time and date.

T   F   4. Classifying a file with the **file** command prevents other users from accessing it.

T   F   5. To create a new file called **foo**, you begin by keying in **cat > foo**.

Completion Questions

Write the correct answer in each blank space.

6. The **less** command is often used to open and display the contents of a file instead of the _____ command.

7. When writing commands, a dot (.) represents the _____ directory and the dot-dot (..) represents the _____ directory.

8. To create an empty file, you may use the _____ command.

9. Files in the same _____ may not have the same file name.

10. A temporary storage area for print jobs that are pending is called a/an _____.

Multiple Choice Questions

For each question, write the letter for the correct answer in the blank space.

11. Wildcards are often used with the cp command in order to
   a. copy multiple files with different file extensions.
   b. copy multiple files with the same file extension.
   c. display multiple files with the same file extension.
   d. display multiple files with different file extensions.

12. Which command/s can be used to display file contents a screenful at a time?
   a. **cat**
   b. **more**
   c. **less**
   d. both b and c

13. The **mv** command is used for both moving files and
   a. renaming files.
   b. copying directories recursively.
   c. deleting files.
   d. classifying files.

14. If you key in **rm -r *.txt**, you will
   a. be prompted before removing the *.**txt** files.
   b. be prompted for your user password.
   c. delete all the *.**txt** files recursively.
   d. delete all the *.**txt** files only in the current directory.

15. The **cat** command cannot be used to
   a. change the name of a file.
   b. combine the contents of multiple text files.
   c. create and name a new file.
   d. display the contents of a file.

Writing Commands

Write the correct steps or commands to perform the required action as if you were at the computer. You will assume that there is a terminal window open. The prompt will indicate the current working directory.

16. You want to copy the *.**txt** files to the **/home/lin/test** directory, but you wanted to be prompted if you are going to overwrite any files in the **/home/lin/test** directory.

   `[lin@RedHat9 lin]`

17. You want to know if **fan.tif**, located in the **/public** directory, is really a graphic file.

   `[stuttle@RedHat9 stuttle]`

18. You wish to view the contents of the file called **longfile**, located in the **/mnt/floppy** directory, one screen at a time, but you want the ability to scroll forward and backwards in the file.

   `[mhall@RedHat9 mhall]`

19. Your structure is **/home/Jimenez/school/classes/math**. You want to copy all the files in the math directory to the **school** directory. Use dot addressing techniques.

   `[jimenez@RedHat9 math]`

20. You want to print the text file called **testing** located in your home directory.

   `[xu@RedHat9 floppy]`

Application Assignments

Problem Set I—At the Computer: Multiple Choice

Note: For all problems, your work (files and directories) will be saved to the floppy disk labeled BOOK. Do not save any items to your home directory.

Problem A

- Mount the BOOK disk.
- Open a terminal window and use the terminal window for Problem A.
- Change the default directory to **/mnt/floppy**.
- Make a copy of the file called **grammy.rec** and call the new file **grammy.tap**.
- Display only the **grammy.*** files so you may see the file dates.

  1. Are the file dates the same?
     - a. yes
     - b. no

  2. What are the sizes of the grammy files in bytes?
     - a. **grammy.rec** = 1569 and **grammy.tap** = 1339
     - b. **grammy.rec** = 1596 and **grammy.tap** = 1496
     - c. both files are 1334 bytes.
     - d. **grammy.rec** = 569 and **grammy.tap** = 596

- Make a copy of the **grammy.rec** file and call the new file **gram:rec**.

  3. What was displayed?
     - a. **cp: cannot create regular file 'gram:rec' : Invalid file name**
     - b. **cp: cannot create regular file 'gram:rec' : Invalid argument**
     - c. **cp: cannot create regular file 'gram:rec' : Invalid option**
     - d. no message was displayed.

Problem B

- Open a terminal window and use the terminal window for Problem B.
- Display only the files with a ***.99** extension so you may see the file dates.

  4. What date is listed for **ast.99**?
     - a. **Oct 31   2001**
     - b. **Oct 14   2000**
     - c. **Oct 30   22:30**
     - d. **Oct 30   2001**

- If there is not a directory on the BOOK disk called **files**, create it now.
- Copy all the files from the **/mnt/floppy** directory with a **.99** file extension to the **files** directory. Use an option with the command that allows you to see how many files were copied.

  5. What option did you use?
     - a. **-p**
     - b. **-r**
     - c. **-v**
     - d. **-x**

  6. How many files were copied?
     - a. two
     - b. four
     - c. six
     - d. eight

Problem C

* Using the terminal window, display the contents of the file called **grammy.rec** so that it appears one screen at a time.

    7. What command could you have used?

        a. **more**

        b. **less**

        c. either a or b

        d. neither a nor b

    8. What was the record of the year?

        a. *Brand New Day*

        b. *Smooth*

        c. *American Woman*

        d. *Put Your Lights On*

* With **mnt/floppy** as the default directory, display the contents of the file **gold_old.mov** located in the **media/movies** directory using a relative path.

    9. What command did you use?

        a. **cat /mnt/floppy/media/movies/gold_old.mov**

        b. **cat /floppy/media/movies/gold_old.mov**

        c. **cat media/movies/gold_old.mov**

        d. **cat gold_old.mov**

    10. What movie title is displayed?

        a. *Gone with the Wind*

        b. *An Officer and a Gentleman*

        c. *North by Northwest*

        d. *Overboard*

* With **mnt/floppy** as the default directory, display the contents of the file **ame-lit.bks** located in the **media/books** directory.

    11. What author is *not* displayed?

        a. Mark Twain

        b. John Steinbeck

        c. William Faulkner

        d. Edgar Allen Poe

Problem D

* Using the terminal window, find out what kind of file **mime-magic** is. It is located in the **etc** directory.

    12. What command did you use?

        a. **cat /etc/mime-magic**

        b. **ls /etc/mime-magic**

        c. **file /etc/mime-magic**

        d. none of the above

13. The file, **mime-magic**, is a(n)
     a. **ASCII C++ program text**
     b. **ASCII English text**
     c. **ASCII English text, with CRLF line terminators**
     d. **ASCII text, with no line terminators**

* You want to find out what kind of file **5report** is on the BOOK disk.

14. The file, **5report** is a/an
     a. **ASCII C++ program text**
     b. **ASCII English text**
     c. **ASCII English text, with CRLF line terminators**
     d. **ASCII text, with no line terminators**

* You want to change the date of the file called **venus.tmm** on the BOOK disk to the current date.

15. What is the easiest way to change the date of the **venus.tmm** file?
     a. **cp venus.tmm ven.tmm**
     b. **file venus.tmm**
     c. **touch venus.tmm**
     d. **ls venus.tmm**

* Using the correct command, change the date of the **venus.tmm** file to the current date.

Problem E

* Open a terminal window and use the terminal window for Problem E.

* Change the default directory to **/mnt/floppy**.

* You want to create a text file called **states** using the **cat** command in the **/mnt/floppy** directory.

16. What command will you use?
     a. **cat states**
     b. **cat > states**
     c. **cat < states**
     d. **none of the above**

* Create the **states** file and enter the following data:

  California
  Michigan
  Arizona
  Florida
  Texas
  Oregon
  Washington
  Louisiana
  New York
  Ohio

17. In order to write the file to disk, you had to press the **Ctrl** key and the _____ key.
   a. **d**
   b. **s**
   c. **t**
   d. **y**

* Create a text file called **dances.new** and enter the following data:

BALLROOM DANCES

Waltz
Two-Step
Swing
West Coast Swing

* Combine the contents of the file called **dances.new** and **dances.txt** into a new file called **dances.all**.

18. The command you used was
   a. **cat dances.new > dances.all; cat dances.txt > dances.all**
   b. **cat dances.new dances.txt > dances.all**
   c. **cat dances.new dances.txt < dances.all**
   d. **cat dances.all > dances.new dances.txt**

Problem F

* Open a terminal window and use the terminal window for Problem F. Be sure the default directory is **/mnt/floppy**.

* Rename the file called **dress.up** to **dress.down**.

19. Which command did you use?
   a. **cp dress.up dress.down**
   b. **cp dress.down dress.up**
   c. **cat dress.up dress.down**
   d. **mv dress.up dress.down**

* Use the **ls** command to locate **dress.up**.

20. What message is displayed?
   a. **ls:dress.up: File renamed**
   b. **ls:dress.up: File moved**
   c. **ls:dress.up: No such file or directory**
   d. **ls:dress.up: No such file**

* With **/mnt/floppy** as the default, create a directory called **fun**.

* Move all the files that have **dances** in their name to the **fun** directory.

21. All the files that have **dances** in their name are
   a. only in the **/mnt/floppy/fun** directory.
   b. only in the **/mnt/floppy** directory.
   c. in both the **/mnt/floppy/fun** and the **/mnt/floppy** directory.
   d. none of the above

Problem G

* Open a terminal window and use the terminal window for Problem G.

Note: If you accidentally deleted the **class** directory, you can recreate it. The **class** directory has one directory in it, **place**. The files in the **class** directory are **ast.tmp**, **bonjour.tmp**, **galaxy.tmp**, **jupiter.tmp**, **jup.tmp**, **mercury.tmp**, and **ven.tmp**. The files in the **place** directory are **ast.99** and **jup.99**.

* With **/mnt/floppy** as the default directory, delete the file called **ast.tmp** in the **class** directory.

> 22. What command did you use?
>   a. **rm   ast.tmp**
>   b. **rm   /class/ast.tmp**
>   c. **rm   class/ast.tmp**
>   d. **rm   /home/ast.tmp**

* Copy all the files in the **fun** directory to the **class** directory.

* With **/mnt/floppy** as the default directory, you want to retain only **dances.all** in the **class** directory.

> 23. Which command can you use that will query you whether or not you want to delete a file?
>   a. **rm   class/dances*.***
>   b. **rm -i   class/dances*.***
>   c. **rm -v   class/dances*.***
>   d. **rm -r   classes/dances*.***

* With **/mnt/floppy** as the default directory, retain only **dances.all** in the **class** directory using the option in Question 23.

* You wish to delete the directory **work** with all its directories and files in the *fastest* way.

> 24. Which command will accomplish this fast deletion of **work**?
>   a. **rm   work**
>   b. **rm -i   work**
>   c. **rm -v   work**
>   d. **rm -r   work**

* Delete **work** using the command you chose in Question 24.

* Close all open windows. If you are ending your work session, be sure to unmount the floppy disk and remove it from the drive.

Problem Set II—At the Computer: Short Answer

1. Create a directory called **practice5** in your home directory. Change directories to the **practice5** directory.
2. Create two directories under **practice5** called **dir1** and **dir2**.
3. Create three files called **temp1**, **temp2**, and **temp3** in the **practice5** directory. The contents of **temp1** should be **This is temporary file 1**. The contents of **temp2** should be **This is temporary file 2**. The contents of **temp3** should be **This is temporary file 3**.
4. Copy **temp1** to **temp4**, **temp2** to **temp5**, and **temp3** to **temp6**.
5. Copy only the **temp3**, **temp4**, and **temp5** files to **dir1**.
6. Copy only the **temp1**, **temp2**, and **temp6** to **dir2**.
7. Copy the **/etc/passwd** file to the **practice5** directory.
8. Rename the **passwd** file to **PASSWORD**. Use **more** and **less** to look at the contents.
9. What kind of file is **PASSWORD**?

10. Interactively delete **temp1**, **temp2**, and **temp6** from the **practice5** directory. Use a wildcard (globbing).

11. Move the remaining **temp** files to **dir2**. Use a wildcard (globbing).

12. Use **find** to discover how many **temp** files you have. How many temp files are there?

13. Create the following files and include the colons in the file contents:

File Name	File Contents
book1	Mystery:Women. Grafton:Sue:Q:is:for:Quarry. Baker:Susan:My:First:Murder.
book2	Mystery:Men. Coben:Harlan:Gone:For:Good. Allyn:Doug:Black:Water.
book4	Science:Fiction Heinlein:Robert:The:Door:Into:Summer. Asimov:Issac:I:Robot.
book5	Horror. Koontz:Dean:The:Watchers. King:Stephen:Carrie
book9	American:Literature. Steinbeck:John:The:Grapes:of:Wrath. Twain:Mark:Tom:Sawyer.
book10	English:Literature. Dickens:Charles:The:Pickwick:Papers. Thackeray:William:Vanity:Fair.

14. Create a directory called **mybooks** under the **practice5** directory.

15. Under **mybooks**, create three directories: **mystery**, **scifi**, and **literature**.

16. Move **book1** and **book2** to **mybooks/mystery**.

17. Move **book4** and **book5** to **mybooks/scifi**.

18. Move **book9** and **book10** to **mybooks/literature**.

19. Change your directory to **dir1**. While in **dir1**, using dot addressing techniques, rename **book1** to **Book1**.

20. While in **dir1**, using dot addressing techniques, combine the contents of **Book1** and **book2** into a new file to be called **book3** to be saved to the **mystery** directory.

21. While in **dir1**, using dot addressing techniques, combine the contents of **book4** and **book5** into a new file to be called **book6** in the **scifi** directory.

22. While in **dir1**, using dot addressing techniques, combine the contents of **book9** and **book10** into a new file to be called **book8** in the **literature** directory.

23. Change directories to the **mybooks** directory. Using dot addressing techniques, combine all the **book** files you have created into a new file to be called **book7** to be located in the **mybooks** directory. Use wildcards.

24. Compare and contrast using **cat**, **more**, and **less** to view **book7**.

25. Change directories to **dir1**. While in **dir1**, use **find** to discover how many **book** files you have starting with the **practice5** directory. You want to be sure and include any **book** files, including **Book1**. Use brackets with your wildcards. How many files did you find?

26. Change the time of all the files in the **dir1** directory to the current time. Confirm that you changed the time.

27. Change directories to **practice5**. Move the **dir1** directory under the **dir2** directory.

28. In the **dir2** directory, create a new file called **temp7**. The contents are **THIS IS A TEMPORARY FILE**. Overwrite **temp4** with **temp7**. Confirm that you did overwrite **temp4** with **temp7**.

29. Create a directory under **practice5** called **backup5**. Copy all the files and directories you created to the **backup** directory. Hint: Remember recursive. Did you get any messages? If so, what was the message? List the directories in the **backup5** directory. Explain why each is there. Does every directory in **backup5** have files? Why or why not?

30. With one command, completely remove **dir2** in the **practice5** directory but not in the **backup5** directory.

31. Get a blank floppy disk. Label it PRACTICE disk. Do not use the BOOK disk. Mount it. Copy everything in the **practice5** directory under your home directory to the floppy disk to a directory called **practice5**. When you have finished, unmount the floppy disk and remove it from the drive.

Problem Set III—Brief Essay

Use gEdit or OpenOffice.org Writer to write and print your response. Be sure to put your name as well as what day and time your class is. Include the number of the question you are answering.

a. Compare and contrast moving and copying files and directories. Explain when and why you would choose to move files and when and why you would choose to copy files. Support your explanation. In addition, name and describe the purpose of one option that you might use with the **cp** command and one option you might use with the **mv** command.

b. *Deleting files and directories can have serious consequences. You should therefore never delete directories, only files.* Agree or disagree with this statement and explain your answer. In addition, describe what commands you would use and why.

c. *Only system administrators need to learn file management commands. It is unnecessary for ordinary users to learn file management commands.* Agree or disagree with this statement. Support your answer. Include in your explanation the types of commands that administrators or ordinary users might use and why.

CHAPTER 6

Editors

Chapter Overview

Linux relies heavily on simple text files—most of the Linux configuration files are plain ASCII text files. A plain text file is a file without any font or style formatting applied to it. Remember, in Linux, everything is a file. When you begin to create shell scripts, which are also simple text files, you need a tool to create them. You will find that you need to create or edit files at the character-based log in. In fact, to configure the X Window System, which allows you to run Linux graphics, you may need to edit configuration files.

Furthermore, if you are a system administrator or a root user, you must learn some type of text editor because in an emergency situation, such as when booting Linux from a maintenance disk, you will have no graphic editor available to you. Thus, it is imperative that you learn to use a text editor. You will learn to use both vi (vim) and Emacs, which are provided with Red Hat Linux. Either of these can be used at the command line or in the GUI.

Learning Objectives

1. Compare and contrast a graphic editor with a text editor.
2. Explain the purpose and function of the vi editor.
3. Explain the purpose and function of the Last Line mode.
4. Explain how to move and search within a file using vi search commands and vi cursor movement keys.
5. Explain how to use the built-in help for vi.
6. Explain how to make text corrections and how add text to a file when in insert mode.
7. Explain how to correct or edit text using delete and change commands.

287

8. Explain the purpose and function of the substitute command.
9. Explain the purpose and function of the work buffer, the undo buffer, and registers and how these buffers can be manipulated.
10. Explain how multiple files and multiple windows can be used to read information from one file into another and how to copy and paste from one window to another.
11. Explain the purpose and function of Emacs.

Student Outcomes

1. Use the basic set of vi commands to create and edit documents and place vi in Last Line mode.
2. Move within a file using movement command keys.
3. Move through the help window using normal vi movement and editing keys.
4. Using vi, add text to a file using insert commands.
5. Using vi, delete and change commands to correct text.
6. Replace text using substitute commands and then print the changed file.
7. Copy, paste, and move text using copy and move commands.
8. Use multiple files and windows to read information from one file into another and to copy and paste data from one window to another.
9. Use Emacs to edit a file.

6.1 ● Editors

Traditionally, most Linux and Unix distributions include and install at least one cursor-based editor because you will need to know how to create and edit text files. An *editor* is program that allows you to create and edit documents. A *text editor* uses simple cursor- and keyboard-based operations to give you the opportunity to edit and create text files in a full-screen environment. You may use these editors from the command line without any kind of X Window System support.

An editor is like a very simple word processor, but there are no menus, scroll bars, or the ability to use a mouse at the command line. Although an editor allows you to create and edit documents, a text editor has no text formatting features that allow you to use different font styles such as bold or italic, nor can you perform simple formatting tasks such as centering text or creating and modifying margins. If you are using the GNOME desktop, there is a graphical text editor called **gedit**. In the GNOME desktop **gedit** does offer GUI type features such as mouse action, menus, and scroll bars. However, there are still no formatting features. Red Hat Linux installs different word processors—if you do a full installation—such as AbiWord and OpenOffice.org Writer. Both of these application programs allow you to save your documents in a plain text format, stripping all formatting from the documents. But if you are going to be creating and modifying text files, the best tool to use is a plain text editor.

6.2 ● The vi Editor

vi, pronounced "vee-eye," was the first screen-based editor for Unix systems. It is the standard editor on every Linux and Unix system. Prior to vi, the standard Unix editor was ed. The ed editor was a line-oriented editor, which meant you could see only one line at a time, making it difficult to use. The next editor was ex, which was a superset of ed. It had the advantage of having a vi command that allowed you to see the entire screen (visual mode). Since most users, when using ex, far preferred using the visual mode, the developers of ex simply created the program vi. The original vi program is not available to use with Red Hat or any free version of

Unix or Linux due to copyright issues. However, every version of Linux/Unix provides a clone of vi. The most popular clones are elvis, nvi, and vim. vim (Vi Improved) is the editor supplied with Red Hat Linux, but it is simply referred to as vi. In the text, it will be referred to as **vi**, even though in fact, you are using the **vim** clone. If your distribution of Linux or Unix did not include vim, you may go to **http://www.vim.org** and download a free copy.

The vi editor is designed to be fast and efficient, once you learn to use it. However, you may find initially that the commands are cryptic and typically tend to be one-letter commands. Thus, for text movement, you use **h** to move up and **k** to move right. When editing, characters are deleted with **x**, to copy and paste you use **y** and **p**.

Furthermore, vi is a modal editor. A modal editor is an editor that has modes. A mode is a general state, usually used with an adjective describing the state such as "I am in study mode," indicating that the individual is totally focused on studying. More technically, a mode is a special state that user interfaces must pass into in order to perform certain functions. For example, in order to insert characters into a document in vi, one must key in i to invoke the "Insert" command. The effect of this command is to put vi into "Insert mode," at which point keying in i has a completely different effect, which is to place the character i in your document. You must then press another key to leave Insert mode and enter another mode. The two major modes of operation in vi are Command mode and Insert mode. In Command mode, you give vi commands such as delete, which is usually a one-letter command: **d**. The vi editor is very powerful, so not all features of vi will be demonstrated. Instead, you will learn the basic set of vi commands that allow you to edit and create documents.

6.3 ● Activity: Creating a File

Note: The activities in this book assume Linux is installed at run level 3. See the Installation
         section of Appendix A for details.

STEP 1   Mount the BOOK disk. Open a terminal window.

STEP 2   Key in the following: **cd /mnt/floppy** Enter

STEP 3   Key in the following: **vi vimeditor** Enter

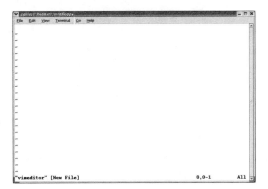

WHAT'S **HAPPENING?** You have opened a new file called vimeditor that can be saved to the BOOK disk. You could have also keyed in **vim vimeditor**. When you create a file with the vi editor, all your keystrokes are saved to a work buffer. A work buffer is a place in memory where data is temporarily stored. vi does not create the file until you tell it to write the data to disk.

Currently, the cursor in the upper left hand corner indicates your current location in the file. At the bottom of the screen is the name of the new file, vimeditor. The numbers indicate the cursor position, and **All** indicates that all the file is shown. The ˜s (tildes) are not text but indicate lines on the screen. vi always starts in Command mode. This means that everything you key in is considered a command. In order to place data in the file, you must issue the insert command (i).

STEP 4   Key in the following: **i**

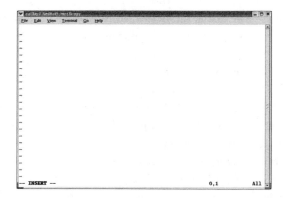

WHAT'S HAPPENING? You did not see **i** as a command displayed on the screen, nor did you press **Enter** because you simply are issuing vi a command to change modes to insert. At the bottom of the screen, you now see the word **INSERT**. At this point, everything you key in is considered text in the file. This is not a word processor and lines will not wrap. You must press **Enter** at the end of each line to move to the next line.

STEP 5   Key in the following, pressing **Enter** where indicated:

> **What is Vim? Enter**
> **Enter**
> **Vim is a highly configurable text editor built to enable efficient text editing.**
> **Enter**

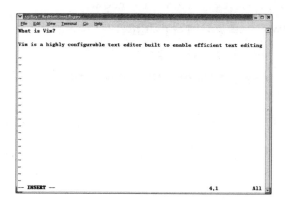

WHAT'S HAPPENING? You are still in Insert mode. Note that the numbers at the bottom of the screen indicate that you are on the first characters on the fourth line (4,1). Depending on the size of your screen and what characters you pressed, your position could be different. You do have some editing capabilities in Insert mode. Pressing the **Backspace** key deletes the previous character. Pressing the **Delete** key deletes the forward character. Pressing **Ctrl** + **w** will delete the previous word. However, to use vi to edit, you must go to Command mode. You enter Command mode by pressing the **Esc** key, usually once, but at least until you no longer see INSERT at the bottom of the window.

STEP 6   Press **Esc**. Press **.** (the period).

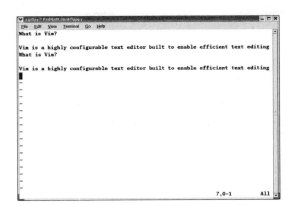

WHAT'S HAPPENING? Pressing **Esc** returned you to Command mode. While you are editing, vi keeps the text you are working on in a work buffer so you may edit it. In Command mode, pressing the . inserts the last text you keyed in below the current line. When you issue a command in Command mode, you do not need to press **Enter**. Merely pressing the key for the command will execute the command. When you finish editing, you must save what is in the work buffer to a file if you wish to keep the data. However, there are times you do not want to save what you have written. vi allows you to exit the program without saving the data. To handle this, vi uses a Last Line mode. *Last Line mode* moves you to the bottom of the document where you enter a last line command. Last Line mode is always preceded by a colon (:). In addition, with all Last Line mode commands, you must press **Enter** to execute the command.

STEP 7   Key in **:q!** **Enter**

STEP 8   Key in the following: **ls vimeditor** **Enter**

```
[cgillay@linux72   floppy]$   ls   vimeditor
ls: vimeditor: No such file or directory
[cgillay@linux72   cgillay]$ _
```

WHAT'S HAPPENING? When you used the **:q!**, you told vi to exit without saving changes. In Command mode, any keystroke is a command. In Insert mode, any keystroke is considered text that is placed in the file. You must be in command mode—then any time you precede a keystroke with a :, you are placing vi in Last Line mode. The colon then moves the cursor to the bottom of the screen where any keystroke following the : is considered a command.

STEP 9   Key in the following: **vi vimeditor** **Enter**

STEP 10   Key in the following: **i**

STEP 11   Key in the following, including the errors. Do not key in **Enter**, but simply press **Enter** where indicated:

What is Vim? **Enter**
Enter
Vim is a highly configurable text editor built to enable efficient text editing. **Enter**
It is a better version of the vi editorss sent with most UNIX distributions. **Enter**
Vimis often called a "programmer's editor," and so useful for programming **Enter**
that some consider it an entire IDE.

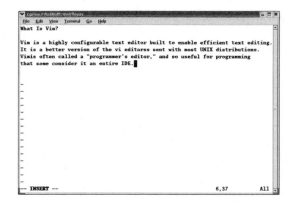

WHAT'S HAPPENING? You are still in Insert mode. You want to change to Command mode. This time, you do want to save the file to disk. In Command mode, pressing ZZ saves the file to disk and exits vi. Remember, case matters.

STEP 12 Press the [Esc] key. Key in the following: **ZZ**

STEP 13 Key in the following: **cat   vimeditor** [Enter]

```
[cgillay@linux72   floppy]$   vi   vimeditor
[cgillay@linux72   floppy]$   cat   vimeditor
What is Vim?


Vim is a highly configurable text editor built to enable efficient text editing.
It is a better version of the vi editorss sent with most UNIX distributions.
Vimis often called a "programmer's editor," and so useful for programming
that some consider it an entire IDE.
[cgillay@linux72   floppy]$
```

WHAT'S HAPPENING? You saved your file to disk. You may also use a last line command to save the file to disk. The **:wq** command will write the file to disk and quit vi. The command **:w** will write the file to disk without exiting vi, and **:w** *newfilename* will save the file to a new name and change your editing session to the new file.

STEP 14 Key in the following: **vi   vimeditor** [Enter]

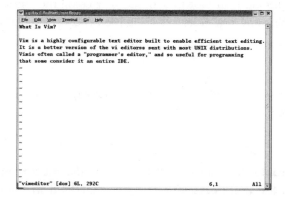

WHAT'S HAPPENING? You have used vi to open an existing file. You are in Command mode. At the bottom of the screen is listed the name of the file (**vimeditor**), the number of lines (6L), and the number of characters (283c). The number of lines or characters may vary if you added a space or another carriage return. When you begin a session with the vi editor using an existing file, vi reads the existing file into the work buffer. During your editing, vi makes all the changes to the file in the work buffer. The file saved on disk is not altered unless you write the contents of the work buffer to disk.

STEP 15 Key in the following: **:q** `Enter`

```
[cgillay@linux72   floppy]$   vi vimeditor
[cgillay@linux72   floppy]$
```

WHAT'S HAPPENING? You have returned to the terminal window.

6.4 • Moving and Searching in a File

When you are in Command mode, you may move the cursor to any location in the file. Many commands in vi operate on blocks of text ranging from a character to paragraphs. These defined blocks of text include the following:

character	One character. This includes nonprinting characters as well as spaces and tabs.
word	A word is comprised of characters up to a space, a tab, a number, or a punctuation mark. vi considers a group of punctuation marks as one word, thus **?]** and **don't** would be counted as one word. A delimited word is one that includes the adjacent punctuation marks, so **don't** would be considered one word. Delimited words are separated from one another by a space, a tab, or a new line (A new line is created when you press `Enter`.)
line	A string of characters followed by a new line. This means that if you enter a line of text that continues on to the next lines, unless you have pressed `Enter`, it is considered one line.
sentence	A sentence is a block of text that ends with a period, a question mark, or an exclamation point and must be followed either by two spaces or by pressing `Enter`. When you select a word, it counts the word up to a punctuation mark (. !?) followed by two spaces.
paragraph	A paragraph is preceded and followed by one or more blank lines. A blank line is not really blank. It is created by pressing `Enter` two times. A paragraph is then comprised of a group of sentences up to the next blank line.
screen	The terminal screen displays all or a portion of what is in the work buffer. You may scroll through the display, or you may move through sections of the screen display.

Table 6.1, "Cursor Movement Keys in vi," lists the keys you can use to move the cursor when in command mode. A number preceding the command will move you in numerical increments so that, for instance, **7w** would move you seven words forward.

Block of text	Command	Movement
Character	h or left arrow	Left one character.
	l or right arrow	Right one character.
	[Space Bar]	Right one character.
Word	w	Forward one word.
	W	Forward one delimited word.
	b	Back one word.
	B	Back one delimited word.
	e	Forward to end of word.
	E	Forward to end of delimited word.
Line	k or up arrow	Up one line.
	j or down arrow	Down one line.
	0 (zero)	Beginning of current line.
	$	End of current line.
	[Enter]	Beginning of next line.
	-	Beginning of previous line.
	+	Beginning of next line.
	^	First nonblank character of current line.
	G	Beginning of last line.
	nG	Go to the line number specified by n.
Sentence	)	Beginning of sentence
	(	end of sentence.
Paragraph	}	Beginning of paragraph.
	{	End of paragraph.
Screen	H	Upper left corner of the screen.
	nH	after top line, go to line number specified by n.
	L	Last line of screen.
	nL	After bottom line, go to line number specified by n.
	M	Middle line of screen.
	[Ctrl] + U	Up one half screen.
	[Ctrl] + D	Down one half screen.

Ctrl + F or **PgDn**	Forward one screen.
Ctrl + B or **PgUp**	Back one screen.
Ctrl + E	Shows one more line at bottom of screen.
Ctrl + Y	Shows one more line at top of screen.

Table 6.1 • Cursor Movement Keys in vi

You may also use various search commands to locate a particular line, string, or character. If you are not doing a line search, the search will begin at your current cursor location and continue searching through the rest of the file. If the search does not find what you specified, it will start at the beginning of the file and end at your current cursor location. A line search searches the line you are on. Table 6.2, "Search Commands in vi," lists the commands to locate text in a file.

Command	**Result**
/*text*	Search forward for specified text. Command must be followed by **Enter**.
/	Repeats forward search. Command must be followed by **Enter**.
/*text*/+n	Go forward to line number specified by n after search *text* found.
?*text*	Search forward for specified text. Command must be followed by **Enter**.
?	Repeat previous search backwards. Command must be followed by **Enter**.
n	Repeat previous search.
N	Repeat search in opposite direction.
f*x*	Move forward on current line to character specified by *x*.
F*x*	Move backward on current line to character specified by *x*.
t*x*	Move forward on current line to character just before character specified by *x*.
T*x*	Move backwards on current line to character just before character specified by *x*.
,	Reverse search direction for last f, F, t or T.
;	Repeat last character search for last f, F, t, or T.

Table 6.2 • Search Commands in vi

6.5 ● Activity: Moving and Searching in a File

Note 1: The BOOK disk is mounted. A terminal window is open. The default directory is
/mnt/floppy.

Note 2: If your terminal window is a different size than the one shown in the examples, the
screen movement keys will place you in a different location. To match the examples,
size your terminal window to match the example.

Note 3: Remember that case matters. Also pay attention to whether or not you press `Enter`.
Do not press `Enter` automatically.

STEP 1   Key in the following: **cd /mnt/floppy; vi newprson.fil** `Enter`

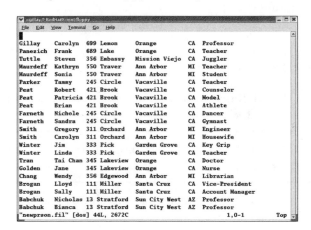

WHAT'S HAPPENING? ► You first confirmed that your default directory was **/mnt/floppy**. You
then opened an existing file on the BOOK disk. You are in Command mode. You may move
around the file using the movement command keys.

STEP 2   Key in the following: **1G**

STEP 3   Press **H**. Press the `Space Bar`. Press the right arrow. Press **w** three times.

```
Gillay      Carolyn     699 Lemon       Orange          CA   Professor
Panezich    Frank       689 Lake        Orange          CA   Teacher
Tuttle      Steven      356 Embassy     Mission Viejo   CA   Juggler
```

WHAT'S HAPPENING? ► This version of **vim** remembers the last place you were in the file when
you last exited it. So you began by pressing 1G which took you to the top of the file, then you
pressed the uppercase **H** which insured you were at the top of the screen. Then, as you saw, you
moved one character, then another character forward, then three words forward.

STEP 4   Key in the following: **L**

```
Brogan      Sally       111 Miller      Santa Cruz      CA   Account Manager
Babchuk     Nicholas    13 Stratford    Sun City West   AZ   Professor
Babchuk     Bianca      13 Stratford    Sun City West   AZ   Professor
"newprson.fil" [dos] 44L, 2672C
```

WHAT'S HAPPENING? ► Now you moved to the last line of the screen. If you did not size your
terminal screen to match the example, you may not see the "newprson.fil" [dos] 44L, 2672C
line and the cursor position, 23,1. **Top** indicates that you are at the top of the file.

STEP 5   Key in the following: **H**. Key in the following: **M**.

```
Peat       Robert    421 Brook      Vacaville       CA  Counselor
Peat       Patricia  421 Brook      Vacaville       CA  Model
Peat       Brian     421 Brook      Vacaville       CA  Athlete
Peat       Brian     421 Brook      Vacaville       CA  Athlete
Farneth    Nichole   245 Circle     Vacaville       CA  Dancer
Farneth    Sandra    245 Circle     Vacaville       CA  Gymnast
```

WHAT'S **HAPPENING?** You moved first to the top of the screen and then to the middle of the screen.

STEP 6   Key in the following: **b**. Key in the following: **8b.**

```
Peat       Robert    421 Brook      Vacaville       CA  Counselor
Peat       Patricia  421 Brook      Vacaville       CA  Model
Peat       Brian     421 Brook      Vacaville       CA  Athlete
Farneth    Nichole   245 Circle     Vacaville       CA  Dancer
Farneth    Sandra    245 Circle     Vacaville       CA  Gymnast
```

WHAT'S **HAPPENING?** You moved back one word, then you moved back eight words.

STEP 7   Key in the following: **G**.

```
Perez      Sergio    134 Seventh    Ann Arbor       MI  Editor
Yuan       Suelin    56 Twin Leaf   Orange          CA  Artist
Markiw     Nicholas  12 Fifth       Glendale        AZ  Engineer
```

WHAT'S **HAPPENING?** You moved to the beginning of the last line. Note the screen now states **Bot** at the bottom of it.

STEP 8   Key in the following: **5G**

```
Gillay     Carolyn   699 Lemon      Orange          CA  Professor
Panezich   Frank     689 Lake       Orange          CA  Teacher
Tuttle     Steven    356 Embassy    Mission Viejo   CA  Juggler
Maurdeff   Kathryn   550 Traver     Ann Arbor       MI  Teacher
Maurdeff   Sonia     550 Traver     Ann Arbor       MI  Student
```

WHAT'S **HAPPENING?** Now you moved to the fifth line of the file.

STEP 9   Key in the following: **$.** Then key in the following: **)**.

```
Perez      Sergio    134 Seventh    Ann Arbor       MI  Editor
Yuan       Suelin    56 Twin Leaf   Orange          CA  Artist
Markiw     Nicholas  12 Fifth       Glendale        AZ  Engineer
```

WHAT'S **HAPPENING?** You moved to the end of the current line and then asked to move forward to the end of the sentence. Since there is no punctuation in this file, you moved to the end of the file.

STEP 10   Key in the following: **H**. Then key in **e** four times.

```
Babchuk    Nicholas  13  Stratford  Sun City West  AZ    Professor
Babchuk    Bianca    13  Stratford  Sun City West  AZ    Professor
Rodriguez  Bob       20  Elm            Ontario    CA    Systems Analyst
```

WHAT'S HAPPENING? You moved to the top of the screen and then moved to the end of the fourth word.

STEP 11 Press Ctrl + b. Press Ctrl + e.

```
Babchuk    Nicholas  13  Stratford  Sun City West  AZ    Professor
Babchuk    Bianca    13  Stratford  Sun City West  AZ    Professor
Rodriguez  Bob       20  Elm            Ontario    CA    Systems Analyst
```

WHAT'S HAPPENING? You went back one screen and then asked to see one more line at the bottom of the screen.

STEP 12 Key in the following: **/Carolyn** Enter

WHAT'S HAPPENING? You asked to move to the string of data, Carolyn. The message at the bottom of the screen told you that you hit BOTTOM and then the search continued at the top. In the newest version of **vim**, when you search, it highlights in color all occurrences of the text you are searching for. Right now, your cursor should be at the first occurrence of **Carolyn**.

STEP 13 Key in the following: / Enter

```
Smith      Gregory   311  Orchard   Ann Arbor      MI    Engineer
Smith      Carolyn   311  Orchard   Ann Arbor      MI    Housewife
Winter     Jim       333  Pick      Garden Grove   CA    Key Grip
```

WHAT'S HAPPENING? Using the / continued your search forward for the next occurrence of the string, **Carolyn**.

STEP 14 Key in the following: / Enter

```
cgillay:2:RedHat8:/mnt/floppy
File  Edit  View  Terminal  Go  Help
Gillay      Carolyn   699 Lemon     Orange         CA  Professor
Panezich    Frank     689 Lake      Orange         CA  Teacher
Tuttle      Steven    356 Embassy   Mission Viejo  CA  Juggler
Maurdeff    Kathryn   550 Traver    Ann Arbor      MI  Teacher
Maurdeff    Sonia     550 Traver    Ann Arbor      MI  Student
Parker      Tammy     245 Circle    Vacaville      CA  Teacher
Peat        Robert    421 Brook     Vacaville      CA  Counselor
Peat        Patricia  421 Brook     Vacaville      CA  Model
Peat        Brian     421 Brook     Vacaville      CA  Athlete
Farneth     Nichole   245 Circle    Vacaville      CA  Dancer
Farneth     Sandra    245 Circle    Vacaville      CA  Gymnast
Smith       Gregory   311 Orchard   Ann Arbor      MI  Engineer
Smith       Carolyn   311 Orchard   Ann Arbor      MI  Housewife
Winter      Jim       333 Pick      Garden Grove   CA  Key Grip
Winter      Linda     333 Pick      Garden Grove   CA  Teacher
Tran        Tai Chan  345 Lakeview  Orange         CA  Doctor
Golden      Jane      345 Lakeview  Orange         CA  Nurse
Chang       Wendy     356 Edgewood  Ann Arbor      MI  Librarian
Brogan      Lloyd     111 Miller    Santa Cruz     CA  Vice-President
Brogan      Sally     111 Miller    Santa Cruz     CA  Account Manager
Babchuk     Nicholas  13 Stratford  Sun City West  AZ  Professor
Babchuk     Bianca    13 Stratford  Sun City West  AZ  Professor
Rodriguez Bob         20 Elm        Ontario        CA  Systems Analyst
search hit BOTTOM, continuing at TOP                    2,11          4%
```

WHAT'S HAPPENING? You went to the next occurrence of the string Carolyn. Again, the message at the bottom of the screen told you that you hit BOTTOM and then the search continued at the top. In this file, there are only two occurrences of **Carolyn**.

STEP 15 Key in the following: **n**

```
Smith       Gregory   311 Orchard   Ann Arbor      MI  Engineer
Smith       Carolyn   311 Orchard   Ann Arbor      MI  Housewife
Winter      Jim       333 Pick      Garden Grove   CA  Key Grip
```

WHAT'S HAPPENING? Keying in n continued your search. If you wanted to go in the opposite direction, you would have keyed in N. You may have already noticed that the upper- and lowercase command change direction. You may also become tired of the highlighting. You can turn it off.

STEP 16 Key in the following: **:nohlsearch** Enter

```
Smith       Gregory   311 Orchard   Ann Arbor      MI  Engineer
Smith       Carolyn   311 Orchard   Ann Arbor      MI  Housewife
Winter      Jim       333 Pick      Garden Grove   CA  Key Grip
```

WHAT'S HAPPENING? Now the highlighting is turned off. You cursor is on the **C** in **Carolyn**.

STEP 17 Key in the following: **fn**

```
Smith       Gregory   311 Orchard   Ann Arbor      MI  Engineer
Smith       Carolyn   311 Orchard   Ann Arbor      MI  Housewife
Winter      Jim       333 Pick      Garden Grove   CA  Key Grip
```

WHAT'S HAPPENING? Keying in **f** followed by the **n** took you to the first occurrence of the character **n**.

STEP 18 Key in the following: **fn**. Key in the following: **fn**. Key in the following: **fn**.

```
Smith       Gregory   311 Orchard   Ann Arbor      MI  Engineer
Smith       Carolyn   311 Orchard   Ann Arbor      MI  Housewife
Winter      Jim       333 Pick      Garden Grove   CA  Key Grip
```

WHAT'S HAPPENING? Each time you keyed in **fn** you were taken to the next occurrence of the character **n**. However, when you press the last **fn**, the system beeped at you because their were no more "n's" in the current line. To move back, you would key in **Fn** to move backwards through the line.

STEP 19 Key in the following: **1G**

```
▪
Gillay      Carolyn   699 Lemon     Orange         CA  Professor
Panezich    Frank     689 Lake      Orange         CA  Teacher
Tuttle      Steven    356 Embassy   Mission Viejo  CA  Juggler
```

WHAT'S **HAPPENING?** Since vi remembers the last place you were in the file, you went to the first line in the file so when you open the file, you will be at top of the file.

STEP 20 Press **ZZ**.

```
[cgillay@linux72   floppy]$   cd /mnt/floppy; vi newprson.fil
[cgillay@linux72   cgillay]$  ▪
```

WHAT'S **HAPPENING?** You have closed the file.

6.6 ● Getting Help

As you can see, using vi requires knowledge of a plethora of commands. In order to assist you, Red Hat's Linux version of vi, vim, comes with some built-in help. You use the Last Line command, **:help** Enter to enter help. You may move through the Help window using the normal vi movement and editing keys. To return to your document, you simply key in **:q** Enter . Table 6.3, "Help in vi," lists some of the help available.

Command	Result
:help	Enter vi help. Must be followed by Enter .
:help quickref	Lists all vi commands. This is a complete list and is a very large file. Must be followed by Enter .
:help howto	Lists HOWTOs on a variety of subjects. Must be followed by Enter .
:help *topic*	Displays help for a specific topic that was keyed in. Must be followed by Enter , for example, **:help scrolling** Enter .
:help *command*	Displays help for a specific command as indicated by a command. Must be followed by Enter , for example, **help ZZ** Enter .
:help *keystrokes*	Enters help and gives help on what keystrokes means in Command mode. For example, you would key in **:help ctrl-D** followed by an Enter . This is a case where you actually key in Ctrl followed by the keystroke of interest, for example, **:help ctrl-D** Enter . Note the hyphen between **ctrl** and the character.

:help i_*keystrokes*   Enters help and gives help on what keystrokes mean in Insert mode. You would key in **:help ctrl-D** followed by an [Enter]. This is a case where you actually key in **i-ctrl** followed by the keystroke of interest, for example, **:help i_ctrl-D** [Enter]. Note the underscore and the hyphen.

Table 6.3 • Help in vi

6.7 • Activity: Using Help

Note 1:   The BOOK disk is mounted. A terminal window is open. The default directory is **/mnt/floppy**.

Note 2:   If your terminal window is a different size than the one shown in the examples, the screen movement keys will place you in a different location. To match the examples, size your terminal window to match the example.

Note 3:   Remember that case matters. Also pay attention to whether or not you press [Enter]. Do not press [Enter] automatically.

STEP 1   Key in the following: **vi** [Enter]

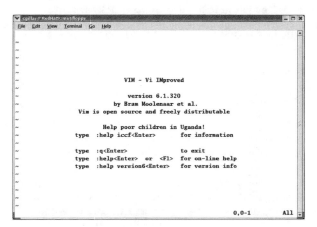

WHAT'S HAPPENING? Using vi with no file name brings you to the introductory screen of vi. It gives you the steps to take for getting help.

STEP 2   Key in the following: **:help howto** [Enter]

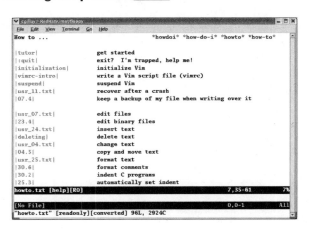

WHAT'S HAPPENING? You may use the vi editing and movement keys to move within this document. Items within the vertical bars such as |:quit| are called vi tags. You may go to the subject of interest by placing your cursor within the vertical bars and pressing Ctrl +].

STEP 3   Move the cursor inside |:quit| Press Ctrl +]

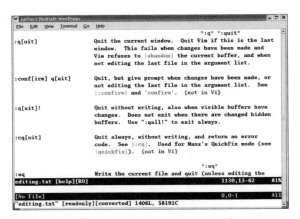

WHAT'S HAPPENING? You were taken to the subject **quit**. To return to your previous location, you press Ctrl + o.

STEP 4   Press Ctrl + o. Key in the following: **:help quickref** Enter

WHAT'S HAPPENING? By keying the command :**help quickref**, you were taken to a complete list of the vi commands. You could use the vi movement keys to move through the document.

STEP 5   Key in the following: **:help scrolling** Enter

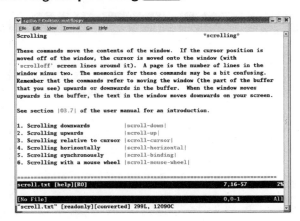

WHAT'S HAPPENING? > By keying the topic of **scrolling**, you were taken to information about scrolling in general.

STEP 6   Key in the following: **:help G** [Enter]

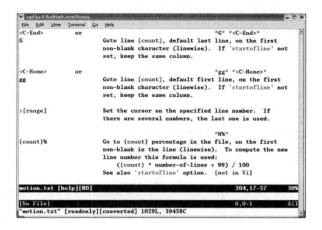

WHAT'S HAPPENING? > Now you were taken to help about a specific command, the **G** or Go To command. If you want help about keystroke combinations, you can also receive this help. Be sure to actually key in the word **ctrl**. Do not press the [Ctrl] key.

STEP 7   Key in the following: **:help ctrl-b** [Enter]

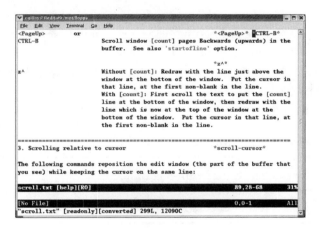

WHAT'S HAPPENING? > You now know what [Ctrl] + **b** key does. However, this is using [Ctrl] + **b** in Command mode. If you want to know what [Ctrl] + **b** does in Insert mode, you can also find out that information. Be sure to actually key in the word **i_ctrl**. Do not press the [Ctrl] key.

STEP 8   Key in the following: **:help i_ctrl-b** [Enter]

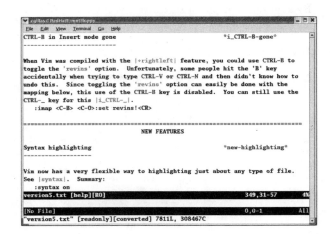

WHAT'S **HAPPENING?** ╳ Now you see that **Ctrl** + **b** in Insert mode is no longer available.

STEP 9   Key in the following: **:q** **Enter**.

STEP 10   Key in the following: **ZZ**. Close the terminal window.

WHAT'S **HAPPENING?** ╳ **:q** took you out of help. **ZZ** ended your vi session.

6.8 ● **Adding Text to a File**

You may add text to any file with vi. But once again, there are a series of commands that you may use. With vim, once you are in Insert mode, you may simply key in data as you do with any editor. However, when you are using vi or vim, and you are in command mode, you can use the following insertion keys. Once you use these keys, they place you in insert mode. These are listed in Table 6.4, "Adding Text in vi."

Command	Result
i	Inserts text before cursor.
I	Inserts text at the beginning of line.
a	Inserts text after cursor.
A	Append text at end of line.
o	Opens a new line below current line.
O	Opens a new line above current line.
r	Replaces current single character.
R	Replaces characters, beginning with current character. Will overwrite characters in line until **Esc** is pressed.

Table 6.4 ● Adding Text in vi

6.9 ● Activity: Adding Text to a File

Note: The BOOK disk is mounted. A terminal window is open. The default directory is
/mnt/floppy.

STEP 1   Key in the following: **vi vimeditor** Enter

STEP 2   Move the cursor on the period after **IDE**. Press **i**. Press the → key.
Press the Space Bar.

STEP 3   Enter the following text, including errors. Do not key in Enter at the end of the text.
Just press Enter where indicated in the file.

An IDE (Integrated Development Enter
Environment) is a programming environment that has been packaged as an Enter
application program. The abbreviation IDE also stands for Integrated Drive Enter
Electornics. Enter
What VIM is Not? Enter
Vim isn't an editor designed to hold users' ahnds. It is a tool of which Enter
must be learned. Vim is not a word processor. Although it can display text Enter
with various forms of highlighting and formatting, it is not there to Enter
provideWYSIWYG editing of documents.

STEP 4   Press Esc to return to Command mode.

STEP 5   Place the cursor on the period immediately after the word Electornics. Press **o**.

```
Environment) is a programming environment that has been packaged
as an application program. The abbreviation IDE also stands for
Integrated Drive   Electornics.
█
What VIM is Not?
Vim isn't an editor designed to hold users' ahnds. It is a tool of
which
```

WHAT'S HAPPENING? By returning to Command mode, positioning your cursor on the period
and pressing **o**, you opened a line below the current line. You are now in Insert mode.

STEP 6   Press Enter.

STEP 7   Key in the following:

Vim is not just for programmers, though. Vim is perfect for all kinds Enter
of text editing, from composing email to editing configuration files. Enter

```
Environment) is a programming environment that has been packaged as an
application program. The abbreviation IDE also stands for Integrated
Drive   Electornics.

Vim is not just for programmers, though. Vim is perfect for all kinds
of text editing, from composing email to editing configuration files.
█
What VIM is Not?
Vim isn't an editor designed to hold users' ahnds. It is a tool of which
```

WHAT'S HAPPENING? You inserted text. You may also use the **a** command. The **a** command is similar to the **i** command, except **a** inserts text after the cursor.

STEP 8   Press Esc to return to Command mode. Place the cursor on the *s* in *isn't* in the second line of the fourth paragraph. Press **i**. Press the Space Bar.

```
What VIM is Not?
Vim i sn't an editor designed to hold users' ahnds. It is a tool
of which
```

WHAT'S HAPPENING? The *space* character was placed before the "*s*" in *isn't.*

STEP 9   Press the Backspace key. Press Esc. Place the cursor on the "*s*" in *isn't*. Press **a**. Press the Space Bar.

```
What VIM is Not?
Vim is n't an editor designed to hold users' ahnds. It is a tool
of which
```

WHAT'S HAPPENING? Since you used the **a** command, your data insertion—the space—was placed after the cursor.

STEP 10   Press the right arrow. Press the Delete key. Key in the following: **o**.

```
What VIM is Not?
Vim is not an editor designed to hold users' ahnds. It is a tool
of which
```

WHAT'S HAPPENING? You deleted the apostrophe and added the letter o.

STEP 11   Press Esc Position the cursor on the "a" in *ahnds* in the second line of the last paragraph. Press **R**.

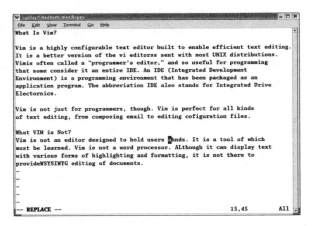

WHAT'S HAPPENING? Your cursor is now positioned on the **a**. At the bottom of the screen, you see the —REPLACE— command. Each character you key in will replace an existing character. If you had used the lower case **r**, you would have only replaced one character.

STEP 12   Key in the following: **ha**

```
What VIM is Not?
Vim is not an editor designed to hold users' hands. It is a tool of which
```

WHAT'S **HAPPENING?** ⟩ Each character you keyed in replaced an existing character.

STEP 13   Press ⟨Esc⟩. Key in the following: **1G**.

STEP 14   Press ⟨Esc⟩. Press **ZZ**.

WHAT'S **HAPPENING?** ⟩ You have moved to the top of the file and then saved your file and returned to the terminal window.

6.10 ● Correcting Text

Although you can enter Insert mode and move within the document to correct errors, you may also correct or edit a text file using the Delete and Change commands. Once you learn these commands, you will find them faster and easier to use in editing a file. The Undo and Redo commands are included here, as they are helpful when you are editing. The Delete (**x**) command works with single characters. The Delete (**d**) command removes text from the work buffer. The Change (**c**) command works like the Delete command, except you are left in Insert mode. All of these commands (**x**, **d** and **c**) also work with blocks of text. Thus, if you wanted to delete five characters, you would key in **5x**. If you wanted to delete five words, you would key in **d5w**. These commands are listed in Table 6.5, "Delete and Change Commands in vi."

Command	Result
u	Undoes what you just did. It only restores the most recently deleted text.
⟨Ctrl⟩ + **R**	Redoes the previous undo.
cw*newword*	Deletes the existing word and places you in Insert mode for the new word.
cc*newline*	Deletes the existing sentence and places you in Insert mode for the new sentence.
dd	Deletes a line.
dw	Deletes a word.
D	Deletes from the cursor to the end of the line.
d0	Deletes from the cursor to the beginning of the line.
x	Deletes current cursor position.
X	Deletes back one character.

Table 6.5 ● Delete and Change Commands in vi

6.11 ● Activity: Correcting Text

Note: The BOOK disk is mounted. A terminal window is open. The default directory is **/mnt/floppy**.

STEP 1   Key in the following: **vi newprson.fil** ⟨Enter⟩

STEP 2   Key in the following: **7G**. Press ⟨Ctrl⟩ + **g**

```
gillay@RedHat9:/mnt/floppy
File  Edit  View  Terminal  Go  Help
Gillay     Carolyn   699 Lemon     Orange        CA  Professor
Panezich   Frank     689 Lake      Orange        CA  Teacher
Tuttle     Steven    356 Embassy   Mission Viejo CA  Juggler
Maurdeff   Kathryn   550 Traver    Ann Arbor     MI  Teacher
Maurdeff   Sonia     550 Traver    Ann Arbor     MI  Student
Parker     Tammy     245 Circle    Vacaville     CA  Teacher
Peat       Robert    421 Brook     Vacaville     CA  Counselor
Peat       Patricia  421 Brook     Vacaville     CA  Model
Peat       Brian     421 Brook     Vacaville     CA  Athlete
Farneth    Nichole   245 Circle    Vacaville     CA  Dancer
Farneth    Sandra    245 Circle    Vacaville     CA  Gymnast
Smith      Gregory   311 Orchard   Ann Arbor     MI  Engineer
Smith      Carolyn   311 Orchard   Ann Arbor     MI  Housewife
Winter     Jim       333 Pick      Garden Grove  CA  Key Grip
Winter     Linda     333 Pick      Garden Grove  CA  Teacher
Tran       Tai Chan  345 Lakeview  Orange        CA  Doctor
Golden     Jane      345 Lakeview  Orange        CA  Nurse
Chang      Wendy     356 Edgewood  Ann Arbor     MI  Librarian
Brogan     Lloyd     111 Miller    Santa Cruz    CA  Vice-President
Brogan     Sally     111 Miller    Santa Cruz    CA  Account Manager
Babchuk    Nicholas  13 Stratford  Sun City West AZ  Professor
Babchuk    Bianca    13 Stratford  Sun City West AZ  Professor
"newprson.fil" 44 lines --15%--                        7,1        Top
```

WHAT'S HAPPENING? You move to the seventh line. Using [Ctrl] + **G** showed you what file you are in, what line number you are in, and what percent of the file is in the work buffer you are looking at.

STEP 3   Key in the following: **4w**. Key in the following: **dew.** Key in **X** six times.

Maurdeff	Sonia	550 Traver	Ann Arbor	MI	Student
Parker	Tammy	245 Circle	CA		Teacher
Peat	Robert	421 Brook	Vacaville	CA	Counselor

WHAT'S HAPPENING? You moved to the fourth word and deleted it. You then deleted the "empty" spaces prior to CA with the **X**.

STEP 4   Key in the following: **i**. Key in the following: **Tustin** [Space Bar] [Tab]

Maurdeff	Sonia	550 Traver	Ann Arbor	MI	Student
Parker	Tammy	245 Circle	Tustin	CA	Teacher
Peat	Robert	421 Brook	Vacaville	CA	Counselor

WHAT'S HAPPENING? You went to Insert mode and added the word *Tustin*, a space, and then a tab.

STEP 5   Press [Esc]. Key in the following: **8u**.

Maurdeff	Sonia	550 Traver	Ann Arbor	MI	Student
Parker	Tammy	245 Circle	Vacaville	CA	Teacher
Peat	Robert	421 Brook	Vacaville	CA	Counselor

WHAT'S HAPPENING? You returned to Command mode and undid your last eight changes.

STEP 6   Key in the following: **2G**. Key in the following: **2w**. Key in **x** two times.

Gillay	Carolyn	9 Lemon	Orange	CA	Professor
Panezich	Frank	689 Lake	Orange	CA	Teacher

WHAT'S HAPPENING? You moved to the second line, second word, and deleted two characters.

STEP 7   Key in the following: **cw450**

Gillay	Carolyn	450 Lemon	Orange	CA	Professor
Panezich	Frank	689 Lake	Orange	CA	Teacher

WHAT'S HAPPENING? ⟩ By using the Change Word command (**cw**), you were placed in Insert mode and could add the new text. It is useful to know where you are in the file. There is a command, **:set number**, that will display the line numbers. These numbers are for reference only and are not part of the file.

STEP 8   Press **Esc** to return to Command mode. Key in the following: **:set number** **Enter**

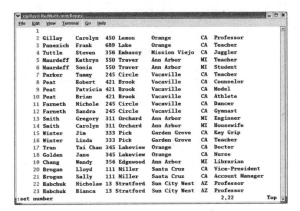

WHAT'S HAPPENING? ⟩ Now that you can see your line numbers, you can use them for reference. But realize that each time you delete or add lines, the numbers will change.

STEP 9   Key in the following: **18G**. Key in the following: **dd**

17 Tran	Tai Chan 345 Lakeview	Orange	CA	Doctor
18 Chang	Wendy	356 Edgewood	Ann Arbor	MI	Librarian
19 Brogan	Lloyd	111 Miller	Santa Cruz	CA	Vice-President

WHAT'S HAPPENING? ⟩ You moved to line 18 and then deleted it so that line 19 became line 18.

STEP 10   Key in the following: **D**

17 Tran	Tai Chan 345 Lakeview	Orange	CA	Doctor
18				
19 Brogan	Lloyd	111 Miller	Santa Cruz	CA	Vice-President

WHAT'S HAPPENING? ⟩ You have deleted the text from the cursor to the end of the line.

STEP 11   Key in the following: **5dd**

16 Winter	Linda	333 Pick	Garden Grove	CA	Teacher
17 Tran	Tai Chan 345 Lakeview	Orange	CA	Doctor
18 Rodriguez	Bob	20 Elm	Ontario	CA	Systems Analyst
19 Helm	Milton	333 Meadow	Sherman Oaks	CA	Consultant
20 Suzuki	Charlene 567 Abbey	Rochester	MI	Day Care Teacher
21 Markiw	Nicholas 354 Bell	Phoenix	AZ	Engineer
22 Markiw	Emily	10 Zion	Sun City West	AZ	Retired
23 Nyles	John	12 Brooks	Sun City West	AZ	Retired
5 fewer lines				

WHAT'S HAPPENING? ⟩ You deleted the next five lines and the message at the bottom of the screen told you so. You may also turn off an option that you set.

STEP 12   Key in the following: **:set nonumber** **Enter**

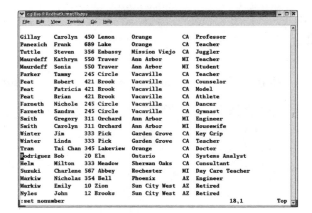

WHAT'S HAPPENING? You no longer have line numbers

STEP 13 Key in the following: **:q!** **Enter**

WHAT'S HAPPENING? You moved to the top of the file. You then exited vi and did not save any of your changes.

6.12 • Searching and Replacing

Searching and replacing is a useful feature that most word processors possess. Rather than searching for a word, deleting it, and then replacing it with another word, you can search and replace with one command. In vim, you may do so using the Substitute command. The Substitute command is a combination of the Search and Change commands. Just as you used the / to find a string of text, the Substitute command does the same. The difference is that when it finds a match, it changes it. The syntax of the command is:

```
: [location] s/string/replacement/ [option]
```

The command will be executed in the current line unless you state otherwise. The location is what you want to be searched. If you do not specify where to search, only the current line will be used. A period (.) within the location indicates the current line, and a $ represents the last line. If you wish to use a range of numbers, you must separate them with a comma (,). Some examples of how to interpret the Location command are listed in Table 6.6, "Location Command Results."

Location	Result
3	line 3
5,10	line 5 through line 10
1,.	beginning of file through the current line
.,$	current line through end of file
1,$	entire file
.,.+5	current line through fifth following line (six lines in all)

Table 6.6 • Location Command Results

The string is what you are looking for, and the replacement is what will replace the string. Note that the string and the replacement are set off by delimiters. In the example, the forward slash is used as a delimiter, although in fact any character other than a letter, a number, a space, or the forward slash can be used. Some useful options include **g**, **i**, **I**, and **c**. The global (**g**) option replaces all occurrences in the line or block of text. Ignore case (**i**) ignores the case for the search pattern. The do-not-ignore (**I**) option means that no replacement will occur unless the string is the correct case. The confirm (**c**) option asks you to confirm each substitution prior to its occurring. You key in **y** if you wish the substitution to occur and **n** to skip this match and continue on. You may use **Esc** to skip this match, **a** to substitute this and all remaining matches, and **q** to quit substituting. **Ctrl** + **E** will scroll the screen up and **Ctrl** + **Y** will scroll the screen down.

6.13 • Activity: Replacing Text and Printing the File

Note: The BOOK disk is mounted. A terminal window is open. The default directory is **/mnt/floppy**.

STEP 1   Key in the following: **vi newprson.fil** **Enter**

STEP 2   Key in the following and note the colon preceding the command:
:13s/Smith/Goldberg **Enter**

```
Farneth    Sandra    245 Circle    Vacaville    CA  Gymnast
Goldberg    Gregory  311 Orchard   Ann Arbor     MI  Engineer
Smith       Carolyn  311 Orchard   Ann Arbor     MI  Housewife
```

WHAT'S HAPPENING? You went to Line 13 and substituted the string Goldberg for Smith. The spacing became incorrect because Goldberg has more character than Smith. The highlighted search is on the next Smith but the cursor is on the "G" in **Goldberg**.

STEP 3   Key in the following: **w**. Key in **X** three times.

```
Farneth    Sandra    245 Circle    Vacaville    CA  Gymnast
Goldberg  Gregory   311 Orchard   Ann Arbor     MI  Engineer
Smith       Carolyn  311 Orchard   Ann Arbor     MI  Housewife
```

WHAT'S HAPPENING? You moved to the next word (**Gregory**) and used the **X** to delete the characters (spaces) before the cursor.

STEP 4   Key in the following and note the colon before the command:
:1,$s/Brogan/Brogin/c **Enter**

```
Chang     Wendy     356 Edgewood  Ann Arbor      MI  Librarian
Brogan    Lloyd     111 Miller    Santa Cruz    CA  Vice-President
Brogan    Sally     111 Miller    Santa Cruz    CA  Account Manager
Babchuk   Nicholas  13 Stratford  Sun City West AZ  Professor
replace with Brogin (y/n/a/q/^E/^Y)?_
```

WHAT'S HAPPENING? Your command asked that you begin at the first line and continue to the end of the file and replace every occurrence of **Brogan** with **Brogin**, but be queried before the replacement occurs. The first **Brogan** (**Lloyd**) is the character string you are trying to change. It is highlighted in gray. Search found all the **Brogan**s as indicated by the next **Brogan** (**Sally**) highlighted in red. The ^ represents pressing the [Ctrl] key.

STEP 5   Key in the following: **n**

```
Chang     Wendy     356 Edgewood    Ann Arbor       MI   Librarian
Brogan    Lloyd     111 Miller      Santa Cruz      CA   Vice-President
Brogan    Sally     111 Miller      Santa Cruz      CA   Account Manager
Babchuk   Nicholas  13 Stratford    Sun City West   AZ   Professor
replace with Brogin (y/n/a/q/^E/^Y)?_
```

WHAT'S HAPPENING? The first Brogan was not replaced and is now highlighted in red. You have moved to the next occurrence of the string Brogan (now highlighted in gray) again, being queried whether or not you want the replacement to occur.

STEP 6   Key in the following: **y**

```
Chang     Wendy     356 Edgewood    Ann Arbor       MI   Librarian
Brogan    Lloyd     111 Miller      Santa Cruz      CA   Vice-President
Brogin    Sally     111 Miller      Santa Cruz      CA   Account Manager
Babchuk   Nicholas  13 Stratford    Sun City West   AZ   Professor
```

WHAT'S HAPPENING? Since you answered **y** for yes, the replacement occurred. There are no more occurrences of **Brogan**, so your search ceased. Global search and replaces are very useful but can be traumatic if you are not careful.

STEP 7   Key in the following and note the colon preceding the command: **:1,$s/i/J/g** [Enter]

```
cgillay@RedHat9:/mnt/floppy                                          _ □ ✕
File  Edit  View  Terminal  Go  Help
Babchuk     NJcholas  13 Stratford   Sun CJty West   AZ   Professor
Babchuk     BJanca    13 Stratford   Sun CJty West   AZ   Professor
RodrJguez   Bob       20 Elm         OntarJo         CA   Systems Analyst
Helm        MJlton    333 Meadow     Sherman Oaks    CA   Consultant
SuzukJ      Charlene  567 Abbey      Rochester       MI   Day Care Teacher
MarkJw      NJcholas  354 Bell       PhoenJx         AZ   EngJneer
MarkJw      EmJly     10 ZJon        Sun CJty West   AZ   RetJred
Nyles       John      12 Brooks      Sun CJty West   AZ   RetJred
Nyles       SophJe    12 Brooks      Sun CJty West   AZ   RetJred
MarkJw      NJck      10 ZJon        Sun CJty West   AZ   RetJred
WashJngon   Tyrone    345 Newport    Orange          CA   Manager
Jones       Steven    32 North       PhoenJx         AZ   Buyer
SmJth       DavJd     120 CollJns    Orange          CA   Chef
Babchuk     Walter    12 VJew        Thousand Oaks   CA   PresJdent
Babchuk     Deana     12 VJew        Thousand Oaks   CA   HousewJfe
Jones       Cleo      355 Second     Ann Arbor       MI   Clerk
Gonzales    AntonJo   40 Northern    OntarJo         CA   EngJneer
JONES       JERRY     244 East       MJssJon VJejo   CA   Systems Analyst
Lo          OphelJa   1213 WJck      PhoenJx         AZ   WrJter
Jones       ErvJn     15 Fourth      Santa Cruz      CA   Banker
Perez       SergJo    134 Seventh    Ann Arbor       MI   EdJtor
Yuan        SuelJn    56 TwJn Leaf   Orange          CA   ArtJst
MarkJw      NJcholas  12 FJfth       Glendale        AZ   EngJneer
95 substitutions on 41 lines                        44,1        Bot
```

WHAT'S HAPPENING? As you can see, global indeed means global. You replaced every letter "i" with the letter "J". Fortunately, you can undo your changes

STEP 8   Key in the following: **u**

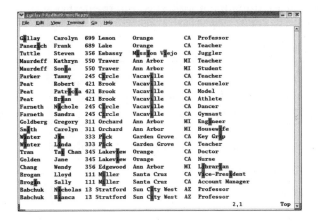

WHAT'S HAPPENING? You undid your changes and they are highlighted in red. Another way to make global changes is to use the Repeat Edit (.) command in conjunction with a Search (**/text**), a Change Word (**cw**) and a Next (**n**) command, which allows you to move through a file and change all occurrences of a word or phrase.

STEP 9 Key in the following: **1G**. Key in the following: **/Markiw** Enter

Suzuki	Charlene	567	Abbey	Rochester	MI	Day Care Teacher
Markiw	Nicholas	354	Bell	Phoenix	AZ	Engineer

STEP 10 Key in the following: **cwMarket**. Press the Esc key

Suzuki	Charlene	567	Abbey	Rochester	MI	Day Care Teacher
Market	Nicholas	354	Bell	Phoenix	AZ	Engineer

WHAT'S HAPPENING? You went to the top of the file, searched for the text string **Markiw**, and used **cw Market** to change the text, which then placed you in Insert mode. You pressed the Esc key to change to Command mode.

STEP 11 Key in the following: **n**. Key in the following, which is the period: **.**

Suzuki	Charlene	567	Abbey	Rochester	MI	Day Care Teacher
Market	Nicholas	354	Bell	Phoenix	AZ	Engineer
Market	Emily	10	Zion	Sun City West	AZ	Retired

WHAT'S HAPPENING? Using the **n** moved you to the next occurrence of **Markiw**. Pressing the **.** (period) repeated the last edit. Remember, in the next steps, you will press the **n**, then the period.

STEP 12 Key in the following: **n**. Key in the following: **.**

Nyles	Sophie	12	Brooks	Sun City West	CA	Retired
Market	Nick	10	Zion	Sun City West	AZ	Retired

WHAT'S HAPPENING? Using the **n** moved you to the next occurrence of **Markiw**. Pressing the **.** (period) repeated the last edit.

STEP 13 Key in the following: **n**. Key in the following: **.**

Yuan	Suelin	56	Twin Leaf	Orange	CA	Artist
Market	Nicholas	12	Fifth	Glendale	AZ	Engineer

WHAT'S HAPPENING? Again, using the **n** moved you to the next occurrence of **Markiw**. Pressing the **.** (period) repeated the last edit.

STEP 14 Key in the following: **n.**

```
Yuan        Suelin    56 Twin Leaf   Orange        CA   Artist
Market      Nicholas  12 Fifth       Glendale      AZ   Engineer
Pattern not found: Markiw
```

WHAT'S HAPPENING? Now there are no further occurrences of **Markiw**.

STEP 15 Press Esc. Key in the following: **1G**.

STEP 16 Key in the following: **ZZ**

STEP 17 Be sure the printer is on. Key in the following: **lpr newprson.fil** Enter

WHAT'S HAPPENING? You moved to the top of the file then you exited the file, saving your changes. You then printed your file. You should have a hard copy of your file.

6.14 • Copying, Pasting, and Moving Text

When you key in **u** for undo, the text comes from the buffer. Remember, a buffer is an area in memory used for temporary storage. Actually, vi maintains more than one buffer. Remember, the text you are working in is not saved to disk until you write it to disk. All your work occurs in the work buffer. In addition to this work buffer, vi also has an additional buffer, which for purposes of clarity will be called the "undo buffer." vi uses the undo buffer for text you delete, cut, or change. Whenever text is altered, it is stored in the undo buffer. Thus, each time you place something in the undo buffer, it replaces what was there. In addition to the work buffer and the undo buffer for editing changes, vi also provides up to 26 named buffers, or registers, that can hold text while you are in an editing session.

You may manipulate these buffers with the Delete, Put, and Yank commands. The Yank command (**y**) differs from the Delete commands in that it does not delete the text in the work buffer but copies it to the undo buffer. The Put command (**p, P**) copies text from the undo buffer into the work buffer.

You may create a named buffer or register. The register's name is a letter of the alphabet. You indicate that you are naming the buffer when you use the Yank command by preceding it with a " (quotation mark). Thus, if you keyed in **"cyy**, you are naming your buffer **c** and are storing the contents of the current line in the **c** buffer. Naming the buffer **"c**, vi will overwrite the contents of the **c** buffer each time it deletes or yanks text into the buffer. If instead you name your buffer **"C**, this will append the newly yanked or deleted text to the end of the **"C** buffer.

The Put command copies text from the undo buffer into your work buffer. Using **p**, (lowercase p) inserts the text after the current character, whereas **P** (uppercase P) inserts the text before the current character. If you do not use the Put command immediately after a Yank or Delete command, you should use a named buffer. Thus to use text in the **c** buffer, your command would be **"cp**. These commands are listed in Table 6.7, "Copying and Moving Commands in vi"

Command	Result
"*x*d <cm>	Places deleted text up to location specified by <cm> into named buffer indicated by **x**.
"*X*d <cm>	Appends deleted text up to location specified by <cm> into named buffer indicated by **X**.
p	Inserts last deleted text after cursor
P	Inserts last deleted text before cursor
"*x*p	Inserts last deleted text after cursor from the named buffer as indicated by **x**.
"*x*P	Inserts last deleted text before cursor from the named buffer as indicated by **x**.
y <cm>	Copies text up to location specified by **<cm>**.
"*x*y <cm>	Copies text up to location specified by <cm> and places it in a named buffer indicated by **x**.
"*X*y <cm>	Appends text up to location specified by **<cm>** to a named buffer indicated by **X**.
yy	Copies current line.
"*x*yy	Copies current line into named buffer as indicated by **x**.
"*X*yy	Appends current line to a named buffer indicated by **X**.

Table 6.7 • Copying and Moving Commands in vi

6.15 • Activity: Copying, Pasting, and Moving Text

Note: The BOOK disk is mounted. A terminal window is open. The default directory is **/mnt/floppy**.

STEP 1   Key in the following: **vi newprson.fil** [Enter]

STEP 2   Key in the following: **3G**. Key in the following: **yy**.

STEP 3   Key in the following: **35G**. Key in the following: **p**

```
Babchuk    Walter     12 View        Thousand Oaks  CA   President
Panezich   Frank      689 Lake       Orange         CA   Teacher
```

WHAT'S HAPPENING? You moved to Line 3. You yanked Line 3. You then moved to line 35 and pasted the text after the line.

STEP 4   Move the cursor up two lines and place the cursor on **S** in **Smith**.

STEP 5   Key in the following: **P**

```
Jones       Steven    32 North    Phoenix        AZ  Buyer
Panezich    Frank     689 Lake    Orange         CA  Teacher
Smith       David     120 Collins Orange         CA  Chef
Babchuk     Walter    12 View     Thousand Oaks  CA  President
```

WHAT'S HAPPENING? You moved to two lines above. Your **P** command pasted the text before the current line. Thus, the lowercase p pastes text after the current line and the uppercase P pastes text before the current line.

STEP 6   Move up three lines to **Market**. Key in the following: **4w**.

```
Nyles       Sophie    12 Brooks    Sun City West  CA  Retired
Market      Nick      10 Zion      Sun City West  AZ  Retired
Washingon   Tyrone    345 Newport  Orange         CA  Manager
```

WHAT'S HAPPENING? Your cursor is now positioned on the **S** in **Sun City West**.

STEP 7   Key in the following: **"x4dw**

```
Nyles       Sophie    12 Brooks    Sun City West  CA  Retired
Market      Nick      10 Zion      Retired
Washingon   Tyrone    345 Newport  Orange         CA  Manager
```

WHAT'S HAPPENING? You have deleted four words and placed them in a buffer named **x**.

STEP 8   Move the cursor to the **O** in **Orange** immediately beneath the current line.

```
Nyles       Sophie    12 Brooks    Sun City West  CA  Retired
Market      Nick      10 Zion      Retired
Washingon   Tyrone    345 Newport  Orange         CA  Manager
```

WHAT'S HAPPENING? You have positioned your cursor.

STEP 9   Key in the following: **D**

```
Nyles       Sophie    12 Brooks    Sun City West  CA  Retired
Market      Nick      10 Zion      Retired
Washingon   Tyrone    345 Newport
```

WHAT'S HAPPENING? You deleted from the cursor position to the end of the line.

STEP 10   Key in the following: **p**

```
Nyles       Sophie    12 Brooks    Sun City West  CA  Retired
Market      Nick      10 Zion      Retired
Washingon   Tyrone    345 Newport  Orange         CA  Manager
```

WHAT'S HAPPENING? You pasted the text from the buffer back into the line. The undo buffer is holding the text **Orange   CA   Manager**. You want to return the text from your named buffer called **x**.

STEP 11   On the line above **Washington, Tyrone**, position your cursor on the space just before **Retired.**

```
Nyles      Sophie     12 Brooks      Sun City West   CA   Retired
Market     Nick       10 Zion        ▓Retired
Washingon  Tyrone     345 Newport    Orange          CA   Manager
```

WHAT'S HAPPENING? You are now going to use your named buffer **x**, where you saved the text **Sun City West AZ**.

STEP 12 Key in the following: **"xp**

```
Nyles      Sophie     12 Brooks      Sun City West   CA   Retired
Market     Nick       10 Zion        Sun City West   AZ ▓ Retired
Washingon  Tyrone     345 Newport    Orange          CA   Manager
```

WHAT'S HAPPENING? Instead of copying the last deleted text (**Orange CA Manager**) into your file, you copied the information from the buffer called **x**.

STEP 13 Key in the following: **1G**

STEP 14 Key in the following: **:q!** Enter

WHAT'S HAPPENING? You moved to the top of the file and then you exited the file without saving your changes.

6.16 • Multiple Windows and Multiple Files

Sometimes the text you want to include in one file already exists in another file. vi allows you to read in the information from one file into another with **:r**, the Read command. You may also exit vi temporarily to another Linux command. You may do so by keying in **:!** followed by the command you wish to execute.

The vi editor that comes with Linux (vim) also provides what is called a visual mode. When you are in visual mode the character under the cursor is displayed in inverse video. *Inverse video* is a display method that causes a portion of the display to appear like a negative of the regular display. If the display screen normally displays light images against a dark background, putting it in reverse or inverse video mode will cause it to display dark images against a light background. You may use the cursor movement keys to extend the display, making it easier to see text you wish to copy or delete.

You may also use multiple windows in vi by using the **:split** command. The **:split** command splits the current window into two separate windows and displays the current file in both windows. By default, you are in the top window. You can move in the default window without affecting what is being displayed in the bottom window. However, any changes you make in either window will affect the entire file. You may also have a split window with two different files, allowing you to copy and paste from one window to another. Table 6.8, "Window Commands," gives you these commands as well as the cursor movement keys between windows.

Command	Result
:r *filename*	Reads the indicated file into the current file.
:!command	Exits vi temporarily and allows you to execute the specified command.
v	Places your vi window in visual mode.

:split	Splits the current vi window into two windows.
:split filename	Splits the current vi window into two windows with the other window opening the named file.
Ctrl + **Wj**	Goes down one window.
Ctrl + **Wk**	Goes up one window.
ZZ	Closes a window.

Table 6.8 • Window Commands

6.17 • Activity: Manipulating Files and Windows

Note 1: The BOOK disk is mounted. A terminal window is open. The default directory is **/mnt/floppy**.

Note 2: The **cities** file was created in Chapter 5, Activity 5.17. If you do not have this file, create it now.

STEP 1 Key in the following: **vi cities** **Enter**

STEP 2 Key in the following: **L**. Key in the following: **:r state.cap** **Enter**

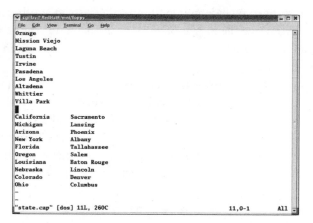

WHAT'S HAPPENING? You have combined the contents of two files. The file, **state.cap**, still exists as a separate file.

STEP 3 Key in the following: **:!cat state.cap** **Enter**

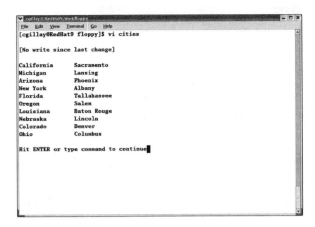

WHAT'S HAPPENING? You have temporarily exited vi by using the **:!** Command. Now you are using the **cat** command. As you can see, the **state.cap** file still exists. However, you have changed the contents of the **cities** file. What if you only wanted information from the **state.cap** file to paste into the **cities** file? You can do that with the **split** command.

STEP 4 Press [Enter]. Key in the following: **:q!** [Enter]

STEP 5 Key in the following: **vi cities** [Enter]

STEP 6 Key in the following: **:split** [Enter]

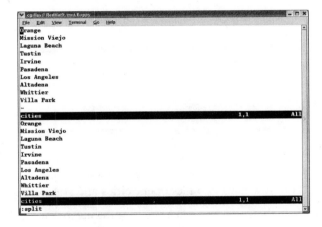

WHAT'S HAPPENING? Your screen is split into two sections. Both sections show the same file because it is the same file. Any change made in either window will affect the entire file, since you are only dealing with one file.

STEP 7 Press [Ctrl] + **wj**. Press [Ctrl] + **wk**

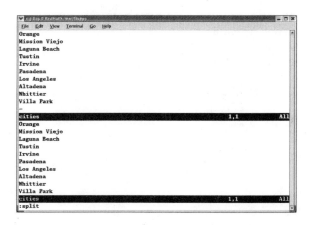

WHAT'S HAPPENING? The combination keys allowed you to move from one window to another.

STEP 8   Key in the following: **ZZ**.

STEP 9   Key in the following: **:split state.cap** [Enter]

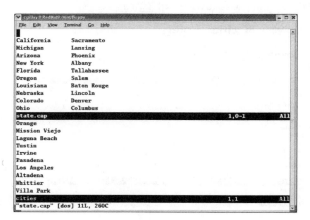

WHAT'S HAPPENING? By keying in **ZZ**, you closed one window. Then you opened a new file, **state.cap** in a window. You now have two files open: **cities** and **state.cap**.

STEP 10   Be sure you are in the **state.cap** window. Place the cursor on the **C** in **California**.

STEP 11   Key in the following: **v**

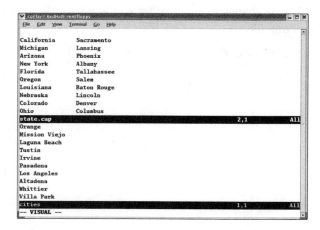

WHAT'S HAPPENING? > You are now in the visual editor. The word **VISUAL** is at the bottom of the screen. You may use the cursor movement keys to select items.

STEP 12 Key in the following: **e**

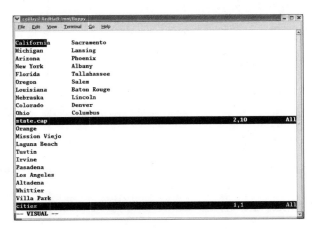

WHAT'S HAPPENING? > The visual editor allows you to see that you selected **California** because it is in inverse video.

STEP 13 Key in the following: **y**. Press **Ctrl** +wj to move to the bottom window.

STEP 14 Position your cursor on the **O** in **Orange**.

STEP 15 Key in **i**. Press **Enter**. Press **Enter** Press **Esc**. Press **H**.

STEP 16 Key in the following: **p**

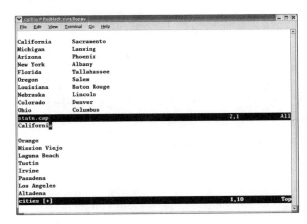

WHAT'S HAPPENING? > You moved to the **cities** window, added some blank lines, and then copied text from the **state.cap** file to the **cities** file.

STEP 17 Key in the following: **ZZ**

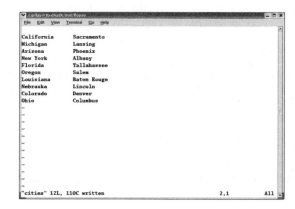

WHAT'S HAPPENING? You closed the **cities file** and saved your changes. Your **state.cap** file is still open.

STEP 18 Key in the following: **ZZ**

STEP 19 Key in the following: **cat cities** [Enter]

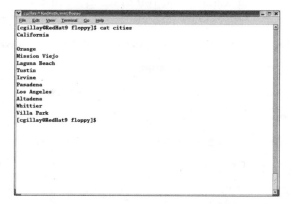

WHAT'S HAPPENING? You closed the **state.cap** file and opened the **cities** file. You see that your change was incorporated into the cities file.

STEP 20 Close the terminal window.

6.18 ● Emacs

Originally Emacs was developed as a series of editor commands or macros. A macro is a series of commands that allow you to automate a complicated task. The name Emacs is an acronym for **Editor Macros**. It is another popular editor. It fully supports the X Window System and allows for mouse interaction. Emacs is not a modal editor. It does not require you to track whether you are in Insert or Command mode. Instead, commands use key combinations such as the [Ctrl] or other special keys such as the [Alt] key and a letter to issue commands. When you use a special control character on the keyboard , Emacs always inserts text. Emacs is also more consistent than vi, as most commands are accessed via using the [Alt] or [Ctrl] keys. Although Emacs supports mouse action and various keys such as the [→] and [PgUp] keys, there is also a series of keyboard controls that allow you to accomplish tasks within Emacs. Table 6.9, "Basic Editing Commands," gives a list of the common commands. Note that most of the commands are a two-step series—first you press [Ctrl] + **x**, and then you press the appropriate key combination to accomplish the task.

Key Combinations	Purpose
Ctrl + x, **Ctrl** + f *filename*	Loads existing file.
Ctrl + x + i	Inserts existing file into current text.
Ctrl + x, **Ctrl** + s	Saves current file.
Ctrl + x, **Ctrl**, s, !	Saves all open files.
Ctrl + x, **Ctrl** + w *filename*	Saves file under a new name.
Ctrl + x, s	Saves all open files with a confirmation request.
Ctrl + x, **Ctrl** + c	Exits Emacs.
Ctrl + h + c	Gives help about a particular key.
Ctrl + h + t	Provides a tutorial about Emacs.
Ctrl + x, u	Undoes the last change.
Ctrl + g	Aborts current command.

Table 6.9 • Basic Editing Commands

When you save a file, Emacs automatically creates a backup copy *name"*, which is the original file you began with. Furthermore, Emacs does regular saves with the file named *#name#*. You can return to this file if you are unable to exit Emacs properly. Table 6.10, "Other Emacs Keys," lists cursor movement and text manipulation keys.

Alt Keys	Purpose	**Ctrl** keys	Purpose
Alt + <	Moves cursor to start of file	**Ctrl** + @	Marks cursor location. After moving cursor, can move or copy text to mark.
Alt + >	Moves cursor to end of file.	**Ctrl** + a	Moves cursor to start of line.
Alt + b	Moves cursor back one word.	**Ctrl** + b	Moves cursor back one character.
Alt + d	Deletes current word.	**Ctrl** + d	Deletes character under cursor.
Alt + f	Moves cursor forward one character.	**Ctrl** + e	Moves cursor to end of line.
Alt + q	Reformats paragraph to fill lines.	**Ctrl** + f	Moves cursor forward one character.
Alt + t	Transposes two words.	**Ctrl** + h	Accesses help.

Alt + **u**	Capitalizes all letters of current word.	**Ctrl** + **k**	Deletes text to end of line.
Alt + **w**	Scrolls up one screen.	**Ctrl** + **n**	Moves cursor to next line.
		Ctrl + **Delete**	Deletes character under cursor.
		Ctrl + **w**	Deletes marked text.
		Ctrl + **y**	Inserts text from buffer and places it after the cursor.
		Ctrl + **p**	Moves cursor to preceding line.
		Ctrl + **t**	Transposes characters.
		Ctrl + **v**	Scrolls down one screen.
		Ctrl + **w**	Deletes marked text.

Table 6.10 • Other Emacs Keys

In Emacs you also edit a file in a buffer and have the choice of writing this buffer back to the file on disk when you have completed your work. You may have many work buffers. When you delete text it is saved in an ordinary buffer that you can recall to your file. In addition, Emacs also allows the use of multiple registers, which are identified by a character (letter or number). These named registers can be inserted into your text as needed.

6.19 • Activity: Using Emacs

Note: The BOOK disk is mounted.

STEP I   Click the Main Menu button. Point to **Programming**. Click **Emacs**.

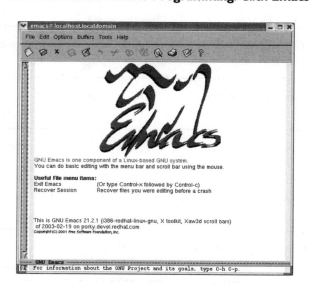

WHAT'S HAPPENING? You have opened Emacs. The opening screen gives you information about Emacs, such as how to Exit and what version.

STEP 2   Press F1. Key in the following: **?**

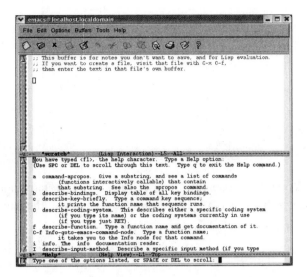

WHAT'S HAPPENING? Pressing F1 took you to help. The **?** then led you to the help options.

STEP 3   Press Ctrl + x. Press Ctrl + x. Press Ctrl + f.

WHAT'S HAPPENING? The prompt at the bottom of the screen is asking you which file you want to load.

STEP 4   Press the Backspace key twice to delete the ~/ and key in the following:

/mnt/floppy/media/books/mystery.bks Enter

WHAT'S HAPPENING? You see the contents of an existing file. The status line at the bottom of the window lets you know that this is a DOS file and also gives you the name of the file.

STEP 5   Press **Ctrl** + **f**. Press the **→** key. Press **Ctrl** + **e**.

WHAT'S HAPPENING? The **Ctrl** + **f** and the right arrow key moved you forward one character. The **Ctrl** + **e** moved you to the end of the line.

STEP 6   Press **Alt** + **>**. *Note:* This is tricky—you have to hold the **Shift** key, since the **>** is the uppercase character.

WHAT'S HAPPENING? The **Alt** + > moved you to the end of the file. However, although you cannot see the characters, there are two tab marks following **Choosers**.

STEP 7   Press the **Backspace** key twice. Press **Enter**

WHAT'S HAPPENING? You deleted the two tab marks and added an **Enter** (a carriage return, line feed) to move to the next line.

STEP 8   Press **Alt** + <. *Note:* This is tricky—you have to hold the **Shift** key, since the < is the uppercase character.

STEP 9   Press **Ctrl** + f. Press the **→** key. Press **Ctrl** + e.

WHAT'S HAPPENING? The **Alt** + < moved you to the top of the file. Again, the **Ctrl** + f and the right arrow key moved you forward one character. The **Ctrl** + e moved you to the end of the line.

STEP 10   Press the **↓**. Press **Ctrl** + b. Press the **←** key. Press **↓** once. Press **Ctrl** + a.

WHAT'S HAPPENING? You moved around the document with these keys. The **Ctrl** + **b** and left arrow moved you back a character at a time. The down arrow key moved you down one line and the **Ctrl** + **a** moved you to the beginning of the line. You may delete text and undo the deletion. **Ctrl** + **k** deletes the current line. Press **Ctrl** + **x**, and **u** will undo the last change.

STEP 11 Press **Ctrl** + **k**. Press **Ctrl** + **x**. Press **u**.

WHAT'S HAPPENING? You deleted a line and then "undid" your deletion. You may also restore the text repeatedly, even after making many changes. To do this, you would press **Ctrl** + **x** and then **u**. You can use this combination in sequence to undo your editing commands changes. This is an advantage over vi in that vi only restores your most recent changes. You may insert text just by keying in data. You may also copy and paste or cut and paste.

STEP 12 Press **Ctrl** + **a**. Press **Ctrl** + **Space Bar**.

WHAT'S **HAPPENING?** You have just marked the starting point for the block of text you want to copy. You see the words **Mark set** in the status bar.

STEP 13 Press the ⬇ key twice to move the cursor to the second line down, which begins with **Connelly**.

STEP 14 Press **Alt** + w.

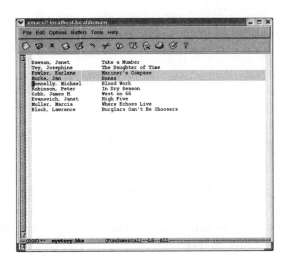

WHAT'S **HAPPENING?** You have just marked the end of the text you want to copy.

STEP 15 Press **Alt** + >. *Note:* This is tricky—you have to hold the **Shift** key, sincethe > is the uppercase character.

STEP 16 Press **Ctrl** + y.

WHAT'S HAPPENING? `Alt` + > moved you to the end of the file and `Ctrl` + y pasted the text your marked. If you wanted to "cut" instead of copy, you would have used `Ctrl` + w instead of `Alt` + w.

STEP 17 Press `Ctrl` + x. Press `Ctrl` + s.

WHAT'S HAPPENING? You have just saved the file. The message at the bottom of the window told you that Emacs wrote the file to disk.

STEP 18 Press `Ctrl` + x. Press `Ctrl` + c.

WHAT'S HAPPENING? You exited Emacs and have returned to the desktop.

STEP 19 Open a terminal window. Key in the following: **ls -a /mnt/floppy/media/books** `Enter`

```
[cgillay@linux72  cgillay]$  ls -a /mnt/floppy/media/books
ame-lit.bks  mystery.bks mystery.bks~ pulitzer.bks
[cgillay@linux72  cgillay]$ _
```

WHAT'S HAPPENING? You can see that you have another copy of **mystery.bks**, called **mystery.bks ~ **. The copy with a tilde is the backup copy that Emacs created.

STEP 20   The file **crops.txt** was created in Activity 5.21, where you renamed **states.usa** to **crops.txt**. In the terminal window, key in the following:

emacs /mnt/floppy/crops.txt Enter

STEP 21   Press Ctrl + s.

WHAT'S **HAPPENING?** You see the **I-search** prompt at the bottom of the screen. Now you key in the text you are looking for.

STEP 22   Key in the following: **cotton**

WHAT'S **HAPPENING?** As you keyed in your search word, emacs found the first occurrence of **c** in **CHIEF**, then the first occurrence of **cotton** and highlighted it and highlighted all the other occurrences of **cotton**.

STEP 23   Press Ctrl + s.

WHAT'S HAPPENING? You searched for and located the next occurrence of **cotton**. You can reformat the document as well.

STEP 24 Press [Alt] + **q**.

WHAT'S HAPPENING? You have reformatted your lines so there are no tabs or carriage returns.

STEP 25 Press [Ctrl] + **x**. Press **u**.

WHAT'S **HAPPENING?** You undid your formatting.

STEP 26   Press [Ctrl] + **x**. Press [Ctrl] + **s**.

WHAT'S **HAPPENING?** Since you made no changes, Emacs told you that the file did not need to be saved in the status area.

STEP 27   Press [Ctrl] + **x**. Press [Ctrl] + **c**

WHAT'S **HAPPENING?** You exited Emacs.

STEP 28   Unmount the BOOK disk. Remove it from the drive.

STEP 29   Close the terminal window.

Chapter Summary

In this chapter you were introduced to the following:

- Opening and using the vi editor.
- Using the command mode in vi.
- Using the last line mode in vi.
- Using the insert mode in vi.
- Creating files with vi.
- Moving and searching within vi.
- Using vi help
- Adding, correcting, and replacing text in a file when using vi.
- Copying, pasting, and moving text in vi.
- Using multiple files and windows in vi.
- Printing a file created with vi.
- Using the Emacs editor.
- Opening and using the Emacs editor to create and save a file.
- Using Emacs help.
- Opening an existing file in Emacs.

Key Terms

Command mode
delimited word
editor
insert mode
inverse video
last line mode
modal editor
mode
text editor
work buffer

Discussion Questions

1. Compare and contrast a graphical editor with a text editor.
2. Why is it important to learn how to use a text editor?
3. vi is a modal editor. Explain.
4. List and describe the two major modes of operation in vi.
5. What is the function of a *work buffer*?
6. What is the function of the last line mode?
7. Many commands in vi operate on blocks of text. List and describe three of these defined blocks.
8. What is the difference between using **fn** and **Fn** in vi?
9. How can you enter the help window? Move through the help window? Return to your document?
10. List and explain how three insert commands can be used when adding text in vi.
11. Explain the functions of each of the following delete commands: **dd**, **dw**, **D**, and **d0**.

12. Explain the function of the **x,d**, and **c** commands and explain how these commands work with blocks of text.
13. What is the function of the substitute command?
14. Write the proper command syntax for the substitute command and briefly explain each part.
15. When using the substitute command, a comma (**,**) or period (**.**) may be used as part of the location. Explain the functions of these two symbols.
16. What is the function of the **g** (global) option, used with the Substitute command?
17. How can you exit and print a file while keeping the changes you made to the file?
18. What is a buffer?
19. The Delete (**d**), Yank (**y**), and Put (**p, P**) commands allow users to manipulate what is in a buffer. Explain the unique function of each of these commands.
20. What is the function of the Put command? How do the **p** and put **P** commands differ?
21. What command would you use to indicate that you want to name a buffer? What command indicates the name that you wish to use?
22. Compare and contrast the Yank command with the Delete command.
23. When would you use the **:r** command? The **:!** command?
24. Explain the purpose and function of the **:split** command.
25. Explain the purpose and function of Emacs.

True/False Questions

For each question, circle the letter T if the question is true and the letter F if the question is false.

T   F   1. When using a modal editor, insert mode allows you to use the cursor to move to within the file and operate on blocks of text.

T   F   2. In the vi editor, the **r** command is used to replace a current single character.

T   F   3. If a location is not specified when issuing the search command, vi will automatically assume to search the entire text.

T   F   4. Buffers are specified or named by a letter of the alphabet

T   F   5. You cannot print a file while you are in vi.

Completion Questions

Write the correct answer in each blank space.

6. When using a modal editor, such as vi, the user must be in the _____ mode to delete and the _____ mode to add text the document.
7. When in command mode, keying in the cursor movement keys of **9w** will move the cursor _____ _____ forward
8. The vi editor allows you to display multiple windows at the same time using the _____ command.
9. A non-modal editor that supports the X Window System and allows for mouse interaction is _____.
10. A series of commands that automates a complicated task is called a(n) _____.

Multiple Choice Questions

For each question, write the letter for the correct answer in the blank space.

11. When using command mode in vi, a user would use which of the following commands to copy?
    a. b
    b. h
    c. x
    d. y

12. Which of the following is not a vi clone?
    a. elvis
    b. evim
    c. nvi
    d. vim

13. To insert text before the cursor use the ____ key.
    a. a
    b. A
    c. i
    d. I

14. Instead of using arrow keys to move up and down in vi, you could use
    a. d and u
    b. h and l
    c. j and k
    d. t and b

15. To list many of the vi commands in the help window, key in
    a. :help how to
    b. :help quickref
    c. both a and b
    d. neither a nor b

Writing Commands

Write the correct steps or commands to perform the required action as if you were at the computer. You will assume that you are in vi.

16. You want to exit vi and save the changes you made in the file.

17. You are in command mode. You want to move forward seven words.

18. You are in command mode. You want to locate the string of data **May**.

19. You are in command word. You want to delete 5 words.

20. You are in command mode. You want to see your line numbers.

Application Assignments

Problem Set I—At the Computer: Multiple Choice

For problems A and C, you may use either vi or Emacs to create these documents. For problems B, D, and E, use vi. For all documents, put your name, day and time, and the problem number.

Setup   Take the following steps to free up room on the Book disk.

        Do not worry if you do not have these files to delete.

- Mount the BOOK floppy disk.
- Key in the following: **cd /mnt/floppy** <kbd>Enter</kbd>
- Key in the following: **rm -r .thumbnails**
- Key in the following: **rm -r .Trash-*yourusername***

Problem A

Note: Since vi does not support word wrap, press <kbd>Enter</kbd> where appropriate. You do not need to match the line endings in the example. However, do press <kbd>Enter</kbd> for the separation of paragraphs.

- Open the **vimeditor** file located on the BOOK disk.
- Edit it as follows:

> Your name
> *Class number*
> Class day and class time
> Chapter 6, Problem A

What Is Vim?

Vim is a highly configurable text editor built to enable efficient text editing. It is an improved version of the vi editor distributed with most UNIX systems.

Vim is often called a "programmer's editor," and it is so useful for programming that many consider it an entire IDE. An IDE (Integrated Development Environment) is a programming environment that has been packaged as an application program. The abbreviation IDE also stands for Integrated Drive Electronics.

Vim is not just for programmers, though. Vim is perfect for all kinds of text editing, from composing email to editing configuration files.

What Vim Is Not?

Vim is not an editor designed to hold its users' hands. It is a tool, the use of which must be learned. Vim is not a word processor. Although it can display text with various forms of highlighting and formatting, it is not there to provide WYSIWYG (what-you-see-is-what-you-get) editing of documents.

The Vim Community

Some people say that vi users are a rabid pack of fanatical lunatics. We prefer
to think of ourselves as a community of users who have found a piece of software
that perfectly meets our needs. We like to help our fellow users whenever we can.

Help Files

Vim's online documentation system, accessible via the :help command, is an
extensive cross-referenced and hyperlinked reference. It is kept up to date
with the software and can answer almost any question about Vim's functionality.
The VimDoc project maintains an online, hyperlinked copy of the documentation.

This information was taken from *The vim Editor*, September 12, 2002, **http://www.vim.org**.

- Save and print this file.

Problem B

- Create a file called **jhelp** on the BOOK disk.
- At the top of the file, include the following information:

        Your name
        Class Number
        Class day and class time
        Chapter 6, Problem B

- In vi, get help on **J**.
- In the **jhelp** document, briefly describe the purpose of **J**.
- Save and print **jhelp**.

Problem C

- Copy the file **exp01jan.dta** to a new file called **exp02oct.dta** on the BOOK disk.
- Edit the **exp02oct.dta** file.
- At the top of the file, include the following information:

        Your name
        Class Number
        Class day and class time
        Chapter 6, Problem C

- In the top line, change **JANUARY, 2001** to **October 2002.**
- Change **RENT** from **1175** to **1275**
- Change **HEAT** from **185** to **250**
- Change **ELECTRICITY** from **95** to **295**
- Change **PHONE** from **30** to **50**

- Change **FOOD** from **390** to **425**.
- After **PERSONAL CARE** and before **MISC**, add a line called **ENTERTAINMENT** with an amount of **200**.
- Change **TOTAL** from **2255** to **2875**
- Save and print **exp02oct.dta**

Problem D

- Copy **personal.fil** to a new file called **myperson.fil** on the BOOK disk.
- Using vi, edit the new file.
- At the top of the file, include the following information:

> Your name
> *Class number*
> Class day and class time
> Chapter 6, Problem D

- Change every occurrence of **Carolyn** to **Marilyn**.
- Change every occurrence of **Winter** to **Summer**.
- Change every occurrence of **Sun City West** to **Sun City East**.
- Delete lines 8 though 12 in the file.
- On lines 10 and 15, add your name, your address, city and state, and your profession (*Note:* Your address and profession information can be imaginary).
- Save and print **myperson.fil**.

Problem E

- Copy the file **/media/movies/bestsong.mov** to **/mnt/floppy**.
- Using vi, open **bestsong.mov** in the **/mnt/floppy** directory.
- At the top of the file, include the following information:

> Your name
> *Class number*
> Class day and class time
> Chapter 6, Problem E

- At the end of the **bestsong.mov** file, read in the **award.mov** file.
- After **YEAR SONG TITLE,** add a blank line.
- Before 2000, add the song, **2001   IF I DIDN'T HAVE YOU   MONSTERS, INC.**
- After **YEAR SONG TITLE**, and before **2000**, add **2001 A BEAUTIFUL MIND**.
- Save and print **bestsong.mov**.
- Unmount your BOOK disk. Remove it from the drive. Close any open windows.

Problem Set II—At the Computer: Short Answer

Note: To minimize keying in data, Chapter 5 Short Answers need to have been completed.

Cursor Movement

1. Create a directory called **practice6** in your home directory. How did you accomplish this task?
2. If you are in a lab environment that allowed you to retain the **practice5** directory activities on your computer, completed in Chapter 5, Problem Set II: At the Computer—Short Answer, copy recursively all the files and directories from **practice5** to **practice6**. Otherwise, use the PRACTICE disk you created at the end of the Chapter 5, Problem Set II: At the Computer—Short Answer from the **practice5** directory to the **practice6** directory located in your home directory. How did you accomplish this task?
3. You should be in your home directory. Change directories to **practice6/mybooks**. How did you accomplish this task?
4. Copy the file called **book7** to a file called **bigfile**, also to be located in the **mybooks** directory. How did you accomplish this task?
5. Using **vi**, open **bigfile**. Be sure you are in command mode. How did you accomplish this task?
6. Move to the top of the file. How did you accomplish this task?
7. In the next steps, you are going to use the keyboard, not the cursor movement keys.
8. Using the keyboard, not the cursor movement keys, move to the next line of text. What key did you press?
9. Move to the "n" in **Grafton**, the sixth character. How did you accomplish this?
10. Move the cursor back to the beginning of the line. How did you accomplish this?
11. Move to the sixth character with one command. How did you accomplish this?
12. Move the cursor down three lines. How did you accomplish this?
13. Move the cursor to the beginning of the current line. How did you accomplish this?
14. Move to the end of the line. How did you accomplish this?
15. Move the cursor to the **F** in **For**. How did you accomplish this?
16. Move up one line and then to the beginning of the line. How did you accomplish this?
17. Move forward five sentences. How did you accomplish this?
18. Press }. Where does it take you? Why?
19. Press {. Where does it take you? Why?
20. Repeat 9–19 using the cursor movement keys, **Home**, **End**, etc. Which do you prefer?
21. Go to the top of the file. How did you accomplish this?
22. Quit vi without saving the data. How did you accomplish this?

More Cursor Movement

1. Open **bigfile** in the **practice/mybooks** directory. How did you accomplish this?
2. Go to the top of the file. How did you accomplish this?
3. Press **8w**. Where does it take you? Why?
4. Press **8W**. Where does it take you? Why?
5. Press **W**. Press **w**. Where does it take you? Why?
6. Press **3b**. Press **b** twice. Press **B**. Where does it take you? Why?
7. Press **e**. Press **E**. Where does it take you? Why?
8. Go to the beginning of the line the quickest way. Press **15l**. Press **15l**. (It is the number 1, then the number 5, then the letter l.) What happened?

9. Display the status line. How did you accomplish this? What line are you on? How many total lines are there in the file?

10. Move the cursor a full screen forward. Display the status line. What line are you on? How did you accomplish this?

11. Go to the top of the file. How did you accomplish this?

12. Quit **vi** without saving the data. How did you accomplish this?

Adding and Editing Text

1. Move to the **practice6/mybooks/mystery** directory. Copy **Book1** to **women**. Open **women**. How did you accomplish this?

2. Move to the end of the file the quickest way. How did you accomplish this?.

3. Press **a**. Press **Enter**. What happened? Why?

4. Key in the following: **Peters:Elizabeth:Crocodile:on:the Sandbank.**

5. Return to command mode. How did you accomplish this? Move to the line beginning with **Grafton**. Place yourself in visual mode. Select **Grafton:Sue:**. Place **Grafton:Sue** in a buffer. Paste your selection above the Grafton line. At the end of the new line, add **G:is:for:Gumshoe.** How did you accomplish this?

6. Return to command mode. Select the two Grafton lines including the last period. Copy both lines between Baker and Peters. How did you accomplish this?

7. Return to command mode. Delete the first two Grafton lines. Undo your deletion. Redo your deletion. How did you accomplish this?

8. Go to the top of the file. How did you accomplish this?

9. Save the file and exit **vi**.

Searching and Replacing Text

1. Open **bigfile** in the **practice/mybooks** directory. Be sure you are in command mode. Be sure you are at the top of the file. How did you accomplish this?.

2. Find all occurrences of **King**. How many are there? How did you accomplish this?

3. Search back thought the file for all occurrences of **Grafton**. How many are there? How did you accomplish this?

4. Turn off the search highlighting. How did you accomplish this?

5. Move to the top of the file. Change **Mystery:Women** to **MYSTERY:WOMEN**. How did you accomplish this?

6. Place the new **MYSTERY:WOMEN.** in a named buffer. How did you accomplish this?

7. Locate the first occurrence of **Mystery:Men**. Change it to **MYSTERY:MEN.**

8. Place the new **MYSTERY:MEN** in a different named buffer. How did you accomplish this?

9. Move to the next occurrence of **Mystery:Women.** Replace it with your first named buffer. How did you accomplish this?

10. Move to the next occurrence of **Mystery:Men.** Replace it with your second named buffer. How did you accomplish this?

11. Move to the top of the file. How did you accomplish this?

12. Save the file and exit **vi**.

13. Get the disk labeled PRACTICE disk. Do not use the BOOK disk. Mount it. Copy everything in the **practice6** directory under your home directory to the floppy disk to a directory called **practice6**. When you have finished, unmount the floppy disk and remove it from the drive.

Problem Set III—Brief Essay

Use vi or Emacs to write and print your response. Please be sure to put your name as well as what day and time your class is and which problem you are answering.

    a. Compare and contrast Emacs, vi, and gEdit. Identify at least two advantages and two disadvantages of each tool.

    b. *Since word processors are so much more powerful than text editors, they will replace all test editors in Linux.* Agree or disagree with this statement. Support your answer.

    c. In vi, compare and contrast Insert mode, Command mode, and Last Line mode. Give two examples of how you would use each mode.

CHAPTER 7

Pipes, Filters, and Redirection

Chapter Overview

The operating system usually expects to read information from the keyboard. The keyboard is the standard input device. The standard output device, where the results of commands and the output of programs is displayed, is the screen. However, there are times when it is desirable to redirect input and output. Changing the standard input or standard output from one device to another is a process known as redirection.

In addition, Linux has many commands that can take standard input, modify it, and write the results to standard output. These types of commands are known as filters. Linux also provides the ability to pipe commands. Pipes allow the standard output from one command to be used as standard input to the next command. Pipes, used with filters, allow the user to link commands. Pipes, filters, and redirection give the user choices in determining where information is read from (input) and written to (output). Many of the commands that you will learn to use in this chapter were designed to be used with pipes and redirection. You will also learn about regular expressions and extended regular expressions that allow you to search for information in files using various ambiguous file references. Furthermore, you will learn about file compression and archiving.

Learning Objectives

1. Explain why and how standard input, standard output, and the terminal are treated as files at the operating system level.
2. Explain the purpose and function of standard I/O (input/output).
3. List and explain the four major file categories found in Linux.
4. Explain the purpose and function of the **cut** and **paste** commands.
5. Explain the purpose and function of filters and filter commands.

343

6. Explain the purpose and function of pipes.
7. Compare and contrast the search abilities of **grep**, **egrep**, and **fgrep**.
8. Explain how the **pr** command can be used to convert a text file into a paginated, columned version.
9. Explain the purpose and function of the **tee**, **tr**, and **ispell** commands.
10. Explain why and how the **head** and **tail** commands are used.
11. Compare and contrast the **uniq**, **diff**, and **comm** commands, which are used to display or exclude similar lines within documents.
12. Explain the purpose and function of the **File Roller**, **bzip2**, **bunzip2**, **gzip**, **gunzip**, **zip**, **unzip**, **zcat**, and **tar** commands.

Student Outcomes

1. Use standard input, standard output, and the terminal as files.
2. Use redirection symbols to modify the standard output of a file.
3. Create files and use the **cut** and **paste** commands to manipulate information in these files.
4. Use the **sort** and **wc** filter commands to manipulate information and then display the modified output.
5. Use pipes to create pipelines.
6. Use the search capabilities of **grep**, **egrep**, and **fgrep**, with and without options, to locate uninterrupted strings and/or regular expressions.
7. Will format and print a document using the **pr** and **lpr** commands.
8. Modify a document using the **tee**, **tr**, and **ispell** commands.
9. Use the **head** and **tail** commands to display a specific number of lines at the top and at the bottom of a text file.
10. Use the **uniq**, **diff**, and **comm** commands to compare files.
11. Use the **File Roller**, **bzip2**, **bunzip2**, **gzip**, **gunzip**, **zcat**, **zip**, **unzip**, and **tar** commands to compress, extract, read, and archive the contents of a file.

Commands Introduced

|	diff	paste	uniq
<	egrep	pr	unzip
>	fgrep	sort	wc
>>	grep	tail	who
bzip2	gunzip	tar	whoami
bunzip2	gzip	tee	zcat
comm	head	tr	zip
cut	ispell	tty	

7.1 • Standard Input and Output—The Terminal as a File

You have already used standard input, standard output, and standard error. If you key in a command on the keyboard, the shell recognizes it as standard input. After the input is processed, it is written to standard output—usually the monitor. If there is an error completing the command, the output is written to standard error—again, usually the monitor. In reality, a command does not know where it is sending or receiving information. It could be from or to a file, to a printer, or to the monitor. A command simply uses standard input, standard output, and standard error. The shell directs where standard output and standard error is to go and where standard input is to come from. Thus, three standard files are involved when you execute a command in Bash: **stdin**, **stdout**, and **stderr**. The term *file* is slightly misleading. Actually, these are not true files but file descriptors which can be treated as files at the operating system level. The file descriptors are listed in Table 7.1, "File Descriptors."

File Descriptor	Name	Common Abbreviation	Usual Default
0	Standard input	stdin	Keyboard
1	Standard output	stdout	Terminal
2	Standard error	stderr	Terminal

Table 7.1 • File Descriptors

When the term *terminal* is used, it includes a keyboard and a monitor. In previous chapters, you have been working with ordinary files and directories. Remember, Linux has another type of file, a device file, usually located in the **/dev** directory, which represents a peripheral device such as a printer, a terminal, or a disk drive. Thus, your terminal is a named file such as **/dev/tty1**.

Normally, when you log in, the shell directs the standard output from a command you key in to the device file for your terminal. Thus, what you key in is displayed on the screen. The shell also directs the standard input to come from the same device file so that your commands expect standard input to come from the keyboard. In other words, if you keyed in **cat myfile**; it would copy the output to the screen. The input was the file name (argument) you used. See Figure 7.1, "Standard Input and Output and the Terminal."

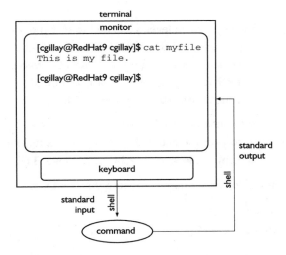

Figure 7.1 • Standard Input and Output and the Terminal

If, however, you use **cat** with no arguments, (file name), followed by **Enter**, you are directing the shell to take its input from the keyboard (standard input). Then, each line you key in would simply display on the screen until you pressed **Ctrl** + **D**, indicating that you were done keying in data. Pressing **Ctrl** + **D** is an EOF (end-of-file) signal that tells **cat** there is no more input coming from the keyboard, and to return you to the shell. You know you are returned to the shell, because you see a prompt. You may use several commands to identify your terminal. These include **who**, **who am i**, and **tty**.

The syntax for the **who** command is as follows:

```
who [options] [arguments]
who am i
```

and the syntax for the **tty** command is as follows:

```
tty
```

Table 7.2, "who Options," lists some of the major options used with the **who** command.

Option	Result
-am i	Displays on the terminal the name of the invoking user.
-m	Same as **who am i**.
-q	Displays only the user name and local number of users on the terminal.
-H	Prints the headings.

Table 7.2 • who Options

7.2 • Activity: Using Standard Input and Output and the Terminal as a File

Note 1:   If your system is set up to automatically execute startx, prior to executing Step 1, you will need to open a terminal window. Your results will not be the same as those shown. If you have root privileges and your lab environment allows it, you can alter the way your system boots.

WARNING: To change your run level, you need to edit the **/etc/inittab** file. This can be a very dangerous procedure as this is the initilization file that starts your entire system. If you make a mistake, you will not be able to boot your system at all. Hence, it is a good idea to make a backup copy of your original **inittab** file. Then to alter it, you will see that there is a line in **inittab** that states **id:5:initdefault:**

This boots your system into the X environment immediately. To boot into a text-based interfaced, you need to alter the line in the file so it reads **id:3:initdefault:** (You are changing the system from run level of 5 (X11) to run level 3 (Full mulituser mode)).

STEP 1   Boot the system and log in but do not execute the **startx** command.

```
Red Hat Linux release 92 (Shrike)
Kernel 2.4.20-6 on an I686

RedHat9 login: cgillay
Password:
Last login: Sun Jun 29 17:34:04 on tty1
[cgillay@RedHat9   cgillay]$
```

WHAT'S **HAPPENING?** You have logged in to your system but not started X. **Last login:** tells you your terminal—in this case **tty1**. The **who** command can always tell you who is logged in.

STEP 2   Key in the following: **who** Enter

```
[cgillay@RedHat9   cgillay]$ who
cgillay   tty1            Jun 29 22:42
[cgillay@RedHat9   cgillay]$
```

WHAT'S HAPPENING? Your display will differ. The **who** command tells you "who" is logged onto the system as well as what the file name is for your terminal. In this example, since this is a "stand-alone" system, there is only one user logged on. The term *tty* comes from the antiquated term *teletype terminal*, which is characterized by a noisy mechanical printer, a very limited character set, and poor print quality. However, in the Linux and Unix world, it is any terminal at all. **tty** is also a command which tells you the name of the current controlling terminal. The names of your devices are kept in the **/dev** directory.

STEP 3   Key in the following: **who -H** [Enter]

```
[cgillay@RedHat9   cgillay]$   who -H
NAME           LINE    TIME              COMMENT
cgillay        tty1    Jun 29 22:48
[cgillay@RedHat9   cgillay]$
```

WHAT'S HAPPENING? Here you see the header information for your terminal.

STEP 4   Key in the following: **who -q** [Enter]

```
[cgillay@RedHat9   cgillay]$ who -q
cgillay
# users=1
[cgillay@RedHat9   cgillay]$
```

WHAT'S HAPPENING? Here you get a quick count of the user names and the total number of users on the system.

STEP 5   Key in the following: **who am i; who -m** [Enter]

```
[cgillay@RedHat9   cgillay]$ who am i; who -m
cgillay      tty1     Jun 29 4 22:48
cgillay      tty1     Jun 29 4 22:48
[cgillay@RedHat9   cgillay]$
```

WHAT'S HAPPENING? Here you can see that **who am i** and **who -m** produce the same results—the name of the current user. If you want to see your actual device name, you can use the **tty** command.

STEP 6   Key in the following: **tty** [Enter]

```
[cgillay@RedHat9   cgillay]$ tty
/dev/tty1
[cgillay@RedHat9   cgillay]$
```

WHAT'S HAPPENING? Again, your actual terminal name—the device name is **/dev/tty1**—is displayed. What you have been doing is using the shell which has executed the command you used and then directed the output of the command to standard output—the terminal. If you use a command such as **cat** (a utility) with an argument (a file name) what it actually does is copy the file to standard output or display the contents of a file on the terminal.

STEP 7   Place the BOOK disk in the floppy drive.

STEP 8   Key in the following: **mount /mnt/floppy; cat /mnt/floppy/bye.txt** [Enter]

```
[cgillay@RedHat9  cgillay]$ mount /mnt/floppy; cat /mnt/floppy/
bye.txt

GOODBYE ALL.
IS THIS ALL THERE IS?
YES!
[cgillay@RedHat9  cgillay]$
```

WHAT'S HAPPENING? The **cat** command used with an argument (the file called **bye.txt** located on the BOOK disk in the directory **/mnt/floppy**), copies the contents to standard output. But if you have no argument, the **cat** command will copy standard input (the keyboard) to standard output (the monitor).

STEP 9   Key in the following: **cat** [Enter]

STEP 10 Key in the following: **testing standard input and output** [Enter]

```
[cgillay@RedHat9  cgillay]$ cat
testing standard input and output
testing standard input and output
_
```

WHAT'S HAPPENING? You keyed in the **cat** command without an argument. You then keyed in a line of text. That same line of text was displayed under what you entered. This is because the **cat** command read standard input (your keyboard entry) and then the **cat** command copied the output to standard output (the monitor). There is not a prompt returned because the command is expecting more input from standard input (the keyboard). It will continue to copy your keyboard input to the monitor until you send the command a signal ([Ctrl] + **D**). This signal sends an EOF (end-of-file) signal, which tells the **cat** command that there is no more standard input coming, and thus no more text to copy to standard output. When you press [Ctrl] + **D**, **cat** is done executing and returns you to the shell, which is indicated by the prompt indicating that the shell is ready for a new command.

STEP 11 Press [Ctrl] + **d**.

```
[cgillay@RedHat9  cgillay]$ cat
testing standard input and output
testing standard input and output
[cgillay@RedHat9  cgillay]$
```

WHAT'S HAPPENING? You have indeed been returned to the prompt.

STEP 12 Key in the following: **startx** [Enter]

STEP 13 Open a terminal window. Key in the following: **who** [Enter]

```
[cgillay@RedHat9  cgillay]$ who
cgillay  tty1           Jun 29 22:48
cgillay  pts/0          Jun 29 23:01 (:0.0)
[cgillay@RedHat9  cgillay]$
```

WHAT'S HAPPENING? You seemed to have two users logged on when you used the **who** command. However, remember that now you are in the GUI—the GNOME desktop. Looking at the above example, **pts/0** is a pseudo terminal. It is a pseudo device. A device normally directly corresponds to a hardware entity such as a serial port. However, a device may not have a hardware component, so the kernel creates pseudo devices that can be accessed as devices but have no physical existence. Often, a hardware entity may correspond to several devices, just as do pseudo terminals in X.

A pseudo terminal is used as a *terminal emulator* for X Window System and to telnet into a system. Telnet is the Internet standard protocol for remote logins. A terminal emulator is a program that allows a computer to act like a specific brand of terminal. Telnet is an actual program in Linux that uses this as a protocol and acts as a terminal emulator for the remote login session. The computer, then, appears as a terminal to the host computer and behaves as if you were logged on locally.

In X Window System, you can have many different invocations of xterm running at once on the same terminal, each of which has independent input and output processes running in it, which will then be directed to the actual physical device. Thus, each terminal window you open is the device for that window. It is a pseudo device and not attached to a real physical port.

STEP 14   Key in the following: **tty** `Enter`

```
[cgillay@RedHat9   cgillay]$   tty
/dev/pts/0
[cgillay@RedHat9   cgillay]$
```

WHAT'S **HAPPENING?** This is the pseudo terminal for the terminal window you opened.

STEP 15   Open a new terminal window. Key in the following: **tty** `Enter`

```
[cgillay@RedHat9   cgillay]$   tty
/dev/pts/1
[cgillay@RedHat9   cgillay]$
```

WHAT'S **HAPPENING?** This is the pseudo terminal for this window. You are using two terminals for only one physical device. Both terminals are pointing to **/dev/tty1**.

STEP 16   Close the terminal windows.

7.3 ● Standard Input and Output—Standard I/O

Standard I/O (input/output) allows the shell used with all text-based Linux utilities to control and direct the program input, output, and error information. Whenever you key in a command in the shell, you are launching it or starting a process. When you start a process, it is automatically provided with the three file descriptors as described in Table 7.1, "File Descriptors." Standard input is a text input stream, and by default it is attached to the keyboard. Standard output is a text output stream, and by default it is attached to your terminal or terminal window. Standard error is also a text output stream, but it is used for errors or other information unrelated to the successful results of your command. By default, it is attached to your terminal or terminal window. If a process opens additional files for input or output, they are assigned to the next available file descriptor.

However, the result or output of many of the commands you have used has been some action that occurred, such as copying a file with the **cp** command or removing a file with the **rm** command. In those cases, there was no standard output written to the screen unless you had an error message (**stderr**) such as **bash: rm: cannot lstat "nofile": No such file or directory.**

On the other hand, the output of command like **ls** or **cat** has been a screen display of the contents of the file that you asked to be displayed. The shell directed the standard output of the command to be written to the screen. Redirection means that you tell the shell you want information read from or written to a device *other than* the standard ones. With any command that deals with standard output, such as the **cat** command, you can write the output to some other place such as another file. This process is called redirecting the output of a command. See Figure 7.2, "Redirecting Standard Output."

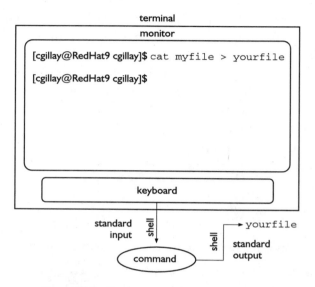

Figure 7.2   Redirecting Standard Output

In this example, you have overwritten the contents of the file **yourfile** with the contents of the file **myfile**. Redirection works only when the command expects to send its output to standard devices or receive the information from standard input.

The symbols used for redirection are:

> The greater-than symbol redirects the output of a command to some other device or file.

< The less-than symbol tells the shell to get its input from somewhere other than the keyboard.

>> The double greater-than symbol redirects the output of a command but does not overwrite the existing file. It appends the output to the end of the existing file.

You have already used some of these redirection symbols. When you keyed in **cat > cities**, in Chapter 5, you were telling the shell to redirect standard input to a file called **cities**.

7.4 • Activity: Using the Redirection Symbols

Note: You are in the GNOME desktop. The BOOK disk is mounted.

STEP 1   Open a terminal window.

STEP 2   Key in the following: **cd /mnt/floppy; rm .nau*.* class/.nau*.*** [Enter]

STEP 3   Key in the following: **mkdir work; mv inv*.* exp*.* work** [Enter]

STEP 4   Key in the following: **mv LON*.* pro* work** [Enter]

STEP 5 Key in the following: **mv ast*.* earth*.* jup*.* astronomy** Enter

STEP 6 Key in the following: **mv mer*.* ven*.* astronomy**

```
[cgillay@RedHat9  gillay]$  cd /mnt/floppy; rm .nau*.* class/.nau*.*
rm: cannot lstat `.nau*.*': No such file or directory
rm: cannot lstat `class/.nau*.*': No such file or directory
[cgillay@RedHat9  floppy]$  mkdir work; mv inv*.* exp*.* work
[cgillay@RedHat9  floppy]$  mv LON*.* pro* work
[cgillay@RedHat9  floppy]$  mv ast*.* earth*.* jup*.* astronomy
[cgillay@RedHat9  floppy]$  mv mer*.* ven*.* astronomy
[cgillay@RedHat9  floppy]$
```

WHAT'S **HAPPENING?** In this example, there are no files placed by Nautilus on your BOOK disk. If there had been, you would have removed the hidden files that Nautilus had placed on your BOOK disk and you would see no message. These hidden files are a function of which version of Linux you are running. Remember, you may not have all the files on your disk if you did not do all the activities or homework or if you did not use the Nautilus file manager and depending on which version of Linux you are running. In addition, you moved various files to various directories. On a FAT floppy disk, the maximum number of files that can be placed in the root directory is 224. Although there is plenty of physical room left on your disk, and you have not exceeded the 224 file limit, you will still run out of room on the BOOK disk. The BOOK disk has files with long file names and file names with spaces in them. When you use long file names or file names with spaces, those entries count for more than one entry in the Root Directory Table. This is how you will quickly exceed the 224 file name limit in the root directory. By creating directories and moving files to those directories, you have freed up space for new files in the root directory.

STEP 7 Key in the following: **cd astronomy; ls ast*.*** Enter

```
[cgillay@RedHat9  floppy]$  cd astronomy; ls ast*.*
ast.99    ast.new    astro.tmp    astro.txt    ast.tmp
[cgillay@RedHat9  astronomy]$
```

WHAT'S **HAPPENING?** You changed directories to the **astronomy** directory, then used the **ls** command. The **ls** command behaved in the "normal" way. You asked for a display of all the files on the BOOK disk in the **astronomy** directory that began with **ast** and had anything else in their names. The selected files were displayed on the screen. Because the **ls** command writes its results to the screen, a standard output, redirection can be used with this command.

STEP 8 Key in the following: **cd ..** Enter

STEP 9 Key in the following: **ls astronomy/ast*.* > happy; cat happy; ls happy** Enter

```
[cgillay@RedHat9  floppy]$  ls astronomy/ast*.* > happy; cat happy; ls happy
astronomy/ast.99
astronomy/ast.new
astronomy/astro.tmp
astronomy/astro.txt
astronomy/ast.tmp
happy
[cgillay@RedHat9  floppy]$
```

WHAT'S HAPPENING? You changed directories to **/mnt/floppy**. The output of the **ls** command has been sent to the file called **happy**. Nothing appears on the screen. When you key in **ls astronomy/ast*.***, you normally see the directory listing of all the **ast*.*** files in the **astronomy** directory on the screen, as you did in the display following Step 6. The **>** sign tells the shell that instead of sending the standard output to the screen, you want to redirect that output elsewhere. **happy** is the name of the file where you sent the output. When you used the **cat happy** command, you saw the output that would have normally gone to the screen saved in a file called **happy**. To show that it existed, you then displayed the file name **happy** using the **ls** command.

You may also use the file descriptors to your advantage. You used this feature in Chapter 2 when you used the **find** command and "filtered" out the error messages by sending them to a null device (**find / -iname gedit 2>/dev/null**). In that example, you redirected the standard error—file descriptor 2—to a null device or nowhere, sometimes called the byte bucket. You can redirect error messages to a file as well. This can be useful when you want to keep error messages separate from the information sent to standard output. You can then differentiate between output and errors.

STEP 10   Key in the following: **cat nofile** [Enter]

```
[cgillay@RedHat9   floppy]$   cat nofile
cat: nofile: No such file or directory
[cgillay@RedHat9   floppy]$
```

WHAT'S HAPPENING? Since **nofile** does not exist, you got an error message. You are going to redirect that error message to a file.

STEP 11   Key in the following: **cat nofile 2> errors** [Enter]

```
[cgillay@RedHat9   floppy]$   cat nofile 2> errors
[cgillay@RedHat9   floppy]$
```

WHAT'S HAPPENING? You used the file descriptor (2—standard error) and redirected that error message (**>**) to a file called **errors**.

STEP 12   Key in the following: **clear; cat errors** [Enter]

```
[cgillay@RedHat9   floppy]$ clear; cat errors
cat: nofile: No such file or directory
[cgillay@RedHat9   floppy]$
```

WHAT'S HAPPENING? You first cleared the screen, then displayed the contents of the file called **errors**. The error message was saved to a file called **errors**. If you use the ampersand (**&**), you may redirect both the output of a command and any error messages to a file.

STEP 13   Key in the following: **cat carolyn.fil nofile** [Enter]

```
[cgillay@RedHat9   floppy]$   cat carolyn.fil nofile

Hi, my name is Carolyn.
What is your name.
cat: nofile: No such file or directory
[cgillay@RedHat9   floppy]$
```

WHAT'S HAPPENING? Here you have both standard output (the contents of the file **carolyn.fil**) as well as an error message telling you that **nofile** does not exist.

STEP 14 Key in the following: **cat carolyn.fil nofile >& errors; cat errors** Enter

```
[cgillay@RedHat9  floppy]$  cat Carolyn.fil nofile >& errors; cat errors

Hi, my name is Carolyn.
What is your name.
cat: nofile: No such file or directory
[cgillay@RedHat9  floppy]$
```

WHAT'S HAPPENING? You see the same information that you saw following Step 12 but instead of the information being displayed on the screen, it was saved to a file called **errors**. You displayed the contents of the **errors** file using **cat**.

If you want to append text to the end of the file, rather than overwriting, you may do so using **>>**.

STEP 15 Key in the following: **cat bye.txt hello.txt** Enter

```
[cgillay@RedHat9  floppy]$  cat bye.txt hello.txt

GOODBYE ALL.
IS THIS ALL THERE IS?
YES!

HELLO, EVERYONE.
HOW ARE YOU?
ISN'T THIS FUN???
[cgillay@RedHat9  floppy]$
```

WHAT'S HAPPENING? You have two separate files. You want to add **bye.txt** to the end of **hello.txt**. If you keyed in **cat bye.txt > hello.txt**, you would overwrite the contents of **hello.txt** with the contents of **bye.txt**. Again, to *append* to the end of an existing file, you use the double **>>**.

STEP 16 Key in the following: **cat bye.txt >> hello.txt** Enter

STEP 17 Key in the following: **cat hello.txt** Enter

```
[cgillay@RedHat9  floppy]$  cat bye.txt >> hello.txt
[cgillay@RedHat9  floppy]$ cat hello.txt

HELLO, EVERYONE.
HOW ARE YOU?
ISN'T THIS FUN???

GOODBYE ALL.
IS THIS ALL THERE IS?
YES!
[cgillay@RedHat9  floppy]$
```

WHAT'S HAPPENING? Instead of overwriting the contents of **hello.txt** with the contents of **bye.txt**, the contents of **bye.txt** were added to the end of the **hello.txt** file.

You may also redirect standard input to a program or a command using the **<** symbol. Thus, a command or program that normally expects to get its input from the keyboard can be redirected to instead get the information from a file. You learned to use the commands that are specific to vi. When you used the editor, you gave it the commands (input from the keyboard—standard input). You can tell vi to get the input from a file instead of getting it from the keyboard. First you must create the file from which **vi** can get commands.

STEP 18 Key in the following, pressing ⟨Enter⟩ at the end of each line:

    cat > commands

    dd

    G

    p

    p

    :wq

```
[cgillay@RedHat9  floppy]$  cat > commands
dd
G
p
p
:wq
_
```

WHAT'S HAPPENING? You have created a file with vi commands in it (**dd**—delete a line, **G**—go to the bottom, **p**—paste the line twice, and then write the file to disk and quit—**:wq**). Now you need to save the file.

STEP 19 Press ⟨Ctrl⟩ + **d.**

Note: The **cities** file was created in Chapter 5, Activity 5.17.

STEP 20 Key in the following: **cat cities** ⟨Enter⟩

```
[cgillay@RedHat9   floppy]$ cat cities
California

Orange
Mission Viejo
Laguna Beach
Tustin
Irvine
Pasadena
Los Angeles
Altadena
Whittier
Villa Park
[cgillay@RedHat9   floppy]$
```

WHAT'S HAPPENING? You see the contents of the **cities** file.

STEP 21 Key in the following: **vi cities < commands** Enter

```
[cgillay@RedHat9  floppy]$  vi cities < commands
Vim: Warning: Input is not from a terminal
[cgillay@RedHat9  floppy]$
```

WHAT'S **HAPPENING?** The editor warned you that you are not getting the input from standard input (terminal). vi then took its input from the command file. Remember, in the **commands** file you had vi commands.

STEP 22 Key in the following: **cat cities** Enter

```
[cgillay@RedHat9  floppy]$ cat cities

Orange
Mission Viejo
Laguna Beach
Tustin
Irvine
Pasadena
Los Angeles
Altadena
Whittier
Villa Park
California
California
[cgillay@RedHat9  floppy]$
```

WHAT'S **HAPPENING?** vi took the commands from your file (standard input) and altered the file.

7.5 • Linux Files and File Structures

The Linux file system is designed to be looked at as one massive folder that holds other files and folders. Files are very specialized, as files contain information. Different types of files are found on the Linux system. The various types of files fall under some major categories—ordinary files (or regular files), special files, links, and directories.

Ordinary files consist of programs (executable files), word processing files, shell scripts, and other such files. These files contain information you create or manipulate. Most files are ordinary files. You generally spend your time using and dealing with ordinary files. Special files fall into two categories—block special and character special. Remember, all physical devices are associated with the file system. *Character special files* produce a stream of bytes, one character at a time. This produces something called raw data. These types of files are related to serial input/output devices such as a printer. *Block special files*, as their name indicates, process their data a block at a time and are used for the reading or writing of data to devices such as a disk. There are other special device files such as **/dev/null**. A *linked file* is a special directory entry that can specify that one file points to another file (link). Whenever an operation is performed on the link, the actual file is what is operated on. And last, a directory is a container for files.

Ordinary files can be structured in several ways. These include unstructured ASCII characters, records, and trees. An ASCII file is simply a file that has no structure and is regarded merely as a sequence of bytes. For instance, in the file **newprson.fil**, the following data is considered character strings:

```
G
i
l
l
a
y

C
a
r
o
l
y
n
```

Text files give you the most flexibility in entering data because you enter any kind of data in any order. But there is no way to retrieve the information if, for instance, you only wanted to retrieve last names. You can only view or print the entire file, not just the last names.

A second type of data storage stores data as a sequence of fixed-length records. The records have some sort of internal structure, and the data must be entered as records. However, once entered, the data can be manipulated and retrieved.

```
G
i
l
l
a
y
C
a
r
o
l
y
n
```

```
P
a
n
e
z
i
c
h
F
r
a
n
k
```

The next type of file is structured as a tree of records that do not have to be the same length. Each record has a key field such as record number in a fixed location in the record. The key field sorts the tree so that you can quickly locate a record with a particular key. In the following example, you could quickly locate the record for Frank Panezich by looking for Record 3.

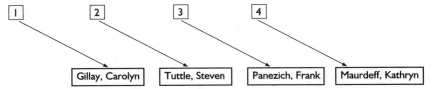

Throughout this text, you have primarily been dealing with ordinary files. You have been processing your files in some way. One of the features of the Linux file system is that you can manipulate files to produce the results you need. Since ordinary files are fundamentally character sequences, you can manipulate these files in a variety of ways. Many of the commands that you have been using are intended to be filters. Filters modify text in some meaningful way to the user. Text is fed into the command's standard input or read from a file or files, modified in some useful way, and then sent to standard output or to a new file. You may combine multiple commands to produce text streams, which are modified at each step.

As a Linux user or as a Linux administrator, you will constantly be manipulating your files. Pipes, filters, and redirection allow you the tools and flexibility to maintain and manage your system. Although almost all commands allow the use of pipes, filters, and redirection, the following group of commands will allow you to see how you can effectively manage your system.

7.6 • The cut and paste Commands

When you used the **cat** command to combine files, you appended one file to another. The **paste** command allows you to combine files; it will take the first line of the first file and follow it by the first line in the second file and place it in the third file. It will write lines consisting of sequentially corresponding lines from each file separated by tabs to standard output. The **paste** command is most useful when you combine files with columns of information. The syntax is

```
paste  file1  file2
```

Table 7.3, "**paste** Options," lists some of the major options used with the **paste** command.

Option	Name	Result
-		Replaces a file name with standard input.
-d*char*	Delimiter	Separates columns with the *char* defined in *char* instead of a tab.
-s	Serial	Merges lines from a file one file at a time.

Table 7.3 • paste Options

The **cut** command allows you to retrieve some, but not all fields in a file. You can use the **cut** command to remove specific columns or fields from a file. The syntax is

```
cut  [options]  ...[files]...
```

Table 7.4, "**cut** Options," lists some of the major options used with the **cut** command. In the following table, *list* is a sequence of integers. You use a command if you wish separate values. You use a hyphen to specify a range.

Option	Name	Result
-b *list*	Bytes *list*	Specifies a *list* of positions. Only bytes located in those positions will be displayed.
-c *list*	Characters *list*	Cuts the columns' positions that you have identified in your *list*.
-d *c*	Delimiter *c*	Used with the -f option to specify which field delimiter you want to use that is defined by c. The default delimiter is the tab.
-f *list*	File *list*	Cuts the fields that you have identified in your *list*.

Table 7.4 • cut Options

To look at the syntax in another way, if you use **cut -f** *list* [**-d** *char*] *file1 file2* or **cut -c** *list file1 file2* when you use the -f option, you are referring to a field. Using *list* refers to a comma- or hyphen-separated list of numbers or range of numbers that specifies a field. Thus, **-f 1** means you are looking for Field 1. If you use **-f 1,3**, that means you are looking for Fields 1 and 3, and if you use **-f 1-3**, you are looking for Fields 1 through 3. The **-d** option refers to what specific character is separating the fields, and *char* is the character that you used to separate the fields. When you use the **-c** option, you are referring to character position, so that if you use **-c1**, you are asking for the first character, whereas **-c 1,14** is asking for the first and fourteenth character. If you use **-c 4-6**, you are asking for the fourth through sixth character position in the file.

7.7 • Activity: Using the cut and paste Commands

Note: The BOOK disk is mounted and **/mnt/floppy** is the default directory with a terminal window open.

STEP 1 Create a file called **dogs** with the following data:
Cocker Spaniel
Beagle
Collie
Great Dane
Boxer

STEP 2 Create a file called **cats** with the following data:
Russian Blue
Manx
Bombay
American Shorthair
Persian

STEP 3   Create a file called **birds** with the following data:

African Grey

Cockatiel

Parrot

Parakeet

Canary

WHAT'S **HAPPENING?** You have created three files. All of the data in each file is in a single column. If you used the **cat** command to combine these files, the data would be combined sequentially with the contents of one file following the contents of another. Instead, you can use the **paste** command to paste the information side by side.

STEP 4   Key in the following: **paste dogs cats** Enter

```
[cgillay@RedHat9    floppy]$   paste dogs cats
Cocker Spaniel          Russian Blue
Beagle  Manx
Collie  Bombay
Great Dane      American Shorthair
Boxer    Persian
[cgillay@RedHat9    floppy]$
```

WHAT'S **HAPPENING?** As you can see, the files are combined line by line and side by side, and the output is displayed on the screen.

STEP 5   Key in the following: **paste -d',' dogs cats birds**

```
[cgillay@RedHat9    floppy]$ paste -d',' dogs cats birds
Cocker Spaniel,Russian Blue,African Grey
Beagle,Manx,Cockatiel
Collie,Bombay,Parrot
Great Dane,American Shorthair,Parakeet
Boxer,Persian,Canary
[cgillay@RedHat9    floppy]$
```

WHAT'S **HAPPENING?** You redirected the output to the screen. The **-d ','** allowed the substitution of the comma for the Tab character.

STEP 6   Key in the following: **paste dogs cats birds > pets; cat pets** Enter

```
[cgillay@RedHat9     floppy]$ paste dogs cats birds > birds; cat pets
Cocker Spaniel          Russian Blue African Grey
Beagle    Manx          Cockatiel
Collie    Bombay        Parrot
Great Dane              American Shorthair  Parakeet
Boxer      Persian Canary
[cgillay@RedHat9    floppy]$
```

WHAT'S **HAPPENING?** Now you have combined the three files into one by using redirection. You can extract fields from the **pets** file.

STEP 7   Key in the following: **cut -f2 pets** ⟨Enter⟩

```
[cgillay@RedHat9  floppy]$  cut -f2 pets
Russian Blue
Manx
Bombay
American Shorthair
Persian
[cgillay@RedHat9  floppy]$
```

WHAT'S HAPPENING? If you look at the output following Step 6, you can see that you extracted the second column of information.

STEP 8   Key in the following: **cut -f1,3 pets** ⟨Enter⟩

```
[cgillay@RedHat9  floppy]$  cut -f1,3  pets
Cocker Spaniel    African Grey
Beagle    Cockatiel
Collie  Parrot
Great Dane          Parakeet
Boxer      Canary
[cgillay@RedHat9  floppy]$
```

WHAT'S HAPPENING? You extracted the first and third column from the **pets** file. You can also use the **cut** command to cut data from fixed-length records or an ASCII file.

STEP 9   Key in the following: **cp newprson.fil persons** ⟨Enter⟩

STEP 10   Key in the following: **vi persons** ⟨Enter⟩

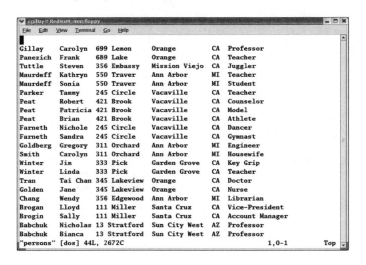

WHAT'S HAPPENING? You have created a new file called **persons**. You are going to make this file smaller by deleting data in the file.

STEP 11   Key in the following: **1G**

STEP 12   Key in the following: **dd**

STEP 13   Move the cursor to **Parker**.

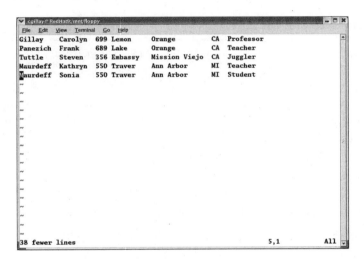

WHAT'S HAPPENING? You deleted the first blank line. You are going to delete the next 38 lines.

STEP 14 Key in the following: **38dd**

WHAT'S HAPPENING? Your file now contains only five lines.

STEP 15 Press **ZZ**.

STEP 16 Key in the following: **cat persons** [Enter]

```
[cgillay@RedHat9  floppy]$  cat persons
Gillay     Carolyn   699 Lemon      Orange          CA  Professor
Panezich   Frank     689 Lake       Orange          CA  Teacher
Tuttle     Steven    356 Embassy    Mission Viejo   CA  Juggler
Maurdeff   Kathryn   550 Traver     Ann Arbor       MI  Teacher
Maurdeff   Sonia     550 Traver     Ann Arbor       MI  Student
[cgillay@RedHat9  floppy]$
```

WHAT'S HAPPENING? You have a smaller file.

STEP 17 Key in the following: **cut -c1-19,51-62 persons** [Enter]

```
[cgillay@RedHat9   floppy]$   cut   -c1-19,51-62   persons
Gillay     Carolyn   Professor
Panezich   Frank     Teacher
Tuttle     Steven    Juggler
Maurdeff   Kathryn   Teacher
Maurdeff   Sonia     Student
[cgillay@RedHat9   floppy]$
```

WHAT'S **HAPPENING?** You extracted the first 19 characters and the characters from 51 through 62. Although this data may appear to be in columns, it actually is not. It is a straight ASCII file and does not have fields. The data in the file is separated by spaces, not by assigned fields. This means you must extract the data by character position. Now you can combine these commands using redirection to create a file that will contain a report of people and pets—extracting specific data from two separate files.

STEP 18 Key in the following: **cut -c1-19 persons > t2** [Enter]

STEP 19 Key in the following: **cut -f1,3 pets > t1** [Enter]

STEP 20 Key in the following: **cat t2 t1** [Enter]

```
[cgillay@RedHat9   floppy]$   cut   -c1-19 persons > t2
[cgillay@RedHat9   floppy]$   cut -f1,3  pets > t1
[cgillay@RedHat9   floppy]$   cat t2 t1
Gillay     Carolyn
Panezich   Frank
Tuttle     Steven
Maurdeff   Kathryn
Maurdeff   Sonia
Cocker Spaniel   African Grey
Beagle     Cockatiel
Collie     Parrot
Great Dane       Parakeet
Boxer      Canary
[cgillay@RedHat9   floppy]$
```

WHAT'S **HAPPENING?** You have extracted data from two files and created two new files, **t1** and **t2**. You are now going to combine them into a third file called **t3**, again using redirection.

STEP 21 Key in the following: **paste t2 t1 > t3; cat t3** [Enter]

```
[cgillay@RedHat9   floppy]$   paste   t2   t1 > t3; cat t3
Gillay     Carolyn   Cocker Spaniel African Grey
Panezich   Frank     Beagle    Cockatiel
Tuttle     Steven    Collie    Parrot
Maurdeff   Kathryn   Great Dane            Parakeet
Maurdeff   Sonia     Boxer         Canary
[cgillay@RedHat9   floppy]$
```

WHAT'S HAPPENING? You now have a new file called **t3** that contains data extracted from different files.

7.8 ● Filters

When you do not specify a command line argument, many Linux commands read their input from standard input and write their output to standard output. Linux has many of these commands, which may also generate modified output. Commands that output a modified version of their input are referred to as *filters*. Many commands and programs are meant to be used this way. Filter commands manipulate information on input and produce modified output. Two such utilities are **sort** and **wc**.

sort simply sorts lines of text and writes the output to the screen. The **sort** filter command arranges or sorts lines of input text and sends them to standard output (the screen), unless you redirect it. The default sort is in ascending order (A to Z or lowest to highest numbers), starting in the first column. The syntax for sort is:

```
sort [options] [files]
```

Table 7.5, "**sort** Options," lists some of the major options used with the **sort** command.

Option	Name	Result
-b	Blank	Ignores leading spaces and tabs.
-c	Check	Checks whether *files* are already sorted and if so, produces no output.
-d	Dictionary	Sorts in dictionary order.
-f	Fold	Ignores upper/lowercase differences.
-g	General numeric	Sorts according to general numeric value.
-n	Numeric	Sorts according to string numeric value.
-r	Reverse	Sorts in reverse order (descending Z-A).
-t*c*	Separate	Separates fields with character defined by *c*. Default is tab.
-u	Unique	Sorts so that identical files in input file appear only once in output.

Table 7.5 ● sort Options

wc counts the number of bytes, words, and lines of input. It will print a total line for multiple files. If no files are listed, then it will read standard input. The syntax for **wc** is as follows:

```
wc [options]... [file]...
```

Table 7.6, "**wc** Options," lists some of the major options used with the **wc** command.

Option	Name	Result
-c	Bytes	Displays the character count only.
-l	Line	Displays the line count only.
-w	Words	Displays the word count only.

Table 7.6 • wc Options

7.9 • Activity: Using sort and wc

Note 1: The BOOK disk is mounted with **/mnt/floppy** as the default directory with a terminal window open.

Note 2: Remember, when you see [Ctrl] + **d**, it means to hold down the [Ctrl] key and press the letter **d**.

STEP 1   Key in the following:
sort [Enter]
BETA [Enter]
OMEGA [Enter]
CHI [Enter]
epsilon [Enter]
beta [Enter]
ALPHA [Enter]
chi [Enter]
[Ctrl] + **d**

```
[cgillay@RedHat9   floppy]$   sort
BETA
OMEGA
CHI
epsilon
beta
ALPHA
chi
ALPHA
beta
BETA
chi
CHI
epsilon
OMEGA
[cgillay@RedHat9   floppy]$
```

WHAT'S HAPPENING? The **sort** command took input from the keyboard. When you pressed [Ctrl] +**D**, you told the **sort** command that you were finished entering data. Then, the **sort** command "filtered" the data and wrote the keyboard input alphabetically to the standard output device (the screen). Depending on what version of Linux you have, your sort order may be different. In the older sort sequence, uppercase words came first and then lowercase words, based on the characters' numerical value. However, later versions of Linux sort more intelligently so that identical words are placed together. Regardless of what version you have, if you wanted to intermix upper- and lowercase letters, you may use the **-f** option. The **-f** option "folds" lowercase and uppercase together.

STEP 2   Key in the following:

    sort -f [Enter]
    BETA [Enter]
    OMEGA [Enter]
    CHI [Enter]
    epsilon [Enter]
    beta [Enter]
    ALPHA [Enter]
    chi [Enter]
    [Ctrl] + **d**

```
[cgillay@RedHat9   floppy]$   sort
BETA
OMEGA
CHI
epsilon
beta
ALPHA
chi
ALPHA
beta
BETA
chi
CHI
epsilon
OMEGA
[cgillay@RedHat9   floppy]$
```

WHAT'S **HAPPENING?** Now your words are in alphabetical order, regardless of case. You may see no difference in the sort sequence since generally, by default, **sort** will "fold" in upper and lower case characters.

STEP 3   Key in the following:

    sort [Enter]
    333 [Enter]
    3 [Enter]
    23 [Enter]
    124 [Enter]
    [Ctrl] + **d**

```
[cgillay@RedHat9  floppy]$   sort
333
3
23
124
124
23
3
333
[cgillay@RedHat9  floppy]$
```

WHAT'S HAPPENING? The **sort** command does not seem very smart because these numbers are not in order. Numbers, in this case, are really character data and not numeric values that are manipulated mathematically. Numbers are often used as character data. For instance, a zip code or a phone number—although they use numbers—really are character data and are not treated mathematically. You would not think of adding your address to your phone number and dividing by your zip code, for example.

Character data is sorted from left to right. Numeric data is sorted by units. Thus, if you look at "Smith" and "Smythe," you read character data from left to right and would place "Smith" before "Smythe." If you had the numbers "124," "222," "22," "23," "31," "9," and "6," the numeric order would be 6, 9, 22, 23, 31, 124, and 222. You first sort all the single-digit numbers. You then sort the two-digit numbers by first looking at the first digit—thus you know that 22 and 23 come before 32. Since 22 and 23 have the same first digit, you then look at the second digit to determine that the 2 in 22 comes before the 3 in 23.

A human knows that "12" comes before "13" because a person has learned how numbers work. The shell is different. It relies on something called the ASCII sort sequence. ASCII is a standard code that assigns values to letters, numbers, and punctuation marks—all the characters. The ASCII sort sequence is determined by the number assigned to the ASCII character. The sort order is punctuation marks, including spaces, then numbers, then letters (lowercase preceding uppercase). If you had a series of characters such as BB, aa, #, 123, bb, 13, and AA, the ASCII sort order would be:

    #   123   13   aa   AA   bb   BB

Notice with the new sort sequence, the relative positions of aa and AA did not change, but the relative positions of BB and bb did change.

There is another point about using the **sort** command. Not only does it follow the ASCII sort sequence, but it also sorts entire lines from left to right. Thus, the sort sequence of "Carolyn Smith" and "Robert Nesler" is:

```
Carolyn Smith
Robert Nesler
```

Because the sort command looks at the entire line, "Carolyn" comes before "Robert."

In the numeric example, **sort** looked at the entire line, and, since the "1" in "124" preceded the "2" in "23," it placed the "124" before the "23." You can force the shell to sort numbers by using the **-g** option or the **-n** option, which sorts based on general numeric values.

STEP 4   Key in the following:

        sort -g `Enter`

        333 `Enter`

        3 `Enter`

        23 `Enter`

        124 `Enter`

        `Ctrl` + **d**

```
[cgillay@RedHat9  floppy]$  sort -g
333
3
23
124
3
23
124
333
[cgillay@RedHat9  floppy]$
```

WHAT'S HAPPENING? By using the **-g** option, you are now sorted in correct numerical order. The **wc** command is another command that uses standard input and writes to standard output.

STEP 5   Key in the following: **wc** `Enter`

        One. Two. ? `Enter`

        Three. ? `Enter`

        Four. Five. `Enter`

        Six. `Enter`

        `Ctrl` + **c**

```
[cgillay@RedHat9  floppy]$  wc
One. Two. ?
Three. ?
Four. Five.
Six.
      4   8      38
[cgillay@RedHat9  floppy]$
```

WHAT'S HAPPENING? There are 4 lines, 8 words, and 38 bytes in the text you keyed in. Note that the command counts words. Thus, **One** followed by a period was considered one word, but the **?** by itself also counted as a word. In addition, the `Enter` that you do not see is also counted as a byte. You may use redirection with these commands using a file as input.

STEP 6   Key in the following: **sort state.cap; wc state.cap** `Enter`

```
[cgillay@RedHat9  floppy]$  sort state.cap; wc state.cap

Arizona        Phoenix
California      Sacramento
Colorado       Denver
Florida        Tallahassee
```

```
Louisiana          Baton Rouge
Michigan           Lansing
Nebraska           Lincoln
New York           Albany
Ohio               Columbus
Oregon             Salem


     11       22      260 state.cap
[cgillay@RedHat9    floppy]$
```

WHAT'S HAPPENING? You keyed in the **sort** command. The **sort** command expects its input either from the keyboard or from a file. You used the **sort** command with the argument of a file name, **state.cap**. Displayed on your screen (the standard output) is the **state.cap** file arranged in alphabetical order. **wc** also expects either keyboard input or a file argument. If you do not use the redirection symbol <, the command would wait for input from the keyboard. It expects a file name or input from the keyboard. If you had used **wc < state.cap**, it would have worked, but it would not have displayed the file name, **state.cap**, in the output. The **sort -r** options allows you to sort in reverse or descending order (Z to A). **wc** also has an option, the **-l** (el, not one), which simply prints the new line count; and the **-w** option, which counts only the words.

STEP 7   Key in the following: **sort -r state.cap; wc -l state.cap** [Enter]

```
[cgillay@RedHat9    floppy]$ sort -r state.cap; wc -l   state.cap
Oregon             Salem
Ohio               Columbus
New York           Albany
Nebraska           Lincoln
Michigan           Lansing
Louisiana          Baton Rouge
Florida            Tallahassee
Colorado           Denver
California          Sacramento
Arizona            Phoenix

     11 state.cap
[cgillay@RedHat9    floppy]$
```

WHAT'S HAPPENING? The file **state.cap** that the **sort** command used as input is displayed on the screen in reverse alphabetical order. The standard output, the result of the **sort** command, is written to the screen. The **wc** command, using **-l**, told you that there are 11 lines in this file. Note that the "blank" line counts as a line.

In these examples, you have been "massaging the data." The actual data in **state.cap** has not changed at all. It remains exactly as it was written. The only thing that has changed is the way it is displayed—the way you are looking at the data. This alphabetic arrangement is temporary. If you want to change the data in the file, you need to use redirection to save the altered data to a new file.

STEP 8   Key in the following: **sort state.cap > sorted.cap; cat sorted.cap** [Enter]

```
[cgillay@RedHat9  floppy]$ sort  state.cap > sorted.cap; cat sorted.cap

Arizona        Phoenix
California      Sacramento
Colorado       Denver
Florida        Tallahassee
Louisiana      Baton Rouge
Michigan       Lansing
Nebraska       Lincoln
New York       Albany
Ohio           Columbus
Oregon         Salem
[cgillay@RedHat9   floppy]$
```

WHAT'S HAPPENING? You saved the sorted output to a new file called **sorted.cap**. The standard output of the command **sort state.cap** will normally be written to the screen (standard output). Since standard output is written to the screen, you redirected it to a file called **sorted.cap**, or the command line **sort state.cap > sorted.cap**.

7.10 • Pipes

Pipes allow the standard output of one program to be used as the standard input to the next program. When you use pipes, you are not limited to two programs. You may pipe together many programs. The term *pipe* reflects the flow of information from one command to the next. Thus, you can create a pipeline using many commands. This makes it possible to use Linux utility programs as building blocks for larger programs. Many of these utility programs were designed to be used in this way. These utilities perform a specific kind of filtering operation on input text. You may take any command that has standard output and pipe it to a filter or another command. The filter will "do" something to the standard output of the previous command, such as sort it. Since filters always write to standard output, you may use pipes and filters to further refine your data. Essentially, you may use filters to transform data to your needs.

The pipe symbol is the vertical bar | used between two commands. On the keyboard, a typical location for the pipe symbol is above the [Enter] key, combined with the \. This means you must use the [Shift] key to access the pipe symbol. If you have a notebook computer, the location of the pipe will vary.

The syntax of a command line using pipes is:

```
command_1 [options][arguments] ¦ command_2 [options] [arguments] ¦ command_3...
```

You are not limited to two or three commands but may continue the pipeline. You may also redirect the final output to a file or a device.

7.11 • Activity: Using Pipes

Note 1:   The BOOK disk is mounted with **/mnt/floppy** as the default directory with a terminal
            window open.

Note 2:   You will use the pipe symbol |, so be sure you locate it on the keyboard.

STEP 1   Key in the following: **more ls** [Enter]

```
[cgillay@RedHat9  floppy]$  more ls
ls: No such file or directory
[cgillay@RedHat9  floppy]$
```

WHAT'S HAPPENING? The **more** command is designed to work with files. **ls** is a command and not a file. However, since **ls** writes standard output, you can pipe it as input to the **more** command.

STEP 2   Key in the following: **ls | more** Enter

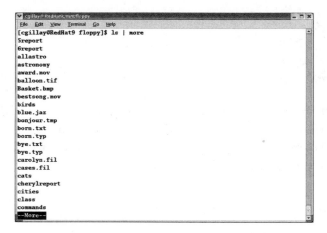

WHAT'S HAPPENING? Your files may vary. By using the pipe symbol, you asked that the output of the **ls** command be used as input to the **more** command. The **-- More --** on the bottom of the screen tells you that there are "more" screens of data. Press Enter to scroll a line at a time and the Space Bar to scroll a screen at a time. You can use **q** to stop the display and return to the prompt. You can combine commands using pipes.

STEP 3   Press **q**

STEP 4   Key in the following: **ls | sort -r | more** Enter

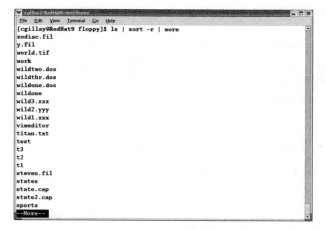

WHAT'S HAPPENING? You now have a list of your files sorted in reverse alphabetical order displayed one screenful at time. The **lpr** utility is also a command that will accept input from either a file or standard input. You have used **lpr** *filename* so that you could print a file. However, if you wanted to print your listing of files, you could not key in **ls lpr**, again because

ls is a command and not a file. You may pipe the output of **ls** to the **lpr** command. In fact, any command with standard output can be piped to **lpr**.

STEP 5 Press **q**.

Note: The option is 1 (one) not the letter l (ell).

STEP 6 Key in the following: **ls -1 *.txt** Enter

```
[cgillay@RedHat9  floppy]$  ls -1 *.txt
born.txt
bye.txt
crops.txt
galaxy.txt
good.txt
hello.txt
NEW AUTOS.txt
planets.txt
Sandy and Nicki.txt
Sandy and Patty.txt
titan.txt
[cgillay@RedHat9  floppy]$
```

WHAT'S HAPPENING? You have listed all the files that have **.txt** as an extension in the **/mnt/floppy** directory, one line per file. Now, to print this output, you pipe it to **lpr**.

STEP 7 Key in the following: **ls -1 *.txt | lpr** Enter

WHAT'S HAPPENING? You should have a hard copy of files that were listed following Step 6. You can combine commands as well in the pipeline. You can find out how many lines are in a set of files by using **wc** and the **-l** option (ell not 1) and the piping the output of that command as input to the **sort** command, using the **-g** option to sort in numeric order.

STEP 8 Key in the following: **wc -l *.txt | sort -g** Enter

```
[cgillay@RedHat9  floppy]$ wc -l *.txt | sort -g
2   Sandy and Nicki.txt
2   Sandy and Patty.txt
4   born.txt
4   bye.txt
4   good.txt
7   galaxy.txt
8   hello.txt
10  planets.txt
11  NEW AUTOS.txt
14  titan.txt
20  crops.txt
86 total
[cgillay@RedHat9  floppy]$
```

WHAT'S HAPPENING? Your total files could vary if you did not do all the activities or did additional activities. The number of lines in each file is counted for all the files on the BOOK disk that have a **.txt** extension, and then that output was piped as input to the **sort** command.

You used the **-g** option so that the numbers would sort in general numeric order and be treated as numeric data rather than as character data. You then got a total number of lines for all of the **.txt** files.

7.12 • Introducing grep, egrep, and fgrep

The **grep** command (global regular expression print) utility will search through one or more files to see if any of the files contain a string of characters that is specified on the command line. The output is written to standard output. The syntax is:

```
grep [options] pattern [file...]
grep [options] [-e patterns | -f file] [file...]
```

grep searches for what are called regular expressions (RE). ***Regular expressions*** are wildcard patterns built using special characters. A regular expression is a pattern that describes a set of strings. Some common ones are listed in Table 7.7, "Common Regular Expressions."

Expression	Result
*	Matches all characters.
?	Matches a single character.
[a-z]	Matches a range of characters. In this example, anything that is **a** through **z**.
[abcd]	Matches a range of characters specified within the brackets. In this example, it would match any **a**, **b**, **c**, or **d** or combination thereof.
\?	Matches the **?**. Since **?** is a special character, if you actually want to locate a **?**, you precede it with the backslash. This would be true of any special character that has meaning to the shell. The backslash character is used as an "escape character" to escape the pattern.
^abc	Matches **abc** at the beginning of the line.
$abc	Matches **abc** at the end of the line.

Table 7.7 • Common Regular Expressions

In addition to regular expressions, there are extended regular expressions, also called full regular expressions. ***Extended regular expressions*** include all the regular expressions as well as other special characters. These include the **+**, the **?**, and the **|** to give special meaning to your search pattern. The plus allows you to add items to your search pattern. The question mark allows you to have zero or one occurrence of a string, and the vertical bar acts as an "or" operator. An or operator means that either string on each side of the vertical bar can be matched. This means that using a vertical bar between two regular expressions will match either the first or the second expression, or both. Table 7.8, "Extended Regular Expressions," gives examples of the use of these characters.

Extended Regular Expression	Matches	Examples
ab+c	a followed by one or more **b**'s followed by a **c**	yab<u>c</u>x **abbbbc94**
'ab?c'	a followed by nothing or one **b** followed by a **c**	back **abcdef**
'(ab)+c'	One or more occurrences of the string **ab** followed by a **c**	zabcd **abcabcxy**
'(ab)?c'	No or one occurrence of the string **ab** followed by **c**	xc **abccc**
'ab|ac'	Either **ab** or **ac**	**ab ab ab**ac
'^Exit|^Quit'	Any line that begins with **Exit** or **Quit**	**Exit Quit** No Exit
'(D|N)|.Jones'	**D.Jones** or **N.Jones**	P.**D. Jones N.Jones**

Table 7.8 ◦ Extended Regular Expressions

Thus, **grep** is a command for searching files for lines matching a given regular expression. The **fgrep** command searches only for fixed, uninterrupted strings rather than regular expressions. The **egrep** command (extended version of **grep**) searches for regular and extended regular expressions. **egrep** is usually the fastest of the three commands. When looking at syntax, usually **grep**, **egrep**, and **fgrep** are grouped together. Table 7.9, "**grep**, **egrep**, and **fgrep** Options," lists some of the major options used with the **grep**, **egrep**, and **fgrep** command.

Option	Name	Result
-c	Count	Displays only a count of matched lines.
-d *action*	Directories	Defines an action for processing directories. Possible actions are **read** to read directories like ordinary files; **skip** to skip directories; and **recurse** to read all files under each directory—same as **-r**.
-E	Extended	Same as **egrep**.
-F	Fixed strings	Same as **fgrep**.
-I	Ignore case	Ignores distinction between upper- and lowercase characters.
-n	Line numbers	Displays the lines and their line numbers.
-r	Recursive	Reads all files under each directory.
-v	Not match	Displays all lines that *do not* match pattern.
-w	Word	Displays match only on whole words. Words are divided by characters that are not letters, digits, or underscores.

| -x | Except | Displays lines only if pattern matches entire line. |

Table 7.9 • grep, egrep, and fgrep Options

7.13 • Activity: Using grep, egrep, and fgrep

Note: The BOOK disk is mounted with **/mnt/floppy** as the default directory. A terminal window is open.

STEP 1   Key in the following: **grep Teacher personal.fil** [Enter]

```
[cgillay@RedHat9   floppy]$   grep Teacher personal.fil
Panezich   Frank      689 Lake      Orange        CA  Teacher
Maurdeff   Kathryn    550 Traver    Ann Arbor     MI  Teacher
Winter     Linda      333 Pick      Garden Grove  CA  Teacher
Suzuki     Charlene   567 Abbey     Rochester     MI  Day Care Teacher
[cgillay@RedHat9   floppy]$
```

WHAT'S **HAPPENING?** You searched for the character string **Teacher** in the **personal.fil**. Each occurrence was found and written to the screen. You have not changed the data in the **personal.fil**, only what you are displaying.

STEP 2   Key in the following: **grep ^Bab personal.fil** [Enter]

```
[cgillay@RedHat9   floppy]$   grep ^Bab personal.fil
Babchuk    Nicholas 13 Stratford   Sun City West  AZ  Professor
Babchuk    Bianca   13 Stratford   Sun City West  AZ  Professor
Babchuk    Walter   12 View        Thousand Oaks  CA  President
Babchuk    Deana    12 View        Thousand Oaks  CA  Housewife
[cgillay@RedHat9   floppy]$
```

WHAT'S **HAPPENING?** You used a regular expression—locate all the occurrences of any line that has **Bab** as its first characters (**^Bab**) followed by any other characters. You may also use **grep** to search through files.

STEP 3   Key in the following: **grep Carolyn *.fil** [Enter]

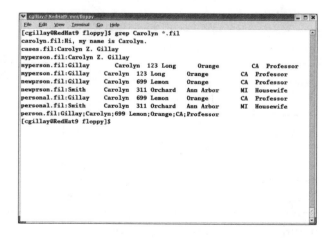

WHAT'S HAPPENING? Here you asked for any occurrence of the string **Carolyn** in any file that had **.fil** as an extension. If you want a count of each time **Carolyn** occurred in the specified files (*.**fil**), you can use the **-c** option.

STEP 4   Key in the following: **grep -c Carolyn *.fil** [Enter]

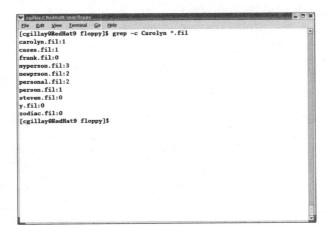

```
[cgillay@RedHat9 floppy]$ grep -c Carolyn *.fil
carolyn.fil:1
cases.fil:1
frank.fil:0
myperson.fil:3
newprson.fil:2
personal.fil:2
person.fil:1
steven.fil:0
y.fil:0
zodiac.fil:0
[cgillay@RedHat9 floppy]$
```

WHAT'S HAPPENING? Here you see that the string **Carolyn** did not appear in **frank.fil**, **steven.fil**, **y.fil**, or **zodiac.fil**. There are many options with **grep**, such as **-v** for every occurrence except the one you asked for (in the above example, this would find every line *except* a line that contained **Carolyn**), **-n** to display the line numbers, and so on. You can see the differences between **egrep** and **grep** in the following command set.

STEP 5   Key in the following: **grep 'Carolyn|Smith' personal.fil** [Enter]

```
[cgillay@RedHat9  floppy]$  grep 'Carolyn|Smith' personal.fil
[cgillay@RedHat9  floppy]$ ▉
```

WHAT'S HAPPENING? You were asking for any occurrence of **Carolyn** *or* **Smith** in the **personal.fil**. The **grep** command found nothing because the "or" construct—the pipe—is not a regular expression.

STEP 6   Key in the following: **egrep 'Carolyn|Smith' personal.fil** [Enter]

```
[cgillay@RedHat9  floppy]$  egrep 'Carolyn|Smith'personal.fil
Gillay    Carolyn  699 Lemon      Orange       CA  Professor
Smith     Gregory  311 Orchard    Ann Arbor    MI  Engineer
Smith     Carolyn  311 Orchard    Ann Arbor    MI  Housewife
Smith     David    120 Collins    Orange       CA  Chef
[cgillay@RedHat9  floppy]$ ▉
```

WHAT'S HAPPENING? Since **egrep** does allow the use of extended regular expressions, either **Carolyn** or **Smith** matched the criteria. You must be careful about spacing. If you had keyed in the command as **egrep 'Carolyn | Smith' personal.fil**, with a space after **Carolyn** and a space before **Smith**, you would have gotten different results. The names with **Carolyn** would have been displayed, but neither **Gregory Smith** nor **David Smith** would have been displayed. This is because in **personal.fil**, the last names are not preceded by a space. Thus, no **Smith**s would have found. **Carolyn**s are preceded by a space, so all **Carolyn**s would have been found. **grep -E** is the same as **egrep**.

STEP 7   Key in the following: **grep -E 'Carolyn|Smith' personal.fil** [Enter]

```
[cgillay@RedHat9  floppy]$  grep -E 'Carolyn|Smith' personal.fil
Gillay      Carolyn   699 Lemon      Orange         CA  Professor
Smith       Gregory   311 Orchard    Ann Arbor      MI  Engineer
Smith       Carolyn   311 Orchard    Ann Arbor      MI  Housewife
Smith       David     120 Collins    Orange         CA  Chef
[cgillay@RedHat9  floppy]$
```

WHAT'S HAPPENING? As you can see, **grep -E** behaved the same way as **egrep**. Again, remember that the vertical bar indicates a search for either item or both.

STEP 8   Key in the following: **egrep 'Markiw|Nicholas' personal.fil** [Enter]

```
[cgillay@RedHat9  floppy]$  egrep  'Markiw|Nicholas'  personal.fil
Babchuk     Nicholas 13 Stratford   Sun City West  AZ  Professor
Markiw      Nicholas 354 Bell       Phoenix        AZ  Engineer
Markiw      Emily    10 Zion        Sun City West  AZ  Retired
Markiw      Nick     10 Zion        Sun City West  AZ  Retired
Markiw      Nicholas 12 Fifth       Glendale       AZ  Engineer
[cgillay@RedHat9  floppy]$
```

WHAT'S HAPPENING? Since **egrep** does allow the use of extended regular expressions, it found the text that matched your criteria—either **Nicholas** *or* **Markiw**. **fgrep** does not allow the use of wildcards or regular expressions.

STEP 9   Key in the following: **fgrep Carolyn personal.fil** [Enter]

```
[cgillay@RedHat9  floppy]$  fgrep Carolyn personal.fil
Gillay      Carolyn   699 Lemon      Orange         CA  Professor
Smith       Carolyn   311 Orchard    Ann Arbor      MI  Housewife
[cgillay@RedHat9  floppy]$
```

WHAT'S HAPPENING? Since you used a specific string of data, **fgrep** could find the occurrence of **Carolyn** in **personal.fil**. However, if you use a wildcard, **fgrep** will not find any occurrences of your request.

STEP 10   Key in the following: **fgrep Car* personal.fil** [Enter]

```
[cgillay@RedHat9  floppy]$  fgrep Car* personal.fil
[cgillay@RedHat9  floppy]$
```

WHAT'S HAPPENING? Again, **fgrep** cannot use wildcards. **grep** would have worked in the above step. Again, **grep -f** is the same as **fgrep**.

STEP 11   Key in the following: **grep -F Car* personal.fil** [Enter]

```
[cgillay@RedHat9  floppy]$  grep -F Car* personal.fil
[cgillay@RedHat9  floppy]$
```

WHAT'S HAPPENING? You got the same results using **fgrep**. Since the **grep** family of commands writes to standard output, you can pipe the output to another command.

STEP 12   Key in the following: **grep AZ personal.fil | sort** [Enter]

```
[cgillay@RedHat9    floppy]$   grep AZ personal.fil | sort
Babchuk     Bianca     13 Stratford   Sun City West   AZ   Professor
Babchuk     Nicholas   13 Stratford   Sun City West   AZ   Professor
Jones       Steven     32 North       Phoenix         AZ   Buyer
Lo          Ophelia    1213 Wick      Phoenix         AZ   Writer
Markiw      Emily      10 Zion        Sun City West   AZ   Retired
Markiw      Nicholas   12 Fifth       Glendale        AZ   Engineer
Markiw      Nicholas   354 Bell       Phoenix         AZ   Engineer
Markiw      Nick       10 Zion        Sun City West   AZ   Retired
Nyles       John       12 Brooks      Sun City West   AZ   Retired
[cgillay@RedHat9    floppy]$
```

WHAT'S HAPPENING? You asked **grep** to locate all occurrences of **AZ** in the file called **personal.fil**. You then piped (had the standard output of the **grep** command sent as standard input to the **sort** command because you wanted the output sorted in alphabetical order).

If you had wanted a permanent copy of this list, you could have redirected the standard output (normally displayed on the screen) to a file. If you wanted only a printout, you could have redirected the standard output (normally displayed on the screen) to the printer. You could not do both. For instance, if you had keyed in the command as

```
grep  AZ personal.fil  |  sort  >  az.fil  >  lpr
```

you would have an empty file called **az.fil**, but it would not print. Also, you should realize that if you keyed in

```
grep  AZ personal.fil  |  sort  >  az.fil  |  lpr
```

it also would not work. You would get an error message of **printer: nothing to print**. However, you would have created the sorted file **az.fil**. It would not print because no command was issued. **az.fil** is not a command and **lpr** needs a command as input. You were, in essence, keying in the command **az.fil | lpr**. Just because you use pipes, filters, and redirection, the rules of the operating system are not suspended.

Perhaps the easiest way to remember the rules of pipes, filters, and redirection is that, when you use a pipe, there must be a command on either side of the pipe. Remember, you are taking the standard output of a command and using it as standard input to the next command. Remember also that not every command has standard output that is displayed on the screen. For instance, when you key in **rm** *filename* at the system level, there is no output that appears or is written to the screen. The file is simply deleted. Conversely, when you use redirection, it is an "instead of" action. Instead of the standard output being written to the screen, you are redirecting (sending) it somewhere else, such as a file or a device. You get only one "somewhere else." Since it is an "instead of" action, you cannot say instead of displaying the output of the **ls** command on the screen, redirect the output to a file and redirect the output to the printer. Your choice is either the printer or a file, not both. The primary use of pipes and filters is manipulating the standard output and standard input of commands. You also have to be aware of what you are asking for it to interpret your results correctly.

STEP 13 Key in the following: **grep -c CA personal.fil** Enter

STEP 14 Key in the following: **grep -ci CA personal.fil** Enter

STEP 15 Key in the following: **grep -ciw CA personal.fil** Enter

```
[cgillay@RedHat9    floppy]$    grep -c CA personal.fil
20
[cgillay@RedHat9    floppy]$    grep -ci CA personal.fil
23
[cgillay@RedHat9    floppy]$    grep -ciw CA personal.fil
20
[cgillay@RedHat9    floppy]$
```

WHAT'S HAPPENING? Here in the first command, you were asking for all the people who lived in California (**CA**). You used the **-c** option to count, and you received a count of 20. In the next command, you thought you were asking the same question, but you added the **-i** option (ignore case). In this case, you got a count of 23. The difference is that in this file, there are some character strings that matched **CA** (**Carolyn** as well as **CA**). In the last iteration of the command, you added the **-w** option (only match whole word), then you saw the correct number of 20. **grep** and its variant forms (**egrep** and **fgrep**) will be an often-used command. For instance, if you wanted to know how many people on this system were using Bash as their shell, you find that information with **grep**.

STEP 16 Key in the following: **grep -c /bin/bash /etc/passwd** [Enter]

```
[cgillay@RedHat9    floppy]$    grep -c /bin/bash    /etc/passwd
16
[cgillay@RedHat9    floppy]$
```

WHAT'S HAPPENING? You used **grep** to count (**-c**) all the users who use the Bash shell (**/bin/bash**) by searching the **/etc/passwd** file that lists what the default shell is for each user. In this example, there are 16 users who are using Bash as their shell.

7.14 • Formatting a Document with pr

So far, whenever you have printed a file, it printed in its "raw" form. In other words, however the document appeared on the screen is how it printed. There is a utility program called **pr** that will convert a text file to a paginated, columned version. If you do not specify any files, **pr** will read standard input. By default, **pr** formats the specified files into single-column pages of 66 lines. Each page has a five-line header. The default values are the current file's name, its last modification date, the current page, and a five-line trailer that consists of blank lines. Once you have formatted the document, you may pipe it to **lpr** so it prints in its formatted form. The syntax is **pr [options] [arguments]**. The **pr** command has over 20 options. Some of the most useful are listed in Table 7.10, "pr Options."

Option	Result
+*num_page*	Discards the first page number and begins printing on specified page.
-*num_col*	Prints in the number of columns specified by num_col.
-a	Displays columns across rather than down.
-d	Displays in double-spaced format.

-f, -F	Separates pages with form feed, not new lines. Linux uses line feed as its text line terminator. This means to move the cursor down to the same column on the next line. Originally this would have been done by feeding the paper through the printer. A form feed is the character used to start a new page on a printer.
-h *header*	Uses your text in as specified by header instead of the file name.
-l *lines*	Sets the page length to lines specified by *lines*.

Table 7.10 • pr Options

7.15 • Activity: Using pr

Note: The BOOK disk is mounted with **/mnt/floppy** as the default directory. A terminal window is open.

STEP 1   Key in the following:
pr Enter
This is text. Enter

```
[cgillay@RedHat9  floppy]$ pr
This is text.



2003-06-30  18:18                                    Page 1


This is text
 —
```

WHAT'S **HAPPENING?** The **pr** command is taking your input and displaying it in a formatted form on your screen.

STEP 2   Press Ctrl + **c** to return to the prompt.

STEP 3   Key in the following: **pr titan.txt | more** Enter

```
[cgillay@RedHat9  floppy]$  pr titan.txt | more

2001-10-31  13:43            titan.txt            Page 1



Saturn's largest moon is Titan. Titan is about
40% the diameter of earth. Saturn has 18 moons,
all named after the Titans. In Greek mythology,
the Titans were the children and the grandchildren
of the god Uranus and Gaea, the goddess of Earth.

Their names are:
```

Pan	Atlas	Prometheus	Pandora
Epimetheus	Janus	Mimas	Enceladus
Telesto	Calypso	Dione	Helene
Rhea	Tethys	Titan	Hyperion
Iapetus	Phoebe		

--More--

WHAT'S HAPPENING? Your output is now formatted. If you wanted to print it in this form, you could pipe it to the printer so that the command line would be **pr titan.txt | lpr**.

STEP 4   Press ⌈Ctrl⌉ + **c** to return to the command line.

STEP 5   Key in the following: **pr -dh "My formatted file" personal.fil | more** ⌈Enter⌉

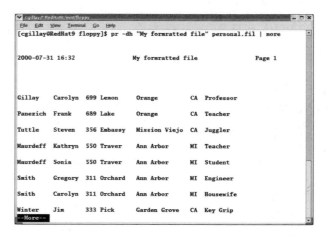

WHAT'S HAPPENING? Here you double-spaced your document as well as created a personalized header. Since your header information had spaces, you needed to enclose it with quotation marks.

STEP 6   Press ⌈Ctrl⌉ + **c** to return to the command line.

STEP 7   Key in the following: **ls *.txt | pr -3a | more** ⌈Enter⌉

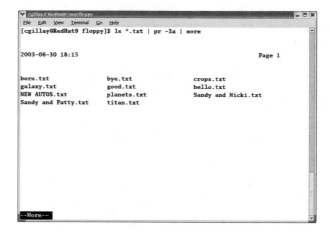

WHAT'S HAPPENING? Here you used the **ls** command to locate all the files with a **.txt** extension. You then piped the output to the **pr** command and asked that the output be displayed in three columns across the screen. You then piped it to **more** so you could see it on the screen. Again, if you wanted to print your output, rather than piping it to **more**, you would have piped it to **lpr (ls *.txt | pr -3a | lpr)**.

STEP 8   Press ⌷Ctrl⌷ + **c** to return to the command line.

7.16 ● Introducing tee, tr, and ispell

The **tee** utility is a means to accept output from another command and send it both to standard output and to a file. The **tee** command takes a single input and sends the output in two directions. It is like a fork in the road, except that the command allows you to go in both directions. **tee** allows you to watch the progress of a program on the screen and save the output to a file. Essentially, **tee** reads from standard input and writes to both standard output and to files. The syntax is

```
tee [options] files
```

tee has minimal options. One useful option is **-a**, which appends the output to a file, rather than overwriting the file.

The **tr** command "translates" and/or deletes characters from standard input, writing to standard input. The **tr** utility takes its input only from standard input. The syntax is

```
tr [options] string1 [string2]
```

Table 7.11, "**tr** Options," lists some of the major options used with the **tr** command.

Option	Name	Result
-d	Delete	Deletes characters in *string 1*.
-s	Squeeze	Squeezes out repeated output characters in *string 2*.
-t	Truncate	Truncates *string 1* to length of *string 2* b.

Table 7.11 ● tr Options

Table 7.12, "Special Characters Options," lists some of the special characters used with the **tr** command. See Appendix B for the standard ASCII table.

Special Character	Keystroke	Meaning
\a	^ G	bell
\b	^ H	backspace
\f	^ L	form feed
\n	^ J	new line
\r	^ M	carriage return
\t	^ I	horizontal tab
\v	^ K	vertical tab
\nnn		characters with octal value of *nnn*

Table 7.12 ● Special Characters Options

The **tr** command translates each character in *string1* in standard input to the corresponding character in *string2*. **tr** does not change the contents of the original file. It allows you to substitute or delete characters specified by the options and patterns. The patterns are strings, and the strings are character sets. In its most basic use, **tr** literally translates each character in *string1* into the character in the corresponding position in *string2*. Strings are "quoted" with either single or double quotation marks. It is not possible to replace a single character with several characters. The most common options used are **-d** (delete a character) and **-s** (substitute a character or squeeze out repeated output characters in *string2*). A common use of **tr** is to convert lowercase characters to uppercase characters or to remove an incorrect character in a file.

Most Linux distributions come with an interactive spell checker program, **ispell**. You can use the program as a stand-alone or with an editor. The **ispell** program compares the words of one or more files with the dictionary. It will display unrecognized words with possible correct spellings, and it does allow for editing with its own set of commands. The syntax is **ispell [options] [files]**.

7.17 • Activity: Using tee, tr, and ispell

Note 1:   The BOOK disk is mounted with **/mnt/floppy** as the default directory. A terminal window is open.

Note 2:   The **crops.txt** file was created in Activity 5.21.

STEP 1   Key in the following: **grep South crops.txt | tee south.fil** [Enter]

```
[cgillay@RedHat9  floppy]$  grep South crops.txt | tee south.fil
Georgia          South       peanuts, cotton, corn
Florida          South       citrus fruits, vegetables, potatoes
North Carolina   South       tobacco, soybeans, corn, peanuts
Louisiana        South       soybeans, sugar cane, rice
Alabama          South       peanuts, cotton, soybeans
[cgillay@RedHat9  floppy]$
```

WHAT'S HAPPENING? Here you found every occurrence of **South** in the **crops.txt** file. You then piped it to the **tee** command, which placed the contents of the file in a new file called **south.fil** and also displayed the output on the screen.

STEP 2   Key in the following: **cat south.fil** [Enter]

```
[cgillay@RedHat9  floppy]$  cat south.fil
Georgia          South    peanuts, cotton, corn
Florida          South    citrus fruits, vegetables, potatoes
North Carolina   South    tobacco, soybeans, corn, peanuts
Louisiana        South    soybeans, sugar cane, rice
Alabama          South    peanuts, cotton, soybeans
[cgillay@RedHat9  floppy]$
```

WHAT'S HAPPENING? The file does exist and it holds the contents of what you extracted from the **crops.txt** file with the **grep** command. Now you want to translate every occurrence of **South** to SOUTH.

STEP 3   Key in the following: **tr "South" "SOUTH" < south.fil** [Enter]

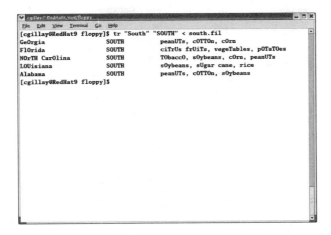

WHAT'S HAPPENING? You could have also written the command as

cat south.fil | tr South SOUTH. However, as you look at your output, you see that **tr** translated every occurrence of your selected letters. It did distinguish words from characters. The **tr** utility is for translating every character. The original file is not impacted. If you wanted to save the output, you could redirect it to a file.

STEP 4   Key in the following:

cat south.fil; tr [a-z] [A-Z] < south.fil | tee southern.fil [Enter]

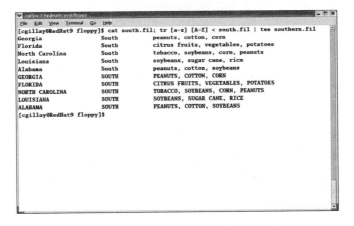

WHAT'S HAPPENING? Here you looked at the contents of **south.fil** with the **cat** command and saw it did not change. You then used the **tr** utility to translate all lowercase letters to uppercase letters. You used brackets because you had a range, although the command would have worked as well without brackets. You used **south.fil** as input to **tr**. You then piped the output to the **tee** command so that you could see the output on the screen while saving it to a file called **southern.fil** at the same time. If you only wanted to save the output to the file, you could have written the command as **tr [a-z] [A-Z] < south.fil > southern.fil**. Again, the brackets are not necessary since you specified a range. However, using brackets clarifies what you are translating. To delete characters, you use the **-d** option.

STEP 5   Key in the following: **tr -d RICE < southern.fil** [Enter]

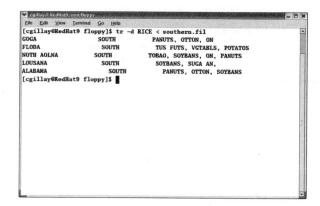

WHAT'S HAPPENING? Again, every occurrence of **R, I, C,** and **E** was deleted in the output displayed on the screen. However, since you did not save this output to a file but only wrote it to the screen, the original file is still intact. You may also use special characters with the **-s** command. For instance. **\012** is the octal number for blank lines. If you wanted to strip blank lines from a file, you could use the octal value.

Note: Press the ⟨SpaceBar⟩ between the first and second and the second and third quote.

STEP 6   Key in the following: **tr -s " " "\012" < work/exp01jan.dta** ⟨Enter⟩

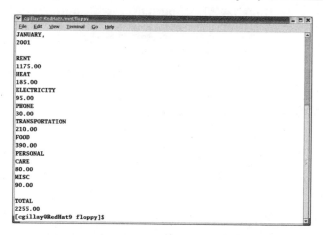

WHAT'S HAPPENING? You stripped the file of blank lines, and now every line in the file is on a new line. The **-s** command is especially useful when you need to remove a character that is repeated several times. The **-s** option checks for sequences of the specified *string 1* character repeated several consecutive times. When this happens, it replaces the sequence of repeated characters with one occurrence of the corresponding character from *string 2*.

STEP 7   Key in the following:
    cat > this.fil ⟨Enter⟩
    This:is:a:test:of:using:-s:with:tr. ⟨Enter⟩
    ⟨Ctrl⟩ + **d**

Note: The first quote encloses the :. The second quote encloses a space. Be sure to press the ⟨SpaceBar⟩ in the second series of quotes.

STEP 8   Key in the following: **cat this.fil; tr ":" " " < this.fil** ⟨Enter⟩

```
[cgillay@RedHat9  floppy]$  cat this.fil; tr ":" " " < this.fil
This:is:a:test:of:using:-s:with:tr.
This is a test of using -s with tr.
[cgillay@RedHat9  floppy]$
```

WHAT'S HAPPENING? When you used **cat this.fil**, : appeared between each word. When you used the **tr**, you asked it to find every occurrence of the : and substitute it with a space.

STEP 9   Key in the following:
    cat > spelling Enter
    This is a file wiht misspelled words Enter
    tht I can corect with the dictoonary. Enter
    Ctrl + d

STEP 10   Key in the following: **ispell spelling** Enter

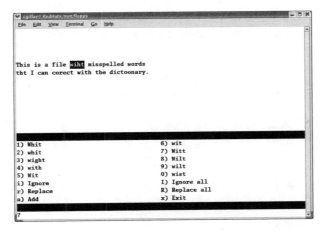

WHAT'S HAPPENING? You created a file with some misspelled words. You then began checking it with the **ispell** utility. It found your first incorrect word. Your choices are at the bottom of the screen. In this case, you want to use word number 4, so you key in 4. Note that your number may be different.

STEP 11   Key in the following: **4** (or the correct number).

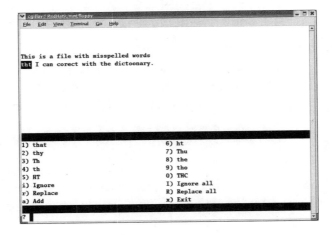

WHAT'S HAPPENING? The word **wiht** was replaced with the correct spelling of **with**. It then moved on to the next incorrect word, **tht** and again gives you choices. In this case, 1 is the correction you want.

STEP 12 Key in the following: **1**

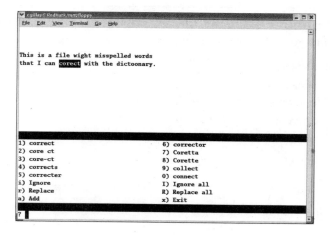

WHAT'S HAPPENING? The word **tht** was corrected to **that**. It then moved to the next error, **corect**. The choice you want is again 1. You also can replace words, insert a new word, look up a word, and so on.

STEP 13 Key in the following: **1**.

STEP 14 Key in the following: **1**. Press **x** if necessary.

Note: In some versions of ispell, if there are no more words to correct, you are returned to the prompt.

STEP 15 Key in the following: **cat spelling**

```
[cgillay@RedHat9  floppy]$  cat spelling
This is a file with misspelled words
that I can correct with the dictionary.
[cgillay@RedHat9  floppy]$
```

WHAT'S HAPPENING? Your text file was corrected.

7.18 • Introducing head and tail

The **head** and **tail** commands are used to display a specific number of lines at the top of a file (**head**) or the bottom of the file (**tail**). By default, both commands display 10 lines. **head** displays the first 10 lines in a file and **tail** displays the last 10 lines in a file unless otherwise specified.

The syntax for **head** is

```
head [options] [files].
```

With no files defined, **head** uses standard input. If more than one file is listed, a header is displayed for each file. Table 7.13, "**head** Options," lists some of the major options used with the **head** command.

Option	Name	Result
-n *num*	Number	Displays first lines defined by *num*.
-q	Quiet	Never displays print headers giving file name.
-v	Verbose	Displays file name headers for even one file.

Table 7.13 • head Options

The syntax for **tail** is

```
tail [options] [file]
```

Table 7.14, "**tail** Options," lists some of the major options used with the **tail** command.

Option	Name	Result
-n *num*	Number	Displays last lines defined by *num*.
-q	Quiet	Never displays print headers giving file name.
-v	Verbose	Displays file name headers for even one file.

Table 7.14 • tail Options

7.19 • Activity: Using head and tail

Note: The BOOK disk is mounted with **/mnt/floppy** as the default directory. A terminal window is open.

STEP 1   Key in the following: **head personal.fil; tail personal.fil** [Enter]

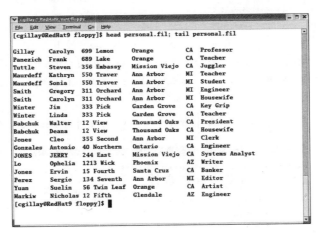

WHAT'S HAPPENING? **head** displayed the first ten lines of the **personal.fil** file, whereas **tail** displayed the last ten lines of the same file. In the above example, you do not see the file name listed.

STEP 2   Key in the following: **head -20v personal.fil** [Enter]

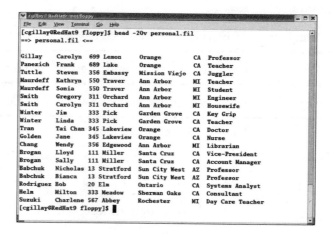

```
[cgillay@RedHat9 floppy]$ head -20v personal.fil
==> personal.fil <==

Gillay      Carolyn   699 Lemon     Orange        CA  Professor
Panezich    Frank     689 Lake      Orange        CA  Teacher
Tuttle      Steven    356 Embassy   Mission Viejo CA  Juggler
Maurdeff    Kathryn   550 Traver    Ann Arbor     MI  Teacher
Maurdeff    Sonia     550 Traver    Ann Arbor     MI  Student
Smith       Gregory   311 Orchard   Ann Arbor     MI  Engineer
Smith       Carolyn   311 Orchard   Ann Arbor     MI  Housewife
Winter      Jim       333 Pick      Garden Grove  CA  Key Grip
Winter      Linda     333 Pick      Garden Grove  CA  Teacher
Tran        Tai Chan  345 Lakeview  Orange        CA  Doctor
Golden      Jane      345 Lakeview  Orange        CA  Nurse
Chang       Wendy     356 Edgewood  Ann Arbor     MI  Librarian
Brogan      Lloyd     111 Miller    Santa Cruz    CA  Vice-President
Brogan      Sally     111 Miller    Santa Cruz    CA  Account Manager
Babchuk     Nicholas  13 Stratford  Sun City West AZ  Professor
Babchuk     Bianca    13 Stratford  Sun City West AZ  Professor
Rodriguez   Bob       20 Elm        Ontario       CA  Systems Analyst
Helm        Milton    333 Meadow    Sherman Oaks  CA  Consultant
Suzuki      Charlene  567 Abbey     Rochester     MI  Day Care Teacher
[cgillay@RedHat9 floppy]$
```

WHAT'S HAPPENING? Now you see the first 20 lines of the file as well as the file name.

STEP 3   Key in the following: **head -2 *.fil** [Enter]

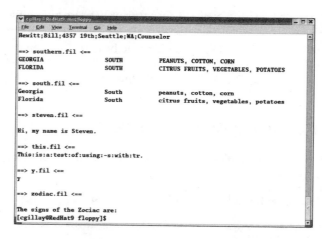

```
Hewitt;Bill;4357 19th;Seattle;WA;Counselor

==> southern.fil <==
GEORGIA              SOUTH           PEANUTS, COTTON, CORN
FLORIDA              SOUTH           CITRUS FRUITS, VEGETABLES, POTATOES

==> south.fil <==
Georgia              South           peanuts, cotton, corn
Florida              South           citrus fruits, vegetables, potatoes

==> steven.fil <==

Hi, my name is Steven.

==> this.fil <==
This:is:a:test:of:using:-s:with:tr.

==> y.fil <==
y

==> zodiac.fil <==

The signs of the Zociac are:
[cgillay@RedHat9 floppy]$
```

WHAT'S HAPPENING? You saw the first two lines of every file that has **.fil** as an extension. The file name was automatically printed. If you wanted to see the last two lines of every file that had **.fil** as an extension, you would key in **tail -2 *.fil**. You can also use pipes with the **head** and **tail** commands.

STEP 4   Key in the following: **grep CA personal.fil | sort | head -5** [Enter]

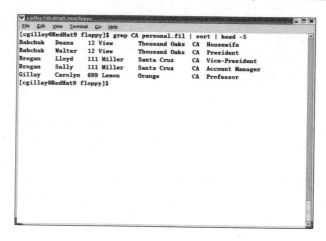

```
[cgillay@RedHat9 floppy]$ grep CA personal.fil | sort | head -5
Babchuk    Deana    12 View     Thousand Oaks CA  Housewife
Babchuk    Walter   12 View     Thousand Oaks CA  President
Brogan     Lloyd    111 Miller  Santa Cruz    CA  Vice-President
Brogan     Sally    111 Miller  Santa Cruz    CA  Account Manager
Gillay     Carolyn  699 Lemon   Orange        CA  Professor
[cgillay@RedHat9 floppy]$
```

WHAT'S HAPPENING? Here you found every occurrence of **CA** in the **personal.fil**. You then sorted it and displayed the first five lines of the file.

STEP 5   Key in the following: **grep CA *.fil | sort | tail -20 Enter**

```
cgillay @ RedHat9:/mnt/floppy
 File  Edit  View  Terminal  Go  Help
[cgillay@RedHat9 floppy]$ grep CA *.fil | sort | tail -20
personal.fil:Gonzales  Antonio  40 Northern   Ontario       CA  Engineer
personal.fil:Helm      Milton   333 Meadow    Sherman Oaks  CA  Consultant
personal.fil:Jones     Ervin    15 Fourth     Santa Cruz    CA  Banker
personal.fil:JONES     JERRY    244 East      Mission Viejo CA  Systems Analyst
personal.fil:Nyles     Sophie   12 Brooks     Sun City West CA  Retired
personal.fil:Panezich  Frank    689 Lake      Orange        CA  Teacher
personal.fil:Rodriguez Bob      20 Elm        Ontario       CA  Systems Analyst
personal.fil:Smith     David    120 Collins   Orange        CA  Chef
personal.fil:Tran      Tai Chan 345 Lakeview  Orange        CA  Doctor
personal.fil:Tuttle    Steven   356 Embassy   Mission Viejo CA  Juggler
personal.fil:Washingon Tyrone   345 Newport   Orange        CA  Manager
personal.fil:Winter    Jim      333 Pick      Garden Grove  CA  Key Grip
personal.fil:Winter    Linda    333 Pick      Garden Grove  CA  Teacher
personal.fil:Yuan      Suelin   56 Twin Leaf  Orange        CA  Artist
person.fil:Gillay;Carolyn;699 Lemon;Orange;CA;Professor
person.fil:Hall;Mary;111 Meadow;Altadeana;CA;Principal
person.fil:Panezich;Frank;689 Lake;Orange;CA;Teacher
person.fil:Tuttle;Steven;356 Embassy;Mission Viejo;CA;Juggler
southern.fil:LOUISIANA           SOUTH        SOYBEANS, SUGAR CANE, RICE
southern.fil:NORTH CAROLINA      SOUTH        TOBACCO, SOYBEANS, CORN, PEANUTS
[cgillay@RedHat9 floppy]$
```

WHAT'S HAPPENING? Now you found every occurrence of **CA** in all the files with a **.fil** extension. You piped the output to **sort** and then showed the last 20 lines of each file.

7.20 • Introducing uniq, diff, and comm

The **uniq** command displays a file, skipping any adjacent lines. If, for instance, a file contained a list of names and had adjacent identical entries, only one of those identical entries would be displayed. The power of **uniq** is its ability to remove duplicate lines from a sorted file. However, the file must be sorted, since **uniq** compares adjacent lines only. Thus, **uniq** removes duplicate adjacent lines from the sorted *file 1* and sends one copy of each line to *file 2* or to standard output. The syntax of **uniq** is

```
uniq [options] file1 file2
```

Table 7.15, "**uniq** Options," lists some of the major options used with the **uniq** command.

Option	Name	Result
-c	Count	Displays each line once, but prefixes it with the number of occurrences.
-d	Duplicate	Displays duplicate lines one time, but shows no unique lines.
-D	All duplicate	Displays all duplicate lines.
-i	Ignore	Ignores case differences when comparing.
-u	Unique	Displays only unique lines.

Table 7.15 • uniq Options

The **diff** command compares two files and displays a list of differences between them. The **diff** command does not change either file; instead, it displays the actions you need to take to convert one file into the other. The output from the command displays the lines that differ. You would see a notation, such as **3d2**, above a line. This means that you need to delete the third line in the first file, so File 1 is identical to File 2. The **diff** command assumes that you want to convert the first file into the second file. You may also use **diff** to compare the contents of directories. If both arguments are directories, then **diff** will report the lines that are different. The syntax is **diff [options] [diroptions]** *file 1 file 2.*

The **comm** command compares lines that are common to the sorted files—**file1** and **file2**. The output is displayed in three columns. The three columns are comprised of lines that are unique to **file1** and **file2** and lines that are common to both files. The **comm** command selects duplicate or unique lines between two sorted files, whereas **uniq** selects duplicated or unique lines within the same sorted file. The syntax is **comm [options] file1 file2**. A useful option is a column number (**-1**, **-2**, or **-3**). If you use one of those numbers, only that column will print.

7.21 • Activity: Using uniq, diff, and comm

Note: The BOOK disk is mounted with **/mnt/floppy** as the default directory. A terminal window is open.

STEP 1   Key in the following:
　　　　　 cat newprson.fil personal.fil | sort > dupe.fil; cat dupe.fil | more Enter

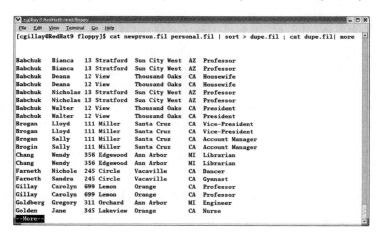

WHAT'S HAPPENING? You have created a sorted file with duplicate lines called **dupe.fil**.

STEP 2   Press **q.**

STEP 3   Key in the following: **uniq dupe.fil | more** Enter

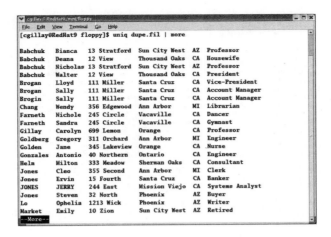

WHAT'S HAPPENING? The **uniq** command displayed on standard output only the nonduplicated lines. If you only wanted to see the lines in the file that are not duplicated, you could use the **-u** option.

STEP 4   Press **q**.

STEP 5   Key in the following: **uniq -u dupe.fil | more** [Enter]

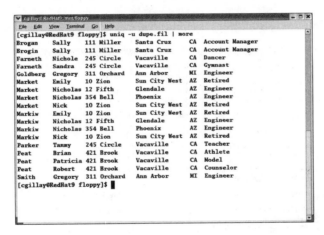

WHAT'S HAPPENING? Here you see the nonduplicated lines. If you wanted to see one copy of each duplicated line, you could use the **-d** option.

STEP 6   Key in the following: **uniq -d dupe.fil | more** [Enter]

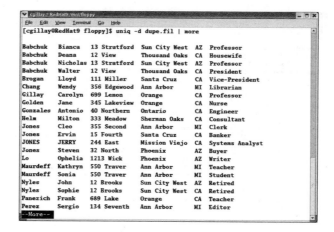

```
[cgillay@RedHat9 floppy]$ uniq -d dupe.fil | more

Babchuk    Bianca     13 Stratford   Sun City West  AZ  Professor
Babchuk    Deana      12 View        Thousand Oaks  CA  Housewife
Babchuk    Nicholas   13 Stratford   Sun City West  AZ  Professor
Babchuk    Walter     12 View        Thousand Oaks  CA  President
Brogan     Lloyd      111 Miller     Santa Cruz     CA  Vice-President
Chang      Wendy      356 Edgewood   Ann Arbor      MI  Librarian
Gillay     Carolyn    699 Lemon      Orange         CA  Professor
Golden     Jane       345 Lakeview   Orange         CA  Nurse
Gonzales   Antonio    40 Northern    Ontario        CA  Engineer
Helm       Milton     333 Meadow     Sherman Oaks   CA  Consultant
Jones      Cleo       355 Second     Ann Arbor      MI  Clerk
Jones      Ervin      15 Fourth      Santa Cruz     CA  Banker
JONES      JERRY      244 East       Mission Viejo  CA  Systems Analyst
Jones      Steven     32 North       Phoenix        AZ  Buyer
Lo         Ophelia    1213 Wick      Phoenix        AZ  Writer
Maurdeff   Kathryn    550 Traver     Ann Arbor      MI  Teacher
Maurdeff   Sonia      550 Traver     Ann Arbor      MI  Student
Nyles      John       12 Brooks      Sun City West  AZ  Retired
Nyles      Sophie     12 Brooks      Sun City West  CA  Retired
Panezich   Frank      689 Lake       Orange         CA  Teacher
Perez      Sergio     134 Seventh    Ann Arbor      MI  Editor
--More--
```

WHAT'S HAPPENING? Here only the duplicated lines are displayed but each is shown only once. In each of these examples, you displayed the output to the screen (standard output) rather than saving it to a file. In every case, you could have used the > symbol to save the output to a file. The **diff** command shows where you need to make changes in a file to make one file identical to the other.

STEP 7   Press **q**.

STEP 8   Key in the following: **diff personal.fil newprson.fil** [Enter]

```
> Peat       Patricia  421 Brook    Vacaville     CA  Model
> Peat       Brian     421 Brook    Vacaville     CA  Athlete
> Farneth    Nichole   245 Circle   Vacaville     CA  Dancer
> Farneth    Sandra    245 Circle   Vacaville     CA  Gymnast
> Goldberg   Gregory   311 Orchard  Ann Arbor     MI  Engineer
15c21
< Brogan     Sally     111 Miller   Santa Cruz    CA  Account Manager
---
> Brogin     Sally     111 Miller   Santa Cruz    CA  Account Manager
21,22c27,28
< Markiw     Nicholas  354 Bell     Phoenix       AZ  Engineer
< Markiw     Emily     10 Zion      Sun City West AZ  Retired
---
> Market     Nicholas  354 Bell     Phoenix       AZ  Engineer
> Market     Emily     10 Zion      Sun City West AZ  Retired
25c31
< Markiw     Nick      10 Zion      Sun City West AZ  Retired
---
> Market     Nick      10 Zion      Sun City West AZ  Retired
38c44
< Markiw     Nicholas  12 Fifth     Glendale      AZ  Engineer
---
> Market     Nicholas  12 Fifth     Glendale      AZ  Engineer
[cgillay@RedHat9 floppy]$
```

WHAT'S HAPPENING? Looking at the last lines, the display states:

```
38c44
< Markiw    Nicholas    12 Fifth    Glendale    AZ    Engineer
---
> Market    Nicholas    12 Fifth    Glendale    AZ    Engineer
```

The < indicates this line is from the first file, **personal.fil**. The > indicates that this line is from the second file, **newprson.fil**. The 38 means Line 38 in the first file must be changed (c) in Line 44 of the second file for the two files to be identical. The other instructions are **a** for add and **d** for delete. You can also use **diff** with directories.

STEP 9   Key in the following: **ls files astronomy** [Enter]

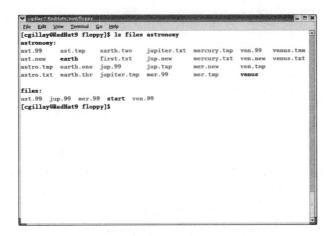

WHAT'S HAPPENING? The **files** directory has four files with the **.99** extension and a directory called **start**. The **astronomy** directory has four **.99** files, as well as other files, and no directory called **start**.

STEP 10 Key in the following: **diff files astronomy** Enter

WHAT'S HAPPENING? You can see the differences between the two directories. The **comm** commands show you the differences between files.

STEP 11 Create two files, **stuff** and **stuff2**. The contents of **stuff** is:

> **fork**
> **knife**
> **spoon**

The contents of **stuff2** is:
> **fork**
> **knife**
> **spoon**
> **teaspoon**

STEP 12 Key in the following: **comm stuff stuff2** Enter

```
[cgillay@RedHat9    floppy]$    comm stuff stuff2
                    fork
                    knife
                    spoon
         teaspoon
[cgillay@RedHat9    floppy]$
```

WHAT'S HAPPENING? The first column shows lines found only in the first file. There are none. The second column shows lines found only in the second file. There is one, **teaspoon**. The third column shows lines that are found in both. Each file contains **fork**, **knife**, and **spoon**. If you wanted to see only the differences, you could use the option **-3**.

STEP 13 Key in the following: **comm -3 stuff stuff2** [Enter]

```
[cgillay@RedHat9    floppy]$    comm -3 stuff stuff2
         teaspoon
[cgillay@RedHat9    floppy]$
```

WHAT'S HAPPENING? You see only the differences. If you wanted to see the lines in common, you could use the **-2** option.

STEP 14 Key in the following: **comm -2 stuff stuff2** [Enter]

```
[cgillay@RedHat9    floppy]$    comm -2 stuff stuff2
         fork
            knife
            spoon
[cgillay@RedHat9    floppy]$
```

WHAT'S HAPPENING? You now see what lines the two files have in common.

7.22 • File Compression and Archiving

You have been using the BOOK disk with many files and directories on it. These files are quite small, for the most part. However, in general, you will find that files tend to be much larger, particularly graphic files. Large files take much room on a disk. If you need to save space on a disk, one way to save room is to compress the file. Also, if you are planning on sending a large file or files over the Internet or to another computer system on your network, large files obviously take longer to send, so compressing files is advantageous. In addition, you will often download files from the Internet or receive files from another computer on your system. These files also will often be compressed.

You will also find that it is often useful to store a group of files and a directory structure in one file so that they can be easily backed up or moved to another computer. This is known as archiving. An archive file is different than a compressed file. An *archive file* is a group of files and directories that are stored in one file. An archive file uses the same amount of space that the original files and directories use. An archive file is not compressed. A *compressed file*, sometimes called a zipped file, is one or more files and/or directories that are stored in a single file that uses less disk space than the original files and/or directories. However, an archive file can be compressed. Thus, an archive file is not compressed but a compressed file can be an archive file. Linux offers several utilities that assist you in these endeavors. For file compression, the utility programs are **gzip**, **bzip2**, and **zip**. Red Hat recommends using **bzip2** because it offers the most compression. The **gzip** tool is common to most Unix and Linux distributions. If you need to transfer files between a Linux system and other operating systems, particularly MS Windows, then **zip** is the preferred tool as it is more compatible with the compression utilities in Windows. For archiving files and directories, **tar** is the recommended tool. In addition, Red Hat Linux includes a graphical utility called **File Roller** that can compress, decompress, and archive files.

7.23 • File Compression and Archiving Tools

The **bzip2** utility can compress a file or files and directories. The **bunzip2** utility will uncompress the files or directories. When you use **bzip2**, it will compress the specified files or read from standard input, and it will rename the compressed file to **filename.bz2**. Your file(s) will no longer exist under the original name. To uncompress the files, you use **bunzip2**, which will delete the **.bz2** files and replace it with the original file names. The **bzip2** family of commands are **bzip2**, **bunzip2**, **bzcat**, and **bzip2recover**. **bzip2** compresses the files, **bunzip2** uncompresses the files, **bzcat** decompresses all the specified files to standard output, and **bzip2** will try to recover data from damaged files. The syntax is:

```
bzip2 [options] [filenames . . .]
bunzip2 [options] [filenames . . .]
bzcat [options] [filenames . . .]
bzip2recover filename
```

Table 7.16, "bzip2 Options," lists some of the major options used with these commands.

Option	Name	Result
-c		Writes output to standard output keeping original files unchanged.
-d	Decompress	Forces decompression
-f	Force	Forces compression or decompression even if the file has hard links
-k	Keep	Keep—do not delete input files during compression or decompression.
-v	Verbose	Displays the name and percentage reduction for each file compressed or decompressed.
-V	Version	Displays the version number and quits.

Table 7.16 • bzip2 Options

The **gzip** utility can compress a file or files, and the **gunzip** utility will uncompress the file or files. When you use **gzip**, it will compress the specified files or read from standard input, and it will rename the compressed file to **filename.gz**. To uncompress the files, you use **gunzip**, which will take all of **gzip**'s options. The **zcat** utility will read one or more files that have been compressed with **gzip** and write them to standard output. The **zcat** command is identical to

gunzip -c and uses the options **-fhLV**, which are described in the **gzip/gunzip** options. The syntax is

```
gzip [options] [files]
gunzip [options] [files]
zcat [options] [files]
```

Table 7.17, "**gzip, gunzip**, and **zcat** Options," lists some of the major options used with these commands.

Option	Name	Result
-c		Writes output to standard output keeping original files unchanged. Same as **gunzip -c.**
-d	Decompress	Uncompresses file.
-f	Force	Forces compression or decompression even if the file has multiple links or the corresponding file already exists.
-h	Help	Displays a help screen and then quits.
-l	List	Lists compressed size, uncompressed size, ratio, and uncompressed name.
-L	License	Displays the **gzip** license and quits.
-n	No name	When compressing, does not save the original file name and time stamp. When decompressing, does not restore the original file name if present (remove the **gzip** suffix from compressed file name). This is the default.
-N	Name	When compressing, always saves the original file name and time stamp. This is the default. When decompressing, restores the original file name and time.
-r	Recursive	Travels the directory structure recursively. If any of the file names on the command line are directories, **gzip** will descend into the directory and compress all the files it finds or decompress them with **gunzip**.
-v	Verbose	Displays the name and percentage reduction for each file compressed or decompressed.
-V	Version	Displays the version number and quits.

Table 7.17 • gzip, gunzip, and zcat Options

The **zip** and **unzip** utilities are compatible with the **pkzip** and **pkunzip** programs in the Windows world. These utilities also compress and uncompress files. However, the original file or files remain in place. You simply create a new file that contains the contents of the files that you compressed. The syntax is

```
zip [options] compressedfilename files
unzip [options] compressedfilename
```

The compression and uncompression programs and the file extensions used are shown in Table 7.18, "File Compression Tools."

Compression Tool	Uncompression Tool	Extension Used
bkzip2	bkunzip2	.bz2
gzip	gunzip2	.gz
zip	unzip	.zip

Table 7.18 • File Compression Tools

The **tar** utility program is used for archiving files. Its name comes from "tape archive," as the original use of this command was to back up multiple files on tape devices. You can use **tar** to create an archive of multiple files into a single file. Thus, it is used to create a single file that, when unpacked, create a directory structure with all the files and directories beneath that directory. Often **tar** files are compressed with **gzip** or **bzip2** to make storing and handing the archives easier. Software that has been processed by **tar** and compressed by **gzip** usually has the extension **.tar**, **.gz**, or **.tgz**. The syntax is

```
tar [options] [tarfile] [other-files]
```

Table 7.19, "**tar** Options," lists some of the major options used with **tar**.

Option	Name	Result
-c	Create	Creates a new tar archive file.
-f	File	Archives the files to a tar file rather than a tape device, or extracts from a tar archive rather than a tape device.
-t	List	Produces a table of contents of all the files in an archive.
-v	Verbose	Displays all the names of the files being added to the archive.
-x	Extract	Extracts from a tar archive file.
-z	Zip	Causes **tar** to use **gzip** automatically to compress the archive while the archive is being created, and to decompress the archive when extracting files from it.

Table 7.19 • tar Options

7.24 • Activity: Using bzip2, bunzip2, gzip, gunzip, zcat, tar, and File Roller

Note: The BOOK disk is mounted with **/mnt/floppy** as the default directory. A terminal window is open.

STEP 1   Key in the following: **cp italy.tif plane.bmp quasars.doc *.fil ~** [Enter]

STEP 2   Key in the following: **cd; ls -l** [Enter]

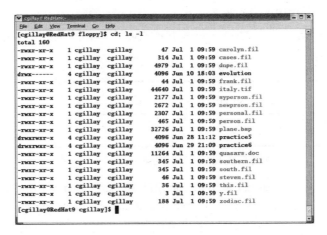

WHAT'S HAPPENING? You may have more files and directories in your home directory than shown here. You have copied some large files to your home directory. You then changed directories to your home directory. You are going to see the results of compressing the files.

STEP 3   Key in the following: **bzip2 -v italy.tif plane.bmp quasars.doc** [Enter]

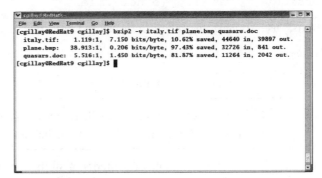

WHAT'S HAPPENING? The percentage that the file was compressed is dependent on the type of file. As you can see, **.bmp** and **.doc** files compress at a greater ratio than **.tif** files. Each file that you compressed was replaced by a file with a **.bz2** extension. These files no longer exist in your home directory by their original name.

STEP 4   Key in the following: **ls -l *.bz2** [Enter]

STEP 5   Key in the following: **ls -l italy.tif plane.bmp quasars.doc** [Enter]

STEP 6   Key in the following: **ls -l /mnt/floppy/italy.tif** [Enter]

STEP 7   Key in the following: **ls -l /mnt/floppy/plane.bmp** [Enter]

STEP 8   Key in the following: **ls -l /mnt/floppy/quasars.doc** [Enter]

WHAT'S HAPPENING? You can see how much smaller the files are when compressed. To uncompress the files and return them to their original names, you can use the **bzip2** utility.

STEP 9 Key in the following: **bunzip2 *.bz2; ls *.bz2** Enter

STEP 10 Key in the following: **ls italy.tif plane.bmp quasars.doc** Enter

```
[cgillay@RedHat9   cgillay]$ bunzip2 *.bz2; ls *.bz2
ls: *.bz2: No such file or directory.
[cgillay@RedHat9   cgillay]$ ls italy.tif plane.bmp quasars.doc
italy.tif    plane.bmp    quasars.doc
[cgillay@RedHat9   cgillay]$
```

WHAT'S HAPPENING? Your files have been uncompressed. The **gzip** utility works in much the same way.

STEP 11 Key in the following: **gzip -v italy.tif plane.bmp quasars.doc** Enter

```
[cgillay@RedHat9   cgillay]$ gzip -v italy.tif plane.bmp quasars.doc
italy.tif              12.7%         -replaced with italy.tif.gz
plane.bmp             97.3%         -replaced with plane.bmp.gz
quasars.doc           83.3%         -replaced with quasars.doc.gz
[cgillay@RedHat9   cgillay]$
```

WHAT'S HAPPENING? Each file that you compressed was replaced by a file with a **.gz** extension. These files no longer exist in your home directory by their original name. The percentage that the file was compressed is dependent on the type of file. As you can see, **.bmp** and **.doc** files compress at a greater ratio than **.tif** files.

STEP 12 Key in the following: **ls -l *.gz** Enter

STEP 13 Key in the following: **ls -l /mnt/floppy/italy.tif** Enter

STEP 14 Key in the following: **ls -l /mnt/floppy/plane.bmp** Enter

STEP 15 Key in the following: **ls -l /mnt/floppy/quasars.doc** Enter

```
[cgillay@RedHat9 cgillay]$ ls -l *.gz
-rwxr-xr-x   1 cgillay  cgillay      38995 Jul  1 09:59 italy.tif.gz
-rwxr-xr-x   1 cgillay  cgillay        901 Jul  1 09:59 plane.bmp.gz
-rwxr-xr-x   1 cgillay  cgillay       1907 Jul  1 09:59 quasars.doc.gz
[cgillay@RedHat9 cgillay]$ ls -l /mnt/floppy/italy.tif
-rwxr-xr-x   1 cgillay  cgillay      44640 Jul 27  2000 /mnt/floppy/italy.tif
[cgillay@RedHat9 cgillay]$ ls -l /mnt/floppy/plane.bmp
-rwxr-xr-x   1 cgillay  cgillay      32726 Nov 27  1998 /mnt/floppy/plane.bmp
[cgillay@RedHat9 cgillay]$ ls -l /mnt/floppy/quasars.doc
-rwxr-xr-x   1 cgillay  cgillay      11264 Oct 31  2001 /mnt/floppy/quasars.doc
[cgillay@RedHat9 cgillay]$
```

WHAT'S HAPPENING? You can see how much smaller the files are when compressed. You can see the size of what the file would be uncompressed by using **zcat** and the **wc** commands.

STEP 16 Key in the following: **zcat -c plane.bmp.gz | wc -c** Enter

```
[cgillay@RedHat9  cgillay]$  zcat -c plane.bmp.gz  |  wc -c
32726
[cgillay@RedHat9  cgillay]$
```

WHAT'S HAPPENING? By piping the output from **zcat** to the **wc** command, you saw the size of the file when uncompressed. If you want full details, you can use the **-l** option.

STEP 17 Key in the following: **zcat -l plane.bmp.gz** Enter

```
[cgillay@RedHat9  cgillay]$  zcat -l plane.bmp.gz
      compressed          uncompressed        ratio uncompressed_name
          901                  32726          97.3% plane.bmp
[cgillay@RedHat9  cgillay]$
```

WHAT'S HAPPENING? You received full information about your compressed file. If you wish to retain your original files and yet have a compressed file, you may also do that by piping the output of the **cat** command to the **gzip** command.

STEP 18 Key in the following: **cat *.fil | gzip > new.gz; ls -l** Enter

```
[cgillay@RedHat9 cgillay]$ cat *.fil | gzip > new.gz; ls -l
total 124
-rwxr-xr-x   1 cgillay  cgillay         47 Jul  1 09:59 carolyn.fil
-rwxr-xr-x   1 cgillay  cgillay        314 Jul  1 09:59 cases.fil
-rwxr-xr-x   1 cgillay  cgillay       4979 Jul  1 09:59 dupe.fil
drwx------   4 cgillay  cgillay       4096 Jun 10 18:03 evolution
-rwxr-xr-x   1 cgillay  cgillay         44 Jul  1 09:59 frank.fil
-rwxr-xr-x   1 cgillay  cgillay      38995 Jul  1 09:59 italy.tif.gz
-rwxr-xr-x   1 cgillay  cgillay       2177 Jul  1 09:59 myperson.fil
-rw-rw-r--   1 cgillay  cgillay       2243 Jul  1 10:37 new.gz
-rwxr-xr-x   1 cgillay  cgillay       2672 Jul  1 09:59 newprson.fil
-rwxr-xr-x   1 cgillay  cgillay       2307 Jul  1 09:59 personal.fil
-rwxr-xr-x   1 cgillay  cgillay        465 Jul  1 09:59 person.fil
-rwxr-xr-x   1 cgillay  cgillay        901 Jul  1 09:59 plane.bmp.gz
drwxrwxr-x   4 cgillay  cgillay       4096 Jun 28 11:12 practice5
drwxrwxr-x   4 cgillay  cgillay       4096 Jun 29 21:09 practice6
-rwxr-xr-x   1 cgillay  cgillay       1907 Jul  1 09:59 quasars.doc.gz
-rwxr-xr-x   1 cgillay  cgillay        345 Jul  1 09:59 southern.fil
-rwxr-xr-x   1 cgillay  cgillay        345 Jul  1 09:59 south.fil
-rwxr-xr-x   1 cgillay  cgillay         46 Jul  1 09:59 steven.fil
-rwxr-xr-x   1 cgillay  cgillay         36 Jul  1 09:59 this.fil
-rwxr-xr-x   1 cgillay  cgillay          3 Jul  1 09:59 y.fil
-rwxr-xr-x   1 cgillay  cgillay        188 Jul  1 09:59 zodiac.fil
[cgillay@RedHat9 cgillay]$
```

WHAT'S HAPPENING? You see all the files that have **.fil** as an extension, but now you have a file called **new.gz**. Note that it is displayed in bright red. A bright red color indicates a compressed or archived file. You can also look at the contents of a **.gz** file, presuming it is a text file, with the **zcat** command.

STEP 19 Key in the following: **zcat new.gz | head** Enter

```
[cgillay@RedHat9   cgillay]$ zcat new.gz  |  head

Hi, my name is Carolyn.
What is your name?


November 23, 1999


This activity is a practice exercise in creating or
making a text file with exercise as the
file name and txt as the selected file
extension. All the data, starting with
[cgillay@RedHat9   cgillay]$
```

WHAT'S HAPPENING? You see the contents of the files but no file name is given for each display. You can also use the **tar** command to create an archive of multiple files in a single file. Tar files usually have a **tar** extension .

STEP 20 Key in the following: **tar -cvf floppy.tar /mnt/floppy** Enter

STEP 21 Key in the following: **ls -l floppy.tar** Enter

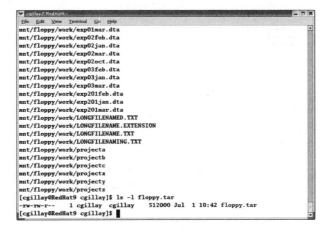

WHAT'S HAPPENING? You used the **tar** command to create an archive of all the files and directories on the BOOK disk (**/mnt/floppy**). You used the **c** option to create the **tar** file, the **v** option to see what files were being created, and the **f** option to archive the file to a **tar** file rather than to a tape device. You then used the **ls** command to see the size of the file. Note again that the color for a **tar** file is red. You may list the contents of an archived file.

STEP 22 Key in the following: **tar -tvf floppy.tar | head; tar -tvf floppy.tar | tail** Enter

```
[cgillay@RedHat9 cgillay]$ tar -tvf floppy.tar | head; tar -tvf floppy.tar | tail
drwxr-xr-x cgillay/cgillay    0 2003-07-01 08:42:04 mnt/floppy/
-rwxr-xr-x cgillay/cgillay   93 2003-06-30 09:36:08 mnt/floppy/happy
-rwxr-xr-x cgillay/cgillay  121 2001-10-30 13:10:56 mnt/floppy/born.txt
-rwxr-xr-x cgillay/cgillay   86 2003-06-30 10:07:26 mnt/floppy/errors
-rwxr-xr-x cgillay/cgillay   13 2003-06-30 10:12:16 mnt/floppy/commands
-rwxr-xr-x cgillay/cgillay  138 2001-10-31 15:50:24 mnt/floppy/file2.swt
-rwxr-xr-x cgillay/cgillay  137 2001-10-31 15:51:24 mnt/floppy/file4.fp
-rwxr-xr-x cgillay/cgillay   98 2003-06-30 10:10:18 mnt/floppy/hello.txt
-rwxr-xr-x cgillay/cgillay   46 2003-06-30 10:36:28 mnt/floppy/dogs
-rwxr-xr-x cgillay/cgillay   52 2003-06-30 10:36:48 mnt/floppy/cats
-rwxr-xr-x cgillay/cgillay   97 2001-12-05 23:15:58 mnt/floppy/work/LONGFILENAMED.TXT
-rwxr-xr-x cgillay/cgillay  122 2001-05-27 22:09:36 mnt/floppy/work/LONGFILENAME.EXTE
NSION
-rwxr-xr-x cgillay/cgillay   81 2001-05-27 22:08:40 mnt/floppy/work/LONGFILENAME.TXT
-rwxr-xr-x cgillay/cgillay   99 2001-12-05 23:16:06 mnt/floppy/work/LONGFILENAMING.TX
T
-rwxr-xr-x cgillay/cgillay   18 1999-05-07 22:31:46 mnt/floppy/work/projecta
-rwxr-xr-x cgillay/cgillay   18 1999-05-07 22:31:58 mnt/floppy/work/projectb
-rwxr-xr-x cgillay/cgillay   18 2000-08-02 22:23:20 mnt/floppy/work/projectc
-rwxr-xr-x cgillay/cgillay   18 2000-04-11 22:33:38 mnt/floppy/work/projectx
-rwxr-xr-x cgillay/cgillay   18 2000-04-11 22:33:42 mnt/floppy/work/projecty
-rwxr-xr-x cgillay/cgillay   18 2000-08-02 22:23:34 mnt/floppy/work/projectz
[cgillay@RedHat9 cgillay]$
```

WHAT'S HAPPENING? You used the **t** option (list the files in an archive) and the **v** option to see the file details. Had you not used **v**, you would have only seen the file names. The **f** indicated a file. You then piped the command to the **head** and **tail** commands and saw that the **tar** command did archive all the files and all the directories on the floppy disk. You can uncompress the file with **tar** as well.

STEP 23 Key in the following: **tar -xvf floppy.tar; ls** [Enter]

```
mnt/floppy/work/exp02jan.dta
mnt/floppy/work/exp02mar.dta
mnt/floppy/work/exp02oct.dta
mnt/floppy/work/exp03feb.dta
mnt/floppy/work/exp03jan.dta
mnt/floppy/work/exp03mar.dta
mnt/floppy/work/exp201feb.dta
mnt/floppy/work/exp201jan.dta
mnt/floppy/work/exp201mar.dta
mnt/floppy/work/LONGFILENAMED.TXT
mnt/floppy/work/LONGFILENAME.EXTENSION
mnt/floppy/work/LONGFILENAME.TXT
mnt/floppy/work/LONGFILENAMING.TXT
mnt/floppy/work/projecta
mnt/floppy/work/projectb
mnt/floppy/work/projectc
mnt/floppy/work/projectx
mnt/floppy/work/projecty
mnt/floppy/work/projectz
carolyn.fil   floppy.tar    myperson.fil   person.fil     quasars.doc.gz  this.fil
cases.fil     frank.fil     new.gz         plane.bmp.gz    southern.fil    y.fil
dupe.fil      italy.tif.gz  newprson.fil   practice5       south.fil       sodiac.fil
evolution     mnt           personal.fil   practice6       steven.fil
[cgillay@RedHat9 cgillay]$
```

WHAT'S HAPPENING? By using the **x** option, you extracted the archived file. The **v** displayed what work was being done, and the **f** indicated that it was a file. Note that you now have an **mnt** directory in your home directory.

STEP 24 Key in the following: **ls mnt** [Enter]

```
[cgillay@RedHat9   cgillay]$ ls mnt
floppy
[cgillay@RedHat9   cgillay]$
```

WHAT'S HAPPENING? You created your entire directory structure from the BOOK disk in your home directory. You can also compress the files at the same time that you archive them. Usually compressed, tarred files use the extension **tgz**.

STEP 25 Key in the following: **rm -r mnt** [Enter]

STEP 26   Key in the following: **tar -czvf floppy.tgz /mnt/floppy** Enter

STEP 27   Key in the following: **ls -l floppy.tgz** Enter

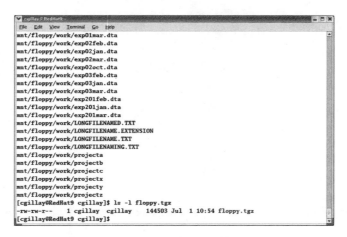

WHAT'S HAPPENING? You compressed and tarred (archived) at the same time. You can see the difference in size. You can use **tar -tzvf floppy.tzg** to see a listing of what files are in your tar file. When you extract the tarred and zipped file, it too will create an entire directory structure.

STEP 28   Key in the following: **tar -xzvf floppy.tgz** Enter

STEP 29   Key in the following: **ls** Enter

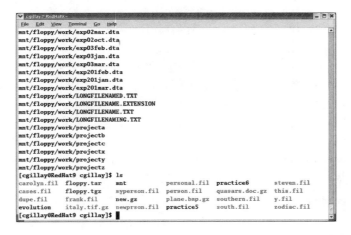

WHAT'S HAPPENING? Again, you created your entire directory structure in your home directory under the directory called **mnt**. The **File Roller** utility is simply a graphical interface to tarring and zipping files and directories.

STEP 30   Click the **Main Menu**. Point to **Accessories**. Click **File Roller**.

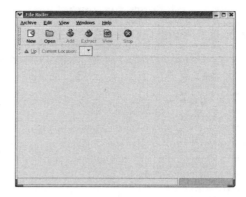

WHAT'S HAPPENING? As you can see from the menu choices, you can Archive, Edit, or View archived files.

STEP 31   Click **New**. Click the down arrow on the **Archive type** drop-down list box.

WHAT'S HAPPENING? In the File Roller, as you can see, you can call on all the file compression and archiving tools.

STEP 32   Click outside the menu to close it. Click **Cancel**. Click **Open**.

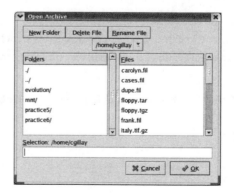

WHAT'S HAPPENING? Since this a utility for arching and compressing files, only those files that are archived or compressed are listed. You could also in your home directory window simply double-click the file name and it would automatically invoke the appropriate utility program. Now you are going to clean up your home directory.

STEP 33 Click **Cancel**. Close the **File Roller** window.

STEP 34 Make the terminal window active. Key in the following:

    rm -r mnt fl*.* *.gz *.fil [Enter]

WHAT'S HAPPENING? You have removed all the files that you created in this activity.

STEP 35 Unmount your BOOK disk. Remove it from the drive. Close any open windows.

Chapter Summary

In this chapter you were introduced to the following:
- Standard input, standard output, and standard error.
- The terminal as a file.
- Using the **who** and **whoami** commands.
- Redirection with the redirection symbols: **>**, **<**, and **>>**.
- Linux file types and the structure of their data including ordinary files, character files, and block files.
- The **cut** and **paste** commands.
- The purpose of pipes and filters and how to create a pipeline of commands.
- Using the **sort** and **wc** commands.
- Regular and extended regular expressions.
- Using **grep**, **fgrep**, and **egrep** with regular and extended regular expressions.
- Formatting your output with the **pr** command.
- Modifying file output with the **tee** command.
- Using the **tr** command using standard input that is modified and written to standard output and to a file.
- Using the **ispell** utility to spell check documents.
- Using the **head** and **tail** commands to limit the lines that are displayed in a file.
- Comparing file contents with the **uniq**, **diff**, and **comm** commands.
- Creating and extracting compressed files and archives with **bzip2**, **bunzip2**, **gzip**, **gunzip**, **zcat**, **tar**, and **File Roller**.

Key Terms

archive file	extended regular expressions	pipe
block special files	filters	regular expressions
character special files	linked file	terminal emulator
compressed file	ordinary files	

Discussion Questions

1. What is the function of the **who** command? What is its syntax?
2. Define standard input, standard output, and standard error.
3. What is a pseudo device?
4. Explain the purpose and function of standard input and output.
5. Define standard error.
6. What is the difference between **>** and **>>** when redirecting output?

7. How is the symbol < used in redirection?
8. Define redirection.
9. List and explain the purpose of the types of files found on the Linux system.
10. What is the advantage of using an ASCII data file? The disadvantage?
11. Explain the purpose and function of filters.
12. Compare and contrast combining files using the **cat** command with the **paste** command.
13. Explain the purpose and function of the **cut** command.
14. What is a filter command?
15. List and explain the function of **sort** and **wc**.
16. How does the **sort** command sort numeric information? Character data?
17. Explain the purpose and function of pipes.
18. Pipes change Linux utility programs. Explain.
19. Why could you not key in **ls lpr**?
20. What is the purpose and function of the **grep** command?
21. Compare and contrast the **grep, fgrep**, and **egrep** commands.
22. What is a regular expression?
23. What is the purpose of an extended regular expression?
24. Explain the purpose and function of the **pr** command.
25. Give the syntax of the **pr** command and list and explain the use of at least four options that can be used with this command.
26. Explain the functions of the **tee** command and the **tr** command in reference to standard input and output.
27. Explain the purpose and function of the **ispell** program.
28. Compare and contrast the **head** command with the **tail** command.
29. Compare and contrast the **comm** command with the **uniq** command and **diff** command.
30. What is the function of the **gzip** command? The **gunzip** command? The **zcat** command? The **bzip2** command? The **bunzip2** command? **File Roller**?

True/False Questions

For each question, circle the letter T if the question is true and the letter F if the question is false.

T	F	1. Standard output can be directed to a file.
T	F	2. The **uniq** command compares two files and displays a list of differences between them.
T	F	3. The **tty** command tells you the name of the current controlling terminal.
T	F	4. For the **uniq** command to work properly, you must use sorted files.
T	F	5. The **zcat** command will compress files.

Completion Questions

Write the correct answer in each blank space.

6. When a command is executed, the three standard files that are involved are _____, _____, and _____.

7. Special files that produce raw data and are related to serial devices such as printers are often called _____ special files; those that process data a block at a time are used to read/write to devices such as a disk are called _____ special files.

8. The **grep** command will search through one or more files looking for a character string that is a _____ expression.

9. If you wanted to know how many lines were in a file, you would use the ____ command.

10. "Zipping" a file with **gzip** implies that you will use _____ to uncompress it.

Multiple Choice Questions

For each question, write the letter for the correct answer in the blank space.

11. The command **cat newreport >> oldreport** would
    a. overwrite **oldreport** with **newreport**.
    b. overwrite **newreport** with **oldreport**.
    c. add the contents of **newreport** to **oldreport**.
    d. display the contents of **oldreport** and **newreport** in the terminal window.

12. The command **cut -c1-3 resources** would extract the _____ from the **resources** file and write the output to the terminal window.
    a. first through third characters
    b. first and third characters
    c. first through third fields
    d. first and third fields

13. The command **grep "movies | films" cinema** would locate _____ in the **cinema** file.
    a. every occurrence of **movies** or **films**
    b. only **movies**
    c. only **films**
    d. none of the above

14. The command **ls news* | pr -5a | lpr** would locate all the files that begin with **news** and have any other characters and format the output
    a. in five columns and display the output in the terminal window.
    b. in five columns across and print the output.
    c. either a nor b
    d. neither a nor b

15. The extension usually given to a file that has been compressed with **gzip** and processed by **tar** is
    a. **.gz**.
    b. **.gzip**.
    c. **.tar, .gz,** or **.tgz**.
    d. **.zp**.

Writing Commands

Write the correct steps or commands to perform the required action as if you were at the computer. You will assume that there is a terminal window open. The prompt will indicate the current working directory.

16. You have two files, **singers** and **songs**. You want to substitute the **:** (colon) for the Tab character and you want the data combined side by side. You want to save the output to a file called **music**.

```
[markiw@RedHat9 markiw]$
```

17. You have a file called **states**. You want to sort the file in descending order (**z-a**) and save the sorted file to a new file called **sortedstates**. You also want to see the output displayed on the screen.

    [phan@RedHat9 phan]$

18. You want to count how many lines are in each file that is located in the **/public** directory that has the extension of **.fil**. You want this output sorted numerically, in descending order, and the output displayed on the screen.

    [janchez@RedHat9 jsanchez]$

19. You want to locate any occurrence of **rock** or **roll** in the **music** file. The **music** file is in the **/mnt/floppy** directory. You want to save the output to file in your home directory that will be called **rockers**.

    [LaKeisha@RedHat9 school]$

20. You want to archive multiple files in your **bin** directory (**/home/cgillay/bin**) and place them in a single file that you will save to your current working directory (**/home/cgillay/ archive**). You want to be able to see which files are being created. You will name the new file **bin.tar**.

    [cgillay@RedHat9 archive]$

Application Assignments

Problem Set I—At the Computer: Multiple Choice

Note: For all problems, your work (files and directories) will be saved to the floppy disk labeled BOOK unless otherwise specified.

Problem A

- Mount the BOOK disk if it is not already mounted.
- Open a terminal window.
- Open a second terminal window.
- Find the name of each of your terminal windows.
    1. What command could you use?
        a. **who**
        b. **tty**
        c. **who am I**
        d. all of the above
- Close one of the terminal windows.
- Key in the following: **cd** [Enter]
- Key in the following: **cat /mnt/floppy/music/Id*hits.* > idols** [Enter]
    2. You have
        a. used redirection.
        b. created a file called **idols** in your home directory.
        c. both a and b
        d. neither a nor b

* Key in the following: **cat /mnt/floppy/music/id*.* > idols2** [Enter]

* You should see an error message. You want to save the error message in a file called **idolerrors**.

     3. Which command did you use?

         a. **cat /mnt/floppy/music/id*.* 1> idolerrors**

         b. **cat /mnt/floppy/music/id*.* 2> idolerrors**

         c. **cat /mnt/floppy/music/id*.* 3> idolerrors**

         d. **cat /mnt/floppy/music/id*.* > idols2 > idolerrors**

* Delete the files **idols**, **idols2**, and **idolerrors** from your home directory.

Problem B

* Open a terminal window.

* Change your directory to **/mnt/floppy**.

* On the BOOK disk, you will use the **pets** and **persons** file created in Activity 7.7.

* In the **persons** file, cut out characters 10–19 and 48–51 and save the output on the BOOK disk in a file called **h1**.

     4. Which command did you use to extract this information?

         a. **cut -c 10-19,48-51 persons > h1**

         b. **cut -f 1 10-19, f2 48-51 persons > h1**

         c. **cut -d 10-19,48-51 persons > h1**

         d. **cut -b 10-19,48-51 persons > h1**

     5. In the **h1** file, which items are listed?

         a. first name and occupation.

         b. first name and state.

         c. last name and occupation.

         d. last name and state.

* In the **pets** file, cut out Columns 1 and 2 and save the output on the BOOK disk in a file called **h2**.

     6. Which command did you use to extract this information?

         a. **cut -f1,2 pets > h2**

         b. **cut -f1,f2 pets > h2**

         c. **cut -c1-14,18-25 pets > h2**

         d. **cut -b1-14,18-25 pets > h2**

* Using the **paste** command, create a sorted file called **h3** comprised of **h2** and **h1** (in that order).

     7. Which command could you use to achieve these results?

         a. **paste h2 h1 | sort > h3**

         b. **paste h2 h1 > h3; cat h3 | sort**

         c. **paste h2 h1 > h3; sort h3**

         d. all of the above

     8. What is the first name and state that appears in the first line?

         a. **Carolyn CA**

         b. **Frank   CA**

         c. **Kathryn MI**

         d. **Sonia   MI**

Problem C

* Your default directory is **/mnt/floppy**.

* Without saving the output to a separate file, find out which automobile appears first in a sorted list of the two files, **NEW AUTOS.txt** and **oldauto.mak**.

  9. What command could you have used?
     a. **cat "NEW AUTOS.txt" oldauto.mak | sort**
     b. **sort "NEW AUTOS.txt" oldauto.mak**
     c. either a or b
     d. neither a nor b

  10. Which automobile was listed first?
      a. **BMW**
      b. **Buick Roadmaster**
      c. **Buick Skylark**
      d. **Chrysler PT Cruiser**

  11. How many words are there in the **oldauto.mak** file?
      a. **12**
      b. **22**
      c. **182**
      d. **216**

  12. What command could you have used?
      a. **wc -c oldauto.mak**
      b. **wc -m oldauto.mak**
      c. **wc -l oldauto.mak**
      d. **wc -w oldauto.mak**

* Using **vi,** edit the file **award.mov**.

* Delete the first blank line.

* Add a blank line under **YEAR TITLE** and add the following:

  2002   A BEAUTIFUL MIND

* Adjust the years below so that the file reads:

YEAR	TITLE
2002	A BEAUTIFUL MIND
2001	GLADIATOR
2000	AMERICAN BEAUTY
1999	SHAKESPEARE IN LOVE
1998	TITANIC
1997	THE ENGLISH PATIENT

* In **vi,** key in **1G,** then save the file to disk and exit **vi**.

* Use the **commands** file created in Activity 7.4 to edit the **award.mov** file.

  13. What command did you use?
      a. **vi award.mov < commands**
      b. **vi award.mov | commands**
      c. **commands > vi award.mov**
      d. **commands | vi award.mov**

14. What difference do you see in the newly edited **award.mov** file?
   a. **A BEAUTIFUL MIND** is displayed twice at the end of the file.
   b. **A BEAUTIFUL MIND** is displayed twice at the beginning of the file.
   c. **YEAR   TITLE** is displayed twice at the end of the file.
   d. **YEAR   TITLE** is displayed twice at the beginning of the file.

Problem D

- Your default directory is **/mnt/floppy**.
- Using one command line, combine all the files that begin with **file*.*** into a single file called **mixer.fil** and display the line(s) that are duplicated on the screen.

15. What command could you use?
   a. **sort | cat file*.* | tee mixer.fil | uniq -d**
   b. **cat file*.* | sort | tee mixer.fil | uniq -d**
   c. **sort | cat file*.* | tee mixer.fil | uniq -u**
   d. **cat file*.* | sort | tee mixer.fil | uniq -u**

16. Is the line **This is file 2.** a duplicate line?
   a. Yes.
   b. No.

- You want to find out how many people live in **AZ** in the **personal.fil**.

17. What command could you use?
   a. **grep -c AZ personal.fil**
   b. **egrep -c AZ personal.fil**
   c. **fgrep -c AZ personal.fil**
   d. any of the above

18. In the **personal.fil** file, how many times does **Engineer** appear?
   a. 0
   b. 2
   c. 4
   d. 6

- You want to find out how many people live in **AZ** in all the files that have **.fil** as an extension.

19. What command could you have used?
   a. **grep AZ *.fil**
   b. **grep AZ *.fil | wc**
   c. **grep AZ *.fil > wc**
   d. any of the above

20. How many people live in **AZ** in all the files that have .**fil** as an extension?
   a. 45
   b. 365
   c. 3273
   d. 3683

- Spell check the **venus.txt** located in the **astronomy** directory.

21. What command did you use?
   a. **ispell astronomy/venus.txt**
   b. **spell astronomy/venus.txt**
   c. **spelling astronomy/venus.txt**

22. Based on the results from the above command, what was the first misspelled word found?
    a. **terrestrial**
    b. **Venusquakes**
    c. **moon-lit**
    d. **atmosphere**

- Translate all the uppercase characters in the **blue.jaz** file to a number ranging from 0–9 and display the output on the screen.

23. What command did you use?
    a. **tr a-z 0-9   blue.jaz**
    b. **tr a-z 0-9   < blue.jaz**
    c. **tr A-Z 0-9   blue.jaz**
    d. **tr A-Z 0-9   < blue.jaz**

24. Based on the result from the above command, what was the first number to appear?
    a. 9
    b. 6
    c. 3
    d. 0

- Unmount your BOOK disk. Remove it from the drive. Close any open windows.

Problem Set II—At the Computer: Short Answer

Note: To minimize keying in data, the "Short Answers" section in Chapter 6 needs to have been completed.

1. Create a directory called **practice7** in your home directory. How did you accomplish this task?

2. If you are in a lab environment that allowed you to retain the **practice6** directory activities on your computer—completed in Chapter 6, Problem Set II, At the Computer: Short Answer—copy recursively all the files and directories from **practice6** to **practice7**. Otherwise, use the PRACTICE disk you created at the end of Chapter 6, Problem Set II, At the Computer: Short Answer from the **practice6** directory to the **practice6** directory located in your home directory. How did you accomplish this task?

3. You should be in your home directory. Change directories to **practice7/mybooks**. How did you accomplish this task?

4. How many users are logged on to your system? How did you accomplish this task?

5. What is your actual terminal name? What command did you use to find this information?

6. Key in **cat one**. What happened? Why?

7. Key in **cat**. Press **Enter**. Key in **one**. Press **Enter**. Press **Ctrl** + D. What happened? Why?

8. In the **backup5/dir2** directory are files that begin with **temp**. Redirect all the contents of those files into a file called **newest** located in the **practice7** directory. How did you accomplish this task?

9. Create a file called **commands** with **vi** in the **practice7** directory. The commands you are going to enter will have you move to the fourth line, then delete three lines,

then go to the fourth line, then copy the current line, then paste the current line three times, and then write the file to disk and quit **vi**. What are the contents of the **commands** file?

10. Open the **newest** file and look at the contents. Then, use **commands** as input to **vi** to make changes to the **newest** file. Use **cat** to view the contents of **newest**. What changes were made? Why?

11. Append the contents of the file **book4** to the end of the **newest** file. **book4** is in the **mybooks/scifi** directory. How did you accomplish this task?

12. Copy the file **Book1** located in the **mybooks/mystery** directory to your current directory and name it **w1**. Copy the file called **book2** located in the **mybooks/mystery** directory to your current directory and call it **m1**. How did you accomplish this task?

13. Look at the contents of **w1** and **m1**. You see that the author's last name is listed first in both files. You want to create a new file where the author's first name is first and the last name is last. The first line will read **Women. Mystery** and **Men. Mystery**. Hint: Use the **cut** command. Also remember that the : is a delimiter (-**d**) for each field (-**f**). You will have to create some intermediate files using the **paste** command to get the final output. Name the intermediate files anything you choose but the final files will be called **w2** for the women and **m2** for the men. How did you accomplish these tasks?

14. Create a file that will be called **both** from **w2** and **m2** so that the columns are side by side. Have the men appear in the first column. What command did you use?

15. Create a file that will be called **both2** from **w1** and **m1** so that the columns are side by side. Have the men appear in the first column. What command did you use?

16. Sort the file called **book7** located in the **mybooks** directory so it displays one screen at a time. What command did you use? Whose name appeared first?

17. How many words, lines, and characters are in **book7**? What command did you use? How can you explain that the line count and the word count are the same number? How many words, lines, and characters are in **both** and **both2**? Explain the difference in the count.

18. Locate and count the number of times the letter **m** appears in the file called **bigfile** located in the **mybooks** directory. What command did you use? Locate and count the number of times either **m** or **M** appears in **bigfile**. What command did you use? Are there any differences? Why?

19. Locate every occurrence of the word **mystery** or **MYSTERY** recursively in the **practice7** directory. What command did you use?

20. Locate any line that has **Susan** or **Sue** in **bigfile**. You want to create a new file with the results called **sue** but you also see the results on the screen. What command did you use?

21. In the file **m1**, you want to replace every occurrence of a colon with a space and display the output on the screen. The octal value for a space is **\040**. What command did you use? Now you want to replace every colon with a horizontal tab and display the output on the screen. The **\t** is the symbol for horizontal tab. What command did you use?

22. You want to know how many lines are duplicated in the file **bigfile** located in the **mybooks** directory. You only want to display the output to the screen. You do not want to create any new files. What command did you use? How many lines are duplicated? Now you want to know how many lines are unique in **bigfile**. You only want to display the output to the screen. You do not want to create any new files. What command did you use? How many lines are unique? Hint: remember to use the command; the file must be sorted.

23. How big is the file called **book7** in the **mybooks** directory? Compress it using **gzip** and display the name and percent reduction as you zip the file. What command did you use? Now, find out what the compressed size, uncompressed size, and ratio compression are. What command did you use? Now unzip the file. What command did you use?

24. Archive the **temp** files in the **backup5** directory to the current directory to a file called **temping.tar**. What command did you use? Are the **temp** files still in the **backup5/dir2** directory?

25. Get the disk labeled PRACTICE disk. Do not use the BOOK disk. Mount it. Copy everything in the **practice7** directory under your home directory to the floppy disk to a directory called **practice7**. When you have finished, unmount the floppy disk and remove it from the drive.

Problem Set III—Brief Essay

Note: If you are saving your homework files to the floppy disk, you could run out of room on the disk. There are several solutions:

1. Create a directory called **homework** on your floppy disk and save all your written assignments to that directory.

2. When you have finished your assignment and printed it, delete the file from your floppy disk.

3. Create your homework assignments in your home directory. Then save your homework assignments to a new floppy disk, not the BOOK or BOOK2 disk.

Use gEdit or OpenOffice.org Writer to write and print your response. Be sure to put your name as well as what day and time your class is. Include the number of the question you are answering.

a. Compare and contrast standard input, standard output, and standard error. In your answer, explain the purpose and function of file descriptors. Give one example of how you might use a file descriptor.

b. Explain the purpose and function of pipes as they refer to shell capabilities, and demonstrate your understanding by using an example of two or more filter programs.

c. Compare and contrast **bzip2**, **bunzip2**, **gzip**, **gunzip**, **zcat**, **zip**, **unzip**, and **tar**. Give one example of when and how you would use each command.

CHAPTER 8

File Systems, File Ownership, Permissions, and Links

Chapter Overview

In a multi-user operating system such as Linux, the security of user and system data is critical. You only want to give access to data to those users who need to use it. In order to provide this type of security and the ability to manage the users and their files, Linux first ensures that every user is an authorized user through the logon process. Next, permissions are assigned to each file and directory on the system. Permissions that can be granted are read, write, and execute. They may be assigned symbolically or numerically. Permissions determine the ways in which files and directories can be accessed. There are default permissions assigned to every file and directory. Since every file and directory on the system is owned by someone, permissions can be modified by the owner of the files and directories. In addition, permissions are usually granted to groups rather than on a user-by-user basis. However, permissions only apply if you are working with a secure file system such as the ext2 or ext3m, the native file system for Linux. Thus, not only must a disk or partition be formatted, but a secure file system must be placed on the device. Since the available space on a disk is of concern, Linux provides commands that monitor disk space. Linux also provides the ability to link files, either a hard link or a symbolic link. Links are references to files. A link associates a file name with a location on the disk. Whenever you specify a file name in a command line, you are pointing to the place on the disk. Using links, the same file can be accessed from different places in the directory structure without having to store the file more than one time.

In this chapter, you will learn how to format disks and place a file system on a disk, as well as monitor your available disk space. Furthermore, you will learn to view, assign, and modify permissions for files and directories. Last, you will learn how to link files and directories.

415

Learning Objectives

1. Explain the concept of file ownership and use of permissions to access files and directories.
2. Compare and contrast formatting and creating a file system.
3. Describe how to create a file system.
4. Discuss the importance of and methods of monitoring disk space.
5. Explain the relationship that exists among permissions, file ownership, and groups.
6. List and explain the three types of permissions and how they are applied to files and directories.
7. Explain the purpose and function of symbolic permissions.
8. Explain the purpose and function of octal permissions.
9. Explain the purpose and function of hard links.
10. Explain the purpose and function of soft (symbolic) links.
11. Compare and contrast hard links with soft links.

Student Outcomes

1. View permissions of files and directories.
2. Format a disk and create an ext2 file system on a floppy disk.
3. Display free space and used space on a disk using the **du** and **df** commands.
4. View and change user and group information.
5. Display permission information on files and directories using **ls -1**.
6. Use the **chmod** command to manage permissions of files and directories.
7. Use the **umask** command to view umask values and to calculate the mask for files and directories.
8. Learn to change file and directory permissions using symbolic and absolute mode.
9. Learn to view links and display inode numbers.
10. Create hard and soft links using the **ln** command.

Commands Introduced

chgrp	echo $USER	mkfs
chmod	format	su
chown	fsck	tune2fs
df	groups	umask
du	id	user
echo $GROUPS	mke2fs	

8.1 • File Ownership and Permissions

Linux, as an operating system based on Unix, is designed as a multi-user system. A multi-user system is, of course, a system where many users can work with the system at one time. If you have multiple users on a system, security of user and system data is of paramount concern. Access should be given only to users who need to access the data. Since Linux is essentially a server operating system, good and efficient file security is built into Linux. Thus, to provide this security, every user must be a valid or authorized user. You are considered an authorized user if you can successfully log on. If you can log on, then the system administrator (super user/root) has created an account for you with a user name and password that indicates that you have access to the system and are an authorized user. The kind of access you have to the system is also determined by the system administrator and depends on the groups you belong to and the permissions you and the groups you belong to have been assigned.

In a secure system, you do not want an individual user to be able to modify, add, or delete files of another user. In fact, you may not even want an individual user to be able to read another user's files. In a secure multi-user environment like Linux, file and directory permissions access rights are defined. If you are using Linux on a computer as a stand-alone operating system, obviously you will not have several users logged at the same time. Nonetheless, you are still bound by the architecture of a multi-user system that provides security for all users. Furthermore, even if you are working on a stand-alone Linux computer, if you have more than one user using the system, you may want to define who has access to which files and directories.

In order to provide this type of security and the ability to manage the users and their files, Linux/Unix assigns permissions to each file and directory . A *permission* is the ability to access (read, write, execute, traverse, etc.) a file or directory. Depending on the operating system and the file system, each file may have different permissions for different kinds of access and different users or groups of users. Permissions are granted by the owner of the files and directories. Every file and directory on the system is owned by someone. Usually, the owner of the file or directory is the user who created it. Although permissions could be granted on a user-by-user basis, this would be logistically difficult to manage. Hence, permissions are usually granted to groups. A *group* is a set of users to whom the owner can grant permissions.

One user, the super user (the root), has special privileges because the super user, in a sense, owns everything. The super user has the power to change file ownerships and bypass permissions that the actual owner of the file or directory may have set. The super user also uses his root account to provide administrative functions, such as maintenance of the system. There are also other accounts on the system not intended for human interaction at all. These types of accounts are used generally by system daemons, which access files on the system through a specific system user ID other than the root or an ordinary user account.

In addition to regular files and directories, there are also special files such as devices and sockets. Each type of special file has its own rules regarding permissions and ownership. A *device* is a unit of hardware inside or outside the system unit. It is capable of providing input, receiving output, or both. *Sockets* provide a method for communication between a client program and a server program in a network. A socket is defined as "the endpoint in a connection." Sockets are created and used with a set of programming requests sometimes called the sockets application programming interface (API). The most common sockets API is the Berkeley Unix interface for sockets. Sockets can also be used for communication between processes within the same computer.

"Permissions" refers to the way a file can be used by an individual user. There are three file permissions: read (r), write (w) and execute (x). A read permission gives you the right to look at a file's contents. A write permission gives you the right to alter or delete a file. An execute permission gives you the right to execute a program. For directories, the permissions are the same—read/write/execute—but have different meaning. A read permission gives you the right to list the contents of a directory. A write permission gives you the right to add or remove files in that directory. You may not separate these permissions, i.e., you cannot give rights to add files to a directory but deny permission to remove a file in that directory. An execute permission gives you the right to list information about files in that directory (traverse the directory tree). Normally in a directory both read and execute permissions are paired, and either both are given or denied to a user.

Whenever a file or directory is created, the operating system assigns a set of default permissions. Many utility programs, as well, assign permissions based on certain default criteria. To determine who gets what permissions, Linux allows three levels of permissions: user (owner), group, and other. Every valid user is assigned to a group (or groups). Each user (owner) can assign permissions to the three groups. Each file has a user (owner) and a group. The user (owner) is generally the user who created the file. Each user also belongs to a default group, and that group is also assigned to every file the user creates. Many groups can be created, however, and users can belong to multiple groups. The super user (root) is generally the creator of new groups. The user (owner) of the file or directory is typically one person—the person who created it. The group is the group that the owner belongs to and is assigned to every file that the user creates. Other is everyone else or, colloquially, the world. Thus, you have three types of permissions (r, w, x) that can be assigned to three groups (user, group, other), for a total of nine access bits. Although the owner is the user, become accustomed to using the word user. The permissions are u,g, and o (o is "other," not "owner").

8.2 • Activity: Looking at Permissions

Note 1:   In order for these activities to work correctly, the users, accounts, directories and files need to be established as defined in Appendix A.

Note 2:   Sometimes, when using the terminal window in the GUI or in the GUI, you may get a message telling you the device is busy and cannot be unmounted. If this happens, try closing the terminal window and retry it or simply unmount on the GNOME desktop.

Note 3:   The activities in this book assume Linux is installed at run level 3. See the Installation section of Appendix A for details.

STEP 1   Mount the BOOK disk. Open a terminal window.

STEP 2   Key in the following: **ls -l /mnt/floppy** Enter

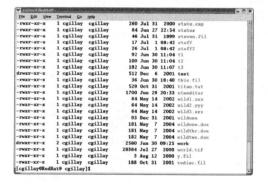

WHAT'S **HAPPENING?** When you mounted the floppy disk, you became the "owner" of the files. If you logged on as a different user, such as **alincoln**, and then mounted the floppy, you would see the owner and group listed as **alincoln**, not **cgillay**. Since you used the -l option with ls, you also see that you read, write, and execute permissions for these files. The first three bits are the permissions for the owners, the next three are permissions for the group, and the last three are for others. However, this disk has been formatted as a FAT (file allocation table, the formatting system used by MS-DOS and MS-Windows) disk and although you can alter permissions, it is meaningless to do so since the FAT file system does not recognize permissions.

You are logged in as your user name. You are the user who mounted the disk and no one can unmount that disk but the user (owner). You can prove this by logging on as another user and trying to unmount the disk. You may log on as another user by using the **su** command. The **su** command allows you to spawn a shell with the effective user ID of another user. If no user is specified, the command will create a shell for the privileged or root user, provided that you give the correct superuser password.

STEP 3 Key in the following: **su   alincoln** `Enter`

STEP 4 For the password, key in **president** `Enter`

STEP 5 Key in the following: **cd** `Enter`

STEP 6 Key in the following: **whoami** `Enter`

```
[cgillay@linux72  cgillay]$  su alincoln
Password:
[alincoln@linux72  cgillay]$  cd
[alincoln@linux72 alincoln]$  whoami
alincoln
[alincoln@linux72 alincoln]$
```

WHAT'S HAPPENING? You logged on as **alincoln** but remained in your home directory. You then used the **cd** command, which took you to the home directory of **alincoln**. The **whoami** command told you who you are logged in as.

STEP 7 Key in the following: **cp   /mnt/floppy/award.mov   ~** `Enter`

STEP 8 Key in the following: **ls -l award.mov** `Enter`

```
[alincoln@linux72 alincoln]$   cp /mnt/floppy/award.mov ~
[alincoln@linux72 alincoln] $ ls -l award.mov
-rwxrwxr-x 1  alincoln  alincoln  162  Oct 12 19:25 award.mov
[alincoln@linux72 alincoln]$
```

WHAT'S HAPPENING? You were allowed to copy the file award.mov from the floppy disk that was mounted by **cgillay** (or your user name) to alincoln's home directory. Once the file was copied, alincoln became the owner of the file.

STEP 9 Key in the following: **rm award.mov** `Enter`

STEP 10 Key in the following: **umount /mnt/floppy** `Enter`

```
[alincoln@linux72 alincoln]$  umount  /mnt/floppy
umount: only cgillay can umount /dev/fd0 from /mnt/floppy
[alincoln@linux72 alincoln]$
```

WHAT'S HAPPENING? Although you could delete the **award.mov** file as **alincoln** in alincoln's home directory you, as **alincoln**, cannot unmount the floppy disk. You will see the user name that you logged in as instead of **cgillay**. Since **cgillay** (or your user na me) mounted the floppy, only that same user can unmount that floppy.

STEP 11 Key in the following: **exit** `Enter`

STEP 12 Key in the following: **whoami** `Enter`

```
[alincoln@linux72 alincoln]$   exit
exit
[cgillay@linux72  cgillay]$  whoami
cgillay
[cgillay@linux72  cgillay]$
```

WHAT'S HAPPENING? You exited the shell you spawned and returned to the shell you were running as the user you logged in as. Now you want to copy the files from the BOOK disk to a new directory in your home directory called **book.** You will then format a new disk and copy these files back to the new disk. Be patient. It takes time to copy files from a floppy disk to the hard disk.

STEP 13 Key in the following: **mkdir book** [Enter]

STEP 14 Key in the following: **cd /mnt/floppy** [Enter]

STEP 15 Key in the following: **cp -r --parents * ~/book** [Enter]

STEP 16 Key in the following: **cd; ls book** [Enter]

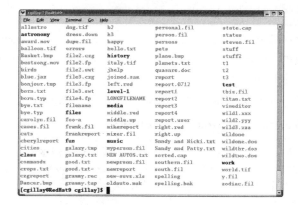

WHAT'S HAPPENING? You have created a directory called **book** in your home directory. You then copied all the files and directories from the BOOK floppy disk to a directory called **book.** Be patient, it takes time to copy from a floppy disk.

STEP 17 Key in the following: **ls -l book** [Enter]

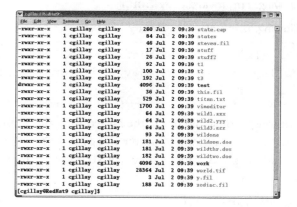

WHAT'S HAPPENING? You are looking at the long listing of your files in the book directory under your home. When you copied the files to the book directory, you became the owner of the files. The dates also changed and are now the current date. You also have a set of permissions associated with each file, and again, you have the same permissions. You now want to format a new floppy disk and place the ext2 file system on it. You will copy the files from the book directory back to the newly formatted disk. Since you are placing the native Linux file system on the floppy disk, you will be able to change permissions and groups on the disk. The current BOOK disk is a FAT disk that does not recognize permissions and rights. But first, you need to learn about formatting a disk and placing a file system on it.

8.3 • File Systems

Permissions only apply if you are working with a secure file system such as the ext2 file system for Linux. If you are using another file system, such as FAT, there are no available permissions or file ownership, even though those permissions are displayed. Although the hard disk, and hence, your home directory has been formatted as a Linux file system, the BOOK disk (the floppy disk that came with the textbook) uses a FAT file system. In order to test ownership and permissions, you want to create a floppy disk that has a Linux file system on it. This means you must place the Linux file system on a newly formatted floppy disk.

There are two parts to creating a file system on any device. First it is formatted, which is considered a low-level format (laying of the track and sector information), and second, the file system of choice is put into place on the disk.

The syntax for the format command for a floppy disk is: **fdformat [-n]** *device*. The available option is **-n**, which is "no verify." This option will disable the verification that is performed after the format. You must know the actual name of the device, sometimes called the raw device file name. Usually, the floppy device name is **/dev/fd0** although it could be **/dev/fd1**. In order to format a floppy disk, it *must not be mounted*. If the disk is mounted, Linux considers the device busy and cannot format it. You may also specify a code for the type of disk that you are using. Table 8.1, "Disk Types," lists the various options.

Name	Disk Type	Actual Disk Size	Number Used
d	low density—a 5¼-inch disk	360 KB	360
D	low-density—a 3½-inch disk	720 KB	720
h	high-density—a 5¼-inch disk.	1.2 MB	1200
H	high-density—a 3½-inch disk.	1.44 MB	1440

Table 8.1 • Disk Types

Thus, to use the command to format a 5¼-inch low-density floppy disk on a floppy disk designated as **/dev/fd1**, you would key **fdformat /dev/fd1d360**. To format a 3½-inch high-density disk designated as **/dev/fd0**, you would key in **fdformat /dev/fd0H1440**. However, since virtually all floppy disks today are 3½-inch high-density disks, you do not need to add the type or size information. Furthermore, since most people purchase pre-formatted disks, you really do not have to low-level format the disk. But, in the interest of using the command, you will low-level format your floppy disk.

To create a file system, you use the mkfs or the mke2fs command. Remember, a file system is what determines how files are named, stored, and retrieved on a device. With the release of Red Hat Linux 7.2, the native or default file system changed from ext2 to ext3. This continues in the later versions of Linux. The ext3 file system is what is referred to as journaling file system. Journaling file systems are designed to recover quickly from a system crash. With a journaling file system, a log is kept of all system actions and placed in a journal file. In the event of a system crash, Linux only needs to read the journal file to restore the system to its previous state. Files that were in the process of being written to disk can then be restored to their original state. The ext3 file system is really ext2 with the ability to recover faster after the system goes down. If you install Red Hat Linux 9.0 on a new hard disk, the default file system assigned to the Linux partitions will be ext3. If you upgrade from an earlier version of Red Hat Linux that was using ext2 partitions, the installation process will allow you to convert from ext2 to ext3 without data loss. You may also convert to an ext3 file system at a later date by using tune2fs, a program that can add a journal to an existing ext2 file system without data loss. You may also use the tune2fs program to revert to an ext2 file system. These conversions, however, are limited to the root user and are beyond the scope of this text. In addition, on a floppy disk, you really do not need journaling capabilities, so you will create the ext2 files system using mkfs on your floppy disk.

Every file system has its own **mkfs** command associated with it. Thus, for instance, for an MS-DOS file system, the command is **mkfs.msdos**, and for the ext2 Linux file system, (ext2) the command is **mkfs.ext2**. The command **mke2fs** is equivalent to **mkfs.ext2**. To create an ext3 file system, you would still use the **mke2fs** command but use the **-j** or **-J** option for journaling.

The program mkfs is actually a front-end program that creates a file system of any type by executing the correct version of mkfs for that type of file system. The command mkfs, fs-type tells mkfs to execute the correct version of mkfs. You may directly use **mke2fs**, **mkfs.ext2**, or **mkfs.ext3**. If you use **mkfs.ext3**, then a journal is automatically created as if you specified the **-j** option. Major file systems are listed in Table 8.2, "Major Linux File System Types."

Type	File System	Description
ext3	third extended file system	Native Red Hat Linux file system.
ext2	second extended file system	Native Linux file system for versions of Red Hat Linux prior to 7.2.
nfs	network file system	Allows access to remote files on a network.
umsdos	UMSDOS file system	MS-DOS file system with extensions that allow features that are similar to Linux, including long file names.
msdos	DOS-FAT file system	Accesses MS-DOS files.
vfat	VFAT file system	Accesses Windows 95/98/2000 files.
ntfs	NT file system	Accesses Windows NT files.
iso9660	ISO9660 file system	Used by most CD-ROMs.
hfs	Apple Mac file system	Accesses files from Apple Macintosh.
ncpfs	Novell file system	Access files from a Novell server.
smbfs	SMB file system	Accesses files from a Windows for Workgroups or Windows NT server.

Table 8.2 · Major Linux File System Types

The syntax for the command is:

```
mkfs [ -v ] [ -t  fstype ] [fs-options] device  [ blocks]
```

Table 8.3, "**mkfs** Options," lists some of the major options used with the **mkfs** command.

Option	Name	Result
-v	Verbose	Displays all commands executed to create the specific file system.
-t *fstype*	File system type	Type is the type of file system you wish to create, as listed in Table 8.2. If not specified, ext2 is used.
-fs -options	File system options	Options that are passed to the real file system builder. Most file system builders support **-c** (check for bad block) and **-v** (verbose).
device	Device name	This must be a "real" device name, such as /dev/fd0, the raw device name You cannot use /**mnt**/**floppy**, the logical device name.
blocks	Blocks	Blocks refers to the size of the file system in 1024-byte blocks.

Table 8.3 • mkfs Options

Thus, using the above command to format a 3½-inch floppy disk in the Linux file system, you could issue the command as simply **mkfs** /**dev**/**fd0** and assume that **mkfs** will get the correct version of **mkfs** for ext2. If you wanted to be more specific, you could issue the command as

```
mkfs  -t  ext2  /dev/fd0  1440
```

In this example, you are saying use the **mkfs** command; the type of file system you wish to make is the **ext2** file system. You want to create it on the device named /**dev**/**fd0** and the total block size is **1440** (1.44 MB). However, only the root user can use the command in this format.

If you wanted the 3½-inch floppy disk to be formatted with the MS-DOS file system, you would issue the command as **mkfs -t msdos** /**dev**/**fd0** **1440**. Once the disk is formatted and has a file system on it, it can be mounted. Again, only the root user can use the command in this format.

8.4 • Activity: Creating an ext2 File System

Note: The BOOK disk is mounted. Your home directory is the default directory.

STEP 1 Key in the following: **umount** /**mnt/floppy** [Enter]

```
[cgillay@linux72  cgillay]$  umount /mnt/floppy
[cgillay@linux72  cgillay]$
```

WHAT'S HAPPENING? Once again, if a disk is mounted, Linux feels the device is busy and in use, and will not let you format a device in use. You must unmount it prior to formatting or placing a file system on a disk.

STEP 2   Remove the BOOK disk. *Do Not* use the BOOK disk. Get a new disk and label it BOOK2. Place it in the disk drive. *Do not* mount the disk.

STEP 3   Key in the following: **cat /etc/fstab; whereis fdformat mkfs** Enter

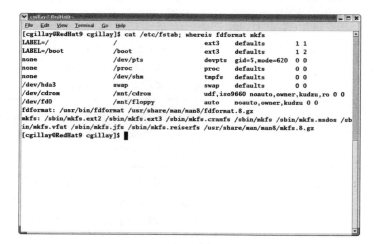

WHAT'S HAPPENING? You placed the disk that you want to format in the drive. You did not mount it. You then checked the **fstab** file for the actual name of your floppy drive. In this example, it is **fd0**. Remember, you must know the actual device name to format it and place a file system on it. You also verified the location of the two programs you want to use, **fdformat** and **mkfs**. The **fdformat** program is located in the **/usr/bin** directory and the **mkfs** front end, and the specific format type programs are located in the **/sbin** directory. You need to know this information so you may format the disk and place a file system on it. *Note:* If the command **fdformat /dev/fd0** does not work, try **fdformat /dev/fd0H1440** instead.

STEP 4   Key in the following: **fdformat /dev/fd0** Enter

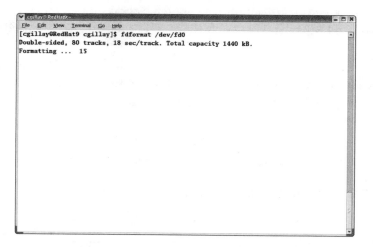

WHAT'S HAPPENING? If you got the message, **bash: fdformat: command not found,** you would need to key in the absolute path to the program. For instance, in this example, the absolute path would be **/usr/bin/ fdformat,** and then the command to be keyed in would be

/usr/bin/ fdformat /dev/fd0. Again, note that you are using the actual name of the device, **/dev/fd0** and you let **fdformat** decide on the size of the disk. You could key in **fdformat /dev/fd0H1440**, which would specify a high-density 1.44 MB disk. When the command is finished executing, you see the following screen:

```
[cgillay@linux72  cgillay]$  fdformat /dev/fd0
Double-sided, 80 track, 18 sec/track. Total capacity 1440 kB.
Formatting... done
Verifying...done
[cgillay@linux72  cgillay]$
```

WHAT'S **HAPPENING?** Now you are ready to place the ext2 file system on this disk.

STEP 5 Key in the following: **mkfs /dev/fd0** Enter

```
[cgillay@linux72  cgillay]$  mkfs /dev/fd0
bash: mkfs: command not found
[cgillay@linux72  cgillay]$
```

WHAT'S **HAPPENING?** Your command is correct—you are going to create a file system (**mkfs**) on the device, **/dev/fd0**. You are letting the **mkfs** decide on the file type and size of the disk. You could key the command in as **mkfs -t ext2 /dev/fd0 1440**. This would specify the Linux type (**-t ext2**) and the floppy disk (**/dev/fd0**), and you would assign it a block size (**1440**). Here blocks specifies a 1.44-MB high-density 3½-inch floppy disk. In this example, the **mkfs** command is not in the search path. You must give it the absolute path. *Note:* If the location of your **mkfs** file is in a directory other than the example, substitute that path name for the one given in the step.

STEP 6 Key in the following: **/sbin/mkfs /dev/fd0** Enter

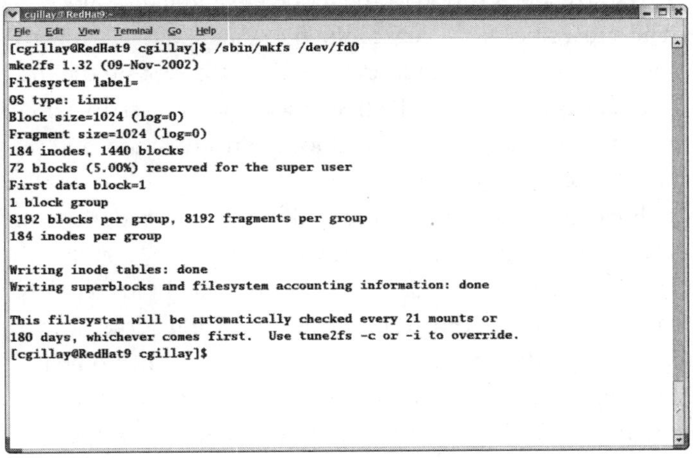
cgillay@RedHat9:~
File Edit View Terminal Go Help
[cgillay@RedHat9 cgillay]$ /sbin/mkfs /dev/fd0
mke2fs 1.32 (09-Nov-2002)
Filesystem label=
OS type: Linux
Block size=1024 (log=0)
Fragment size=1024 (log=0)
184 inodes, 1440 blocks
72 blocks (5.00%) reserved for the super user
First data block=1
1 block group
8192 blocks per group, 8192 fragments per group
184 inodes per group
Writing inode tables: done
Writing superblocks and filesystem accounting information: done
This filesystem will be automatically checked every 21 mounts or
180 days, whichever comes first. Use tune2fs -c or -i to override.
[cgillay@RedHat9 cgillay]$

WHAT'S **HAPPENING?** You see the **mke2fs** command was used. You also see information about block sizes and inodes. The starting point for any disk is ordinarily several hundred megabytes of linear storage space. In order to manage this space, it is subdivided into a "chunk" of data called a block, normally 1024 bytes (1 Kbyte). It then numbers these blocks sequentially. Then the blocks are arranged into several groups, designed to store a different data type. Block devices, such as disks, transfer information in blocks (as opposed to devices such as a keyboard, which transfers data one character at a time). Thus, an ext2 or ext3 file system has several structural components: inodes, superblocks, a map of the disk blocks in the file system, a summary of the block usage, and the data blocks.

Inodes (information nodes) administer the data. The *inode* is a computer-stored description of an individual file. It is a data structure that holds information about every file. There is an inode for each file, and a file is uniquely identified by the file system on which it resides and its inode number on that system. Each inode contains the following information: the device where the inode resides, locking information, mode and type of file, the number of links to the file, the owner's user and group ids, the security settings, the number of bytes in the file, access and modification times, the time the inode itself was last modified, and the addresses of the file's blocks on disk. The file name is not stored in the inode but in the directory. The number of inodes is fixed at the time the file system is created, and once the inodes are used, you no longer have room on the disk, regardless of the physical space remaining.

A file, then, consists of an inode with all the management information and several blocks that actually contain the data itself. The management information is separated from the data so that the data and the management information can be handled separately. For instance, if you move a file to a different directory, only the management information changes, without affecting the data. The number of data blocks required depends on the size of the file. An important function in the inode is where the data in the file is stored. The numbers of the first 12 data blocks are stored in the inode. If the file is bigger than 12 Kbytes, then another inode points to a block that does not contain data but can reference up to 256 further data blocks. This scheme continues for larger files.

Directories are managed like files. A directory is like a file that lists all the files and directories. Each line in the file contains the name of the file along with its inode number. This is also where the directory references itself (.) and references its parent directory (..). This means, then, that the first inode points to the root directory, which contains all the information about the names and inodes of the files and directories stored in it.

A *superblock* is a record that describes the characteristics of a file system. It has information about disk block size, the size and location of the inode table, the disk block map, usage information, and so on. The superblock is the key to the file system, and if damaged could result in a file system that was unreadable. To this end, several copies are kept on the file system.

The map of the disk blocks is a table of the free blocks the file system contains, the summary of the block usage records information about the blocks already in use, and the data blocks where the data is actually stored.

This file system architecture has consequences for how your system performs. Linux is an extremely fast and secure operating system. When you access a file, it caches the necessary inode information in buffers. A *cache* is a small, fast memory area that holds recently accessed data. It is designed to speed up subsequent access to the same data. Linux does not write to disk until either the buffer is full or a pre-determined time has elapsed, at which time it flushes the buffer (does a write to disk). This is one reason you must log out. Part of the log-out procedure is flushing the buffers. If you do not log out and let Linux shut down properly, the buffers are not flushed and you crash your system.

Now that you have placed the file system on the disk, you are going to move the files from the **book** directory to the floppy and work with permissions. However, first you might like some information about disk use.

8.5 ● Disk Use

The space available on disk is always of concern. Eventually, no matter what size your disk is, you will run out of room. In addition, Linux runs most efficiently with at least 5 to 30 per cent of the disk space free in each type of file system. This is generally true of all operating systems. The minimum amount of disk space you should leave free is machine-dependent. Using the maximum amount of disk space will degrade performance and, obviously, if you fill a disk, you will not be able to add any more files to it.

The reason you need free disk space is that when Linux processes run, they generate a number of housekeeping files to track what is being done. Furthermore, in any operating system, to maintain the file system—as well as perform other system-related tasks—there is always overhead. *Overhead* includes the needed resources (usually processing time or storage space), that are used for purposes incidental to, but also necessary to, the main one. In a retail business, for instance, overhead consists of items like the cost of heating and cooling the building and the cost of electricity and supplies. None of these items has anything directly to do with selling merchandise, but the business cannot be run without the overhead items. It is part of the "cost" of doing business. The same analogy works with computers—there is a "cost" for doing the business of running and maintaining the system, which includes the file system. There are always cost trade-offs. For instance, if you keep a program running all the time, you save the overhead costs of loading and initializing the program for each transaction. But by running the program all the time, you now have introduced a space overhead consideration. For instance, in Linux, a directory can hold any number of files; it is generally a good use of space to keep the number of files in any single directory reasonably small. Too many files in a directory degrade performance and increase the size of the directory file. Deleting files shrinks the size of the directory file.

Two programs that can help you monitor disk space are **du** (disk usage) and **df** (disk free). The **du** command reports how much space is used by a directory, including its subdirectories, or a specific file. It displays the number of blocks that are occupied by the directory or file. The syntax for **du** is **du [options] [file]**. Table 8.4, "**du** Options," lists some of the major options used with the **du** command.

Option	Name	Result
-a	All	Displays the count for all files, not just directories.
-b	Bytes	Displays the size in bytes.
-c	Total count	Displays a grand total.
-h	Human readable.	Displays output in bytes, kilobytes or megabytes.
-k	Kilobytes	Displays output in kilobytes.
-m	Megabytes	Displays output in megabytes.
-s	Summarize	Displays a total.

Table 8.4 ● du Options

The syntax for **df** is **df [options] [file]**. Table 8.5, "**df** Options," lists some of the major options used with the **df** command.

Option	Name	Result
-a	All	Displays all file systems, including those with 0 blocks.
-h	Human readable	Displays output in bytes, kilobytes, or megabytes.
-i	Inodes	Displays inode information instead of block usage.
-k	Kilobytes	Displays output in block sizes of 1024.
-l	Local	Limits display to local file system.
-m	Megabytes	Displays output in block sizes of 1,048,576.
-t *type*	Type	Limits display to files systems of the type specified by type.
-T	Display type	Displays the file system type.

Table 8.5 • df Options

8.6 • Activity: Using du and df

Note 1:   The BOOK2 disk is in the drive. A terminal window is open. Your home directory is the default directory.

Note 2:   If you do not have a book directory in your home directory, you need to create it now. Make your home directory the default directory. Remove any disks in the floppy drive. Insert the BOOK disk into the drive. Mount it. Then, return to Activity 8.2 and do steps 13, 14, and 15. When you have completed those steps, unmount the BOOK disk and remove it from the drive.

STEP 1   If the **BOOK2** disk is not in the floppy drive, insert it now.

STEP 2   Key in the following: **mount /mnt/floppy** Enter

```
[cgillay@linux72    cgillay]$   mount /mnt/floppy
[cgillay@linux72    cgillay]$
```

WHAT'S HAPPENING? Now that the BOOK2 disk has been formatted and had a file system placed on it, you may mount it so you may access it.

STEP 3   Key in the following: **du -ch /mnt/floppy; ls -l /mnt/floppy** Enter

```
[cgillay@linux72    cgillay]$   du -ch /mnt/floppy
12k       /mnt/floppy/lost+found
13k       /mnt/floppy
13k       total
total 12
drwxr-xr-x 2     root   root   12288   Nov 17 21:50 lost+found
[cgillay@linux72    cgillay]$
```

WHAT'S **HAPPENING?** Even though this disk is "empty," Linux still has some administrative information that it places on the disk. The lost+found directory, owned by root, is used by certain utilities such as fsck (file system check). As an ordinary user, you cannot change to the **lost+found** directory.

The **fsck** command verifies the integrity of the file system and reports on any problems it finds. It prompts the user to either repair or ignore the problem. If, for instance, when running **fsck**, it discovers a file that has lost its link to its file name, it will ask you if you want to fix the problem. If you agree, it places the file in the **lost+found** directory and gives its inode number as its file name. The **fsck** command should be run on unmounted file systems *only*. This is because if any errors are found and corrected, you will have to reboot the system because the changes made by **fsck** may not be sent back to the system's internal knowledge of the file system layout. Although you can unmount most file systems, you cannot unmount the root file system while you are running the system. If you needed to run **fsck** on the root file system, you would need to use the installation floppies and boot floppy. In general, when you boot the system, the file system is checked. *Never* run **fsck** on your mounted root file system.

STEP 4   Key in the following: **du -ch book** [Enter]

WHAT'S **HAPPENING?** You see a list of files in the **book** directory and the total disk usage. You can see that the total is 1.3M. It appears that your files from the **book** directory will fit on the **BOOK2** disk since a floppy disk has 1.44M of space available. *Note:* Your total number may vary, depending on what files you placed on the original **BOOK** disk.

STEP 5   Key in the following: **cd book; cp -r * /mnt/floppy** [Enter]

```
cp: cannot create regular file '/mnt/floppy/states': No space left on device
cp: cannot create regular file '/mnt/floppy/steven.fil': No space left on device
cp: cannot create regular file '/mnt/floppy/stuff': No space left on device
cp: cannot create regular file '/mnt/floppy/stuff2': No space left on device
cp: cannot create regular file '/mnt/floppy/t1': No space left on device
cp: cannot create regular file '/mnt/floppy/t2': No space left on device
cp: cannot create regular file '/mnt/floppy/t3': No space left on device
cp: cannot create directory '/mnt/floppy/test': No space left on device
cp: cannot create regular file '/mnt/floppy/this.fil': No space left on device
cp: cannot create regular file '/mnt/floppy/titan.txt': No space left on device
cp: cannot create regular file '/mnt/floppy/vimeditor': No space left on device
cp: cannot create regular file '/mnt/floppy/wild1.xxx': No space left on device
cp: cannot create regular file '/mnt/floppy/wild2.yyy': No space left on device
cp: cannot create regular file '/mnt/floppy/wild3.zzz': No space left on device
cp: cannot create regular file '/mnt/floppy/wildone': No space left on device
cp: cannot create regular file '/mnt/floppy/wildone.dos': No space left on device
cp: cannot create regular file '/mnt/floppy/wildthr.dos': No space left on device
cp: cannot create regular file '/mnt/floppy/wildtwo.dos': No space left on device
cp: cannot create directory '/mnt/floppy/work': No space left on device
cp: cannot create regular file '/mnt/floppy/world.tif': No space left on device
cp: cannot create regular file '/mnt/floppy/y.fil': No space left on device
cp: cannot create regular file '/mnt/floppy/zodiac.fil': No space left on device
[cgillay@RedHat9 book]$
```

WHAT'S HAPPENING? You can see that all the files and directories in the book disk did not fit on the floppy disk that you labeled **BOOK2**. This appears contradictory. As you know, the **BOOK** disk and **BOOK2** disk are both 1.44M; files and directories that once fit on a 1.44M disk no longer fit on a 1.44M disk. How can this be? It is because of the file system. Remember, the **BOOK** disk is a disk that has the FAT file system, whereas the **BOOK2** disk has the ext2 file system.

STEP 6   Key in the following: **cd; df -ih /mnt/floppy** [Enter]

```
[cgillay@linux72  cgillay]$  df -ih /mnt/floppy
Filesystem      Inodes    Iused    Ifree    Iuse%    Mounted on
/dev/fd0        184       184      0        100%     /mnt/floppy
[cgillay@linux72  cgillay]$
```

WHAT'S HAPPENING? Although the floppy disk holds 1.44M, space is taken on the floppy not only by the **lost+found** directory, but also by the superblocks and other accounting information. The superblocks are overhead and are necessary for maintaining the file system because they contain file system information. But most important, you have used up all your inodes. There are not enough inodes available to allow all the files and directories to be "recopied" to the same floppy. It may seem strange that the same sized disk cannot hold all the information that it did before. Again, this has to do with the file system structure and the overhead that the ext2 file system requires. Remember, the original BOOK disk used a FAT file system. A FAT file system on a floppy disk has a block size of 512. The ext file system uses a block size of 1024. Different file system architectures have different space requirements.

STEP 7   Key in the following: **df -ih book** [Enter]

```
[cgillay@RedHat9  cgillay]$  df -ih book
Filesystem             Inodes    Iused    Ifree    Iuse%  Mounted on
/dev/hda2              9.3M      291      9.0M     4%     /
[cgillay@RedHat9  cgillay]$
```

WHAT'S HAPPENING? The **df** command shows total disk usage on a device, not for a specific directory.

STEP 8   Key in the following: **du -s book /mnt/floppy** [Enter]

```
[cgillay@linux72  cgillay]$  du -s book /mnt/floppy
1316            book
331             /mnt/floppy
[cgillay@linux72  cgillay]$
```

WHAT'S HAPPENING? You see a summary of the usage of the BOOK2 disk and the **book** directory. You want to move the files from this directory to your floppy disk. However, you are going to have to be selective, as you can see all the files will not fit on the floppy disk. But first, you are going to recreate your file system on the BOOK2 disk. Remember, you *must* unmount a floppy disk (or any disk) before you create a file system on it.

STEP 9   Key in the following: **umount /mnt/floppy** [Enter]

STEP 10   Key in the following: **/sbin/mkfs /dev/fd0** [Enter]

STEP 11   Key in the following: **mount /mnt/floppy** [Enter]

```
cgillay@RedHat9:~
File  Edit  View  Terminal  Go  Help
[cgillay@RedHat9 cgillay]$ umount /mnt/floppy
[cgillay@RedHat9 cgillay]$ /sbin/mkfs /dev/fd0
mke2fs 1.32 (09-Nov-2002)
Filesystem label=
OS type: Linux
Block size=1024 (log=0)
Fragment size=1024 (log=0)
184 inodes, 1440 blocks
72 blocks (5.00%) reserved for the super user
First data block=1
1 block group
8192 blocks per group, 8192 fragments per group
184 inodes per group

Writing inode tables: done
Writing superblocks and filesystem accounting information: done

This filesystem will be automatically checked every 33 mounts or
180 days, whichever comes first.  Use tune2fs -c or -i to override.
[cgillay@RedHat9 cgillay]$ mount /mnt/floppy
[cgillay@RedHat9 cgillay]$ █
```

WHAT'S HAPPENING? You unmounted your floppy disk so that you could place a file system on it. You then used **mkfs /dev/fd0** to place a file system on the disk. This process removed the files that had been copied to the **BOOK2** disk. You then remounted it so you can copy files and directories from the **book** directory to the BOOK2 disk. But in order to copy the files from the **book** directory, you need to eliminate some files and directories. And, to make some activities work, you are going to add some files. You are first going to copy the **.99** files from the **astronomy** directory to the **book** directory using the dot (.) as the destination. Remember, the dot represents the current directory. Then you are going to eliminate the extra files that **emacs** created—**good.txt ~** and **mystery.bks ~** located in the **media/books** directory. Be sure to include the ~. If you did not do all the activities or missed a step in the activities, you may be missing files. Since you are deleting files, if the files are missing it is all right.

Note: Some versions Red Hat will ask for verification each time you try to delete a file. If this happens to you, just confirm each deletion by pressing **y**.

STEP 12 Key in the following: **cd book** [Enter]

STEP 13 Key in the following: **cp astronomy/*.99 .** [Enter]

STEP 14 Key in the following: **rm good.txt ~** [Enter]

STEP 15 Key in the following: **rm media/books/mystery.bks ~** [Enter]

```
[cgillay@linux72   book]$   cd book
[cgillay@linux72   book]$   cp astronomy/*.99  .
[cgillay@linux72   book]$   rm good.txt~
[cgillay@linux72   book]$   rm media/books/mystery.bks~
[cgillay@linux72   book]$
```

WHAT'S HAPPENING? You have added the **.99** files to the book directory and removed the files **good.txt ~** and **mystery.bks ~**.

STEP 16 Key in the following: **rm my*.* report.0712 report.user *.mov; cd** [Enter]

```
[cgillay@RedHat9   book]$   rm   my*.*   report.0712   report.user
*.mov; cd
[cgillay@RedHat9   cgillay]$ _
```

WHAT'S HAPPENING? You have removed files and returned to your home directory. *Note:* Remember, you may see an error message (**rm: cannot remove *'filename'*: No such file or**

directory). If you did not create all the files in the activities or homework, do not be concerned. If you do not have the files to delete, that is OK. If you never created the file, then it is not there. You may also use Nautilus file manager to remove files and directories. Using a GUI interface such as the Nautilus file manager in removing files and directories is an advantage here. Since it is a graphical display, it is easier to see the files and directories than when you using the command prompt. You need to eliminate some directories and files so that you can fit the files and directories on the **BOOK2** floppy disk.

STEP 17   Minimize the terminal window. Double-click your home directory icon on the desktop. Click **Information**. Click **Tree**. Make the **book** directory the default directory. Be in Icon view.

STEP 18   Click **Edit**. Click **Preferences**. Click the **Views** tab. Enable **Show hidden and backup files**. Click **Close**. Expand the **book** directory.

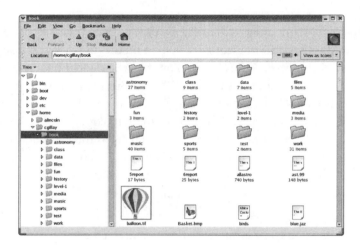

WHAT'S HAPPENING? When you asked to see the hidden files and folders, a new directory may have appeared—**.thumbnails**. If it appeared, this directory keeps an image of your graphical items. You are going to delete that directory along with others you no longer will need.

STEP 19   If you have a **.thumbnails** directory, click it to select it and press the Delete key.

STEP 20   Select the directories **astronomy, class, files, history, test,** and **work**. (Remember to hold the Ctrl key when you click each item.) Press the Delete key.

STEP 21   Select the files **balloon.tif** and **Basket.bmp**. Press the Delete key.

STEP 22   Change to list view. Scroll so that **Dancer.bmp** is at the top of the window. Select the files **Dancer.bmp**, **dog.tif**, and **dupe.fil**. Press the Delete key.

STEP 23   Scroll so errors is at the top of the window. Select **errors**, **filename** and **foo-a**. Press the Delete key.

STEP 24   Scroll so **italy.tif** is at the top of the window. Select the files **italy.tif**, **LONGFILENAME**, **mixer.fil**, and **NEW AUTOS.TXT**. Press the Delete key.

STEP 25   Scroll until **Old Automobiles** is at the top of the window. Select the files **Old Automobiles**, **plane.bmp**, **quasars.doc**, **report**, **report1**, and **report2**. Press Delete.

STEP 26   Scroll so **report3** is at the top of the window. Select the files **report3**, **report4**, **Sandy and Nicki.txt**, **Sandy and Patty.txt**, and **spelling.bak**. Press the Delete key.

STEP 27   Scroll until you locate **world.tif**. Select it. Press the Delete key. Click **View**. Click **View as Icons**. Scroll to the top of the window.

STEP 28   Click **Edit**. Click **Select All Files**. Click **Edit**. Click **Copy Files**.

STEP 29   Double-click the floppy disk icon on the desktop. In the right pane of the floppy disk icon, right-click and then click **Paste files**.

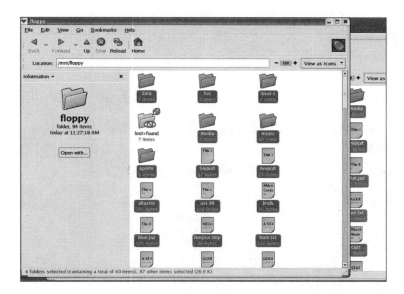

WHAT'S HAPPENING? ⟫ You have your floppy disk window open, as well as the **book** directory window. The files and directories have been copied. However, you may see that the **.thumbnails** directory was created on the floppy disk.

STEP 30   In the floppy window, click in the window to deselect the files. If you have a **.thumbnails** directory, select and delete it. Close the **floppy** window.

STEP 31   If it is not active, make the **book** window active. If all the files are not selected, select them now. Press the Delete key. Close the window.

STEP 32   Activate your terminal window. Key in the following: **ls -l /mnt/floppy/ast.99** Enter

```
[cgillay@linux72  cgillay]$  ls -l /mnt/floppy/ast.99
-rwxrwxr-x  1      cgillay  cgillay  148  Oct 13 10:18 /mnt/floppy/ast.99
[cgillay@linux72  cgillay]$
```

WHAT'S HAPPENING? ⟫ When you copied the files, you retained ownership and the same permissions. The date is the date that you copied the files to the disk.

STEP 33   Key in the following: **rm -r book** Enter

STEP 34   Key in the following: **du -cha /mnt/floppy** Enter

```
cgillay@RedHat9 -                                                    _ □ x
File  Edit  View  Terminal  Go  Help
1.0K    /mnt/floppy/media/books/mystery.bks
5.0K    /mnt/floppy/media/books
13K     /mnt/floppy/media
1.0K    /mnt/floppy/level-1/hello.txt
1.0K    /mnt/floppy/level-1/level-2/hello.txt
1.0K    /mnt/floppy/level-1/level-2/level-3/hello.txt
2.0K    /mnt/floppy/level-1/level-2/level-3
4.0K    /mnt/floppy/level-1/level-2
6.0K    /mnt/floppy/level-1
1.0K    /mnt/floppy/fun/dances.all
1.0K    /mnt/floppy/fun/dances.new
1.0K    /mnt/floppy/fun/dances.txt
4.0K    /mnt/floppy/fun
1.0K    /mnt/floppy/data/bonjour.txt
1.0K    /mnt/floppy/data/good.txt
1.0K    /mnt/floppy/data/highest.txt
1.0K    /mnt/floppy/data/mother.let
1.0K    /mnt/floppy/data/tea.tax
1.0K    /mnt/floppy/data/thank.you
1.0K    /mnt/floppy/data/thin.est
8.0K    /mnt/floppy/data
190K    /mnt/floppy
190K    total
[cgillay@RedHat9 cgillay]$ █
```

WHAT'S HAPPENING? On your BOOK2 disk, you see all of your files (**a**) with a grand total (**c**) in human-readable form (**h**).

STEP 35 Key in the following: **df -ih /mnt/floppy** Enter

```
[cgillay@RedHat9   cgillay]$  df -ih /mnt/floppy
Filesystem            Inodes     Iused   Ifree   Iuse%  Mounted on
/dev/fd0                 184       175       9     96%   /mnt/floppy
[cgillay@RedHat9   cgillay]$
```

WHAT'S HAPPENING? Even though your files are not large, you can see that your inode usage is causing your disk to be almost full. *Note:* Your numbers could be slightly different.

STEP 36 Key in the following: **cd /mnt/floppy; ls -l dress.down; rm dress.down** Enter

STEP 37 Key in the following: **df -ih /mnt/floppy** Enter

```
[cgillay@RedHat9 cgillay]$ cd /mnt/floppy; ls -l dress.down; rm
dress.down
-rwxr-xr-x    1  cgillay  cgillay      284  Jul 2 09:38 dress.down
[cgillay@RedHat9   floppy]$ df -ih /mnt/floppy
Filesystem         Inodes    Iused   Ifree   Iuse%  Mounted on
/dev/fd0              184      174      10     95%   /mnt/floppy
[cgillay@RedHat9   floppy]$
```

WHAT'S HAPPENING? Although you removed a file, you did not gain much disk space. You are going to delete a directory with other directories in it.

STEP 38 Key in the following: **du -sh media; rm -r media; df -ih /mnt/floppy** Enter

```
[cgillay@RedHat9   floppy]$ du -sh media; rm -r media; df -ih /mnt/
floppy
13K      media
Filesystem          Inodes    Iused   Ifree   Iuse%  Mounted on
/dev/fd0               184      162      22     89%   /mnt/floppy
[cgillay@RedHat9   floppy]$
```

WHAT'S HAPPENING? Because of file management, you freed up more space when you deleted a directory.

STEP 39 Key in the following: **cd** Enter

```
[cgillay@linux72   floppy]$  cd
[cgillay@linux72   cgillay]$
```

WHAT'S **HAPPENING?** You have returned to your home directory.

8.7 ● Groups

Permissions, file ownership, and groups are dependent on one another. Permissions refer to the ways that a user can access, use, and manipulate a file or directory. Remember, a directory is just a special type of file and there are three permissions—read, write and execute—that can be assigned to a file. Ownership defines who has the right to assign permissions to the file. The groups are who receive the assigned file permissions. Groups are a convenient way to organize user accounts so that users may share files within their group. Thus, each user belongs to one or more sets of groups. These sets of users are the groups. There are three categories of groups used to assign file and directory permissions: *user*, *group*, and *other*. The last group (**other**) is anyone else who can log onto the system. Different types of permissions can be assigned to the different levels of groups.

Every Linux file and directory has an owner. The owner of the file is usually the creator of the file. The owner of the file (or the super user) can assign the permissions for the file. When a new user account is created, such as **student**, that account is assigned a numeric user id (UID) as well. In Red Hat Linux, the default is to use a number that is greater than 500 and greater than all other existing user IDs.

When Red Hat Linux creates a new user account, by default it also creates a new group for every new user, and that group name is the user's login name. By default, each user belongs to that group. That group is assigned to every file the user creates. Again, that group name is the same as the user name. If the user name were **student**, that user's group name would also be **student** and the user, **student**, would belong to the group, **student**. Red Hat Linux also assigns a numeric value to that group (GID). The default is to use the smallest number greater than 500 that is greater than all other group IDs. Thus, if **cgillay** were the first user, then **cgillay**'s user id would be **500** and there would be a group **cgillay** with a group id of **500**. If **student** were the second user, the user id would be **501** and **student** would belong to the student group with an group id of **501**. Supplementary groups can be created and users can belong to multiple groups.

All the information about users and groups is kept in two files. User information is stored in the **/etc/passwd** file. Group information is kept in the **/etc/group** file. Only the super user (root) may create users and groups. These files can be edited directly by the root user as well.

There are several commands to manage and view groups and ownership of files and directories. These include **chgrp**, **chown**, **groups**, and **id**.

The **chgrp** command changes which groups can access a file or directory. Only the owner of the file or the root can use this command. The syntax for **chgrp** is

```
chgrp [options] newgroup [file]
```

where *newgroup* is either a group name or group ID number. Table 8.6, "**chgrp** Options," lists some of the major options used with the **chgrp** command.

Option	Name	Result
-c	Change	Displays information only about files that were changed.
-R	Recursive	Traverses the directory tree making changes in the tree.
-v	Verbose	Displays all information about changes that are made.

Table 8.6 • chgrp Options

The **chown** command changes the ownership of one or more files. Only the root may use this command. Ordinary users cannot. The syntax for **chown** is

```
chown [options] newowner [:group]] file
```

where *newowner* is either a user ID number or a login name that is located in the **/etc/passwd** file. Table 8.7, "**chown** Options," lists some of the major options used with the **chown** command.

Option	Name	Result
-c	Change	Displays information only about files that were changed.
-R	Recursive	Traverses the directory tree making changes in the tree.
-v	Verbose	Displays all information about changes that are made.

Table 8.7 • chown Options

The **groups** command allows you to see to which groups you belong to as well as what groups others users belong to. The syntax is **groups** [*options*] [*users*]. The groups and members of the groups are located in the **/etc/passwd** and **/etc/group** files.

The **id** command will display information about yourself or another user. It will display your user name; **uid** (user id number); **gid** (group id number); and additional group IDs. The syntax is as follows:

```
id [options] [username]
```

Table 8.8, "**id** Options," lists some of the major options used with the **id** command.

Option	Name	Result
-g	Group	Displays only group id.
-G	Supplementary groups	Displays only the additional groups you or another user belong to.
-n	Name	When used with **-u**, **-g**, or **-G**, displays the user name, not the group number.
-u	User id	Displays only the user id number.

Table 8.8 id Options

You may also find the value of the environmental variables for users and groups by using the **echo $USER** or **echo $GROUPS** command.

8.8 ● Activity: Looking at Users and Groups

Note: The BOOK2 disk mounted. Your home directory is the default directory. A terminal window is open.

STEP 1   Key in the following: **ls -l /etc/passwd /etc/group** Enter

```
[cgillay@linux72  cgillay]$  ls -l /etc/passwd  /etc/group
-rw-r—r-- 1      root  root    732    Aug 6   09:41 /etc/group
-rw-r—r-- 1      root  root    1578   Aug 17  22:54 /etc/passwd
[cgillay@linux72  cgillay]$
```

WHAT'S HAPPENING? By looking at the long listing, you can see that the owner and group ownership of these files is root. You also see that no one but the **root** has read and write (**rw**) permissions.

STEP 2   Key in the following: **cat /etc/passwd** Enter

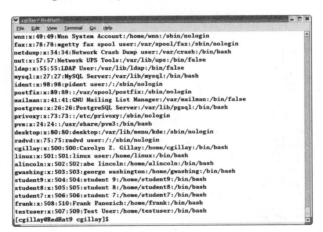

WHAT'S HAPPENING? Your screen display will be different. However, each entry in this file has the format of *username :password :uid :gid :comments :homedir :shell*. Details about each field include the following:

- *username*   A unique character string identifying the account. Usually it is the name that the user logs in with. For special accounts such as **bin** or **daemon**, it would be the name of the account.
- *password*   The password is encrypted and represented by an **x**. If the character is an *, the account is disabled and that user cannot log in. The password may be changed only by root or by the user with the **passwd** command.
- *uid*   The user id, which is a unique number the system uses to identify the account. The system uses this number internally when dealing with processes and file permissions. The **uid** is more convenient for the system, whereas the user name is more convenient for the human user.
- *gid*   The group id, which is a unique number referring to the user's default group.

- *comments*   Miscellaneous information that appears about the user, such as the user's real name. Other information can be kept here as well, such as the user's address or phone number. Programs such as **mail** and **finger** use this information to identify users.
- *homedir*   The user's home directory. When the user logs on, the shell finds the current working directory named in **homedir**.
- *shell*   The name of the program to run when the user logs in. Usually this is the full path name of a shell.

Table 8.9, "/etc/**passwd** Entries," breaks down one user

```
cgillay:x:500:500:Carolyn Z. Gillay:/home/cgillay:/bin/bash
```

username	password	uid	gid	comments	homedir	shell
cgillay:	x:	500:	500:	Carolyn Z. Gillay:	/home/cgillay:	/bin/bash

Table 8.9 • /etc/passwd Entries

STEP 3   Key in the following: **cat /etc/group** Enter

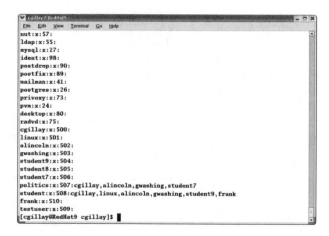

WHAT'S **HAPPENING?**   Your screen display will be different. However, each entry in this file has the format of *groupname:password:gid:members*. Details about each field include the following:

- *groupname*   A unique character string identifying the group. This is what is displayed when you issue the **ls -l** command.
- *password*   Usually left blank, as groups normally do not have passwords. If there were a password, it would be encrypted.
- *gid*   The group id, used by the system to refer to the group.
- *members*   A list of all users who belong to the group but who have a different **gid** in **/etc/password.** That is to say, this list does not contain those users who have this group set as their default group in **/etc/password**; it is only for users who are additional members of the group. The list is delimited by commas with no spaces.

Table 8.10, "/etc/**group** Entries," breaks down two groups, **alincoln** and **student**.

groupname	password	gid	members
alincoln:	x:	502	
student:	x:	504	alincoln, cgillay, gwashing, linux, student9

Table 8.10 • /etc/group Entries

WHAT'S HAPPENING? When you log in, you are automatically assigned to the group id given in the **/etc/passwd** file, as well as to any additional groups that you belong to in **/etc/group**. For a user, this means that you have access to any files on the system with a group id contained in one of these lists. There can be an additional assigned group password so that the user has to know his own password to log in and the group password to access any files or directories protected by a group password. In the example above, **alincoln** has a group called **alincoln** assigned the gid of **502**. The **student** group is a little different. It still has a **gid** of **504**. However, note that there is no user called **student** who is a member of the **student** group. This is an example of a group that was created without a corresponding user. This is a common practice when managing a computer system. For instance, you may have files that you want to allow access to for all the users who are salespeople. Each salesperson has a user logon name such as **cgillay** and **alincoln**. But rather than adding **cgillay** to **alincoln's** group and vice versa, instead, you create a group (not user) called **sales**. Then all sales people get assigned to their own group and to the **sales** group. You may see what groups you are a member of by using the **groups** command.

STEP 4   Key in the following: **groups** [Enter]

```
[cgillay@linux72  cgillay]$  groups
cgillay  politics  student
[cgillay@linux72  cgillay]$
```

WHAT'S HAPPENING? Your display will be different. In this example, **cgillay** belongs to the group **cgillay** and to the groups called **student** and **politics**. This means that any file that has group permissions for **student, politics,** or **cgillay** is available to the user **cgillay**. Groups are often used to limit use of hardware. For instance, if you had a color printer that you accessed via **/dev/color** and you wanted to allow only certain users to print to that printer, you could create a group called **color**, assign the device to this group, and make this special file readable only for the **color** group and not readable for any other user. You would then add anyone who was allowed to use the color printer to the **color** group in the **/etc/group** file. You may also see the environmental value of **GROUPS** by using the **echo** command to display the value.

STEP 5   Key in the following: **echo $GROUPS** [Enter]

```
[cgillay@RedHat9  cgillay]$  echo $GROUPS
500
[cgillay@RedHat9  cgillay]$
```

WHAT'S HAPPENING? This tells you your group number, 500. However, this information is not as complete as you might like. The **id** command can give you more specific information.

STEP 6   Key in the following: **id** [Enter]

```
[cgillay@linux72  cgillay]$  id
uid=500(cgillay)  gid=500(cgillay)  groups=500(cgillay),504  (student),508(politics)
[cgillay@linux72  cgillay]$
```

WHAT'S HAPPENING? Here you see the user id number (**uid**) and group id number (**gid**) of the current user, **cgillay**. You also see all the groups that this user belongs to with both the group name and group number displayed. You can display the supplemental groups of the current user.

STEP 7   Key in the following: **id -nG** Enter

```
[cgillay@linux72   cgillay]$   id -nG
cgillay  politics  student
[cgillay@linux72   cgillay]$
```

WHAT'S HAPPENING? You see the groups that this user belongs to in human readable form. You can even see what groups other users belong to.

STEP 8   Key in the following: **id student9** Enter

```
[cgillay@linux72   cgillay]$   id student9
uid=504(student9)  gid=509(student9)  groups=509(student9),504(student)
[cgillay@linux72   cgillay]$
```

WHAT'S HAPPENING? The identification information for **student9** indicates that he has a user id of **504**, a group id of **504**, and he belongs to two groups: **student9** and **student**. The **student** group is a group without a corresponding user.

STEP 9   Key in the following: **id student** Enter

```
[cgillay@linux72   cgillay]$ id student
id: student: No such user
[cgillay@linux72   cgillay]$
```

WHAT'S HAPPENING? Although there is a group called **student** that several users on this system belong to, there is no user called **student**. You may change group memberships using the Nautilus file manager.

STEP 10   Double-click your home directory icon on the desktop. Click **Information**. Click **Tree**. Make **/mnt/floppy** the default directory.

STEP 11   Right-click **sports**. Click **Show Properties**. Click the **Permissions** tab.

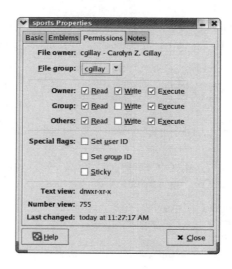

WHAT'S HAPPENING? The **Properties** sheet **Permissions** tab shows that the **Owner (User)** has **Read**, **Write**, and **Execute** permissions, whereas the **Group** and **Others** have only **Read** and **Execute** permission. The owner of the file is **cgillay**. Whenever you see **Owner**, think **User**. You will see that the three types of users are **User** (**u**), **Group** (**g**), and **Others** (**o**). At the command line, **u**, **g**, and **o** are used. **Others** is the "world." The graphical permissions are shown in check boxes to indicate what the valid permissions are, whereas the text permissions are shown as they appear in the command line: **drwxrwxr-x**. The **d** represents a directory and the **-** means there is no write permission for **Groups** and **Others**.

If this user belongs to more than one group, the user can change the group to one of the groups listed by clicking the down arrow in the **File group** drop-down list box and selecting a different group. Note that the owner of the file cannot be changed in this property sheet.

STEP 12 If available, click the down arrow in the **File group** drop-down list box.

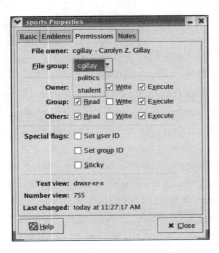

WHAT'S HAPPENING? In this example, there are three groups available: **cgillay**, **politics**, and **student**. By changing the group to a group other than **cgillay**, the user **cgillay** is allowing access to this directory to anyone who is a member of the alternate group. The permissions can be the same as those of the owner, or they can be altered for the group.

STEP 13 Click outside the drop-down list box. Close the dialog box. Right-click **ast.99**. Click **Properties**. Click the **Permissions** tab.

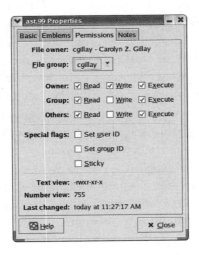

WHAT'S HAPPENING? The **Properties** sheet **Permissions** tab shows that the **Owner** (**User**) and **Group** have **Read**, **Write**, and **Execute** permission, whereas the **Group** and **Others** have only **Read** and **Execute** permission. In this case, both the owner and group are **cgillay**.

STEP 14 Close the dialog box. Close the Nautilus file manager window. Activate the terminal window.

STEP 15 Key in the following: **cd /mnt/floppy; ls -dl sports -l ast.99** [Enter]

```
[cgillay@linux72  cgillay]$  cd /mnt/floppy; ls -dl sports  ast.99
-rwxrwxr-x    1    cgillay      cgillay       148    Oct 13 10:18 ast.99
drwxrwxr-x    2    cgillay      cgillay      1024    Oct 12 21:21 sports
[cgillay@linux72  floppy]$
```

WHAT'S HAPPENING? The permissions are identical to those displayed in the Nautilus file manager window. In addition to the nine permissions for user, group, and other, there are three more permissions that control special attributes for executable files and directories. These are *SUID (Set User ID)*, *SGID (Set Group ID)*, and the *sticky bit*. Each of these items is a bit in a file that can be on or off. The SUID bit is for executable files only.

When a program is executed, normally its process is "owned" by the user who launched the program. However, if the executable file has its SUID bit set, then the file's original owner owns the process no matter which user launched the program. Typically, when the SUID is set, the file's owner is the root. This offers anyone temporary root access for the entire time the program is executing. Thus, when the SUID is on, the person running the program inherits the permissions granted to the program. The owner of the program remains root (or the original owner), who actually owns the program. This means that the user running the program has the effective ID of the program's original owner, who remains the same no matter who executes the program. If, for instance, the program has the ability to read, write, and delete files, the user running that program has the same rights, regardless of what his normal permissions are. An example of this is the **passwd** command. The **/etc/passwd** file can be modified only by root. However, you want to grant users the right to change their password, which means the **/etc/passwd** file must be updated. By setting the SUID on, any user can execute the **passwd** program, which then, for that specific time of execution only, inherits the permissions of the root so the **/etc/passwd** file can be updated.

The SGID (Set Group ID) works the same way for groups. When the SGID is on, it sets the process group owner to the file's group owner. When SGID is on, the effective group ID of the person running the program is the group ID assigned to the program. The person running the program has all the permissions assigned to the group that owns the program. The SGID has a special effect on directories. When the SGID is set on a directory, any new files created in that directory are assigned the same group ownership as the directory itself. This means that if you have a directory called **/politics** with the group **politicians** and the SGID is set, then all files created in that directory will have the group **politicians** assigned to it, regardless of the of the creator's group. This can be very valuable for a team that is sharing files because all files in directory then provide access to all members of the group.

At one time, the sticky bit, when applied to executable files, told the operating system to save a copy of the program in memory after the program finished executing. In this way, a frequently used program would execute faster, since the program would not need to be loaded every time it was used. It was useful for large programs or programs that were run frequently. However, today, with memory being relatively inexpensive and with modern virtual memory techniques, sticky bits are rarely placed on executable programs.

However, the sticky bit is used with directories. For a directory, the sticky bit has a different meaning. If the sticky bit is set on a directory, only the owner of a file within that directory can rename or delete that file. Any other user may not delete or rename files in that directory, even if he has write access to the directory. To look at SUID, you can look at the permissions of the **mount** command or the **passwd** commands as examples. Normally, the **passwd** program is located in the **/usr/bin** directory, and the **mount** command is located in the **/bin** directory.

STEP 16   Key in the following: **ls -l /usr/bin/passwd /bin/mount** Enter

```
[cgillay@linux72   floppy]$   ls -l /usr/bin/passwd /bin/mount
-rwsr-xr-x 1       root   root   57628 Jul 24 2001 /bin/mount
-r-s--x--x 1       root   root   13476 Aug 6 2001 /usr/bin/passwd
[cgillay@linux72   floppy]$
```

WHAT'S **HAPPENING?** Here, the owner is **root** and the group is **root** for both programs. In the **/bin/mount** program, the first set of permissions (**rws**) indicates that the **SUID** is on. The **s** replaces the **x.** Thus, when you mount a device, you have the effective permissions of the root during the execution of the **mount** program, but root never gives up ownership. If you look at the second program, **/usr/bin/passwd**, the first set of permissions (**r-s**) indicate that the **SUID** is on. The **s** replaces the **x.** Again, when you change your password with the **passwd** command, you have the effective permissions of the root during the execution of the **passwd** command, but root never gives up ownership. If colors are set, files that have on **SUID** are highlighted in red.

STEP 17   Key in the following: **ls -ld /politics** Enter

```
[cgillay@linux72   floppy]$   ls -ld /politics
drwxrxsr-t       2 root   politics       4096  Aug  6 09:47 /politics
[cgillay@linux72   floppy]$
```

WHAT'S **HAPPENING?** In this example, the **/politics** directory has its sticky bit set on. The last set of permissions (**r-t**) tells you that. The **t** replaces the **x.** This means that in this directory, only the owner of a file within the directory can rename or delete that file. Any other user may not delete or rename files of other users in that directory, even if he has write access to the directory.

STEP 18   Key in the following: **ls -l ast.99; chown alincoln ast.99** Enter

```
[cgillay@linux72   floppy]$ ls -l ast.99; chown alincoln ast.99
-rwxr-xr-x     1  cgillay  cgillay    148  Jul 4 11:06 ast.99
chown: changing ownership of 'ast.99': Operation not permitted
[cgillay@linux72   floppy]$
```

WHAT'S **HAPPENING?** You issued the command **chown.** You then keyed in **alincoln** (new owner) for the file **ast.99.** Here you see that you do not have permission to change owners. Remember, only root can execute the **chown** command. However, you can change groups, but you must belong to the group to do so.

STEP 19   Key in the following: **chgrp student ast.99; ls -l ast.99** Enter

```
[cgillay@linux72  floppy]$  chgrp student ast.99; ls -l ast.99
-rwxr-xr-x     1  cgillay  student        148  Jul 4 11:06 ast.99
[cgillay@linux72  floppy]$
```

WHAT'S **HAPPENING?** Since **cgillay** belongs to the **student** group, she could change the group access.

STEP 20 Key in the following: **chgrp alincoln ast.99** [Enter]

```
[cgillay@linux72  floppy]$  chgrp  alincoln  ast.99
chgrp: changing group of 'ast.99'"  Operation not permitted
[cgillay@linux72  floppy]$
```

WHAT'S **HAPPENING?** Since **cgillay** is not a member of the **alincoln** group, she cannot change the group to **alincoln** for the file **ast.99**.

STEP 21 Key in the following: **cd** [Enter]

WHAT'S **HAPPENING?** You have returned to your home directory.

8.9 • Permissions

As stated previously, there are three permission types—read, write and execute. When these permissions are applied to files, they grant the user the rights to:

read (r)   look at the file's contents.
write (w)   change the contents of the file or delete the file.
execute (x)   run the file as a program (if it is a program).

When these permissions are applied to directories, they grant the user the rights to:

read (r)   list the contents of a directory.
write (w)   add or remove files from a directory.
execute (x)   access file and subdirectories, which is the ability to change into this directory with **cd**. Within a directory structure, normally **r** and **x** are paired.

When a user creates a file or a directory, the operating system normally assigns a default set of permissions. These defaults are established either by accepting what is set by the installation of Red Hat or changes that are made by the root (system administrator). The user can change these default permissions for files and directories he has created and assign different levels of permissions to the different types of users in his groups. Thus, the elements that make up the security system for files and directories in Linux can be summarized as follows: there are three levels of permissions (read, write, and execute), and those permissions may be assigned to three types of users (user, group, and other). For example, if you look at a file such as april.txt, using the ls-l command, you would see the following display:

```
-rwxr-x-- 1  cgillay   student  86  Jan 21 10:30   april.txt
```

Using what you have learned, you can see the breakdown of permissions and ownership as exemplified in Table 8.11, "Ownership and Permissions."

File Type	User(Owner) Permissions	Group Permissions	Other Permissions	User (Owner)	Group
-	rwx	r-x	---	cgillay	student
Ordinary file	The user (owner) can read, write, and execute the file.	The group can read and execute the file.	All others have no access to the file.	The user (owner) is cgillay.	The group that can access the file is student. student has the permissions specified under group permissions.

Table 8.11 • Ownership and Permissions

There are some differences when you look at directory entries—a home directory and one that you might create. A typical directory entry might be

```
drwxr-xr-x    2   cgillay     cgillay  4086   Jan 21 10:30   cgillay
```

The breakdown of the listing is shown in Table 8.12, "Directory Ownership and Permissions."

File Type	User(Owner) Permissions	Group Permissions	Other Permissions	User (Owner)	Group
d	rwx	r-x	r-x	cgillay	cgillay
Directory	The user (owner) can add or remove files from the directory, list the contents of the directory, and change to the directory, i.e., traverse the directory structure.	The group can list the contents of the directory but may not add or delete files in it. The group member can change to the directory, i.e., traverse the directory structure.	All others can list the contents of the directory but may not add or delete files in it. Others can change to the directory, i.e., traverse the directory structure.	The user (owner) is cgillay.	The group that can access the directory is cgillay.

Table 8.12 • Directory Ownership and Permissions

A typical home directory entry might be

```
drwx --- ---   2   cgillay     cgillay  4086   Oct 21 10:30   cgillay
```

The breakdown of the listing is shown in Table 8.13, "Home Directory Ownership and Permissions."

File Type	User(Owner) Permissions	Group Permissions	Other Permissions	User (Owner)	Group
d	rwx	---	---	cgillay	cgillay
Directory	The user (owner) can add or remove files from the directory, list the contents of the directory, and change to the directory, i.e., traverse the directory structure.	The group cannot add or delete files in the directory. In fact, they cannot even list the contents of the directory, nor can they change to the directory, i.e., they cannot traverse the directory structure.	All others cannot add or delete files in the directory. In fact, they cannot even list the contents of the directory, nor can they change to the directory, i.e., they cannot traverse the directory structure.	The user (owner) is **cgillay**.	The group that can access the directory is **cgillay**.

Table 8.13 • Home Directory Ownership and Permissions

The primary command to manage the permissions on files and directories is **chmod**.

chmod   Change permissions for a file or directory. Only the owner or root can use this command. The syntax is

```
chmod [options]  mode[,mode].. file..or chmod [options]  octal-mode file.
```

To use the **chmod** command, you use a + (plus) to add permissions and a - (minus) to remove permissions. An = (equal) sets the permissions to exactly what was specified and removes permissions for fields that are unspecified. You may assign those permissions to **u** (user/owner), **g** (group), **o** (other), or **a** (all). In Tables 8.11, 8.12, and 8.13, note that the term "user" is used instead of "owner." In fact, you are talking about ownership. However, you do not want to mix up permissions assigned to **o** (other) with those assigned to **u** (user/owner).

You use the same syntax to apply permissions to directories, but remember that **x** (execute) has a different meaning. In a directory, execute permission means that a user has the right to navigate through the directory structure and change to that directory. Thus, the user could have a file that was readable by all users, but if he placed it in a directory that had no execute privileges, then no user could read the file even though each user had read and write permissions to the file.

Table 8.14, "**chmod** Options," lists some of the major options used with the **chmod** command.

Option	Name	Result
-c	Change	Displays information only about files that were changed.
-R	Recursive	Traverses the directory tree, making changes in the tree.
-v	Verbose	Displays all information about changes that are made.

Table 8.14 • chmod Options

8.10 • Activity: Using Permissions

Note: The BOOK2 disk mounted. Your home directory is the default directory. A terminal window is open.

STEP 1   Key in the following: **cd   /mnt/floppy** [Enter]

STEP 2   Key in the following: **ls -l jup.99; chmod -x jup.99; ls -l jup.99** [Enter]

```
[cgillay@RedHat9   floppy]$   ls -l jup.99; chmod -x jup.99; ls -l
jup.99
-rwxr-xr-x    1   cgillay   cgillay         190   Jul 4   11:06 jup.99
-rw-r--r--    1   cgillay   cgillay         190   Jul 4   11:06 jup.99
[cgillay@RedHat9   floppy]$
```

WHAT'S **HAPPENING?** You may change file and directory permissions on those files you own with the **chmod** command. By using the **-x** option, you removed execute permission for all levels of users. You may also be specific when assigning permissions.

STEP 3   Key in the following: **ls -l mer.99; chmod -v o-xr mer.99; ls -l mer.99** [Enter]

```
[cgillay@RedHat9   floppy]$   ls -l mer.99; chmod -v o-xr mer.99; ls
-l mer.99
-rwxr-xr-x    1   cgillay   cgillay       406   Jul 4   11:06   mer.99
mode of 'mer.99' changed to 750 (rwxr-x--)
-rwxr-x--    1   cgillay   cgillay       406   Jul 4   11:06   mer.99
[cgillay@RedHat9   floppy]$
```

STEP 4   Key in the following: **ls -l ven.99; chmod og-rwx ven.99; ls -l ven.99** [Enter]

```
[cgillay@RedHat9 floppy]$ ls- l ven.99; chmod og-rxw ven.99; ls
-l ven.99
-rwxr-xr-x 1 cgillay cgillay 478 Jul 4 11:06 ven.99
-rwx------ 1 cgillay cgillay 478 Jul 4 11:06 ven.99
[cgillay@RedHat9 floppy]$
```

WHAT'S **HAPPENING?** Here you removed all the permissions (**rwx**) for the group and for **others** for the **ven.99** file.

STEP 5   Key in the following: **ls -l jup.99; cp jup.99 jupiter.99; ls -l jupiter.99** [Enter]

```
[cgillay@RedHat9    floppy]$   ls -l jup.99; cp jup.99 jupiter.99; ls
-l jupiter.99
```

```
-rw-r--r--  1  cgillay  cgillay       190  Jul 4  11:06   jup.99
-rw-r--r--  1  cgillay  cgillay       190  Jul 4  19:24   jupiter.99
[cgillay@RedHat9   floppy]$
```

WHAT'S HAPPENING? When you copied the file, you retained the same permissions as the original file. However, **jupiter.99** did not exist. What happens to permissions when there is an existing file that you are going to overwrite?

STEP 6   Key in the following: **ls -l jupiter.99 ast.99** (Enter)

STEP 7   Key in the following: **cp ast.99 jupiter.99; ls -l ast.99 jupiter.99** (Enter)

```
[cgillay@RedHat9 floppy]$ ls -l jupiter.99 ast.99
-rwxr-xr-x    1  cgillay  student   148  Jul 4  11:06   ast.99
-rw-r—r—     1  cgillay  cgillay   190  Jul 5  19:24   jupiter.99
[cgillay@RedHat9 floppy]$ cp ast.99 jupiter.99; ls -l ast.99
jupiter.99
-rwxr-xr-x    1  cgillay  student   148  Jul 4  11:06   ast.99
-rw-r—r—     1  cgillay  cgillay   148  Jul 5  19:28   jupiter.99
[cgillay@RedHat9   floppy]$
```

WHAT'S HAPPENING? When you copy a file to a file that already exists, the file retains its original permissions and does not take on the permissions of the file that overwrote it. However, if you want to preserve the permissions and ownership, you can use the **-p** option with the **cp** command.

STEP 8   Key in the following: **cp -p ast.99 jupiter.99; ls -l ast.99 jupiter.99** (Enter)

```
[cgillay@RedHat9   floppy]$  cp -p ast.99 jupiter.99; ls -l ast.99
jupiter.99
-rwxr-xr-x    1  cgillay  student   148  Jul 4  11:06   ast.99
-rwxr-xr-x    1  cgillay  student   148  Jul 4  11:06   jupiter.99
[cgillay@RedHat9   floppy]$
```

WHAT'S HAPPENING? As you can see, even though **jupiter.99** existed, the permissions and group ownership were taken from the **ast.99** file.

STEP 9   Key in the following:

    chmod -wx jupiter.99; ls -l jupiter.99; rm jupiter.99 (Enter)

```
[cgillay@RedHat9   floppy]$   chmod -wx jupiter.99; ls -l
jupiter.99; rm jupiter.99
-r--r--r--    1  cgillay  student    148  Jul 4  11:06  jupiter.99
rm: remove write-protected regular file 'jupiter.99'?
```

WHAT'S HAPPENING? You removed the write and execute permissions from the **jupiter.99** file. However, since you are the owner of the file, even though it is write-protected, you may still delete it. In this case, you are not going to delete it.

STEP 10 Key in the following: **n** (Enter)

STEP 11 Key in the following: **ls -l *.99** [Enter]

```
[cgillay@RedHat9  floppy]$  ls -l *.99
-rwxr-xr-x  1  cgillay  student    148  Jul 4  11:06  ast.99
-rw-r--r--  1  cgillay  cgillay    190  Jul 4  11:06  jup.99
-r--r--r--  1  cgillay  student    148  Jul 4  11:06  jupiter.99
-rwxr-x---  1  cgillay  cgillay    406  Jul 4  11:06  mer.99
-rwx------  1  cgillay  cgillay    478  Jul 4  11:06  ven.99
[cgillay@RedHat9  floppy]$
```

WHAT'S HAPPENING? Here you have a set of files with different permissions you have set. The ast.99 file has a standard set of permissions, but the student group has access to it. You altered jup.99 so that the group and others can only read the file. You altered jupiter.99 to make it a read-only file for all levels of users. The file mer.99 has full privileges for the user (owner) and read and execute permission for the group, but others have no permission. The ven.99 file has permissions only for the user (owner). How do file permissions work if another user tries to manipulate these files and if the new user belongs to a common group?

STEP 12 Key in the following: **chmod g+w ast.99; ls -l ast.99** [Enter]

```
[cgillay@RedHat9  floppy]$  chmod g+w ast.99; ls -l ast.99
-rwxrwxr-x  1  cgillay  student      148  Jul 4  11:06  ast.99
[cgillay@RedHat9  floppy]$
```

WHAT'S HAPPENING? You have now given the **student** group write permission for the **ast.99** file.

Note 1: If you do not have another user that you may log in as, you cannot do the next steps.

Note 2: Check with your instructor for the user ID you may log in as if they are different than the textbook as assigned in Appendix A.

STEP 13 Key in the following: **cd; umount /mnt/floppy** [Enter]

STEP 14 Close the terminal window. Click the Main Menu button. Click **Log Out**. Click **OK**.

WHAT'S HAPPENING? You have logged out of GNOME, but not out of your original user login.

STEP 15 Key in the following: **exit** [Enter]

```
Red Hat Linux release 7.2 (Enigma)
Kernel 2.4.7-10 on an i686

Linux72  login:
```

WHAT'S HAPPENING? You do not have to reboot to log in as a different user.

STEP 16 Use **student9** as your login name and **student9** as your password.

STEP 17 Key in the following: **mount /mnt/floppy** [Enter]

STEP 18 Key in the following: **cd /mnt/floppy; ls -l *.99** [Enter]

```
[student9@RedHat9  floppy]$  ls -l *.99
-rwxrwxr-x 1  cgillay   student        148  Jul 4  11:06  ast.99
-rw-r--r-- 1  cgillay   cgillay        190  Jul 4  11:06  jup.99
-r--r--r-- 1  cgillay   student        148  Jul 4  11:06  jupiter.99
-rwxr-x--- 1  cgillay   cgillay        406  Jul 4  11:06  mer.99
-rwx------ 1  cgillay   cgillay        478  Jul 4  11:06  ven.99
[student9@RedHat9  floppy]$
```

WHAT'S HAPPENING? You are now logged in as **student9**. Note that you are not using GNOME; you are at the command prompt. You mounted the BOOK2 floppy. The owner and permissions remain the same as they were in the previous steps. In this example, **cgillay** is still the owner of these files. Your user name should be the owner of these files.

STEP 19 Key in the following: **groups; cat jupiter.99 ven.99** Enter

```
[student9@RedHat9 floppy]$ groups; cat jupiter.99 ven.99
student9 student

Jupiter is the largest planet
in our Solar System.  It has a
giant red spot on it.  Huge storms
larger than our earth that last
more than a century take place
on the planet Jupiter.
cat ven.99: Permission denied
[student9@RedHat9  floppy]$
```

WHAT'S HAPPENING? Although you belong to the **student9** and **student** group, only the owner of the file can access the file **ven.99**. Your owner name will vary. In this example, the owner is **cgillay**. You could open **jupiter.99** because everybody has read privileges for that file.

STEP 20 Key in the following: **rm ven.99** Enter

```
[student9@linux72 floppy]$  rm ven.99
rm: remove write-protected regular file 'ven.99'?
```

WHAT'S HAPPENING? The system is waiting for a response.

STEP 21 Key in the following: **y** Enter

```
[student9@RedHat9 floppy]$  rm ven.99
rm: remove write-protected file 'ven.99'? y
rm: cannot remove 'ven.99' Permission denied
[student9@RedHat9  floppy]$
```

WHAT'S HAPPENING? As you can see, the permissions work very effectively.

STEP 22 Key in the following: **ls -l ast.99; rm ast.99** Enter

```
[student9@RedHat9 floppy]$  ls -l ast.99; rm ast.99
-rwxrwxr-x      1 cgillay  student       148 Jul 4  11:06  ast.99
rm: cannot remove 'ast.99' Permission denied
[student9@RedHat9  floppy]$
```

WHAT'S HAPPENING? Although you are not the owner of the file, **student** is a member of the **cgillay** (or user login) group. Why, then, since the group has **w** permissions, can you not delete the file? The **w** permissions allow you to add or remove files in a directory. Remember directory permissions. Note that there is a period in the next command. The period is dot notation for the current directory, **/mnt/floppy**.

STEP 23   Key in the following: **ls -l -d .** [Enter]

```
[student9@linux72 floppy]$  ls -l -d .
drwxr-xr-x 8  cgillay   student     2048   Oct 15 15:41.
[student9@linux72   floppy]$
```

WHAT'S HAPPENING? Although **student9** is a member of the student group, which does have read, write, and execute (**rwx**) permissions for the file called **ast.99**, the directory permissions are only read and execute (**r-x**). This means that only the owner (or root user) may delete a file from the directory. Therefore you, as user **student9**, cannot remove the file. Thus, directory permissions override file permissions.

STEP 24   Key in the following: **cp   *.99   /public** [Enter]

STEP 25   Key in the following: **cd   /public; ls -l -d   .; ls -l** [Enter]

```
[student9@linux72 floppy]$   cp *.99 /public
cp: cannot open 'mer.99' for reading: Permission denied
cp: cannot open 'ven.99' for reading: Permission denied
[student9@linux72 floppy]$   cd /public; ls -l -d .; ls -l
drwxrxr-    2     root   student     4096   Oct 16 09:27   .
total 12
-rwxrwxr-x 1    student9 student9    148    Oct 16   09:27   ast.99
-rw-rw-r-- 1    student9 student9    190    Oct 16   09:27   jup.99
-r--r--r-- 1    student9 student9    148    Oct 16   09:27   jupiter.99
[student9@linux72   public]$
```

WHAT'S HAPPENING? You copied the ***.99** files to the **/public** directory. Because you did not preserve the permissions or ownership, the files are now owned by **student9**. The file **mer.99** could not be copied because only the owner and group could copy the file (using read permission), and you are neither the owner, nor a member of the **cgillay** (or user) group. The file **ven.99** could not be copied because only the owner could copy the file (using read permission). You then changed directories to the **public** directory. This directory has a different set of permissions. The owner is **root**, but the group **student** has write permission. **student9** is a member of the **student** group. Write permission in a directory gives you the permission to add or delete files from a directory. Now you should be able to delete all the **.99** files.

STEP 26   Key in the following: **rm   *.99** [Enter]

```
[student9@linux72 public] $ rm *.99
rm: remove write-protected file 'jupiter.99'?
```

STEP 27   Key in the following: **y** [Enter]

```
[student9@linux72   public]$   $ rm *.99
rm: remove write-protected file 'jupiter.99'? y
[student9@linux72   public]$
```

WHAT'S HAPPENING? Since you are a member of both your login name group (**student9** in this example) and a member of the **student** group, you have the directory permission to remove files, even a read-only file.

STEP 28 Key in the following: **cd /politics; ls -l** [Enter]

```
[student9@linux72 public] $ cd /politics; ls -l
total 8
-rwxrwxr-- 1      alincoln  alincoln  17 Aug 6  09:45 test.fil
-rwxrwxr-- 1      alincoln  student   23 Aug 6  09:47 testing.fil
[student9@linux72  politics]$
```

WHAT'S HAPPENING? You are in a different directory, the **politics** directory. It would seem clear that you cannot delete **test.fil** since you are not the user **alincoln**, nor are you a member of the **alincoln** group. However, since you are logged on as **student9**, and thus a member of the **student** group, you do have delete privileges for the **testing.fil** file.

STEP 29 Key in the following: **rm testing.fil; ls -ld . [Enter]**

```
[student9@linux72 politics]$ rm testing.fil, ls -ld .
rm: cannot unlink 'testing.fil': Permission denied.
drwxrwxr-t 2    root    politics 4096  Aug 6 09:47 .
[student9@linux72  politics]$
```

WHAT'S HAPPENING? You could not remove the file. Directory permissions override file permissions. This directory has a sticky bit set. Note the **t** at the end of the directory permissions. When the sticky bit is set in a directory, only the owner of the file may remove or rename the file. However, since you are a member of the **student** group, you could edit the **testing.fil** file and save your changes to the **politics** directory.

STEP 30 Key in the following: **cd; umount /mnt/floppy** [Enter]

STEP 31 Key in the following: **exit** [Enter]

```
Red Hat Linux release 7.2 (Enigma)
Kernel 2.4.7-10 on an i686

Linux72 login: ]
```

WHAT'S HAPPENING? You do not have to reboot to log in as a different user.

STEP 32 Log in your usual way.

STEP 33 Key in the following: **mount /mnt/floppy; cd /mnt/floppy; rm jupiter.99** [Enter]

```
[cgillay@linux72  floppy]$ mount /mnt/floppy; cd /mnt/floppy; rm jupiter.99
rm: remove write-protected file 'jupiter.99'?
[cgillay@linux72  floppy]$
```

WHAT'S HAPPENING? You are now logged in as the owner of the file. You may remove it.

STEP 34 Key in the following: **y** [Enter]

STEP 35 Key in the following: **ls jupiter.99; cd** [Enter]

```
rm: remove write-protected file 'jupiter.99'? y
[cgillay@linux72 floppy] $ ls jupiter.99; cd
ls: jupiter.99: No such file or directory
[cgillay@linux72   floppy]$
```

WHAT'S HAPPENING? Since you are the owner, you can do what you wish with the file. You then changed directories to your home directory.

8.11 • Octal Permissions

To alter permissions, you have been using *symbolic mode*. It was symbolic because you were using letters such as **-r**. There is another mode called *numeric mode*, *octal mode*, or *absolute mode*, in which you use bits and octal notation. You need to understand both modes because there are some occasions where symbolic mode will not work. You will often find that absolute mode rather than symbolic mode is used in documentation. Furthermore, at times you may find absolute mode more convenient.

A typical mode contains three characters, matching the three levels of permissions (user, group, and other). In addition, within each level there are three bits matching read, write, and execute permissions. Table 8.15, "Absolute Mode," demonstrates this.

User			Group			Other		
read	write	execute	read	write	execute	read	write	execute
400	200	100	40	20	10	4	2	1

Table 8.15 • Absolute Mode

You sum each number in each column to give octal permissions. Thus, for a file called **ast.99**, if you wanted to give read permission to everyone, you would choose the correct number from each column - 400 for the user, + 40 for the group, + 4 for everyone else. The command would then read **chmod 444 ast.99**. If you were using symbolic mode, you could issue the command as **chmod =r ast.99**. If you keyed in **chmod +r ast.99**, you would be granting read permission to everyone, but not removing other permissions. Using **=r** will assign read permission for everyone and at the same time, removing all other permissions.

Another way to look at the numeric mode of setting permissions is to assume read permissions are equal to 4, write permissions are equal to 2, execute permissions are equal to 1, and no permissions is equal to 0. You could then build a table and sum the permissions to reach the correct number to use with chmod. For instance, if you keyed in **chmod ug=rw,o=r ast.99** for the file **ast.99**, you would be assigning read and write permissions to both user and group and read permission only to others symbolically. However, you can use numeric permissions. Table 8.16, "Numeric Permissions," gives an example of this.

Permission	Owner	Group	Other
Read	4	4	4
Write	2	2	0
Execute	0	0	0
Total	6	6	4

Table 8.16 • Numeric Permissions

The command could then be issued as **chmod 664 ast.99**. If you use the table in Table 8.15, it also will derive the number 664 (read 400 + write 200 for user = 600; read 40 + 20 write for group = 60; and read =4 for others, which still totals 664). Another example might be if you install a program and want to make it available to everyone to execute on the system. You want to retain read, write, and execute permissions for the user, but execute only permissions for members of the group and the rest of the world. Symbolically, you could write the command as **chmod u=rwx,g=x,o=x ast.99** or you could derive the numeric value as exemplified in Table 8.17, "Numeric Permissions."

Permission	Owner	Group	Other
Read	4	0	0
Write	2	0	0
Execute	1	1	1
Total	7	1	1

Table 8.17 • Numeric Permissions

The command would then be **chmod 711 ast.99**. If you use the table in Table 8.15, it also will derive the number 711 (read 400 + write 200 + execute 100 for user = 700; execute 10 group = 10; and execute =1 for others, which still totals 711). As you work with numeric values, you will find common numeric codes that are most often used. See Table 8.18, "Commonly Used Absolute Modes."

Absolute Permission	Symbolic Permission	Meaning
600	u=rw,g=,o=	Owner has read and write permission.
644	u=rw,g=r,o=r	Owner has read and write permission. Group and others have read-only permission.
666	u=rw,g=rw,o=rw	Everyone has read and write permissions.
700	u=rwx,g=,o=	Owner has read, write, and execute permissions. If applied to a directory, only the owner has read and write to the directory. Directories must have the execute bit set.

710	u=rwx,g=x,o=	Owner has read, write, and execute permissions. Group has execute permission.
711	u=rwx,g=x,o=x	Owner has read, write, and execute permissions. Group and others have execute permission. This can be used with directories so that the group or others may not list the contents of a directory but would be able to retrieve a file from the directory if they knew the file name.
751	u=rwx,g=rx,o=x	Owner has read, write, and execute permissions. Group has read and execute permission, and others have execute permission.
755	u=rwx,g=rx,o=rx	Owner has read, write, and execute permissions. Group and others have read and execute permission. Only the owner can change the contents of the directory, but everyone may view the contents.
777	u=rwx,g=rwx,o=rwx	Everyone has read, write, and execute permissions.

Table 8.18 • Commonly Used Absolutes Mode

To further talk about permissions, whenever you create a file or a directory, Linux will assign default permissions to the file or directory. To disclose the default permission, you may use the **umask** command. The **umask** command is a "mask" that determines which permissions are on or off. The syntax is

```
umask [nnn]
```

where *nnn* is the umask value you are setting. You may view the values symbolically rather than numerically by using the **-S** option with **umask**. The default protections for your directories are set using a startup script (**/etc/profile**) when you boot the system. You may also place the **umask** command in your shell's startup file if you want a different default value from what the default permissions are. In Bash, the file is called **.bashrc**.

If you wanted to find the default permissions assigned to files, you would subtract the value found with **umask** from 666 (read/write permissions for owner, group, and others). If you wanted to find the default permissions assigned to directories, you would subtract the value found with **umask** from 777 (read/write/execute permissions for owner, group, and other). Thus, if you keyed in **umask** and the value 027 was returned, the results would be 640 (read/write permissions for the owner, read permissions for the group, and no permissions for the other). If applied to a directory, the result would be 750 (read/write/execute permission for the owner, read and execute permissions for the group, and no permissions for others). However, when doing the subtraction, use zero as the digit for each number less than zero. In the two examples, then, Table 8.19, "umask Values permissions," shows the results:

umask Applied to File	umask Applied to Directory
666	777
-027	-027
640	750

Table 8.19 • umask Values permissions

There is an even easier way to determine the mask. You can use the **-S** option with **umask**, which will print the symbolic form. The **umask** command allows you to set certain file permissions without having to set individual permissions for every file you create. For security reasons, when you create a file, the execute permission is left off; however, the execute permission is included in the directory permissions. If you want to change your umask values, you can use Table 8.20, "umask Values."

umask	File Permissions	Directory Permissions
7	None	None
6	None	Execute (x)
5	Write (w)	Write (w)
4	Write (w)	Write and Execute (wx)
3	Read (r)	Read (r)
2	Read (r)	Read and Execute (rx)
1	Read and Write (rw)	Read and Write (rw)
0	Read and Write (rw)	Read, Write, and Execute (rwx)

Table 8.20 • umask Values

Each **umask** value would be placed in the corresponding position: user, group, and other. So if you assigned an **umask** of 001, files that were created would be assigned read and write permissions for the user, group, and others. The directories that were created would be assigned read, write, and execute permissions for the owner and group, and read and write permissions for others.

8.12 • Activity: Using Numeric Permissions

Note: You are logged on as your usual user account. The BOOK2 disk mounted. Your home directory is the default directory. A terminal window is open.

STEP 1   Key in the following: **cd /mnt/floppy**

STEP 2   Key in the following: **umask; umask -S; umask 002; umask -S** [Enter]

```
   [cgillay@linux72   floppy]$   cd /mnt/floppy
   [cgillay@linux72   floppy]$   umask; umask -S; umask 002; umask -S
   0002
   u=rwx,g=rwx,o=rx
   u=rwx,g=rwx,o=rx
   [cgillay@linux72   floppy]$
```

WHAT'S HANGING? Your initial value may have been a different number. By keying in **umask** and **umask -S**, you saw what your default umask value was. In this case, it was **0002**. You may ignore the first 0 as it indicates that an octal number follows. You then changed the **umask** value to 002 and looked at it symbolically (**u=rwx,g=rwx,o=rx**). So, to calculate the default values that now will be assigned to files in the directory, subtract this number from 666. If you take 666 and subtract 002, the value becomes the absolute mode of 664. This should mean that for new files, user would have read and write permissions; group would have read and write permissions, and others would have read permission only. This matches the symbolic mode if you remember that the execute permission is always left off. Table 8.21, "Translating **umask** Values for Files," shows this graphically.

Permission	Owner	Group	Other
Read	4	4	4
Write	2	2	0
Execute	0	0	0
Total	6	6	4

Table 8.21 • Translating umask Values for Files

You also see this using the absolute mode values. Table 8.22, "Absolute Mode and **umask**," demonstrates this.

User			Group			Other		
read	write	execute	read	write	execute	read	write	execute
400	200	100	40	20	10	4	2	1
400	200		40	20		4		

Table 8.22 • Absolute Mode and umask

Again, 400 + 200 = 600 for the user (read and write); 40 + 20 = 60 for the group (read and write) and 4 = 4 for others equals a total of 664. So files in this directory should be assigned the default permissions of **-rw-rw-r--**. To test this, you can create a file and see what permissions are assigned.

STEP 3   Key in the following:
   cat > abc.def Enter
   This is a test. Enter
   Ctrl + d

STEP 4   Key in the following: **ls -l abc.def** Enter

```
[cgillay@linux72  floppy]$  cat > abc.def
This is a test.
[cgillay@linux72 floppy] $ ls -l abc.def
-rw-rw-r--      1       cgillay cgillay  16  Oct 16  20:24 abc.def
[cgillay@linux72  floppy]$
```

WHAT'S HAPPENING? Here the **umask** value did assign the "664" (**-rw-rw-r--**) set of permissions to the new file, **abc.def**, and did leave off the execute permission. You may also test the directory permissions. In this case, the **umask** value of 002 would be subtracted from 777. If you take 777 and subtract 002, the value becomes the absolute mode of 775. This should mean that a new directory would have the permissions of owner having read, write, and execute permission; group having read, write, and execute permissions; and others having read and execute permissions. Table 8.23, "Translating **umask** Values for Directories," shows this graphically.

Permission	Owner	Group	Other
Read	4	4	4
Write	2	2	0
Execute	1	1	1
Total	7	7	5

Table 8.23 • Translating umask Values for Directories

You also see this using the absolute mode values. Table 8.24, "Absolute Mode and **umask** Directory Values," demonstrates this.

User			Group			Other		
read	write	execute	read	write	execute	read	write	execute
400	200	100	40	20	10	4	2	1
400	200	100	40	20	10	4		1

Table 8.24 • Absolute Mode and umask Directory Values

Again, 400 + 200 + 100 = 700 for the user (read, write and execute); 40 + 20 + 10 = 70 for the group (read, write, and execute); and 4 + 1 = 5 for others equals a total of 775. So a new directory should be assigned the default permissions of **drwxrwxr-x.** This should match the symbolic mode executed in Step 2 (**u=rwx,g=rwx,o=rx**). To test this, you can create a directory and see what permissions are assigned.

STEP 5   Key in the following: **mkdir abc; ls -ld abc** Enter

```
[cgillay@linux72  floppy]$  mkdir; ls -ld abc
drwxrwxr-x   2      cgillay cgillay 1024  Oct 16    20:53 abc
[cgillay@linux72  floppy]$
```

WHAT'S HAPPENING? Here the **umask** value did assign the "775" (**drwxrwxr-x**) set of permissions to the directory **abc**. You may change the permission mode of any file or directory you own.

STEP 6   Key in the following: **chmod 700 abc; ls -ld abc** [Enter]

```
[cgillay@linux72   floppy]$   chmod 700 abc; ls -ld abc
drwx------     2    cgillay      cgillay      1024   Oct 16    20:53 abc
[cgillay@linux72   floppy]$
```

WHAT'S HAPPENING? You made the directory **abc**, to which only the owner may write files. No other user will be able to even list the contents of this directory. What happens to permissions when files are copied to a directory?

STEP 7   Key in the following: **ls -l *.dos; cp *.dos abc; ls -l abc** [Enter]

```
[cgillay@linux72 floppy]$ ls -l *.dos; cp *.dos abc; ls -l abc
-rwxrwxr-x 1 cgillay cgillay 181 Oct 12 21:21 wildone.dos
-rwxrwxr-x 1 cgillay cgillay 181 Oct 12 21:21 wilthr.dos
-rwxrwxr-x 1 cgillay cgillay 182 Oct 12 21:21 wildtwo.dos
total 3
-rwxrwxr-x 1 cgillay cgillay 181 Oct 16 20:56 wildone.dos
-rwxrwxr-x 1 cgillay cgillay 181 Oct 16 20:56 wilthr.dos
-rwxrwxr-x 1 cgillay cgillay 182 Oct 16 20:56 wildtwo.dos
[cgillay@linux72 floppy]$
```

WHAT'S HAPPENING? The permissions remained as they were. They did not take the **umask** default of 664. The default is only for new files.

STEP 8   Key in the following: **cd abc**

STEP 9   Key in the following:
    cat > happy.txt [Enter]
    This is a test. [Enter]
    [Ctrl] + **d**

STEP 10 Key in the following: **ls -l happy.txt** [Enter]

```
[cgillay@linux72   abc]$   ls -l happy.txt
-rw-rw-r-- 1     cgillay     cgillay 16  Oct 16 21:00 happy.txt
[cgillay@linux72   abc]$
```

WHAT'S HAPPENING? When you created a new file, it got the **umask** value of 664: **-rw-rw-r--**. However, since you made this directory available only to the owner, it does not matter what permissions you gave the files, as no one but the owner will be able to access the directory. If you cannot access the directories, you cannot manipulate the files.

STEP 11 Key in the following: **cd ..; chmod 775 abc; chmod 647 abc/happy.txt** [Enter]

STEP 12 Key in the following: **ls -ld abc; ls -l abc** [Enter]

```
[cgillay@RedHat9   abc]$ cd ..; chmod 775 abc; chmod 667 abc/
happy.txt
[cgillay@RedHat9   floppy]$  ls -ld abc; ls  -l abc
drwxrwxr-x    2   cgillay    cgillay   1024   Jul  5 23:27   abc
total 4
-rw-r--rwx    1   cgillay    cgillay     16   Jul  5 23:27   happy.txt
-rwxr-xr-x    1   cgillay    cgillay    181   Jul  5 23:20   wildone.dos
-rwxr-xr-x    1   cgillay    cgillay    181   Jul  5 23:20   wilthr.dos
-rwxr-xr-x    1   cgillay    cgillay    182   Jul  5 23:20   wildtwo.dos
[cgillay@RedHat9   floppy]$
```

WHAT'S HAPPENING? You have changed the directory **abc** so that permissions are read, write, and execute for the owner and the group; but read and execute for others. The files in the directory have a mix of permissions. In this example, by using 647, **happy.txt** has read and write permissions for the owner; read for the group: and read, write, and execute for all others. You gave **happy.txt** a strange set of permissions so that you can demonstrate the use of permissions. You have a conflict for the file **happy.txt**. The file permissions allow the deletion of this file by others, but the directory permissions do not. Which takes precedence? As you recall, unless the sticky bit is set, the directory permissions are the permissions that allow addition or deletion of files in the directory.

STEP 13 Key in the following: **cd; umount /mnt/floppy** [Enter]

STEP 14 Log off and the log back on as **student9**. Mount the floppy.

STEP 15 Key in the following: **umask 002; cd /mnt/floppy** [Enter]

STEP 16 Key in the following: **ls -ld abc; cd abc; ls -l** [Enter]

STEP 17 Key in the following: **rm happy.txt** [Enter]

```
[student9@RedHat9   floppy]$  ls -ld abc; cd abc; ls -l
drwxrwxr-x   2  cgillay    cgillay   1024  Jul   5 23:27   abc
total 4
-rw-r--rwx   1  cgillay    cgillay     16  Jul  5 23:27  happy.txt
-rwxr-xr-x   1  cgillay    cgillay    181  Jul  5 23:20   wildone.dos
-rwxr-xr-x   1  cgillay    cgillay    181  Jul  5 23:20   wilthr.dos
-rwxr-xr-x   1  cgillay    cgillay    182  Jul  5 23:20   wildtwo.dos
[student9@RedHat9   abc]$  rm happy.txt
rm: cannot remove 'happy.txt': Permission denied
[student9@RedHat9   abc]$
```

WHAT'S HAPPENING? Since, as **student9** (others) you have read and execute privileges for the directory **abc**, you could move to it. Now you tried to delete the file **happy.txt**. For the file **happy.txt** you, as a member of the others group, do have write privilege, but for the directory **abc**, you do not have write privileges. You could not delete the file **happy.txt**, so directory permissions ruled.

STEP 18 Key in the following: **cd; umount /mnt/floppy** [Enter]

STEP 19 Logout as **student9** and log back in as your usual user name.

STEP 20 Mount the BOOK2 disk.

8.13 • Linking Files—Hard Links

A *link* is a pointer to a file. Every time you create a file, you are placing a pointer in a directory. The pointer associates a file name with a location on the disk. Whenever you specify a file name in a command line, you are pointing to the place on the disk. Links, then, are references to files. Using links, the same file can be accessed from different places in the directory structure without having to store the file more than one time.

Again, every file is written to a physical location on your drive, which is called the inode, and each inode has a unique number to identify it. When you key in a command, such as **ls** for a directory listing, you are really looking at the index that tells the file system which inode number matches each file. When you create a *hard link*, you are creating another directory listing that points to the same inode. This means that you can create as many hard links on your system to one file without occupying additional disk space. If you make any changes to a hard-linked file, those changes will be reflected in the "original" file, since all the linked files are pointing to the same inode (or file). Only one actual file exists, the one referenced by the inode number. On the other hand, if you delete one of these files (pointers), the other hard-linked files remain because you have not deleted the inode to which they point. If you had multiple hard links to a file, the only way you could actually delete the file would be to delete every hard link that points to that file. Hard links to a file may only exist on the same disk and partition as the original file. Hard links do not work with networked file systems, other partitions, any mounted devices, or any other file system.

Links allow you to define more than one name for a file. This is not the same as copying a file. You are actually referencing the same file. This is especially valuable in a multi-user system. For instance, if two users were collaborating on a project, they might have a file in common, such as **report**. If each user had a separate copy of the **report** file, it would be difficult to identify which **report** is the most current version. If, instead, the **report** file is linked, each user is working on the identical file. When the **report** file gets modified, this modifies the **report** file for everyone (because only one **report** file actually exists). In Figure 8.1, "Linked File in a Multi-User System," **cgillay** is the owner of the report file, but **fpanezich** can access it and make changes to it. All changes will be reflected in cgillay's **report** file because it is the same file.

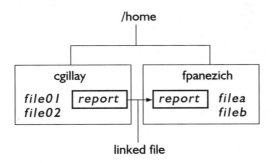

Figure 8.1 • *Linked File in a Multi-User System*

Linking files can also be useful to a user who is running Linux as a stand-alone system. For instance, a user might have an elaborate directory structure. If the user wanted to be able to access a file quickly in his home directory, without traversing through the directory structure, he could link the file. For instance, in Figure 8.2, "Linked Files in a Single-User System," **cgillay** is a teacher who keeps her syllabi in the **class** directory. If it was the beginning of the semester, and she needed to prepare her syllabi, she could link each syllabus file and place the link in her home directory.

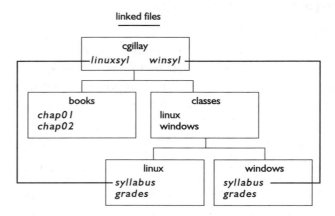

Figure 8.2 • Linked File in a Single-User System

The **ln** command is used to create an additional link to an existing file. The syntax is

```
ln [options] exisitingfile [destinationname]
```

If *destinationname* is an existing file, it is overwritten. If *destinationname* is an existing directory, the link is named *existingname* and is created in that directory. In order for links to work, the user must have read, write, and execute permissions to the directory where the link will exist.

8.14 • Activity: Using Hard Links

Note: You are logged on as your usual user account. The BOOK2 disk is mounted. Your home directory is the default directory. A terminal window is open.

STEP 1   Key in the following: **umask 002** [Enter]

STEP 2   Create two files called **file01** and **file02** in your home directory. The contents of **file01** will be **This is my first file.** The contents of **file02** will be **This is my second file.**

STEP 3   Key in the following: **cat file01 file02; ls -l file01 file02** [Enter]

```
[cgillay@linux72  cgillay]$   cat file01 file02; ls -l file01 file02
This is my first file.
This is my second file.
-rw-rw-r-- 1    cgillay cgillay    23    Oct 16 23:10     file01
-rw-rw-r-- 1    cgillay cgillay    24    Oct 16 23:10     file02
[cgillay@linux72   cgillay]$
```

WHAT'S **HAPPENING?** The number **1**, following the permissions, indicates that there are no links.

STEP 4   Key in the following: **ln file01   fileA; ln file02 fileB; ls -l fil*** [Enter]

```
[cgillay@RedHat9   cgillay]$   ln file01 fileA; ln file02 fileB; ls
-l fil*
-rw-rw-r--    2   cgillay   cgillay    23    Jul   6 00:12   file01
-rw-rw-r--    2   cgillay   cgillay    24    Jul   6 00:12   file02
-rw-rw-r--    2   cgillay   cgillay    23    Jul   6 00:12   fileA
-rw-rw-r--    2   cgillay   cgillay    24    Jul   6 00:12   fileB
[cgillay@RedHat9   cgillay]$
```

WHAT'S HAPPENING? ▷ Now you can see that the number following the permissions shows two links for each file. However, you do not know from this display which file is linked to which. You can check the inode numbers to see which files are linked.

STEP 5   Key in the following: **ls -i1 fil*** [Enter]

```
[cgillay@linux72   cgillay]$ ls -i1 fil*
5865678    file01
5865680    file02
5865678    fileA
5865680    fileB
[cgillay@linux72   cgillay]$
```

WHAT'S HAPPENING? ▷ Your inode numbers will be different. You used the **i** (inode) and **1** (number 1 for one column) with the **ls** command. You can see that **file01** and **fileA** have the same inode number as do **file02** and **fileB**, indicating they are identical files. Any changes made to **file01** will be reflected in **fileA**, and any changes made to **fileA** will be reflected in **file01** because they are the same file. The same is true with **file02** and **fileB**. You can prove this by making changes to **file01**.

STEP 6   Using vi, add a line to the bottom of **file01** stating **THIS IS MY CHANGE**. Save the file with the changes.

STEP 7   Key in the following: **cat file01 fileA** [Enter]

```
[cgillay@linux72   cgillay]$   cat file01 fileA
This is my first file.
THIS IS MY CHANGE.

This is my first file.
THIS IS MY CHANGE.

[cgillay@linux72   cgillay]$
```

WHAT'S HAPPENING? ▷ You can see that the change you made to **file01** was reflected in the linked file, **fileA**. This would not be true if you had merely copied **file01** to **fileA**. If you had copied, instead of linked, **file01** and **fileA** would have different contents.

STEP 8   Key in the following: **cd; cp /mnt/floppy/*.99   ~; ls -l** [Enter]

```
cgillay@RedHat9:~                                                    _ □ x
File  Edit  View  Terminal  Go  Help
[cgillay@RedHat9 cgillay]$ cd; cp /mnt/floppy/*.99 ~; ls -l
total 48
-rwx--x--x   1 cgillay  cgillay      148 Jul  6 00:29 ast.99
drwx------   4 cgillay  cgillay     4096 Jun 10 18:03 evolution
-rw-rw-r--   2 cgillay  cgillay       43 Jul  6 00:24 file01
-rw-rw-r--   2 cgillay  cgillay       24 Jul  6 00:12 file02
-rw-rw-r--   2 cgillay  cgillay       43 Jul  6 00:24 fileA
-rw-rw-r--   2 cgillay  cgillay       24 Jul  6 00:12 fileB
-rw-r--r--   1 cgillay  cgillay      190 Jul  6 00:29 jup.99
-rwxr-x---   1 cgillay  cgillay      406 Jul  6 00:29 mer.99
drwxrwxr-x   4 cgillay  cgillay     4096 Jun 28 11:12 practice5
drwxrwxr-x   4 cgillay  cgillay     4096 Jun 29 21:09 practice6
drwxrwxr-x   4 cgillay  cgillay     4096 Jul  1 19:51 practice7
-rwx------   1 cgillay  cgillay      478 Jul  6 00:29 ven.99
[cgillay@RedHat9 cgillay]$
```

WHAT'S HAPPENING? You have ensured that your home directory is your default directory and copied the files with the **.99** extension from the BOOK2 disk to your home directory. You may have other directories or files in your home directory than those that are shown here, and the dates may vary. In this case, you are the owner of the files and the files have different permissions. You are going to create a link to files in different directories. However, the first step is to give read, write, and execute permissions so that you may link the files for other users. In a multi-user environment, you would most likely give read, write, and execute permissions to members of your group rather than the entire world. In this example, you are going to give read, write, and execute privileges to groups and to others for purposes of demonstration.

STEP 9   Key in the following: **chmod 777 *.99; ls -l *.99** [Enter]

```
[cgillay@linux72  cgillay]$  chmod 777 *.99; ls -l *.99
-rwxrwxrwx 1    cgillay cgillay        148    Oct 16 23:15    ast.99
-rwxrwxrwx 1    cgillay cgillay        190    Oct 16 23:15    jup.99
-rwxrwxrwx 1    cgillay cgillay        406    Oct 16 23:15    mer.99
-rwxrwxrwx 1    cgillay cgillay        478    Oct 16 23:15    ven.99
[cgillay@linux72  cgillay]$
```

WHAT'S HAPPENING? Now that your ***.99** files are available to everyone, there is still one more step to take. The other user would need to make his/her directory available to you by giving you write and execute permissions. Since you are also the "other" user, you need to change the permissions of the directory of the other user. For purposes of demonstration, you will become the other user and give full rights to everyone.

Note 1:   If you do not have another user that you may log in, you cannot do the next steps.

Note 2:   Check with your instructor for the user name you may log in as and the password if you did not follow the setup instructions in Appendix A.

STEP 10   Key in the following: **whoami; who am i; su student9** [Enter]

```
[cgillay@linux72  cgillay]$  whoami; who am i; su student9
cgillay
linux72!cgillay    pts/0    Oct 17    10:22 (0:)
Password:
```

WHAT'S HAPPENING? The **whoami** command with no spaces shows the name of the current user logged onto the system. **who am i**, with spaces, displays the name and current status of the invoking user. The **su** command runs a shell with a substitute user and group ids. If you key it in with no argument, it allows you to log in as the super user, if you know the root password. When you followed **su** by a user name (**student9**), it prompted you for that user's password. You are spawning another shell. When you enter a command at the shell prompt, the shell process calls the **fork** system call to create a copy of itself (spawn a child) and then uses the **exec** system call to overlay that copy in memory with a different program (the command you asked it to run).

STEP 11   Key in the following: **student9** [Enter]

STEP 12   Key in the following: **whoami** [Enter]

```
[cgillay@linux72   cgillay]$   whoami
student9
[student9@linux72   cgillay]$
```

WHAT'S HAPPENING? Your default directory is still **cgillay** (your login user name), but you are now effectively the user you logged in as—in this case, **student9**.

STEP 13 Key in the following: **cd /home; ls -l** Enter

```
student9@RedHat9:/home                                          _ □ x
File  Edit  View  Terminal  Go  Help
[cgillay@RedHat9 cgillay]$ whoami; who am i; su student9
cgillay
cgillay   pts/0        Jul  6 00:11 (:0.0)
Password:
[student9@RedHat9 cgillay]$ whoami
student9
[student9@RedHat9 cgillay]$ cd /home; ls -l
total 36
drwx------   12 alincoln  alincoln   4096 Jul  2 09:36 alincoln
drwx------   31 cgillay   cgillay    4096 Jul  6 00:43 cgillay
drwx------   12 frank     frank      4096 Jun 25 18:32 frank
drwx------    4 gwashing  gwashing   4096 Jun  9 09:26 gwashing
drwx------   13 linux     linux      4096 Jun 26 10:07 linux
drwx------    4 student7  student7   4096 Jun  9 09:27 student7
drwx------    4 student8  student8   4096 Jun  9 09:27 student8
drwx------   12 student9  student9   4096 Jul  6 00:43 student9
drwx------   13 testuser  testuser   4096 Jun 25 23:16 testuser
[student9@RedHat9 home]$ ▮
```

WHAT'S HAPPENING? You may have more or fewer users on your system. In this case, all the directories listed have **rwx** permissions only for the owner. You are going to change the permissions for **student9** (or your other user) to full access.

STEP 14 Key in the following: **chmod 777 student9; ls -ld student9** Enter

```
[student9@linux72    home]$   chmod  777  student9; ls -ld  student0
drwxrwxrwx  3      student9     student9    4096    Oct 17 11:29 student9
[student9@linux72    home]$
```

WHAT'S HAPPENING? You have given full access to the **student9** directory.

STEP 15 Key in the following: **cd student9** Enter

STEP 16 Create and save a file called **mars.99** with the contents of **This is my Mars file.**

STEP 17 Key in the following: **cat mars.99; chmod 777 mars.99; ls -l mars.99** Enter

```
[student9@linux72   student9]$ cat mars.99; chmod 777 mars.99; ls -l mars.99
This is my Mars file.
-rwxrwxrwx   1      student9      student9     22  Oct 17 11:40 mars.99
[student9@linux72   student9]$
```

WHAT'S HAPPENING? In the **student9** directory you have created a file owned by **student9**. You changed the permissions so any user can read, write, or execute the file. *Note:* In the next step, use your usual user name instead of **cgillay**.

STEP 18 Key in the following: **ln mars.99   /home/cgillay** Enter

```
[student9@linux72    student9]$   ln   mars.99 /home/cgillay
ln: accessing 'home/cgillay/mars.99': Permission denied
[student9@linux72    student9]$
```

WHAT'S HAPPENING? You do not have permissions for the **cgillay** (or your user directory).

STEP 19 Key in the following: **exit** [Enter]

STEP 20 Key in the following: **whoami** [Enter]

```
[student9@linux72   student9]$   exit
[cgillay@linux72   cgillay]$   whoami
cgillay
[cgillay@linux72   cgillay]$
```

WHAT'S HAPPENING? Since you spawned another shell, you did not have to change users to return to who you were logged in as.

STEP 21 Key in the following: **ln /home/student9/mars.99; ls -l mars.99** [Enter]

```
[cgillay@linux72   cgillay]$   ln /home/student9/mars.99; ls -l mars.99
-rwxrwxrwx   2      student9      student9      22 Oct 17 11:40   mars.99
[cgillay@linux72   cgillay]$
```

WHAT'S HAPPENING? You now show two links to this file. You also see that **mars.99** is still owned by **student9**, not by you. What about the inode number for this file?

STEP 22 Key in the following: **ls -l mars.99 /home/student9/mars.99** [Enter]

```
 [cgillay@linux72   cgillay]$   ls -il mars.99 /home/student9/mars.99
1851556 /home/student/mars.99       1851556 mars.99
 [cgillay@linux72   cgillay]$
```

WHAT'S HAPPENING? You can see that you are referencing the same file. The file, **mars.99**, has the identical inode number in both directories. What happens if you change the contents of the file?

STEP 23 Using **vi**, add a line to the **mars.99** file that states **THIS IS A CHANGE**. Save the changes.

STEP 24 Key in the following: **cat mars.99** [Enter]

```
[cgillay@linux72   cgillay]$   cat mars.99
This is my Mars file.
THIS IS A CHANGE.

[cgillay@linux72   cgillay]$
```

WHAT'S HAPPENING? You have changed the file. Now you are going to see the results of those changes to **mars.99** in the **student9** directory.

STEP 25 Key in the following: **su student9** [Enter]

STEP 26 Key in the correct password.

STEP 27 Key in the following: **cd; cat mars.99; ls -l mars.99** [Enter]

```
[cgillay@linux72  cgillay]$  cd; cat mars.99; ls -l mars.99
This is my Mars file.
THIS IS A CHANGE.


-rwxrwxrwx     2     student9 student9      40 Oct 17 11:48  mars.99
[student9@linux72   student9]$
```

WHAT'S HAPPENING? You see your change to **mars.99** reflected.

STEP 28 Key in the following: **rm mars.99; ls; cd /home; chmod 700 student9; exit** [Enter]

```
[student9@linux72   student9]$ rm mars.99;cd /home; chmod 700 student9; exit
exit
[cgillay@linux72   cgillay]$
```

WHAT'S HAPPENING? You deleted the **mars.99** file in the **student9** directory. You then assigned the **student9** directory read, write, and execute permissions for only the owner, and then you exited the process.

STEP 29 Key in the following: **cd; cat mars.99; ls -l mars.99; ls -i mars.99** [Enter]

```
[cgillay@linux72  cgillay]$ cd; cat mars.99; ls -l mars.99; ls -i mars.99
This is my Mars file.
THIS IS A CHANGE.


-rwxrwxrwx   1      student9       student9       40 Oct 17 11:48  mars.99
1851556 mars.99
[cgillay@linux72   cgillay]$
```

WHAT'S HAPPENING? You keyed in **cd** to be sure you were in your home directory. You also can see that now there is only one link, but the file's owner is still **student9**. But the reason you still have the file in your directory, even though you deleted it as **student9**, is that in reality, there was only one file (remember the inode number). Linux simply had a pointer for that file to two directories (the link). When **student9** deleted the file, Linux deleted the link to **student9**, but not the file **mars.99**. It still has the same inode number.

STEP 30 Key in the following: **rm mars.99** [Enter]

STEP 31 Key in the following: **exit** [Enter]

WHAT'S HAPPENING? You should have returned to the GNOME desktop. If you are still in the terminal window, keep keying in **exit** until the terminal window closes.

8.15 • Linking Files—Symbolic Links

In addition to hard links, Linux also allows the use of symbolic links, sometimes called soft links. A *symbolic link* is an indirect pointer to a file and is a directory entry that contains the path name to the linked file. A symbolic link is not a direct hard link, but rather provides information on how to locate a specific file. A symbolic link is another way to write the file's path name. Symbolic links can be used with any physical drive or directory. Symbolic links to a file or a directory do not have to exist on the same disk and partition as the original file. Symbolic links do work with networked file systems, other partitions, any mounted devices, or any other file system.

A symbolic link is a small file that you create, and the content of this file is the path to the file you are linking it to. Symbolic links are similar to shortcuts in the Windows environment. By default, Linux creates a number of symbolic links when it is installed. For instance, **ex** is actually a link to **vi**; **sh** is a link to **bash**, and some of your devices may have a symbolic link, such as **cdrom - > hdc**. When you use **ls** with a symbolically linked file, you will see where the original file is located. However, the counter, unlike hard links, does not show how many symbolic links exist. Furthermore, with hard links, the inode is stored, as you saw in the last activity, but with symbolic links that path name is stored. Because of this, when you delete the original file, the symbolic link (or links) is not deleted, but now the symbolic link points to a non-existent file. Symbolic links can also be created for directories.

The **ln -s** command is used to create a symbolic link to an existing file. The syntax is **ln -s** *source destination.* The source is the absolute or relative path to the original file, and the destination is the name of the link you choose. In general, relative paths are preferred to absolute paths, which can help minimize problems if directories are relocated. In fact, in practice, symbolic links are almost exclusively used. This is not only because of the flexibility but because of accuracy. With a symbolic link you can check what is being pointed to—this is much more difficult with hard links.

8.16 • Activity: Using Symbolic Links

Note: You are logged on as your usual user account. The BOOK2 disk is mounted. Your home directory is the default directory. The **.99** files have been copied to your home directory.

STEP 1   Open a terminal window. Key in the following: **ls -l /usr/bin/consolehelper** [Enter]

STEP 2   Key in the following: **ls -l /usr/bin/reboot** [Enter]

STEP 3   Key in the following: **ls -l /usr/bin/poweroff** [Enter]

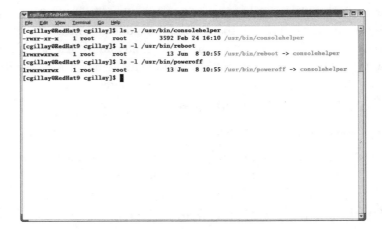

WHAT'S HAPPENING? In this example, you can see that **reboot** and **poweroff** are links that point to **consolehelper** (/usr/bin/reboot -> consolehelper and /usr/bin/poweroff -> consolehelper.) In the permissions, the first character is an "l," indicating a linked file with a pointer to **consolehelper**. **Consolehelper** is a tool that makes it easier for users to run system programs. It is intended to be transparent to the user, which means the user never runs the **consolehelper** program directly. Instead, programs such as **reboot** or **shutdown** are linked to **consolehelper**, so that if a non-root user calls the **reboot** program, **consolehelper** will be invoked to authenticate the action (verify that the user has the correct permissions to reboot the system), and then, if the user does have the correct permissions, will actually invoke the **reboot** command.

STEP 4   Key in the following: **ln -s   /mnt/floppy/sports/foot-col.tms   college**

STEP 5   Key in the following : **ls -l college** ⸢Enter⸣

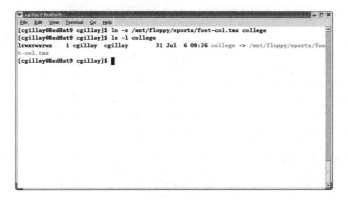

WHAT'S HAPPENING? You can see that you using a symbolic link saves you the trouble of keying in a long path name. Note that the permissions first show the "l" for link.

STEP 6   Key in the following: **ls -l   /mnt/floppy/sports/foot-col.tms** ⸢Enter⸣

```
[cgillay@linux72   cgillay]$ ls -l /mnt/floppy/sports/foot-col.tms
-rwxrwxr-x  1 cgillay cgillay 227 Oct 12 21:21 /mnt/floppy/sports/foot-col.tms
[cgillay@linux72   cgillay]$
```

WHAT'S HAPPENING? You can also see that the permissions are different. However, since you are the owner of the file, you can make any change you wish. Any change will be reflected in the original file as well as the one in your home directory.

STEP 7   At the end of the **college** file, using **vi**, add the line **Alabama's Crimson Tide**. Save the changes.

STEP 8   Key in the following: **cat   college   /mnt/floppy/sports/foot-col.tms** ⸢Enter⸣

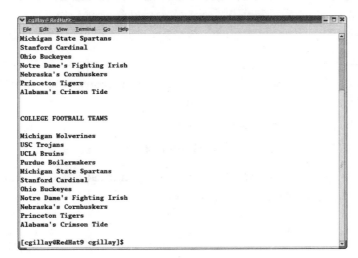

WHAT'S **HAPPENING?** The file contents are identical. You may also use a link for a directory name.

STEP 9   Key in the following: **ln -s /mnt/floppy/sports; ls -ld sports** [Enter]

```
[cgillay@linux72  cgillay]$  ln -s  /mnt/floppy/sports; ls -ld sports
lrwxrwxrwx   1  cgillay  cgillay 18 Oct 17 12:34 sports -> /mnt/floppy/sports
[cgillay@linux72   cgillay]$
```

WHAT'S **HAPPENING?** You have now accessed a directory on your floppy disk with a short name. You used an absolute path. A relative path would have looked like **ln -s ../mnt/floppy/sports**. If you use the **..** instead of the /, if the **mnt** directory changes location, your symbolic link would still work. If you used an absolute path, it would no longer be available to you. Once you have created a symbolic link to a directory, it is much easier to copy or look at files in this directory on the floppy disk.

STEP 10   Key in the following: **cp ast.99 sports; ls sports** [Enter]

```
[cgillay@linux72  cgillay]$ cp ast.99 sports; ls sports
ast.99 basketbl.tms bsball-a.tms  bsball-n.tms foot-col.tms foot-pro.tms
[cgillay@linux72   cgillay]$
```

WHAT'S **HAPPENING?** You easily copied a file to the **/mnt/floppy/sports** directory by using the symbolic link, **sports**. You can also change directories using symbolic links.

STEP 11   Key in the following: **cd sports; pwd** [Enter]

```
[cgillay@linux72   cgillay]$   cd sports; pwd
/home/cgillay/sports
[cgillay@linux72    sports]$
```

WHAT'S **HAPPENING?** You have changed directories to **sports**, but note that your working directory is the directory that holds the symbolic link; in this case, your home directory, not **/mnt/floppy/sports**, which is the absolute path.

STEP 12   Key in the following: **cd ..; pwd** [Enter]

```
[cgillay@linux72    cgillay]$   cd ..; pwd
/home/cgillay
[cgillay@linux72    cgillay]$
```

WHAT'S **HAPPENING?** When you used the double dot, the parent was not **/mnt/floppy**, but the location of the symbolic link, your home directory.

STEP 13   Key in the following: **rm sports** [Enter]

STEP 14   Key in the following: **ln -s ast.99 sat.99; ls -l ast.99 sat.99** [Enter]

```
[cgillay@linux72    cgillay]$   ln -s ast.99 sat.99; ls -l ast.99 sat.99
-rwxrwsrwx    1    cgillay   cgillay   148  Oct 16 23:15 ast.99
lrwxrwxrwx    1    cgillay   cgillay   6    Oct 17 12:38 sat.99 -> ast.99
[cgillay@linux72    cgillay]$
```

WHAT'S HAPPENING? You have linked **ast.99** to the **sat. 99** file. The dates are not the same as they would be with a hard link, and nor is the size. However, if you just copied the **ast.99** file to your home directory, the dates and sizes would be the same. But what about the inodes?

STEP 15 Key in the following: **ls -il ast.99 sat.99** **Enter**

```
[cgillay@RedHat9  cgillay]$  ls -i ast.99 sat.99
311426 -rwxrwxrwx  1 cgillay  cgillay 148 Jul 6 00:29 ast.99
312981  lrwxrwxrwx 1 cgillay  cgillay   6 Jul 6 09:48 sat.99 -> ast.99
[cgillay@RedHat9  cgillay]$
```

WHAT'S HAPPENING? The inode number for each file is different, indicating that each file—the original file and the link—is being treated as separate entities by the operating system. What happens if you delete the file that the link is pointing to?

STEP 16 Key in the following: **rm ast.99; ls -l sat.99** **Enter**

```
[cgillay@linux72  cgillay]$  rm ast.99; ls -l sat.99
lrwxrwxrwx   1  cgillay  cgillay  6 Oct 17  12":38 sat.99 ->ast.99
[cgillay@linux72  cgillay]$
```

WHAT'S HAPPENING? Since you deleted the original file, **ast.99**, the link, **sat.99**, points to nowhere. Hence, it is highlighted in your listing.

STEP 17 Key in the following: **rm *.99 college file*** **Enter**

```
[cgillay@linux72  cgillay]$  rm *.99 college file*
[cgillay@linux72  cgillay]$
```

WHAT'S HAPPENING? You removed the symbolically linked file, **sat.99** as well as **college**. You also removed all the files your created in your home directory.

STEP 18 Unmount the BOOK2 disk. Remove it from the drive.

Chapter Summary

In this chapter you were introduced to the following:
- File ownership
- File and directory permissions.
- Types of file systems and how they impact permissions.
- The ability to determine disk usage and free space on a disk.
- An understanding of how groups are used in Linux and how you may assign permissions to groups.
- Who may assign permissions and the types of permissions available.
- How to assign file permissions symbolically and numerically.
- An understanding of how default permissions are assigned.
- The ability to create hard and soft links to files and directories.

Key Terms

absolute mode	journaling file systems	permission
cache	link	sockets
device	numeric mode	superblock
group	octal mode	symbolic link
hard link	other	symbolic mode
inode	overhead	user

Discussion Questions

1. Explain the concept of file ownership and the need of permissions to access files and directories.
2. List and explain the levels of permissions assigned by default. What makes a user a part of each level?
3. List and explain the types of permissions assigned to files or directories.
4. What do these permissions mean when applied to a file? A directory?
5. What command allows you to log on as another user, given that you have the proper password.
6. What type of disk are you formatting if you use the following command:

   ```
   fdformat /dev/fd0h1200.
   ```

7. There are two parts to creating a file system on any device. Explain.
8. What is a journaling file system? What was it designed for and how does it work?
9. What is an inode?
10. What is a superblock? What happens if this part of a file system is damaged?
11. To maintain the file system there is always "overhead." Explain.
12. Explain how **du** and **df** help monitor disk space.
13. Why should the **fsck** command be run only on unmounted file systems?
14. Define permissions, file ownership, and groups.
15. List and explain the three categories of groups.
16. List and explain two of the commands that are used to manage and view groups and ownership of files and directories.
17. Why would you create a group without a corresponding user?
18. List and explain two of the three permissions that control special attributes for executable files and directories.
19. How is a sticky bit used?
20. Explain each part of the following entries in the **/etc/group** file: **groupname**, **password**, **members**.
21. List and explain the three permission types as they apply to files. As they apply to directories.
22. Using the **ls-1** command, you display the following information:

    ```
    -rwxr----- 1 cgillay student 86 Oct 15 11:30 joanne.txt
    ```

    What permissions are given to the owner? What permissions are given to the group? What permissions are given to the other users?
23. What is a symbolic mode?
24. What is an absolute mode?
25. What is the function of the **umask** command? What does the **–S** option allow this command to do?

26. Explain one way to compute the absolute mode to find numeric permissions.
27. What is a hard link?
28. Describe how a link is useful on a multi-user system?
29. How are hard links useful on a stand-alone system?
30. What is the function of the **ln** command with hard links? Write the command syntax for this command. What happens if the destination name is the same as the existing file when you use a link?
31. What is a symbolic link?
32. How are symbolic links different from hard links?
33. What happens to soft links if you delete the original file that they link to? What happens to the hard links if you delete the original file that they link to?
34. What is the function of the **ln** command with soft links? Write the command syntax for the **ln** command and identify the parts.

True/False Questions

For each question, circle the letter T if the question is true and the letter F if the question is false.

T   F   1. The super (root) user is able to access files that are not intended for human interaction.

T   F   2. Once a device is mounted, only the user that mounted the device has permission to unmount the device.

T   F   3. When formatting a floppy drive, it is imperative that you first mount the device.

T   F   4. The **chgrp** command is used to change which groups can access a file or directory and can only be used by the root user.

T   F   5. Links allow a user to give a single file multiple names and is the same as copying a file.

Completion Questions

Write the correct answer in each blank space.

6. The _____ and _____ are items that can be changed to protect access to files.

7. Details about the user, such as the users full name, can be found in the _____ field of the **/etc/passwd** file.

8. To calculate the default permissions assigned to a file, you simply subtract the value found with **umask** from _____.

9. The terms *octal* and *numeric* refer to _____ mode.

10. If files are linked, you may determine if they are identical by comparing the _____ displayed in the results of the **ls –i** command.

Multiple Choice Questions

For each question, write the letter for the correct answer in the blank space.

11. The power to change file ownerships or bypass permissions that may have already been set belongs to the
    a. authorized user.
    b. owner of the file.
    c. super user.
    d. group.

12. A user looking for user or group information can often find it in the _____ file(s).
     a. /etc/group
     b. /etc/passwd
     c. /etc/user
     d. either a or b

13. Which command would assign read, write, and execute permissions to the **grad.99** file for both the user and the group, while assigning no permissions to other users.
     a. **chmod 770 grad.99**
     b. **chmod 774 grad.99**
     c. **chmod 440 grad.99**
     d. **chmod 330 grad.99**

14. You are logged in as **cgillay**. You want to change users to **wclinton**. Which command would you use?
     a. **su**
     b. **su wclinton**
     c. **switch user**
     d. **switch wclinton**

15. The file report has the following permissions: **-rwxrwxrw-**. Using the command **chmod og=rw,o= report** will result in the report file having the following permissions.
     a. **-rw-rw-rw-**
     b. **-rw-rw----**
     c. **-rwxrwx---**
     d. **-rwxrw-rw-**

Writing Commands

Write the correct steps or commands to perform the required action as if you were at the computer. You will assume that there is a terminal window open. The prompt will indicate the current working directory.

16. You want to estimate the file space usage of the **/home/chen/images** directory. You want to display all the files and directories in the images directory and you want it to be displayed in human readable form. You also want to display the output one screen at a time.

```
[chen@linux72 chen]$_
```

17. You want to change the group membership of the **finalreport** file, located in your home directory, from **bpeat** to **sales**.

```
[bpeat@linux72 bpeat]$_
```

18. You want to assign file permissions to the **movies** file located in the **/home/jschmidt/fun** directory so that the owner has read, write, and execute permissions, the group has read and execute permissions, and others have read only permissions. You want to be sure that those are the only permissions on the file. You want to see the change as it occurs. Use symbolic mode.

```
[jschmidt @linux72 jschmidt]$_
```

19. You want to assign file permissions to the **movies** file located in the **/home/jschmidt/fun** directory so that the owner has read, write and execute permissions, the group has read and execute permissions and others have read only permissions. You want to be sure that those are the only permissions on the file. You want to see the change as it occurs. Use octal mode.

```
[jschmidt @linux72 jschmidt]$_
```

20. You want to change your **umask** value in your terminal window so that, for directories, the owner will be able to read, write, and execute, the group will be able to read and execute, and others will only be able to read. For files, the owner will be able to read and write, and the group and others will be able to read only. You then want to display the values in the **umask** symbolically.

```
[xu@linux72 xu]$_
```

Application Assignments

Problem Set I—At the Computer: Short Answer

Note: See the note on page 414 for information about disk usage.

Use vi or any editor to create a document called **Chapter8.HW**. In this document, you will answer the questions that follow. You do not need to rekey in the questions but be sure to number them. *Do not hand in any hand-written answers*. The actual questions to be answered are indicated by the problem number. Please use the following format and use **pr** to print the document:

> *Name*
> *Class number*
> *Class Day and Time*
> Chapter 8 Homework
> 1.
> 2.
> etc.

You may also use a word processor to answer the questions, but be sure to include the above information.

Problem A

* Open a terminal window.
* Mount the BOOK2 disk.
* Determine which directory on the BOOK2 disk is the largest in kilobytes.

    1. Excluding the **/mnt/floppy** directory itself, which directory was the largest?
    2. What command did you use to determine the largest directory on the BOOK2 disk?
    3. If you wanted a sorted display, in numeric order, of the information requested in Question 2, what command could you use?
    4. How many total inodes are on your BOOK2 disk?
    5. What command did you use to determine the total inodes on the BOOK2 disk?

6. How many 1k blocks are on your BOOK2 disk?

7. What command did you use to determine the total number of 1k blocks on the BOOK2 disk?

Problem B

8. What is your user id number? Do you belong to any groups? If you do, what groups do you belong to and what is/are their number(s)?

9. How did you locate this information?

10. What is alincoln's user id number? What groups does he belong to?

11. How did you locate this information?

Problem C

* For all the files on the BOOK2 disk that begin with **w** and have any name or extension, change the permissions so that only the user (owner) and group can read, write, and execute these files. Do not use the numeric permissions. *Use symbolic permissions.*

12. What command did you use?

* For all the files on the BOOK2 disk that begin with **c** and have any name or extension, change the permissions so that only the owner can read, write, and execute the files; the group can read and execute; and all others can only execute. *Use numeric permissions.*

13. What command did you use?

Problem D

* On the BOOK2 disk, change the permissions on the directory called **data** so that only the user (owner) can read, write, and execute the directory.

14. Which command did you use?

* Change the group for **frank.fil** to **student**.

15. What command did you use?

16. What permissions does **frank.fil** have?

* Copy the file called **frank.fil** to the **data** directory.

17. Which permissions does **frank.fil** have in the **data** directory?

18. Why were those permissions assigned?

19. What is the group assigned to the **frank.fil** in the **data** directory?

20. What is your **umask** value?

21. What permissions will be assigned to any directories you create?

22. What permissions will be assigned to any files you create?

* Change your **umask** value to **033**.

* In the **data** directory, create a new file called **test**. The contents of the file is **THIS IS A TEST.**

* In the **data** directory, create a directory called **what**.

* Copy the file **test** to the **what** directory.

23. What permissions were assigned to **test** in the **data** directory? Why?

24. What permissions were assigned to **test** in the **what** directory? Why?

25. What permissions were assigned to the **what** directory? Why?

- Change your umask value to **002**.
- Unmount the BOOK2 disk. Remove it from the drive.

Problem Set II—At the Computer: Short Answer

Note 1:   To minimize keying in data, Chapter 5, 6, and 7 Short Answers need to have been completed.

Note 2:   Unless specified, do not save files to disk. Use standard output for results.

Note 3:   It is assumed your login name is **linux** and you have all the accounts in Appendix A.

1. Create a directory called **practice8** in your home directory. How did you accomplish this task?

2. If you are in a lab environment that allowed you to retain the **practice7** directory activities on your computer, completed in Chapter 7, Problem Set II: At the Computer—Short Answer, copy recursively all the files and directories from **practice7** to **practice8**. Otherwise, use the PRACTICE disk you created at the end of the Chapter 7, Problem Set II: At the Computer—Short Answer from the **practice7** directory to the **practice8** directory located in your home directory. How did you accomplish this task?

3. Change directories to **practice8**. You want to know, sorted in numerical order, from smallest block to largest block, an estimate of how much space your file system occupies, and you want to display the output to the screen. What command did you use?

4. Now you want to know how many bytes each directory and file occupies in **practice8**— again, sorted in numerical order with output displayed to the monitor. What commands did you use? What did you deduce about file and directory sizes? *Hint:* you need to use several options and do a little math.

5. Change directories to you r home directory. Issue the same command as you did in question 2. Are there any differences in the display? If there are, why did this occur?

6. While in your home directory, find out how much free disk space you have. What command did you use? Change to the **practice8** directory. Issue the same command. Are there any differences? Why or why not?

7. How many inodes do you have? Which file system occupies the largest amount of space? Why? What command did you use?

8. For the file named **both**, what permissions does it have? Who is the owner? What group does it belong to? What command did you use?

9. For the directory named **mybooks** what permissions does it have? Who is the owner? What group does it belong to? What command did you use?

10. What is your user name and to which groups do you belong? What command did you use? What id number is assigned to your login name and to each group to which you belong? Identify two commands that allow you to display this information. What command could you use to display only the group numbers? group names?

11. What groups do users **alincoln**, **student7**, and **student8** belong to? What command did you?

12. Copy the file called **both** from the **practice8** directory to the /**politics** and /**public** directories. What happened? Why?

13. What permissions does **both** have in the **public** directory? Who is the owner? What is the group membership?

14. Change the permissions for the **both** file in the /**public** directory so that only the current owner has read, write, and execute permissions. Use symbolic mode. What command did you use?

15. Change group ownership for the **both** file in /**public** directory to **student**. What command did you use?

16. Log out and log on as **student8**. Change directories to /**public**. What happened? Why? Log out and log on as **student9**. Change directories to /**public**. What happened? Why?

17. While logged on as **student9**, what are the permissions of the /**public** directory? the **both** file? Copy the **both** file in the **public** directory to your home directory—**student9**. What happened? Why? Now delete the **both** file in the /**public** directory. What happened? Why? What have you learned about file and directory permissions? Remove the **both** file from the /**home/student9** directory.

18. Log out and log on as **linux**. Change directories to the **practice8** directory. Copy the **both** file and the **both2** file to the /**public** directory. What permissions do these files have in the /**public** directory. Why?

19. Change the permissions for the **both** file in the **practice8** directory so that the user has read, write, and execute permissions, the **group** and **other** has read only permissions. Use octal mode. Change the **group** to **student** for the **both** file. What commands did you use? Change the permissions for the **both2** file so that it is read only for user, group and other. Use octal mode. Copy **both** and **both2** from the **practice8** directory to the /**public** directory. What happened to the permissions? Why? Remove the **both** and **both2** file from the /**public** directory.

20. Create a directory under **practice8** called **test**. Copy **both** and **both2** to the **test** directory. What permissions does the **test** directory have? What permissions do these files have in the **test** directory? Why? Create a new file in the **test** directory called **both3**. Its contents are **THIS IS A TEST**. What permissions does **both3** have? Why?

21. Log out and log back on as **student9**. Create a file called **linkfile**. The contents are **This is a linked file**. Move **linkfile** to the /**public** directory. Change the group to **student**. Log out and log in as **linux**. Change directories to **practice8**. Create a symbolic link to /**public/linkfile** calling it **elvis** in the **practice8** directory. What commands did you use? Add your name to the contents of **elvis**. Is that change reflected in **linkfile**? Why or why not? Delete the **linkfile** in /**public**. Is **elvis** a viable file; for instance, can you view the contents of **elvis**? Why or why not? Delete **elvis**.

22. Get the disk labeled **PRACTICE** disk. Do not use the BOOK or BOOK2 disk. Mount it. Copy everything in the **practice8** directory under your home directory to the floppy disk to a directory called **practice8**. When you have finished, unmount the floppy disk and remove it from the drive.

Problem Set III—Brief Essay

Use gEdit or OpenOffice.org Writer to write and print your response. Be sure to put your name as well as what day and time your class is. Include the number of the question you are answering.

a. Compare and contrast hard links and symbolic links. Include in your discussion when you would choose to use a hard link and when you would choose to use a symbolic link.

b. Compare and contrast **fdformat** and **mkfs**. In your discussion, include a discussion of the purpose and function of inodes.

c. What advantages and disadvantages are there to assigning permissions to files and directories? In your discussion, include the types of permissions that can be assigned and to whom they can be assigned.

CHAPTER 9

Processes, Shell Scripts, Variables, and Command Line Substitution

---

Chapter Overview

A shell is simply a program with which the user can interact to issue commands. Commands you use are loaded into memory from disk, except those commands that are called built-ins. The shell is a very powerful tool and is responsible for executing programs, interpreting ambiguous file references and variable file substitution, handling pipes and redirection, controlling your environment, and writing shell scripts with the built-in interpreted programming language.

When you issue a command in Linux, you are starting a process. There are several commands to assist you in seeing what processes are running. Among these are **ps, pstree, uptime**, and **top**. You may also end processes by using the **kill** and **killall** command. Furthermore, you may run a command in either foreground or background using the **fg** and **bg** command. The **jobs** command lets you use what foreground and background programs are running.

You may also create an alias, which is usually a user-defined abbreviation for a command. There are also keywords that have special meaning to the shell. To see what kind of command you are using, you will use the **type** command. The **help** command is like the man pages for a built-in command. You may also store a list of directories and recall them with the **popd** and **pushd** commands. The **dirs** commands lets you know what is in your list of directories.

You may also use and create variables and make them available to child shells using the **export** or **declare -x** commands, which are built-in commands. Command line expansion is what the shell must do to the command line before it passes arguments and options to the program being called.

The shell interprets quote characters. It also has an order in which it executes other types of command substitution.

The Bash shell has a number of startup files that are sourced. The **source** command is a built-in command. The **dot** command (.) is another name for **source**. Both commands take a script name as an argument. The script will be executed in the environment of the current shell, and no child process will be started.

In this chapter, you will use all these commands to further enhance your use and understanding of Linux. You will also have an opportunity to write your first shell scripts.

Learning Objectives

1. Explain the purpose and function of the kernel.
2. Explain the responsibilities of the shell.
3. Explain the purpose and function of a process.
4. Explain the login cycle.
5. Explain the purpose and function of the **kill** and **killall** commands.
6. Explain when and how you would use the **job**, **fg**, and **bg** commands.
7. Explain the purpose and function of a shell script and how to execute a script.
8. List and explain the order in which commands are executed.
9. Explain how built-in commands can be used to manipulate directory stacks.
10. Compare and contrast local and global environmental variables.
11. List naming restrictions when naming variables.
12. Explain the purpose and function of the **export** and **declare** commands.
13. Define command line expansion and explain the use of quoting when entering commands.
14. Explain the purpose and function of sourcing and determine if an initialization file should be sourced.

Student Outcomes

1. Use the **ps**, **pstree**, **uptime**, and **top** commands to view and interpret information given about the processes that are currently running.
2. Use **kill** and **killall** commands, as well as their available options, to terminate processes.
3. Use the **jobs** command to see what commands are running and the **fg** and **bg** commands to send processes to the background or to the foreground.
4. Use the vi editor to write a shell script, and then use the **chmod** command to make the file executable.
5. Use the **type** and **help** commands to see the kind and purpose of the command being used, and then use the **alias** command to create shortcuts to selected commands.
6. Use the built-in commands **dirs**, **pushd**, and **popd** to manipulate the directory stack.
7. Create and remove variables.
8. Use **export** and **declare -x** commands with environmental variables.
9. Use the single quote, double quote, and backslash with variables.
10. Explain the order in which the shell processes command line expansion.
11. Revise the **.bashrc** file and source it.

Commands Introduced

$?	dirs	exit
alias	dot	export
bg	echo	fg
declare	exec	fork

help	ps	top
if	pstree	type
jobs	pushd	unalias
kill	set	unset
killall	source	uptime
popd		

9.1 • The Shell

When you log into your Linux system, you are typically at the shell prompt. You may issue commands from here or start the GUI by using the **startx** command. However, the shell is simply a program with which the user can interact to issue commands. In reality, the Linux operating system is divided into two pieces: the kernel and the utilities. See Figure 9.1, "The Linux System."

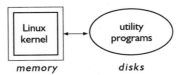

memory   *disks*

Figure 9.1 • The Linux System

The *kernel* is the heart of any operating system. It is responsible for such tasks as resource allocation and low-level hardware interfaces. Typically, the kernel includes an interrupt handler that handles all requests or completed I/O (input/output) operations that compete for the kernel's services, a scheduler that determines which programs share the kernel's processing time and in which order, and a supervisor that gives use of the computer to each process when it is scheduled. A kernel usually includes a manager of the operating system's address spaces in memory or storage. This manager shares the memory or storage among all components and other users of the kernel's services. A kernel's services are requested by other parts of the operating system or by application programs through a specified set of program interfaces sometimes known as system calls. The kernel is the part of the operating system that loads first, and it remains in main memory until you turn off the computer.

The utilities reside on the disk and are brought into memory only when you request that a command be executed. Nearly every command you have used has been a utility brought from disk to memory, including the shell itself.

9.2 • The Role of the Shell

The shell is a very powerful tool. There are many things for which the shell is responsible. These include the following:

• **Execution of programs**

This is how you have been interacting with the shell. You key in a command with options and arguments. The shell reads the command and the options and arguments, and then it has the job of determining which program to execute and locating the program on disk. The shell also has the job of passing the options and arguments to the program that is to be executed. These commands brought from disk into memory require that a new process be created for them to run in, referred to as "forking," which uses the **fork** command. These commands can also be called external commands since they are "external" to memory and must be brought into memory to execute. However, not all commands are brought from disk to memory. There is another set of commands called *built-in* commands. Also known as internal commands, these are commands that are "built into" the shell, which knows how to execute and run them within the environment of the current shell. When the shell runs a built-in, it does not have to fork a new process. Thus, built-ins run more quickly and can affect the environment of the current shell.

- **Ambiguous file references and variable substitution**

    When you use ambiguous file references—i.e, wildcards such as the * and ?—the shell, prior to running the program, first interprets the special character and finds the files that match that character so it may pass the arguments to the selected command. For instance, if you have files called **my.txt**, **your.txt**, and **his.txt** and if you key in the command **ls** *.txt, the shell locates all the files that have **.txt** as an extension. It then passes each of those file names to the **ls** command. The **ls** command never sees the *, but the shell passes the arguments of **my.txt**, **your.txt**, and **his.txt** to the **ls** command. As far as the **ls** command is concerned, it is as if you keyed in **ls   my.txt your.txt his.txt** on the command line. The same is true with variable substitution. You can, as you will learn later, assign a value to a variable. When you precede the variable name with a dollar sign ($), the shell will substitute the value that was assigned to that variable. You have used this feature with predetermined variables such as **PATH** or **PS1**. When you keyed in **echo $PATH**, the shell substituted the value for **PATH** on your system.

- **Redirection**

    It is the shell's responsibility to recognize the special redirection symbols (>, >>, and <). When it reads the command line and encounters a redirection symbol, it takes the next word on the command line as the name of the file (or device—remember that in Linux a device is a file) that the standard output is to be redirected to. Before the shell starts the execution of the requested program, it redirects the standard output to the named file. As far as the program is concerned, it runs in the usual way. It is unaware that its standard output is being redirected to a file. The same would be true for the >> and the < symbols.

- **Pipes**

    It is the shell's responsibility to recognize the special pipe symbol (|). When it reads the command line and encounters the pipe symbol, it takes the standard output from the command before the pipe and gives it as standard input to the command following the pipe. It then executes both (or more) programs on the command line. Again, as far as the program is concerned, it writes standard output in the usual way, unaware that its output is not being written to the terminal but is being used as input to the next command. The next command that wants standard input is also unaware that its standard input is not coming from the keyboard but is coming from the output of the preceding command.

- **Controlling the environment**

    When you log onto your system, you are given your own copy of the shell. This is your environment. Your environment includes such items as your home directory and your search path. You may customize this environment.

- **Interpreted Programming Language**

    The shell has its own built-in programming language which allows you to create shell scripts (write your own programs). The shell language is an interpreted language; that is, the shell analyzes your script one line at a time and executes it one line at a time. This differs from other programming languages like C or Visual Basic, which provide a compiled program. When you buy software or run executable programs, you typically purchase or use an executable version of a program. This means that the program is already in machine language—it has already been compiled and assembled and is ready to execute. A compiler is a special program that processes statements written in a particular programming language and turns them into machine language or "code" that a computer's processor uses. Compiled programs take less time to run than interpreted programs.

9.3 ● Process Structure

A *process* is an executing program. The operating system tracks every process through an identification number called the process identification (PID). The process structure is hierarchical, like the file system. There is a root process that is the parent to all processes. A process has a parent and can have children. When you turn on your computer, a single process begins called **init**. The **init** process is the root process; it is created when you initialize or start your system. All other processes are created by the **fork** and **exec** commands, also referred to as system routines or system calls. A system call is used by a process (the parent) to make a copy (the child) of itself. The child process is identical to the parent except it has a different process identifier and a zero return value from the **fork** call. A **fork** followed by an **exec** can be used to start a different process. See Figure 9.2, "**fork** and **exec**."

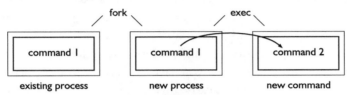

Figure 9.2 ● fork and exec

When you turn on your computer, **init** starts and gets a program called **getty**. The purpose of **getty** is to determine the speed of your terminal and other such information and display the login message at the assigned terminal. It then waits until you key something in. As soon as you key in your login name, the **getty** program goes away but before it does, it starts a program called **login**, which presents the password prompt. The **login** program then has the job of verifying your login name and your password against the **/etc/passwd** file. Once **login** determines that you are a valid user, it then looks for which program to load. In Red Hat Linux, it is normally **/bin/bash**. But the shell could be any of the various shells provided in the Unix/Linux world, such as the korn shell (**ksh**) or the Bourne shell (**sh**). Once the chosen shell is loaded, you are then are presented with the command prompt.

When you are in the shell, you key in the command you wish to execute. The shell has the job of analyzing what you keyed in and processing your request. If you key in a command such as **ls**, the shell looks for the command on disk. When the shell locates the command, it asks the kernel to start the execution of the selected program. At that point the shell goes to sleep until the program execution is complete. The kernel copies the program, such as **ls**, into memory and then **ls** executes. In this example, **ls** is copied into memory and is executing. Now **ls** is a process. You can think of **ls** as a program when stored on disk and a process when running in memory. When **ls** has completed execution, you are returned to the shell, which waits for your next command. There are, obviously, other scenarios. If, for instance, you execute a program such as **cat** and press **Enter**, the shell will wait for input from the keyboard (standard input). This cycle continues until you log off. When you log off, then **init** starts a new **getty**, and the cycle continues. See Figure 9.3, "The Login Cycle."

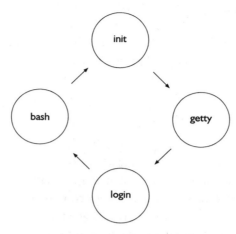

Figure 9.3 • The Login Cycle

9.4 • Processes

Whenever you issue a command, it creates or starts a new process. This consists of the program code (which may be shared with other processes that are executing the same program) and private data. The process may have other associated resources such as a process identifier, open files, CPU time limits, shared memory, or child processes. A multitasking operating system can run processes concurrently or in parallel. If you have only one processor, then two or more processes have access to the CPU and are carried out nearly simultaneously. Concurrent processes appear to occur at the same time, but they really do not. Each program is assigned some CPU time in turn. Thus, each program runs more slowly, but without visible interruption. The kernel of the operating system controls and manages the processes. Among its tasks is a determination of what the priority is for use of the CPU. If you had multiple CPUs, the operating system could divide up the instructions and perform them at the same time (in parallel).

When you have issued a command such as **ls**, you begin a process. The operating system must create an environment for the program to run in. The operating system must allocate resources for the program to use, such as allocation of memory to store the program's instructions and data. Processes can assume different states. The most frequent states are R (running), S (sleeping—when the program has nothing to do and is waiting for input), and T (temporarily interrupted or stopped). You may also see Z, so called zombies, that remain because their parent has not destroyed them properly. The processes managed by Linux are mapped to the **/proc** directory. The entries in this directory do not correspond to actual files on a disk. Instead, they are just items of information that can be displayed by using the file system. With many commands, you are not aware that the system is operating concurrently until you run a time-consuming command. For instance, when you formatted a disk, you had to wait until the process was complete before you could key in another command. However, you could have opened another terminal and continue working, or if you are running X Window System, you would achieve the same results by opening another terminal window and keying in your new command.

When you successfully log in, you launch the shell. The shell belongs to a process group identified by the group's PID. The shell is in charge of the terminal and waits for you to key in a command.

The shell can spawn (create) other processes. When you *spawn* a process, you create a child process in a multitasking operating system such as Linux. The child program is spawned from the parent program. When you enter a command at the prompt or from a shell script, the shell must find the command you asked for, either from the built-in commands or from disk. It then arranges for the command to be executed by system calls to the kernel. A system call is a request for kernel services and is the only way a process can access the hardware of the system. Figure 9.4, "Shell and Command Execution," shows the processes that occur.

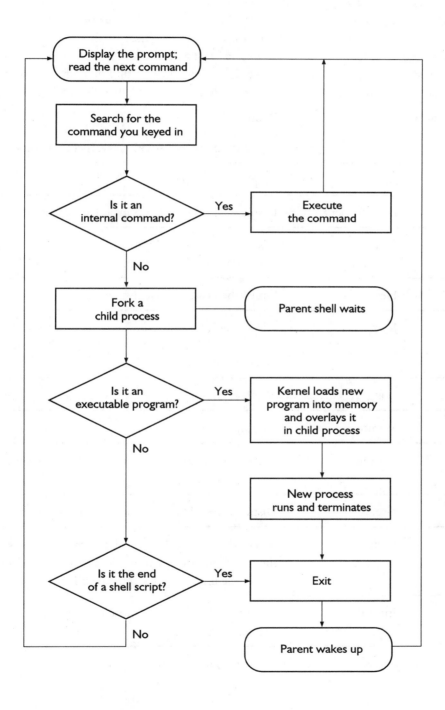

Figure 9.4 • Shell and Command Execution

There are several commands to assist you in seeing what processes are running. Among these are **ps**, **pstree**, **uptime**, and **top**. The **ps** command will report on active processes. The **pstree** command is another way to see what processes are running and to see what processes are child processes. The **uptime** command will report the current time, the amount of time logged in, the number of users logged in, and the system load averages. The *load average* is a number based on the number of processes waiting to run at a given time. The higher the load average, the less CPU time each process gets. The **top** command will report on the most CPU-intensive processes running. The **top** command is dynamic and essentially combines the output of several commands, allowing you to sort processes by the percentage of processor time they use, memory the processes use, or the total time they have run on the system.

The **ps** syntax is **ps** *[options] process-numbers*. The **ps** command accepts options without a hyphen; however, it is good practice to include it. You may also find different results when you use or do not use the hyphen. For useful options for **ps**, see Table 9.1, "ps Options."

Option	Name	Result
a	All with tty	Displays all processes with a tty, including other users.
A	All	Displays all processes.
e	Environment	Displays all processes and includes environment.
f	Full	Displays process information in a tree format (a forest), the parent process, and their relations.
h	Header	Omits the header in the display.
j	Jobs	Displays job information. Lists the processes of users and group users in numerical format and will include the parent process IDs.
l	Long	Displays a long listing.
m	Memory	Displays details on memory use for each process.
t	Terminal	Displays only the process attached to the terminal name that follows.
u	User	Displays user ID and memory use information.
w	Wide	If you have a long display, **ps** truncates the lines when they reach the right side of the display. Use of this option causes the lines to wrap to the next line.
x	Includes	Displays processes, even those not owned by the controlling terminal.

Table 9.1 • ps Options

The **top** command has both options that can be run at the command line, and, once you have started the **top** command, you may toggle different interactive commands. For useful options for **top**, see Table 9.2, "**top** Command Line Options."

Option	Name	Result
d *time*	Delay	Specifies the delay between screen updates. **d** is followed by a time.
P *pid*	Processes	Specifies which pid to monitor. **p** is followed by the process id number.
q	No delay	Refreshes the display without any delay.
S	Cumulative	Displays total CPU time of each process, including dead children.

Table 9.2 • top Command Line Options

Table 9.3 lists the interactive options for the **top** interactive command.

Toggle	Result
Space Bar	Immediately updates display.
A	Sorts task by age with newest listed first.
f or F	Adds or removes fields from the display.
h	Displays help screen.
k	Kills a process. You will be prompted for the pid number of the process you want to kill and the signal to send to it. A normal signal is 15.
M	Sorts processes by memory used in descending order.
n	Changes the number of processes to display.
N	Sorts tasks by pid numerically.
o or O	Changes the order of displayed fields.
s	Changes the delay between updates. You will be prompted to enter the time.
S	Toggles cumulative mode on or off.
q	Quit.
T	Sorts by the amount of processor time the process has used in descending order, either cumulatively or since the last refresh of the top screen.

Table 9.3 • Interactive top Options

9.5 • Activity: Looking at Processes

Note: You are logged in and have started X Window System (**startx**).

STEP 1   Open a terminal window. Key in the following: **ps** Enter

```
[cgillay@RedHat9    cgillay]$  ps
  PID   TTY            TIME          CMD
 2723  pts/0          00:00:00      bash
 2805  pts/0          00:00:00      ps
[cgillay@RedHat9    cgillay]$
```

STEP 2   Open another terminal window. Key in the following: **ps** Enter

```
[cgillay@RedHat9    cgillay]$  ps
  PID   TTY            TIME          CMD
 2708  pts/1          00:00:00      bash
 2840  pts/1          00:00:00      ps
[cgillay@RedHat9    cgillay]$
```

WHAT'S **HAPPENING?** Each terminal window has a process id assigned to it. Your pid numbers will, of course, be different. The **ps** command shows you a list of all processes owned by the current user with the process identification number, the CPU time used by the process, and the command line itself. The **ps** command is itself listed, since it is a process. In Linux, all the resources of the system are managed by the program called the kernel. Everything else that runs on the system is a process. The shell then creates a new process each time you enter a command. Remember, when a new process is created, it is called *forking* since one process splits into two. If you are running X Window System, each process starts in one or more windows. The window where you are entering commands is owned by an **xterm** process, which in turn forks a shell to run within the window, and that shell forks even more processes as you continue your work.

STEP 3   Close the second terminal window. In the open terminal window, key in the following:
ps -a Enter

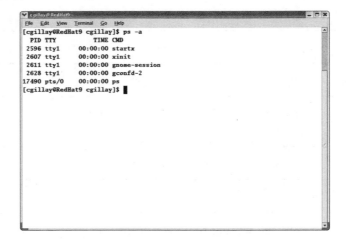

WHAT'S **HAPPENING?** When you use the **-a** option, you see a list of all the processes owned by this specific tty.

STEP 4   Key in the following: **ps x** Enter

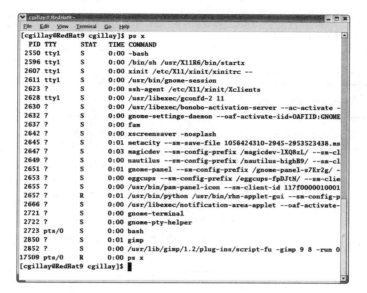

WHAT'S **HAPPENING?** > In this case, when you used the **x** option, you did not preface it with a hyphen. When you use the **x** option, you see all the processes, even those without a controlling tty. The first entry (**-bash**) indicates the bash shell that was started by the logon process. You also see the status. In this example, most of these processes are sleeping.

STEP 5   Key in the following: **ps -af** Enter

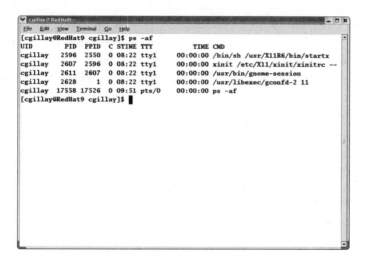

WHAT'S **HAPPENING?** > Here you did use the hyphen preceding the options. When you used the hyphen, you selected all the processes with a tty. If you do not use the hyphen, you would get a display limited to this terminal window. See Table 9.4, "**ps** Descriptions."

Name	Description
UID	User identification—the login id of the user who owns the process, in this case **cgillay**.

PID	The process ID number for the process you are running.
PPID	The parent process ID number for the parent of the current process you are running.
C	The CPU utilization of the process.
STIME	The time the process began to run
TTY	The terminal ID that the process is associated with.
TIME	Refers to how much time the process has run. This can be deceiving, as in this example it appears that none of the processes have used any time at all. However, the number refers to how much time the process has required from the operating system. At this point, these processes have required little time from the operating system.
CMD	The command that is the process.

Table 9.4 • ps Descriptions

When you key in a command, the shell parses the command. To *parse* is to analyze something in an orderly way. In linguistics, to parse is to divide words and phrases into different parts in order to understand relationships and meaning. In general, to parse someone's writing or speech simply means to interpret it. When used in computer terminology, to parse is to divide a computer language statement into parts that can be made useful for the computer, or actually for the operating system. The shell has to interpret what you keyed in on the command line.

The shell evaluates what you have keyed in. It first has to determine whether or not the first word is a built-in command or an executable program. Remember, some commands are built directly into the shell; they are part of the shell. The shell always tries to execute a built-in before it tries to find a command with the same name in your search path. Furthermore, to execute a built-in, the shell does not have to fork a process. If the command is not a built-in, the shell invokes the fork system call to make a copy of itself. Its child will search the path for the command you requested as well as handle other details, such as setting up the file descriptors. While the child works, the parent process normally sleeps.

The parent shell is in a wait state. **wait** is also a system call. Remember, the child is handling the details of the command you keyed in. The wait system call causes the parent process to suspend until one of its child processes ends. If the wait is a successful one, it will return the pid of the child and the exit status. The wait system call not only puts a parent to sleep, but also ensures that the process terminates correctly. For instance, if the parent dies before the child, the *init* process adopts any orphaned zombie processes.

After you have keyed in a command, the shell forks off a child process. The child searches for the program you asked to execute. If it finds it, the child calls the **exec** system call with the name of the command as the argument. The kernel loads the new program in place of the shell that called it. The child is then overlaid with the new program. The new program now becomes the child process and begins to execute. When the process is complete, the parent shell awakens. The child shell normally sends a signal to the parent and waits for the parent to accept the child's exit status. Figure 9.5, "System Calls," shows an example of this process using the **grep** command.

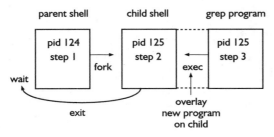

Figure 9.5 • System Calls

In Step 1 of this example, the parent process creates a copy of itself with the **fork** system call, which is called the child shell. The parent is in a wait state. Then, in Step 2, the child shell has a new pid and will share the CPU with its parent. The kernel loads the **grep** program into memory and executes it (**exec**) in place of the child shell. In Step 3, the **grep** program exits, sending a signal to the parent, the kernel cleans up, and the parent is awakened.

Going back to the display, in this example the top line has a process id of 2596 (**/bin/sh**). The second line has a process id of 2607, but its parent process is 2596, or the original shell that was launched. By using the **e** and **l** options, you will be able to see that the parent process of many of the processes is 1 (*init*).

STEP 6   Key in the following: ps -el | more [Enter]

```
cgillay@RedHat9:~
File  Edit  View  Terminal  Go  Help
[cgillay@RedHat9 cgillay]$ ps -el | more
F S   UID   PID  PPID  C PRI  NI ADDR    SZ WCHAN  TTY        TIME CMD
4 S     0     1     0  0  75   0  -     343 schedu ?      00:00:04 init
1 S     0     2     1  0  75   0  -       0 contex ?      00:00:00 keventd
1 S     0     3     1  0  75   0  -       0 schedu ?      00:00:00 kapmd
1 S     0     4     1  0  94  19  -       0 ksofti ?      00:00:00 ksoftirqd_
CPU0
1 S     0     9     1  0  75   0  -       0 bdflus ?      00:00:00 bdflush
1 S     0     5     1  0  75   0  -       0 schedu ?      00:00:00 kswapd
1 S     0     6     1  0  75   0  -       0 schedu ?      00:00:00 kscand/DMA
1 S     0     7     1  0  75   0  -       0 schedu ?      00:00:00 kscand/Nor
mal
1 S     0     8     1  0  75   0  -       0 schedu ?      00:00:00 kscand/Hig
hMem
1 S     0    10     1  0  75   0  -       0 schedu ?      00:00:00 kupdated
1 S     0    11     1  0  85   0  -       0 md_thr ?      00:00:00 mdrecovery
d
1 S     0    15     1  0  75   0  -       0 end    ?      00:00:00 kjournald
1 S     0    73     1  0  85   0  -       0 end    ?      00:00:00 khubd
1 S     0  1717     1  0  75   0  -       0 end    ?      00:00:00 kjournald
1 S     0  2085     1  0  83   0  -     491 schedu ?      00:00:00 dhclient
5 S     0  2125     1  0  75   0  -     362 schedu ?      00:00:00 syslogd
5 S     0  2129     1  0  75   0  -     342 do_sys ?      00:00:00 klogd
--More--
```

WHAT'S HAPPENING? Here you can see that the parent process (1) is **init**. When you start up your system, the **init** process is the first process. Its job is to initialize the system, then begin other processes to open terminals. It also sets up your standard input, standard output and standard error, and so on. Since it is the first process, it is the parent process of many other processes. Another way to see what processes are running is to use the **pstree** command. This command displays all the processes as a tree with the root being the first process run, **init**.

STEP 7   Press **q**. Key in the following: **pstree** | more [Enter]

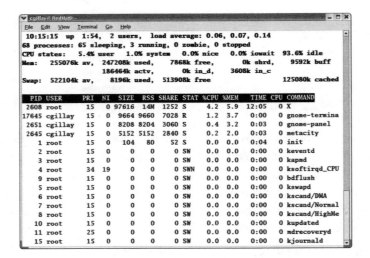

WHAT'S HAPPENING? Here you see the **init** process at the top of the tree with the other processes listed in a hierarchical fashion. If you want to know what the load is on your system, you can use the **uptime** command. The load average is a number that measures the number of processes waiting to run at some given time. The higher the load average, the less CPU time each process is getting.

STEP 8   Press **q**. Key in the following: **uptime** [Enter]

```
[cgillay@RedHat9  cgillay]$  uptime
10:12:43  up    1:51  2 users, load average 0.04, 0.10, 0.16
[cgillay@RedHat9  cgillay]$
```

WHAT'S HAPPENING? Since not much is happening on this system, the load average is quite low. There are two users, since you are running are terminal window in GNOME. The **top** command is a dynamic utility; it combines the output of several other utilities and shows all processes that are running.

STEP 9   Key in the following: **top** [Enter]

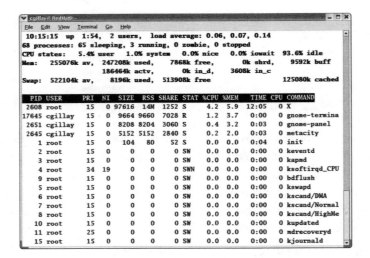

WHAT'S HAPPENING? You see information such as how many users, the load average, and so on. It is interesting to note how many processes are running, even though you are not "doing"

much at this point. The display is ranked by CPU usage so you can tell what processes are using the most resources.

STEP 10   Press **M**

WHAT'S HAPPENING? ⊱ You used **M** to sort the display by memory usage. You can see that in this example, X takes the most memory, followed by the various GNOME applications. In general, graphical displays and environments take the most memory.

STEP 11   Press **q**.

WHAT'S HAPPENING? ⊱ You have returned to the terminal window.

9.6 ● **The kill and killall Commands**

A signal sends a message to a process and normally causes the process to end or terminate. Signals can be sent to a process by certain key sequences such as **Ctrl** + **C**. All processes sharing the terminal are affected by the signal sent. You may also use a command, the **kill** command, to send a signal to terminate a process. If no signal is specified, the **TERM** signal is sent, which normally kills the process. A process can choose to ignore the signal or use it to begin an orderly shut down, including flushing buffers, closing files, and so on. You may only kill processes that your user id owns. However, the root user can kill any process. The syntax of kill is **kill** [*option*] *pid*. Table 9.5, "**kill** Options," lists some major options used with the **kill** command.

Option	Name	Result
-s	Signal	Specifies which signal to send. Signal may be a signal name or number.
-l	List	Displays a list of signal names.
-p	Print	Only displays the process id of the named process and does not send any signals.
pid	Process ID	Specifies the list of processes that **kill** should signal.

Table 9.5 ● kill Options

You may also use the **killall** command, which will kill a process by name if you do not know the process id number. The **killall** command sends a signal to all processes running any of the specified commands. If more than one process is running the specified command, it will kill all of them. It will treat command names that contain a / as files and will kill all processes that are executing that file. The syntax is **killall** [*options*] *names.* Table 9.6, "**killall** options," lists some major options used with the **killall** command.

Option	Name	Result
-signal	Signal	Sends a signal to the process. Signal may be name or number.
-I	Interactive	Prompts for confirmation before killing a process.
-l	Lists	Displays a list of known signal names.
-v	Verbose	After killing a process, displays success and process id.

Table 9.6 • killall Options

9.7 • Activity: Using the kill and killall Commands with Processes

Note: A terminal window is open and your home directory is your default directory.

STEP 1   Key in the following: **kill -l** [Enter]

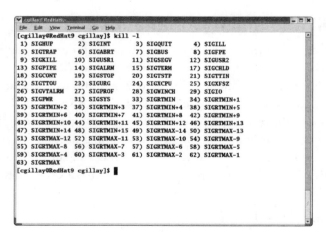

WHAT'S HAPPENING? Here you see a list of all the available signals and their signal id number. **SIGTERM (15)** is normally what is sent when you kill a process.

STEP 2   Open another terminal window. In the new window, key in the following:
find /bin/m* /etc/p* /e* /etc/p* /bin/m* | more [Enter]

STEP 3   Activate the first terminal window. Key in the following: **ps -a** [Enter]

WHAT'S HAPPENING? You first looked for files by running the **find** command, and you piped the result to the **more** command. You then asked for all the processes running. If you had keyed in **ps**, you would have only seen the processes in the current terminal window. In this example, **more** has a process number of 17869. You want to kill **more**. Your process number will be different. To kill **more**, substitute your process id number for pidmore.

STEP 4   Key in the following: **kill** *pidmore* [Enter]

WHAT'S HAPPENING? If you look at the second terminal window, you can see that **more** was terminated and you have been returned to the prompt. If you run **ps** and the list is too long and you know the process name, you can pipe the output to the **grep** command to obtain the process id. Thus, the command would be **ps -a | grep more**, substituting the name of the command you were looking for. You may also use the **killall** command with the process name.

STEP 5   Close one open terminal window. Click the Main Menu button. Point to **Accessories**.
Click **Text Editor**.

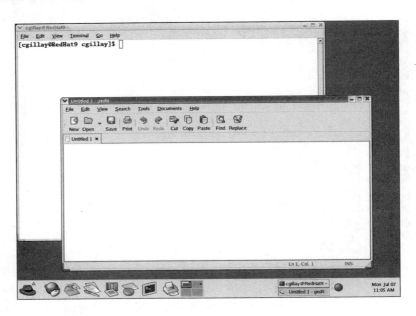

WHAT'S **HAPPENING?** You have two programs open: **shell** and **gedit**.

STEP 6   In the terminal window, key in the following: **killall gedit** ⌈Enter⌋

WHAT'S **HAPPENING?** You used the **killall** command with the process name and thus closed **gedit**.

STEP 7   Close the terminal window.

WHAT'S **HAPPENING?** You have returned to the desktop.

9.8 • The fg, bg, and jobs Commands

In the examples you have so far used, your commands have been run in foreground. A command run in foreground must be completed before the shell returns you to a prompt. A command that runs in the background can continue running while you run other commands. If you append a **&** (ampersand) to the end of a command, you are placing that command in background. When you do, the shell (not the operating system) assigns a job number to that command. Job numbers refer to background processes that are currently running under your shell. A job number is different from a process number. Processes number refer to all processes running on the entire system for all users. A job is simply a command line that was executed from your shell. If you continue issuing background commands while the first background command is running, the shell will sequentially number those additional jobs. If you only have one background command running, the **fg** command will bring that background job to the foreground. If you have more than one background job running, the shell will select the most recent program that is running in the background to bring to the foreground. If you want to bring another background job to the foreground, you must use **fg** with the command name, preceded by a **%** (percent) sign or **fg** with the job number, also preceded by a **%** sign. You may also invoke the job most recently placed in background by keying in **fg %+**. If you key in **fg %-**, you will bring into foreground the next most recently placed job that was placed in the background.

You may also place a command running in foreground in background with the **bg** command. However, you need to suspend the currently running job so you may regain control of the terminal. You do so by pressing ⌷Ctrl⌷ + Z. The **jobs** command lists your jobs that are running. The **jobs**, **fg**, and **bg** commands are all built-in commands.

9.9 • Activity: Using the fg, bg, and jobs Commands

STEP 1   Open a terminal window. Key in the following: **stty -a** ⌷Enter⌷

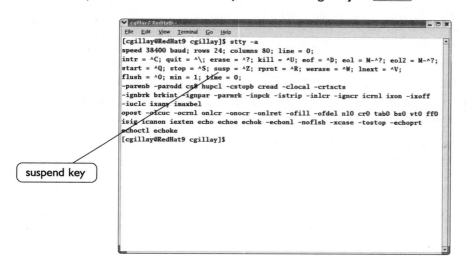

suspend key

WHAT'S HAPPENING? ⟩ The **stty** command allows you to print and change your terminal line settings. The **-a** option shows all your settings. If you look at your display, you should see a setting for **susp = ^Z**. This confirms that pressing the ⌷Ctrl⌷ and **Z** key will suspend a job.

STEP 2   Key in the following: **cal 10 2004&** ⌷Enter⌷

STEP 3   Key in the following: **cal 10 2004&** Enter

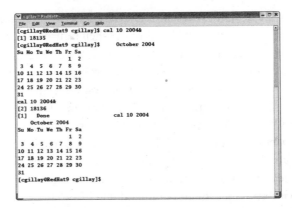

WHAT'S HAPPENING? You ran the **cal** command twice in background. The number in brackets [1], is the job number. Since this is a very quick command, the program responded with [1] Done. The second command has a job number of [2].

STEP 4   Key in the following: **jobs** Enter

```
[cgillay@RedHat9  cgillay]$  jobs
[2]+  Done                          cal 10 2004
[cgillay@RedHat9  cgillay]$
```

WHAT'S HAPPENING? You have no jobs running so the **jobs** command shows you the completed state of job 2.

STEP 5   Key in the following: **vi test.fil&** Enter

```
[cgillay@RedHat9  cgillay]$  vi test.fil&
[1] 18151
[cgillay@RedHat9  cgillay]$
```

WHAT'S HAPPENING? Your process number will be different. In this example, [1] is the job number and 18151 is the process id. You are not in vi, but you were returned to the prompt as you are running vi in the background. Since you have only one job running, you can bring it to foreground by keying in **fg**. However, if you want to select which job to bring forward, you can use the job number preceded by the percent sign (%).

STEP 6   Key in the following: **fg %1** Enter

WHAT'S HAPPENING? The vi program is now in foreground.

STEP 7   Key in the following: **:q!** Enter

```
[cgillay@RedHat9   cgillay]$   fg %1
vi test.fil
[cgillay@RedHat9   cgillay]$
```

WHAT'S HAPPENING? You brought vi to the foreground and then exited vi without saving the file.

STEP 8   Mount the BOOK2 floppy disk.

STEP 9   Key in the following: **gedit &** Enter

STEP 10   Click the terminal window to return the keyboard focus to it. Key in the following:
vi & Enter

STEP 11   Key in the following: **vi test &** Enter

STEP 12   Key in the following: **find / -iname '*.fil' 2>/dev/null | grep personal.fil &** Enter

STEP 13   Key in the following: **jobs** Enter

```
[cgillay@RedHat9 cgillay]$ gedit &
[1] 18496
[cgillay@RedHat9 cgillay]$ vi &
[2] 18497
[cgillay@RedHat9 cgillay]$ vi test &
[3] 18498

[2]+  Stopped                vim
[cgillay@RedHat9 cgillay]$ find / -iname '*.fil' 2>/dev/null | grep personal.fil
&
[4] 18500

[3]+  Stopped                vim test
[cgillay@RedHat9 cgillay]$ jobs
[1]   Running                gedit &
[2]-  Stopped                vim
[3]+  Stopped                vim test
[4]   Running                find / -iname '*.fil' 2>/dev/null | grep personal.
fil &
[cgillay@RedHat9 cgillay]$ ▊
```

WHAT'S HAPPENING? You opened a copy of the **gedit** program. You then opened two copies of **vi**. You then ran a **find** command. The output from the **find** command is running. Then you saw the status of your jobs. The **find** command is running as well as the other three programs. You see a job number as well as a **+** for the most recent job and a **-** for the last job placed in background. You cannot abort a process you are running in background with the interrupt key, usually ⌷**Ctrl** + **C**. You can use the **kill** command to end these processes.

STEP 14 Key in the following: **ps** ⌷**Enter**⌷

```
[cgillay@RedHat9 cgillay]$ find / -iname '*.fil' 2>/dev/null | grep personal.fil
&
[4] 18500

[3]+  Stopped                 vim test
[cgillay@RedHat9 cgillay]$ jobs
[1]   Running                 gedit &
[2]-  Stopped                 vim
[3]+  Stopped                 vim test
[4]   Running                 find / -iname '*.fil' 2>/dev/null | grep personal.
fil &
[cgillay@RedHat9 cgillay]$ /home/cgillay/.Trash/personal.fil
/mnt/floppy/personal.fil
/IMAGES/book2ch08/personal.fil
ps
  PID TTY          TIME CMD
18464 pts/0    00:00:00 bash
18496 pts/0    00:00:00 gedit
18497 pts/0    00:00:00 vim
18498 pts/0    00:00:00 vim
18516 pts/0    00:00:00 ps
[4]   Done                    find / -iname '*.fil' 2>/dev/null | grep personal.
fil
[cgillay@RedHat9 cgillay]$
```

WHAT'S HAPPENING? By this time, the **find** command may be completed. Each **vim** and the **gedit** has a process number. In this example 18496 was the **gedit** placed in background. Then **vim** was assigned 18497 and 18498 as process numbers. Use your own process id number. *1pidnumber* will represent your first process number.

STEP 15 Key in the following: **kill *1pidnumber   2pidnumber 3pidnumber*** ⌷**Enter**⌷

```
[cgillay@RedHat9  cgillay]$  kill 18496 18497 18498
[cgillay@RedHat9  cgillay]$
```

WHAT'S HAPPENING? You have returned to the prompt and closed all open **gedit** windows. In the X Window System environment, in the GNOME desktop, you could have also simply opened multiple terminal windows so that if you had a long running job, you could have it run in one terminal window while you did work in the other terminal window.

9.10 ● Shell Scripts

A shell script is a file that contains commands that can be executed by the shell. Any command that you can run at the command line can be placed in a shell script. Anything that you may do on a command line such as use wildcards or pipes and filters may also be placed in a shell script. The simplest way to execute a shell script is to give its file name on the command line, presuming the script is in a directory that is included in the search path. The shell then reads and executes the commands in the script, one after another because it is an interpreted language. A shell script allows you to initiate a complex series of commands or commands that are repetitive in nature.

In order to execute a shell script, the user must have permission to read and execute the file that is the shell script. The execute permissions tell the shell and the operating system that the owner, group, or others have permission to execute the shell script. Of course, the shell script must be a viable series of Linux commands. If the command does not work on the command line, it will not work in a shell script either. When you create the shell script in an editor such as vi, you will need to use the **chmod** command to make the file executable.

9.11 ● Activity: Writing Shell Scripts

Note: The BOOK2 disk is mounted. A terminal window is open. Your default directory is your home directory.

STEP 1   Key in the following: **vi a**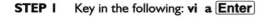

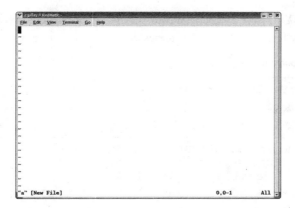

WHAT'S **HAPPENING?** ◌ You are going to create a file that will display the letter "a" fifteen times per line. When writing the file, remember the **yy** command in vi. You can enter "a" fifteen times in insert mode, then return to command mode, use **yy** and then **p** to paste the line four times.

STEP 2   Enter the following lines in **vi**.
>   **echo aaaaaaaaaaaaaaa**
>   **echo aaaaaaaaaaaaaaa**
>   **echo aaaaaaaaaaaaaaa**
>   **echo aaaaaaaaaaaaaaa**
>   **echo aaaaaaaaaaaaaaa**

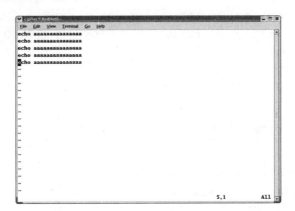

WHAT'S **HAPPENING?** ◌ You have created a shell script that will display the letter "a" fifteen times per line. This script does not do anything but **echo** each line of characters on the screen. You are going to create four "alphabet" files so you may see how shell scripts work and how to place the different scripts in background and foreground.

STEP 3   Save the file and exit vi.

STEP 4   Create three more files, **b**, **c**, and **d**, which will be the same as "**a**" except that **b** will **echo b**, **c** will **echo c**, and **d** will **echo d**.

STEP 5   Key in the following: **ls** [Enter]

```
[cgillay@RedHat9  cgillay]$  ls
a  b  c  d  evolution  practice5  practice6  practice7  practice8
[cgillay@RedHat9  cgillay]$
```

WHAT'S HAPPENING? You have at least the four files you just created in your home directory. You may have more or fewer files and directories depending on your system.

STEP 6   Key in the following: **a** [Enter]

```
[cgillay@RedHat9  cgillay]$  a
bash: a: command not found
[cgillay@RedHat9  cgillay]$
```

STEP 7   Key in the following: **ls -l a** [Enter]

```
[cgillay@RedHat9  cgillay]$  ls -l a
-rw-rw-r--  1  cgillay  cgillay         105  Jul 7 12:07 a
[cgillay@RedHat9  cgillay]$
```

WHAT'S HAPPENING? Remember, when you key in text, it is the shell's job to read the text and determine what to do with what you keyed in. The shell has the job of first determining which program to execute, and then locating the program on disk so it may be executed. However, **a** is not yet a program that the shell recognizes. You must make it executable. For the purposes of the exercises, you are going to give everyone permissions to execute this file.

STEP 8   Key in the following: **chmod 777 a b c d; ls -l a b c d** [Enter]

```
[cgillay@RedHat9  cgillay]$  chmod  777 a b  c d; ls -l a b  c d
-rwxrwxrwx 1  cgillay  cgillay         105  Jul 7 12:07 a
-rwxrwxrwx 1  cgillay  cgillay         105  Jul 7 12:07 b
-rwxrwxrwx 1  cgillay  cgillay         105  Jul 7 12:07 c
-rwxrwxrwx 1  cgillay  cgillay         105  Jul 7 12:07 d
[cgillay@RedHat9  cgillay]$
```

WHAT'S HAPPENING? You have made your "alphabet" files executable.

STEP 9   Key in the following: **a** [Enter]

```
[cgillay@RedHat9  cgillay]$  a
bash: a: command not found
[cgillay@RedHat9  cgillay]$
```

WHAT'S HAPPENING? Your logon shell is not set up to search for executable programs in your home directory. You can verify this by looking at your path.

STEP 10   Key in the following: **echo $PATH** [Enter]

```
[cgillay@RedHat9   cgillay]$   echo $PATH
/usr/kerberos/bin:/usr/local/bin:/bin:/usr/bin:/usr/X11R6/bin:
/home/cgillay/bin
[cgillay@RedHat9   cgillay]$
```

WHAT'S HAPPENING? In this example, the search path does not include your home directory but does include a directory called **/home/**_username_**/bin**.

STEP 11 Key in the following: **ls; ls -d .*** Enter

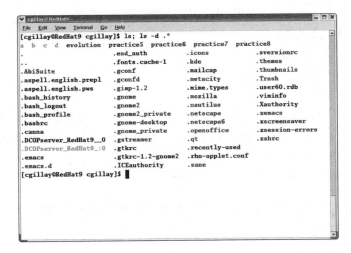

WHAT'S HAPPENING? You see that normally, by default, a directory called **/home/**_username_**/bin** is included in the search path. You just looked for a directory called **bin** in your home directory. The **.*** looked for any hidden directories. Remember, anything that is hidden is preceded by a . (period). In this example, even though the directory called **/home/**_username_**/bin** is in your search path, as of yet the **bin** directory does not exist. You must create it.

STEP 12 Key in the following: **mkdir bin; cp a b c d bin; cd bin; ls** Enter

```
[cgillay@RedHat9    cgillay]$ mkdir  bin;  cp  a  b  c  d bin;  cd bin;  ls
a  b  c  d
[cgillay@RedHat9    cgillay]$
```

WHAT'S HAPPENING? You changed permissions on your alphabet files in an earlier step to make them executable. You then created a **bin** directory where the shell, in the search path, looks for executable programs. You copied your alphabet scripts to the **bin** directory. You should now be able to execute your shell scripts.

STEP 13 Key in the following: **a; b; c; d** Enter

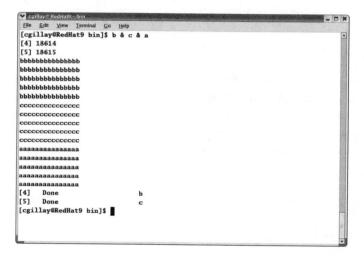

```
cgillay@RedHat9:~/bin
File  Edit  View  Terminal  Go  Help
[cgillay@RedHat9 cgillay]$ mkdir bin; cp a b c d bin; cd bin; ls
a   b   c   d
[cgillay@RedHat9 bin]$ a; b; c; d
aaaaaaaaaaaaaa
aaaaaaaaaaaaaa
aaaaaaaaaaaaaa
aaaaaaaaaaaaaa
aaaaaaaaaaaaaa
bbbbbbbbbbbbbb
bbbbbbbbbbbbbb
bbbbbbbbbbbbbb
bbbbbbbbbbbbbb
bbbbbbbbbbbbbb
cccccccccccccc
cccccccccccccc
cccccccccccccc
cccccccccccccc
cccccccccccccc
dddddddddddddd
dddddddddddddd
dddddddddddddd
dddddddddddddd
dddddddddddddd
[cgillay@RedHat9 bin]$
```

WHAT'S HAPPENING? You executed your scripts. Each script displayed ("echoed") the character to the screen. You executed the scripts in sequence. You did not get a prompt back until **d** was finished running. You may run these scripts in background.

STEP 14   Key in the following: **b & c & a** [Enter]

```
cgillay@RedHat9:~/bin
File  Edit  View  Terminal  Go  Help
[cgillay@RedHat9 bin]$ b & c & a
[4] 18614
[5] 18615
bbbbbbbbbbbbbb
bbbbbbbbbbbbbb
bbbbbbbbbbbbbb
bbbbbbbbbbbbbb
bbbbbbbbbbbbbb
cccccccccccccc
cccccccccccccc
cccccccccccccc
cccccccccccccc
cccccccccccccc
aaaaaaaaaaaaaa
aaaaaaaaaaaaaa
aaaaaaaaaaaaaa
aaaaaaaaaaaaaa
aaaaaaaaaaaaaa
[4]   Done                    b
[5]   Done                    c
[cgillay@RedHat9 bin]$
```

WHAT'S HAPPENING? Here you got a job number for **b** and **c** and your prompt was returned as soon as **a** was finished executing. Note that when you placed commands in background, you did not need to enter a **;** (semi-colon) to separate the commands. Also, since these are such small programs, the programs hardly needed to be in background.

STEP 15   Key in the following: **b& c& d&** [Enter]

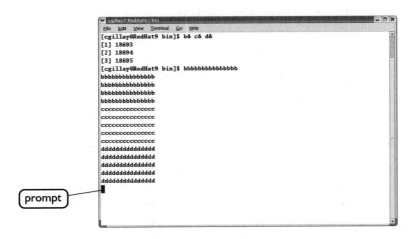

WHAT'S HAPPENING? You got your command prompt back immediately since all jobs were being run in background. It may appear as though you do not have your prompt back. However, the location of the cursor is your prompt. You may have gotten your prompt back depending on the speed of your processor.

STEP 16 Key in the following: **ls Enter**

```
ls
a   b   c   d
[1]      . Done              b
[2] -      Done              c
[3] +      Done              d
[cgillay@RedHat9  bin]$
```

WHAT'S HAPPENING? The + following the job number is the current job. The - following the job number was the previous job. You may also group commands with parentheses. The shell creates a copy of itself for each group, treating each group as a job and creating a new process to execute each of the commands.

STEP 17 Key in the following: **(ls .. /mnt/floppy;b; a)& ls /mnt/floppy/*.txt; c Enter**

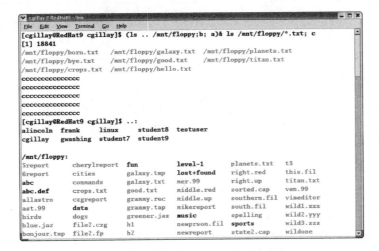

WHAT'S HAPPENING? To see the display as the command executed, you may need to scroll to the top of the terminal window. The commands **ls /mnt/floppy** and **c** ran immediately. The commands **ls /mnt/floppy**, **b**, and **a** did run in the background.

STEP 18   Press ⟨Enter⟩. Key in the following: **cd; rm -r bin; a** ⟨Enter⟩

```
[cgillay@RedHat9  bin]$  cd; rm -r bin; a
bash: a: command not found
[cgillay@RedHat9  cgillay]$
```

WHAT'S HAPPENING? You moved to your home directory. You then removed your **bin** directory. Your program no longer works because the shell is looking only in the **bin** directory for an executable file. You can still execute a program without its being in the search path, but you must key in the command a little differently. You preface the command you want to run with a period, followed by a forward slash, then the command.

STEP 19   Key in the following: **./a** ⟨Enter⟩

```
[cgillay@RedHat9  cgillay]$  ./a
aaaaaaaaaaaaaaa
aaaaaaaaaaaaaaa
aaaaaaaaaaaaaaa
aaaaaaaaaaaaaaa
aaaaaaaaaaaaaaa
[cgillay@RedHat9  cgillay]$
```

WHAT'S HAPPENING? As you can see, you can run the command even without having the command in the **bin** directory (or a directory that your path searches for executable files).

STEP 20   Be sure the BOOK2 disk is mounted.

STEP 21   Key in the following: **mv a b c d /mnt/floppy; ls** ⟨Enter⟩

```
[cgillay@RedHat9  cgillay]$  mv a b c d ; ls
evolution   practice5   practice6   practice7   practice8
[cgillay@RedHat9  cgillay]$
```

WHAT'S HAPPENING? You moved your shell scripts to your floppy disk so that they are no longer in your home directory.

9.12 • Command Types

You have been keying commands and they have executed. You have used built-in commands, executable programs, and now a shell script. There is an order in which commands are executed. The order is:

1. aliases
2. keywords
3. functions
4. built-in commands
5. executable programs

An *alias* is a shorthand name for a command or a series of commands. It is usually a user-defined abbreviation for a command. Aliases are particularly useful if there are certain options you use. The user may define an alias. Aliases may also be defined by the root and become part of your startup configuration files that start your shell. *Keywords* are words that have special meaning to the shell such as **if, while,** and **until.** These words are typically used in shell scripts. *Functions* are groups of commands organized as separate routines. Functions are similar to aliases, but typically functions are more complex than aliases. You can add parameters to the function you use. Aliases and functions are defined within the shell's configuration files. *Built-in* commands are internal routines in the shell, and executable programs reside on disk and must be called into memory to be used. The shell uses the path variable to locate the executable programs on a disk and forks a process before the command can be executed. The built-in commands and functions are defined within the shell and therefore are faster to execute because they require no disk operations. Shell scripts and executable programs such as **ls** and **date** are stored on disk, and the shell must locate them via the search path to execute them. You may use the **type** command to see what kind of command you are using. You may use the **help** command to see the purpose and syntax of a built-in command. You may also use the **alias** command to create shortcuts to commonly used commands.

9.13 • Activity: Using alias, type, and help

Note: Be sure the BOOK2 disk is mounted. Your default directory is your home directory.

STEP 1   Key in the following: **alias** [Enter]

```
[cgillay@RedHat9 cgillay]$ alias
alias l.='ls -d .* --color=tty'
alias ll='ls -l --color=tty'
alias ls='ls --color=tty'
alias mc='. /usr/share/mc/bin/mc-wrapper.sh'
alias vi='vim'
alias which='alias | /usr/bin/which --tty-only --read-alias --show-dot --show-tilde'
[cgillay@RedHat9 cgillay]$
```

WHAT'S **HAPPENING?** Your aliases may vary. On this system, there are several aliases—one is **l.**, which will list all the hidden files and directories, and another is **ll**, which will do a long listing.

STEP 2   If you have an **ll** alias, key in the following: **ll** [Enter]

```
[cgillay@RedHat9  cgillay]$ ll
total 20
drwx------   4  cgillay   cgillay   4096 Jun  10  18:03 evolution
drwxrwxr-x   4  cgillay   cgillay   4096 Jun  28  11:12 practice5
drwxrwxr-x   4  cgillay   cgillay   4096 Jun  29  21:09 practice6
drwxrwxr-x   4  cgillay   cgillay   4096 Jul   1  19:51 practice7
drwxrwxr-x   4  cgillay   cgillay   4096 Jul   6  10:59 practice8
[cgillay@RedHat9  cgillay]$
```

WHAT'S **HAPPENING?** Your display may be different. However, the **alias** displayed a new command with **ll** that gave you a long listing of your directory. You may create your own aliases.

STEP 3   Key in the following: **alias m=more lF='ls -alF' lsf='ls /mnt/floppy'; alias** Enter

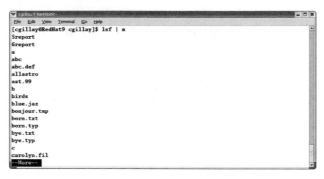

```
[cgillay@RedHat9 cgillay]$ alias m=more lF='ls -alF' lsf='ls /mnt/floppy'; alias
alias l.='ls -d .* --color=tty'
alias lF='ls -alF'
alias ll='ls -l --color=tty'
alias ls='ls --color=tty'
alias lsf='ls /mnt/floppy'
alias m='more'
alias mc='. /usr/share/mc/bin/mc-wrapper.sh'
alias vi='vim'
alias which='alias | /usr/bin/which --tty-only --read-alias --show-dot --show-tilde'
[cgillay@RedHat9 cgillay]$
```

WHAT'S HAPPENING? You created three aliases: **m**, **lF**, and **lsf**. Since both **lF** and **lsf** had spaces in them, you needed to use quotation marks to ensure the entire command was captured.

STEP 4   Key in the following: **lsf | m** Enter

```
[cgillay@RedHat9 cgillay]$ lsf | m
5report
6report
a
abc
abc.def
allastro
ast.99
b
birds
blue.jaz
bonjour.tmp
born.txt
born.typ
bye.txt
bye.typ
c
carolyn.fil
--More--
```

WHAT'S HAPPENING? You executed your new aliases and with the new commands got a listing of the files on the BOOK2 disk that paused when the screen was full.

STEP 5   Press Ctrl + **c** to return to the command prompt.

STEP 6   Key in the following: **unalias m; alias** Enter

```
[cgillay@RedHat9 cgillay]$ unalias m; alias
alias l.='ls -d .* --color=tty'
alias lF='ls -alF'
alias ll='ls -l --color=tty'
alias ls='ls --color=tty'
alias lsf='ls /mnt/floppy'
alias mc='. /usr/share/mc/bin/mc-wrapper.sh'
alias vi='vim'
alias which='alias | /usr/bin/which --tty-only --read-alias --show-dot --show-tilde'
[cgillay@RedHat9 cgillay]$
```

WHAT'S HAPPENING? Using the **unalias** command followed by the name of the alias removes it from your alias list. You can find out what kind of command you are using by using the **type** command followed by the name of the command that you are interested in.

STEP 7   Key in the following: **type lsf** Enter

```
[cgillay@RedHat9  cgillay]$  type lsf
lsf is aliased to `ls /mnt/floppy'
[cgillay@RedHat9  cgillay]$
```

WHAT'S HAPPENING? You now know that **lsf** is an alias. You may use the **type** command with any command for which you want to know the type.

STEP 8   Key in the following: **type pwd clear lsf find if** Enter

STEP 9   Key in the following: **type -path cal** Enter

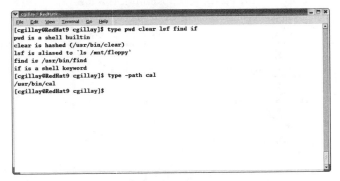

WHAT'S HAPPENING? You can see by your display that the type of command is listed for each command that you entered. In this example, the **clear** command is hashed. In this series of activities, the user, **cgillay**, constantly used the **clear** command. Because of this, **clear** was hashed. *Hashing* is the transformation of a string of characters into a usually shorter fixed-length value or key that represents the original string. Hashing is used to index and retrieve items in a database because it is faster to find the item using the shorter hashed key than to find it using the original value. As you can see, hashing is used to retrieve commands that are constantly used so that they can be retrieved more quickly. You may also use the **type** command with the **-path** option. When you do, **type** will show you the directory location of the requested command. When you try to use a man page for a built-in command, you will not get the syntax or a description, but only a list of the built-in commands.

STEP 10   Key in the following: **man cd** Enter

WHAT'S HAPPENING? You only see a list of the built-in commands. If you wanted a full tutorial on **bash**, you could key in **man bash**. However, for a quick description, you can use the **help** command.

STEP 11 Press **q**. Key in the following: **help pwd cd bg logout** [Enter]

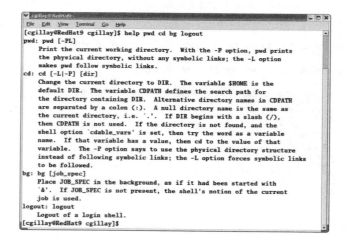

WHAT'S HAPPENING? Each of the commands you asked for help on was displayed with a brief description of its purpose.

STEP 12 Key in the following: **help if** [Enter]

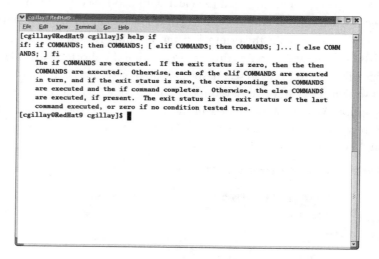

WHAT'S HAPPENING? The **if** command is a keyword. It is a conditional statement that can be used at the command line or in a shell script. The brief description shows you the syntax and includes the keyword. The example **if** allows you to make decisions. These types of commands control the flow of a program by allowing decision making based on whether an expression is true or false—*if command is true, then do that command.* **if** begins the statement, and **fi** ends the statement. When a process stops executing for any reason, it returns an ***exit status*** to its parent's process. The exit status can also be called a condition code or return code. The shell stores the exit status of the last command in a variable called **$?**. By convention, an exit status that is not zero represents a false value and means a command has failed. A zero exit status represents a true value and means the command was successfully executed.

STEP 13 Key in the following: **ls /mnt/floppy/personal.fil; echo $?** Enter

STEP 14 Key in the following: **ls nofile; echo $?** Enter

```
[cgillay@RedHat9  cgillay]$  ls /mnt/floppy/personal.fil; echo $?
/mnt/floppy/personal.fil
0
[cgillay@RedHat9  cgillay]$  ls nofile; echo $?
ls: nofile: No such file or directory
1
[cgillay@RedHat9  cgillay]$
```

WHAT'S HAPPENING? In the first example, the **personal.fil** did exist, so the exit code was **0** (true) because the command successfully executed. In the second case, **nofile** does not exist, so the exit code was **1** (false) and the command was not successfully executed.

STEP 15 Close the terminal window. Open a terminal window.

STEP 16 Key in the following: **alias** Enter

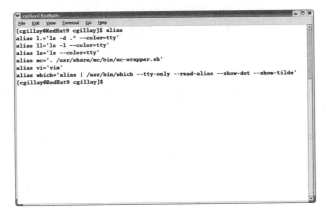

WHAT'S HAPPENING? The aliases that you created are no longer available. The aliases kept from one terminal session to another are in a file called **.bashrc**, which is located in the user's home directory. Because **.bashrc** is executed each time you start a new shell, any aliases set at the command line are not inherited by new shells. Only aliases that are kept in the **.bashrc** file will be reset for new shells that are executed.

9.14 • Manipulating the Directory Stack with Built-in Commands

If you find that as you work you move up and down the directory tree to the same directories using the **cd** command, you can store a list of those directories. This list is called a *stack*. You may manipulate the stack. The **pushd** (push directory) command pushes directories onto a stack. The **popd** (pop directory) command removes them from the stack. The **dirs** command displays the currently remembered directories that were placed on the stack with the **pushd** command.

The syntax of the **pushd** command is

```
pushd  [dir ]  [ +N | -N ]
```

For useful options for **pushd**, see Table 9.7, "**pushd** Options."

Option	Name	Result
dir	Directory name	Adds a directory to the directory stack at the top, making it the current working directory.
+*N*	Number	Places the *N*th directory in the directory stack at the top of the stack. Count from the left, beginning with zero from the directory stack.
-*N*	Number	Places the *N*th directory in the directory stack at the top of the stack. Count from the right from the directory stack.

Table 9.7 ▫ pushd Options

The syntax of the **popd** command is

```
popd   [ +N  |  -N ]
```

For useful options for **popd**, see Table 9.8, "**popd** Options."

Option	Name	Result
+*N*	Number	Removes the *N*th directory in the directory stack at the top of the stack. Count from the left, beginning with zero from the directory stack.
-*N*	Number	Removes the *N*th directory in the directory stack at the top of the stack. Count from the right from the directory stack.

Table 9.8 ▫ popd Options

The syntax of the **dirs** command is

```
dirs   [ clpv ]  [ +N ]  [ -N ]
```

For useful options for **dirs**, see Table 9.9, "**dirs** Options."

Option	Name	Result
-c	Clears	Clears the directory stack.
-l	Long	Specifies that the **dirs** command should display the full path name, relative to your home directory.
-p	Preface	Displays the directory stack one line at a time and does not display the position in the stack.
-v	Verbose	Displays the directory stack one line at a time and displays the directory name with its position in the stack.

Table 9.9 ▫ dirs Options

The **pushd** command allows you to change directories and at the same time build a list of the directories you are working with. You may add a directory to the top of the directory stack, or you may rotate the stack, making the new top of the stack the current working directory. If you provide no arguments to the **pushd** command, the two top directories are exchanged. The **popd** command removes directories from the directory stack. If you provide no arguments, it removes the top directory from the stack and changes directories to the new top directory. You may list the directories in the stack with the **dirs** command. The **dirs** command displays what is in the stack.

9.15 • Activity: Using the Built-in Commands dirs, pushd, and popd

Note: The BOOK2 disk is mounted. Your default directory is your home directory.

STEP 1   Key in the following: **dirs** Enter

```
[cgillay@RedHat9   cgillay]$   dirs
~
[cgillay@RedHat9   cgillay]$
```

WHAT'S **HAPPENING?** Since your directory stack is empty, only the home directory, represented by ~, is displayed.

STEP 2   Key in the following: **dirs -l** Enter

```
[cgillay@RedHat9   cgillay]$   dirs -l
/home/cgillay
[cgillay@RedHat9   cgillay]$
```

WHAT'S **HAPPENING?** When you used the -l option, the full path name of your directory was displayed. To change directories, and at the same time add a directory to the top of the stack, you may use the **pushd** command with a directory name.

STEP 3   Key in the following: **pushd /mnt/floppy/sports** Enter

STEP 4   Key in the following: **pushd /mnt/floppy/data** Enter

STEP 5   Key in the following: **dirs -l** Enter

```
[cgillay@RedHat9    cgillay]$   pushd /mnt/floppy/sports
/mnt/floppy/sports  ~
[cgillay@RedHat9    sports]$   pushd /mnt/floppy/data
/mnt/floppy/data   mnt/floppy/sports   ~
[cgillay@RedHat9    data]$  dirs -l
/mnt/floppy/data   /mnt/floppy/sports   /home/cgillay
[cgillay@RedHat9    data]$
```

WHAT'S **HAPPENING?** With the first **pushd** command you added the /**mnt/floppy/sports** directory to the stack and at the same time changed the working directory to **sports**. The second **pushd** command added the directory /**mnt/floppy/data** to the top of the stack and also made the working directory **data**. The stack now consists of three directories: /**mnt/floppy/data**, /**mnt/floppy/sports**, and your home directory. The leftmost directory, in this case /**mnt/floppy/data**, is the most recent directory pushed onto the stack. You verified that by using the **dirs -l** command to see the order of the directory stack.

STEP 6 Key in the following: **pushd** [Enter]

```
[cgillay@RedHat9  data]$  pushd
/mnt/floppy/sports /mnt/floppy/data ~
[cgillay@RedHat9  sports]$
```

WHAT'S HAPPENING? The **pushd** command with no options swapped the two top directories on the stack so that your working directory changed to **/mnt/floppy/sports**.

STEP 7 Key in the following: **dirs -v** [Enter]

STEP 8 Key in the following: **pushd /mnt/floppy/fun** [Enter]

```
[cgillay@RedHat9  sports]$  dirs -v
     0  /mnt/floppy/sports
     1  /mnt/floppy/data
     2  ~
[cgillay@RedHat9  sports]$  pushd /mnt/floppy/fun
/mnt/floppy/fun /mnt/floppy/sports /mnt/floppy/data ~
[cgillay@RedHat9  fun]$
```

WHAT'S HAPPENING? By using **dirs** with the **-v** option, you saw your directory stack in numerical order. You added another directory to your stack, the **/mnt/floppy/fun** directory. It is in the leftmost position, as it is the most recent directory. When you used the **pushd** command, you changed your current working directory to **/mnt/floppy/fun**.

STEP 9 Key in the following: **pushd** [Enter]

```
[cgillay@RedHat9  fun]$  pushd
/mnt/floppy/sports /mnt/floppy/fun /mnt/floppy/data ~
[cgillay@RedHat9  sports]$
```

WHAT'S HAPPENING? Again, the **pushd** command swapped the two top directories so that **/mnt/floppy/sports** became your working directory and it also moved to the top of the stack. You may also use a plus with a number (**+n**) as an option. When you use a numerical value, the **pushd** command will rotate the stack so that the "nth" directory from the left will be pushed on top of the stack. If you use a minus with a number (**-n**), the **pushd** command will rotate the stack so that the "nth" directory from the right will be pushed on top of the stack.

STEP 10 Key in the following: **dirs -v** [Enter]

```
[cgillay@RedHat9  sports]$ dirs -v
     0  /mnt/floppy/sports
     1  /mnt/floppy/fun
     2  /mnt/floppy/data
     3  ~
[cgillay@RedHat9  sports]$
```

WHAT'S HAPPENING? You see that your home directory is in numerical position number 3. Thus, if you use **pushd** with the numerical value of 3, your working directory should become your home directory.

STEP 11 Key in the following: **pushd +3** [Enter]

```
[cgillay@RedHat9  sports]$   pushd +3
~ /mnt/floppy/sports /mnt/floppy/fun /mnt/floppy/data
[cgillay@RedHat9  cgillay]$
```

WHAT'S HAPPENING? Indeed your default directory is now your home directory. It became the top of the stack. The third directory was the third directory from where you were in the stack (**/mnt/floppy/sports** was the "0" directory, **/mnt/floppy/fun** was the first directory, and **/mnt/floppy/data** was the second directory; your home directory was the third directory in the stack).

STEP 12 Key in the following: **pushd** [Enter]

```
[cgillay@RedHat9  cgillay]$  pushd
/mnt/floppy/sports ~ /mnt/floppy/fun /mnt/floppy/data
[cgillay@RedHat9  sports]$
```

WHAT'S HAPPENING? Again, **pushd** rotated the two directories from the left so that **/mnt/floppy/sports** became your working directory.

STEP 13 Key in the following: **pushd /mnt/floppy/abc** [Enter]

```
[cgillay@RedHat9  sports]$  pushd /mnt/floppy/abc
/mnt/floppy/abc /mnt/floppy/sports ~ /mnt/floppy/fun /mnt/floppy/data
[cgillay@RedHat9  abc]$
```

WHAT'S HAPPENING? You added another directory to the stack and **/mnt/floppy/abc** became the working directory.

STEP 14 Key in the following: **dirs -v** [Enter]

```
[cgillay@RedHat9  abc]$ dirs -v
    0  /mnt/floppy/abc
    1  /mnt/floppy/sports
    2  ~
    3  /mnt/floppy/fun
    4  /mnt/floppy/data
[cgillay@RedHat9  abc]$
```

WHAT'S HAPPENING? You may use negative numbers with the **pushd** command. When you do so, you rotate the bottom directories to the top.

STEP 15 Key in the following: **pushd -2** [Enter]

```
[cgillay@RedHat9  abc]$  pushd -2
~ /mnt/floppy/fun /mnt/floppy/data /mnt/floppy/abc /mnt/floppy/sports
[cgillay@RedHat9  cgillay]$
```

WHAT'S HAPPENING? Your home directory is now your working directory. Your stack was rotated so that the last three directories became the first three directories and the "third" directory (number 2 in the list) became the working directory. In addition, the third directory (number 4 in the list) **/mnt/floppy/fun** became the second directory and **/mnt/floppy/data** became the third directory in the stack.

STEP 16 Key in the following: **pushd** [Enter]

```
[cgillay@RedHat9  cgillay]$  pushd
/mnt/floppy/fun ~ /mnt/floppy/data /mnt/floppy/abc /mnt/floppy/sports
[cgillay@RedHat9  fun]$ _\
```

WHAT'S HAPPENING? You swapped the top two directories. You may remove a directory from the stack by using the **popd** command.

STEP 17 Key in the following: **popd** [Enter]

```
[cgillay@RedHat9  fun]$  popd
~ /mnt/floppy/data /mnt/floppy/abc /mnt/floppy/sports
[cgillay@RedHat9  cgillay]$
```

WHAT'S HAPPENING? The **popd** command with no options removes the directory at the top of the stack—starting from the left—and changes your current working directory to the next in the stack. In this case, your working directory became your home directory because it was next in the stack. If you want to remove a specific directory, you use the **+n** option. Again, in the example, it is easier to start with 0 (computer count from 0). In that case, your home directory is 0, **/mnt/floppy/data** is 1, and **/mnt/floppy/abc** is 2. Thus, to remove **/mnt/floppy/abc**, you would use the number 2.

STEP 18 Key in the following: **popd +2** [Enter]

```
[cgillay@RedHat9  cgillay]$  popd +2
~ /mnt/floppy/data /mnt/floppy/sports
[cgillay@RedHat9  cgillay]$
```

WHAT'S HAPPENING? You removed the **/mnt/floppy/abc** directory from the stack, but your working directory remained your home directory.

9.16 • Variables and the set Command

The shell can define two types of variables, local and environmental. The variables contain information used for customizing the shell and also information required by other processes. Local variables are private to the shell that they are created in and are not passed on to any processes spawned from that shell. Environmental variables are often called global variables and are passed from parent process to child process to child process and so on. Some environmental variables are inherited by the login shell from the **/bin/login** program or are gotten from user-initialization files, shell scripts, or even at the command line. Any environmental variable set in a child process is not passed back to the parent process. By convention, environmental variables are usually given names in uppercase, such as **PATH**, **HOME**, whereas locally defined variables are usually given names that are lowercase. A variable can contain any mix of letters, numbers, or underscores but can never begin with a number. In addition, the shell itself has a number of predefined options that can be enabled or disabled. The **set** command with no options will print the values of all known variables to the shell. Options can be enabled with *-option*, or disabled with *+option*. The shell also has modes that may also be turned on or off with the **set** command. For instance, the **noclobber** option, if on, will not allow a user that uses redirection to overwrite an existing file. Table 9.10, "Common Shell Modes," displays the more commonly used options. To see a fully defined list, you may use the man bash command.

Shell Options	Purpose
noclobber	Does not allow output redirection to overwrite an existing file.
noglob	Does not allow the use of wildcards.
nounset	Indicates an error when trying to use an undefined variable.
vi	Enters vi editing mode.

Table 9.10 • Common Shell Modes

9.17 • Activity: Using the set Command

Note: Your default directory is your home directory. You have a terminal window open.

STEP 1   Key in the following: **set -o** Enter

WHAT'S HAPPENING? The following are the modes set in this shell. In this example, **noclobber** is set to off. This means you can overwrite an existing file with redirection. If it was set to on, you could not overwrite a file. You can test this assumption.

STEP 2   Create a file called **file1** with the following contents: **This is file 1.**

STEP 3   Create another file called **file2** with the following contents: **This is file 2.**

STEP 4   Key in the following: **cat file1 > file2; cat file1 file2** Enter

```
[cgillay@RedHat9   cgillay]$  cat file1 > file2; cat file1 file2
This is file 1.
This is file 1.
[cgillay@RedHat9   cgillay]$
```

WHAT'S HAPPENING? Since **noclobber** is off, you were allowed to overwrite **file2** with **file1**. To prevent this, you can turn on the **noclobber** option.

STEP 5 Key in the following: **set -o noclobber** [Enter]

STEP 6 Create a new file called **file3** with the contents **This is file 3.**

STEP 7 Key in the following: **cat file3 > file1** [Enter]

```
[cgillay@RedHat9  cgillay]$  cat file3 > file1
bash: file1: Cannot overwrite existing file.
[cgillay@RedHat9  cgillay]$
```

WHAT'S HAPPENING? Since **noclobber** is now on, you cannot overwrite a file. However, this is set only for this session of the shell (terminal window) and only prevents overwriting when you use redirection. If you use a command such as **cp**, you can overwrite the file even with **noclobber** on. In addition, when you exit this shell (terminal window) and open a new shell, the options will be returned to their default value.

STEP 8 Key in the following: **cp file3 file1; cat file3 file1** [Enter]

```
[cgillay@RedHat9  cgillay]$ cp file3 file1; cat file3 file1
This is file 3.
This is file 3.
[cgillay@RedHat9  cgillay]$
```

WHAT'S HAPPENING? As you can see, **noclobber** only prevents overwriting with redirection. It does not prevent copying over a file.

STEP 9 Key in the following: **rm file*** [Enter]

```
[cgillay@RedHat9  cgillay]$  rm file*
[cgillay@RedHat9  cgillay]$
```

WHAT'S HAPPENING? You have removed the files you created.

9.18 • User-created Variables

You may create a variable and name it anything you wish, provided that the first character is not a number. In addition, when you assign a value to a variable, you must not precede or follow the equal sign with a blank space or a tab mark. In order to see the value of the variable you have set, you may use the **echo** command with $ and the name of the variable. The syntax is *variablename =value*. Again, case matters. The variable settings remain in place only for that work session with the terminal window.

9.19 • Activity: Creating and Removing User-created Variables

Note: Your default directory is your home directory. You have a terminal window open.

STEP 1 Key in the following: **student=Carolyn** [Enter]

STEP 2 Key in the following: **echo student** [Enter]

```
[cgillay@RedHat9   cgillay]$   echo student
student
[cgillay@RedHat9   cgillay]$
```

WHAT'S HAPPENING? The **echo** command simply copies the argument you supplied (**student**) to standard output (the terminal screen). Thus, when you keyed in **echo student**, the command simply displayed the argument (**student**) to the screen. The $ (dollar sign) preceding the **echo** command informs it that you want to see the value of the requested variable name.

STEP 3   Key in the following: **echo $student** [Enter]

```
[cgillay@RedHat9   cgillay]$   echo $student
Carolyn
[cgillay@RedHat9   cgillay]$
```

WHAT'S HAPPENING? Now you can see that the variable **student** has the value **Carolyn**. Preceding the variable *student* with the $ sign indicated that you wanted the value of **student**, not that you wanted the string **student** echoed to the screen. If you want to see the variable name, you may use either single quotation marks or the backslash preceding the variable name.

STEP 4   Key in the following: **echo '$student' \$student** [Enter]

```
[cgillay@RedHat9   cgillay]$   echo '$student'   \$student
$student   $student
[cgillay@RedHat9   cgillay]$
```

WHAT'S HAPPENING? Here you set off your request with delimiters, and the **echo** command displayed what the variable name was. However, if you use double quotation marks as your delimiters, the value of the variable will be displayed.

STEP 5   Key in the following: **echo "$student"** [Enter]

```
[cgillay@RedHat9   cgillay]$   echo "$student"
Carolyn
[cgillay@RedHat9   cgillay]$
```

WHAT'S HAPPENING? The double quotation marks allowed the **echo** command to provide the value of the variable. Double quotation marks turn off any special meanings of other characters. Thus, if you want to assign spaces or tabs to a variable name, you must use double quotation marks.

STEP 6   Key in the following: **students=Carolyn and Frank** [Enter]

```
[cgillay@RedHat9   cgillay]$   students=Carolyn and Frank
bash: and: command not found
[cgillay@RedHat9   cgillay]$
```

WHAT'S HAPPENING? The Bash shell reads the "**and**" as a command and not part of the variable value of **Carolyn and Frank**. Since **and** is not a Bash command, you received an error message.

STEP 7   Key in the following: **students="Carolyn and Frank"; echo $students** [Enter]

```
[cgillay@RedHat9  cgillay]$  students="Carolyn and Frank"; echo $students
Carolyn and Frank
[cgillay@RedHat9  cgillay]$
```

WHAT'S HAPPENING? The **echo** command read your variable value (**Carolyn and Frank**) as one character string. You may also use double quotation marks if you wish to preserve any spacing considerations.

Note: Where you see `Space Bar`, press the `Space Bar` key five times.

STEP 8   Key in the following: **students="Carolyn `Space Bar` and `Space Bar` Frank"**
`Enter`

STEP 9   Key in the following: **echo $students** `Enter`

```
[cgillay@RedHat9  cgillay]$  students="Carolyn        and        Frank"
[cgillay@RedHat9  cgillay]$  echo $students
Carolyn and Frank
[cgillay@RedHat9  cgillay]$
```

WHAT'S HAPPENING? Although you used spaces in your variable value, they were not retained when you used **echo**. To view them with the spacing, you surround your variable name with double quotation marks.

STEP 10 Key in the following: **echo "$students"** `Enter`

```
[cgillay@RedHat9  cgillay]$  echo "$students"
Carolyn        and        Frank
[cgillay@RedHat9  cgillay]$
```

WHAT'S HAPPENING? You retained the spacing by using the double quotation marks. In the above example, you used "hard" spaces. You may use escape sequences as well. *Escape sequences* are a series of characters that start with the escape character and are often used to control display devices. If, in naming a variable, you wish to use special keys on the keyboard such as `Tab` or `Enter`, simply pressing those keys on the keyboard will not work. By using an escape sequence, you can enter those characters. In order for **echo** to read those escape sequences correctly, you must include the **-e** option. Table 9.11, "Escape Sequences," lists the escape sequences that **echo** recognizes.

Characters	Meaning
\a	bell
\b	`Backspace`
\c	Prints the line without a new line.
\f	Form feed
\n	New line
\r	Return

\t	**Tab**
\v	Vertical tab
\\	Backslash
\nnn	An octal code represented by *nnn*.

Table 9.11 • Escape Sequences

Note: Where you see **Tab**, press the **Tab** key.

STEP 11   Key in the following: **students="carolyn Tab**

```
[cgillay@RedHat9   cgillay]$   students="carolyn
```

WHAT'S HAPPENING? When you pressed the **Tab** key, the system simply beeped at you. You did not tab over to the next tab stop. The **Tab** key had no meaning.

STEP 12   Press the **Ctrl** + **c** key to break out of this command.

STEP 13   Key in the following: **students="carolyn\t\tand\t\tfrank\n"** **Enter**

STEP 14   Key in the following: **echo $students** **Enter**

STEP 15   Key in the following: **echo -e $students** **Enter**

```
[cgillay@RedHat9   cgillay]$   students="carolyn\t\tand\t\tfrank\n"
[cgillay@RedHat9   cgillay]$   echo $students
carolyn\t\tand\t\tfrank\n
[cgillay@RedHat9   cgillay]$   echo -e $students
carolyn      and          frank

[cgillay@RedHat9   cgillay]$
```

WHAT'S HAPPENING? In naming your variable, **students**, you used the **\t** to add tabs to your variable name. You also added a **\n** which will produce a new line. When you keyed in **echo $students**, that line only produced what you literally keyed in. You wanted **echo** to interpret your escape sequences, so when you added the **-e** option, your statement was correctly interpreted and the tabs and new line were included in your output.

When you execute a command using a variable as an argument, the shell will replace the name of the variable with the value of the variable and pass it to the program that is executing. You may also use special characters such as * or the ?. However, you need to be aware that the shell parses a command line in a specific order. Within this order, it will find the "value" of the wildcard and will pass it to the program being executed. But if you enclose the variable name with double quotation marks, it will pass only the value specified in the variable name. If you do not enclose the variable name in quotation marks, the shell will find all occurrences of what you requested and pass those values to the command.

STEP 16   Create a new file called **carolyn.report.0712** with the contents **This is a July report.**

STEP 17   Create a new file called **carolyn.report.user** with the contents **This is a user report.**

STEP 18   Key in the following: **cp carolyn.report.user frank.report.user** **Enter**

STEP 19 Key in the following: **ls *rep*** [Enter]

```
[cgillay@RedHat9  cgillay]$  ls *rep*
carolyn.report.0712    carolyn.report.user    frank.report.user
[cgillay@RedHat9  cgillay]$
```

WHAT'S HAPPENING? You have three new files.

STEP 20 Key in the following: **report=carolyn*** [Enter]

STEP 21 Key in the following: **echo "$report"** [Enter]

```
[cgillay@RedHat9  cgillay]$  echo "$report*)
carolyn*
[cgillay@RedHat9  cgillay]$
```

WHAT'S HAPPENING? Because you quoted the variable name, the shell did not interpret the * as a wildcard, but merely returned the actual value of what the variable contained and thus displayed the *. But, if you do not quote the variable, the shell will interpret the * as a wildcard and will display any files that match the wildcard criteria.

STEP 22 Key in the following: **echo $report; ls $report** [Enter]

```
[cgillay@RedHat9  cgillay]$  echo $report; ls $report
carolyn.report.0712    carolyn.report.user
carolyn.report.0712    carolyn.report.user
[cgillay@RedHat9  cgillay]$
```

WHAT'S HAPPENING? Both the **echo** command and the **ls** command used the variable **report**, and the shell interpreted the * and then passed the expanded value of **report** to the commands. It matched the value of **carolyn*** to the files that matched the criteria. Instead of keying in **ls carolyn*** (which would have gotten the same results), you keyed in the variable name without quotation marks. The advantage to setting up a variable that can be interpreted is that you can limit your **report** files to only those with **carolyn** in their name. If you had keyed in **ls *rep***, you would have gotten the **frank** report file as well. By setting up the variable, you have limited your report files to only those with **carolyn** in their name.

The variables you created will last until you exit the terminal window. You may also remove the value of a variable at any time during a work session. You may either set the value of the variable to nothing (*variablename =*   ) or use the unset command (**unset** *variablename*).

STEP 23 Key in the following: **student=; unset students** [Enter]

STEP 24 Key in the following: **echo $student $students** [Enter]

```
[cgillay@RedHat9  cgillay]$  student=;  unset students
[cgillay@RedHat9  cgillay]$  echo $student  $students

[cgillay@RedHat9  cgillay]$
```

WHAT'S HAPPENING? You no longer have any variables set.

STEP 25 Key in the following: **rm *rep*; ls *rep*** [Enter]

```
[cgillay@RedHat9   cgillay]$   rm *rep*; ls *rep*
ls *rep*: No such file or directory
[cgillay@RedHat9   cgillay]$
```

WHAT'S HAPPENING? You have removed the **report** files from your home directory.

9.20 ● export and declare

You may create your own environmental variables by using the **export** or **declare -x** commands. Both **declare** and **export** are built-ins. Environmental variables are available to the shell in which they were created and are also available to any subshells or processes spawned from the parent shell. Many environmental variables such as **HOME, PATH,** or **PS1** are set by the **/bin/ login** program before you log on. Normally those environmental variables are defined and stored in **.bash_profile**, which is kept in the user's home directory. Environmental variables are those that have been exported with the **export** or **declare -x** command and will be available in a subshell that has been spawned from the parent shell.

The shell in which a variable is created is the parent shell. Any shell started from the parent shell is the child shell. Environmental variables can be passed to any child process started from the shell where the environmental variables were created, and those variables can be passed to any other shells spawned from that child. A child shell can create a variable and pass it to a child shell it creates, but cannot pass it back to its parent. The syntax for **export** is export *variable=value*. You may also create the variable and at any time export it. (*variablename=value;* **export** *variablename*). To see the exported variables in your shell, you may key in **export** with no options or use **export** with the -p option. The output from **export** or **export -p** will display all variable names that are exported in this shell. The syntax for the **declare** is **declare -x** *variablename=value*. If you use no options or variable names are given, then the values of the variables are displayed.

9.21 ● Activity: Using export and declare

Note: Your default directory is your home directory. You have a terminal window open.

STEP 1   Key in the following: **export -p** [Enter]

WHAT'S HAPPENING? You are looking at a display of all the names that were exported for this shell. In this example, the values were exported using the **declare -x** command.

STEP 2   Key in the following: **student=carolyn; echo $student; echo $$** [Enter]

```
[cgillay@RedHat9   cgillay]$ student=carolyn; echo $student; echo $$
carolyn
3194
[cgillay@RedHat9   cgillay]$
```

WHAT'S HAPPENING? You have created a variable called **student** with the value of **carolyn**. You also found out the process id (pid) of this shell. When you use **echo $$**, it will display the current running pid. Your pid number will be different from the one shown in the example.

STEP 3   Key in the following: **bash** [Enter]

STEP 4   Key in the following: **echo $$; echo $student** [Enter]

```
[cgillay@RedHat9   cgillay]$ bash
[cgillay@RedHat9   cgillay]$  echo $$; echo $student
3345
[cgillay@RedHat9   cgillay]$
```

WHAT'S HAPPENING? You spawned a shell by starting a second Bash shell, which is a child to the parent shell. You can see that the new shell has a different pid, indicating that it is a different process. You also can see that your environmental variable **$student** was not passed to the child shell. In order to pass an environmental variable to a child process, you must export or declare it.

STEP 5   Key in the following: **exit** [Enter]

STEP 6   Key in the following: **echo $$** [Enter]

```
[cgillay@RedHat9   cgillay]$  exit
[cgillay@RedHat9   cgillay]$  echo $$
3194
[cgillay@RedHat9   cgillay]$
```

WHAT'S HAPPENING? You have returned to the parent shell. You are going to pass some environmental variables to the child shell.

STEP 7   Key in the following: **STUDENT=frank; export STUDENT** [Enter]

STEP 8   Key in the following: **declare -x STUDENTS="Carolyn and Frank"** [Enter]

```
[cgillay@RedHat9   cgillay]$  STUDENT=frank; export STUDENT
[cgillay@RedHat9   cgillay]$  declare -x STUDENTS="Carolyn and Frank"
[cgillay@RedHat9   cgillay]$
```

WHAT'S HAPPENING? You created two environmental variables, **STUDENT** and **STU-DENTS**. You exported them so that any child shells should have access to these variables.

STEP 9   Key in the following: **bash** [Enter]

STEP 10   Key in the following: **echo $STUDENT $STUDENTS** [Enter]

```
[cgillay@RedHat9    cgillay]$    echo $STUDENT  $STUDENTS
frank Carolyn and Frank
[cgillay@RedHat9    cgillay]$
```

WHAT'S HAPPENING? You have passed the value of your environmental variables to the child shell.

STEP 11 Key in the following: **declare -x STUDENT=carolyn; echo $STUDENT** `Enter`

```
[cgillay@RedHat9    cgillay]$ declare -x STUDENT=carolyn; echo
$STUDENT
carolyn
[cgillay@RedHat9    cgillay]$
```

WHAT'S HAPPENING? In your child shell, you have changed the value of the environmental variable **STUDENT** from **frank** to **carolyn**. However, this is a child process. You can pass this value to a child shell but not to a parent.

STEP 12 Key in the following: **bash** `Enter`

STEP 13 Key in the following: **echo $STUDENT** `Enter`

```
[cgillay@RedHat9    cgillay]$    bash
[cgillay@RedHat9    cgillay]$    echo $STUDENT
carolyn
[cgillay@RedHat9    cgillay]$
```

WHAT'S HAPPENING? You launched or spawned another child shell, and the environmental value of **STUDENT** was passed to the child shell.

STEP 14 Key in the following: **exit** `Enter`

STEP 15 Key in the following: **exit** `Enter`

STEP 16 Key in the following: **echo $STUDENT** `Enter`

```
[cgillay@RedHat9    cgillay]$    bash
[cgillay@RedHat9    cgillay]$    echo $STUDENT
frank
[cgillay@RedHat9    cgillay]$
```

WHAT'S HAPPENING? You keyed in **exit** twice to return to the parent shell. Your **declare** statement passed the changed variable only to the child process, not to the parent process.

9.22 ● Command Line Expansion and Quoting

Command line expansion is what the shell must do to the command line before it passes it on to the program that is being called. Each line of a shell script also undergoes this expansion. In reality, what is happening is you are using a shorthand way to provide information to a command that makes it easier to correctly key in a command. You can use these kinds of special notations so when they are expanded, they can replace variables with the values you want the variables to have, such as replace wild cards with a list of specific files, and so on. Thus, when you key in a command like **ls *.txt**, you are using a shorthand way to refer to a group of files.

The shell must interpret and expand the *.txt notation so it knows what files to pass to the ls command.

When you key in a command, the command does not immediately execute. The shell must parse the command and break it into separate parts and interpret each part. The shell must then scan each part of the command line looking for special characters and patterns that tell the shell what to do. If you key in a command such as cp *.txt ~, there are three parts to the command: cp, *.txt, and ~. Before the command cp can be executed, the other parts of the command must be expanded. The *.txt must be expanded so that all files that end in .txt are located, and the ~ must be expanded to the user's home directory.

To further complicate matters is the whole issue of how the shell interprets quote characters. There are essentially three types of quote characters that the shell recognizes: the single quote ('), the double quote ("), and the back quote (`). Quotes must be matched; that is, you cannot begin a phrase with a single quote and end it with a double quote. The Bash shell will let you know if you have mismatched quotation marks. You may also use the backslash character (\), which is nearly equivalent to placing single quotes around a character to prevent the shell from attempting to interpret what follows the backslash. Thus, if you wanted to display the * character and not have the shell treat it as a wildcard, you would need to either quote it ("*") or use the backslash character preceding the asterisk (*). This tells the shell that you literally want to display the * character and not have the shell interpret it as a wildcard and expand it.

9.23 ● The Single Quote, the Double Quotes, and the Backslash

You have already used single quotes so that the shell would interpret a character string with spaces as a single unit. Remember, whenever the shell sees a white space—a blank—it will interpret the next item in the command line as an option or an argument. Thus, by using the single quotation mark, you are asking the shell to treat the argument on the command line as a single unit. Furthermore, when you use special characters such as * or ?, when a special character is enclosed in single quotes, the shell does not treat it as a special character and tries to expand it. Instead, the shell simply displays the special character as an ordinary character. The purpose of using the single quotation mark is that it stops all types of expansion. If you want to protect special characters from being interpreted or to prevent parameter expansion, you must use single quotes.

The double quotes are similar to single quotes, except that they are not as restrictive as single quotes. Single quotes tell the shell to ignore *anything* enclosed in the quotes. Double quotes, also known as weak quotes, tell the shell to ignore most special characters in the quoted statement. However, what is ignored depends on what you are doing with the double quotes. When you use double quotes, the shell will ignore pipes, aliases, tilde substitution, wildcard expansion, and blank spaces in a character string. But double quotes do allow parameter substitution, command substitution, and arithmetic expression evaluation. When you use double quotes with parameter substitution, command substitution, and arithmetic expression evaluation, the following three characters are not ignored:

- dollar sign
- backslashes
- back quotes

This means that the shell will perform expansion on those items within double quotes that are preceded by the above special characters. Thus, if you have a variable called **name** with a value of **Carolyn**, then keying in '**$name**' would return the literal text—**$name**—whereas keying in "**$name**" would return the value of the variable—**Carolyn**.

Essentially, using the backslash tells the shell not to interpret what follows the backslash. It is almost identical to using the single quotes. But when text is enclosed in double quotes, then you must use the \ instead of single quotes if you do not want the item expanded. If you use a backslash as the last character at the end of a line, the shell then treats that backslash as a continuation of that line. It removes the *newline* character and does not treat *newline* as an argument. You use this if you have a very long command line that cannot be keyed in. Remember, if you press [Enter] at the end of a line, the shell assumes you have completed your command and will attempt to execute it. By keying in the backslash, the shell will continue to the next line without executing your command until you press [Enter].

9.24 ● Activity: The Single Quote, the Double Quotes, and the Backslash

Note: Your default directory is your home directory. You have a terminal window open. The BOOK2 disk is mounted.

STEP 1   Key in the following: **cp /mnt/floppy/personal.fil ~** [Enter]

STEP 2   Key in the following: **grep Smith personal.fil** [Enter]

```
[cgillay@RedHat9   cgillay]$   cp /mnt/floppy/personal.fi ~
[cgillay@RedHat9   cgillay]$   grep Smith personal.fil
Smith    Gregory   311 Orchard Ann Arbor      MI     Engineer
Smith    Carolyn   311 Orchard Ann Arbor      MI     Housewife
Smith    David     120 Collins Orange         CA     Chef
[cgillay@RedHat9   cgillay]$
```

WHAT'S HAPPENING? First you copied **personal.fil** to your home directory. Then, you used the **grep** command. The **grep** command worked in the usual way. You extracted all the **Smith**s, but if you only wanted to extract only **Smith Gregory**, you would key in the command differently. Note that in the next command you will press the [Space Bar] five times between **Smith** and **Gregory** to account for the spaces between the last name and first name.

STEP 3   Key in the following: **grep Smith   Gregory personal.fill**

```
[cgillay@RedHat9   cgillay]$   grep Smith     Gregory personal.fil
grep: Gregory:      No such file or directory
personal.fil:Smith    Gregory    311 Orchard    Ann Arbor    MI    Engineer
personal.fil:Smith    Carolyn    311 Orchard    Ann Arbor    MI    Housewife
personal.fil:Smith    David      120 Collins    Orange       CA    Chef
[cgillay@RedHat9   cgillay]$
```

WHAT'S HAPPENING? The **grep** command assumed that **Gregory** was a second argument (**Smith** was the first argument and **personal.fil** was the third argument). You did get all the other **Smith**'s but you only wanted **Gregory**. You want the shell to treat **Smith Gregory** as one argument. To do so, you enclose it in quotation marks. Note that in the next command you will press the [Space Bar] five times between **Smith** and **Gregory** to account for the spaces between the last name and first name.

STEP 4   Key in the following: **grep 'Smith   Gregory' personal.fil**

```
[cgillay@RedHat9    cgillay]$   grep 'Smith      Gregory' personal.fil
Smith    Gregory   311 Orchard Ann Arbor    MI      Engineer
[cgillay@RedHat9    cgillay]$
```

WHAT'S HAPPENING? Now you extracted the information you wanted. By enclosing your name in quote marks, you told the shell to treat the name as one argument.

STEP 5   Create three files as follows:

File name	Contents
test1	THIS IS TEST 1.
test2	THIS IS TEST 2.
test3	THIS IS TEST 3.

STEP 6   Key in the following: **echo test*** Enter

STEP 7   Key in the following: **ls test*** Enter

STEP 8   Key in the following: **cat test*** Enter

```
[cgillay@RedHat9    cgillay]$   echo test*
test1    test2    test3
[cgillay@RedHat9    cgillay]$   ls test*
test1   test2   test3
[cgillay@RedHat9    cgillay]$   cat test*
THIS IS TEST 1.
THIS IS TEST 2.
THIS IS TEST 3.
[cgillay@RedHat9    cgillay]$
```

WHAT'S HAPPENING? You have used the special character (*) with various commands. Now you are going to create a variable to see how the quote marks work.

STEP 9   Key in the following: **a='This is text.'**

STEP 10   Key in the following: **b='test* will display the test files.'**

STEP 11   Key in the following: **echo $a** Enter

STEP 12   Key in the following: **echo $b** Enter

```
[cgillay@RedHat9    cgillay]$   echo $a
This is text.
[cgillay@RedHat9    cgillay]$   echo $b
test1   test1    test3   will display the test files.
[cgillay@RedHat9    cgillay]$
```

WHAT'S HAPPENING? When you viewed variable **a**, using **echo $a**, the quotes indicated that the entire phase should be treated as a unit. However, when you viewed variable **b**, using **echo $b**, the wildcard (*) was interpreted and expanded so that the all the file names that began with **test** were displayed. The shell interpreted the * and expanded it before it passed the values to echo. If you do not want the shell to interpret the * and treat is simply as a character, you can use the double quotation marks.

STEP 13 Key in the following: **echo "$b"** [Enter]

```
[cgillay@RedHat9  cgillay]$  echo $b
test* will display the test files.
[cgillay@RedHat9  cgillay]$
```

WHAT'S **HAPPENING?** In this case, with the use of the double quotes, the * was not interpreted and all the **test** files were not displayed.

STEP 14 Key in the following: **echo Don't you like Linux?** [Enter]

```
[cgillay@RedHat9  cgillay]$  echo Don't you like Linux?
>
```

WHAT'S **HAPPENING?** The shell is waiting for the second quote mark. Since it did not find one, it provided you with a secondary prompt waiting for you to provide a matching quote.

STEP 15 Key in the following: **'** [Enter]

```
>'
Dont you like Linux?

[cgillay@RedHat9  cgillay]$
```

WHAT'S **HAPPENING?** You provided the second quotation mark, and the shell could continue. However, it interpreted the second quotation mark as a completion. If you want **Don't** to be read as one word, you must quote it with either the \ or double quotation marks, since the word has a single quotation mark within it. If you used a single quotation mark, it would read the second quotation mark as closure.

STEP 16 Key in the following: **echo Don\'t you like Linux? "Don't you like Linux?"** [Enter]

```
[cgillay@RedHat9 cgillay]$ echo Don\t you like Linux?"Don't you like Linux?"
Don't you like Linux? Don't you like Linux?
[cgillay@RedHat9  cgillay]$
```

WHAT'S **HAPPENING?** You quoted the apostrophe in **Don't** using two methods, the \ and the double quotation marks. The backslash has another purpose when used as the last character on a line. It allows you to continue a line. Remember, it will remove the *newline* character.

STEP 17 Key in the following: **echo This is a long line** [Enter]

```
[cgillay@RedHat9  cgillay]$  echo This is a long line\
>
```

WHAT'S **HAPPENING?** Since you used the backslash as the last character (even though you pressed [Enter]) the **echo** command was not executed. Instead, you were presented with the secondary prompt.

STEP 18 Key in the following: **to type.** [Enter]

```
>to type.
This is a long lineto type.
[cgillay@RedHat9  cgillay]$
```

WHAT'S HAPPENING? Note that since there was no space between the word **line** and **to** (a continuation of the line), it was displayed as one word: **lineto**.

9.25 • More on Command Line Expansion

As you have learned, when the shell processes a command, it does not immediately execute it. It first parses the command and breaks the command into separate words. The shell then looks at each word looking for special characters that tell the shell to take certain actions. Before the shell executes the command, it performs any command-line expansion it needs to pass the proper items to the command. You have used many of these command-line expansions, such as having the shell substitute a list of file names for a wildcard. There are other types of command substitution. The shell has a specific order in which it must process the command line expansion. The order is:

1. brace expansion
2. tilde expansion
3. parameter expansion.
4. variable substitution
5. command substitution
6. arithmetic expansion
7. word splitting
8. pathname expansion

In the next activity, you will look at some examples of how these other command expansions work.

9.26 • Activity: More on Command Line Expansion

Note 1: Your default directory is your home directory. You have a terminal window open. The BOOK2 disk is mounted.

Note 2: If **personal.fil** is not in your home directory, copy it from the BOOK2 disk to your home directory.

STEP 1   Key in the following making sure to use the curly braces:
ls /mnt/floppy/file?.{czg,fp,swt} [Enter]

```
[cgillay@RedHat9   cgillay]$   ls /mnt/floppy/file?.{czg,fp,swt}
/mnt/floppy/file2.czg  /mnt/floppy/file3.czg   /mnt/floppy/file4.fp
/mnt/floppy/file2.fp   /mnt/floppy/file3.fp
/mnt/floppy/file2.swt  /mnt/floppy/file3.swt
[cgillay@RedHat9   cgillay]$
```

WHAT'S HAPPENING? You have just used curly braces. Curly braces are another means of expansion. When you use curly braces ({ }) for a list of comma-separated strings, they will match what is within the curly braces. There can be no spaces within the curly braces. Any characters that precede the curly braces are called *preambles*, and any characters following the curly braces are called *postambles*. Here, **/mnt/floppy/file?.** was the preamble. There was no postamble. Before the shell passed the values to the **ls** command, it expanded the items in the curly braces so it knew what to pass.

STEP 2 Key in the following, making sure to use the curly braces:
mkdir {1,2,3}test; ls -d *test [Enter]

```
[cgillay@RedHat9  cgillay]$  mkdir {1,2,3}test; ls -d *test
1test    2test     3test
[cgillay@RedHat9  cgillay]$
```

WHAT'S HAPPENING? Here you used a postamble—test—and you created three directories using the expanded items within the curly braces, followed by **test**. You then used the **ls** command with the **-d** option to list those directories.

STEP 3 Key in the following: **mkdir czg{1,2,3}test; ls -d czg*test** [Enter]

```
[cgillay@RedHat9  cgillay]$  mkdir czg{1,2,3}test; ls -d czg*test
czg1test   czg2test     czg3test
[cgillay@RedHat9  cgillay]$
```

WHAT'S HAPPENING? Here you used both a preamble (**czg**) and a postamble (**test**), and you created three more directories using the expanded items within the curly braces.

STEP 4 Key in the following: **rm -r *test*** [Enter]

STEP 5 Key in the following: **cd /mnt/floppy** [Enter]

STEP 6 Key in the following: **cd data** [Enter]

STEP 7 Key in the following: **echo ~ ~student9 ~+ ~-** [Enter]

```
[cgillay@RedHat9  cgillay]$  cd /mnt/floppy
[cgillay@RedHat9  cgillay]$  cd data
[cgillay@RedHat9  cgillay]$  echo ~  ~student9  ~+  ~-
/home/cgillay  /home/student9   /mnt/floppy/data /mnt/floppy
[cgillay@RedHat9  data]$
```

WHAT'S HAPPENING? Here you used tilde expansion. The **echo ~** displayed the fully expanded home directory (**/home/cgillay**). The **echo ~student9** expanded the full path name of the home directory of **student9**. The **echo ~+** expanded to the full path name of the working directory. The **echo ~-** expanded to the previous working directory.

STEP 8 Key in the following: **cd ~-** [Enter]

```
[cgillay@RedHat9  data]$  cd ~-
[cgillay@RedHat9  floppy]$
```

WHAT'S HAPPENING? When you keyed in the command **cd ~-**, the tilde expansion changed directories to the last working directory, in this case the **/mnt/floppy** directory. You may also test and modify variables when you use special modifiers. The modifier can check to see if a variable is set and then assigns a value to the variable based on what the result of the test is. These special variable modifiers are listed in Table 9.12, "Special Modifiers."

Special Modifier	Meaning
${*variable*:-*word*}	If the variable is set and is not empty, substitute its value. Otherwise substitute the value of *word*.

${variable:=*word*)	If the variable is set and is not empty, substitute its value. Otherwise set it to the value of *word*. This is a permanent setting.
${variable:+*word*}	If the variable is set and is not empty, substitute the value of *word*. Otherwise substitute nothing.
${*variable*:?*word*}	If the variable is set and is not empty, substitute the value of *word*. Otherwise print the value of word and exit the shell.

Table 9.12 • Special Modifiers

STEP 9   Key in the following: **cd** Enter

STEP 10   Key in the following: **music=rock; echo ${music:-classical}** Enter

```
[cgillay@RedHat9   floppy]$   cd
[cgillay@RedHat9   cgillay]$   music=rock; echo ${music:-classical}
rock
[cgillay@RedHat9   cgillay]$
```

WHAT'S HAPPENING? You changed directories to your home directory. You then set the variable **music** to **rock**. The next statement was a test. The first part of the test was the question, "Was the variable **music** empty?" The answer is false—it has a value of **rock**. Since it was not empty, simply leave it as is and display the value—**rock**.

STEP 11   Key in the following: **unset music; echo ${music:-classical}** Enter

```
[cgillay@RedHat9   cgillay]$ unset music; echo ${music:-classical}
classical
[cgillay@RedHat9   cgillay]$
```

WHAT'S HAPPENING? In this example, the variable **music** had no value. Therefore, the special modifier (**-classical**) set the value of **music** to **classical**.

When you use command substitution, it makes it possible to use the standard output of command in a shell script as well as on the command line. It is used when you want to assign the output of a command to a variable or when you want to substitute the value of a command within a string. All shells use the back quotes to perform command substitution. The back quotes are *not* the single quotation mark ('). The back quote (`) is usually the lowercase position on the ~ key. The Bash shell also allows the new form, which is where the command is placed within a set of parentheses preceded by the dollar sign ($). The bash shell performs the expansion by executing the command and returns the standard output of the command without any trailing lines. All characters within the parentheses make up the command; none are treated in any special fashion. Remember to use the back quotes, not the single quotation mark.

STEP 12   Key in the following: **echo "The date is `date`"** Enter

STEP 13   Key in the following: **d=$(date); echo $d** Enter

```
[cgillay@RedHat9  cgillay]$  echo "The date is `date`"
The date is Mon Jul 7 21:23:25 PST 2003
[cgillay@RedHat9  cgillay]$  d=$(date); echo $d
Mon Jul 7 21:23:42 PST 2003
[cgillay@RedHat9  cgillay]$
```

WHAT'S HAPPENING? In the "old" style, the output of the **date** command is substituted in the string. In the "new" style, the output of the **date** command is substituted into the expression and then assigned to the variable **d** and displayed on the screen.

STEP 14 Key in the following: **echo "The month is `cal 7 2003`"** [Enter]

STEP 15 Key in the following: **echo $(cal) "$(cal)"** [Enter]

```
[cgillay@RedHat9  cgillay]$  echo "The month is `cal 7 2003`"
The month is       July 2003
Su  Mo  Tu  We  Th  Fr  Sa
        1   2   3   4   5
 6   7   8   9  10  11  12
13  14  15  16  17  18  19
20  21  22  23  24  25  26
27  28  29  30  31.
[cgillay@RedHat9  cgillay]$  echo $(cal)  "$(cal)"
July 2003  Su  Mo Tu We Th  Fr Sa Su 1 2 3 4 5 6 7 8 9
10 11 12 13 14 15 16 17 18 19 20 21 22 23 24 25 26 27 28 29 30 31
July 2003
Su  Mo  Tu  We  Th  Fr  Sa
        1   2   3   4   5
 6   7   8   9  10  11  12
13  14  15  16  17  18  19
20  21  22  23  24  25  26
27  28  29  30  31
[cgillay@RedHat9  cgillay]$
```

WHAT'S HAPPENING? The first example was the "old" way. The second, the "new" way. Note that if you do not quote the command, you lose all the new lines.

STEP 16 Key in the following:
       x="You have ` ls /mnt/floppy | wc -l ` files on the BOOK2 disk." [Enter]

STEP 17 Key in the following: **echo $x** [Enter]

```
[cgillay@RedHat9  cgillay]$ x="You have ` ls /mnt/floppy | wc -l`
files on the BOOK2 disk."
[cgillay@RedHat9  cgillay]$  echo $x
You have 98 files on the BOOK2 disk.
[cgillay@RedHat9  cgillay]$
```

WHAT'S HAPPENING? Your number may vary. Here you assigned the variable **x** to a quoted statement, and within the statement you used the back quotes to obtain the output of a command.

The shell will perform arithmetic expansion by calculating an arithmetic expression and substituting the result of the calculation. The expression is treated as if you used double quotation marks. You may use either the square brackets—[*expression*]—or double parenthesis— ((expression)).

STEP 18   Key in the following: **echo $[9 + 5 + 11] $((5 * 10))** ⌢Enter⌣

```
[cgillay@RedHat9  cgillay]$  echo $[ 9 + 5 + 11]   $(( 5 * 10 ))
25  50
[cgillay@RedHat9  cgillay]$
```

WHAT'S HAPPENING? Your expression was calculated and displayed. You can nest calculations as well.

STEP 19   Key in the following: **echo $[(25 + 4) * 2 * (3 + 3)]** ⌢Enter⌣

```
[cgillay@RedHat9  cgillay]$  echo $[ (25 + 4 ) * 2 * ( 3 + 3) ]
348
[cgillay@RedHat9  cgillay]$
```

WHAT'S HAPPENING? You can see that you can do various mathematical calculations. You can also use arithmetic expansions with other kinds of commands. For instance, if you wanted to know how many pages were in a document, you could set a variable and do a calculation.

STEP 20   Key in the following: **pages=$[$(wc -l < personal.fil)/10]** ⌢Enter⌣

STEP 21   Key in the following: **echo $pages** ⌢Enter⌣

```
[cgillay@RedHat9  cgillay]$ pages=$[ $(wc -l < personal.fil)/10 ]
[cgillay@RedHat9  cgillay]$ echo $pages
3
[cgillay@RedHat9  cgillay]$
```

WHAT'S HAPPENING? Here you calculated the number of pages in the document **personal.fil** in your home directory if you allowed 10 lines per pages. That value was calculated and placed in the variable **pages**. When you asked for the value of **$pages**, **3** was returned, which is the number of pages that would be printed if you allowed 10 lines per page.

You may also use the **IFS** (Internal Field Separator) shell variable to specify which characters you want to use to separate arguments on a command line. When you assign an IFS the value of a new character (provided you do not quote or escape the character), this character can separate fields, but only if they undergo some type of expansion. This interpretation of the command line is called *word splitting*.

STEP 22   Key in the following: **cd /mnt/floppy; a=ast.99:jup.99; cat $a** ⌢Enter⌣

```
[cgillay@RedHat9  cgillay]$ cd /mnt/floppy; a=ast.99:jup.99; cat $a
cat: ast.99:jup.99: No such file or directory
[cgillay@RedHat9  floppy]$
```

WHAT'S HAPPENING? You changed your working directory to **/mnt/floppy**. You then set a variable called **a** that had the value of **ast.99** and **jup.99**. You separated the variables by a colon. However, the colon is not recognized as a delimiter. Thus, when you tried to use the variable **$a**, it could not be read.

STEP 23 Key in the following: **IFS=":"; cat $a** ⎡Enter⎤

```
[cgillay@RedHat9  floppy]$  IFS=":"; cat  $a; cd



The study of Astronomy came from Astrology.
Most scientists no longer believe in
Astrology.  The science of Astronomy is
changing every day.This is my January file.


Jupiter is the largest planet
in our Solar System.  It has a
giant red spot on it.  Huge storms
larger than our earth that last
more than a century take place
on the planet Jupiter.
[cgillay@RedHat9  floppy]$
```

WHAT'S HAPPENING? You told the shell that the colon (:) was an assigned delimiter. Now you could use your variable name with the **cat** command.

STEP 24 Key in the following: **cd** ⎡Enter⎤

STEP 25 Key in the following: **rm personal.fil** ⎡Enter⎤

WHAT'S HAPPENING? You have returned to your home directory and deleted **personal.fil** from your home directory.

9.27 ● The Initialization Files and Sourcing

The Bash shell has a number of startup files that are sourced. *Sourcing* a file causes all the settings in the file to become part of the current shell, and a subshell is not created. The **source** command is a built-in command. The dot command (.) is another name for **source**. Both commands take a script name as an argument. The script will be executed in the environment of the current shell, and no child process will be started. All variables that are set in the shell script will become part of the shell's environment. The **source** or **dot** command can be used to reexecute any of the initialization files if they have been modified. This allows you to make those changes without having to log out and log back in.

The initialization files are sourced depending on whether or not the shell is a login shell, an interactive shell (but not the login shell), or a shell script. When you log on, before you see the shell prompt, the **/etc/profile** script is sourced. Then the shell looks for a file called **.bash_profile** in the user's home directory, and if it exists, it is sourced. This file sets up the user's aliases and then sets up any user-specified environmental variables. If, however, the user has no file called **.bash_profile**, but does have a file called **.bash_login**, that file will be sourced. If the user does not have a **.bash_profile** file, but does have a file called **.profile**, then that file will be sourced.

9.28 ● Activity: Altering the .bashrc File

Note: Your default directory is your home directory. You have a terminal window open. The BOOK2 disk is mounted.

STEP 1   Key in the following: **ls -l .b*** Enter

```
[cgillay@RedHat9  cgillay]$  ls -l  .b*
-rw------  1 cgillay  cgillay  15176  Jul  7  21:59 .bash_history
-rw------  1 cgillay  cgillay     24  Feb 11  05:34 .bash_logout
-rw------  1 cgillay  cgillay    191  Feb 11  05:34 .bash_profile
-rw------  1 cgillay  cgillay    124  Feb 11  05:34 .bashrc
[cgillay@RedHat9  cgillay]$ _
```

WHAT'S **HAPPENING?** In this example, there are four Bash initialization files. Note that you already have read and write permissions for these files. They do not need to have execute permissions. You are going to alter your **.bashrc** file and add some aliases and environmental variables, but first you are going to make a copy of the **.bashrc** file so that you can return to your original **.bashrc** file before you log off.

STEP 2   Key in the following: **cp .bashrc .bashrc.old** Enter

STEP 3   Key in the following: **vi .bashrc** Enter

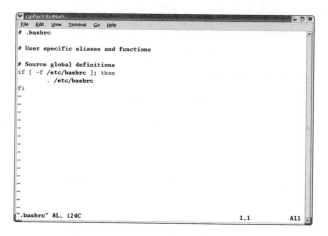

WHAT'S **HAPPENING?** Those items in the file preceded by a **#** are comments and will not be executed.

STEP 4   Move the cursor below **# User specific aliases and functions**.

STEP 5   In Insert mode, key in the following:

    set -o noclobber
    student=Carolyn
    alias m=more
    alias lf='ls /mnt/floppy'
    alias lF='ls -alF'

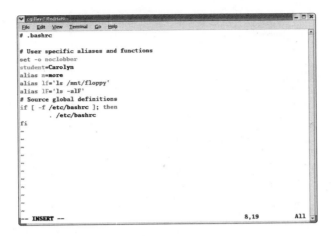

```
# .bashrc

# User specific aliases and functions
set -o noclobber
student=Carolyn
alias m=more
alias lf='ls /mnt/floppy'
alias lF='ls -alF'
# Source global definitions
if [ -f /etc/bashrc ]; then
        . /etc/bashrc
fi
~
~
~
~
~
~
~
~
~
~
~
-- INSERT --                                    8,19        All
```

WHAT'S HAPPENING? You have added some variables, aliases, and options to your **.bashrc** file.

STEP 6   Save the file.

STEP 7   Key in the following: **echo $student; lf** Enter

```
[cgillay@RedHat9   cgillay]$   echo $student; lf


bash: lf: command not found
[cgillay@RedHat9   cgillay]$
```

WHAT'S HAPPENING? Since you have not executed your **.bashrc** file, none of your changes have taken effect.

STEP 8   Key in the following: **source .bashrc** Enter

STEP 9   Key in the following: **echo $student** Enter

```
[cgillay@RedHat9   cgillay]$   echo $student
Carolyn
[cgillay@RedHat9   cgillay]$
```

WHAT'S HAPPENING? Your variable **student** now displays a value. This value will also exist in all child processes.

STEP 10 Key in the following: **bash** Enter

STEP 11 Key in the following: **echo $student** Enter

```
[cgillay@RedHat9   cgillay]$   bash
[cgillay@RedHat9   cgillay]$   echo $student
Carolyn
[cgillay@RedHat9   cgillay]$
```

WHAT'S HAPPENING? Your child process retains the value of **Carolyn** for the variable **student**.

STEP 12 Key in the following: **exit** Enter

STEP 13 Key in the following: **lf | m** Enter

WHAT'S HAPPENING? Your aliases now work.

STEP 14 Press [Ctrl] + **c**. Key in the following: **cp /mnt/floppy/personal.bin ~** [Enter]

STEP 15 Key in the following: **cp /mnt/floppy/ast.99 ~** [Enter]

STEP 16 Key in the following: **cat ast.99 > personal.fil** [Enter]

```
[cgillay@RedHat9  cgillay]$ cat ast.99 > personal.fil
bash: personal.fil: cannot overwrite existing file
[cgillay@RedHat9  cgillay]$
```

WHAT'S HAPPENING? Since you set **noclobber** on, you cannot use redirection to overwrite a file, but remember, you could have overwritten it with the **cp** command.

STEP 17 Key in the following: **cp .bashrc.old .bashrc; rm .bashrc.old** [Enter]

STEP 18 Key in the following: **rm personal.fil ast.99** [Enter]

```
[cgillay@RedHat9  cgillay]$ cp bashrc.old .bashrc; rm .bashrc.old
[cgillay@RedHat9  cgillay]$ rm personal.fil ast.99
[cgillay@RedHat9  cgillay]$
```

WHAT'S HAPPENING? You returned your **.bashrc** to its original state and removed the **personal.fil** and the **ast.99** files.

STEP 19 Unmount the BOOK2 disk and remove it from the drive. Close the terminal window.

Chapter Summary

In this chapter you were introduced to the following:

- The role of the shell and its responsibilities.
- A definition of a process and how the operating systems tracks processes with a pid.
- The available commands to look at processes with the commands **ps**, **pstree**, **uptime** and **top**.
- The ability to control processes with the **kill**, **killall**, **fg, bg**, and **jobs** commands.
- What a shell script is and how to write and execute a shell script.
- How to determine what type of command you want to use with the **type** and **help** commands.
- Using directory stacks and the built-ins: **dirs**, **pushd**, and **popd**.
- An in-depth look at variables, both user-created and environmental variables.
- How to make your user-created variables available to child shells with the **export** and **declare** commands.

* The explanation of what command line substitution is
* A detailed look at quoting, including the single quotes, the double-quotes and backquotes and the effective use of quoting.
* The explanation and use of command line expansion including the order in which they are processed.
* A description of the initialization files and how sourcing is used with them as well as the ability to customize your own environment with sourcing.

Key Terms

alias	hashing	preambles
built-in	kernel	process
escape sequences	load average	sourcing
exit status	parse	stack
forking	postambles	word splitting

Discussion Questions

1. What is the main function of the shell?
2. Explain the purpose and function of the kernel.
3. Explain the functions of the interrupt handler, scheduler, and supervisor that reside within the Linux kernel.
4. What are utilities?
5. What are external commands? Built-in commands? How are each type of these commands executed by the shell?
6. List the six responsibilities of the shell. Briefly explain two of these responsibilities.
7. What is a process?
8. Describe the hierarchical structure that the process adheres to.
9. Explain the function of the pid.
10. Explain the login cycle. What processes occur? What does each process do before going to the next process?
11. Processes can assume different states to allocate their resources better. Explain. List the symbol and meaning for each of these states.
12. What does it mean to *spawn* a process?
13. How can you determine what processes are owned by the current tty?
14. In computer terminology, what does it mean to "parse a command"?
15. What is the function of the **pstree** command? The **uptime** command? The **top** command?
16. Compare and contrast the **kill** and **killall** commands.
17. What is the function of the **jobs** command? What kind of command is it?
18. Compare and contrast the **fg** command with the **bg** command.
19. Compare and contrast a job number with a process identification number.
20. What is a shell script?
21. How do you execute a shell script?
22. What is an alias? When does the shell execute the alias?
23. Give the order in which commands are executed.
24. What is the function of the **type** command? The **help** command? The **alias** command?
25. What is a stack? What command builds the directory stack?
26. What command is used to remove directories from a stack? What command is used to display directories that were placed on a stack?

27. Name two types of variables and define each.
28. When naming a variable are there any rules that must be followed?
29. What are escape sequences?
30. How can you find the value of a variable?
31. If you spawn a child process, what happens to the variable created in the parent process?
32. How may you pass variables to a child process. Why would you do so?
33. What is the purpose and function of command line expansion?
34. What is the function of quote characters?
35. Explain the function of single and double quotes and the backslash. What types of expansions do they stop? What types of expansions do they allow?
36. Compare and contrast the use of single quotes, double quotes, and back quotes.
37. Compare using the backslash with using single quotes.
38. List the shell order in which a command line expansion is processed.
39. What are preambles and postambles?
40. Why would you source a file?

True/False Questions

For each question, circle the letter T if the question is true and the letter F if the question is false.

T   F   1. The shell is responsible for program execution, redirection, pipes, and controlling the environment.

T   F   2. The **uptime** command can be used to display system load averages; the higher the average, the more time available for each process.

T   F   3. The **dirs** command can be used to display the directory stack.

T   F   4. To create a variable called **house** with a value of **ranch**, key in **echo $house=ranch**.

T   F   5. **1fruit** is an acceptable name for a variable.

Completion Questions

Write the correct answer in each blank space.

6. The heart of the Linux operating system, which loads when the computer is turned on and remains in main memory until it is turned off is the _____.
7. A program being executed by the shell is considered to be a(n) _____.
8. The **fg** command is used to bring a command to the _____, while the **bg** command can be used to bring a command to the _____.
9. If you do not want the shell to overwrite files when you use redirection, you may set _____ to on.
10. If you are constantly moving between two directories, rather than use the **cd** command, use the ____ command.

Multiple Choice Questions

For each question, write the letter for the correct answer in the blank space.

11. If no signal is specified when you issue the **kill** command, then the signal sent is
   a. **TERMINAL**
   b. **TERM**
   c. **kill**
   d. **killall**

12. In Linux a file that allows you to initiate a complex series of commands or commands that are repetitive in nature is called a(n)
    a. alias.
    b. shell.
    c. shell script.
    d. built-in.

13. If you want to know if a command is a built-in or a keyword, you may use the ___ command.
    a. **echo**
    b. **list**
    c. **fg**
    d. **type**

14. You set a variable so that **h='ls -l hi'**. You then key in **echo $h**. What will be displayed?
    a. A long listing of the **hi** file.
    b. **ls -l hi**
    c. **$h**
    d. **h**

15. You set a variable so that **h='ls -l hi'**. You then key in **echo '$h'**. What will be displayed?
    a. A long listing of the hi file.
    b. **ls -l hi**
    c. **$h**
    d. **h**

Writing Commands

Write the correct steps or commands to perform the required action as if you were at the computer. You will assume that there is a terminal window open. The prompt will indicate the current working directory.

16. You have a graphics program running call **gimp**. You want to kill the process.

    ```
    [ifujiwara@RedHat9 ifujiwara] $
    ```

17. You have four programs running in background in the following order. **vi**, **ages**, **happy**, **testing**. You want to bring **happy** to the foreground.

    ```
    [jthibodeaux@RedHat9 jthibodeaux] $
    ```

18. You have just written a shell script called **mytest**, located in your home directory. What is the first thing that you must do so that you may run this script?

    ```
    [ggonzales@RedHat9 ggonzales] $
    ```

19. You are constantly issuing the command **ls -l /public/accounts/phone/714**. You are tired of keying in this long command. You would to simply key in **714** to display a long listing of the **/public/accounts/phone/714**. What can you do?

    ```
    [fpanezich@RedHat9 fpanezich] $
    ```

20. The variable **history** has a value of **ancient**. You want to echo a statement so that if the variable **history** is not empty, you substitute the value **modern**.

    ```
    [jweir @RedHat9 jweir] $
    ```

Application Assignments

Problem Set I—At the Computer: Short Answer

Note: See the note on page 414 for information about disk usage.

Use vi or any editor to create a document called **Chapter9.HW**. In this document, you will answer the questions that follow. You do not need to rekey in the questions but be sure to number them. *Do not hand in any hand-written answers.* The actual questions to be answered are indicated by the problem number. Use **pr** to print the document and use the following format:

> *Name*
> *Class number*
> *Class Day and Time*
> Chapter 9 Homework
> > 1.
> > 2.
> > etc.

You may also use a word processor to answer the questions, but be sure to include the above information.

Problem A

* Be sure you are using the GNOME desktop.
* Open a terminal window.
* Determine the ownership of the processes owned by this tty.
    1. What command did you use?
    2. Is **xinit** one of the processes listed?
* Determine the status of all processes, even those without a controlling tty.
    3. What command did you use?
    4. What is the status of the command you just executed?
* Determine the load average and number of users.
    5. What command did you use?
    6. How many users are there?
    7. What is the load average?
* Determine, with a dynamic display, all processes that are running.
    8. What command did you use?
* With the above command running, press **h** (help).
    9. What key can you press to sort the list by pid (process id number)?
    10. What key can you press to sort the list by CPU usage?
    11. Using one of the above, determine which user owns the number 1 process.

Problem B

* You wish to determine the signal id for **SIGQUIT**.
    12. What command did you use?
    13. What is the signal id for **SIGQUIT**?

* In a terminal window, key in the following: **gedit** [Enter]
* You want to kill the **gedit** process.

    14.   What steps did you take to kill the process?

Problem C

* In your home directory, create two subdirectories—one called **abc** and the other called **czg**.
* Using an editor, create the following shell script called **data** in your home directory:

> **oldir=$(pwd)**
> **echo "Starting directory was " $olddir**
> **gohome**
> **echo "Current default directory is now $(pwd)**

* Using an editor, create the following shell script called **gohome** in your home directory:

> **cd**
> **echo "New default directory is now " $(pwd)**
> **echo "Last default directory was oldir.**

    15.   What do you first have to do to make these shell scripts work?

    16.   What command did you use in answer to Question 15 to accomplish your task?

* Change directories to **czg**. Execute the **data** script.

    17.   What command did you use to execute **data**?

* Your scripts did not work! You need to figure out what is wrong with them.
* Rewrite the **data** and **gohome** scripts so that they work correctly. The scripts must be in your home directory. You also want to test them. Test each, first in the **abc** and then in the **czg** directories.

    18.   Provide your new working shell scripts in your answer for both **data** and **gohome**.

* Remove the **czg** and **abc** directories and any other directories you might have created.
* Delete the files **data** and **gohome**.

Problem D

* Mount the BOOK2 disk.
* Create an alias called **lfda** that will list all the directories in **/mnt/floppy** *including* child directories, but only list directories and not files. (*Hint:* Remember **find**.)
* Create an alias called **lfdo** that lists all the directories in only **/mnt/floppy** *not including* child directories, but does not list files. (*Hint:* remember **egrep** and **piping**.)
* Test your aliases.

    19.   Write out the command you used to create **lfda** and **lfdo**.

* You want to know what kind of commands **popd**, **dirs**, and **noclobber** are.

    20.   What command did you use?

    21.   What was the output from the command you used in Question 20?

* You want to know how to use **dirs** including the syntax for the command.

    22.   What command did you use?

    23.   What does the -l flag do when used with **dirs**?

Problem E

- Create a variable called **president** with **John F. Kennedy** as the value.
- Create a variable called **presidents** with **Harry S. Truman** and **Rutherford B. Hayes** as the values.

    24.   How did you create these two variables?

- You want to see the value for **presidents**.

    25.   What command did you use?

- Key in the following: **bash** Enter

    26.   What value does the variable **presidents** have? Why does it have the value it does?

- Key in the following: **exit** Enter
- You want to pass the variable **president** to the child shell.

    27.   What command did you use?

- Key in the following: **bash** Enter

    28.   What value does the variable **president** have?

- Change the value of the variable **president** to **George Washington**.
- Make **president** available to the child shell.
- Key in the following: **bash** Enter

    29.   What value does the variable **president** have?

- Key in the following: **exit** Enter

    30.   What value does the variable **president** have?

- Key in the following: **exit** Enter

    31.   What value does the variable **president** have?

Problem F

- In your home directory, using command line expansion, and using the postamble **yyy**, create two directories, one of which begins with **a** and the other beginning with **b**.

    32.   What command did you use?

- In your home directory, using command line expansion, and using the preamble **xxx**, create two more directories, one of which ends with **A** and the other that ends with **B**.

    33.   What command did you use?

- Remove the directories you created.
- Create the following shell script called **demo**. The contents are as follows:

```
twolines="This is line 1.
This is line 2."
echo "$twolines"
echo $twolines
```

- Execute **demo**.

    34.   What is the output from **demo**?

- Redefine the **IFS** variable so that the output of the second **echo** is the same as the first **echo** in your shell script.

35. What command did you use?

* Remove any files or directories you created in your home directory.
* Be sure to unmount your BOOK2 disk and remove it from the drive.

Problem Set II—At the Computer: Short Answer

Note: To minimize keying in data, the Short Answers in Chapters 5, 6, 7, and 8 need to have been completed.

1. Create a directory called **practice9** in your home directory. How did you accomplish this task?
2. If you are in a lab environment that allowed you to retain the **practice8** directory activities on your computer, completed in Chapter 8, Problem Set II—At the Computer: Short Answer, copy recursively all the files and directories from **practice8** to **practice9**. Otherwise, use the PRACTICE disk you created at the end of the Chapter 8, Problem Set II—At the Computer: Short Answer from the **practice8** directory to the **practice9** directory located in your home directory. How did you accomplish this task?
3. Change directories to **practice9**. What shell are you running? How did you find out this information? What shells are available to you? How did you find out this information?
4. You want to know what processes are running only under your current terminal window. What command did you use? You want to know the status of those running processes under your current terminal window. What command did you use?
5. You want to know all processes that are running on your system. What command did you use? You want to know the status all processes that are running on your system. What command did you use?
6. What is the process number of your shell? What is the parent process of this subshell? Spawn a subshell. What is its parent process? Why? Terminate the second shell. What commands did you use?
7. The **yes** command will continually display the **y** (or the command line argument) separated by spaces and then followed by a new line (Enter). This can be a useful command in scripts and background processes as its output can be piped to a program that issues prompts. With that knowledge, execute the **yes** command and then suspend the process. Then resume the process. Then suspend the process. Then kill the process. What commands did you use?
8. Now redirect the output of the **yes** command to the **/dev/null** device and place the command in background. Then list all of the files in your home directory and redirect the output to a file called **thefile**. In addition, redirect the error messages from this output to a file called **errors**. Place this command in background as well. What commands did you use? What is the status of all these processes? What command did you use? How could you bring a process into foreground when there are multiple processes running? Kill all the running processes. How did you accomplish this task?
9. Create a shell script called **sample** in the **practice9** directory that will copy all the files in the **/home/practice9/mybooks/scifi** directory that begin with **b** to the **practice9** directory. Then the shell script will display the contents of each file you copied. What are the commands in the shell script? How did you execute it? What, if anything, did you have to do to execute it?
10. Create an alias that will allow you to key in **DIR** and see a long listing of all the files in your home directory. How did you create the alias?

11. What kind of command is **history**? What is its syntax? What is the purpose of the **history** command? How did you find out this information?

12. In the following activity, you will use the **pushd** and **popd** commands. Change directories to the **mybooks** directory. Then change directories to the **literature** directory. Then change directories to the **scifi** directory. What directory is listed first in the directory stack? What command did you use to locate this information? Key in **pushd +2**. What directory are you in? Why? Key in **popd +2**. What directory are you in? Was any directory removed from the directory stack? If so, which directory? Return to the **practice9** directory.

13. Create a variable called **scifi** that has the value of **/home/**_username_**/practice9/mybooks/scifi**. Create another variable called **mystery** that has the value of **/home/**_username_**/practice9/mybooks/mystery**. Remember _username_ is the name you logged in as. How did you create the variables? Using the variable name, list the contents of the **scifi** directory; the **mystery** directory. What command did you use? Create a new directory under the **practice9** directory called **newbooks**. Using the variable name, copy all the files from the **scifi** and **mystery** directory to the **newbooks** directory. What command did you use?

14. Create a variable called **Coben** that has the value of **Tell No One**. Make this variable available to the child shell. What command(s) did you use? Open a child shell. What is the value of **Coben**? Change the value of **Coben** to **No Second Chance**. Open a child shell. What is the value of **Coben**? Key in **exit** twice. What is the value of **Coben**? Why?

15. Create a variable **number** that will display the following statement: **There is/are** _nnn_ **user(s) logged in**. The _nnn_ is a count of how many users are logged in and results from the output of a command. How did you create this variable? Create another variable called **name** that will display the following statement: **The current user's name is** _loginname_. The _loginname_ is the name of the currently logged in user. How did you create this variable? Using the variables **number** and **name**, determine how many users are logged in and the current user's name.

16. Get the disk labeled **PRACTICE** disk. Do not use the BOOK or BOOK2 disk. Mount it. Copy everything in the **practice9** directory under your home directory to the floppy disk to a directory called **practice9**. When you have finished, unmount the floppy disk and remove it from the drive.

Problem Set III—Brief Essay

Use gEdit or OpenOffice.org Writer to write and print your response. Be sure to put your name as well as what day and time your class is. Include the number of the question you are answering.

a. Describe the purpose and function of the shell. Include in your discussion a comparison of the types of commands available to you.

b. Compare and contrast single quotes, double quotes, back quotes, and the backslash. Give examples on how each could be used on the command line.

c. Compare and contrast background and foreground jobs. Include the syntax you would use to place a command in foreground and in background.

CHAPTER 10

Shell Scripts

Chapter Overview

Shell programming is a skill often demanded of Linux system administrators, Web authors, and those who work in a Linux/Unix world. By learning to script, administrators will have skills that allow them to solve system administration problems and automate routine administration tasks. But even ordinary users find that shell scripts increase their flexibility in solving problems, automating routine tasks and customizing their environment, not to mention enhancing their understanding of Linux concepts. Shell programs, usually referred to as a *shell scripts*, are used on every Unix- and Linux- based system. An important function of shell scripts is controlling the initialization of Linux when you first boot the system as well as automating repetitive tasks.

This chapter will introduce you to the logic of building shell scripts, as well as applying documentation standards to those scripts. You will also learn how to use the test process to evaluate different types of data in your scripts. You need to understand the flow of shell scripting to effectively write shell scripts. You will learn the basic components of a script. You will learn how to allow your script to accept values from the command line and interact with the user. You will learn programming structures that allow you to change the sequential flow and build decision structures that test for a condition and, based on that condition, execute the appropriate statements, using **if** and **case** statements. You will also learn about looping structures using **while**, **until**, and **for** commands.

547

Learning Objectives

1. Explain the purpose and function of shell programming.
2. Explain how to create, document, and execute shell scripts.

3. Explain the purpose and function of the **read** command.
4. Explain the purpose and function of the **shift** command.
5. Explain how the **set** command can be used to reset the positional parameters.
6. Explain the purpose and function of the **exit** status.
7. Explain the purpose and function of the **test** and **let** commands.
8. Explain the purpose and function of the **if-then** command construct.
9. Explain the purpose and function of the **if-then-else** command construct.
10. Explain the purpose and function of the **if-then-elif** command construct.
11. Explain the purpose and function of the **case** command.
12. Explain how loops can be used to execute a set of commands repeatedly, a set number of times, or until a condition is met.

Student Outcomes

1. Write a shell script.
2. Use the **read** command to incorporate user input.
3. Create a script that uses positional parameters.
4. Use the **shift** command in a shell script.
5. Use the **set** command to reset positional parameters.
6. Use the exit status in programming a script.
7. Use the **test** command to check the validity of conditions formulated in loops and branches.
8. Use the **set** command to perform operations on arithmetic values.
9. Use the **if-then-else** command construct to allow a two-way decision making process.
10. Use the **if-then-elif** command constructs to facilitate a multiway decision making process.
11. Use the **case** command to provide a way to make multiway decisions.
12. Use the **for**, **while**, and **until** commands to construct loops to execute a set of commands.

Commands Introduced

case	if/then/elif	shift
exit	let	test
exec	read	until
for	set	while

10.1 • Commands, Comments, and Executing Shell Scripts

A shell script combines Linux commands to perform specific tasks. It contains commands that the shell can execute. It can contain any commands that you can enter at the shell prompt. A command in a shell script can use wildcards, redirection, pipes, filters, and the use of variables. As a matter of fact, when you have keyed in commands at the command line, such as **grep "Teacher" personal.fil | sort > teacher.fil**, you could have placed those commands in a shell script. The advantage of a script is that you can save one command or a series of commands into a file and then simply have the shell execute the file. Using the example above, you could save the commands in a file called **teacher**, and every time you needed the above information, you would only need to key in **teacher**.

However, typically shell scripts are a series of commands rather than a single command. The Bash shell, like most shells, provides many programming tools you can use to create your scripts. You can define variables and assign values to those variables. You may also define variables in a script and have the user enter the values for those variables when the script is executed. You may create loops as well as create conditional control structures in a shell script. A *loop* repeats Linux commands. Loops allow the use of specific key words such as **for**, **while**, and **until**. In addition, you can use what are called *conditional control structures*, sometimes called conditional flow, which allows you to make decisions on the commands you wish to execute in the shell script. A control structure consists of two major components, a *test* and *commands*. If the test is successful, the command will execute. If the test is unsuccessful, the command will not execute. This allows you to change the order of execution of commands in a script. You can also create expressions that perform arithmetic operations, as well as create expressions that can do comparison operations. In this chapter, you will develop and create shell scripts using basic Linux commands as well as using tests such as **if-then-else**.

10.2 • Commands, Comments, and Executing Shell Scripts

A shell script is a text file that contains Linux commands. You usually create a shell script using any standard editor such as **vi**, **emacs**, or **gEdit**. One of the most important things to do when you are writing shell scripts is to provide complete documentation within the script. *Documentation* is the information that describes the script to its users. The purpose of documentation is so that you, and others who might use the script, have relevant information about the script. Complete documentation should contain the following:

- The script name.
- The purpose of the script.
- Any syntax usage; i.e., how to use the script.
- The name of the author of the script.
- The date the script was written.
- The date(s) the script was modified, and the name of the person who modified the script, if modified by other than the original author.

The way that you document a shell script is through comments. *Comments* are short explanations that describe the above items. Those items are normally placed at the beginning of the shell script. In addition, comments can be interspersed throughout the script and include information such as the definition of variables. Comments can appear in any line or any part of a line. Comments are always preceded by the pound sign (**#**). A comment indicates to the Bash shell that the items on the line are not to be executed. The first line of the shell script, however, cannot be a comment. The first line of the shell script is used to identify the program that is to be used to execute the lines in the script. This line, called the *shebang* line is written as **#!/bin/bash** when using Bash. If you were using another interpreter, such as tcsh, it would be written as **#!/bin/tcsh**. The **#!** is called a magic number and is used by the kernel to identify the program that should interpret the lines in your script file. This line *must* be the top line in your script. There are two explanations for origin of the term "shebang"—one from The Jargon Dictionary is as follows:

> *The character sequence "#!" that frequently begins executable shell scripts under Unix probably derived from "shell bang" under the influence of American slang "the whole shebang" (everything, the works).*

And the other, from **searchSolaris.com**, is this:

Among Unix shell (user interface) users, a shebang is a term for the "#!" characters that must begin the first line of a script. In musical notation, a "#" is called a sharp and an exclamation point—"!"—is sometimes referred to as a bang. Thus, shebang becomes a shortening of sharp-bang.

As has been discussed earlier, when you key in a command, the shell forks (or spawns) a child process that executes the command. While the child process is executing the command, the parent process sleeps. When a process sleeps, it uses no computer time; it is waiting to wake up. When the child process finishes executing the command, it dies. Then, the parent process, which is running the subshell, wakes up and prompts you for another command. However, for commands that are built into the shell (built-ins) such as **echo**, **cd**, and so on, the shell does not need to fork a process.

When the shell forks, it creates a duplicate of the shell process or a subshell. This new process tries to **exec** (execute) the command. Both **fork** and **exec** are system calls that are routines executed by the operating system. If what you keyed in is an executable program, then **exec** succeeds and the operating system overlays the new subshell with the executable program. If the command is a shell script, **exec** fails. When **exec** fails, the system assumes that the command is a shell script, and the subshell runs the commands in the script. The subshell takes its input from a file, the shell script. What this means is that you may run a shell script in a variety of ways. For instance, if you had a shell script called **hi**, you could execute it in the following ways:

```
bash  hi
. hi
```

Entering the commands in this way means that the script does not have to have execute permission. However, the script will run more slowly, so normally, shell scripts are given execute permissions. If the shell script does have execute permissions, you may run the script, in this instance called **hi,** by keying in **./hi**, provided the script is located in your home directory. If you want the shell script to behave like any other command, you would need to look at your path statement to know where Linux looks for executable programs. Normally, one of these locations is the **bin** directory located in the user's home directory (**/home/**_username_**/bin**). By placing your shell script in that location, and with your shell script having execute permissions, you may invoke the shell script—no matter what your default directory is—by simply keying in the shell script name, i.e., **hi**.

10.3 • Activity: Writing a Shell Script

Note 1:   If you are going to take more than one work session to complete this chapter, and if you are working in a lab environment and your files are not saved from one session to the next, you may want to save each shell script you write to your floppy disk (BOOK2 disk). You can then copy the scripts back to your home directory each time you log in.

Note 2:   Your default directory is your home directory.

STEP 1   Mount the BOOK2 floppy and open a terminal window.

STEP 2   Create the following shell script in your home directory, but substitute your name for my name and the current date for the date displayed. The script will be called **first**:

#!/bin/bash
 # Script name: first
 # Purpose: Writing a shell script using variables and quoting.

Written by Carolyn Z. Gillay on July 8, 2003
echo "Good day $LOGNAME."
echo "Your current default directory is `pwd`."
echo "The name of your computer is `uname -n`."
echo "A list of files on the BOOK2 disk that have 99 as an extension."
ls -l /mnt/floppy/*.99   # Listing 99 files in a single column.
echo "The time is `date +%r`! "
echo "Your script is ended $LOGNAME."

STEP 3   Key in the following: **cat first** [Enter]

```
[cgillay@RedHat9  cgillay]$  cat first
#!/bin/bash
#  Script name: first
#  Purpose: Writing a shell script using variables and quoting.
#  Written by Carolyn Z. Gillay on July 8, 2003.
echo  "Good day $LOGNAME."
echo "Your current default directory is `pwd` ."
echo "The name of your computer is `uname -n`."
echo "A list of files on the BOOK2 disk that have 99 as an
extension."
ls  -1  /mnt/floppy/*.99  # Listing 99 files in a single column.
echo  "The time is `date +%r`!"
echo Your script is ended $LOGNAME.
[cgillay@RedHat9  cgillay]$
```

WHAT'S HAPPENING? You began your script with the shebang, **#!/bin/bash**. The magic number **#!** told the system that this is a shell script with **/bin/bash** being the specific shell you are planning to use to run the script. The next three lines are comments and will be ignored (not executed) when you execute the script. These lines are important information. You are documenting your script with the name of the script, the purpose and the author, and the date of creation.

The next line—**echo "Good day $LOGNAME."**—uses the variable **LOGNAME.** It is a variable that the login utility assigned a value when you logged in. You asked for the value of the variable because you preceded it with $. The value is the name that you logged in as. You enclosed the entire statement with double quotation marks (") to set it off. The quotation marks are not actually needed. However, they are useful because they definitely set off what you want displayed.

The next line—**echo "Your current default directory is `pwd`."**—has several important elements. **echo** is going to display on the screen whatever you have keyed in enclosed by the quotations marks ("). However, note that **pwd** is enclosed not by single quotation marks but by the back quotes (`). Remember, the back quote is located under the ˜ on the keyboard. When you use back quotes, the shell will replace the command, including the back quotes, with the output of the command. Remember, this is command substitution. If you use the single (') or double (") quotation marks, the shell will interpret what is in quotes as merely a character string and instead of seeing your current directory, you would simply see **pwd** displayed.

The next line—**echo "The name of your computer is `uname -n`."**—is again a quoted statement with the command **uname -n** enclosed with back quotes. The command **uname** displays system information and the **-n** option asks for the name of your computer, or technically, the network node hostname. Remember, when you enclose a command with back quotes, you are asking for the output of the command.

The next line—**echo "A list of files on the BOOK2 disk that have 99 as an extension."**—is simply a description of what you are doing. The only command is **echo**. The next line—**ls -1 /mnt/floppy/*.99 # Listing 99 files in a single column.**—executes the **ls** command with the **-1** option for a single column display. Note that there is a comment within the line, again preceded by the **#**. The comment will not display when the script is executed.

The next line—**echo "The time is `date +%r` ! "**—again contains a command enclosed in back quotes. You have used the **date** command in prior exercises. The **+** sign indicated that you want the date in a specific format. The **%** indicates how the sequence will be interpreted. The **r** indicates that you want the time displayed only in a 12-hour format, using A.M. or P.M.

The last line—**echo Your script is ended $LOGNAME.**—again uses the login variable. In this case, you did not use quotation marks to set off your display. Now you want to execute your script.

STEP 4 Key in the following: **first** [Enter]

```
[cgillay@RedHat9 cgillay]$ first
bash: first: command not found
[cgillay@RedHat9 cgillay]$
```

WHAT'S **HAPPENING?** The shell only looks in directories set in the path to execute commands. Your home directory is not in the path.

STEP 5 Key in the following: **ls -l first; ./first; bash first** [Enter]

```
[cgillay@RedHat9 cgillay]$ ls -l first;./first; bash first
-rw-rw-r--   1 cgillay   cgillay        470  Jul   8 10:00 first
bash: ./first: Permission denied
Good day cgillay.
Your current default directory is /home/cgillay.
The name of your computer is RedHat9.
A list of files on the BOOK2 disk that have 99 as an extension.
/mnt/floppy/ast.99
/mnt/floppy/jup.99
/mnt/floppy/mer.99
/mnt/floppy/ven.99
The time is 10:13:13 AM!
Your script is ended cgillay.
[cgillay@RedHat9 cgillay]$
```

WHAT'S **HAPPENING?** The **first** script does not have execute permissions. When you tried to execute **first** using **./first**, it could not run, as the proper permissions were not assigned to the file. When you executed the command as **bash first**, since **bash** expects input from a file, you did not need execute permissions. You could also execute the command with **. first**. In this case there would be a space between the period and the script name. Running a script in this manner also does not require that the file have execute permissions.

Usually, users want to run a shell script as they would run any command. There are two things that must occur for this to happen. First, execute permissions must be granted to the shell script (file). Secondly, the shell script must be located in a directory that is in the **PATH** statement.

STEP 6   Key in the following: **echo $PATH** [Enter]

```
[cgillay@RedHat9   cgillay]$   echo $PATH
/user/kerberos/bin:/usr/local/bin:/bin:/usr/bin:/usr/X11R6/bin:
/home/cgillay/bin
[cgillay@RedHat9   cgillay]$
```

WHAT'S **HAPPENING?** Your path statement may be different, but usually, the default search path includes **/home/*username*/bin**. In the example above, you can see that the last directory to be searched for executable programs is **/home/cgillay/bin.** You have confirmed that **/home/cgillay/bin** was in the search path. However, as of yet, there is no **bin** directory in **/home/cgillay.** Usually the **/home/*username*/bin** directory must be created; it is not created by default. Once the **bin** directory is created in your home directory, you will want to keep all your script files. If shell script files are given execute permissions and then moved (or created) in the **/home/*username*/bin** directory, then the script becomes a command like any other command.

STEP 7   Key in the following: **mkdir bin; chmod +x first** [Enter]

STEP 8   Key in the following: **mv first bin; first** [Enter]

```
[cgillay@RedHat9   cgillay]$   mkdir bin; chmod +x first
[cgillay@RedHat9   cgillay]$   mv first bin; first
Good day cgillay.
Your current default directory is /home/cgillay.
The name of your computer is RedHat9.
A list of files on the BOOK2 disk that have 99 as an extension.
/mnt/floppy/ast.99
/mnt/floppy/jup.99
/mnt/floppy/mer.99
/mnt/floppy/ven.99
The time is 10:21:00 AM!
Your script is ended cgillay.
[cgillay@RedHat9   cgillay]$
```

WHAT'S **HAPPENING?** You created a **bin** directory in your home directory and then changed permissions on the **first** file so that it was executable. You then moved **first** to **/home/cgillay/bin.** Then you keyed in **first**. Now your shell script ran as an ordinary command.

10.4 • The read Command

As you begin to create shell scripts, you will want to prompt the user for information. Then you will want to be able to store this information in a user-created variable. The **read** command allows your script to accept input from the user and then store that information in one or more variables. The **read** command is a built-in command used to read input from the terminal or from a file. You can use the **echo** command to output data and the **read** command to read input into variables. It allows a user to interactively input a value for a variable. The **read** command literally reads the next line in standard input. Everything entered as standard input up to pressing [Enter] is read in and assigned to a variable. If the variable is preceded by a **$**, or if double quotes are used, the value will be interpreted by the shell for variable expansion. If the variable is enclosed in single quotes, variable expansion will not occur. Table 10.1, "The **read** Command," lists the available options.

Pressing **Enter** is the standard used in this text. Technically, it is a *newline* character. There are actually keyboards that have a newline key or use other keys to indicate the end of a line. The newline character is a command separator. It initiates the execution of the command that preceded your pressing the newline key—in this text, the **Enter** key.

Syntax	Operation
read *uservariable*	Reads a line from standard input and assigns it to the named *uservariable*. *uservariable* is named within the script.
read *one two three*	Reads a line from standard input to the first white space and places the first word keyed into the variable named *one*, the second word into the variable named *two* and the rest of the line into the variable *three*. *one*, *two*, and *three* are examples of names that can be used. Any word can be used.
read	Reads a line from standard input and assigns it to the built-in variable *REPLY*.

Table 10.1 • The read Command

10.5 • Activity: Using the read Command

Note: You have a terminal window open. Your default directory is your home directory. The BOOK2 disk is mounted.

STEP 1   Key in the following: **bash -version** **Enter**

```
[cgillay@RedHat9  cgillay]$  bash -version
GNU bash, version 2.05b.0(1)-release (i386-redhat-linux-gnu)
Copyright 2002 Free Software Foundation, Inc.
[cgillay@RedHat9  cgillay]$
```

WHAT'S HAPPENING? It is useful to know what software version you are running. Each release of software will usually include more options and enhancements. In this example, you are running the 2.05b.0(1) version of **bash**. You may have a different release.

STEP 2   Create the following shell script in your home directory, but substitute your name for my name and the current date for the date given in the script. The script will be called **readinfo**:

#!/bin/bash
 # Script name: readinfo
 # Purpose: Using read.
 # Written by Carolyn Z. Gillay on July 8, 2003
echo -n "What is your full name? "
read first middle last
echo "I am glad you are in my class, $first. "
echo -n "Do you like this class? "

read answer
echo "$answer is the right answer. "
echo -n "What is your favorite class? "
read REPLY
echo I thought you might like $REPLY best.
echo -n "Name three of your friends. "
read friend1 friend2 friend3
echo I had $friend2 in one of my classes.
echo I also think I may have had $friend1 in another class.
echo Bye $first.

STEP 3 Key in the following: **bash readinfo** Enter

```
[cgillay@RedHat9 cgillay]$ bash readinfo
What is your full name?
```

WHAT'S **HAPPENING?** The first executable line states **echo -n "What is your full name? "** The **-n** following **echo** suppresses a new line and prompts the user for information. At the prompt, you are going to answer the question and provide your first, middle, and last names.

STEP 4 Key in your first, middle, and last names and press Enter

```
[cgillay@RedHat9 cgillay]$ bash info
What is your full name? Carolyn Zonia Gillay
I am glad you are in my class, Carolyn.
Do you like this class?
```

WHAT'S **HAPPENING?** When you keyed in your information, the next line in the script, **read first middle last**, read the characters you keyed in by position so that, in this example, **Carolyn** is the value for the variable **first**, **Zonia** is the value for the variable **middle**, and **Gillay** is the value for the variable **last**. Then, the next line in the script, **echo "I am glad you are in my class, $first. "** used the value in the variable **$first** (**Carolyn**) and displayed it on the line. The script then read the next line, **echo -n "Do you like this class? "** prompting the user for input.

STEP 5 Key in the following: **Yes** Enter

```
[cgillay@RedHat9 cgillay]$ bash readinfo

What is your full name? Carolyn Zonia Gillay
I am glad you are in my class, Carolyn.
Do you like this class? Yes
Yes is the right answer.
What is your favorite class?
```

WHAT'S **HAPPENING?** When you provided an answer, **Yes**, the line, **echo "$answer is the right answer. "** used **Yes** as the value in the variable **$answer**. The script then read the next line, **echo -n "What is your favorite class? "** prompting the user for input.

STEP 6 Key in the following: **Linux** Enter

```
[cgillay@RedHat9  cgillay]$  bash readinfo
What is your full name? Carolyn Zonia Gillay
I am glad you are in my class, Carolyn.
Do you like this class? Yes
Yes is the right answer.
What is your favorite class? Linux
I thought you might like Linux best.
Name three of your friends.
```

WHAT'S **HAPPENING?** When you provided an answer, **Linux**, the line **read REPLY** used **Linux** as a value for the built-in variable **$REPLY.** The script then read the next line, **echo I thought you might like $REPLY best.** using **Linux** as the value for the built-in variable **REPLY.** The next line, **echo -n "Name three of your friends. "** is prompting the user for input.

STEP 7   Key in three of your friends' names and press Enter

```
[cgillay@RedHat9  cgillay]$  bash info
What is your full name? Carolyn Zonia Gillay
I am glad you are in my class, Carolyn.
Do you like this class? Yes
Yes is the right answer.
What is your favorite class? Linux
I thought you might like Linux best.
Name three of your friends. Frank Steven Emily
I had Steven in one of my classes.
I also think I might have had Frank in another class.
Bye Carolyn.
[cgillay@RedHat9  cgillay]$
```

WHAT'S **HAPPENING?** When you provided the input—in this case, **Frank, Steven,** and **Emily**— the next line in the script **read friend1 friend2 friend3**, assigned the value **Frank** to **friend1**, the value **Steven** to **friend2**, and the value **Emily** to **friend3**. The next two lines (**echo I had $friend2 in one of my classes** and **echo I also think I may have had $friend1 in another class.**) used **Steven** for **$friend2** and **Frank** for **$friend1**. The last line—**echo Bye $first.**— used the value for the variable **$first** defined earlier in the script. You have been quoting special characters. Remember, placing special characters in quotes prevents special characters from being evaluated. Sometimes, however, you want your special characters (regular expressions) to be evaluated.

STEP 8   Create the following shell script in your home directory, but substitute your name for my name. The script will be called **files**:
        #!/bin/bash
        # Script name: files
        # Purpose: Evaluating special characters.
        # Written by Carolyn Z. Gillay on July 8, 2003.
        echo -n "Please enter the files you are looking for: "
        read looking
        echo "The files you asked for are: " $looking

STEP 9   Key in the following: **chmod +x files; ./files** Enter

```
[cgillay@RedHat9  cgillay]$  chmod +x files; ./files
Please enter the files you are looking for:
```

WHAT'S HAPPENING? Here you are going to use a special character, the *, which you want the shell to evaluate. You are going to provide **/mnt/floppy/*.99** as the variable. In this case, you do want the shell to interpret or "expand" the * to represent any file name that has a **.99** extension located in the **/mnt/floppy** directory. If you quoted the *, then the shell would not expand that variable.

STEP 10 Key in the following: **/mnt/floppy/*.99** ⟨Enter⟩

```
[cgillay@RedHat9  cgillay]$  chmod +x files; ./files
Please enter the files you are looking for: /mnt/floppy/*.99
The files you asked for are: /mnt/floppy/ast.99
/mnt/floppy/jup.99 /mnt/floppy/mer.99 /mnt/floppy/ven.99
[cgillay@RedHat9  cgillay]$
```

WHAT'S HAPPENING? The shell could expand the * and showed you all the files in **/mnt/floppy** that had any file name but had the extension **.99**.

10.6 • Positional Parameters

In the same way that you use arguments with commands, arguments can be used effectively in script files. A *command line argument* follows a command and is passed to it. You will sometimes hear options referred to as arguments. The difference between the two is subtle. Arguments are all the separate words that appear on the command line after the command. Options are only those arguments that change the behavior of the command. Arguments to a program are usually given after the command name, usually separated by spaces. For instance, look at the command **ls -l test.fil**

```
Command           Command Line Arguments
ls        -l  test.fil
```

In the above example, the spaces are delimiters. First the command is issued, **ls**. Then the **-l** is still an argument but it is considered an option passed to the **ls** command because it will tell the shell that you want to change the behavior of the **ls** command (long listing). The second argument is **test.fil**, which is passed to the **ls** command, so it knows which file you want the option to apply to. Arguments give the command additional instructions. When you key in a command followed by argument, you are parsing a command. Remember, to parse is to analyze something in an orderly way. In linguistics, to parse is to divide words and phrases into different parts in order to understand relationships and meanings. In computers, to parse is to divide the computer language statement into parts that can be made useful for the computer. In the above example, the **ls** command had two arguments passed to it(**-l** and **test.fil**)so that the **ls** command can display a long listing of the **test.fil.**

Command line arguments can be referenced in a script with *positional parameters*. When you key in the name of the script file to execute, you can also key in, at the same time, additional information on the command line that your script can use. When you write the script file, you supply the markers or place holders within the script to let the script know that something (an argument) will be keyed in with the script name. The place holder or marker used in a script file is the dollar sign ($) followed by a number. The shell uses **$0** to store the name of the command used to call a script. The **$** sign is the signal to the shell that an argument is coming. The numbers indicate what position the argument is on the command line. Thus, in the command **ls -l test.fil**, the command **ls** occupies the first position, which will be referenced in the script as **$0**. The **-l** occupies the second position on the command line and will be referenced in the script as **$1**. **test.fil** occupies the third position on the command line and will be referenced in the script as **$2**. When you exceed **$9**, you must use curly braces so that the number is kept as one number. Thus, 10 would be referenced as **${10}**. Table 10.2, "Positional Parameters," lists some other special uses of positional parameters.

Command Line Arguments	Description
$0	Linux command
$*n*	The number of the position on the command line, where *n* represents a number.
${*nn*}	Any number that exceeds a single digit.
$#	The count of command line arguments.
$*	All the command line arguments beginning with the first argument.
$@	The command line arguments individually quoted. Is the same as $*, except when enclosed in double quotation marks.
$?	The return status of the most recently executed command.
$$	The process id of the current process.
$!	The process id of the last background command.
"$*"	All the command line arguments beginning with 1 and expanded to a single argument, i.e. "$1 $2 $3".
"$@"	The command line arguments individually quoted and expanded to separate arguments, i.e., "$1" "$2" "$3".

Table 10.2 • Positional Parameters

10.7 • Activity: Using Positional Parameters

Note: You have a terminal window open. Your default directory is your home directory.

STEP I Create the following shell script in your home directory, but substitute your name for my name and the current date for the date given in the script. The script will be called **getargs**:

```
#!/bin/bash
# Script name: getargs
# Purpose: Using positional parameters.
# Written by Carolyn Z. Gillay on July 8, 2003.
# Arguments are passed to the command based on position.
echo $0  #Name of command is always $0
echo 1st position on command line that is passed to echo is $1.
echo 2nd position on command line that is passed to echo is $2.
echo 3rd position on command line that is passed to echo is $3.
ls  $4 $5  #4th and 5th position on command line are passed to ls.
echo $3  $1  $2
```

STEP 2 Key in the following: **. getargs apple bette carolyn -I files** Enter

```
[cgillay@RedHat9  cgillay]$ . getargs  apple bette carolyn -l
files
bash
1st position on command line that is passed to echo is apple.
2nd position on command line that is passed to echo is bette.
3rd position on command line that is passed to echo is carolyn.
-rwxrwxr-x   1 cgillay  cgillay    236 Jul  8 11:34  files
carolyn  apple  bette
[cgillay@RedHat9  cgillay]$
```

WHAT'S HAPPENING? Look at a breakdown of the command line:

Position 0	Position 1	Position 2	Position 3	Position 4	Position 5
bash	apple	bette	carolyn	-l	files

When you executed the script, position 0 is not **getargs** but **bash**. When you execute a shell script using *. command name*, you are really running or invoking another shell, which then runs **getargs**. In order not to have invoked another Bash shell, you would have needed to give execute permissions to the file. The script begins counting with the first item after the script name as position 1. The script takes each argument from the command line and places it in the appropriate position. The last line demonstrates that it does not matter in what order or where you place the positional parameters. Whenever the script needs a value for an argument, it locates the item in the specified position on the command line.

STEP 3 Key in the following: **chmod +x getargs; ./getargs A B C -I files** Enter

```
[cgillay@RedHat9  cgillay]$ chmod +x getargs;./getargs A B C -l
files
./getargs
1st position on command line that is passed to echo is A.
2nd position on command line that is passed to echo is B.
3rd position on command line that is passed to echo is C.
```

```
-rwxrwxr-x    1 cgillay  cgillay     236  Jul   8 11:34   files
C  A  B
[cgillay@RedHat9  cgillay]$
```

WHAT'S HAPPENING? Now that you changed the permissions and ran the script using the **./** command, position 0 is occupied by the script name, **./getargs**.

STEP 4 Add the following line to the end of the **getargs** script:

echo 10th position that is passed to echo is ${10}.

STEP 5 Key in the following: **./getargs A B C -l files 6 7 8 9 10 11** Enter

```
[cgillay@RedHat9  cgillay]$ _ ./getargs A B C -l  files 6 7 8 9
10 11
./getargs
1st position on command line that is passed to echo is A.
2nd position on command line that is passed to echo is B.
3rd position on command line that is passed to echo is C.
-rwxrwxr-x    1 cgillay  cgillay     241  Jul   8 11:34   files
C  A  B
10th position that is passed to echo is 10.
[cgillay@RedHat9  cgillay]$
```

WHAT'S HAPPENING? In order to use an argument that is larger than one digit, you must enclose it in curly braces ({   }). Also, although on the command line you had values for positions 6, 7, 8, 9, 10, and 11, only the value for the 10th position was used. Since you did not ask for any of the other values, the script ignored them.

STEP 6 In the **getargs** script, delete the line **echo 10th position that is passed to echo is ${10}.**

STEP 7 Add the following lines to the end of the **getargs** script:

echo $#

echo $*

echo This is a

break for $*.

echo $@

echo This is a

break for $@.

STEP 8 Key in the following: **./getargs A B C -l files 6 7 8** Enter

```
[cgillay@RedHat9  cgillay]$  ./getargs A B C -l  files 6 7 8
./getargs
1st position on command line that is passed to echo is A.
2nd position on command line that is passed to echo is B.
3rd position on command line that is passed to echo is C.
-rwxrwxr-x    1 cgillay  cgillay     236  Jul   8 11:34   files
C  A  B
8
A B C -l files 6 7 8
This is a
```

```
./getargs: line 15: break: only meaningful in a 'for', 'while' or
'until' loop
A B C -l file 6 7 8
This is a
./getargs:line 15: break: only meaningful in a 'for', 'while' or
'until' loop
[cgillay@RedHat9  cgillay]$
```

WHAT'S HAPPENING? The **$#** gives you a count of the command line arguments. The **$*** lists all the command line arguments beginning with the first argument on the command line. The **$@** lists the command line arguments individually quoted. However, since you broke the command line, you did not pass the argument as a single argument. You must enclose that line with double quotation marks. In general, the "**$***" treats the entire list of arguments, including embedded spaces, whereas "**$@**" produces a list of separate arguments. The differences between **$*** and **$@** will become clearer when referencing arguments using the for-in control structure, to be shown later. As you can see, **break** is a special keyword that allows you to exit from a **for, while,** or **until** loop.

STEP 9   Alter the following lines in the **getargs** script by adding double quotes:

> **echo $#**
> **echo $***
> **echo "This is a**
> **break for $*."**
> **echo $@**
> **echo "This is a**
> **break for $@."**

STEP 10   Key in the following: **./getargs A B C -l files 6 7 8** [Enter]

```
[cgillay@RedHat9  cgillay]$ ./getargs A B C -l  files 6 7 8
./getargs
1st position on command line that is passed to echo is A.
2nd position on command line that is passed to echo is B.
3rd position on command line that is passed to echo is C.
-rwxrwxr-x  1 cgillay  cgillay    241  Jul  8 11:34  files
C  A  B
8
A B C -l files 6 7 8
This is a
break for A B C -l files 6 7 8.
A B C -l file 6 7 8
This is a
break for A B C -l files 6 7 8.
[cgillay@RedHat9  cgillay]$
```

WHAT'S HAPPENING? Since you quoted the lines, the script treated the line between the quotes as a single unit.

10.8 • The shift Command

When you have written a script file with positional parameters, you key in the script file name followed by a series of values (arguments). When the script is executed, Bash looks to the command line for the values it needs to plug into the script. It does this based on the position of particular parameters in the command line. In the case of a script file called **list** with the lines **cat $1, cat $2,** and **cat $3**, you would key in the following command line:

```
list    april.txt  may.txt  june.txt
```

With this generic script, you could key in only three file names. If you wanted more file names, you would have to re-execute the script. The **shift** command allows you to shift the parameters to the left, one by one, making the number of parameters on a line limitless. As the **shift** command shifts the contents of the parameters to the left, parameter 2 becomes parameter 1, parameter 3 becomes parameter 2, and so on. The original first argument is discarded as each argument is promoted. The next **shift** again discards the current first argument, and so on. Another way to describe this process is that you are promoting each of the command line arguments. The **shift** command without an argument shifts the parameters once to the left. This allows the script to process all the arguments on the command line. In the original Bourne Shell, you were limited to 9 positional parameters on a command line—**$1** through **$9**. Remember, since **$0** actually represents the command or script, you could have only nine parameters. The Bourne Again Shell (Bash) has no limits on the number of positional parameters you can use, so that **shift** used as a stand-alone command has declined.

10.9 • Activity: Using the shift Command

Note: You have a terminal window open. Your default directory is your home directory.

STEP 1   Key in the following: **echo A B C D E** ⏎Enter⏎

```
[cgillay@RedHat9  cgillay]$  echo A B C D E
A B C D E
[cgillay@RedHat9  cgillay]$
```

WHAT'S HAPPENING? The **echo** on a command line just "echoed" what you keyed in. Thus, the parameters **A, B, C, D,** and **E** on the command line were repeated on the screen. If you wanted to display more than five parameters and place the echoing parameters in a script file, you would need to use the **shift** command.

STEP 2   Create the following shell script in your home directory, but substitute your name for my name and the current date for the date given in the script. The script will be called **alphabet**:

#!/bin/bash
 # Script name: alphabet
 # Purpose: Using shift.
 # Written by Carolyn Z. Gillay on July 8, 2003.
echo $0 $1 $2 $3
shift
echo $0 $1 $2 $3
shift
echo $0 $1 $2 $3

shift
echo $0 $1 $2 $3

WHAT'S HAPPENING? You have created a script file with replaceable parameters. The purpose of the script file is to demonstrate the **shift** command. Remember that **echo** just echoes what you keyed in. In your command line, however, even though you have only four parameters (0 through 3), you want to key in more than four values. If you do not have a directory called **bin** in your home directory, create it now.

STEP 3 Key in the following: **chmod +x alphabet; mv alphabet bin** Enter

STEP 4 Key in the following: **alphabet A B C D E F** Enter

```
[cgillay@RedHat9   cgillay]$   chmod +x alphabet; mv alphabet bin
[cgillay@RedHat9   cgillay]$   $ alphabet A B C D E F
/home/cgillay/bin/alphabet A B C
/home/cgillay/bin/alphabet B C D
/home/cgillay/bin/alphabet C D E
/home/cgillay/bin/alphabet D E F
[cgillay@RedHat9   cgillay]$
```

WHAT'S HAPPENING? You wrote your script, changed the permissions, and moved **alphabet** to the **bin** directory. Then you executed the script. Notice the output. In each case, when the script file read **shift**, it moved each parameter over one position with the exception of **$0**. **$0** always was the name of the shell script.

STEP 5 Edit the **alphabet** script and delete the **$0** wherever it appears.

STEP 6 Key in the following: **alphabet A B C D E F G H** Enter

```
[cgillay@RedHat9   cgillay]$   alphabet A B C D E F G H
A B C
B C D
C D E
D E F
[cgillay@RedHat9   cgillay]$
```

WHAT'S HAPPENING? Notice the output. In each case, when the script file read **shift**, it moved each parameter over one position. You keyed in **alphabet A B C D E F G H.** The following demonstrates what happens.

Script File	Supplied Value from Command Line	Screen Display
echo $1 $2 $3	A is $1 B is $2 C is $3	A B C
shift	A is discarded as $1 B becomes $1 C becomes $2 D becomes $3	

echo $1 $2 $3	B is $1	B C D
	C is $2	
	D is $3	

shift	B is discarded as $1	
	C becomes $1	
	D becomes $2	
	E becomes $3	

echo $1 $2 $3	C is $1	C D E
	D is $2	
	E is $3	

shift	D is discarded as $1	
	E becomes $1	
	E becomes $2	
	F becomes $3	

echo $1 $2 $3	D is $1	D E F
	E is $2	
	F is $3	

WHAT'S HAPPENING? You can see that you are indeed shifting parameters. The last items in the command line (**G** and **H**) were ignored, as they were not used in the script file.

10.10 • The set Command

The **set** built-in command, when used with arguments, allows you to reset the positional parameters. Once you reset the parameters, the old parameters are lost. If you wish to unset the positional parameters, you can use **set --**. You may save your positional parameters in a variable and then clear your current positional parameters. You may also use command substitution in combination with **set** to get output from a command in a form that you can manipulate in a shell script.

10.11 • Activity: Using the set Command

Note: You have a terminal window open. Your default directory is your home directory. You have a directory called **bin** in your home directory.

STEP 1   Key in the following: **cp getargs getargs2** [Enter]

STEP 2   Edit **getargs2** so that it reads:

#!/bin/bash
 # Script name: getargs2
 # Purpose: Using positional parameters with set.
 # Written by Carolyn Z. Gillay on July 8, 2003.
 # Arguments are passed to the command based on position.
echo $0 #Name of command is always $0
echo 1st position on command line that is passed to echo is $1.

echo 2nd position on command line that is passed to echo is $2.

echo 3rd position on command line that is passed to echo is $3.

echo The number of arguments is $#.

echo All the arguments are $*.

oldones=$*

set Carolyn Frank Steven #Resetting the positional parameters.

echo Now the positional parameters are $*.

echo Now the number of positional parameters is $#.

echo Hello there $3.

set $(date) #Resetting positional parameters with a command.

echo $* #Seeing the new positional parameters.

echo The date is $2 $3, $6.

echo The values in \$oldones are $oldones.

set $oldones

echo $3 $1 $2 $4

STEP 3   Key in the following: ./**getargs2 A B C D** [Enter]

```
[cgillay@RedHat9  cgillay]$  ./getargs2  A  B  C  D
./getargs2
1st position on command line that is passed to echo is A.
2nd position on command line that is passed to echo is B.
3rd position on command line that is passed to echo is C.
The number of arguments is 4.
All the arguments are A B C D.
Now the positional parameters are Carolyn Frank Steven.
Now the number of positional parameters is 3.
Hello there Steven.
Mon  Jul  8 20:34:23 PDT 2003
The date is Jul  8, 2003.
The values in $oldones are A B C D.
C A B D
[cgillay@RedHat9  cgillay]$
```

WHAT'S HAPPENING? You begin your script with four positional parameters on the command line: **A B C D**. You had four arguments, and you listed them (**A B C D**). When the script read the line **oldones=$***, it took those four positional parameters and stored the values in a variable named **oldones**. You then changed or set the positional parameters so that now there were now three positional parameters—**Carolyn**, **Frank**, and **Steven**—which were then listed. You used the **$3** positional parameter so that you got the output of **Hello there Steven**. You then set the command **date** to be used as a positional parameter. When you viewed the output of **date**, you saw the current date. The second position in the **date** command, in this example, is **Jul**, the third position is **8**, and the sixth position is **2003**. Then your output used those positional parameters to display **Jul 8, 2003**. Last, you reset the positional parameters using the variable **$oldones** so that once again, your positional parameters are **A**, **B**, **C**, and **D**.

There is also a special modifier, the **:?**, which will check to see if a positional parameter has a value. If it does not have a value, you will get an error message.

STEP 4   Create the following shell script in your home directory, but substitute your name for my name and the current date for the date given in the script. The script will be called **checkit**:

#!/bin/bash
 # Script name: checkit
 # Purpose: Using special arguments.
 # Written by Carolyn Z. Gillay on July 8, 2003.
name=${1:? "You need to supply your first name."}
echo Hello $name
name=${2:? "You need to supply your last name."}
echo $name is a nice last name.

STEP 5   Key in the following: **chmod 777 checkit; mv checkit bin** [Enter]

STEP 6   Key in the following: **checkit** [Enter]

```
[cgillay@RedHat9   cgillay]$   chmod 777 checkit; mv checkit bin
[cgillay@RedHat9   cgillay]$   checkit
/home/cgillay/bin/checkit: line 5: 1: You need to supply your
first name.
[cgillay@RedHat9   cgillay]$
```

WHAT'S HANDLING? You changed the permissions on the file and moved it to the **bin** directory. You then ran the script with no arguments. It tells you that there is no value for the variable called **name**.

STEP 7   Key in the following: **checkit Carolyn** [Enter]

```
[cgillay@RedHat9   cgillay]$   checkit Carolyn
Hello Carolyn
/home/cgillay/bin/checkit: line 7: 2: you need to supply a last
name.
[cgillay@RedHat9   cgillay]$
```

WHAT'S HANDLING? Here it read that you did have a positional parameter in the first position, so it executed the **Hello $1** line, substituting the value **Carolyn** for the variable **name**. It then read the next line. There was no second value for **name**, so you received an error message.

STEP 8   Key in the following: **checkit Carolyn Gillay** [Enter]

```
[cgillay@RedHat9   cgillay]$   checkit Carolyn Gillay
Hello Carolyn
Gillay is a nice last name.
[cgillay@RedHat9   cgillay]$
```

WHAT'S HANDLING? Now you did have two values; the second value of **name** changed from **Carolyn** to **Gillay**. Then the line could execute, **Gillay is a nice last name.**

10.12 • Exit Status

When a process stops executing, it returns an exit status to its parent process. The *exit status* is also referred to as a *condition code* or *return code*. The variable **$?** will store the value of the exit code of the last command processed. An exit status of 0 means that the command was successful or a "true" condition, and an exit status of "not zero" means that the command was not successful—it failed and therefore is a "false" condition. Note that a failure is "not zero," as opposed to a **1**. You will often see a **1** as the return code for a failure, but a failure can be another number, as long as it is not zero.

You may, in a shell script, specify an exit status that you want your shell script to return using the **exit** built-in with the number you wish to be returned. If you do not supply a numeric value, the exit status of the script uses the last exit status of the last command that the script executed.

10.13 • Activity: Using the Exit Status

Note: You have a terminal window open. Your default directory is your home directory. The BOOK2 disk is mounted.

STEP 1   Key in the following: **ls /mnt/floppy/jup.99; echo $?** ⌷Enter⌷

```
[cgillay@RedHat9   cgillay]$   ls /mnt/floppy/jup.99; echo $?
/mnt/floppy/jup.99
0
[cgillay@RedHat9   cgillay]$
```

WHAT'S HAPPENING? Since **jup.99** is a file in the **/mnt/floppy** directory, the command was successful or true. Therefore, the exit status reported a success or the exit code of **0**.

STEP 2   Key in the following: **ls /mnt/floppy/mars.99; echo $?** ⌷Enter⌷

```
[cgillay@RedHat9   cgillay]$   ls /mnt/floppy/mars.99; echo $?
ls: /mnt/floppy/mars.99: No such file or directory
1
[cgillay@RedHat9   cgillay]$
```

WHAT'S HAPPENING? Since **mars.99** is not a file in the **/mnt/floppy directory,** the command was a failure, or false. Therefore, the exit status reported a failure, or the exit code of **1**—not zero.

STEP 3   Key in the following: **name=Sam; grep "$name" /etc/passwd**

STEP 4   Key in the following: **echo $?** ⌷Enter⌷

```
[cgillay@RedHat9   cgillay]$   name=Sam; grep "$name" /etc/password
[cgillay@RedHat9   cgillay]$   echo $?
1
[cgillay@RedHat9   cgillay]$
```

WHAT'S HAPPENING? You set a variable called **name** with the value **Sam**. You then used the **grep** command to try to locate the variable value in the **/etc/passwd** file. Since there is no user name of **Sam**, the **grep** command failed and the exit code was not **0**.

STEP 5   Key in the following: **alphabet A B C D; echo $?** [Enter]

```
[cgillay@RedHat9  cgillay]$  alphabet A B C D; echo $?
A B C
B C D
C D
D
0
[cgillay@RedHat9  cgillay]$
```

WHAT'S HAPPENING? Your **alphabet** script ran successfully, and therefore you received an exit code of **0** (true). However, you can specify what exit code you want returned.

STEP 6   Edit the **alphabet** script located in the **bin** directory. Add a line at the end that states: **exit 5.**

STEP 7   Key in the following: **alphabet A B C D; echo $?** [Enter]

```
[cgillay@RedHat9  cgillay]$  alphabet A B C D; echo $?
A B C
B C D
C D
D
5
[cgillay@RedHat9  cgillay]$
```

WHAT'S HAPPENING? Since you specified the exit code you wanted returned (**5**), that is the value that was stored in the variable **$?**. You now have a user-defined exit code.

10.14 • The test and let Commands

When using Bash, you may not directly specify conditions to test, such as comparing a variable and the value it holds. Because of this, you must use the **test** command to test the conditions you formulate in loops and branches. The **test** command is also a built-in command in the Bash shell. The **test** built-in is used in three areas: to compare two numbers, to compare character strings, and to test whether a file exists or has certain given properties.

The **test** command has the syntax of **test [*expr*]** or **[*expr*]** where *expr* is the expression. The **[*expr*]** with the square brackets may be used instead of the word **test**. If you use **[*expr*]**, you must have a space preceding and following *expr*. In programming, an *expression* is any legal combination of symbols that represents a value. Each language has its own rules for what is legal and illegal. Every expression consists of at least one *operand* and can have one or more *operators*. Operands are values, whereas operators are symbols that represent specific actions. Operands are the objects that are manipulated, and the operators are the symbols that represent specific actions. All expressions have at least one operand. In the expression $x + 5$, x and 5 are operands and + is the operator. Expressions are often classified by the type of value that they represent. Some common examples include the following:

- Boolean expressions that will evaluate to either true or false.
- Integer expressions that will evaluate to whole numbers such as 5 or 100.
- Floating point expressions that will evaluate to real numbers such 1.30 or .002.
- String expressions that will evaluate character strings such as **Carolyn** or **Linux**.

The **test** command evaluates an expression and returns a condition code or exit status indicating that the expression is either true (0) or false (not 0). Expressions may be either binary or unary. Unary expressions are often used to examine file status. Unary has to do with a single element or item. A unary expression is one with only one operand. Table 10.3, "Test Command Operations," lists the major criteria you can use within the expression.

Criteria	Purpose
Integer Comparisons	
-eq	equal
-gt	greater than
-lt	less than
-ge	greater than or equal to
-le	less than or equal to
-ne	not equal
String Comparisons	
-z	Tests for an empty string.
-n	Tests for string value.
=	Equal strings.
!=	Not equal strings.
$tr	Tests to see if string is not a null string.
Logical Operations	
-a	Logical AND—all must be true.
-o	Logical OR—one or other must be true.
!	Logical NOT—none must be true.
File Tests	**Test is true if**
-e *filename*	*filename* exists.
-b *filename*	*filename* exists and is a block special file.
-c *filename*	*filename* exists and is character special file.
-d *filename*	*filename* exists and is a directory.
-f *filename*	*filename* exists and is an ordinary file.

-g *filename*	*filename* exists and its set group ID bit is set.
-k *filename*	*filename* exists and its sticky bit is set.
-L *filename*	*filename* exists and is a symbolic link.
-p *filename*	*filename* exists and is a named pipe.
-r *filename*	*filename* exists and you have read access permissions to it.
-s *filename*	*filename* exists and contains information—has a size greater than 0 bytes.
-u *filename*	*filename* exists and its set user ID bit is set.
-w *filename*	*filename* exists and you have write access permissions to it.
-x *filename*	*filename* exists and you have execute permissions to it.

Table 10.3 ▪ Test Command Operations

The **let** command allows you to perform operations on arithmetic values. You can use **let** to compare two values or to perform arithmetic operations such as multiplication or addition. You use such operations in shell scripts to manage control structures or to perform calculations. The syntax is **let** *arg* **[***arg***]** where each *arg* is an arithmetic expression to be evaluated. An example of this is **let** *arg =value1 operator value2*. The **let** command automatically assumes that the operators are arithmetic or relational. The **let** command will also evaluate any variables and convert their values to arithmetic values. Table 10.4, "Expression Operators," are the valid operators used with **let**.

Arithmetic Operators	**Purpose**
*	multiplication
/	division
+	addition
-	subtraction
%	results in the remainder of a division

Relational Operators

>	greater than
<	less than
>=	greater than or equal to
<=	less than or equal to

=	equal in expr command
= =	equal in let
!=	not equal
&	logical AND
|	logical OR
!	logical NOT

Table 10.4 • Expression Operators

10.15 • Activity: Using the test and let Commands

Note: You have a terminal window open. Your default directory is your home directory. The BOOK2 disk is mounted.

STEP 1   Key in the following: **num=13; test $num -eq 10; echo $?** Enter

STEP 2   Key in the following: **num=13; test $num -eq 13; echo $?** Enter

```
[cgillay@RedHat9  cgillay]$   num=13; test $num -eq 10; echo $?
1
[cgillay@RedHat9  cgillay]$   num=13; test $num -eq 13; echo $?
0
[cgillay@RedHat9  cgillay]$
```

WHAT'S HAPPENING? Here you created a variable called **num** that had a value of 13. You then tested in Step 1 whether the variable stored in **$num** was equal to 10. It was not (false), so the exit code was 1. In Step 2 you tested whether the variable stored in **$num** was equal to 13. It was equal (true), so the exit code was 0.

STEP 3   Key in the following: **[$num -gt 23]; echo $?** Enter

STEP 4   Key in the following: **[$num -lt 23]; echo $?** Enter

```
[cgillay@RedHat9  cgillay]$  [ $num  -gt  23  ]; echo $?
1
[cgillay@RedHat9  cgillay]$  [ $num  -lt  23  ]; echo $??
0
[cgillay@RedHat9  cgillay]$
```

WHAT'S HAPPENING? Here you used the square brackets to evaluate the value in **$num**. In Step 3, you asked if the value stored in **$num** was greater than 23. It was not (false) so the exit code was 1. In Step 4, you asked if the value stored in **$num** was less than 23. It was (true) so the exit code was 0. You have used **test** to compare numbers. You may also use **test** to compare character strings.

STEP 5   Key in the following: **name=Carolyn; test $name != Frank; echo $?** Enter

STEP 6   Key in the following: **test $name != Carolyn; echo $?** Enter

```
[cgillay@RedHat9   cgillay]$ name=Carolyn; test $name != Frank;echo $?
0
[cgillay@RedHat9   cgillay]$   test $name!= Carolyn; echo $?
1
[cgillay@RedHat9   cgillay]$
```

WHAT'S HAPPENING? Here you are testing a character string. You created a variable called **name** with the value of **Carolyn**. In Step 5, you tested whether the value stored in the variable **name** was not equal (!=) to **Frank**. **Carolyn** is not equal to **Frank** (true) so your exit code was 0. In Step 6, you tested whether the value stored in the variable **name** was not equal to **Carolyn**. **Carolyn** is equal to **Carolyn**, therefore the test is false and your exit code was 1. It can also be written as [$name != Frank] or [$name != Carolyn]

STEP 7   Key in the following: **[$name = [Cc]??????]; echo $?** Enter

```
[cgillay@RedHat9   cgillay]$   [ $name = [Cc]?????? ]; echo $?
1
[cgillay@RedHat9   cgillay]$
```

WHAT'S HAPPENING? Here you were attempting to use wildcard expansion. The question mark is treated literally so that the test was looking for question marks. You cannot use wildcard expansion with a simple test. Thus, your exit code was 1, or false. You may also test for whether a file exists or has certain given properties.

STEP 8   Key in the following: **test -e /mnt/floppy/jup.99; echo $?** Enter

STEP 9   Key in the following: **test -e /mnt/floppy/mars.99; echo $?** Enter

STEP 10   Key in the following: **test -d /mnt/floppy/jup.99; echo $?** Enter

STEP 11   Key in the following: **test -d /mnt/floppy/sports; echo $?** Enter

```
[cgillay@RedHat9   cgillay]$   test -e /mnt/floppy/jup.99; echo $?
0
[cgillay@RedHat9   cgillay]$   test -e /mnt/floppy/mars.99; echo $?
1
[cgillay@RedHat9   cgillay]$   test -d /mnt/floppy/jup.99; echo $?
1
[cgillay@RedHat9   cgillay]$   test -d /mnt/floppy/sports; echo $?
0
[cgillay@RedHat9   cgillay]$
```

WHAT'S HAPPENING? Here you are testing for file information. In Step 8, you asked if the file called **jup.99** existed in the **/mnt/floppy** directory. It does exist (true), so the exit code is **0**. In Step 9, you asked if **mars.99** existed in the **/mnt/floppy** directory. It does not exist (false), so the exit code is **1**. In Step 10, you asked if the item called **jup.99** in the **/mnt/floppy** directory was a directory. The item, **jup.99** is a file, not a directory, so the exit code was **1**. In Step 11, you asked if the item called **sports** in the **/mnt/floppy** directory was a directory. It is a directory (true), so the exit code is **0**. The **let** command lets you do arithmetic calculations.

STEP 12   Key in the following: **let x=5*5; echo $x** Enter

STEP 13   Key in the following: **let number=3*5; echo $number** Enter

```
[cgillay@RedHat9   cgillay]$   let  x= 5*5; echo $x
25
[cgillay@RedHat9   cgillay]$   let number=3*5; echo $number
15
[cgillay@RedHat9   cgillay]$
```

WHAT'S HAPPENING? Here you assigned variables called **x** and **number** numeric values arrived by calculations.

10.16 • The if ... then commands and Logical Operators

The order in which the commands execute in a shell script is called the flow of the script. In most scripts, you change the commands that execute depending on some condition provided by the user or by the script itself. When you change the commands that execute based on a condition, you are changing the flow of the script or the conditions, which is why this process is often referred to as conditional flow control or conditional control structures.

The simplest form of providing a condition is by using **if - then**. The **if** command is a Bash built-in. Any command following the **if** construct is tested and its exit code is returned. If the exit status is **0**, the command succeeded and the statements after the **then** keyword are executed. Whatever follows the **if** is a test. It is something that is being evaluated for a true or false status. The **then** is also a bash built-in command. The statement following the **then** may be one command or a block of commands. The commands are executed until the **fi** is reached. Note that **fi** is **if** backwards. **fi** ends the **if** set. If the exit status is a nonzero, meaning the command failed, the statements after **then** are ignored, and control then goes to the line directly after the **fi**.

The structure of the **if-then** construct is shown in Figure 10.1, "**if/then** Construct."

```
if   test-command
     then
          command
          command
          ....
     fi
```

Figure 10.1 • if/then Construct

The **if** evaluates the result of the command following **if**. The exit status is tested. If the exit status is true (0), then the commands between **then** and **fi** are executed; otherwise they are skipped. In the above example, the lines are indented. The shell does not care about whether the lines are indented, but the indention is a form that most people use because it makes reading a script easier. Thus, the **if** and **fi** are lined up. The **then** is indented and the commands that are to be executed after the **then** are further indented. See Figure 10.2, "Flowchart for if-then Construct."

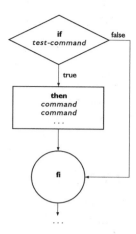

Figure 10.2 • Flowchart for if-then Construct

The logical operators include AND, OR, and NOT. The logical negation operator's symbol is the exclamation point (!), and can be placed in front of any test expression to negate (not) the result of the evaluation of the test. Thus if you have a statement such as **[! -f "$filename"]**, you are evaluating the value of **$filename** so that if the value stored in **$filename** is *not* an ordinary file or it does not exist, the statement will be evaluated as true. The logical AND operator, whose notation is **-a**, requires in its evaluation that both of the two expressions be true in order to return a true value. Thus, if you have a statement such as **[-f "$filename" -a -r "$filename"]**, you are evaluating the value of **$filename** so that if the value stored in **$filename** is an ordinary file *and* is readable by you, then the statement will be evaluated as true. Both statements must be true to be evaluated as true. The logical OR operator, whose notation is **-o**, requires in its evaluation that either of the two expressions must be true in order to return a true value. Thus, if you have a statement such as **[-f "$filename" -o -r "$filename"]**, you are evaluating the value of **$filename** so that if the value stored in **$filename** is an ordinary file *or* is readable by you, then the statement will be evaluated as true. Either statement must be true to be evaluated as true.

There is also another construct you can use—the **&&.** The syntax is

```
command1  &&  command2
```

When you use the **&&** between two commands, **command2** will be executed only if **command1** returns an exit status of **0** (true). If **command1** returns an exit status of a nonzero (false), then **command2** will not be executed. It is like an if/then statement. It is the equivalent of writing

```
if command1 true
      then
               execute command2
fi
```

10.17 • Activity: Using the if ... then commands

Note: You have a terminal window open. Your default directory is your home directory. The BOOK2 disk is mounted. If you have **personal.fil** in your home directory, delete it.

STEP 1   Key in the following: **sort personal.fil > aaa && mv aaa bbb** Enter

```
[cgillay@RedHat9  cgillay]$ sort personal.fil > aaa && mv aaa bbb
sort: open failed: personal.fil: No such file or directory.
[cgillay@RedHat9  cgillay]$
```

WHAT'S HAPPENING? If you had a file called **personal.fil** in your home directory, then the command would work. You tried to sort the **personal.fil** file and redirect the sorted contents to a new file called **aaa** and then rename the **aaa** file to **bbb**. Since **personal.fil** is not in your home directory, the **sort** command failed. Since it failed, the second command (**mv**) never was executed.

STEP 2   Key in the following: **sort /mnt/floppy/personal.fil > aaa && mv aaa bbb** Enter

STEP 3   Key in the following: **ls aaa bbb** Enter

```
[cgillay@RedHat9 cgillay]$ sort /mnt/floppy/personal.fil > aaa && mv aaa bbb
[cgillay@RedHat9  cgillay]$  ls aaa bbb
ls aaa: No such file or directory
bbb
[cgillay@RedHat9  cgillay]$
```

WHAT'S HAPPENING? You sorted the **personal.fil** file on the BOOK2 disk and redirected the sorted contents to a new file called **aaa.** Since the **sort** command succeeded, the **mv** command was executed and the **aaa** file was renamed to **bbb**.

STEP 4   Key in the following: **rm bbb** Enter

WHAT'S HAPPENING? You deleted the file you created. You can use the **&&** construct in a script. However, now you are now going to create more elaborate scripts using the **if/then** construct.

STEP 5   Create the following shell script in your home directory, but substitute your name for my name and the current date for the date given in the script. The script will be called **happy**:

#!/bin/bash
 # Script name: happy
 # Purpose: Using if-then
 # Written by Carolyn Z. Gillay on July 8, 2003.
echo -n "Are you happy? [y/n] "
read answer
if ["$answer" = Y -o "$answer" = y]
        then
                echo That is good to hear.
fi
if ["$answer" = N -o "$answer" = n]
        then
                echo That is too bad.
fi

WHAT'S HAPPENING? In this shell script, you request input from the user that will be stored in the variable called **answer**. The **if** statement then evaluates what the user keyed in that is stored in the variable **answer**. If it is a **Y** or **y** (the **-o** option indicates or), then the statement is true and the command following the **then** will be executed. If it is false, the script does not execute anything between the first **if** and **fi**. It goes to the next line after the first **fi**. In this example, you have another **if** statement. Again, the **if** statement then evaluates what the user keyed in that is stored in the variable **answer**. If it is an **N** or **n** then the statement is true and the command following the **then** will be executed. If it is false, the script does not execute anything between the **if** and **fi** statements, and in this case returns to the command prompt since there are no more commands. If you key in any other value than a **Y**, **y**, **N**, or **n**, the test would be false and you would be returned to the command line.

STEP 6   Key in the following: **chmod 777 happy; mv happy bin** Enter

STEP 7   Key in the following: **happy** Enter

```
[cgillay@RedHat9    cgillay]$    chmod 777 happy; mv happy bin
[cgillay@RedHat9    cgillay]$    happy
Are you happy: [y/n]
```

WHAT'S **HAPPENING?** You gave the **happy** file execute permission and moved it to the **bin** directory. You then executed the file. It read the first line and is asking for input.

STEP 8   Key in the following: **y** Enter

```
[cgillay@RedHat9    cgillay]$    chmod 777 happy; mv happy bin
[cgillay@RedHat9    cgillay]$    happy
Are you happy: [y/n] y
That is good to hear.
[cgillay@RedHat9    cgillay]$
```

WHAT'S **HAPPENING?** Since y was true, the command **echo** was executed and **echo** echoed the line **That is good to hear.** The script then evaluated the variable answer. y was still stored in the variable **answer**. Thus, y was false for the second **if** test, so the lines between the second **if** and **fi** were not executed.

STEP 9   Key in the following: **happy.** Then press **n** Enter

```
[cgillay@RedHat9    cgillay]$    happy
Are you happy: [y/n] n
That is too bad.
[cgillay@RedHat9    cgillay]$
```

WHAT'S **HAPPENING?** In this case, you entered **n**. The script read the first **if** statement and evaluated the value in **answer**. Since it was not y or **Y**, the script did not execute anything between the first **if** and **fi**. It skipped those lines and moved to the next **if** statement. Now **n** is true, and the command echo executed (**That is too bad.**). There were no more lines, so you were returned to the command prompt.

STEP 10   Key in the following: **happy.** Then press **x** Enter

```
[cgillay@RedHat9    cgillay]$    happy
Are you happy: [y/n] x
[cgillay@RedHat9    cgillay]$
```

WHAT'S HAPPENING? In this case, you entered **x**. The script read the first **if** statement and evaluated the value in **answer**. Since it was not **y** or **Y**, the script did not execute anything between the first **if** and **fi.** It skipped those lines and moved to the next **if** statement. Again, it evaluated the value in the variable answer. It was false (not **n** or **N**), so the script did not execute the lines between this **if** and the last **fi**. Since there were no more lines in the script, you were returned to the command prompt. You can also test for a null value.

STEP 11 Create the following shell script in your home directory, but substitute your name for my name and the current date for the date given in the script. The script will be called **name**:

#!/bin/bash
 # Script name: name
 # Purpose: Using if then testing for a null value.
 # Written by Carolyn Z. Gillay on July 8, 2003.
if ["$name" = ""]
   then
      echo The name variable is empty.
fi
echo "$name"

STEP 12 Key in the following: **chmod +x name; name= ; echo $name; ./name** [Enter]

```
[cgillay@RedHat9  cgillay]$  chmod +x name; name= ; echo $name;
./name

The name variable is empty.

[cgillay@RedHat9  cgillay]$
```

WHAT'S HAPPENING? You changed the permissions on the **name** file. You then gave the **name** variable no value and then checked to be sure that it had no value. You then ran the script. The **if** statement evaluated to see if the **name** was empty. It was, so the **then** command was executed. You then asked to display **$name**. Since it was empty, nothing appeared. You are going to create a variable called **name** and place a value in it to test your **name** script.

STEP 13 Key in the following: **name=czg; echo $name** [Enter]

STEP 14 Key in the following: **./name** [Enter]

```
[cgillay@RedHat9  cgillay]$  name=czg; echo $name
czg
[cgillay@RedHat9  cgillay]$  ./name
The name variable is empty.

[cgillay@RedHat9  cgillay]$
```

WHAT'S HAPPENING? You created a variable called **name**. You placed a value in it (**czg**). You then ran your script. The **name** script still stated the **name** variable was empty, when in fact it was not. Remember local and global variables. When you executed your script, the **$name** variable that you created was only local and therefore, as far as the script was concerned, the variable was empty. A false value was returned, and therefore the lines between the **if** and **fi** were executed. What you want to do is make **$name** a global variable. To do so, you need to export it.

STEP 15   Key in the following: **export name=czg; echo $name** [Enter]

STEP 16   Key in the following: **./name** [Enter]

```
[cgillay@RedHat9   cgillay]$   export name=czg; echo $name
czg
[cgillay@RedHat9   cgillay]$   ./name
czg
[cgillay@RedHat9   cgillay]$
```

WHAT'S HAPPENING? Because you exported the variable and made it a global variable, the script knows that there is a value (**czg**) in the variable. It therefore did not execute the lines between the **if** and **fi** lines because the exit status was false. Since the exit code was a nonzero, the script went directly to the line that executed the **echo** statement, the line that followed the **fi**.

STEP 17   Key in the following: **cp   files   ifthen** [Enter]

STEP 18   Edit the **ifthen** script so it reads as follows:

> **#!/bin/bash**
> **# Script name: ifthen**
> **# Purpose: Using the if-then construct.**
> **# Written by Carolyn Z. Gillay on July 8, 2003.**
> **echo -n "Please enter the file you are looking for: "**
> **read looking**
> **if test -e "$looking"**
>   **then**
>   **echo "The file you asked for is " $looking**
> **fi**
> **echo "No file by that name could be found."**

STEP 19   Key in the following: **chmod +x ifthen; mv ifthen bin** [Enter]

STEP 20   Key in the following: **ifthen** [Enter]

```
[cgillay@RedHat9   cgillay]$   chmod +x ifthen; mv ifthen   bin
[cgillay@RedHat9   cgillay]$   ifthen
Please enter the file you are looking for:
```

WHAT'S HAPPENING? You edited the file. You then gave it execute permissions and moved it to the **bin** directory. You executed the file, which is testing for the existence of a file.

STEP 21   Key in the following: **nofile** [Enter]

```
[cgillay@RedHat9   cgillay]$   chmod +x  ifthen; mv ifthen   bin
[cgillay@RedHat9   cgillay]$   ifthen
Please enter the file you are looking for: nofile
No file by that name could be found.
[cgillay@RedHat9   cgillay]$
```

WHAT'S HAPPENING? You tested for the existence of the file called **nofile** in the test. The test failed (false), so the lines between the **if** and **fi** lines were not executed and you went to the next line after the **fi**.

STEP 22 Key in the following: **ifthen** [Enter]

```
[cgillay@RedHat9  cgillay]$  ifthen
Please enter the file you are looking for:
```

STEP 23 Key in the following: **/mnt/floppy/jup.99** [Enter]

```
Please enter the file you are looking for: /mnt/floppy/jup.99
The file you asked for is /mnt/floppy/jup.99
No file by that name could be found.
[cgillay@RedHat9  cgillay]$
```

WHAT'S HAPPENING? You seem to have gotten two responses. You found the file you were looking for, but you also got the message that no file by that name could be found. You tested for the existence of the file called **/mnt/floppy/jup.99**. It did exist, and therefore the statement was true. Because it was true, the lines between the **if** and **fi** lines were executed. When those lines were finished, the script fell through to the next line (**echo "No file(s) by that name could be found.**) and executed it. You need another test.

10.18 • The if ... then ... else commands and the exit Command

The **if-then-else** construct allows a two-way decision process. If the test following the **if** succeeds and thus returns a true status (a zero), the **if** command executes the commands between the **then** and the **else** statements. It then sends the script to the lines following the **fi** and does not execute the lines between **else** and **fi**. If the command after the **if** command fails and thus returns a false status (a nonzero), the script directs the script to the commands between the **else** and **fi** lines to be executed and does not execute the commands between the **then** and **else** commands. The script then sends the script to the lines after the **fi** command. Figure 10.3, "Flowchart for **if-then-else** Construct," shows the flow of the construct.

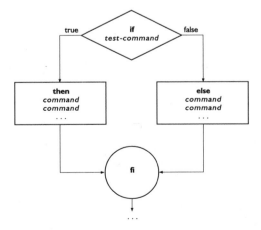

Figure 10.3 • Flowchart for if/then/else Construct

Figure 10.3 demonstrates the flow of the information. You can see that it is a two-way decision process. The structure of **if-then-else** is shown in Figure 10.4, "**if/then/else** Construct."

```
if    test-command
      then
                  command
                  command
                  ...
      else
                  command
                  command
                  ...
fi
```

Figure 10.4 ▪ if/then/else Construct

There is also a built-in command called **exit**. The syntax is **exit [*n*]**, where *n* is the exit status you want returned. The purpose of **exit** is to end the execution of a shell script immediately. *n* can be a **0** (success) or a nonzero (failure). If you do not provide a number, the exit status will be that of the last command you executed. If you use **exit** in a terminal window, it will close the window. However, if you are not in GNOME and key in **exit**, you will log yourself off the system.

There is also another construct you can use, the **||** The syntax is:

```
command1   ||   command2
```

When you use the **||** between two commands, **command2** will only be executed if **command1** returns an exit status of nonzero (false). If **command1** returns an exit status of a zero (true), then **command2** will not be executed. It is like an **if/then/else** statement. It is the equivalent of writing

```
if command1 true
    then
            execute command1
else
    command1 false - now execute command2
fi
```

10.19 ▪ Activity: Using the if ... then ... else commands

Note: You have a terminal window open. Your default directory is your home directory. The BOOK2 disk is mounted.

STEP 1   Key in the following: **name=Carolyn** [Enter]

STEP 2   Key in the following: **grep "$name" /mnt/floppy/personal.fil || echo "No $name."** [Enter]

```
[cgillay@RedHat9  cgillay]$ name=Carolyn
[cgillay@RedHat9  cgillay]$ grep "$name" /mnt/floppy/personal.fil || echo "No $name."
Gillay    Carolyn    699 Lemon     Orange      CA      Professor
Smith     Carolyn    311 Orchard   Ann Arbor   MI      Housewife
[cgillay@RedHat9  cgillay]$
```

WHAT'S HAPPENING? ⇒ You created a variable called **name** with the value of **Carolyn**. You then issued the **grep** command. Since **grep** succeeded, the **echo** command was not executed.

STEP 3   Key in the following: **name=Juan** [Enter]

STEP 4   Key in the following:

        grep "$name" /mnt/floppy/personal.fil || echo "No $name." [Enter]

```
[cgillay@RedHat9 cgillay]$ name=Juan
[cgillay@RedHat9 cgillay]$ grep "$name" /mnt/floppy/personal.fil || echo "No $name."
No Juan
[cgillay@RedHat9 cgillay]$
```

WHAT'S HAPPENING? ⇒ You created a new variable called **name** with the value of **Juan**. You then issued the **grep** command. Since **grep** failed, the **echo** command executed. You can use the **||** construct in a script; however, now you are now going to create more elaborate scripts using the **if/then/else** construct.

STEP 5   Key in the following: **cp bin/ifthen bin/ifthen2** [Enter]

STEP 6   Edit the **ifthen2** script so it reads as follows:

    #!/bin/bash
    # Script name: ifthen2
    # Purpose: Using the if-then-else construct.
    # Written by Carolyn Z. Gillay on July 8, 2003.
    echo -n "Please enter the file you are looking for: "
    read looking
    if test -e "$looking"
        then
            echo "The file you asked for is: " $looking
        else
     echo "No file by that name could be found."
    fi

STEP 7   Key in the following: **ifthen2** [Enter]

```
[cgillay@RedHat9 cgillay]$ ifthen2
Please enter the file you are looking for:
```

WHAT'S HAPPENING? ⇒ You made a copy of the **ifthen** file and named it **ifthen2** in the **bin** directory. You edited the file. You executed the file, which tests for the existence of a file.

STEP 8   Key in the following: **nofile** [Enter]

```
[cgillay@RedHat9 cgillay]$ ifthen2
Please enter the file you are looking for: nofile
No file by that name could be found.
[cgillay@RedHat9 cgillay]$
```

WHAT'S HAPPENING? ⇒ You tested for the existence of the file called **nofile** in the test. The test failed (false), so the script moved to the lines beginning with the **else** statement. The lines between **else** and **fi** were executed. The **fi** terminated the **if** statement.

STEP 9 Key in the following: **ifthen2** [Enter]

```
[cgillay@RedHat9  cgillay]$  ifthen2
Please enter the file you are looking for:
```

STEP 10 Key in the following: **/mnt/floppy/jup.99** [Enter]

```
Please enter the file you are looking for: /mnt/floppy/jup.99
The file you asked for is  /mnt/floppy/jup.99
[cgillay@RedHat9  cgillay]$
```

WHAT'S **HAPPENING?** The **if** statement test was true. It did find a file called **/mnt/floppy/jup.99**. Since the exit status was true, the lines following **then** were executed. But since **then** was true, there was no **else** to execute, so the script terminated at the **fi**. You can have multiple tests and use positional parameters and assign an exit status.

STEP 11 Create the following shell script in your home directory, but substitute your name for my name. The script will be called **argtest**:

#!/bin/bash
 # Script name: argtest
 # Purpose: Using if-then-else
 # Written by Carolyn Z. Gillay on July 8, 2003.
if test $# -eq 0
    then
        echo "You must give one argument."
        exit 1
fi
if test -e "$1"
    then
        echo "$1 exists."
    else
        echo "$1 does not exist."
fi

STEP 12 Key in the following: **chmod +x argtest; mv argtest bin** [Enter]

STEP 13 Key in the following: **argtest** [Enter]

```
[cgillay@RedHat9  cgillay]$  chmod +x argtest; mv argtest bin
[cgillay@RedHat9  cgillay]$  argtest
You must give one argument.
[cgillay@RedHat9  cgillay]$
```

WHAT'S **HAPPENING?** The first **if** statement tests whether or not the user supplied at least one argument on the command line. The **-eq** test operator is used to compare two integers. If you do not supply an argument, the exit code returned is true (equal to 0), and the lines following the **then** statement are executed. You provided an exit code of 1 so that the script will terminate and not execute the next **if** block. This allowed you to immediately exit the script without doing further tests. This kind of test is common for any script that requires the use of arguments. This test prevents the user from receiving useless information from the script, and thus checking for whether the user has provided the appropriate arguments makes the script work in the way the author of the script intended.

STEP 14 Key in the following: **argtest /mnt/floppy/jup.99** [Enter]

```
[cgillay@RedHat9  cgillay]$  argtest /mnt/floppy/jup.99
/mnt/floppy/jup.99 exists.
[cgillay@RedHat9  cgillay]$
```

WHAT'S HAPPENING? Since you provided an argument (**/mnt/floppy/jup.99**) the integer test was false. Since it was false, the commands following the **then** statement were executed.

STEP 15 Key in the following: **argtest nofile** [Enter]

```
[cgillay@RedHat9  cgillay]$  argtest nofile
nofile does not exist.
[cgillay@RedHat9  cgillay]$
```

WHAT'S HAPPENING? Since you provided an argument, the script checked for the existence of a file called **nofile**. Since the test failed, the commands following **then** were not executed, but the statements following **else** were executed.

10.20 • The if ... then ... elif commands

The **if/then/elif** command allows a multi-way decision-making process. Thus, the **elif** command combines the **else** statement, and the **if** statement allows you to create a nested set of **if-then-else** statements. The advantage of using the **elif** statement instead of using the **else** statement is that each **else** statement must be paired with an **fi** statement. You may use multiple **elif** statements which require only a single closing **fi.** The format that demonstrates the use of the **if/then/elif** construct follows as shown in Figure 10.5, "**if/then/elif** Construct."

```
if test-command₁
    then
            command
            command
            ...
    elif test-command₂
        then
                command
                command
                ...
    elif test command₃
        then
                command
                command
                ...
    else
            command
            command
            ...
fi
```

Figure 10.5 • if/then/elif Construct

Looking at the above construct, you can follow its logic. If the command following *test-command1* succeeds, then the commands following **then** are executed, control is passed to **fi**, and your script is ended. If *test-command1* fails, the next **elif** *test-command2* is tested. If it succeeds, the commands following the next **then** are executed, control is passed to the **fi**, and your script is ended. If **elif** *test-command2* fails, the next **elif** *test* **command3** is tested. If it succeeds, the next commands following **then** are executed, control is passed to **fi**, and your script is ended. If the **elif** *test* **command3** fails, control is passed to the **else** statement, the commands following **else** are executed, control is passed to the **fi**, and your script is ended. The **else** block is called the default. You are not limited to a specific number of **elif** statements. Another way to look at the **if/then/elif** construct is seen in Figure 10.6 "Flowchart for the **if/then/elif** Construct."

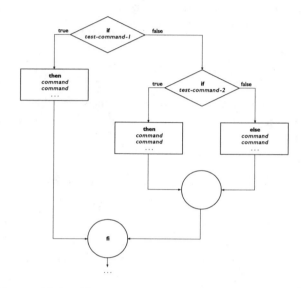

Figure 10.6 • Flowchart for the if/then/elif Construct

10.21 • Activity: Using the if ... then ... elif commands

Note: You have a terminal window open. Your default directory is your home directory.

STEP 1   Create the following shell script in your home directory, but substitute your name for my name and the current date for the date given in the script. The script will be called **guess.**

```
#! /bin/bash
# Script name: guess
# Purpose: Using one if/then/elif to guess the number 3.
# Written by Carolyn Z. Gillay on July 8, 2003.
if test $1 -le 2
     then
          echo "Your guess was too small."
     elif test $1 -ge 4
          then
                echo "Your guess was too big."
     else
          echo "You guessed the right number."
fi
```

STEP 2   Key in the following: **chmod +x guess; mv guess bin** ⎡Enter⎤

STEP 3   Key in the following: **guess 1** ⎡Enter⎤

```
[cgillay@RedHat9  cgillay]$  guess 1
Your guess was too small.
[cgillay@RedHat9  cgillay]$
```

WHAT'S **HAPPENING?** You created a script to guess a number. The correct number is 3. You keyed in **1**. The first test was whether what number you keyed in—the number 1 that was stored in the variable $1—was less than or equal to 2. The test was true so the **then** command was executed and **Your guess was too small.** was echoed to the screen. The script then went to the **fi** and ended.

STEP 4   Key in the following: **guess 5** ⎡Enter⎤

```
[cgillay@RedHat9  cgillay]$  guess 5
Your guess was too big.
[cgillay@RedHat9  cgillay]$
```

WHAT'S **HAPPENING?** Now you keyed in **5**. The first test, whether what you keyed in—the number 5 which was stored in the variable $1—was less than or equal to 2. The test failed (false) so the script went to the next test, the **elif**. The number 5 is greater than or equal to 4, so the test was true. The **then** command was executed and **Your guess was too big.** was echoed to the screen. The script then went to the **fi** and ended.

STEP 5   Key in the following: **guess 3** ⎡Enter⎤

```
[cgillay@RedHat9  cgillay]$  guess 3
You guessed the right number.
[cgillay@RedHat9  cgillay]$
```

WHAT'S **HAPPENING?** Now you keyed in **3**. The first test, whether what you keyed in—the number **3** which was stored in the variable $1—was less than or equal to 2. The test failed (false) so the script went to the next test, the **elif**. The number 3 is not greater than or equal to 4 so the test was false, the **else** command was executed, and **Your guessed the right number.** was echoed to the screen. The script then went to the **fi** and ended. Next you are going to write a more complex **if/then/elif** script.

STEP 6   Create the following shell script in your home directory, but substitute your name for my name and the current date for the date given in the script. The script will be called **ages**:

#!/bin/bash
 # Script name: ages
 # Purpose: Using a more complex if/then/elif.
 # Written by Carolyn Z. Gillay on July 8, 2003.
echo -n "How old are you? "
read age
if [$age -ge 0 -a $age -le 12]
        then

```
                    echo "You are a mere child."
        elif [ $age -ge 13 -a $age -le 19 ]
                then
                            echo "How do you like these teen years?"
        elif [ $age -ge 20 -a $age -le 29 ]
                then
                            echo "Does this make you generation X?"
        elif [ $age -ge 30 -a $age -le 39 ]
                then
                            echo "The thirties are really good years."
        else
                echo "Wow, you don't look that old."
    fi
```

STEP 7   Key in the following: **chmod +x ages; mv ages bin** Enter

STEP 8   Key in the following: **ages** Enter

```
[cgillay@RedHat9  cgillay]$   chmod +x ages; mv ages bin
[cgillay@RedHat9  cgillay]$   ages
How old are you?
```

WHAT'S HAPPENING? The script is asking for input.

STEP 9   Key in the following: **3** Enter

```
[cgillay@RedHat9  cgillay]$   ages
How old are you? 3
You are a mere child.
[cgillay@RedHat9   cgillay]$
```

WHAT'S HAPPENING? The script asked for your input. It then executed the first **if** statement and evaluated the result (3 is greater than 0 and less than or equal to 12). Since it was true, the script went to **then** and executed the next command.

STEP 10   Key in the following: **ages** Enter

```
[cgillay@RedHat9   cgillay]$   ages
How old are you?
```

WHAT'S HAPPENING? The script is asking for input.

STEP 11   Key in the following: **33** Enter

```
[cgillay@RedHat9   cgillay]$   ages
How old are you? 33
The thirties are really good years.
[cgillay@RedHat9   cgillay]$
```

WHAT'S HAPPENING? The script asked for your input. It then executed the first **if** statement and evaluated the result (33 is greater than 0, but it is not less than or equal to 12), then read the next **elif** statement . 33 is greater than or equal to 13, but is not less than or equal to 19, so the next **elif** was read. The input was evaluated. 33 is greater than or equal to 20 but is not less than or equal to 29, so the next **elif** was read. In this case, the **if** evaluated that 33 is greater than or equal to 30, and it is less than or equal to 39. Since it was true, the script went to **then** and executed the **echo** command.

STEP 12 Key in the following: **ages** Enter

```
[cgillay@RedHat9  cgillay]$  ages
How old are you?
```

WHAT'S **HAPPENING?** The script is asking for input.

STEP 13 Key in the following: **60** Enter

```
[cgillay@RedHat9  cgillay]$  ages
How old are you? 60
Wow, you don't look that old!
[cgillay@RedHat9  cgillay]$
```

WHAT'S **HAPPENING?** The script asked for your input. It then executed the first **if** statement and evaluated the result (60 is greater than 0, but it is not less than or equal to 12), then read the next **elif** statement . Each succeeding **elif** statement failed, so the script was directed to the **else** line, which then executed the echo statement, **Wow, you don't look that old!**. The script then terminated.

10.22 • The case Command

The **case** command provides for multi-way decision-making similar to a nested **if**. However, the **case** statement is more readable, particularly if you have several **if**s. The **case** command allows you to compare a single value against other values and to execute one or more commands when a match is found. However, only one of the patterns in the **case** command can match the value given to it. Thus, if you wanted to test multiple conditions, you would not use the **case** command. The **case** statement is good for testing a single variable for multiple possible values. You may use regular expressions to match patterns. The format of the **case** construct is shown in Figure 10.7, "The **case** Construct."

```
case test-string in
      pattern1)
             commands1
             ;;
      pattern2)
             commands2
             ;;
      patternN
             commandsN
             ;;
esac
```

Figure 10.7 • The case Construct

The *test-string* is compared against the values in *pattern 1*, *pattern 2*, and so on until a match is found. When a match is found, the commands listed after the matched value are executed until the double semi-colons (;;) are reached. Once the double semi-colons are reached, the execution of

case is complete. If there is no match, then none of the commands in **case** are executed. It is imperative that the double semi-colons end each *pattern* statement. What you are doing is testing the value of the *test-string* after **case**. If it matches *pattern1* (a regular expression), it executes the commands. If it does not match, it tries matching **pattern2**. If it matches, it executes the commands. It continues trying to match the patterns until there are no more patterns. At that point, control goes out of **case**. However, typically when using **case**, the last statement is represented by *). This wildcard pattern, known as the default case, will match anything. If you do not include the *), and you have no match, then control would pass to the command following the end of the case statement (**esac**) without executing any commands. Using *) allows the execution of a set of commands to handle errors, since *) acts as a catchall where there is no match to the pattern. See Figure 10.8, "Using **case** with a Catchall," to see how the catchall is used.

```
case test-string in
      pattern1)
            commands1
            ;;
      pattern2)
            commands2
            ;;
      *)
            default  commands
            ;;
esac
```

Figure 10.8 • Using case with a Catchall

Pattern	Match
*	Matches any string of characters. Used for the default case.
?	Matches any single character.
[....]	Any characters that are enclosed in the square brackets are tried one at a time for a possible match. If you include a hyphen between two characters, you are specifying a range of characters.
|	Either one choice or the other.

Table 10.5 • Patterns Used with case

Another way to look at the **case** construct is seen in Figure 10.8, "Flowchart for **case** Construct."

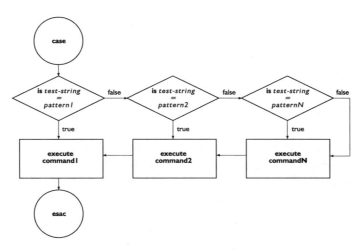

Figure 10.9 • Flowchart for case Construct

10.23 • Activity: Using the case Command

Note: You have a terminal window open. Your default directory is your home directory.

STEP 1   Create the following shell script in your home directory, but substitute your name for my name and the current date for the date given in the script. The script will be called **casing**:

#!/bin/bash
 # Script name: casing
 # Purpose: Using case.
 # Written by Carolyn Z. Gillay on July 8, 2003.
case "$book" in
       biography) echo "I like to read biographies." ;;
       fiction) echo "I like to read fiction even better." ;;
       mystery) echo "I like to read mystery books best of all." ;;
   esac

STEP 2   Key in the following: **chmod +x casing; mv casing bin** [Enter]

STEP 3   Key in the following: **casing** [Enter]

```
[cgillay@RedHat9   cgillay]$   casing
[cgillay@RedHat9   cgillay]$
```

WHAT'S **HAPPENING?** ❯ You created a script to test the **case** command. However, nothing seemed to have happened. You were simply returned to the command prompt. Look at your script. You are using a variable that you have not yet defined.

STEP 4   Key in the following: **book=mystery; echo $book; casing** [Enter]

```
[cgillay@RedHat9   cgillay]$ book=mystery;echo $book; casing
mystery
[cgillay@RedHat9   cgillay]$
```

WHAT'S **HAPPENING?** ❯ You created a variable **book** with the value of **mystery.** You then displayed the value of **$book**, which was correctly displayed as **mystery.** But your script did not use the variable. Remember, if you want a variable to be available to child processes, you need to export it.

STEP 5 Key in the following: **export book; casing** Enter

```
[cgillay@RedHat9   cgillay]$   export book; casing
I like to read mystery books best of all.
[cgillay@RedHat9   cgillay]$
```

WHAT'S **HAPPENING?** Since you exported your **book** variable, the **case** command could check for a pattern match. Note that in this example the double semi-colons followed the pattern. This is allowed, but convention usually places them on a separate line. See Table 10.6, "Execution of **case**," for how **case** was executed.

Command	Process	Result
case "$book" in	case statement read value mystery in the variable $book	
biography) echo "I like to read biographies." ;;	Compared mystery to biography	False—read next pattern.
fiction) echo "I like to read fiction even better." ;;	Compared mystery to fiction.	False—read next pattern.
mystery) echo "I like to read mystery books best of all." ;;	Compared mystery to mystery.	True—a match—executed the echo command.
esac	End of case statement.	

Table 10.6 • Execution of case

You may use commands with **case** statements as well. In the next script, you will create a simple menu.

STEP 6 Create the following shell script in your home directory, but substitute your name for my name and the current date for the date given in the script. The script will be called **casing2**.

```
#!/bin/bash
# Script name: casing2
# Purpose: Using case with commands.
# Written by Carolyn Z. Gillay on July 8, 2003.
clear
echo -e "\n    MY MENU SYSTEM\n"
echo "Please make one of the following choices."
echo " d        Display the date and time. "
echo " w        Display your current working directory. "
echo -e " b      Display the files in your bin directory. "
echo -e "Enter your choice and press <Enter>: \c"
```

```
read answer
echo
case "$answer" in
        d)      date
                ;;
        w)      pwd
                ;;
        b)      ls bin
                ;;
esac
```

STEP 7   Key in the following: **chmod +x casing2** [Enter]

STEP 8   Key in the following: **./casing2** [Enter]

```
       MY MENU SYSTEM

Please make one of the following choices.
        d               Display the date and time.
        w               Display your current working directory.
        b               Display the files in your bin directory.


        Enter your choice and press <Enter>:
```

WHAT'S HAPPENING? You are executing your **casing2** script. It is prompting your for a choice.

STEP 9   Key in the following: **w** [Enter]

```
Enter your choice and press <Enter>: w

/home/cgillay
[cgillay@RedHat9   cgillay]$
```

WHAT'S HAPPENING? Your script worked. What if you keyed in a letter that is not a **pattern**, or what if you used an uppercase letter?

STEP 10 Key in the following: **./casing2** [Enter]

STEP 11 Key in the following: **x**

```
        MY MENU SYSTEM

Please make one of the following choices.
        d               Display the date and time.
        w               Display your current working directory.
        b               Display the files in your bin directory.


Enter your choice and press <Enter>: x

[cgillay@RedHat9   cgillay]$
```

WHAT'S HAPPENING? You were simply returned to your command prompt because you had no pattern to match.

STEP 12 Key in the following: **./casing2** [Enter]

STEP 13 Be sure to use the uppercase letter. Key in the following: **B** [Enter]

```
        MY MENU SYSTEM

Please make one of the following choices.
     d              Display the date and time.
     w              Display your current working directory.
     b              Display the files in your bin directory.


Enter your choice and press <Enter>: B


[cgillay@RedHat9  cgillay]$
```

WHAT'S HAPPENING? Using an uppercase **B** was also invalid. You can test for upper- and lowercase letters, and you can add the *) for any other value the user might key in.

STEP 14 Modify the **casing2** script so it looks as follows. Changes are indicated by underlined text.

> #! /bin/bash
> # Script name: casing2
> # Purpose: Using case with commands.
> # Written by Carolyn Z. Gillay on July 8, 2003.
> clear
> echo -e "\n   MY MENU SYSTEM\n"
> echo "Please make one of the following choices."
> echo " d   Display the date and time. "
> echo " w   Display your current working directory. "
> echo -e " b   Display the files in your bin directory. "
> echo -e "Enter your choice and press <Enter>: \c"
> read answer
> echo
> case "$answer" in
>   <u>d|D)</u>   date
>   ;;
>   <u>w|W)</u>   pwd
>   ;;
>   <u>b|B)</u>   ls bin
>   ;;
>   *)   echo "You did not select a valid letter."
>   ;;
> esac

STEP 15 Key in the following: **./casing2** [Enter]

STEP 16 Be sure to use the uppercase letter. Key in the following: **B** [Enter]

```
    MY MENU SYSTEM

Please make one of the following choices.
    d         Display the date and time.
    w         Display your current working directory.
    b         Display the files in your bin directory.


Enter your choice and press <Enter>: B

ages alphabet argtest casing checkit first guess happy ifthen
ifthen2
[cgillay@RedHat9    cgillay]$
```

WHAT'S HAPPENING? Your files may differ. Since you used the pipe symbol with your characters, you specified a logical operation (B or b).

STEP 17 Key in the following: **./casing2** `Enter`

STEP 18 Key in the following: **x** `Enter`

```
Enter your choice and press Enter: x

You did not select a valid letter.
[cgillay@RedHat9    cgillay]$
```

WHAT'S HAPPENING? As you can see, the **case** command is a very powerful command.

10.24 • Loops—the for, while, and until Commands

Commands entered in a shell script may need to be repeated numerous times. Rather than enter each command multiple times, you can use looping structures to repeat lines of your script. Loops allow you to execute repeatedly a set of commands either a specified number of times or until some condition is met. There are three built-in loop commands. They are **for**, **while**, and **until**.

A **for** loop is used in a shell script to repeat a list of commands once for each item in a list. The list can contain numbers, file names, user names, or words. The format that demonstrates the use of the **for loop** construct is shown in Figure 10.10, "The **for loop** Construct."

```
for variable [ in list ]
do
        command
        command
        ...
done
```

Figure 10.10 • The for loop Construct

The commands between the **do** and **done** are the body of the loop. The commands are executed for as many items as you have in your list. When the **for** loop is executed, the first word in the list is assigned to the variable and the body of the loop is executed. Then the second item in the list is assigned to the variable and the body of the loop is executed. This continues until there are no more items on the list. At that point, the script continues with whatever command follows **done**. If you do not include the **in** within the script, then the script takes the list from the command line. Another way to look at the **for loop** construct is seen in Figure 10.11, "Flowchart for the **for loop** Construct."

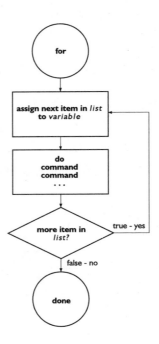

Figure 10.11 • Flowchart for the for loop Construct

A **while** loop is used in a shell script to repeat a list of commands while a specified condition is true. The **while** loop will end as soon as the specified condition evaluates to false. If your first condition evaluates as false, the **while** loop will not execute at all. Also, if your specified condition never evaluates as false, the while loop will never end—an endless loop! In a **while** loop, the condition is tested before the commands are executed. The construct of a **while** loop is like the **for** loop, except that the **while** loop uses a test instead of a variable and a list. The format that demonstrates the use of the **while** loop construct is as shown in Figure 10.12, "The **while** Loop Construct."

```
while test-expression
        do
                commands
done
```

Figure 10.12 • The while Loop Construct

The **test-expression** is evaluated. If it is true, the commands between **do** and **done** are executed. Then the **test-expression** is executed again. If it is true, the commands between **do** and **done** are executed again. This continues until the **test-expression** is evaluated as false. Then the script exits the **while** loop and passes control to the command after **done**. A **while** loop is often used to test the value of user input or the status of a file. It can also be used as a counter. Another way to look at the **while** loop construct is seen in Figure 10.13, "Flowchart for the **while** Loop Construct."

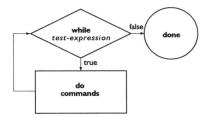

Figure 10.13 • Flowchart for the while Loop Construct

The **until** loop is very similar to the **while** loop, but it reverses the test that controls the loop. In one sense, it is a negative **while** loop. Remember, a **while** loop uses a test or a command to provide a value and then executes the commands as long as the value is true. An **until** loop will continue to loop as long as the **test-expression** is evaluated as false. If your first condition evaluates as true, then the **until** loop will not execute at all. The format that demonstrates the use of the **until** loop construct is as shown in Figure 10.14, "The **until** Loop Construct."

```
until  test-expression
do
        commands
done
```

Figure 10.14 • The until Loop Construct

The **test-expression** is evaluated and if it is true, the **until** loop is exited and passes control to the command following **done**. If the **test-expression** is evaluated as false, the commands between **do** and **done** are executed. Then the **test-expression** is evaluated again and the process continues until the **test-expression** is evaluated as true. Another way to look at the **until** loop construct is seen in Figure 10.15, "Flowchart for the **until** Loop Construct."

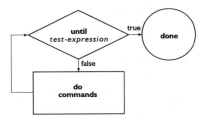

Figure 10.15 • Flowchart for the until Loop Construct

10.25 • Activity: The for, while, and until Commands

Note: You have a terminal window open. Your default directory is your home directory.

STEP 1 Key in the following pressing ⏎Enter at the end of each command:

for i in 1 2 3 4 5 ⏎Enter
do ⏎Enter
echo $i ⏎Enter
done ⏎Enter

```
[cgillay@RedHat9  cgillay]$ for i in 1 2 3 4 5
> do
> echo $i
> done
1
2
3
4
5
[cgillay@RedHat9  cgillay]$
```

WHAT'S HAPPENING? You have constructed a simple **for** loop. Note that since **for** is a key word (and built-in), it can be run at the command line. When you keyed in **for i in 1 2 3 4 5** and pressed **Enter**, you received a secondary prompt, the **>**, waiting for you to enter data. It continued to present the secondary prompt until you keyed in **done**, indicating that your **for** loop was complete. Each time the **for** was read, it changed the variable **$i** to the next item in the list. When there were no more items, the **for** loop concluded and returned you to the ordinary prompt.

STEP 2   Create the following shell script in your home directory, but substitute your name for my name and the current date for the date given in the script. The script will be called **fullname**.

#!/bin/bash
 # Script name: fullname
 # Purpose: Using the for loop.
 # Written by Carolyn Z. Gillay on July 8, 2003.
for name in cgillay gwashing student9 alincoln
do
        echo -n -e $"name: \t"
        grep $(echo $name) /etc/passwd | cut -f5 -d':'
done

STEP 3   Key in the following: **chmod +x fullname; ./fullname** **Enter**

```
[cgillay@RedHat9  cgillay]$  chmod +x fullname; ./fullname
cgillay:        Carolyn Z. Gillay
gwashing:       george washington
student9:       student 9
alincoln:       abe lincoln
[cgillay@RedHat9  cgillay]$
```

WHAT'S HAPPENING? In this example you used a predefined list of user names that will be stored in the variable called **name**. This was the **for .. in** construct. Each name that was in the list first created a new line (**-n**). Since you wanted to use an escape character—the tab (**\t**)—you had to indicate that to the **echo** statement (**-e**). The echo line will display each of the user names in your list. You used the **grep** command to search for each name in the list in the **/etc/password** file. You then cut the fifth field in the **/etc/passwd** file, which is the full user's name, and displayed it. If you eliminate the **in** in your script, you can provide the list at the command line as arguments.

STEP 4 Modify the **fullname** script by deleting the **in** and the list of names.

STEP 5 Key in the following: **./fullname student8 alincoln** Enter

```
[cgillay@RedHat9  cgillay]$  ./fullname  student8  alincoln
student8:       student 8
alincoln:       abe lincoln
[cgillay@RedHat9  cgillay]$
```

WHAT'S HAPPENING? The script performed in the same way except that you provided the arguments at the command line. By doing this, you can have as few or as many arguments as you wish. The **for** command will continue executing until all arguments on the command line have been processed. When you use the while loop, you can use it as a counter with the **let** command. The **let** built-in allows you to evaluate arithmetic expressions and perform mathematical operations.

STEP 6 Create the following shell script in your home directory, but substitute your name for my name and the current date for the date given in the script. The script will be called **counting**:

#!/bin/bash
 # Script name: counting
 # Purpose: Using the while loop with let.
 # Written by Carolyn Z. Gillay on July 9, 2003.
i=0
while ["$i" -lt 5]
     do
              echo "$i"
              let i="$i"+1
     done

STEP 7 Key in the following: **chmod +x counting; ./counting** Enter

```
[cgillay@RedHat9  cgillay]$  chmod +x counting; ./counting
0
1
2
3
4
[cgillay@RedHat9  cgillay]$
```

WHAT'S HAPPENING? You created a variable, the integer "i," which had a value of zero. The **while** loop evaluates whether **i** is less than or equal to **5**. Since you began with **0**, it is less than 5. Since the statement is true, the commands between **do** and **done** are executed. The first iteration displays the value of **i** –(a zero). The next command adds a 1 to the zero, which changes the value of **i** to 1. When control passes to **done**, it returns to the **while** loop, which evaluates whether **1** is less than or equal to **5**. Since the statement is true, control passes to the **do**. The process is repeated until the **i** has a value of **5**. At this point, when the **while** loop evaluates it, **5** is less than or equal to **5**. Thus, you exit the **while** loop.

STEP 8 Create the following shell script in your home directory, but substitute your name for my name and the current date for the date given in the script. The script will be called **baseball**:

```
#!/bin/bash
# Script name: baseball
# Purpose: Using the while loop with user input.
# Written by Carolyn Z. Gillay on July 8, 2003.
winner=Angels
echo "Who won the 2002 World Series? "
echo -n "Enter your choice: "
read choice
    while [ $winner" != "$choice" ]
      do
                echo "You are incorrect. Try another team. "
                echo -n "Enter your choice: "
                read choice
      done
echo "You are correct. The Anaheim Angels won the 2002 World Series."
```

STEP 9   Key in the following: **chmod +x baseball; ./baseball** Enter

```
[cgillay@RedHat9  cgillay]$  chmod +x baseball;./baseball
Who won the 2002 World Series?
Enter your choice:
```

WHAT'S **HAPPENING?** In the first line of the script, you initialized the value of the variable **winner** to **Angels**. You then were asked to key in a choice of what your answer will be. What you keyed in is stored in a variable called **choice**.

STEP 10   Key in the following: **Yankees** Enter

```
[cgillay@RedHat9  cgillay]$  chmod +x baseball;./baseball
Who won the 2002 World Series?
Enter your choice:  Yankees
You are incorrect. Try another team.
Enter your choice:
```

WHAT'S **HAPPENING?** Your guess was not the value in **winner** (**Angels**). The **while** loop evaluated your answer and found the condition to be true. Since the condition was true, the commands between **do** and **done** were executed. The last line before **done** asks for another choice.

STEP 11   Key in the following: **Angels** Enter

```
[cgillay@RedHat9  cgillay]$  chmod +x baseball;./baseball
Who won the 2002 World Series?
Enter your choice:  Yankees
You are incorrect. Try another team.
Enter your choice: Angels
You are correct. The Anaheim Angels won the 2002 World Series.
[cgillay@RedHat9  cgillay]$
```

WHAT'S HAPPENING? Your guess was the value in **winner** (**Angels**). The **while** loop evaluated your answer and found the condition to be false. Since the condition was false, the commands between **do** and **done** were not executed and control passed to the command following **done**.

STEP 12 Modify the **counting** script so it reads as follows. Changes are underlined.

```
#!/bin/bash
# Script name: counting
# Purpose: Using the until loop with let.
# Written by Carolyn Z. Gillay on July 8, 2003.
i=0
until [ "$i" -lt 5 ]
        do
                echo "$i"
                let i="$i"+1
        done
```

STEP 13 Key in the following: **./counting** [Enter]

```
[cgillay@RedHat9   cgillay]$   ./counting
[cgillay@RedHat9   cgillay]$
```

WHAT'S HAPPENING? You were immediately returned to the prompt. You substituted an **until** for a **while**. You created a variable, the integer "**i**," which had a value of zero. The **until** loop evaluated whether the **i** is less than or equal to **5**. Since you began with **0**, it is less than **5**. Since the statement is true, the commands between **do** and **done** are not executed. Thus, you exit the **until** loop.

STEP 14 Modify the **counting** script and change **-lt** to **-ge**.

STEP 15 Key in the following: **./counting** [Enter]

```
[cgillay@RedHat9   cgillay]$   ./counting
0
1
2
3
4
[cgillay@RedHat9   cgillay]$
```

WHAT'S HAPPENING? Now your script ran correctly. The **until** loop evaluated whether the **i** is greater than or equal to **5**. Since the statement is false, the commands between **do** and **done** are executed. The first iteration displays the value of **i** (a zero). The next command adds a 1 to the zero, which changes the value of **i** to **1**. When control passes to **done**, it returns to the **until** loop, which evaluates whether 1 is greater than or equal to **5**. Since the statement is false, control passes to the **do**. The process is repeated until the **i** has a value of **5**. At this point, when the **until** loop evaluates it, **5** is greater than or equal to **5**. Thus, you exit the **until** loop.

STEP 16 Modify the script called **baseball**. Change the **while** to an **until**. Change the **!=** to an **=**.

STEP 17 Key in the following: **./baseball** [Enter]

```
[cgillay@RedHat9  cgillay]$  ./baseball
Who won the 2002 World Series?
Enter your choice:
```

WHAT'S HAPPENING? So far the script is giving you the same result. In the first line of the script, you initialized the value of the variable **winner** to **Angels**. You then were asked to key in a choice of what your answer will be. What you keyed in is stored in a variable called **choice**.

STEP 18   Key in the following: **Yankees** Enter

```
[cgillay@RedHat9  cgillay]$  ./baseball
Who won the 2002 World Series?
Enter your choice:  Yankees
You are incorrect. Try another team.
Enter your choice:
```

WHAT'S HAPPENING? Your guess was not the value in **winner** (**Angels**). The **until** loop evaluated your answer and found the condition to be false. Since the condition was false, the commands between **do** and **done** were executed. The last line before **done** asks for another choice.

STEP 19   Key in the following: **Angels** Enter

```
[cgillay@RedHat9  cgillay]$  ./baseball
Who won the 2002 World Series?
Enter your choice:  Yankees
You are incorrect. Try another team.
Enter your choice: Angels
You are correct. The Anaheim Angels won the 2002 World Series.
[cgillay@RedHat9  cgillay]$
```

WHAT'S HAPPENING? Your guess was the value in **winner** (**Angels**). The **until** loop evaluated your answer and found the condition to be true. Since the condition was true, the commands between **do** and **done** were not executed and control passed to the command following **done**.

Note: If you want to save your scripts created in this chapter, you can copy them to your BOOK2 disk or to a different floppy disk. If you want to save the scripts (and do not forget the ones in the bin directory), remember to unmount the BOOK2 disk first and mount the new floppy disk.

STEP 20   Unmount the BOOK2 disk and remove it from the drive.

Chapter Summary

In this chapter you were introduced to the following:
- The type of documentation you should include in a shell script.
- The use of Linux commands, variables, and variable substitution to write simple shell scripts.
- The use of the **read** command to get and use information from users.
- Developed a script that uses positional parameters.
- The use of the **shift** command in a script to read positional parameters on the command line.
- The use of the **set** command to reset positional parameters.

- The use of the variable $?$ to view the return code (exit code) for a process running in your scripts.
- The use of the **test** to compare numbers, strings, and whether a file exists or has certain properties.
- Identified and used the test operation symbols or values.
- The use of the **let** commands to perform operations on arithmetic values.
- The use of **if** and **then** constructs to provide conditional programming in your scripts.
- The use of **if** and **then** and **else** constructs to provide conditional programming in your scripts.
- The use of **if** and **then** and **elif** constructs to provide conditional programming in your scripts.
- The use of the **case** command to provide multiway decision making capabilities.
- Developed loops using the **for, while,** and **until** commands.

Key Terms

command line argument	documentation	positional parameters
commands	expression	shebang
comments	loop	shell scripts
conditional	operand	test
control structures	operators	

Discussion Questions

1. What is a shell script?
2. Explain the function of a loop.
3. Explain the function of conditional control structures. Name the two components involved in a conditional control structure.
4. In a conditional control structure, what happens if a test is successful? If unsuccessful?
5. Define documentation in reference to a shell script.
6. List at least four types of documentation information that should be provided in a script.
7. Define comments in reference to a shell script.
8. What is the function of the "shebang" line?
9. Explain the term **fork**. What occurs during this process?
10. What is the function of the **read** command? What does it allow a script to do?
11. What is a "command line argument"?
12. Compare and contrast a command line argument with options.
13. What does it mean to "parse a command"?
14. Explain the use of positional parameters. What symbol is used to identify positional parameters?
15. What is the function of the **shift** command? The **set** command?
16. Define *exit status*. What are some other names used for this term?
17. What is the function of the **exit** command?
18. What is an expression?
19. What is the function of the **test** command?
20. What is the function of the **let** command?
21. What does an exit status of **0** (zero) mean when applied to a command? When applied to a condition?
22. What does an exit status of "nonzero" mean when applied to a command? When applied to a condition?

23. Describe the conditional flow control.
24. What happens if **&&** is used between two commands?
25. What happens if **!!** is used between two commands?
26. How does the **if-then-else** command construct allow for a two-way decision process?
27. Compare and contrast the **if-then-elif** construct with the **if-then** construct.
28. What is the function of the **case** command?
29. List the patterns used with the **case** command and explain the function of each.
30. What is the function of the **for** loop? The **while** loop? The **until** loop? When does each loop end?

True/False Questions

For each question, circle the letter T if the question is true and the letter F if the question is false.

T   F   1. All comments must be located at the top of a script and are preceded by a pound sign (**#**).

T   F   2. The **test** command is used to compare numbers or characters.

T   F   3. Operands are used in expressions to represent specific actions.

T   F   4. The **case** command is used to provide a multi-way decision-making process within script.

T   F   5. It is possible for the **until** loop to continue to execute commands without ever stopping.

Completion Questions

Write the correct answer in each blank space.

6. The first line of a script identifying the program used to execute script lines is also referred to as the _____ line.
7. The flow of the script is the order in which commands are _____ in the shell script.
8. When using **if-then**, commands are executed when the test is _____, and stops when _____ is reached.
9. To reset the positional parameters use the _____ command.
10. **if-then** and **if-then-else** allow for a _____- way decision-making process within the script; while the **if-then-elif** allows for a _____- way decision-making process within the script.

Multiple Choice Questions

For each question, write the letter for the correct answer in the blank space.

11. When creating a script, the shell will not allow you to
    a. create loops.
    b. define variables.
    c. set values for variables.
    d. none of the above

12. An exit status of zero (**0**) means that the
    a. condition is true.
    b. command will execute.
    c. both a and b
    d. neither a nor b

13. When using **if-then-else**, if the test following "if" returns a false ("nonzero") status which of the following commands will be executed?
    a. Commands located between **if** and **then**.
    b. Commands located between **then** and **else**.
    c. Commands located between **else** and **fi**.
    d. Commands located between **if** and **fi**.

14. Using the **shift** command allows for _____ to be passed to the script.
    a. a limited number of parameters
    b. an unlimited number of parameters
    c. testing of parameters
    d. three parameters

15. Logical operators include
    a. **-a, -o,** and **!.**
    b. ***, !,** and **$.**
    c. **and, but,** and **or.**
    d. **-gt, -lt** and **-le.**

Writing Commands

The following is a shell script:

```
echo -n "Please enter a value: "
if [-d $value]
        then
                echo "$value is a directory."
elif [-f $value]
then
        if [-r $value -a -w $value -a -x $value]
                echo "You have read, write, and execute permission on $value."
        fi
else
        echo "$file is not a file or directory."
fi
```

Describe what will happen in each of the following cases:

16. **echo -n "Please enter a value: "** For your value, you enter the directory name **bin**.

17. **echo -n "Please enter a value: "** For your value, you enter a file named **report** that has read-only permission.

18. **echo -n "Please enter a value: "** For your value, you enter a file named **report** for which you have read, write and execute permissions.

19. **echo -n "Please enter a value: "** For your value, you enter a file named **report** that does not exist.

20. What is **if [-d $value]** testing for? What is **elif [-f $value]** testing for?

Application Assignments

Problem Set I—At the Computer

Note: See the note on page 414 for information about disk usage.

Use vi or any editor to create your scripts. In your script, in addition to the documentation lines, add the following lines in this order:

> #!/bin/bash
> # Script name: *ages*
> # Purpose: *Using if/else/elif.*
> # Written by *your name* on *current date.*
> # *Class day and time*
> # Chapter 10 Problem *letter* Script.

Obviously, for everything in italics and underlined, substitute the correct information.

Problem A

Write the following shell script called **greet** that will

- greet the user,
- display the current date,
- display a list of files in your **bin** directory,
- display a list of files in your home directory,
- print all the processes that you are running,
- tell the user goodbye.

Save and print this script.

Problem B

Write the following shell script called **change** that will

- take two arguments—the first argument is the name of the original file and the second argument is the new name for the file, and
- if the user does not provide two arguments, an error message will appear telling the user the proper syntax for the command.

The output of the command will look as follows:

```
[cgillay@RedHat9  cgillay]$   change
Syntax is rename oldfilename   newfilename

[cgillay@RedHat9  cgillay]$   change file1   file2
file1 has been renamed file2
```

Save and print this script.

Problem C

Write the following shell script called **asking** that will

- ask the user's full name—first, last, and middle names.

- greet the user by his or her first name.
- ask for the user's login name and print his or her user id (found in **/etc/passwd**).
- if the user does not provide a valid or any user name, the user gets a message and the script is exited.
- display the files in the user's home directory,
- display the processes that the user is running.

Save and print this script.

Problem D

Write the following shell script using **if/then/elif** called **hours** that will

- create a variable called **time** that will contain the current time (remember that in the **date** command, the time always appears in positions 12 through 19 and the hour appears in position 12–13),
- display only the current time with an **echo** statement,
- if the time is less than 12:00 A.M., display a greeting of **Get up**, *username*.
- if the time is between 12:00 P.M. and 5:00 P.M., display a greeting of **Time to nap**, *username*,
- if the time is greater than 5:00 P.M., display a greeting of **Go to bed**, *username*.

Save and print this script.

Problem E

Modify the **hours** script to use **case** instead of **if/then/elif**.

Save and print this script.

Problem F

Modify the **fullname** script (the one that requested user input) so that instead of the full name, you display the group ids for that user in ascending order. *Hint:* All group ids are kept in the **/etc/group** file.

Save and print this script.

Problem G—Challenge Problem

Create a script called **movies** that will ask the user for the name of your favorite movie. After the user correctly names your favorite movie, the script will then ask for the name of your favorite movie star.

Save and print this script.

Cleanup

- If you want to save the scripts you wrote during these activities, save them to the BOOK2 floppy or a new disk.
- Delete all the files you created in your home directory.
- Delete your **/home/usr/bin** directory.

Problem Set II—Brief Essay

Use gEdit or OpenOffice.org Writer to write and print your response. Be sure to put your name as well as what day and time your class is. Include the number of the question you are answering.

a. Use the **cat** command to look at the file called **/etc/bashrc**. There should be an **if** statement for setting the **umask** value. What is the purpose of the **if** statement? Describe the results of the **if** and the **else** statements.

b. Compare and contrast conditional flow controls. What keywords are used for conditional control? How are they used?

c. Describe the purpose and function of positional parameters. How may positional parameters be used with shell scripts? Include in your discussion the purpose and function of the shift command and how it can affect positional parameters.

APPENDIX A

Master Accounts

Installation

In order for the textbook activities and examples to work correctly, Red Hat Linux should be installed at run level 3, not run level 5. Run level 5 takes the user directly into the GUI. This creates problems in exiting to the command line and also creates permission problems. Be sure that when you install Red Hat Linux, you choose the text-based boot process, not the GUI interface boot process. Run levels can be altered by changing **inittab** file located in the **/etc** directory.

WARNING: To change your run level, you need to edit the **/etc/inittab** file. This can be a very dangerous procedure, as this is the initialization file that starts your entire system. If you make a mistake, you will not be able to boot your system at all. Hence, it is a good idea to make a backup copy of your original **inittab** file. Use vi or any editor to alter the **inittab** file. Then to change it, you will see that there is a line in **inittab** that states

    id:5:initdefault:

    This boots your system into the X environment immediately. To boot into a text-based interfaced, you need to alter the line in the file so it reads:

    id:3:initdefault:

    You are changing the system from a run level of 5 (X11) to a run level 3 (Full multiuser mode)

    Once the file is altered and saved, reboot the system. You should then boot into a text mode, and to enter the GUI you will need to key in **startx**.

Accounts

If you are working in a lab environment, these accounts should have already been created for you. However, if you are working on your own computer, and you wish to have your screen displays match those in the text, you must create the following accounts with the matching group membership. Also, later in the text, unless you have these users, you will not be able to do some of the activities. The password for linux and cgillay can be passwords of your own choosing. In order to create users, you must be logged in as root.

Users

User Name	Full Name	Password	Group Membership
cgillay	Carolyn Z. Gillay	zoniagillay	cgillay, politics, student
linux	linux user	generic	linux, student
alincoln	abe lincoln	president	alincoln, politics, student
gwashing	george washington	firstprez	gwashing, politics, student
student9	student 9	student9	student9, student
student8	student 8	student8	student8
student7	student 7	student7	student7, politics

If you are working in a lab environment, these groups should have already been created for you. However, if you are working on your own computer, and you wish to have your screen displays match those in the text, you must create the following groups which do not have a corresponding user. Also, later in the text, unless you have these groups, you will not be able to do some of the activities. In order to create users, you must be logged in as root.

Groups

These are groups that must be created that have no corresponding user name:

politics

student

If you are working in a lab environment, these directories should have already been created for you. However, if you are working on your own computer, and you wish to have your screen displays match those in the text, you must create the following directories. Also, later in the text, unless you have these directories, you will not be able to do some of the activities. In order to create directories off the root, you must be logged in as root.

Directories

These are to be created off the off the root.

Directory Name	Owner	Group	Permissions
politics	root	politics	drwxrwxr-t *Note:* Directory has sticky bit chmod +t /politics
public	root	student	drwxrwxr-

If you are working in a lab environment, these files should have already been created for you. However, if you are working on your own computer, and you wish to have your screen displays match those in the text, you must create the following files in the **politics** directory. Also, later in the text, unless you have these files, you will not be able to do some of the activities. In order to create the files, you must be logged in as root.

Files in Politics Directory

File Name	Permissions	Owner	Group	Contents
test.fil	-rwxrwxr—	alincoln	alincoln	This is a test.
testing.fil	-rwxrwxrwx	alincoln	student	This is another test.

There are no files in the **public** directory.

APPENDIX B

ASCII Collating Sequence

Note: Characters enclosed in braces are usually non-printing characters.

Character	Decimal	Octal	Hex
{NUL}	0	000	00
{SOH}	1	001	01
{STX}	2	002	02
{ETX}	3	003	03
{EOT}	4	004	04
{ENG}	5	005	05
{ACK}	6	006	06
{BEL}	7	007	07
{BS}	8	008	08
{HT}	9	009	09
{LF}	10	010	A
{VT}	11	011	B
{NP}	12	012	C

Character	Decimal	Octal	Hex	Character	Decimal	Octal	Hex
{CR}	13	013	D	& (ampersand)	38	046	26
{SO}	14	014	E	' (apostrophe)	39	047	27
{SI}	15	015	F	((open paren)	40	050	28
{DLE}	16	016	10	) (close paren)	41	051	29
{DC1}	17	017	11	* (asterisk)	42	052	2A
{DC2}	18	018	12	+ (plus)	43	053	2B
{DC3}	19	019	13	, (comma)	44	054	2C
{DC4}	20	020	14	- (hyphen)	45	055	2D
{NAK}	21	021	15	. (period)	46	056	2E
{SYN}	22	022	16	/ (slash or virgule)	47	057	2F
{ETB}	23	027	17	0	48	060	30
{CAN}	24	030	18	1	49	061	31
{EM}	25	031	19	2	50	062	32
{SUB}	26	032	1A	3	51	063	33
{ESC}	27	033	1B	4	52	064	34
{FS}	28	034	1C	5	53	065	35
{GS}	29	035	1D	6	54	066	36
{RS}	30	036	1E	7	55	067	37
{US}	31	037	1F	8	56	070	38
Space	32	040	20	9	57	071	39
! (bang)	33	041	21	: (colon)	58	072	3A
" (double quote)	34	042	22	; (semicolon)	59	073	3B
# (octothorp)	35	043	23	< (left angle bracket)	60	074	3C
$ (dollar sign)	36	044	24	= (equals)	61	075	3D
% (percent)	37	045	25	> (right angle bracket)	62	076	3E

Character	Decimal	Octal	Hex	Character	Decimal	Octal	Hex
? (question mark)	63	077	3F	Y	89	131	59
@ (at sign)	64	100	40	Z	90	132	5A
A	65	101	41	[(left sq. bracket)	91	133	5B
B	66	102	42	\ (backslash)	92	134	5C
C	67	103	43	] (right sq. bracket)	93	135	5D
D	68	104	44	^ (caret)	94	136	5E
E	69	105	45	_ (underscore)	95	137	5F
F	70	106	46	` (grave mark)	96	140	60
G	71	107	47	a	97	141	61
H	72	110	48	b	98	142	62
I	73	111	49	c	99	143	63
J	74	112	4A	d	100	144	64
K	75	113	4B	e	101	145	65
L	76	114	4C	f	102	146	66
M	77	115	4D	g	103	147	67
N	78	116	4E	h	104	150	68
O	79	117	4F	i	105	151	69
P	80	120	50	j	106	152	6A
Q	81	121	51	k	107	153	6B
R	82	122	52	l	108	154	6C
S	83	123	53	m	109	155	6D
T	84	124	54	n	110	156	6E
U	85	125	55	o	111	157	6F
V	86	126	56	p	112	160	70
W	87	127	57	q	113	161	71
X	88	130	58	r	114	162	72

s	115	163	73	z	122	172	7A
t	116	164	74	{ (open French br.)	123	173	7B
u	117	165	75	| (vertical stroke)	124	174	7C
v	118	166	76	} (close French br.)	125	175	7D
w	119	167	77	~ tilde	126	176	7E
x	120	170	78	{DEL}	127	177	7F
y	212	171	79				

What the non-printing characters mean:

Hex	Character	Meaning
00	NUL	Null character.
01	SOH	Start of heading.
02	STX	Start of text.
03	ETX	End of text.
04	EOT	End of transmission.
05	ENG	Enquiry.
06	ACK	Acknowledgment.
07	BEL	Bell (or how to be really annoying).
08	BS	Backspace.
09	HT	Horizontal tab.
A	LF	Line feed.
B	VT	Vertical tab.
C	NP	New page (also called FF or form feed).
D	CR	Carriage return.
E	SO	Shift out.
F	SI	Shift in.
10	DLE	Data link escape.
11	DC1	X-on.

Hex	Character	Meaning
12	DC2	
13	DC3	X-off.
14	DC4	
15	NAK	No acknowledgment.
16	SYN	Synchronous idle.
17	ETB	End transmission block.
18	CAN	Cancel.
19	EM	End of medium.
1A	SUB	Substitute.
1B	ESC	Escape.
1C	FS	File separator.
1D	GS	Group separator.
1E	RS	Record separator.
1F	US	Unit separator.
7F	DEL	Delete or rub out.

GLOSSARY

/dev/null Null device. A fictitious output device for placing output that does not need to be stored or output anywhere else.

~ Tilde. A symbol that represents your home directory.

absolute mode See *octal mode*.

absolute path The exact path to a directory, starting at the root (/) directory.

alias A shorthand name for a command or a series of commands.

ambiguous file reference A wildcard character that represents a character or group of characters.

American Standard Code for Information Interchange (ASCII) ASCII is a code that translates the bits of information into readable letters. An ASCII file is a readable text file.

annihilate/kill Forcibly removing an application from the desktop.

apropos A command that allows you to search for each occurrence of a string of text in the whatis database.

argument A command line argument is anything on a command line following a command that is passed to the previous command. An argument may be a number, letter, file name, directory, or string that gives additional information to the command.

ASCII See *American Standard Code for Information Interchange*.

ASCII sort sequence The ASCII sort sequence is determined by the number assigned to the ASCII character.

authorized user A user who may access the system by successfully logging on.

bash See *Bourne Again Shell*.

Berkeley Software Distribution (BSD) A common version of Unix.

big-endian The order in which a sequence of bytes is stored in memory, where the big end (the most significant value in the sequence) is stored first.

binary A program file that is saved in binary format, as opposed to ASCII (text) format, so that it can be executable.

block special files These files process their data a block at a time and are used for the reading or writing of data to devices such as a disk.

bookmark A reference or place holder for a specific location on the Internet or in a document.

boot See *booting the system*.

booting the system The process of loading the "bootstrap program" that loads the initial files necessary for the operating system to run.

bootstrap programs Programs that contain the commands necessary to load an operating system.

Bourne Again Shell (bash) A command line shell designed after the Bourne shell with added commands and features.

browser A program that allows web navigation and the display of hypertext documents.

BSD See *Berkeley Software Distribution*.

bug A problem in a program that causes the program to not work or to not work correctly.

615

built-in commands Commands that the shell knows how to execute and run within the environment of the current shell.

cache Pronounced "cash," a small fast memory holding recently accessed data, designed to speed up subsequent access to the same data.

capplets Small applications that allow the control of settings.

Carriage Return Line Feed (CRLF) A shorthand way of referring to a carriage return, which moves the cursor to the leftmost part of the line, and the line feed (LF), which drops the cursor to the beginning of the next line.

character special files These files produce a stream of bytes one character at a time. These types of files are typically related to serial input/output devices such as a printer.

child directory A directory that is located within another directory.

child menu A menu in a hierarchical menu structure that is under the parent menu above it. Each subsequent child menu becomes a parent to the next menu in the hierarchy. See also *menu*.

clicking Pressing and releasing the primary (usually left) mouse button once.

close Stopping a window or program.

command line arguments See *argument*.

command mode In vi, you issue cryptic commands typically composed of one or two letters to take an action, such as deleting.

command options See *options*.

comments Short explanations of script file contents.

concatenation To put together.

condition code See *exit status*.

conditional control structures Consists of two major components, a test and a command or commands. If the test is successful, the command will execute. If the test is unsuccessful, the command will not execute.

control Any item that executes a command that "controls" what happens next.

copyleft The Free Software Foundation uses a stipulation called *copyleft,* which states that anyone redistributing the free software must also pass along the freedom to copy and change the program, ensuring that no one can claim ownership for future versions or place restrictions on users.

cp The command that allows you to copy a file from one location to another.

CRLF See *Carriage Return Line Feed*.

cron job A job that is set to run at a specific time.

current directory See *working directory*.

cursor The location where the user can key in information.

daemon Pronounced "demon," a process that executes in the background when called by another program.

debugging Finding and correcting problems in a program.

default What the operating system "falls back to" if no other instructions are given.

delimiter A character used to separate items. Examples of delimiters include a space or the /.

desktop The on-screen work area that emulates the top of a desk.

desktop environment The look and feel of the user environment.

destination The file or directory where you would like to place something.

device A unit of hardware, either inside or outside the system unit, that is capable of providing input, receiving output, or both.

device drivers Software necessary for the use of a hardware device. The program controls the specific peripheral device.

dialog box In a graphical user interface, a box that either conveys information to or requests information from the user.

Digital Subscriber Line (DSL) High-speed constant connection service to the internet provided by the local telephone company.

directory A virtual container that allows the organization of stored files for file systems.

distribution A collection of programs combined with the kernel that allow easier installation and use of the Linux operating system.

documentation Information that describes the purpose of a script to users. Uses comments composed of text preceded by the pound (#) sign.

dot Represents the current directory. See also *dot addressing*.

dot addressing (. and ..) The dot represents the current directory, and the double dot represents the parent directory. You may use the dot and double dot with commands rather than keying in the path name.

dot dot Represents the parent directory. See also *dot addressing*.

drag and drop In a GUI, the process of selecting an object and then, while holding down the mouse button, moving (dragging) the object. When you release the mouse button, the object is "dropped" in its new location.

dragging Placing the pointer over an object, holding down the primary (usually left) mouse button, and moving the object to another location.

drop down See *drop-down menu*.

drop-down menu A menu that presents choices that drop-down from the menu bar when requested and remains open until the user chooses a menu item or closes the menu.

DSL   See *Digital Subscriber Line*.

dummy files   Files that have no particular meaning and are used to test programs and practice file management commands.

echo   The command used to display data to standard output.

editor   A program that allows you to create and edit documents.

egrep   A utility that searches through one or more files to see if any of the files contain a character string that can use extended regular expressions, which are specified on the command line. See also *grep* and *fgrep*.

Emacs   Editor Macros. A text editor developed as a series of editor commands or macros.

emblem   A graphical symbol that the Nautilus file manager adds to icons for files and folders that are read-only, no-read, and no-write, along with any links.

environment   An area in memory where data or other information can be stored.

environment variable   Variables that store information about the characteristics of your work session. Many are read when you log on. You may alter environmental variables. See also *variable*.

escape sequences   A series of characters that start with the escape character and are often used to control display devices.

execute permission (x)   Allows the user to execute the program. When applied to a directory, allows the user to access files and directories and traverse the directory tree.

exit status   The status returned by a process, either successful or unsuccessful.

expression   In programming, any legal combination of symbols that represents a value.

ext2   See *extended file system 2 (ext2)*.

ext3   See *extended file system 3 (ext3)*.

extended file system 2 (ext2)   The native Linux file system for Red Hat Linux for versions prior to 7.2.

extended file system 3 (ext3)   The native Linux file system used in Red Hat Linux 7.2 and above. It is a journaling file system.

extended partition   A partition within a partition. With an extended partition, you can create one or more partitions called logical partitions that reside entirely in the extended partition.

FAQs   See *Frequently Asked Questions*.

fgrep   A utility that will search through one or more files to see if any of the files contain a fixed character string that is specified on the command line. See also *grep* and *egrep*.

FHS   See *File System Hierarchy Standard*.

file   A collection of related information that is stored as a unit.

file descriptors   These are not true files but can be treated as files at the operating system level.

file extension   The last characters that follow a period in a file name. May indicate a file type.

file system   A file system is the way any operating system names, stores, and organizes the files on storage devices such as hard disks or floppy disks.

File System Hierarchy Standard (FHS)   A standard most distributions of Linux follow that determines the location of certain directories and the files contained within them.

filters   Commands that output a modified version of its input.

foreign file system   A file system that is not installed by default but that the operating system can support.

forking   To create a process. When a new process is created, it is called forking since one process splits into two.

Free Software Foundation (FSF)   Coined the term *copyleft* for software that can be distributed for free or for a fee, as long as any copy made allows for free distribution as well. The FREE stands for FREEdom, not necessarily free of charge.

Frequently Asked Questions (FAQs)   A listing of questions about a topic, located online or in a manual.

FSF   See *Free Software Foundation*.

fstab   File System Table located in the /etc directory. A file that keeps track of the block device name given the physical location of the file system, the mount point for the root file system, the device or file system type, any options to be used when mounting a file system, and, if present, a number used to determine whether the dump or fsck utility should be run.

GID   See *group ID*.

GIMP (Graphics and Imaging Program)   A software program included with Red Hat Linux for editing and creating graphic images.

global regular expression print (grep)   A utility that will search through one or more files to see if any of the files contain a string of characters that is specified on the command line.

globbing   A shorthand system that allows you to operate on a group of files rather than a single file using special characters. These special characters are also called wildcards. See also *wildcards*.

GNOME   The desktop provided with Red Hat Linux 7.2 for X Window System.

GNU   See *Gnu's Not Unix*.

Gnu's Not Unix (GNU)   Project created by Richard Stallman to support open and free computing.

graphical user interface (GUI) An interface between the user and the operating system that uses icons, menus, and other graphical objects.

grep See *global regular expression print*, *fgrep*, and *egrep*.

group A specified set of users to whom the owner of a file or directory can grant permissions.

group ID (GID) The number that Red Hat Linux assigns to a user group.

grub Grand Unified Boot Loader. See also *bootstrap program*.

GUI See *Graphical User Interface*.

Guides Full-sized books with detailed information on a given topic.

hard link A hard link is a pointer to an inode. This allows you to create hard links on your system that point to one file without occupying additional disk space.

head A command that displays the first lines of a file.

hide button A way to manipulate the panel so you may choose to hide the taskbar or make it visible by clicking an arrow.

hierarchical menu A menu that opens another menu. A secondary menu will open as a result of a command issued on the first or primary menu. An arrow next to the menu item indicates that another menu will open.

hierarchical structure The directory structure is like an inverted family tree with the root directory at the top and the directories branching off from the root. The hierarchical or tree-structured filing system allows not only for files but also for other directories. The terms directory and subdirectory are used interchangeably.

home directory Each user has a named directory in the /home directory, where, by default, the designated user's files and directories are stored.

homonymous man texts All man pages related to a specific term.

housekeeping tasks The process of file and directory maintenance that encompasses such tasks as copying, renaming, moving, and deleting files and directories.

HOWTOs A set of step-by-step instructions on how to accomplish a specific task.

HTML See *Hypertext Markup Language*.

Hypertext Markup Language (HTML) Text-based program language that browsers use to display web pages.

icon Pictorial representation of an object.

iconify Creates a button on the task list for the current application. Also referred to as minimizing.

IFS See *Internal Field Separator*.

initialization program Stores system settings for a specific computer. It is the first file to be processed when you boot the system.

inode A data structure that contains information about every file on the file system.

insert mode In vi, to add text, you must be in insert mode. You enter insert mode by keying in i.

Integrated Development Environment (IDE) A programming environment that has been packaged as an application program.

Internal Field Separator (IFS) Shell variable that specifies which characters you want to use to separate arguments on a command line.

Internet Service Provider (ISP) Company that provides access to the Internet.

interoperability Allows different computers with different operating systems across a network to communicate.

inverse video A display method that causes a portion of the display to appear like a negative of the regular display. If the display screen normally displays light images against a dark background, putting it in reverse or inverse video mode will cause it to display dark images against a light background.

ISP See *Internet Service Provider*.

ispell An interactive spell-checking program.

journaling file systems A means to recover quickly from a system crash by using a log file of all system actions.

K Desktop Environment (KDE) Alternative GUI desktop provided in Red Hat Linux 7.2.

KDE See *K Desktop Environment*.

kernel The core or lowest level of commands used in an operating system for memory management, process administration, and hardware management.

keyboard focus The area of the desktop that will reflect your keystrokes when you begin keying in data.

LDP See *Linux Documentation Project*.

less A command that allows screen output to be displayed one screen at a time.

lilo Linux Loader. See also *bootstrap program*.

link A pointer to a file.

linked file A special directory entry that can specify when one file points to another file (link). Whenever an operation is performed on the link, the actual file is what is operated on.

Linux Documentation Project (LDP) An effort at documenting and gathering all Linux documentation for easy access and incorporation of the information.

Linux Users Groups (LUGs)   A small local organization created to help people increase awareness of and learn how to use Linux.

little-endian   Describes the order in which a sequence of bytes is stored in computer memory. Little-endian is an order in which the little-end (least significant value in the sequence) is stored first.

load average   A number based on the number of processes waiting to run at a given time.

logical partitions   A partition that resides entirely in the extended partition.

loop   Allows a shell script to repeatedly execute a set of commands either a specified number of times or until some condition is met.

LUGs   See *Linux Users Groups*.

Main menu button   The menu button in GNOME that opens the menu choices. It is represented by a foot, usually in the lower left corner of the screen.

man -f   A command that will display a short description of a command and its purpose. Same as whatis.

man pages   Command-specific help included with Linux.

manpath   A command that lists the directories the man program will search in for the requested man page.

manual pages   See *man pages*.

menu   A list of choices displayed on the screen from which the user chooses a course of action.

menu bar   A rectangular bar, usually in a program, in which the names of the available menus are shown. The user chooses one of these menus and a list of choices for that menu is shown.

message box   A type of dialog box that informs you of a condition.

meta data   Data about data. It is definitional data that provides information about or documentation of other data managed within an application or environment, such as the operating system.

mid-click   Pressing the middle button on the mouse. If you do not have three buttons, you can emulate a three-button mouse by pressing the left and right mouse buttons simultaneously.

MIME   See *Multipurpose Internet Mail Extension*.

Mini HOWTOs   A condensed set of step-by-step instructions for a specific task.

mirror site   A file server that has an exact duplicate of its files located on a different server, which allows access to the files by more people.

mkdir   Command to create a directory.

modal editor   An editor that has modes.

mode   A special state that user interfaces must pass into to perform certain functions.

moderated   Used with newsgroups. In a moderated newsgroup, before anything gets posted, it first goes to the moderator, who decides whether the post is appropriate and makes the decision to post it.

more   A command that limits the screen display to one screenful at a time.

mount   To make a file system available to users.

mount point   The name of the directory where a file system is mounted.

mounting   Associating a partition with a directory.

mouse pointer   An on-screen pointer that is controlled by the movement of the mouse.

mtab   Mount Table located in the /etc directory. A file that lists all of the file systems that are currently mounted and the options they were mounted with.

Multipurpose Internet Mail Extension (MIME)   A MIME type tells Internet applications, such as an email or browser program, what type of file is being exchanged and how to code (sending) and decode it (arrival).

multitasking   Concurrent execution of multiple processes.

multi-user   Concurrent use by many individuals.

multi-user system   A system where many users can work with the system at one time.

native file system   A file system that is installed by default for a specific operating system.

network operating system (NOS)   An operating system that also controls and manages resources and users.

newline character   A command separator that indicates the end of a line and initiates the command that was entered before pressing the newline key.

news reader   A program allowing access to messages posted to a Usenet bulletin board.

newsgroup   Compilation of related material stored for people with related interests.

numeric mode   See *octal mode*.

octal mode   A numeric representation of file and directory permissions, which causes you to use bits and octal notation.

operand   Values.

operating system (OS)   The program that allocates computer resources, schedules tasks, manages the hardware and software, and allows a user to interact with a computer system.

operators   Symbols that represent specific actions.

options   A command line argument that modifies the effects of a command. Most options are preceded by a hyphen and are usually only one character. Many commands allow you to group options following a single hyphen.

ordinary files   Consist of programs (executable files), word processing files, shell scripts, and other such types of files. These files contain information you create or manipulate.

other   Anyone else who can log onto the system. Other is everyone else or colloquially, the world.

overhead   The needed resources that are used for purposes that are incidental to but necessary for the main one. The cost of running and maintaining the operating system, which includes the file system.

panel   The location where you manage your desktop. You may add, delete, or remove items from the panel as well as configure the panel itself.

parent directory   Any directory that contains other (child) directories.

parent menu   A menu in a hierarchical menu structure that is at the top of the menu system. A parent menu may have a child menu; a child menu may become a parent and have child menus of its own. See also *child menu*.

parse   To analyze something in an orderly way.

partition   An area of a fixed disk that has been reserved for a particular file system.

partition table   A list of the partitions created on a fixed disk.

path   A list of the directories that lead to the location of a file.

PDF   See *Portable Document Format*.

permissions   Refers to the rights a user has to perform various actions with a file or a directory. Permissions are read, write, and execute.

pid   See *process identification number*.

pipe   Pipes allow the standard output of one program to be used as the standard input to another program.

plug-in   A small application that is loaded into an existing application to increase or improve its performance.

pointer   An arrow or other indicator on the screen which represents the current cursor (mouse) location.

pointing   Placing the mouse pointer over an object.

portability   Able to be used in a different environment than the native one. Analogous to being "portable."

Portable Document Format (PDF)   Created by Adobe Systems to allow web users access to documents without needing to install the program that created the document on their system.

Portable Operating System Interface for Unix (POSIX)   IEEE standard that allows portability between all variants of Unix.

positional parameters   A number that indicates what position the argument is on the command line. Command line arguments can be referenced in a script. When you write the script file, you supply place holders within the script to let the script know that something (an argument) will be keyed in with the script name. The place holder or marker used in a script file is the dollar sign ($) followed by a number.

POSIX   See *Portable Operating System Interface*.

postambles   Any characters following the curly braces used in expansion.

PostsScript   A language used for printing documents, usually on laser printers.

preambles   Any characters that precede the curly braces used in expansion.

primary mouse button   The mouse button used for most operations, usually configured as the left mouse button.

print job   A print job usually consists of a single document, which can be one page or many pages long.

printenv   Print environment variables   A command that displays on the screen the current environment.

privileged user   See *super user*.

process   An executing program.

process identification number (pid)   Number allocated by the operating system to each process that is being executed.

property sheet   A special kind of dialog box that allows the user to view or change the characteristics of an object.

queue   A line or area where items are stored awaiting their turn; to line up.

r   See *read permission*.

RAM   See *random access memory*.

random access memory (RAM)   Volatile (temporary) location where all work of the operating system is carried out.

read permission (r)   Allows the user to look at the contents of a file and, when applied to directories, gives the right to list the contents of a directory.

recursively   The ability of a routine to literally call back to itself while executing. Within the Linux world, recursively means to apply the command to all directories in the path.

Red Hat Package Manager (RPM)   Application that allows for easy download and installation of upgrades and new software in Red Hat Linux.

redirection A process in which standard output is sent to a location other than the monitor or standard input is received from other than a keyboard—usually a file. The redirection symbols are > < and >>.

regular expression A pattern that describes a set of strings.

relative path The location of a file or directory in a file system that is relative to your current location. It is the path necessary to reach a parent or child of the current working directory.

return code See *exit status*.

right-click menu A menu that opens when you right-click the object. Menu items pertain to that object.

right-clicking Pressing the secondary mouse button, usually the right button.

right-dragging Dragging while holding the secondary mouse button, usually the right mouse button.

rm Command used to remove files. When used with the -r option, will also remove directories with files in them.

rmdir Command used to remove empty directories.

root The administrative account where all functions and settings of the operating system can be accessed and controlled. Also usually the login name of the super user.

root directory The topmost directory of the Linux file system.

RPM See *Red Hat Package Manager*.

script documentation See *documentation*.

search path The set path for searching for program files.

separator line Line displayed between two windows in a split window display.

set Command that displays all the values of all variables known to the shell.

shade/unshade In Gnome, to view the title bar (shade) or the entire window (unshade).

shebang Sharp (#) bang (!) line. The first line of the script that identifies which program will be used to execute the rest of the lines of script.

shell User interface for communicating with the operating system's command interpreter.

shell script A file that stores a combination of commands that run in sequence.

shell scripts A series of commands that has been saved as a file and can be executed as a program.

sockets A method for communication between a client program and a server program in a network; an endpoint in a connection.

source The original file or directory. Where you would like to get your information from.

sourcing Sourcing a file causes all of the settings in the file to become part of the current shell, and a subshell is not created.

spawn Create other processes. See also *forking*.

special files These fall into two categories, block special and character special.

split windows A feature in text editors that allows the viewable areas to be divided, displaying more than one document or area of a document.

stack A list of directories.

standard error Where the operating system expects to write any error messages, usually the monitor.

standard input Where the operating system expects to get its input, usually the keyboard.

standard output Where the operating system expects to write its output, usually the monitor.

Star Office A Linux/Unix office suite of application programs, including a word processor, spreadsheet, and presentation program.

stderr Name of the standard error file. See also *standard error*.

stdin Name of the standard input file. See also *standard input*.

stdout Name of the standard output file. See also *standard output*.

string A group of one or more text characters.

subdirectory See *directory*.

subdirectory markers See *dot addressing*.

submenu A menu that opens another menu.

super user Privileged user who has access to anything on the computer system. See also *root*.

superblock A record that describes the characteristics of a file system.

swap partition Area on the fixed disk allocated for a file used by the operating system.

symbolic link An indirect pointer to a file; a directory entry that contains the path name to the linked file.

symbolic mode Assigning permissions using the characters r, w, and x.

Symmetric Multiprocessing (SMP) Using multiple CPUs.

syntax The strict wording, punctuation, and ordering rules that the shell uses to understand a command.

system administrator The person who manages the computer system or computer network. Also referred to as the super user. The system administrator must have root privileges. See also *super user* and *root*.

system services   System services are services that are run by the computer. These include processes such as those that will mount a file system, start a network, and run scheduled tasks.

tail   A command that displays the bottom lines of a file.

tar   A command that allows you to archive multiple files into a single file.

taskbar buttons   A button on the taskbar (panel) that indicates an open program, file, or window. Clicking the specific button on the taskbar will activate that choice.

telnet   A program that acts as a terminal emulator for a remote login session. The computer then appears as a terminal to the host computer and behaves as if you were logged on locally.

terminal   A named device file listed in the /dev directory, i.e., /dev/tty1.

terminal emulator   A program that allows a computer to act like a specific brand of terminal.

text editor   A very simple word processor that does not provide text-formatting features.

thumbnail   A miniaturized version of an image, commonly used by graphic designers.

title bar   A bar located at the top of a window that contains the name of the program or directory.

typing replaces selection   The process of deleting exisiting characters by selecting them and keying in data. What you key in replaces your selection.

UID   See *user id*.

unary   Like binary (two states), it refers to one state or one thing.

Universal Resource Locator (URL)   The address of a particular website (i.e.: http://www.linux.org)

URL   See *Universal Resource Locator*.

Usenet   Usenet is a distributed bulletin board that is supported by people who post and read articles on the bulletin board. Usenet is probably one of the largest decentralized information utilities available.

user   Every person who wants to access the system must have a user account.

user id (UID)   The unique number that Red Hat Linux assigns to each user.

user interfaces   A user interface allows a user to run programs and to access the file system on the computer. User interfaces are either text based or graphical.

usr   User directory. The shared files that all users in Linux have access to.

variable   A name with an associated value.

vi   Visual mode editor. Pronounced "vee-eye", it was the first screen-based editor for Unix systems.

vim   Vi Improved. vim is a clone of vi, the editor supplied with Red Hat Linux. It is referred to as vi.

virtual terminals   Describes a device that is perceived but not real. Although you have only one physical terminal, Linux can give the appearance of having multiple consoles. Virtual consoles exist outside of the GUI, each with its own shell command prompt.

w   See *write permission*.

whatis   A command that displays a short description of a command and its purpose. Same as man -f.

widgets   Widgets are graphic control elements for specific tasks. There are widgets for items such as text fields or command buttons.

wildcards   The symbols, *, ?, and [ ], also called global file specifications and ambiguous file references, that are used to represent a single character (?), a group of characters (*), or a range of characters that are specified in the square brackets. See also *ambiguous file references* and *globbing*.

window   A defined work area (rectangular frame) on the screen that is moveable and sizeable; information with which the user can interact is displayed in a window.

window manager   Part of the graphical user interface that controls how windows are displayed on the screen.

word splitting   Using argument separators on the command line.

workaround   Something that works for the wrong reason or is a way to "work around" the problem. A workaround is often used to fix bugs.

work buffer   A place in memory where data is temporarily stored.

working directory   Your current location in the file system.

write permission (w)   Gives you the right to alter or delete a file. When applied to directories, allows you to add or remove files in that directory.

X   See *X Window System*.

x   See *execute permission*.

X Window System (X)   A design and set of tools for writing windowing applications.

INDEX

!, 7, 82, 211, 293, 317
#, 12, 78, 211, 366
#!, 549–551
$ prompt, 12
$?, 480, 510, 558, 567
.bash_profile, 214, 523, 535
/dev/null, 111, 355
/etc/group, 435, 436, 439
/etc/passwd, 378, 435, 436, 438, 439, 442, 483

A

absolute mode, 453–455, 457, 458
absolute path, 79, 194
alias, 214, 479, 506–511, 526
ambiguous file references, 94, 100, 272, 343, 482
ampersand, 352, 497
append, 304, 314, 353, 497
apropos, 134, 137–142
argument, 3, 63, 73–74
arithmetic expansion, 530, 534
ASCII file, 243, 244, 355–356, 360
ASCII sort sequence, 366
ASCII text files, 50, 243, 244, 288
ASCII, 50, 243, 244, 355, 366
authorized user, 11, 416

B

back quote, 526, 532, 551, 552
background, 4, 37, 52, 497–498, 502–506

backslash, 73, 372, 519, 521, 526–527, 529
Bash, 9, 72–73
bash -version, 554
bashrc, 455, 511, 535–538
bg, 497, 510
big-endian, 239
bin, 69, 70, 113, 214, 443, 550, 553
block, 101, 103, 238, 423, 425–426
block special files, 355
block special, 355, 569
boot the system, 11–13, 192
browser, 125, 127, 149–150
buffer, 289, 291, 293, 307, 314, 324, 426
bug, 133, 150
built-ins, 73, 124, 481–482, 490, 507, 523
By Type, 186, 428

C

cache, 426
cal, 83–85
case, 587–593
cat, 93, 112, 241
cd, 79, 80, 192
CDPATH, 216–217
changing file names,
   see renaming files
character, 9, 211, 293
character data, 366
character special files, 355
character strings, 73, 356

chgrp, 435–436
child menu, 19
chown, 436
chsh, 77–78
clear, 85, 244, 509
colors, 47, 75–76, 80
comm, 390, 393
command button, 23
command line argument, 210, 363, 557, 558
command line expansion, 525–526, 530
command line, 9, 43, 72, 73
command mode, 289, 291
command substitution, 530, 532, 564
commands, 506–507, 548–549
comments, 536, 548–549
concatenation, 255
concurrent processes, 484
condition code, 510, 567
conditional control structures, 549, 573
conditional flow control, 573
confirm, 23
console, 40
consolehelper, 468
contiguous, 269
control, 23
copy, 231, 232
copying files, 230, 235–236
copyleft, 4, 50
cp, 235–236, 240, 247, 253, 260
cron job, 141

curly braces, 530, 560
cut, 357–358

D

Daemon, 129
daemon, 52, 437
date, 83, 533
declare, 523
defaulted, 249
delete, 307, 314, 382
delimited word, 293
delimiter, 65, 73, 357, 358
desktop, 9–11, 14–17
device, 417
device driver, 3, 12, 45, 71
device file, 133, 178, 345
device names, 45, 179, 347, 423,
    424
df, 427–428
dialog box, 22
diff, 389–390
directories, 9
directory, 65
directory permissions, 417, 451,
    456
directory tree, 65
dirs, 511–513
disk free, 427
dsk management, 89
disk usage, 427
distribution, 5
dot, 73, 191, 200
dot addressing, 200
dot command, 535
dot dot, 200
double dot, 73–74, 191, 200
double quotation marks, 382,
    519, 520
double quote, 526
drop down, 21
du, 427
dummy files, 255

E

echo, 212, 518
ed, 288
editor, 288
egrep, 373–374
elif, 583–584
else, 579, 583
emacs, 322–324
emblem, 26, 185
end of file, 346
environmental, 439
environmental variables, 132,
    133, 210, 212, 516, 523
EOF, 346, 348
escape sequences, 520–521
ex, 288
exclamation point (!), 82, 574

exec, 464, 483, 490, 550
execute (x), 417, 444, 446
execute permission, 66, 103
exit, 14, 41
exit code, 511, 567–568
exit status, 490, 510, 567
export, 479, 523
expression, 133, 568
ext2, 65, 415, 421, 422–423
ext3, 46, 65, 421–422
extended regular expressions,
    372–373

F

FAQs (Frequently Asked
    Questions), 124–125, 157
FAT file system, 351, 418, 421,
    430
fdformat, 421, 424
fdisk, 86
fg, 497
fgrep, 373–374
fi, 510, 573
file, 7–8, 238
file descriptors, 345
file extension, 7, 238
file manager, 10, 11, 23–25
File System Hierarchy Standard
    (FHS), 70, 133
file system, 3, 46, 65–66, 86,
    355, 421–422
file type, 103
file name expansion, 94, 107
filters, 357, 363–364
find, 107–108
focus, 29, 32
foo, 145
for loop, 593–594
foreground, 497
fork, 481, 483
forking, 481, 488
fsck, 45, 46, 429
fstab, 44
full regular expressions, 372
functions, 507

G

gEdit, 50, 288
getty, 483
GID, 435
gid, 436
global, 272, 311
global variables, 516
globbing, 94, 99, 272
GNU, 4
grep, 372–374
group, 416, 417, 425
groupname, 438–439
groups, 435–436
GUI, 3, 6, 9

Guides, 124–125
gunzip, 395–397
gzip, 395–397

H

hard link, 461–462
head, 386–387
help, 142, 300–301, 507
hierarchical, 65, 160, 180
hierarchical menu, 19
highlighting, 20
home directory, 16
homonymous man texts, 140
housekeeping tasks, 230
HOWTOs, 124–125, 157
HTML, 126
hypertext, 125

I

id, 436
if, 507, 510, 573
if - then, 573
if/else, 579–580
if/then/elif, 583–584
IFS (Internal Field Separator),
    534
ignore case, 110, 311, 373
info, 146
Info pages, 125–126, 143–144
init, 12, 483
inodes, 426
insert, 289
Insert mode, 289, 304
internal commands, 481
Internal Field Separator, 534
ispell, 382

J

job, 497
job number, 276, 497
jobs, 497
journaling file system, 65, 421

K

kernel, 3, 481
keywords, 137, 507
kill, 493
killall, 494

L

Last Line mode, 291
LDP, 125
less, 242
let, 570, 597
line, 293, 294
link, 461–467
linked file, 355, 461, 462, 467
Linux Documentation project,
    see LDP
little-endian, 239

ln, 462
ln -s, 468
load average, 486, 492
local variables, 516
logical operators, 573–574
logical partitions, 178, 179
login shell, 516, 535
loop, 549, 593–600
lost+found, 71, 429
low-level format, 421
lpq, 275
lpr, 275–276
lprm, 275, 276
ls, 73, 74
ls -F, 104–105, 191
ls -l, 103–104, 236

M

macro, 322
man, 74, 136–143
man pages, 124–126, 132–134,
    136–137, 139, 142–145, 157,
    479
manpath, 137, 138, 140, 143
manual pages, see man pages
members, 436, 438, 439, 442
menu bar, 21, 24
message box, 23
meta data, 65
metacharacters, 94
MIME, 238
mini-HOWTOs, 124–125,
mirror site, 125
mkdir, 188, 190, 194, 196–201
mke2fs, 421, 422, 425
mkfs, 421–423
mkfs.ext2, 422
mkfs.msdos, 422
modal editor, 289, 322
mode, 289–293
moderated, 160
more, 241–247
mount, 45, 86–87, 92–93, 179
mount point, 45, 46
mounting, 46, 86–94, 179
Move to Trash, 55, 269
move, 31, 36, 262, 264
Mozilla, 15, 16, 19, 127–130,
    149–153, 160, 163
mtab, 93
mv, 202, 204, 260–264

N

named buffers, 314
Nautilus file manager, 11, 15,
    16, 18, 20, 23–32
New Folder, 189, 190, 195, 232
newline, 527, 554
news reader, 149, 150, 160, 163

newsgroup, 150, 159–167
Next, 313
noclobber, 517, 518, 538
noncontiguous, 269,
numeric mode, 453

O

octal mode, 446, 453
one dot, 200,
online, 124
operand, 568, 569
operators, 568, 570–571, 573–
    574
option, 73–74
ordinary files, 355, 357
overhead, 427
overwrite, 251
overwriting, 250–254
owner, 66, 417–418
ownership, 254, 416–418, 435,
    445–446

P

paragraph, 293, 294
parameter expansion, 526, 530
parent menu, 19
parse, 490, 557
partition, 45, 86, 177–179
partition table, 177–179
passwd, 438, 442, 443
password, 437, 438, 439, 442,
    443, 483
paste, 230, 231, 357–363, 230
path, 65
    absolute and relative, 79
pathname expansion, 530
PDF, 54, 158
permissions, 66, 101, 103, 416–
    420, 444–453
    octal permissions (numeric,
    absolute), 453–460
    in a shell script, 550, 552–553,
    563
Permissions tab, 440–442
pid, 52, 483, 484, 487, 490,
    491, 493
pipe, 369–372, 377, 482, 593
popd, 511, 512, 513–516
positional parameters, 557–561,
    565
POSIX, 3–4
postambles, 530
poweroff, 468
pr, 378–381
preambles, 531
print job, 17, 52
print spooler, 52
printenv, 211–212
printing files, 275–276

process id, see pid
processes, 488–493
processes number, 497
PROMPT Variable, 211
property sheet, 33, 48
ps, 486, 488, 489–490
PS1, 210, 211–214
PS2, 211
pseudo device, 349
pseudo terminal, 349
pstree, 486, 491
pushd, 511–516
put, 314
pwd, 79, 82–83, 193

Q–R

quit, 137, 373, 487
raw device, 421
read (r), 417, 444, 456
read permission, 66, 417, 451,
    453, 457
reboot, 14, 19, 468–469
recursive, 101, 107, 207, 235,
    268, 373, 396, 436, 447
redirect, 111, 256, 258, 352,
    354, 363, 377
registers, 314, 324
regular expressions, 372–373,
    376, 587
relative path, 79, 194, 196–201,
    468
remove directory, 204
Repeat Edit command, 313
replacing, 310–314
return code, 510, 567
right-click menu, 32, 33
rm, 204, 207–210, 229–230,
    268, 271–275
rm options, 207, 268
rmdir, 204, 207
rmdir options, 204
root directory, 27, 46, 65, 71,
    86, 179, 180–182, 248, 426
root user, 11, 71, 78, 86, 133

S

screen, 293
scripts, 482, 500–506, 548–553
scrolling, 241, 302–303
Search for Files, 18, 19, 20, 94,
    99
search commands, 295
search path, 111, 113, 425, 482
security, 4, 417, 444
sentence, 293, 294, 307
set, 212, 516–518, 564–566
set number, 309
SGID (Set Group ID), 442
shebang, 549–550

shell, 3, 9, 72–73
  looking at, 74–78
  navigating, 78–83
shell script, 73, 210, 485, 500–506, 548–553
shell variables, 210
shift, 562–564
Show Properties, 440
shutdown, 13, 468
signal id, 494
single quote, 526–530
socket, 417
soft links, 467
sort, 186–188, 363–369
  reverse order, 363
source, 235
sourcing, 535
spam, 161–162
spawn, 418, 419, 464, 485
split, 317, 318
stack, 511–516
standard error, 258
standard input, 344–350
stderr, 110, 345, 349
stdin, 110, 345
sticky bit, 442, 443, 570
string, 82, 94, 137
stty, 497
su, 418, 464
subdirectories, see directories
subdirectory markers, 191
submenu, 19
substitute, 310–311
SUID (Set User ID), 442–443
superblock, 426
symbolic links, 71, 80, 101, 467–471
symbolic mode, 453, 457
symbols, 482
syntax, 73
system calls, 133, 481, 483, 485, 491
system routines, 483
system services, 3

T

tail, 386–389
tar, 395, 397–405
tee, 381–386
TERM, 493
terminal, 20, 40
terminal emulator, 349
test, 568–571
text editor, 43, 44, 50–55
then, 573–587
threaded discussion, 159, 164
thumbnail, 243
tilde, 213, 235, 236
title bar, 21, 24
top, 487
touch, 258–260
tr, 381–386
tty, 346, 347
tune2fs, 422
two dots, 200
type, 479, 507–511
typing replaces selection, 100, 190, 203

U

uid, 435, 437, 489
umask, 455–460
umount, 86, 87
unalias, 508
uname, 551–552
unary, 569
undo, 307
undo buffer, 314, 316
uniq, 389–394
unset, 522
until, 593
until loop, 595
uptime, 486
Usenet, 150, 159–161
User interfaces, 3
user, 435
username, 436, 437

V

variable expansion, 554
variable substitution, 482
variables, 132–133, 210–211
verbose, 188, 240
vi, 288–289
vi tags, 302
View as Icons, 183
View as List, 183
View, 25
vim, 289
virtual consoles, 40
virtual desktop, 37
visual mode, 288, 317

W–Z

wait state, 490, 491
wc, 363–369
whatis, 137, 138–143
whereis, 112–113
while, 593–600
while loop, 594–595
who, 346–348
who am i, 346
whoami, 419, 464
widgets, 10, 29
wildcards, 94, 240–241
window manager, 10
Windows, 3, 5, 7, 8
windows, 17
word splitting, 534
word, 293
work around, 150
work buffer, 289, 291, 293
working directory, 69, 79
write (w), 417, 444
write permission, 66, 188, 417
X Window System, 5–6, 9–10
xterm, 210, 349
Yank command, 314
zcat, 395–396, 398–405
zombies, 484

OTHER TITLES

from **Franklin, Beedle & Associates, Inc.**

To order these books and find out more about Franklin, Beedle & Associates, visit us online at **www.fbeedle.com**

Operating Systems
Linux eTudes (isbn 1-887902-62-7)
Understanding Practical Unix (isbn 1-887902-53-8)
Windows Millennium Edition: Concepts & Examples (isbn 1-887902-49-X)
Windows 98: Concepts & Examples (isbn 1-887902-37-6)
Windows 95: Concepts & Examples (isbn 1-887902-00-7)
Windows 2000 Professional Command Line (isbn 1-887902-79-1)
Windows 2000 Professional: Concepts & Examples (isbn 1-887902-51-1)
Windows User's Guide to DOS: Using the Command Line in Windows 2000 Professional (isbn 1-887902-72-4)
Windows User's Guide to DOS: Using the Command Line in Windows Millennium Edition (isbn 1-887902-64-3)
Windows User's Guide to DOS: Using the Command Line in Windows 95/98 (isbn 1-887902-42-2)
Windows XP Command Line (isbn 1-887902-82-1)
Windows XP: Concepts & Examples (isbn 1-887902-81-3)

Software Applications
Access 97 for Windows: Concepts & Examples (isbn 1-887902-29-5)
Excel 97 for Windows: Concepts & Examples (isbn 1-887902-25-2)
Microsoft Office 97 Professional: A Mastery Approach (isbn 1-887902-24-4)

The Internet & the World Wide Web
Learning to Use the Internet & the World Wide Web (isbn 1-887902-78-3)
Searching & Researching on the Internet & the World Wide Web: Third Edition (isbn 1-887902-71-6)
Web Design & Development Using XHTML (isbn 1-887902-57-0)
The Web Page Workbook: Second Edition (isbn 1-887902-45-7)
Upcoming: JavaScript Concepts & Techniques (isbn 1-887902-69-4)
XML: Learning by Example (isbn 1-887902-80-5)

Computer Science
ASP: Learning by Example (isbn 1-887902-68-6)
Basic Java Programming: A Laboratory Approach (isbn 1-887902-67-8)
Data Structures with Java: A Laboratory Approach (isbn 1-887902-70-8)
DHTML: Learning by Example (isbn 1-887902-83-X)
Computing Fundamentals with C++: Object-Oriented Programming & Design—Second Edition (isbn 1-887902-36-8)
Computing Fundamentals with Java (isbn 1-887902-47-3)
Fundamentals of Secure Computing Systems (isbn 1-887902-66-X)
Guide to Persuasive Programming (isbn 1-887902-65-1)
Modern Programming Languages: A Practical Introduction (isbn 1-887902-76-7)
Persuasive Programming (isbn 1-887902-60-0)
Prelude to Patterns in Computer Science Using Java—Beta Edition (isbn 1-887902-55-4)
Upcoming: Python Programming: An Introduction to Computer Science (isbn 1-887902-99-6)

Professional Reference
The Dictionary of Computing & Digital Media Terms & Acronyms (isbn 1-887902-38-4)
The Dictionary of Multimedia (isbn 1-887902-14-7)

E-Books
Computer Graphics: An Object-Oriented Approach to the Art and Science Implemented in C++ (isbn 1-887902-91-0)
DOS 6: Principles with Practice (isbn 1-887902-93-7)
Internet & Web Essentials: What You Need to Know (isbn 1-887902-92-9)
Operating Systems Bookshelf (isbn 1-887902-94-5)